NLT Desktop Concordance

TYNDALE DESKTOP REFERENCE

Tyndale Desktop Reference

NLT
DESKTOP CONCORDANCE

Tyndale House Publishers, Inc.
Carol Stream, Illinois

Visit Tyndale's exciting Web site at www.tyndale.com

NLT Desktop Concordance, Tyndale Desktop Reference Edition

Cover designed by Erik Peterson

Library of Congress Cataloging-in-Publication Data

NLT desktop concordance.
p. cm. — (Tyndale desktop reference)
ISBN-13: 978-1-4143-2200-1 (sc)
ISBN-10: 1-4143-2200-3 (sc)
1. Bible—Concordances, English—New Living Translation. I. Tyndale House Publishers.
BS425.N583 2008
220.5'20833--dc22 2008009046

Printed in the United States of America

14 13 12 11 10 09 08
7 6 5 4 3 2 1

Contents

How to Use This Book

A concordance is one of the most useful tools a student of the Bible can own. With it you can quickly locate a specific verse or group of related verses to aid your study of a particular passage or your survey of the Bible's message on a topic. This concordance is designed for use with the New Living Translation (second edition).

A concordance is an alphabetical list of words found in the Bible. For each word, it provides a list of Scripture references where that word is found, coupled with a portion of the context. In order to remain handy in size, the *NLT Desktop Concordance* limits the number of words it concords and the number of verses listed per word. Careful thought went into choosing words and verses with the goal of creating a quick and convenient tool for finding important verses.

Unlike many concordances, the *NLT Desktop Concordance* lists each term's part of speech in parentheses, followed by a brief definition for each word. Here is an example of a typical entry:

> **INSPIRED (adj)**
> *influenced, moved; guided or created by divine influence*
> 2 Tim 3:16 . . All Scripture is ***i*** by God

(Note: In order to provide as much context as possible, the term is abbreviated in each reference.)

Because English Bibles vary in how they render the original Greek and Hebrew, this concordance integrates a second type of entry—important traditional or archaic terms with NLT renderings (spelled out rather than abbreviated). Here is an example:

> *SURETY (KJV)*
> Gen 43:9 . . . I ***personally guarantee*** his safety
> Prov 17:18 . . ***put up security*** for a friend
> Heb 7:22 . . . Jesus is the one who ***guarantees***

This feature will help those who are familiar with older or more traditional-sounding translations but who prefer the contemporary language of the NLT find important verses.

This concordance features a third type of entry, devoted to important people in the Bible and their lives. Major characteristics and events are briefly described, followed by references to relevant verses. Here is an example:

> **ISAIAH**
> *Prophet of Judah (southern kingdom) who prophesied during the reigns of four consecutive kings (Isa 1:1); called by God in a vision (Isa 6); prophesied Immanuel's*

coming (Isa 7–11); prophesied to Hezekiah (2 Kgs 19–20; Isa 36–38); recorded history of kings (2 Chr 26:22; 32:32); often quoted in NT (Matt 3:3; 4:14; 8:17; 12:17; 13:14; 15:7; Luke 4:17; John 12:38; Acts 8:28; 28:25; Rom 9:27; 10:16, 20).

(For a list of the abbreviations used for Bible book names and parts of speech, see Abbreviations on page xix.)

On a final note, remember that when using a concordance to study the Bible, the most important concept to keep in mind is the crucial role context plays in determining meaning. The concordance gives small portions of context to help you find verses that are relevant to your study. However, it is important to take the next step and examine each text carefully in its own context. Ask yourself how the entire sentence, verse, paragraph, or even book in which a particular word is used sheds light on what the word means in that particular verse. Taking time to consider Scripture in its context is a significant part of becoming a faithful handler of the Word of God.

Introduction to the New Living Translation

Translation Philosophy and Methodology

English Bible translations tend to be governed by one of two general translation theories. The first theory has been called "formal-equivalence," "literal," or "word-for-word" translation. According to this theory, the translator attempts to render each word of the original language into English and seeks to preserve the original syntax and sentence structure as much as possible in translation. The second theory has been called "dynamic-equivalence," "functional-equivalence," or "thought-for-thought" translation. The goal of this translation theory is to produce in English the closest natural equivalent of the message expressed by the original-language text, both in meaning and in style.

Both of these translation theories have their strengths. A formal-equivalence translation preserves aspects of the original text—including ancient idioms, term consistency, and original-language syntax—that are valuable for scholars and professional study. It allows a reader to trace formal elements of the original-language text through the English translation. A dynamic-equivalence translation, on the other hand, focuses on translating the message of the original-language text. It ensures that the meaning of the text is readily apparent to the contemporary reader. This allows the message to come through with immediacy, without requiring the reader to struggle with foreign idioms and awkward syntax. It also facilitates serious study of the text's message and clarity in both devotional and public reading.

The pure application of either of these translation philosophies would create translations at opposite ends of the translation spectrum. But in reality, all translations contain a mixture of these two philosophies. A purely formal-equivalence translation would be unintelligible in English, and a purely dynamic-equivalence translation would risk being unfaithful to the original. That is why translations shaped by dynamic-equivalence theory are usually quite literal when the original text is relatively clear, and the translations shaped by formal-equivalence theory are sometimes quite dynamic when the original text is obscure.

The translators of the New Living Translation set out to render the message of the original texts of Scripture into clear, contemporary English. As they did so, they kept the concerns of both formal-equivalence and dynamic-equivalence in mind. On the one hand, they translated as simply and literally as possible when that approach yielded an accurate, clear, and natural English text. Many words and phrases were rendered literally and consistently into English, preserving essential literary and rhetorical devices, ancient metaphors, and word choices that give structure to the text and provide echoes of meaning from one passage to the next.

On the other hand, the translators rendered the message more dynamically when the literal rendering was hard to understand, was misleading, or yielded archaic or foreign wording. They clarified difficult metaphors and terms to aid in the reader's understanding. The translators first struggled with the meaning of the words and phrases in the ancient context; then they rendered the message into clear, natural English. Their goal was to be both faithful to the ancient texts and eminently readable. The result is a translation that is both exegetically accurate and idiomatically powerful.

Translation Process and Team

To produce an accurate translation of the Bible into contemporary English, the translation team needed the skills necessary to enter into the thought patterns of the ancient authors and then to render their ideas, connotations, and effects into clear, contemporary English. To begin this process, qualified biblical scholars were needed to interpret the meaning of the original text and to check it against our base English translation. In order to guard against personal and theological biases, the scholars needed to represent a diverse group of evangelicals who would employ the best exegetical tools. Then to work alongside the scholars, skilled English stylists were needed to shape the text into clear, contemporary English.

With these concerns in mind, the Bible Translation Committee recruited teams of scholars that represented a broad spectrum of denominations, theological perspectives, and backgrounds within the worldwide evangelical community. (These scholars are listed at the end of this introduction.) Each book of the Bible was assigned to three different scholars with proven expertise in the book or group of books to be reviewed. Each of these scholars made a thorough review of a base translation and submitted suggested revisions to the appropriate Senior Translator. The Senior Translator then reviewed and summarized these suggestions and proposed a first-draft revision of the base text. This draft served as the basis for several additional phases of exegetical and stylistic committee review. Then the Bible Translation Committee jointly reviewed and approved every verse of the final translation.

Throughout the translation and editing process, the Senior Translators and their scholar teams were given a chance to review the editing done by the team of stylists. This ensured that exegetical errors would not be introduced late in the process and that the entire Bible Translation Committee was happy with the final result. By choosing a team of qualified scholars and skilled stylists and by setting up a process that allowed their interaction throughout the process, the New Living Translation has been refined to preserve the essential formal elements of the original biblical texts, while also creating a clear, understandable English text.

The New Living Translation was first published in 1996. Shortly after its initial publication, the Bible Translation Committee began a process of further committee review and translation refinement. The purpose of this continued revision was to increase the level of precision without sacrificing the text's easy-to-understand quality. This second-edition text was completed in 2004, and an additional update with minor changes was subsequently introduced in 2007. This concordance reflects the updated 2007 text.

Written to Be Read Aloud

It is evident in Scripture that the biblical documents were written to be read aloud, often in public worship (see Nehemiah 8; Luke 4:16-20; 1 Timothy 4:13; Revelation 1:3). It is still the case today that more people will hear the Bible read aloud in church than are likely to read it for themselves. Therefore, a new translation must communicate with clarity and power when it is read publicly. Clarity was a primary goal for the NLT translators, not only to facilitate private reading and understanding, but also to ensure that it would be excellent for public reading and make an immediate and powerful impact on any listener.

The Texts behind the New Living Translation

The Old Testament translators used the Masoretic Text of the Hebrew Bible as represented in *Biblia Hebraica Stuttgartensia* (1977), with its extensive system of textual notes; this is an update of Rudolf Kittel's *Biblia Hebraica* (Stuttgart, 1937). The translators also further compared the Dead Sea Scrolls, the Septuagint and other Greek manuscripts, the Samaritan Pentateuch, the Syriac Peshitta, the Latin Vulgate, and any other versions or manuscripts that shed light on the meaning of difficult passages.

The New Testament translators used the two standard editions of the Greek New Testament: the *Greek New Testament,* published by the United Bible Societies (UBS, fourth revised edition, 1993), and *Novum Testamentum Graece,* edited by Nestle and Aland (NA, twenty-seventh edition, 1993). These two editions, which have the same text but differ in punctuation and textual notes, represent, for the most part, the best in modern textual scholarship. However, in cases where strong textual or other scholarly evidence supported the decision, the translators sometimes chose to differ from the UBS and NA Greek texts and followed variant readings found in other ancient witnesses. Significant textual variants of this sort are always noted in the textual notes of the New Living Translation.

Translation Issues

The translators have made a conscious effort to provide a text that can be easily understood by the typical reader of modern English. To this end, we sought to use only vocabulary and language structures in common use today. We avoided using language likely to become quickly dated or that reflects only a narrow sub-dialect of English, with the goal of making the New Living Translation as broadly useful and timeless as possible.

But our concern for readability goes beyond the concerns of vocabulary and sentence structure. We are also concerned about historical and cultural barriers to understanding the Bible, and we have sought to translate terms shrouded in history and culture in ways that can be immediately understood. To this end:

- We have converted ancient weights and measures (for example, "ephah" [a unit of dry volume] or "cubit" [a unit of length]) to modern English (American) equivalents, since the ancient measures are not generally meaningful to today's readers. Then in the textual footnotes we offer the literal Hebrew, Aramaic, or Greek measures, along with modern metric equivalents.
- Instead of translating ancient currency values literally, we have expressed them in common terms that communicate the message. For example, in the Old Testament, "ten shekels of silver" becomes "ten pieces of silver" to convey the intended message. In the New Testament, we have often translated the "denarius" as "the normal daily wage" to facilitate understanding. Then a footnote offers: "Greek *a denarius,* the payment for a full day's wage." In general, we give a clear English rendering and then state the literal Hebrew, Aramaic, or Greek in a textual footnote.

- Since the names of Hebrew months are unknown to most contemporary readers, and since the Hebrew lunar calendar fluctuates from year to year in relation to the solar calendar used today, we have looked for clear ways to communicate the time of year the Hebrew months (such as Abib) refer to. When an expanded or interpretive rendering is given in the text, a textual note gives the literal rendering. Where it is possible to define a specific ancient date in terms of our modern calendar, we use modern dates in the text. A textual footnote then gives the literal Hebrew date and states the rationale for our rendering. For example, Ezra 6:15 pinpoints the date when the postexilic Temple was completed in Jerusalem: "the third day of the month Adar." This was during the sixth year of King Darius's reign (that is, 515 B.C.). We have translated that date as March 12, with a footnote giving the Hebrew and identifying the year as 515 B.C.
- Since ancient references to the time of day differ from our modern methods of denoting time, we have used renderings that are instantly understandable to the modern reader. Accordingly, we have rendered specific times of day by using approximate equivalents in terms of our common "o'clock" system. On occasion, translations such as "at dawn the next morning" or "as the sun was setting" have been used when the biblical reference is more general.
- When the meaning of a proper name (or a wordplay inherent in a proper name) is relevant to the message of the text, its meaning is often illuminated with a textual footnote. For example, in Exodus 2:10 the text reads: "The princess named him Moses, for she explained, 'I lifted him out of the water.'" The accompanying footnote reads: "*Moses* sounds like a Hebrew term that means 'to lift out.'"
- Sometimes, when the actual meaning of a name is clear, that meaning is included in parentheses within the text itself. For example, the text at Genesis 16:11 reads: "You are to name him Ishmael *(which means 'God hears')*, for the LORD has heard your cry of distress." Since the original hearers and readers would have instantly understood the meaning of the name "Ishmael," we have provided modern readers with the same information so they can experience the text in a similar way.
- Many words and phrases carry a great deal of cultural meaning that was obvious to the original readers but needs explanation in our own culture. For example, the phrase "they beat their breasts" (Luke 23:48) in ancient times meant that people were very upset, often in mourning. In our translation we chose to translate this phrase dynamically for clarity: "They went home *in deep sorrow.*" Then we included a footnote with the literal Greek, which reads: "Greek *went home beating their breasts.*" In other similar cases, however, we have sometimes chosen to illuminate the existing literal expression to make it immediately understandable. For example, here we might have expanded the literal Greek phrase to read: "They went home beating their breasts *in sorrow.*" If we had done this, we would not have included a textual footnote, since the literal Greek clearly appears in translation.
- Metaphorical language is sometimes difficult for contemporary readers to understand, so at times we have chosen to translate or illuminate the meaning of a metaphor. For example, the ancient poet writes, "Your neck is *like* the tower of David" (Song of Songs 4:4). We have rendered it "Your neck is *as beautiful as* the tower of David" to clarify the intended positive meaning of the simile. Another

example comes in Ecclesiastes 12:3, which can be literally rendered: "Remember him . . . when the grinding women cease because they are few, and the women who look through the windows see dimly." We have rendered it: "Remember him before your teeth—your few remaining servants—stop grinding; and before your eyes—the women looking through the windows—see dimly." We clarified such metaphors only when we believed a typical reader might be confused by the literal text.

- When the content of the original language text is poetic in character, we have rendered it in English poetic form. We sought to break lines in ways that clarify and highlight the relationships between phrases of the text. Hebrew poetry often uses parallelism, a literary form where a second phrase (or in some instances a third or fourth) echoes the initial phrase in some way. In Hebrew parallelism, the subsequent parallel phrases continue, while also furthering and sharpening, the thought expressed in the initial line or phrase. Whenever possible, we sought to represent these parallel phrases in natural poetic English.
- The Greek term *hoi Ioudaioi* is literally translated "the Jews" in many English translations. In the Gospel of John, however, this term doesn't always refer to the Jewish people generally. In some contexts, it refers more particularly to the Jewish religious leaders. We have attempted to capture the meaning in these different contexts by using terms such as "the people" (with a footnote: Greek *the Jewish people*) or "the religious leaders," where appropriate.
- One challenge we faced was how to translate accurately the ancient biblical text that was originally written in a context where male-oriented terms were used to refer to humanity generally. We needed to respect the nature of the ancient context while also trying to make the translation clear to a modern audience that tends to read male-oriented language as applying only to males. Often the original text, though using masculine nouns and pronouns, clearly intends that the message be applied to both men and women. A typical example is found in the New Testament letters, where the believers are called "brothers" (*adelphoi*). Yet it is clear from the content of these letters that they were addressed to all the believers—male and female. Thus, we have usually translated this Greek word as "brothers and sisters" in order to represent the historical situation more accurately.

  We have also been sensitive to passages where the text applies generally to human beings or to the human condition. In some instances we have used plural pronouns (they, them) in place of the masculine singular (he, him). For example, a traditional rendering of Proverbs 22:6 is: "Train up a child in the way he should go, and when he is old he will not turn from it." We have rendered it: "Direct your children onto the right path, and when they are older, they will not leave it." At times, we have also replaced third person pronouns with the second person to ensure clarity. A traditional rendering of Proverbs 26:27 is: "He who digs a pit will fall into it, and he who rolls a stone, it will come back on him." We have rendered it: "If you set a trap for others, you will get caught in it yourself. If you roll a boulder down on others, it will crush you instead."

  We should emphasize, however, that all masculine nouns and pronouns used to represent God (for example, "Father") have been maintained without exception. All decisions of this kind have been driven by the concern to reflect accurately the intended meaning of the original texts of Scripture.

Lexical Consistency in Terminology

For the sake of clarity, we have translated certain original-language terms consistently, especially within synoptic passages and for commonly repeated rhetorical phrases, and within certain word categories such as divine names and non-theological technical terminology (e.g., liturgical, legal, cultural, zoological, and botanical terms). For theological terms, we have allowed a greater semantic range of acceptable English words or phrases for a single Hebrew or Greek word. We have avoided some theological terms that are not readily understood by many modern readers. For example, we avoided using words such as "justification" and "sanctification," which are carryovers from Latin translations. In place of these words, we have provided renderings such as "made right with God" and "made holy."

The Spelling of Proper Names

Many individuals in the Bible, especially the Old Testament, are known by more than one name (e.g., Uzziah/Azariah). For the sake of clarity, we have tried to use a single spelling for any one individual, footnoting the literal spelling whenever we differ from it. This is especially helpful in delineating the kings of Israel and Judah. King Joash/Jehoash of Israel has been consistently called Jehoash, while King Joash/Jehoash of Judah is called Joash. A similar distinction has been used to distinguish between Joram/Jehoram of Israel and Joram/Jehoram of Judah. All such decisions were made with the goal of clarifying the text for the reader. When the ancient biblical writers clearly had a theological purpose in their choice of a variant name (e.g., Esh-baal/Ishbosheth), the different names have been maintained with an explanatory footnote.

For the names Jacob and Israel, which are used interchangeably for both the individual patriarch and the nation, we generally render it "Israel" when it refers to the nation and "Jacob" when it refers to the individual. When our rendering of the name differs from the underlying Hebrew text, we provide a textual footnote, which includes this explanation: "The names 'Jacob' and 'Israel' are often interchanged throughout the Old Testament, referring sometimes to the individual patriarch and sometimes to the nation."

The Rendering of Divine Names

All appearances of *'el, 'elohim,* or *'eloah* have been translated "God," except where the context demands the translation "god(s)." We have generally rendered the tetragrammaton (*YHWH*) consistently as "the LORD," utilizing a form with small capitals that is common among English translations. This will distinguish it from the name *'adonai,* which we render "Lord." When *'adonai* and *YHWH* appear together, we have rendered it "Sovereign LORD." This also distinguishes *'adonai YHWH* from cases where *YHWH* appears with *'elohim,* which is rendered "LORD God." When *YH* (the short form of *YHWH*) and *YHWH* appear together, we have rendered it "LORD GOD." When *YHWH* appears with the term *tseba'oth,* we have rendered it "LORD of Heaven's Armies" to translate the meaning of the name. In a few cases, we have utilized the transliteration, *Yahweh,* when the personal character of the name is being invoked in contrast to another divine name or the name of some other god (for example, see Exod 3:15; 6:2-3).

In the New Testament, the Greek word *christos* has been translated as "Messiah" when the context assumes a Jewish audience. When a Gentile audience can be assumed, *christos* has been translated as "Christ." The Greek word *kurios* is consistently translated "Lord," except that it is translated "LORD" wherever the New Testament text explicitly quotes from the Old Testament, and the text there has it in small capitals.

Textual Footnotes

The New Living Translation provides several kinds of textual footnotes, all designated in the text with an asterisk:

- When for the sake of clarity the NLT renders a difficult or potentially confusing phrase dynamically, we generally give the literal rendering in a textual footnote. This allows the reader to see the literal source of our dynamic rendering and how our translation relates to other more literal translations. These notes are prefaced with "Hebrew," "Aramaic," or "Greek," identifying the language of the underlying source text. For example, in Acts 2:42 we translated the literal "breaking of bread" (from the Greek) as "the Lord's Supper" to clarify that this verse refers to the ceremonial practice of the church rather than just an ordinary meal. Then we attached a footnote to "the Lord's Supper," which reads: "Greek *the breaking of bread.*"
- Textual footnotes are also used to show alternative renderings, prefaced with the word "Or." These normally occur for passages where an aspect of the meaning is debated. On occasion, we also provide notes on words or phrases that represent a departure from long-standing tradition. These notes are prefaced with "Traditionally rendered." For example, the footnote to the translation "serious skin disease" at Leviticus 13:2 says: "Traditionally rendered *leprosy.* The Hebrew word used throughout this passage is used to describe various skin diseases."
- When our translators follow a textual variant that differs significantly from our standard Hebrew or Greek texts (listed earlier), we document that difference with a footnote. We also footnote cases when the NLT excludes a passage that is included in the Greek text known as the *Textus Receptus* (and familiar to readers through its translation in the King James Version). In such cases, we offer a translation of the excluded text in a footnote, even though it is generally recognized as a later addition to the Greek text and not part of the original Greek New Testament.
- All Old Testament passages that are quoted in the New Testament are identified by a textual footnote at the New Testament location. When the New Testament clearly quotes from the Greek translation of the Old Testament, and when it differs significantly in wording from the Hebrew text, we also place a textual footnote at the Old Testament location. This note includes a rendering of the Greek version, along with a cross-reference to the New Testament passage(s) where it is cited (for example, see notes on Proverbs 3:12; Psalms 8:2; 53:3).
- Some textual footnotes provide cultural and historical information on places, things, and people in the Bible that are probably obscure to modern readers. Such notes should aid the reader in understanding the message of the text. For example, in Acts 12:1, "King Herod" is named in this translation as "King Herod Agrippa" and is identified in a footnote as being "the nephew of Herod Antipas and a grandson of Herod the Great."
- When the meaning of a proper name (or a wordplay inherent in a proper name) is relevant to the meaning of the text, it is either illuminated with a textual footnote or included within parentheses in the text itself. For example, the footnote

concerning the name "Eve" at Genesis 3:20 reads: "*Eve* sounds like a Hebrew term that means 'to give life.' " This wordplay in the Hebrew illuminates the meaning of the text, which goes on to say that Eve "would be the mother of all who live."

As we submit this translation for publication, we recognize that any translation of the Scriptures is subject to limitations and imperfections. Anyone who has attempted to communicate the richness of God's Word into another language will realize it is impossible to make a perfect translation. Recognizing these limitations, we sought God's guidance and wisdom throughout this project. Now we pray that he will accept our efforts and use this translation for the benefit of the church and of all people.

We pray that the New Living Translation will overcome some of the barriers of history, culture, and language that have kept people from reading and understanding God's Word. We hope that readers unfamiliar with the Bible will find the words clear and easy to understand and that readers well versed in the Scriptures will gain a fresh perspective. We pray that readers will gain insight and wisdom for living, but most of all that they will meet the God of the Bible and be forever changed by knowing him.

The Bible Translation Committee
October 2007

Bible Translation Team
Holy Bible, *New Living Translation*

PENTATEUCH
Daniel I. Block, Senior Translator
Wheaton College

GENESIS
- Allen Ross, *Beeson Divinity School, Samford University*
- Gordon Wenham, *University of Gloucester*

EXODUS
- Robert Bergen, *Hannibal-LaGrange College*
- Daniel I. Block, *Wheaton College*
- Eugene Carpenter, *Bethel College, Mishawaka, Indiana*

LEVITICUS
- David Baker, *Ashland Theological Seminary*
- Victor Hamilton, *Asbury College*
- Kenneth Mathews, *Beeson Divinity School, Samford University*

NUMBERS
- Dale A. Brueggemann, *Assemblies of God Division of Foreign Missions*
- R. K. Harrison (deceased), *Wycliffe College*
- Paul R. House, *Wheaton College*
- Gerald L. Mattingly, *Johnson Bible College*

DEUTERONOMY
- J. Gordon McConville, *University of Gloucester*
- Eugene H. Merrill, *Dallas Theological Seminary*
- John A. Thompson (deceased), *University of Melbourne*

HISTORICAL BOOKS
Barry J. Beitzel, Senior Translator
Trinity Evangelical Divinity School

JOSHUA, JUDGES
- Carl E. Armerding, *Schloss Mittersill Study Centre*
- Barry J. Beitzel, *Trinity Evangelical Divinity School*
- Lawson Stone, *Asbury Theological Seminary*

1 & 2 SAMUEL
Robert Gordon, *Cambridge University*
V. Philips Long, *Regent College*
J. Robert Vannoy, *Biblical Theological Seminary*

1 & 2 KINGS
Bill T. Arnold, *Asbury Theological Seminary*
William H. Barnes, *North Central University*
Frederic W. Bush, *Fuller Theological Seminary*

1 & 2 CHRONICLES
Raymond B. Dillard (deceased), *Westminster Theological Seminary*
David A. Dorsey, *Evangelical School of Theology*
Terry Eves, *Erskine College*

RUTH, EZRA—ESTHER
William C. Williams, *Vanguard University*
H. G. M. Williamson, *Oxford University*

WISDOM BOOKS
Tremper Longman III, Senior Translator
Westmont College

JOB
August Konkel, *Providence Theological Seminary*
Tremper Longman III, *Westmont College*
Al Wolters, *Redeemer College*

PSALMS 1–75
Mark D. Futato, *Reformed Theological Seminary*
Douglas Green, *Westminster Theological Seminary*
Richard Pratt, *Reformed Theological Seminary*

PSALMS 76–150
David M. Howard Jr., *Bethel Theological Seminary*
Raymond C. Ortlund Jr., *Trinity Evangelical Divinity School*
Willem VanGemeren, *Trinity Evangelical Divinity School*

PROVERBS
Ted Hildebrandt, *Gordon College*
Richard Schultz, *Wheaton College*
Raymond C. Van Leeuwen, *Eastern College*

ECCLESIASTES, SONG OF SONGS
Daniel C. Fredericks, *Belhaven College*
David Hubbard (deceased), *Fuller Theological Seminary*
Tremper Longman III, *Westmont College*

PROPHETS
John N. Oswalt, Senior Translator
Wesley Biblical Seminary

ISAIAH
John N. Oswalt, *Wesley Biblical Seminary*
Gary Smith, *Midwestern Baptist Theological Seminary*
John Walton, *Wheaton College*

JEREMIAH, LAMENTATIONS
G. Herbert Livingston, *Asbury Theological Seminary*
Elmer A. Martens, *Mennonite Brethren Biblical Seminary*

EZEKIEL
Daniel I. Block, *Wheaton College*
David H. Engelhard, *Calvin Theological Seminary*
David Thompson, *Asbury Theological Seminary*

DANIEL, HAGGAI—MALACHI
Joyce Baldwin Caine (deceased), *Trinity College, Bristol*
Douglas Gropp, *Catholic University of America*
Roy Hayden, *Oral Roberts School of Theology*
Andrew Hill, *Wheaton College*
Tremper Longman III, *Westmont College*

HOSEA—ZEPHANIAH
Joseph Coleson, *Nazarene Theological Seminary*
Roy Hayden, *Oral Roberts School of Theology*
Andrew Hill, *Wheaton College*
Richard Patterson, *Liberty University*

GOSPELS AND ACTS
Grant R. Osborne, Senior Translator
Trinity Evangelical Divinity School

MATTHEW
Craig Blomberg, *Denver Seminary*
Donald A. Hagner, *Fuller Theological Seminary*
David Turner, *Grand Rapids Baptist Seminary*

MARK
Robert Guelich (deceased), *Fuller Theological Seminary*
George Guthrie, *Union University*
Grant R. Osborne, *Trinity Evangelical Divinity School*

LUKE
Darrell Bock, *Dallas Theological Seminary*
Scot McKnight, *North Park University*
Robert Stein, *The Southern Baptist Theological Seminary*

JOHN
Gary M. Burge, *Wheaton College*
Philip W. Comfort, *Coastal Carolina University*
Marianne Meye Thompson, *Fuller Theological Seminary*

ACTS
D. A. Carson, *Trinity Evangelical Divinity School*
William J. Larkin, *Columbia International University*
Roger Mohrlang, *Whitworth University*

LETTERS AND REVELATION
Norman R. Ericson, Senior Translator
Wheaton College

ROMANS, GALATIANS
Gerald Borchert, *Northern Baptist Theological Seminary*
Douglas J. Moo, *Wheaton College*
Thomas R. Schreiner, *The Southern Baptist Theological Seminary*

1 & 2 CORINTHIANS
Joseph Alexanian, *Trinity International University*
Linda Belleville, *Bethel College, Mishawaka, Indiana*
Douglas A. Oss, *Central Bible College*
Robert Sloan, *Baylor University*

EPHESIANS–PHILEMON
Harold W. Hoehner, *Dallas Theological Seminary*
Moises Silva, *Gordon-Conwell Theological Seminary*
Klyne Snodgrass, *North Park Theological Seminary*

HEBREWS, JAMES, 1 & 2 PETER, JUDE
Peter Davids, *Schloss Mittersill Study Centre*
Norman R. Ericson, *Wheaton College*
William Lane (deceased), *Seattle Pacific University*
J. Ramsey Michaels, *S. W. Missouri State University*

1–3 JOHN, REVELATION
Greg Beale, *Wheaton College*
Robert Mounce, *Whitworth University*
M. Robert Mulholland Jr., *Asbury Theological Seminary*

SPECIAL REVIEWERS
F. F. Bruce (deceased), *University of Manchester*
Kenneth N. Taylor (deceased), *Translator,* The Living Bible

COORDINATING TEAM
Mark D. Taylor, *Director and Chief Stylist*
Ronald A. Beers, *Executive Director and Stylist*
Mark R. Norton, *Managing Editor and O.T. Coordinating Editor*
Philip W. Comfort, *N.T. Coordinating Editor*
Daniel W. Taylor, *Bethel University, Senior Stylist*

Abbreviations

Bible Books

Genesis	Gen
Exodus	Exod
Leviticus	Lev
Numbers	Num
Deuteronomy	Deut
Joshua	Josh
Judges	Judg
Ruth	Ruth
1 Samuel	1 Sam
2 Samuel	2 Sam
1 Kings	1 Kgs
2 Kings	2 Kgs
1 Chronicles	1 Chr
2 Chronicles	2 Chr
Ezra	Ezra
Nehemiah	Neh
Esther	Esth
Job	Job
Psalms	Ps
Proverbs	Prov
Ecclesiastes	Eccl
Song of Songs	Song
Isaiah	Isa
Jeremiah	Jer
Lamentations	Lam
Ezekiel	Ezek
Daniel	Dan
Hosea	Hos
Joel	Joel
Amos	Amos
Obadiah	Obad
Jonah	Jonah
Micah	Mic
Nahum	Nah
Habakkuk	Hab
Zephaniah	Zeph
Haggai	Hag
Zechariah	Zech
Malachi	Mal
Matthew	Matt
Mark	Mark
Luke	Luke
John	John
Acts	Acts
Romans	Rom
1 Corinthians	1 Cor
2 Corinthians	2 Cor
Galatians	Gal
Ephesians	Eph
Philippians	Phil
Colossians	Col
1 Thessalonians	1 Thes
2 Thessalonians	2 Thes
1 Timothy	1 Tim
2 Timothy	2 Tim
Titus	Titus
Philemon	Phlm
Hebrews	Heb
James	Jas
1 Peter	1 Pet
2 Peter	2 Pet
1 John	1 John
2 John	2 John
3 John	3 John
Jude	Jude
Revelation	Rev

Other Abbreviations

(KJV)	King James Version	(n)	noun
(adj)	adjective	(prep)	preposition
(adv)	adverb	(v)	verb

AARON

First high priest of Israel; elder brother and spokesman of Moses (Exod 4:14-31; 7:1-2); confronted Pharaoh with Moses (Exod 5–12); held up Moses' hands during battle (Exod 17:8-15); led Israel while Moses was absent (Exod 24:14); priestly clothing and accessories (Exod 28); his ordination (Exod 29; Lev 8); his failure with the gold calf (Exod 32; Acts 7:40); spoke against Moses, then interceded on behalf of sister, Miriam (Num 12:1-16); helped stop the plague (Num 16:45-48); priesthood confirmed (Num 17; Heb 5:1-4); failed at Meribah and was denied entry to Promised Land (Num 20:1-13); died (Num 20:22-29; 33:38-39).

ABANDON, ABANDONED, ABANDONS (v)

to desert or forsake

Josh 1:5 . . . . will not fail you or ***a*** you.
Josh 24:16 . . We would never ***a*** the LORD
Ezra 9:9 . . . . God did not ***a*** us in our slavery.
Neh 9:31 . . . completely or ***a*** them forever.
Ps 22:1 . . . . . why have you ***a-ed*** me?
Ps 37:25 . . . . never seen the godly ***a-ed***
Ps 37:28 . . . . he will never ***a*** the godly.
Prov 15:10 . . Whoever ***a-s*** the right path
Matt 27:46 . . why have you ***a-ed*** me?
John 16:1 . . . you won't ***a*** your faith.
Rom 1:24 . . . So God ***a-ed*** them to do
Rom 1:28 . . . ***a-ed*** them to their foolish
2 Cor 4:9 . . . down, but never ***a-ed*** by God.
Heb 13:5 . . . I will never ***a*** you.

ABASED (KJV)

Ezek 21:26 . . mighty will be ***brought down.***
Matt 23:12 . . themselves will be ***humbled***
Phil 4:12 . . . how to ***live on almost nothing***

ABEL

Son of Adam and Eve, brother of Cain (Gen 4:1-2); his offering accepted (Gen 4:4; Heb 11:4); murdered by Cain (Gen 4:8; Matt 23:35; Luke 11:51; Heb 12:24; 1 Jn 3:11-12; Jude 1:11); replaced by Seth (Gen 4:25).

ABHOR (v)

to hate or loathe

Ps 119:163 . . I hate and ***a*** all falsehood,

ABIDE(TH), ABIDING (KJV)

Luke 2:8. . . . shepherds ***staying*** in the fields
John 12:46 . . no longer ***remain*** in the dark
John 15:4 . . . be fruitful unless you ***remain***

ABILITY, ABILITIES (n)

talent, aptitude, or skill

Exod 35:34 . the ***a*** to teach their skills
Dan 6:3 . . . . because of Daniel's great ***a,***
Acts 2:4 . . . . Spirit gave them this ***a.***
1 Cor 12:1 . . special ***a-ies*** the Spirit gives
1 Cor 14:1 . . special ***a-ies*** the Spirit gives—
1 Cor 14:12 . special ***a-ies*** the Spirit gives,
2 Cor 1:8 . . . beyond our ***a*** to endure,

ABLE (adj)

marked by power, intelligence, competence, skill, giftedness

Deut 16:17. . must give as they are ***a,***
Dan 3:17 . . . whom we serve is ***a*** to save
Rom 8:39 . . . ever be ***a*** to separate us from
Rom 16:25 . . to God, who is ***a*** to
Eph 3:20 . . . all glory to God, who is ***a,***
Eph 6:13 . . . you will be ***a*** to resist
2 Tim 1:12 . . that he is ***a*** to guard
2 Tim 2:24 . . be ***a*** to teach, and
Jude 1:24 . . . to God, who is ***a*** to keep

ABOLISH (v)
to destroy; to annul
Matt 5:17 . . . did not come to ***a*** the law

ABOUND(ED) (KJV)
Prov 28:20 . . person will ***get a rich reward***
Matt 24:12 . . Sin will ***be rampant everywhere***
Rom 5:15 . . . ***even greater*** is God's wonderful grace
Rom 5:20 . . . grace ***became more abundant***
2 Cor 8:7 . . . ***excel*** also in this gracious act

ABOVE (adv or prep)
in a higher position, superior
Ps 95:3 . . . . . a great King ***a*** all gods.
Ps 99:2 . . . . . exalted ***a*** all the nations.
Luke 12:31 . . Seek the Kingdom of God ***a*** all
Eph 1:21 . . . . far ***a*** any ruler or authority
Phil 2:9 . . . . the name ***a*** all other names,
1 Tim 3:2 . . . a man whose life is ***a*** reproach.
Jas 3:17 . . . . . wisdom from ***a*** is first of all pure.

ABRAHAM (ABRAM)
Father of the nation of Israel (Isa 51:2; John 8:37-59); friend of God (Isa 41:8); father of all people of faith (Gen 12–25; Rom 4; Heb 11); made covenant with the LORD (Gen 12:1-3; 13:14-17; 15:12-21; 22:15-18; 50:24; Exod 2:24; 32:13; Lev 26:42; 2 Kgs 13:23; 1 Chr 13:23; 16:16; Neh 9:8; Ps 105:9; Luke 1:73; Acts 3:25; Gal 3:17-20; Heb 6:13); descendant of Terah from Ur (Gen 11:27-31); husband of Sarah (Sarai) (Gen 11:29); called to leave home (Gen 12:1-9; Acts 7:2-4; Heb 11:8-10); went to Egypt and deceived the Pharaoh (Gen 12:10-20); chose Canaan over the Jordan Plain (Gen 13); rescued Lot from enemies (Gen 14:11-16); blessed by Melchizedek (Gen 14:18-24; Heb 7:1); covenant restated by God (Gen 15); faith counted as righteousness (Gen 15:6; Rom 4:3; Gal 3:6-9; Jas 2:21-23); given son (Ishmael) by Hagar (Gen 16); circumcision commanded (Gen 17; Rom 4:9-12); name changed to "Abraham" (Gen 17:5; Neh 9:7); son promised to Sarah (Gen 17:16; 18:10); welcomed heavenly visitor (Gen 18:1-15); bargained to save Sodom and Gomorrah (Gen 18:16-33); deceived Abimelech (Gen 20); named as a prophet (Gen 20:7); given son (Isaac) by Sarah (Gen 21:1-7; Heb 11:11-12); sent Hagar and Ishmael away (Gen 21:9-14; Gal 4:21-31); offered Isaac as test (Gen 22:1-19; Heb 11:17-19; Jas 2:21); secured burial ground for Sarah (Gen 23); found a wife for Isaac (Gen 24); descendants through wife Keturah (Gen 25:1-6); died (Gen 25:7-11).

ABSTAIN (v)
to refrain from, forgo
Exod 19:15 . then ***a*** from having sexual intercourse.
Acts 15:20 . . ***a*** from eating food offered to idols,

ABUNDANCE (n)
great quantity, affluence; more than ample
Job 36:31 . . . giving them food in ***a.***
Ps 66:12 . . . . a place of great ***a.***
Jer 31:14. . . . The priests will enjoy ***a,***
Matt 13:12 . . have an ***a*** of knowledge.
Matt 25:29 . . they will have an ***a.***
John 1:16 . . . From his ***a*** we have all

ABUNDANT (adj)
marked by great plenty, abounding
Deut 28:11 . . livestock, and ***a*** crops.
Ps 68:9 . . . . . You sent ***a*** rain, O God
Jer 31:12. . . . good gifts—the ***a*** crops
John 16:24 . . you will have ***a*** joy.
2 Cor 8:2 . . . are also filled with ***a*** joy,

ABUSE (n)
strong condemnation or disapproval
Mark 15:29 . shouted ***a,*** shaking their heads

ABUSE (v)
to injure or damage physically or verbally
1 Cor 4:12 . . patient with those who ***a*** us.

ABUSIVE (adj)
using harsh, insulting language; characterized by wrong or improper use or action
1 Cor 5:11 . . worships idols, or is ***a,***
1 Cor 6:10 . . drunkards, or are ***a,*** or
Eph 4:29 . . . use foul or ***a*** language.

ABYSS (KJV)
Luke 8:31. . . send them into the ***bottomless pit***
Rev 9:1. . . . . the shaft of the ***bottomless pit***
Rev 9:11. . . . the angel from the ***bottomless pit***

ACACIA (n)
several species of shrubs and trees, some of which are found in the Holy Land, yielding highly durable wood
Exod 25:10 . make an Ark of ***a*** wood
Exod 27:1 . . ***a*** wood, construct a square altar
Josh 2:1 . . . . the Israelite camp at ***A*** Grove.

ACCEPT, ACCEPTED, ACCEPTS (v)
to receive willingly
Gen 4:4 . . . . The LORD ***a-ed*** Abel
Gen 4:7 . . . . be ***a-ed*** if you do what is right.
Deut 16:19. . Never ***a*** a bribe, for bribes
Job 42:9 . . . . the LORD ***a-ed*** Job's prayer.
Eccl 5:18 . . . to ***a*** their lot in life.
Luke 4:24. . . no prophet is ***a-ed*** in his
Luke 10:16. . who ***a-s*** your message
John 1:12. . . believed him and ***a-ed*** him,
John 17:8 . . . They ***a-ed*** it and know that
Rom 11:12. . when they finally ***a*** it.
Gal 2:9 . . . . . they ***a-ed*** Barnabas and me
Col 2:6 . . . . . just as you ***a-ed*** Christ Jesus
1 Tim 1:15 . . everyone should ***a*** it:
1 Tim 4:9 . . . everyone should ***a*** it.
Jas 1:21. . . . . ***a*** the word God has planted

ACCEPTABLE (adj)
capable or worthy of being accepted; welcome, pleasing, favorable
Mark 7:19 . . every kind of food is ***a***
Rom 4:2. . . . had made him ***a*** to God,
Rom 12:1. . . the kind he will find ***a.***
Rom 14:20. . all foods are ***a,*** but it is
2 Cor 8:12 . . is ***a*** if you give it eagerly.
1 Tim 4:5 . . . made ***a*** by the word of God

ACCIDENTALLY (adv)
unintentionally, by mistake
Josh 20:9 . . . who ***a*** killed another person
Matt 23:24. . so you won't ***a*** swallow a gnat,

ACCOMPLISH, ACCOMPLISHES (v)
to perform, do to completion
Eccl 2:11 . . . to ***a,*** it was all so meaningless
Isa 55:11. . . . fruit. It will ***a*** all I want it to,
Matt 5:17. . . No, I came to ***a*** their purpose.
John 6:63 . . . Human effort ***a-es*** nothing.
Eph 3:20 . . . within us, to ***a*** infinitely more
2 Thes 1:11 . power to ***a*** all the good things

ACCOUNT (n)
description of facts, conditions, or events; a report
Gen 2:4 . . . . This is the ***a*** of the creation
Gen 5:1 . . . . written ***a*** of the descendants
Gen 6:9 . . . . the ***a*** of Noah and his family.
Gen 10:1 . . . This is the ***a*** of the families
Gen 37:2 . . . This is the ***a*** of Jacob and
Rom 14:12. . give a personal ***a*** to God.

ACCOUNTABLE (adj)
subject to giving an account; answerable
Heb 4:13 . . . the one to whom we are ***a.***
Heb 13:17 . . and they are ***a*** to God.

ACCURATE (adj)
conforming exactly to truth or to a standard; free from error, correct
Lev 19:36. . . and weights must be ***a.***
Deut 25:13. . You must use ***a*** scales
Prov 11:1. . . delights in ***a*** weights.
Prov 22:21. . take an ***a*** report to those
John 21:24 . . account of these things is ***a.***

ACCURSED (KJV)
Deut 21:23. . anyone who is hung is ***cursed***
Josh 6:18 . . . things ***set apart for destruction***
1 Cor 12:3 . . will ***curse*** Jesus, and no one
Gal 1:9. . . . . let that person be ***cursed***

ACCUSATION, ACCUSATIONS (n)
a charge of wrongdoing, often false
Ps 4:2 . . . . . . will you make groundless ***a-s?***
Luke 3:14. . . extort money or make false ***a-s.***
1 Tim 5:19 . . Do not listen to an ***a***

ACCUSE, ACCUSED, ACCUSES, ACCUSING (v)
to charge with fault or offense; to blame
Job 22:4 . . . . ***a-s*** you and brings judgment
Ps 27:12 . . . . For they ***a*** me of things
Dan 6:5 . . . . grounds for ***a-ing*** Daniel
Luke 23:14. . ***a-ing*** him of leading a revolt.
John 5:45 . . . it isn't I who will ***a***
John 7:7 . . . . because I ***a*** it of doing evil.
John 8:46 . . . can truthfully ***a*** me of sin?
Acts 18:13 . . ***a-d*** Paul of "persuading
Rom 2:15. . . and thoughts either ***a*** them
Rom 8:33. . . Who dares ***a*** us whom God
Rev 12:10. . . who ***a-s*** them before our God

ACCUSER, ACCUSERS (n)
one who charges another of wrongdoing
Deut 19:18. . If the ***a*** has brought false
Isa 50:8. . . . . Where are my ***a-s?***
Luke 12:58. . the way to court with your ***a,***
Rev 12:10. . . the ***a*** of our brothers

ACKNOWLEDGE, ACKNOWLEDGES (v)
to express a gratitude of debt; to recognize as valid; to confess (wrongdoing)
Jer 3:13. . . . . Only ***a*** your guilt. Admit
Matt 10:32. . Everyone who ***a-s*** me
Luke 12:8. . . Son of Man will also ***a***
Rom 1:28. . . thought it foolish to ***a*** God,
1 Jn 2:23. . . . anyone who ***a-s*** the Son
1 Jn 4:3. . . . . and does not ***a*** the truth

ACQUAINTED (v)
to make familiar; to know firsthand
Isa 53:3. . . . . sorrows, ***a*** with deepest grief.
Acts 18:2 . . . ***a*** with a Jew named Aquila,

ACQUIT, ACQUITTING (v)
to free from the penalty of a guilty action; (used theologically) to justify or make right with God
2 Chr 6:23 . . ***A*** the innocent because of
Prov 17:15. . ***A-ing*** the guilty and

ACT (v)
to behave; to take action or do something
Ps 119:126 . . it is time for you to ***a,***
Eccl 6:8 . . . . how to ***a*** in front of others?

ACTION, ACTIONS (n)
a thing done, deed; an exercise of will
Jer 4:18. . . . . Your own ***a-s*** have brought
Phlm 1:6 . . . put into ***a*** the generosity
Rev 3:2. . . . . ***a-s*** do not meet the requirements

ACTIVITY (n)
a pursuit in which a person is active; quality or state of being active
Eccl 3:1 . . . . for every ***a*** under heaven.

ADAM
First man (Gen 1:26–2:25; Rom 5:14; 1 Tim 2:13-14); son of God (Luke 3:38); sinned (Gen 3:1-19; Hos 6:7; Rom 5:12-21); descendants of (Gen 5); died (Gen 5:5; 1 Cor 15:22-49).

ADD, ADDED (v)
to make or serve as an addition
Deut 4:2. . . . Do not ***a*** to or subtract from
Deut 12:32. . You must not ***a*** anything to
Prov 30:6. . . Do not ***a*** to his words,
Eccl 3:14 . . . Nothing can be ***a-ed*** to it
Matt 6:27. . . worries ***a*** a single moment
Luke 12:25. . worries ***a*** a single moment
Acts 2:47 . . . each day the Lord ***a-ed*** to their
Rev 22:18. . . God will ***a*** to that person

ADEQUATE (adj)
suitable for a task; suitable
2 Cor 2:16 . . who is ***a*** for such a task as this?

ADMIT (v)
to acknowledge, confess
Hos 5:15 . . . until they ***a*** their guilt
John 12:42 . . But they wouldn't ***a*** it

ADMINISTRATOR
Num 3:32 . . chief ***a*** over all the Levites
Isa 37:2. . . . . sent Eliakim the palace ***a***

ADMONISH(ED) (KJV)
Eccl 12:12 . . give you ***some further advice***
Jer 42:19. . . . Don't forget this ***warning*** I
2 Thes 3:15 . ***warn*** them as you would
Heb 8:5 . . . . God ***gave*** him this ***warning***

ADMONITION (KJV)
1 Cor 10:11 . written down ***to warn us***
Eph 6:4 . . . . ***instruction*** that comes from the Lord
Titus 3:10. . . a first and second ***warning***

ADOPT, ADOPTED (v)
to take another's child into one's own family
Rom 8:15. . . when he ***a-ed*** you as his own
Rom 8:23. . . rights as his ***a-ed*** children,
Rom 9:4. . . . to be God's ***a-ed*** children.
Gal 4:5. . . . . so that he could ***a*** us as
Eph 1:5 . . . . decided in advance to ***a*** us

ADULTERER, ADULTERERS (n)
one who commits adultery
Job 24:15 . . . The ***a*** waits for the twilight,
Jas 4:4. . . . . . You ***a-s!*** Don't you realize

ADULTEROUS (adj)
prone to adultery or idolatry
Mark 8:38 . . in these ***a*** and sinful days,

ADULTERY (n)
unlawful sexual relations between a married and an unmarried person; symbolic of idolatry
Exod 20:14 . You must not commit ***a.***
Deut 5:18. . . You must not commit ***a.***
Prov 6:32. . . who commits ***a*** is an utter fool,
Matt 5:27. . . You must not commit ***a.***
Matt 19:18. . You must not commit ***a.***
Mark 10:11 . someone else commits ***a***
Luke 18:20. . You must not commit ***a.***
John 8:4 . . . . caught in the act of ***a.***
1 Cor 6:9 . . . ***a,*** or are male prostitutes,

ADVANTAGE (n)
benefit; upper hand
Exod 17:11 . the Israelites had the ***a.***
Lev 25:17. . . not taking ***a*** of each other.
Rom 3:1. . . . what's the ***a*** of being a Jew?
Rom 7:11. . . Sin took ***a*** of those commands
2 Cor 7:2 . . . astray, nor taken ***a*** of anyone.

ADVERSARY, ADVERSARIES (n)
enemy, opponent
2 Sam 19:22. Why have you become my ***a***
Esth 7:6 . . . . Haman is our ***a*** and our enemy.
Ps 89:23 . . . . beat down his ***a-ies*** before him
Matt 5:25. . . the way to court with your ***a,***

ADVERSITY (n)
affliction, misfortune, woe
Job 36:15 . . . gets their attention through ***a.***
Isa 30:20. . . . ***a*** for food and suffering

ADVICE (n)
recommendation regarding a decision or course of conduct; counsel
1 Kgs 12:8 . . rejected the ***a*** of
2 Chr 10:8 . . rejected the ***a*** of
Prov 12:5. . . ***a*** of the wicked is
Prov 12:26. . godly give good ***a*** to their
Prov 15:22. . Plans go wrong for lack of ***a;***
Isa 44:25. . . . I cause the wise to give bad ***a,***
Rom 11:34. . enough to give him ***a?***

ADVISE (v)
to give advice; to counsel
Ps 32:8 . . . . . I will ***a*** you and watch over
1 Tim 5:14 . . I ***a*** these younger widows
Rev 3:18. . . . I ***a*** you to buy gold from me–

ADVISERS (n)
those who give advice; counselors
1 Sam 28:23. his ***a*** joined the woman in
1 Kgs 12:14 . counsel of his younger ***a.***
Esth 1:13 . . . consulted with his wise ***a,***
Prov 11:14. . safety in having many ***a.***
Prov 29:12. . all his ***a*** will be wicked.

ADVOCATE (n)
one who pleads the cause of another; defender
see also HOLY SPIRIT, COUNSELOR
Job 16:19 . . . My ***a*** is there on high.
John 14:16 . . he will give you another ***A,***
John 14:26 . . the Father sends the ***A***
John 15:26 . . I will send you the ***A***–
John 16:7 . . . if I don't, the ***A*** won't come.
1 Jn 2:1. . . . . an ***a*** who pleads our case

AFFECTION (n)
tender attachment; a positive feeling
Rom 12:10. . each other with genuine ***a,***
2 Pet 1:7. . . . godliness with brotherly ***a,***

AFFIRM (v)
to validate; to confirm
John 3:33 . . . can ***a*** that God is true.
Rom 8:16 . . . ***a*** that we are God's children.
Heb 10:23 . . hope we ***a,*** for God can

AFFLICT, AFFLICTED (v)
relating to, characterized by, or given to persistent suffering or anguish
Deut 28:61. . LORD will ***a*** you
1 Sam 5:12. . were ***a-ed*** with tumors;

AFFORD (v)
to have enough money or other assets for
Lev 5:7. . . . . cannot ***a*** to bring a sheep,
2 Cor 8:3 . . . they could ***a,*** but far more.

AFRAID (adj)
fearful or apprehensive about an unwanted or uncertain situation
Gen 3:10 . . . I was ***a*** because I was naked.
Gen 26:24 . . Do not be ***a,*** for I am
Exod 3:6 . . . he was ***a*** to look at God.
Deut 1:21. . . Don't be ***a!***
Deut 20:1. . . your own, do not be ***a.***
Ps 23:4 . . . . . I will not be ***a,*** for you are
Isa 10:24. . . . do not be ***a*** of the Assyrians
Isa 41:10. . . . Don't be ***a,*** for I am
Isa 43:1. . . . . Do not be ***a,*** for I have
Matt 8:26. . . Why are you ***a?***
Matt 10:31. . So don't be ***a;***
Mark 5:36 . . Don't be ***a.***
John 14:27 . . don't be troubled or ***a.***
2 Tim 4:5 . . . Don't be ***a*** of suffering
1 Pet 3:14. . . don't worry or be ***a***

AFRESH (adv)
from a fresh beginning; anew, again
Lam 3:23 . . . his mercies begin ***a*** each

AGAINST (prep)
in opposition or hostility to; contrary to
Ps 41:9 . . . . . has turned ***a*** me.
Ps 78:19 . . . . even spoke ***a*** God himself,
Matt 6:12. . . those who sin ***a*** us.
Matt 10:35. . to set a man ***a*** his father,
Matt 12:30. . actually working ***a*** me.
Acts 26:14 . . for you to fight ***a*** my will.
Rom 11:30. . Gentiles were rebels ***a*** God,
1 Cor 8:12 . . you are sinning ***a*** Christ.
1 Pet 5:9. . . . Stand firm ***a*** him,

AGED (adj)
showing the effects or characteristics of increasing age
Job 12:12 . . . Wisdom belongs to the ***a,***
Prov 17:6. . . crowning glory of the ***a;***

AGES (n)
long period of time; a generation; a measure of history, geology, or culture
Prov 8:23. . . I was appointed in ***a*** past,
Jer 23:40. . . . infamous throughout the ***a.***
Eph 2:7 . . . . in all future ***a*** as examples

AGGRAVATE (v)
to cause anger by persistent goading; to produce inflammation in
Col 3:21 . . . . do not ***a*** your children,

AGONY (n)
extreme pain and suffering
Ps 6:2 . . . . . . Lord, for my bones are in ***a.***
Luke 22:44. . he was in such ***a*** of spirit that

AGREE, AGREED, AGREEING (v)
to admit, concede
Matt 18:19 . . If two of you ***a*** here on
Luke 7:29. . . ***a-d*** that God's way was right,
Rom 7:16. . . that I ***a*** that the law is good.
Phil 2:2 . . . . make me truly happy by ***a-ing***

AID (v)
to give assistance
Acts 24:17 . . with money to ***a*** my people

AIM (v)
to direct to or toward a specified object or goal
Rom 14:19. . ***a*** for harmony in the church

AIR (n)
empty space, nothingness; atmosphere
1 Thes 4:17 . meet the Lord in the ***a.***

ALABASTER (adj)
a compact, fine-textured, usually white and translucent plaster often carved into vases and ornaments
Matt 26:7. . . with a beautiful ***a*** jar
Mark 14:3 . . with a beautiful ***a*** jar
Luke 7:37. . . she brought a beautiful ***a*** jar

ALARM (n)
a signal that warns or alerts
Num 10:9 . . sound the ***a*** with the trumpets.
2 Cor 7:11 . . such indignation, such ***a,***

ALCOHOL (n)
drink (as wine or beer) containing ethanol
Prov 20:1. . . ***a*** leads to brawls.
Isa 5:22. . . . . boast about all the ***a*** they

ALCOHOLIC (adj)
containing alcohol
Num 6:3 . . . give up wine and other ***a***

ALERT (adj)
quick to perceive and act
Isa 21:7. . . . . the watchman be fully ***a.***
Mark 13:33 . be on guard! Stay ***a!***
1 Pet 5:8. . . . Stay ***a!*** Watch out for

ALIEN (KJV)
Exod 18:3 . . a ***foreigner*** in a foreign
Job 19:15 . . . I am like a ***foreigner*** to them
Eph 2:12 . . . were ***excluded from citizenship***

ALIENATED (KJV)
Ezek 48:14. . traded or ***used by others***
Eph 4:18 . . . ***wander far from*** the life God
Col 1:21 . . . . were once ***far away from God***

ALIVE (adj)
animate, having life; active; aware
Gen 45:7 . . . keep you and your families ***a***
Ps 41:2. . . . . them and keeps them ***a.***
Luke 24:23. . Jesus is ***a!***
Acts 1:3 . . . . ways that he was actually ***a.***
Rom 6:11. . . the power of sin and ***a*** to God
Rev 2:8. . . . . who was dead but is now ***a:***

ALLELUIA (KJV)
Rev 19:1. . . . shouting, "***Praise the Lord!***
Rev 19:3. . . . rang out: "***Praise the Lord!***
Rev 19:4. . . . "Amen! ***Praise the Lord!***"
Rev 19:6. . . . "***Praise the Lord!*** For the Lord

ALLOTMENT, ALLOTMENTS (n)
share, portion, provision
Num 18:21 . Instead of an ***a*** of land, I will
Josh 13:32 . . These are the ***a-s*** Moses had
Jer 13:25. . . . your ***a,*** the portion I have assigned

ALLOWANCE (n)
the act of admitting or conceding; permission
Eph 4:2 . . . . ***a*** for each other's faults

ALLOW, ALLOWED (v)
to admit or concede; to permit
1 Cor 6:12 . . though "I am ***a-ed*** to
1 Cor 10:23 . I am ***a-ed*** to do anything
2 Cor 12:4 . . no human is ***a-ed*** to tell.

ALMIGHTY (n)
having absolute power over all; God
see also (HEAVEN'S) ARMIES
Gen 17:1 . . . I am El-Shaddai—'God ***A.***'
Exod 6:3 . . . as El-Shaddai—'God ***A***'—
Ruth 1:20. . . ***A*** has made life very bitter
Job 6:14 . . . . without any fear of the ***A.***
Job 33:4 . . . . breath of the ***A*** gives me life.
Ps 91:1 . . . . . rest in the shadow of the ***A.***
Rev 4:8. . . . . the ***A***—the one who always was,
Rev 15:3. . . . O Lord God, the ***A.***
Rev 19:6. . . . our God, the ***A,*** reigns.

ALONE (adj)
isolated or solitary; solely or exclusively; without aid or support
John 5:44 . . . the one who ***a*** is God.

ALONGSIDE (adv)
at the side; in parallel position, close by
Gal 3:19 . . . . It was given ***a*** the promise

ALPHA (n)
first letter of Greek alphabet; figurative of beginning or first one
Rev 1:8. . . . . I am the *A* and the Omega—
Rev 21:6. . . . I am the *A* and the Omega—
Rev 22:13. . . I am the *A* and the Omega,

ALTAR, ALTARS (n)
high places of worship on which sacrifices are offered or incense is burned
Gen 8:20 . . . Noah built an ***a*** to the LORD,
Gen 12:7 . . . Abram built an ***a*** there
Gen 22:9 . . . Abraham built an ***a*** and
Gen 26:25 . . Isaac built an ***a*** there
Exod 30:1 . . make another ***a*** of acacia
Exod 37:25 . incense ***a*** of acacia wood.
Josh 8:30 . . . Joshua built an ***a*** to the LORD,
Josh 22:10 . . a large and imposing ***a.***
1 Sam 7:17. . Samuel built an ***a*** to the
2 Chr 4:1 . . . made a bronze ***a*** 30 feet long,
2 Chr 4:19 . . Temple of God: the gold ***a;***
2 Chr 32:12 . only at the ***a*** at the Temple
2 Chr 33:16 . restored the ***a*** of the LORD
Ezra 3:2 . . . . rebuilding the ***a*** of the God
Isa 6:6. . . . . . coal he had taken from the ***a***
Matt 5:23 . . . presenting a sacrifice at the ***a***
Acts 17:23 . . your ***a-s*** had this inscription
Heb 13:10 . . an ***a*** from which the priests
Rev 6:9. . . . . I saw under the ***a*** the souls

ALTERED (v)
to make change or become different; to modify
John 10:35 . . the Scriptures cannot be ***a.***

ALWAYS (adv)
at all times; forever, perpetually
1 Kgs 2:4 . . . will ***a*** sit on the throne
Ps 16:8 . . . . . the LORD is ***a*** with me.
Ps 52:8 . . . . . will ***a*** trust in God's unfailing
Ps 102:27 . . . But you are ***a*** the same;
Ps 106:3 . . . . and ***a*** do what is right.
Prov 23:7. . . They are ***a*** thinking about
Isa 16:5. . . . . He will ***a*** do what is just
Matt 28:20. . I am with you ***a,*** even to
Mark 14:7 . . You will ***a*** have the poor
John 12:8 . . . you will not ***a*** have me.
1 Pet 3:15. . . ***a*** be ready to explain it.

AMAZED (v)
to fill with wonder, astound
Matt 7:28 . . . were ***a*** at his teaching
Mark 7:37 . . They were completely ***a*** and
Mark 10:24 . This ***a*** them. But Jesus
Luke 2:33. . . Jesus' parents were ***a*** at
Acts 2:7 . . . . They were completely ***a.***

AMAZING (adj)
causing amazement, great wonder, or surprise
1 Chr 16:24 . about the ***a*** things he does.
Ps 96:3 . . . . . about the ***a*** things he does.
Ps 126:2 . . . . What ***a*** things the LORD has

AMBASSADOR, AMBASSADORS (n)
an authorized representative or messenger
2 Cor 5:20 . . So we are Christ's ***a-s;***
Eph 6:20 . . . this message as God's ***a.***

AMBITION (n)
aspiration to achieve a particular goal, good or bad
Gal 5:20. . . . anger, selfish ***a,*** dissension,
Phil 1:17 . . . They preach with selfish ***a,***
Jas 3:14. . . . . there is selfish ***a*** in your heart,

ANCESTOR, ANCESTORS (n)
one from whom a person is descended; forefather
Exod 3:15 . . God of your ***a-s***—the God of
Deut 19:14. . markers your ***a-s*** set up
Isa 9:7. . . . . . throne of his ***a*** David for all
Isa 43:27. . . . your first ***a*** sinned against me;
Mark 11:10 . Kingdom of our ***a*** David!
Luke 1:32. . . the throne of his ***a*** David.
Rom 9:5 . . . . Abraham, Isaac, and Jacob are their ***a-s,***
Gal 1:14 . . . . for the traditions of my ***a-s.***
Heb 1:1 . . . . our ***a-s*** through the prophets.

ANCHOR (n)
a reliable or principal support; mainstay
Heb 6:19 . . . trustworthy ***a*** for our souls.

ANCIENT (adj)
having the qualities of age or long existence; old
Dan 7:22 . . . until the *A* One—the Most High—
Mark 7:3 . . . required by their ***a*** traditions.

ANDREW
One of the 12 disciples; listed second (Matt 10:2; Luke 6:14) and fourth (Mark 3:18; 13:3; Acts 1:13); came from Bethsaida (John 1:44); brother of Simon Peter (Matt 4:18); former fisherman

(Mark 1:16); follower of John the Baptist who introduced Peter to Jesus (John 1:40-44).

ANGEL, ANGELS (n)
human or superhuman agent or messenger of God
Exod 23:20 . I am sending an ***a***
2 Sam 24:16. and said to the death ***a,***
Ps 91:11 . . . . will order his ***a-s*** to protect
Matt 4:6. . . . will order his ***a-s*** to protect
Matt 28:2. . . an ***a*** of the Lord came down
Luke 1:26. . . God sent the ***a*** Gabriel
Luke 2:9. . . . an ***a*** of the Lord appeared
Luke 20:36. . they will be like ***a-s.***
Acts 12:7 . . . The ***a*** struck him on the side
1 Cor 6:3 . . . we will judge ***a-s?***
2 Cor 11:14 . disguises himself as an ***a***
Gal 1:8. . . . . or even an ***a*** from heaven,
Heb 1:6 . . . . all of God's ***a-s*** worship him.
Heb 2:7 . . . . a little lower than the ***a-s***
Heb 13:2 . . . entertained ***a-s*** without
1 Pet 1:12. . . the ***a-s*** are eagerly watching
2 Pet 2:4. . . . even the ***a-s*** who sinned.
Jude 1:6 . . . . I remind you of the ***a-s***

ANGELIC (adj)
having or displaying characteristics of an angel
2 Sam 22:11. on a mighty ***a*** being, he flew,
Ps 18:10 . . . . on a mighty ***a*** being, he flew,

ANGER (n)
a strong feeling of displeasure
Exod 34:6 . . slow to ***a*** and filled with
Num 14:18 . slow to ***a*** and filled with
Deut 9:19. . . furious ***a*** of the LORD,
Deut 29:28. . In great ***a*** and fury
2 Kgs 22:13 . LORD's great ***a*** is burning
Ps 30:5 . . . . . his ***a*** lasts only a moment,
Ps 78:38 . . . . Many times he held back his ***a***
Rom 1:18. . . God shows his ***a*** from heaven
Rom 2:5. . . . a day of ***a*** is coming,
Eph 4:26 . . . by letting ***a*** control you.
1 Thes 5:9 . . pour out his ***a*** on us.
Jas 1:20. . . . . Human ***a*** does not produce
Rev 14:10. . . the wine of God's ***a.***

ANGRY (adj)
feeling or showing anger; wrathful
Exod 32:11 . so ***a*** with your own people
Neh 9:17 . . . merciful, slow to become ***a,***
Ps 103:8 . . . . merciful, slow to get ***a***
Prov 22:24. . Don't befriend ***a*** people
Jonah 4:2. . . slow to get ***a*** and filled
Matt 5:22. . . if you are even ***a*** with
Mark 10:14 . he was ***a*** with his disciples.
John 3:36. . . under God's ***a*** judgment.

Acts 4:25 . . . Why were the nations so ***a?***
Jas 1:19. . . . . to speak, and slow to get ***a.***

ANGUISH (n)
extreme pain, distress, or anxiety
Isa 53:11. . . . by his ***a,*** he will be satisfied.
Zeph 1:15 . . of terrible distress and ***a,***
Matt 24:21. . greater ***a*** than at any time
Luke 16:24. . I am in ***a*** in these flames.
Rev 16:10. . . ground their teeth in ***a,***

ANIMAL, ANIMALS (n)
any of a kingdom of living things that typically differ from plants
Gen 1:24 . . . livestock, small ***a-s*** that scurry
Gen 6:19 . . . a pair of every kind of ***a***—
Gen 7:8 . . . . all the various kinds of ***a-s***—
Deut 14:4. . . These are the ***a-s*** you may eat:
1 Kgs 4:33 . . ***a-s,*** birds, small creatures,
Job 12:7 . . . . ask the ***a-s,*** and they will teach
Ps 73:22 . . . . like a senseless ***a*** to you.
Isa 43:20. . . . The wild ***a-s*** in the fields

ANNIHILATED (v)
to cause to cease to exist; to kill
Esth 3:13 . . . and ***a*** on a single day.

ANNOUNCE, ANNOUNCED, ANNOUNCING (v)
to proclaim; to tell news
Jer 51:10. . . . let us ***a*** in Jerusalem
Matt 9:35. . . and ***a-ing*** the Good News
Mark 15:26 . ***a-ed*** the charge against him.
Acts 26:23 . . ***a*** God's light to Jews and
Rev 10:7. . . . as he ***a-d*** it to his servants the prophets.

ANNUAL (adj)
occurring or happening every year or once a year
Exod 30:10 . a regular, ***a*** event
Judg 21:19. . the ***a*** festival of the LORD
1 Sam 1:21. . their ***a*** trip to offer a sacrifice
1 Sam 20:6. . for an ***a*** family sacrifice.
2 Chr 8:13 . . the three ***a*** festivals—

ANOINT, ANOINTED, ANOINTING (v)
to smear or rub with oil; used for healing or consecration to sacred duty; used for grooming or burial; figurative for divine appointment
see also ANOINTED ONE
Exod 30:26 . oil to ***a*** the Tabernacle,
Exod 30:30 . ***A*** Aaron and his sons
Lev 8:12. . . . ***a-ing*** him and making him holy
1 Sam 15:1. . told me to ***a*** you as king

2 Sam 2:4 . . . David and ***a-ed*** him king over
2 Sam 23:1 . . man ***a-ed*** by the God of Jacob,
Ps 23:5 . . . . . honor me by ***a-ing*** my head
Ps 92:10 . . . . You have ***a-ed*** me with
Isa 61:1 . . . . . the LORD has ***a-ed*** me
Dan 9:24 . . . and to ***a*** the Most Holy Place.
Acts 10:38 . . you know that God ***a-ed*** Jesus
Heb 1:9 . . . . your God has ***a-ed*** you,
Jas 5:14 . . . . . over you, ***a-ing*** you with oil

ANOINTED ONE (n)
one chosen by divine election
see also MESSIAH
1 Sam 2:10 . . the strength of his ***a.***"
1 Sam 26:9 . . attacking the LORD's ***a?***
Ps 132:17 . . . my ***a*** will be a light for
Dan 9:25 . . . a ruler—the ***A***—comes.
Isa 45:1 . . . . . the LORD says to Cyrus, his ***a,***

ANSWER, ANSWERED (v)
to reply to a question; to solve a problem
Ps 6:9 . . . . . . the LORD will ***a*** my prayer.
Ps 34:4 . . . . . LORD, and he ***a-ed*** me.
Jonah 2:2 . . . trouble, and he ***a-ed*** me.

ANTICHRIST, ANTICHRISTS (n)
opponent of Christ; the personification of evil
1 Jn 2:18 . . . . heard that the ***A*** is coming,
1 Jn 2:18 . . . . many such ***a-s*** have appeared.
1 Jn 4:3 . . . . . has the spirit of the ***A,***
2 Jn 1:7 . . . . . deceiver and an ***a.***

ANTS (n)
any of a family of colonial hymenopterous insects
Prov 6:6 . . . . from the ***a,*** you lazybones.

ANXIETY, CARE(S) (KJV)
Ps 139:23 . . . know my ***anxious thoughts***
Phil 4:6 . . . . Don't ***worry*** about anything
1 Pet 5:7 . . . . your ***worries and cares*** to God,

APOSTLE, APOSTLES (n)
messengers or "sent ones"; generally but not exclusively applied to the original twelve followers of Christ and to Paul
Mark 3:14 . . and called them his ***a-s.***
Acts 1:26 . . . selected to become an ***a***
Acts 5:2 . . . . part of the money to the ***a-s,***
Acts 8:18 . . . ***a-s*** laid their hands on
Rom 11:13 . . the ***a*** to the Gentiles.
1 Cor 9:1 . . . Am I not an ***a?*** Haven't I seen
1 Cor 9:2 . . . proof that I am the Lord's ***a.***
1 Cor 12:28 . first are ***a-s,*** second are,
2 Cor 12:12 . gave you proof that I am an ***a.***
Eph 2:20 . . . on the foundation of the ***a-s***
Eph 4:11 . . . the ***a-s,*** the prophets,
2 Tim 1:11 . . to be a preacher, an ***a,***
Rev 21:14 . . . of the twelve ***a-s*** of the Lamb.

APPEAR, APPEARED, APPEARING, APPEARS (v)
to come out of hiding and show up in public view; to make one's presence known
Gen 1:9 . . . . so dry ground may ***a.***
Num 14:10 . presence of the LORD ***a-ed***
Deut 33:16 . . ***a-ed*** in the burning bush.
Mal 3:2 . . . . . and face him when he ***a-s?***
Matt 1:20 . . . angel of the Lord ***a-ed*** to him
Matt 24:30 . . will ***a*** in the heavens,
Luke 2:9 . . . . angel of the Lord ***a-ed*** among
Luke 16:15 . . You like to ***a*** righteous
Phil 2:7 . . . . When he ***a-ed*** in human form,
2 Thes 1:7 . . the Lord Jesus ***a-s*** from
2 Tim 1:10 . . by the ***a-ing*** of Christ Jesus,
2 Tim 4:1 . . . ***a-s*** to set up his Kingdom:
Heb 9:24 . . . ***a*** now before God on our
Heb 9:26 . . . ***a-ed*** at the end of the age
1 Pet 5:4 . . . . when the Great Shepherd ***a-s,***
1 Jn 3:2 . . . . . will be like when Christ ***a-s.***

APPEARANCE (n)
external show; the outward or visible aspect
Isa 53:2 . . . . . or majestic about his ***a,***

APPETITE (n)
the desire to eat; an inherent craving
Prov 13:2 . . . have an ***a*** for violence.
Prov 16:26 . . good for workers to have an ***a;***
Phil 3:19 . . . Their god is their ***a,***

APPLES (n)
the fleshy, usually rounded, red, yellow, or green edible fruit of a tree
Prov 25:11 . . golden ***a*** in a silver basket.

APPLY (v)
to bring into action; to put to use especially for some practical purpose
Prov 22:17 . . ***a*** your heart to my instruction.

APPOINT, APPOINTED, APPOINTING (v)
to ordain or designate; to name officially
Deut 1:15 . . . ***a-ed*** them to serve as judges
2 Sam 7:11 . . the time I ***a-ed*** judges to rule
Prov 8:23 . . . I was ***a-ed*** in ages past,
John 15:16 . . I chose you. I ***a-ed*** you
Rom 11:13 . . God has ***a-ed*** me as the
1 Tim 5:22 . . about ***a-ing*** a church leader.
Titus 1:5 . . . . work there and ***a*** elders

APPOINTED (adj)
marked by being fixed or set officially
Exod 23:15 . annually at the ***a*** time
Lev 23:2. . . . the LORD's ***a*** festivals,
Dan 11:27 . . come at the ***a*** time.
Matt 8:29. . . before God's ***a*** time?"
Acts 3:20 . . . Jesus, your ***a*** Messiah.

APPRECIATE (v)
to value or admire highly
Prov 28:23. . people ***a*** honest criticism

APPRECIATION (n)
an expression of admiration, approval, or gratitude
1 Cor 16:18 . must show your ***a*** to all

APPROACH (v)
to draw closer to; to come very near to
1 Tim 6:16. . no human can ***a*** him.

APPROPRIATE (adj)
especially suitable or compatible; fitting
Deut 25:2. . . lashes ***a*** to the crime.
1 Tim 2:9. . . wear decent and ***a*** clothing

APPROVAL (n)
an act or instance of approving
Ps 90:17 . . . . LORD our God show us his ***a***
John 6:27. . . the seal of his ***a.***
Rom 14:4. . . stand and receive his ***a.***
1 Cor 11:19 . you who have God's ***a***
2 Tim 2:15. . and receive his ***a.***
Heb 11:4 . . . God showed his ***a*** of his gifts.

APPROVE, APPROVED, APPROVES (v)
to have or express a favorable opinion of; to attest
Gen 7:2 . . . . animal I have ***a-ed*** for eating
Prov 12:2. . . LORD ***a-s*** of those who
Rom 14:18. . and others will ***a*** of you,
Rom 16:10. . a good man whom Christ ***a-s.***
1 Thes 2:4 . . speak as messengers ***a-ed***

ARARAT (n)
a mountain on the far east border of modern Turkey; the mountain Noah's ark rested on after the Flood
Gen 8:4 . . . . to rest on the mountains of ***A.***

ARCHANGEL, ARCHANGELS (n)
a leader and chief angel; biblically designated as Michael
Dan 10:13 . . one of the ***a-s,*** came to help
Dan 12:1 . . . At that time Michael, the ***a***
1 Thes 4:16 . with the voice of the ***a,***

ARCHER (n)
one who uses a bow and arrow
Prov 26:10. . an ***a*** who shoots at random.

ARCHITECT (n)
a person who designs buildings and advises in their construction; a person who designs and guides a plan or undertaking
Prov 8:30. . . I was the ***a*** at his side.

ARGUE, ARGUING (v)
to contend or disagree in words; to dispute
Job 13:8 . . . . Will you ***a*** God's case
Job 40:2 . . . . to ***a*** with the Almighty?
Prov 25:9. . . ***a-ing*** with your neighbor,
Isa 45:9. . . . . those who ***a*** with their Creator.
Rom 14:1. . . and don't ***a*** with them
1 Cor 11:16 . anyone wants to ***a***

ARGUMENT, ARGUMENTS (n)
the act or process of arguing; discourse intended to persuade
Job 32:3 . . . . to answer Job's ***a-s.***
Job 36:3 . . . . I will present profound ***a-s***
Prov 26:17. . in someone else's ***a***
1 Tim 6:4. . . This stirs up ***a-s***
2 Tim 2:14. . Such ***a-s*** are useless,

ARK (n)
commonly, a portable wooden chest, box, or coffer; specifically, of Noah, a ship the size of a light cruiser; of the Covenant, a sacred housing for the Law of Moses
Exod 25:21 . inside the ***A*** the stone
Deut 10:5. . . tablets in the ***A*** of the
1 Kgs 8:9 . . . Nothing was in the ***A*** except
1 Chr 13:9 . . his hand to steady the ***A.***
Rev 11:19. . . the ***A*** of his covenant

ARM, ARMS (n)
upper limb of the body; extension or projection of; lineage; figurative of power or might
Num 11:23 . Has my ***a*** lost its power?
Deut 4:34. . . a powerful ***a,*** and terrifying
Deut 7:19. . . strong hand and powerful ***a***
Deut 33:27. . everlasting ***a-s*** are under
Ps 44:3 . . . . . it was not their own strong ***a***
Ps 98:1 . . . . . his holy ***a*** has shown
Isa 40:11. . . . carry the lambs in his ***a-s,***
Isa 65:2. . . . . opened my ***a-s*** to a rebellious
Jer 27:5. . . . . powerful ***a*** I made the earth
Mark 10:16 . took the children in his ***a-s***
1 Pet 4:1. . . . you must ***a*** yourselves with

ARMAGEDDON (n)
the gathering place for the final battle between God's forces and Satan's forces associated with Christ's second coming
Rev 16:16. . . with the Hebrew name ***A.***

ARMOR (n)
weapons of war or self-defense; figurative of spiritual resources
Ps 91:4 . . . . . are your ***a*** and protection.
Isa 59:17. . . . righteousness as his body ***a***
Jer 46:4. . . . . and prepare your ***a.***
Rom 13:12. . put on the shining ***a***
Eph 6:11 . . . Put on all of God's ***a***
Eph 6:13 . . . put on every piece of God's ***a***
1 Thes 5:8 . . protected by the ***a*** of faith

ARMY, ARMIES (n)
large band of men organized and armed for war; any large multitude devoted to a cause
Ps 33:16 . . . . best-equipped ***a*** cannot save
Ps 84:12 . . . . LORD of Heaven's ***A-ies,***
Isa 6:3. . . . . . LORD of Heaven's ***A-ies!***
Isa 45:13. . . . LORD of Heaven's ***A-ies,***
Isa 51:15. . . . the LORD of Heaven's ***A-ies.***
Joel 2:2. . . . . great and mighty ***a*** appears.
Joel 2:5. . . . . like a mighty ***a*** moving into
Joel 2:11. . . . This is his mighty ***a,***
Hag 1:5 . . . . LORD of Heaven's ***A-ies*** says:
Zech 8:6. . . . LORD of Heaven's ***A-ies*** says:
Rev 19:14. . . The ***a-ies*** of heaven,
Rev 19:19. . . the horse and his ***a.***

AROMA (n)
a distinctive, pervasive, and usually pleasant or savory smell; a distinctive quality or atmosphere
Gen 8:21 . . . LORD was pleased with the ***a***
Exod 29:18 . it is a pleasing ***a,***
Lev 3:16. . . . a special gift of food, a pleasing ***a***
Eph 5:2 . . . . a pleasing ***a*** to God.

ARREST, ARRESTED, ARRESTING (v)
to take or keep in custody by authority of law
Dan 6:16 . . . orders for Daniel to be ***a-ed***
Matt 10:19. . When you are ***a-ed,*** don't
Mark 14:44 . ***a*** when I greet him with a kiss.
Mark 14:49 . Why didn't you ***a*** me in the Temple?
Luke 20:20. . so he would ***a*** Jesus.
Acts 22:4 . . . to death, ***a-ing*** both men

ARROGANCE (n)
a feeling or an impression of superiority manifested in an overbearing manner or presumptuous claims
1 Sam 2:3. . . Don't speak with such ***a!***
Prov 8:13. . . I hate pride and ***a,***
Isa 16:6. . . . . its pride and ***a*** and rage.
2 Cor 12:20 . slander, gossip, ***a,***

ARROGANT (adj)
exaggerating or disposed to exaggerate one's own worth or importance in an overbearing manner
Ps 31:23 . . . . harshly punishes the ***a.***
Ps 119:78 . . . upon the ***a*** people who lied
1 Tim 6:4 . . . is ***a*** and lacks understanding.
Titus 1:7. . . . not be ***a*** or quick-tempered;

ARROW, ARROWS (n)
a missile weapon shot from a bow and usually having a slender shaft, a pointed head, and feathers at the butt
Ps 64:3 . . . . . their bitter words like ***a-s.***
Ps 64:7 . . . . . with his ***a-s,*** suddenly striking
Ps 91:5 . . . . . the ***a*** that flies in the day.
Ps 127:4 . . . . like ***a-s*** in a warrior's hands.
Eph 6:16 . . . the fiery ***a-s*** of the devil.

ASCEND, ASCENDED (v)
to go or move up
Ps 68:18 . . . . When you ***a-ed*** to the heights,
Isa 14:13. . . . I will ***a*** to heaven
John 6:62 . . . Son of Man ***a*** to heaven again?
John 20:17 . . I haven't yet ***a-ed*** to the Father.
Acts 2:34 . . . never ***a-ed*** into heaven,
Eph 4:8 . . . . When he ***a-ed*** to the heights,

ASHAMED (adj)
feeling shame, guilt, or disgrace
Ps 69:6 . . . . . be ***a*** because of me,
Jer 31:19. . . . I was thoroughly ***a*** of all I did
Jer 48:13. . . . were ***a*** of their gold calf
Mark 8:38 . . If anyone is ***a*** of me
Luke 9:26. . . If anyone is ***a*** of me
Rom 1:16. . . I am not ***a*** of this Good News
2 Tim 1:8 . . . So never be ***a*** to tell others
2 Tim 2:15 . . who does not need to be ***a***

ASHES (n)
burnt residue or remains of the dead, or anything ruined; denotes grief, repentance, or humiliation
Job 42:6 . . . . sit in dust and ***a***
Matt 11:21 . . throwing ***a*** on their heads

ASK, ASKED, ASKING, ASKS (v)
to seek information; to call on for an answer; to make a request
1 Sam 10:22. So they ***a-ed*** the LORD,
Prov 18:6 . . . they are ***a-ing*** for a beating.
Isa 8:19. . . . . Let's ***a*** the mediums
Matt 7:7 . . . . ***a-ing,*** and you will receive
Luke 6:30. . . Give to anyone who ***a-s;***
Luke 11:9. . . will receive what you ***a*** for.
John 17:15 . . I'm not ***a-ing*** you to take them
Eph 3:20 . . . more than we might ***a*** or
Phlm 1:21 . . do what I ***a*** and even more!
1 Jn 5:14. . . . whenever we ***a*** for anything

ASLEEP (adj)
state of bodily rest; figurative for physical death or spiritual dullness
see also DIE, SLEEP
Judg 4:21 . . . Sisera fell ***a*** from exhaustion,
1 Kgs 18:27 . away on a trip, or is ***a*** and
Matt 9:24 . . . isn't dead; she's only ***a."***
Matt 26:40 . . disciples and found them ***a.***
John 11:11 . . Lazarus has fallen ***a,*** but
1 Thes 5:6 . . be on your guard, not ***a*** like

ASSEMBLY (n)
a company of persons gathered for deliberation and legislation, worship, or entertainment
Ps 35:18 . . . . in front of the great ***a.***
Ps 149:1 . . . . praises in the ***a*** of the faithful.

ASSIGN, ASSIGNED (v)
to transfer (property) to another, especially in trust or for the benefit of creditors; to appoint to a duty or task
Gen 47:11 . . So Joseph ***a-ed*** the best land
Deut 32:8. . . the Most High ***a-ed*** lands
Josh 13:14 . . Moses did not ***a*** any allotment

ASSOCIATE (v)
to join as a partner, friend, or companion; to keep company with
Prov 13:20. . ***a*** with fools and get in
Prov 22:24. . or ***a*** with hot-tempered
Prov 24:21. . Don't ***a*** with rebels,
Acts 10:28 . . like this or to ***a*** with you.
1 Cor 5:9 . . . not to ***a*** with people who
1 Cor 5:11 . . are not to ***a*** with anyone

ASSURANCE (n)
the act or action of giving confidence to or making sure or certain
Col 1:27 . . . . This gives you ***a*** of sharing
1 Thes 1:5 . . full ***a*** that what we said

ASSURE (v)
to make certain or reassure
Mark 10:29 . I ***a*** you that everyone who has
Luke 23:43. . I ***a*** you, today you will be with
John 3:5 . . . . I ***a*** you, no one can enter
John 5:25 . . . I ***a*** you that the time is coming,

ASTRAY (adv)
off the right path or route; in error, away from what is desirable or proper
Prov 20:1 . . . Those led ***a*** by drink
Isa 47:10. . . . 'knowledge' have led you ***a,***
Jer 50:6. . . . . shepherds have led them ***a***
1 Jn 2:26. . . . who want to lead you ***a.***

ASTROLOGERS (n)
one who studies the stars and planets to foresee or foretell future events by their positions and aspects
Isa 47:13. . . . all your ***a,*** those stargazers
Dan 2:2 . . . . enchanters, sorcerers, and ***a,***

ATE (v)
to partake of food
see also EAT
Gen 3:6 . . . . some of the fruit and ***a*** it.
Ezek 3:3. . . . And when I ***a*** it, it tasted as
Matt 15:37. . ***a*** as much as they wanted.
Rev 10:10. . . I ***a*** it! It was sweet

ATHLETE, ATHLETES (n)
a person who is trained or skilled in exercises, sports, or games requiring physical strength, agility, or stamina
Ps 19:5 . . . . . like a great ***a*** eager to run
1 Cor 9:25 . . All ***a-s*** are disciplined
1 Cor 9:27 . . body like an ***a,*** training it
2 Tim 2:5 . . . ***a-s*** cannot win the prize unless

ATONE, ATONES (v)
to supply satisfaction for; to make amends; to reconcile
see also FORGIVE
Dan 9:24 . . . their sin, to ***a*** for their guilt,
1 Jn 2:2. . . . . sacrifice that ***a-s*** for our sins—

ATONEMENT (n)
reconciliation; reparation for an offense or injury; cleansing
see also FORGIVENESS
Exod 25:17 . cover—the place of ***a***—
Lev 23:27. . . Day of ***A*** on the tenth day
2 Chr 29:24 . to make ***a*** for the sins
Prov 16:6 . . . faithfulness make ***a*** for sin.

ATTACK, ATTACKED (v)
to set upon or work against forcefully; to assail with unfriendly or bitter words
1 Sam 17:48. Goliath moved closer to ***a,***
Joel 3:19. . . . they ***a-ed*** the people of Judah
Zech 10:2. . . ***a-ed*** because they have no
2 Tim 4:18 . . deliver me from every evil ***a***

ATTENTION (n)
the act or state of applying the mind to an object or thought
Exod 23:13 . Pay close ***a*** to all my
Prov 4:20. . . pay ***a*** to what I say.
Prov 5:1. . . . My son, pay ***a*** to my wisdom;
Acts 18:17 . . Gallio paid no ***a.***
1 Tim 4:15 . . Give your complete ***a*** to

ATTITUDE, ATTITUDES (n)
a mental position with regard to a fact or state; a feeling or emotion toward a fact or state
Eph 4:23 . . . your thoughts and ***a-s.***
Phil 2:5 . . . . have the same ***a*** that Christ
1 Pet 3:8. . . . keep a humble ***a.***
1 Pet 4:1. . . . with the same ***a*** he had,

ATTRACT, ATTRACTED (v)
to pull to or draw toward oneself or itself; to draw by appeal to natural or excited interest, emotion, or aesthetic sense
Isa 53:2. . . . . nothing to ***a*** us to him.
Heb 13:9 . . . ***a-ed*** by strange, new ideas.

ATTRACTIVE (adj)
arousing interest or pleasure; having the power to attract
Prov 19:22. . Loyalty makes a person ***a.***
Col 4:6 . . . . . conversation be gracious and ***a***
1 Tim 2:10 . . make themselves ***a*** by the
Titus 2:10. . . God our Savior ***a*** in every

AUTHORITY, AUTHORITIES (n)
the right to govern; the freedom or ability to act; one entrusted with the right to govern
Matt 28:18 . . been given all ***a*** in heaven
Luke 10:19. . have given you ***a*** over
John 5:22 . . . absolute ***a*** to judge,
Acts 1:7 . . . . ***a*** to set those dates and times,
Rom 13:1 . . . submit to governing ***a-ies.***
Rom 13:1 . . . For all ***a*** comes from God,
Rom 13:2. . . anyone who rebels against ***a***
Rom 13:3. . . without fear of the ***a-ies?***
1 Cor 4:3 . . . by any human ***a.***
1 Cor 15:24 . ruler and ***a*** and power.
Eph 1:22 . . . things under the ***a*** of Christ
Eph 3:10 . . . all the unseen rulers and ***a-ies***
Eph 6:12 . . . against evil rulers and ***a-ies***
Col 2:10 . . . . every ruler and ***a.***
Col 2:15 . . . . the spiritual rulers and ***a-ies.***
1 Tim 2:2 . . . all who are in ***a*** so that
Titus 2:15. . . You have the ***a*** to correct
1 Pet 2:18. . . accept the ***a*** of your masters
1 Pet 3:1. . . . accept the ***a*** of your husbands.
1 Pet 3:22. . . the angels and ***a-ies*** and
1 Pet 5:5. . . . accept the ***a*** of the elders.
Jude 1:6 . . . . the limits of ***a*** God gave them

AVENGE, AVENGES (v)
to take revenge or punish
Deut 32:43. . ***a*** the blood of his servants;
1 Thes 4:6 . . the Lord ***a-s*** all such sins,
Rev 6:10. . . . ***a*** our blood for what they

AVENGER (n)
one who seeks revenge or to punish an evildoer
Num 35:27 . ***a*** finds him outside the city

AVOID, AVOIDING (v)
to keep away from; to depart or withdraw from
Prov 4:24. . . ***A*** all perverse talk;
Prov 14:16. . are cautious and ***a*** danger;
Prov 16:6. . . By fearing the LORD, people ***a***
Prov 20:3. . . ***A-ing*** a fight is a mark
Eccl 7:18 . . . fears God will ***a*** both
Rom 2:3. . . . think you can ***a*** God's

AWAKE (v)
to cease sleeping; to become aroused or active again
see also WAKE
Ps 17:15 . . . . When I ***a,*** I will see
Eph 5:14 . . . "***A,*** O sleeper, rise up

AWARENESS (n)
the state of realization or perception
Hab 2:14 . . . filled with an ***a*** of the glory

AWAY (adv)
in another direction; by a long distance or interval
1 Thes 4:3 . . stay ***a*** from all sexual sin.
2 Tim 3:5 . . . Stay ***a*** from people like that!
1 Pet 2:11. . . keep ***a*** from worldly desires

AWE (n)
an emotion variously combining dread, respect, and wonder that is inspired by authority or the sacred
see also FEAR, REVERENCE
1 Kgs 3:28 . . people were in ***a*** of the king,
Ps 119:120 . . I stand in ***a*** of your
Luke 5:26. . . with great wonder and ***a,***
Acts 2:43 . . . sense of ***a*** came over them
Heb 12:28 . . holy fear and ***a.***

AWESOME (adj)
characterized by reverential fear; expressive of or inspiring awe
see also MARVELOUS, WONDERFUL
Exod 34:10 . the ***a*** power I will display
Deut 7:21. . . a great and ***a*** God.
2 Sam 7:23. . You performed ***a*** miracles
Neh 1:5 . . . . the great and ***a*** God
Job 10:16 . . . display your ***a*** power
Ps 47:2. . . . . Most High is ***a.***
Ps 65:5 . . . . . answer our prayers with ***a***
Ps 106:22 . . . such ***a*** deeds at the Red Sea.
Ps 131:1 . . . . too ***a*** for me to grasp.
Dan 9:4 . . . . a great and ***a*** God!

AX (n)
a cutting tool that is used especially for felling trees and chopping and splitting wood
2 Kgs 6:6 . . . Then the ***a*** head floated
Prov 25:18. . hitting them with an ***a,***

BAAL (n)
a fertility and nature god of the Canaanites and Phoenicians
1 Kgs 18:25 . said to the prophets of ***B,***
1 Kgs 19:18 . bowed down to ***B*** or kissed
Rom 11:4 . . . have never bowed down to ***B!***

BABY, BABIES (n)
infant child; youngest of a group; figurative of new or immature Christians
Exod 2:7 . . . women to nurse the ***b*** for you?
Luke 1:44. . . ***b*** in my womb jumped for
Luke 2:12. . . find a ***b*** wrapped snugly
Luke 2:16. . . the ***b,*** lying in the manger.
Acts 7:19 . . . abandon their newborn ***b-ies***
1 Cor 14:20 . Be innocent as ***b-ies*** when
1 Pet 2:2. . . . Like newborn ***b-ies,*** you must

BABYLON (n)
capital city of the Babylonian Empire; a city devoted to materialism and sensual pleasure; biblical writers used as model of paganism and idolatry
Ps 137:1 . . . . Beside the rivers of ***B,*** we sat
Jer 29:10. . . . will be in ***B*** for seventy years.
Jer 51:37. . . . ***B*** will become a heap of ruins,
Rev 14:8. . . . shouting, "***B*** is fallen—

BACKSLIDERS, BACKSLIDING (KJV)
Prov 14:14. . ***Backsliders*** get what they deserve
Jer 3:22. . . . . heal your ***wayward*** hearts
Jer 31:22. . . . my ***wayward*** daughter
Hos 14:4 . . . heal you of your ***faithlessness***

BAD (adj)
poor, inadequate; morally objectionable; disagreeable, unpleasant
Job 2:10 . . . . of God and never anything ***b?***
Eccl 12:14 . . thing, whether good or ***b.***
Isa 45:7. . . . . good times and ***b*** times.

BALAAM
Pagan prophet, summoned to curse the Israelites but instead blessed them (Num 22–24; also Deut 23:3-5; 2 Pet 2:15-16; Jude 1:11; Rev 2:14); died (Num 31:8; Josh 13:22).

BALANCES (n)
an instrument for weighing; a means of judging or deciding
see also SCALES
Dan 5:27 . . . have been weighed on the ***b***

BALD (adj)
lacking a natural or usual covering (as of hair or vegetation); bare, unadorned
Mic 1:16. . . . yourselves as ***b*** as a vulture,

BALDY (n)
a derogatory nickname for someone who is bald
2 Kgs 2:23 . . "Go away, ***b!***" they chanted.

BANNER (n)
a piece of cloth attached by one edge to a staff and used by a leader as his emblem
Exod 17:15 . "the LORD is my ***b***").
Isa 11:10. . . . will be a ***b*** of salvation

BANQUET, BANQUETS (n)
a sumptuous feast, especially a ceremonious meal in honor of a person, occasion, or achievement
Song 2:4. . . . He escorts me to the ***b*** hall;
Matt 24:38 . . enjoying ***b-s*** and parties

BAPTISM, BAPTISMS (n)
a Christian ordinance; a washing with water to demonstrate cleansing from sin, linked with repentance and admission into the community of faith; figurative of an ordeal or initiation
Matt 3:16 . . . After his ***b,*** as Jesus came up
Luke 3:7. . . . crowds came to John for ***b,***
Acts 19:3 . . . what ***b*** did you experience?

Rom 6:3 . . . . joined with Christ Jesus in ***b,***
Gal 3:27 . . . . united with Christ in ***b***
Eph 4:5 . . . . one Lord, one faith, one ***b,***
Heb 6:2 . . . . further instruction about ***b-s,***
1 Pet 3:21 . . . that water is a picture of ***b,***

BAPTIST (n)
one who baptizes
Matt 11:11 . . greater than John the ***B.***
Mark 1:4 . . . messenger was John the ***B.***

BAPTIZE, BAPTIZED, BAPTIZING (v)
to engage in the ordinance of baptism (see above)
see also WASH
Matt 3:13 . . . River to be ***b-d*** by John.
Matt 28:19 . . of all the nations, ***b-ing***
Mark 1:4 . . . that people should be ***b-d***
Mark 1:8 . . . will ***b*** you with the Holy Spirit!
Mark 10:38 . suffering I must be ***b-d*** with?
Luke 3:3. . . . that people should be ***b-d***
Luke 3:16. . . I ***b*** you with water;
Luke 3:21. . . Jesus himself was ***b-d.***
John 1:28 . . . where John was ***b-ing.***
John 1:31 . . . I have been ***b-ing*** with water
John 1:33 . . . is the one who will ***b*** with
John 3:22 . . . with them there, ***b-ing*** people.
John 3:26 . . . is also ***b-ing*** people.
John 4:1 . . . . was ***b-ing*** and making more
John 4:2 . . . . Jesus himself didn't ***b*** them—
John 10:40 . . where John was first ***b-ing***
Acts 1:5 . . . . be ***b-d*** with the Holy Spirit.
Acts 1:22 . . . time he was ***b-d*** by John
Acts 2:41 . . . ***b-d*** and added to the church
Acts 8:12 . . . and women were ***b-d.***
Acts 8:38 . . . water, and Philip ***b-d*** him.
Acts 11:16 . . will be ***b-d*** with the Holy
Acts 16:15 . . She was ***b-d*** along with
Acts 16:33 . . were immediately ***b-d.***
Acts 19:5 . . . ***b-d*** in the name of the Lord
1 Cor 1:13 . . you ***b-d*** in the name of Paul?
1 Cor 1:14 . . I did not ***b*** any of you
1 Cor 1:16 . . ***b-d*** the household of
1 Cor 10:2 . . were ***b-d*** as followers
1 Cor 15:29 . ***b-d*** for those who are dead?
Col 2:12 . . . . when you were ***b-d.***

BARN (n)
a usually large building for the storage of farm products, feed, animals, and/or equipment
Matt 13:30 . . the wheat in the ***b.***

BARREN (adj)
unproductive, unfruitful, especially in childbearing
Heb 11:11 . . she was ***b*** and was too old.

BASKET (n)
a receptacle made of interwoven material; any of various lightweight, usually wood, containers
Exod 2:3 . . . she got a ***b*** made of papyrus
Acts 9:25 . . . lowered him in a large ***b***
2 Cor 11:33 . in a ***b*** through a window

BARNABAS
Levite believer from Cyprus and generous giver of property (Acts 4:36-37); encourager of Paul (Acts 9:26-29); missionary with Paul (Acts 11:22-30; 12:25; 13:1-3); at Jerusalem council (Acts 15:1-2, 12); disagreed with Paul over John Mark (Acts 15:36-40; see also 1 Cor 9:6; Col 4:10).

BATCH (n)
the quantity baked at one time
Rom 11:16 . . the entire ***b*** of dough is holy
1 Cor 5:6 . . . through the whole ***b*** of dough?
1 Cor 5:7 . . . like a fresh ***b*** of dough
Gal 5:9 . . . . . through the whole ***b*** of dough!

BATH (n)
a washing or soaking (as in water or steam) of all or part of the body
2 Sam 11:2. . unusual beauty taking a ***b.***

BATHED (v)
to take a bath; to give a bath to
John 13:10 . . A person who has ***b*** all over

BATHSHEBA
Committed adultery with King David, widow of Uriah the Hittite (2 Sam 11–12); mother of Solomon, her second son with David (1 Kgs 1–2; 1 Chr 3:5).

BATTLE, BATTLES (n)
a combat between two persons; a general encounter between armies, ships of war, aircraft; an extended contest, struggle, or controversy
1 Sam 17:47. This is the LORD's ***b,***
1 Sam 18:17. the LORD's ***b-s.***
1 Sam 25:28. the LORD's ***b-s.***
2 Kgs 14:8 . . Come and meet me in ***b!***
2 Chr 32:8 . . to fight our ***b-s*** for us!
Ps 24:8 . . . . . LORD, invincible in ***b.***
Rev 16:14. . . gather them for ***b*** against
Rev 20:8. . . . gather them together for ***b***—

BEAR (v)
to carry or support; to give as testimony; to give birth to or produce
see also BORN
Gen 4:13 . . . too great for me to ***b!***
Ps 38:4 . . . . . too heavy to ***b.***

John 15:2 . . . branches that do ***b*** fruit
Heb 13:13 . . and ***b*** the disgrace he bore.

BEAR, BEARS (n)
a large, heavy mammal with shaggy hair, rudimentary tail, and plantigrade feet
2 Kgs 2:24 . . Then two ***b-s*** came out
Isa 11:7. . . . . cow will graze near the ***b.***
Dan 7:5 . . . . it looked like a ***b.***

BEARD, BEARDS (n)
the hair that grows on a man's face often excluding the mustache
Lev 19:27. . . or trim your ***b-s.***
Isa 50:6. . . . . who pulled out my ***b.***

BEAST, BEASTS (n)
devilish creature(s) ravishing the earth during the Tribulation; animals, as distinguished from plants or humans; a contemptible person
Dan 7:3 . . . . Then four huge ***b-s*** came up
Dan 7:6 . . . . authority was given to this ***b.***
1 Cor 15:32 . fighting wild ***b-s***—those
Rev 13:18. . . number of the ***b,*** for it is
Rev 16:2. . . . had the mark of the ***b***
Rev 19:20. . . accepted the mark of the ***b***

BEATEN (v)
to be stricken repeatedly so as to inflict pain
see also FLOGGED, WHIPPED
Acts 16:23 . . They were severely ***b,***
2 Cor 11:25 . Three times I was ***b***
1 Pet 2:20. . . if you are ***b*** for doing wrong.

BEAUTIFUL (adj)
lovely, handsome, or pleasing to the eye; excellent
Gen 2:9 . . . . trees that were ***b***
Gen 6:2 . . . . sons of God saw the ***b***
Prov 11:22. . A ***b*** woman who lacks
Eccl 3:11 . . . everything ***b*** for its own time.
Isa 53:2. . . . . was nothing ***b*** or majestic
Lam 2:15 . . . the city called 'Most ***B***
Acts 3:2 . . . . the one called the ***B*** Gate,
Rom 10:15. . How ***b*** are the feet of

BEAUTY (n)
a particularly graceful, ornamental, or excellent quality; the quality in a person or thing that gives pleasure to the senses
2 Sam 11:2. . a woman of unusual ***b***
Ps 50:2 . . . . . the perfection of ***b,*** God shines
Prov 31:30. . and ***b*** does not last;
Isa 28:1. . . . . but its glorious ***b*** will fade
Jas 1:11. . . . . and its ***b*** fades away.
1 Pet 1:24. . . their ***b*** is like a flower
1 Pet 3:4. . . . ***b*** of a gentle and quiet spirit,

BED (n)
a piece of furniture on or in which to lie and sleep; a place for sleeping
Deut 6:7. . . . when you are going to ***b***
Song 3:1. . . . as I lay in ***b,*** I yearned
Luke 17:34. . will be asleep in one ***b;***

BEDROCK (n)
the solid rock underlying loosely arranged surface materials (as soil)
Matt 7:25. . . it is built on ***b.***

BEG, BEGGED, BEGGING (v)
to ask for charity or mercy; to ask earnestly for
Ps 37:25 . . . . their children ***b-ging*** for bread.
Ps 80:14 . . . . Come back, we ***b*** you,
Mal 1:9. . . . . Go ahead, ***b*** God to
2 Cor 12:8 . . different times I ***b-ged*** the Lord

BEGINNING (n)
the point at which something starts; the first part; the origin, source
Gen 1:1 . . . . In the ***b*** God created
John 1:1 . . . . In the ***b*** the Word already
Rom 16:25. . secret from the ***b*** of time.
1 Jn 1:1. . . . . one who existed from the ***b,***
Rev 21:6. . . . the ***B*** and the End.
Rev 22:13. . . the ***B*** and the End.

BEHEMOTH (n)
Hebrew word that could mean elephant, crocodile, hippopotamus, water buffalo, or mythological monster; a mighty animal created as an example of the power of God
Job 40:15 . . . a look at ***B,*** which I made,

BELIEF (n)
the content of one's conviction on a matter; confidence in or reliance upon the truth of a matter
1 Thes 2:14 . because of their ***b*** in Christ
2 Thes 2:13 . through your ***b*** in the truth.
Titus 1:9. . . . ***b*** in the trustworthy message

BELIEVE, BELIEVED, BELIEVES, BELIEVING (v)
to trust in; to hold a firm conviction about; to accept as true, genuine, or real
see also FAITH, TRUST
Gen 15:6 . . . Abram ***b-d*** the LORD,
Prov 14:15. . simpletons ***b*** everything
Isa 53:1. . . . . Who has ***b-d*** our message?
Matt 27:42. . we will ***b*** in him!
Mark 9:23 . . is possible if a person ***b-s.***
Mark 9:24 . . I do ***b,*** but help me

Mark 15:32 . we can see it and ***b*** him!
Luke 8:12. . . prevent them from ***b-ing***
Luke 24:25. . You find it so hard to ***b***
John 1:7 . . . . so that everyone might ***b***
John 1:12 . . . all who ***b-d*** him and accepted
John 3:16 . . . everyone who ***b-s*** in him
John 4:41 . . . hear his message and ***b.***
John 5:38 . . . because you do not ***b*** me—
John 6:69 . . . We ***b,*** and we know you are
John 7:5 . . . . his brothers didn't ***b*** in him.
John 7:39 . . . to everyone ***b-ing*** in him.
John 9:35 . . . asked, "Do you ***b*** in the Son
John 9:38 . . . Yes, Lord, I ***b!***
John 10:37 . . Don't ***b*** me unless
John 11:25 . . Anyone who ***b-s*** in me
John 11:27 . . ***b-d*** you are the Messiah,
John 11:40 . . see God's glory if you ***b?***
John 12:37 . . did not ***b*** in him.
John 12:38 . . who has ***b-d*** our message?
John 13:19 . . you will ***b*** that I AM
John 14:11 . . Or at least ***b*** because of the
John 14:12 . . anyone who ***b-s*** in me
John 16:30 . . ***b*** that you came from God.
John 17:21 . . world will ***b*** you sent me.
John 19:35 . . so that you also can ***b.***
John 20:8 . . . and he saw and ***b-d***—
John 20:29 . . ***b*** because you have seen
John 20:31 . . and that by ***b-ing*** in him
Acts 10:43 . . that everyone who ***b-s*** in him
Acts 13:8 . . . keep the governor from ***b-ing.***
Acts 16:31 . . ***B*** in the Lord Jesus and
Acts 19:4 . . . ***b*** in the one who would come
Acts 26:27 . . do you ***b*** the prophets?
Acts 27:25 . . For I ***b*** God. I will be just
Rom 1:16 . . . saving everyone who ***b-s***—
Rom 3:22 . . . for everyone who ***b-s,*** no
Rom 3:25 . . . ***b*** that Jesus sacrificed his life,
Rom 4:3 . . . . tell us, "Abraham ***b-d*** God,
Rom 4:20 . . . never wavered in ***b-ing*** God's
Rom 10:9 . . . ***b*** in your heart that God
Rom 10:10 . . For it is by ***b-ing*** in your heart
Rom 10:14 . . unless they ***b*** in him?
Rom 14:23 . . anything you ***b*** is not right,
Rom 16:26 . . they too might ***b*** and obey
1 Cor 1:21 . . to save those who ***b.***
1 Cor 15:2 . . ***b-d*** something that was never
2 Cor 5:7 . . . by ***b-ing*** and not by seeing.
2 Cor 5:14 . . Since we ***b*** that Christ
Gal 3:2 . . . . . because you ***b-d*** the message
Gal 3:6 . . . . . same way, "Abraham ***b-d*** God,
Eph 2:8 . . . . his grace when you ***b-d.***
Col 1:23 . . . . continue to ***b*** this truth
1 Thes 4:14 . For since we ***b*** that Jesus
2 Thes 2:11 . and they will ***b*** these lies.
2 Thes 2:12 . enjoying evil rather than ***b-ing***
1 Tim 3:16 . . He was ***b-d*** in throughout the
Heb 3:14 . . . firmly as when we first ***b-d,***
Heb 11:6 . . . must ***b*** that God exists
Heb 11:13 . . still ***b-ing*** what God had
Jas 2:19. . . . . you ***b*** that there is one God.
1 Jn 3:23. . . . We must ***b*** in the name
1 Jn 4:1. . . . . friends, do not ***b*** everyone
1 Jn 5:1. . . . . Everyone who ***b-s*** that Jesus is
1 Jn 5:10. . . . All who ***b*** in the Son

BELIEVER, BELIEVERS (n)

one who accepts something as true, genuine, or real; one who trusts in or has a firm conviction about

Matt 18:15 . . If another ***b*** sins
Acts 2:44 . . . all the ***b-s*** met together
Acts 4:32 . . . All the ***b-s*** were united
Acts 6:1 . . . . as the ***b-s*** rapidly multiplied,
Acts 6:7 . . . . number of ***b-s*** greatly increased
Acts 13:48 . . for eternal life became ***b-s.***
Acts 14:22 . . they strengthened the ***b-s.***
Acts 15:2 . . . accompanied by some local ***b-s,***
Acts 15:23 . . to the Gentile ***b-s*** in Antioch,
Acts 15:32 . . to the ***b-s,*** encouraging
Acts 16:15 . . I am a true ***b*** in the Lord,
Acts 20:2 . . . there, he encouraged the ***b-s***
Acts 21:25 . . As for the Gentile ***b-s,***
Rom 8:27. . . the Spirit pleads for us ***b-s***
Rom 14:13 . . cause another ***b*** to stumble
Rom 14:15 . . if another ***b*** is distressed
Rom 14:21 . . cause another ***b*** to stumble.
Rom 15:27 . . the ***b-s*** in Jerusalem,
1 Cor 6:2 . . . someday we ***b-s*** will judge
1 Cor 10:27 . who isn't a ***b*** asks you
1 Cor 14:22 . tongues is a sign, not for ***b-s,***
2 Cor 6:15 . . can a ***b*** be a partner with an
2 Cor 11:26 . claim to be ***b-s*** but are not.
Col 4:5 . . . . . among those who are not ***b-s,***
2 Thes 3:6 . . away from all ***b-s*** who live idle
1 Tim 3:6 . . . An elder must not be a new ***b,***
1 Tim 4:12 . . Be an example to all ***b-s***
1 Tim 5:16 . . a woman who is a ***b***
1 Jn 3:10. . . . and does not love other ***b-s***

BELITTLE (v)

to cause (a person or thing) to seem little or less; to speak slightingly of

Prov 11:12 . . foolish to ***b*** one's neighbor;
Prov 14:21 . . a sin to ***b*** one's neighbor;

BELLY (n)

abdomen; the stomach and its adjuncts

Gen 3:14 . . . crawl on your ***b,*** groveling
Dan 2:32 . . . its ***b*** and thighs were bronze,
Matt 12:40 . . in the ***b*** of the great fish

BELONG, BELONGED, BELONGS (v)
to be the property of a person or thing
Lev 25:55. . . people of Israel ***b*** to me.
Lev 27:30. . . ***b-s*** to the LORD and
Ps 22:28 . . . . royal power ***b-s*** to the LORD.
John 8:47 . . . Anyone who ***b-s*** to God
John 15:19 . . if you ***b-ed*** to it, but you
Rom 1:6. . . . called to ***b*** to Jesus
Rom 12:5 . . . we all ***b*** to each other.
2 Cor 10:7 . . who say they ***b*** to Christ
Gal 5:24. . . . Those who ***b*** to Christ
1 Thes 5:5 . . we don't ***b*** to darkness
2 Tim 2:19 . . All who ***b*** to the LORD
1 Pet 3:16. . . because you ***b*** to Christ.
1 Jn 4:6. . . . . If they do not ***b*** to God,

BELOVED (adj)
dearly loved; dear to the heart
Ps 60:5 . . . . . rescue your ***b*** people.
Matt 12:18 . . He is my ***B,*** who pleases me.
1 Cor 4:14 . . as my ***b*** children.
1 Cor 4:17 . . Timothy, my ***b*** and faithful
Eph 6:21 . . . a ***b*** brother and faithful helper
Col 1:7. . . . . Epaphras, our ***b*** co-worker.
Col 4:9 . . . . . a faithful and ***b*** brother,
Col 4:14. . . . Luke, the ***b*** doctor,
Phlm 1:1 . . . to Philemon, our ***b*** co-worker,
Phlm 1:16 . . he is a ***b*** brother,
2 Pet 3:15. . . our ***b*** brother Paul also wrote
Rev 20:9. . . . God's people and the ***b*** city.

BENEFICIAL (adj)
conferring benefits; conducive to personal or social well-being
Titus 3:8. . . . good and ***b*** for everyone.

BENEFIT, BENEFITS (n)
advantages or blessings; something that promotes well-being
Prov 12:14 . . Wise words bring many ***b-s,***
Acts 18:27 . . he proved to be of great ***b*** to
2 Cor 4:15 . . this is for your ***b.***

BENEFIT, BENEFITS (v)
to be useful or profitable to; to favor (another) or gain (for oneself)
Job 36:28 . . . and everyone ***b-s.***
Prov 9:12. . . you will be the one to ***b.***
Luke 9:25. . . what do you ***b*** if you gain
1 Cor 9:14 . . by those who ***b*** from it.

BENJAMIN
Second son of Jacob and Rachel, the youngest of Jacob's 12 sons; never knew his mother (Gen 35:16-20); taken to Egypt against Jacob's wishes (Gen 43:3-17); gave his name to a tribe of Israel; his tribe was blessed (Gen 49:27; Deut 33:12), numbered (Num 1:36-37), allotted land and cities (Josh 18:11-28); civil war nearly wiped them out (Judg 20–21); 12,000 will be marked by God (Rev 7:8).

BESEECH(ING), BESOUGHT (KJV)
Deut 3:23. . . I ***pleaded with*** the LORD
Ps 118:25 . . . LORD, ***please*** give us success
Jon 1:14 . . . . ***pleaded,*** "don't make us die
Matt 8:5. . . . came and ***pleaded with*** him
2 Cor 12:8 . . ***begged*** the Lord to take it away

BESIDE (prep)
by the side of
Ps 16:8 . . . . . he is right ***b*** me.
Ps 109:31 . . . he stands ***b*** the needy,

BEST (adj)
excelling all others
Ps 122:9 . . . . seek what is ***b*** for you,
1 Cor 12:31 . life that is ***b*** of all.
Heb 4:11 . . . do our ***b*** to enter that rest.

BESTOWED (KJV)
Isa 63:7. . . . . he has ***granted*** according

BETHLEHEM (n)
a city about five miles south of Jerusalem in the hill country of Judah; the ancestral home of King David and the birthplace of Jesus Christ
Ruth 1:19. . . When they came to ***B,***
1 Sam 16:1. . go to ***B.*** Find a man named
2 Sam 23:15. the well by the gate in ***B.***
Mic 5:2. . . . . ***B*** Ephrathah, are only a small
Matt 2:1. . . . Jesus was born in ***B*** in Judea,
Matt 2:6. . . . you, O ***B*** in the land of Judah,

BETRAY, BETRAYED (v)
to turn one's back on a friend; to deliver to an enemy by treachery; to lead astray, seduce
Num 5:6 . . . men or women—***b*** the LORD
Deut 32:51. . both of you ***b-ed*** me
Jer 38:22. . . . They have ***b-ed*** and misled
Mal 2:10. . . . Then why do we ***b*** each other,
Matt 10:21 . . A brother will ***b*** his brother
Matt 24:10 . . and ***b*** and hate each other.
Matt 26:21 . . one of you will ***b*** me.
Matt 27:4. . . I have ***b-ed*** an innocent man.
Luke 6:16. . . (who later ***b-ed*** him).
John 18:5 . . . Judas, who ***b-ed*** him,

BETRAYER (n)
one who violates a trust or loyalty
Matt 26:46 . . Look, my ***b*** is here!
John 18:2 . . . Judas, the ***b,*** knew this place,

BETTER (adj)
more attractive, favorable, or commendable; more advantageous or effective
Ps 63:3 . . . . . unfailing love is ***b*** than life
Matt 5:20 . . . unless your righteousness is ***b***
Phil 1:21 . . . and dying is even ***b.***

BEWARE (v)
to take heed or be careful
Mark 8:15 . . ***B*** of the yeast of the Pharisees

BIRD, BIRDS (n)
any of a class of warm-blooded vertebrates distinguished by having the body more or less covered with feathers and the forelimbs modified as wings
Prov 27:8 . . . ***b*** that strays from its nest.
Eccl 10:20 . . ***b*** might deliver your
Matt 8:20 . . . and ***b-s*** have nests,
Luke 9:58. . . and ***b-s*** have nests,

BIRTH (n)
the emergence of a new individual from the body of its parent; beginning, start
Gen 25:24 . . the time came to give ***b,***
Ps 58:3 . . . . . even from ***b*** they have lied
Matt 24:8. . . only the first of the ***b*** pains,
John 3:6 . . . . Spirit gives ***b*** to spiritual life.
Titus 3:5. . . . giving us a new ***b*** and new life
Jas 1:15. . . . . it gives ***b*** to death.

BIRTHRIGHT (KJV)
Gen 25:31 . . your ***rights as the firstborn son***
1 Chr 5:1 . . . ***birthright*** was given to the
Heb 12:16 . . ***birthright as the firstborn son***

BITTER (adj)
expressive of severe pain, grief, or regret; distasteful
Exod 12:8 . . eat it along with ***b*** salad greens
Prov 27:7 . . . ***b*** food tastes sweet to the
Prov 30:23. . a ***b*** woman who finally gets
Jas 3:11. . . . . both fresh water and ***b*** water?

BITTERNESS (n)
an intense or severe expression or feeling of pain, grief, or regret; exhibiting intense animosity
Prov 14:10. . Each heart knows its own ***b,***
Prov 17:25. . ***b*** to the one who gave them
Rom 3:14. . . full of cursing and ***b.***
Eph 4:31 . . . Get rid of all ***b,*** rage,

BLACK (adj)
of the color black; very dark in color
Zech 6:6. . . . The chariot with ***b*** horses
Rev 6:5. . . . . I looked up and saw a ***b*** horse,

BLAME (n)
an expression of disapproval or reproach; responsibility for something believed to deserve censure
1 Cor 1:8 . . . free from all ***b*** on the day
Rev 14:5. . . . they are without ***b.***

BLAMELESS (adj)
characterized by being free from sin and fault
see also INTEGRITY, RIGHTEOUS
Gen 6:9 . . . . only ***b*** person living on earth
Job 1:8 . . . . . ***b***—a man of complete integrity.
Ps 18:23 . . . . I am ***b*** before God;
Prov 13:6. . . guards the path of the ***b,***
Prov 29:10. . The bloodthirsty hate ***b***
Phil 1:10 . . . live pure and ***b*** lives
Col 1:22. . . . and you are holy and ***b***
1 Thes 5:23 . kept ***b*** until our Lord
Titus 1:6. . . . must live a ***b*** life.
2 Pet 3:14. . . pure and ***b*** in his sight.

BLASPHEME, BLASPHEMED, BLASPHEMES, BLASPHEMING (v)
to dishonor or revile God; to speak of or address with irreverence
Lev 24:11. . . son of an Israelite woman ***b-ed***
Lev 24:16. . . Anyone who ***b-s*** the Name
Num 15:30 . have ***b-ed*** the LORD,
Isa 52:5. . . . . My name is ***b-ed*** all day long.
Dan 11:36 . . even ***b-ing*** the God of gods.
Mark 3:29 . . who ***b-s*** the Holy Spirit
Luke 12:10. . who ***b-s*** the Holy Spirit
Acts 6:11 . . . We heard him ***b*** Moses,
Rom 2:24. . . Gentiles ***b*** the name of God
1 Tim 1:13 . . to ***b*** the name of Christ.
1 Tim 1:20 . . learn not to ***b*** God.
Rev 13:1. . . . were names that ***b-ed*** God.

BLASPHEMER (n)
one who dishonors or reviles God; one who speaks or addresses with irreverence
Lev 24:14. . . Take the ***b*** outside the camp,
Lev 24:23. . . took the ***b*** outside the camp

BLASPHEMOUS (adj)
impiously irreverent; profane
2 Kgs 19:6 . . by this ***b*** speech against me
Isa 37:6. . . . . by this ***b*** speech against me

BLASPHEMY, BLASPHEMIES (n)
the words or actions that dishonor God; the act of insulting or showing contempt or lack of reverence for God
Neh 9:18 . . . They committed terrible ***b-ies.***
Mark 3:28 . . all sin and ***b*** can be forgiven,
Mark 14:64 . You have all heard his ***b.***

John 10:33 . . for any good work, but for ***b!***
2 Pet 2:11 . . . a charge of ***b*** against those
Rev 13:5. . . . speak great ***b-ies*** against God.
Rev 13:6. . . . words of ***b*** against God,
Rev 17:3. . . . and ***b-ies*** against God were

BLESS, BLESSED, BLESSES (v)
to confer prosperity or happiness upon; to honor in worship; to offer approval or encouragement; to bring pleasure or divine favor
Gen 1:22 . . . Then God ***b-ed*** them,
Gen 12:3 . . . I will ***b*** those who ***b*** you
Gen 22:18 . . of the earth will be ***b-ed***—
Ps 16:7 . . . . . I will ***b*** the LORD who guides
Prov 31:28 . . Her children stand and ***b***
Matt 5:3. . . . God ***b-es*** those who are poor
Matt 5:7. . . . ***b-es*** those who are merciful,
Matt 5:9. . . . God ***b-es*** those who work for
Matt 5:11 . . . God ***b-es*** you when people
Jas 1:12. . . . . God ***b-es*** those who patiently
Rev 22:7. . . . ***B-ed*** are those who obey
Rev 22:14. . . ***B-ed*** are those who wash

BLESSING, BLESSINGS (n)
happiness; praise; divine favor or heavenly reward; the antidote to cursings
Josh 8:34 . . . ***b-s*** and curses Moses
Prov 13:21 . . ***b-s*** reward the righteous.
John 12:13 . . ***B-s*** on the one who comes in
Acts 4:33 . . . God's great ***b*** was upon them
Acts 11:23 . . evidence of God's ***b,***
Rom 15:27 . . spiritual ***b-s*** of the Good
Eph 3:6 . . . . both enjoy the promise of ***b-s***
Rev 7:12. . . . ***B*** and glory and wisdom

BLIND (adj)
sightless; lacking spiritual discernment
Matt 11:5 . . . the ***b*** see, the lame walk,
Matt 15:14 . . ***b*** guides leading the ***b,***
Mark 10:46 . ***b*** beggar named
Luke 6:39. . . Can one ***b*** person lead

BLINDED (v)
to withhold light from; to be without sight
John 12:40 . . The Lord has ***b*** their eyes
2 Cor 4:4 . . . god of this world, has ***b*** the

BLINK (n)
glimpse, glance; a usually involuntary shutting and opening of the eye
1 Cor 15:52 . moment, in the ***b*** of an eye,

BLOOD (n)
fluid in the circulatory system; signifies human life; kinfolk; of animals, used in priestly sacrifices; of Christ, effective for the forgiveness of sins; on hands or head, symbolic of guilt
Exod 12:13 . When I see the ***b,*** I will pass
Deut 12:23. . But never consume the ***b,***
Isa 1:11. . . . . no pleasure from the ***b*** of bulls
Mark 14:24 . my ***b,*** which confirms the
John 6:53 . . . and drink his ***b,*** you cannot
Acts 15:20 . . and from consuming ***b.***
1 Cor 11:25 . confirmed with my ***b.***
Eph 1:7 . . . . with the ***b*** of his Son
Eph 2:13 . . . through the ***b*** of Christ.
Heb 9:7 . . . . offered ***b*** for his own sins
Heb 9:20 . . . This ***b*** confirms the covenant
1 Pet 1:2. . . . cleansed by the ***b*** of Jesus
1 Pet 1:19. . . the precious ***b*** of Christ,
1 Jn 1:7. . . . . the ***b*** of Jesus, his Son, cleanses
Rev 1:5. . . . . by shedding his ***b*** for us.
Rev 5:9. . . . . your ***b*** has ransomed people
Rev 7:14. . . . in the ***b*** of the Lamb
Rev 12:11. . . by the ***b*** of the Lamb
Rev 19:13. . . He wore a robe dipped in ***b,***

BLOT (v)
to wipe out, destroy; to erase or cover up
Ps 51:1 . . . . . ***b*** out the stain of my sins.
Isa 43:25. . . . I alone—will ***b*** out your sins

BOAST, BOASTED, BOASTING (v)
to puff oneself up in speech, brag
Isa 20:5. . . . . ***b-ed*** of their allies in Egypt!
Jer 9:23. . . . . the wise ***b*** in their wisdom,
Rom 2:17. . . ***b*** about your special
1 Cor 1:31 . . ***b, b*** only about the Lord.
2 Cor 8:24 . . our ***b-ing*** about you is justified.
2 Cor 10:13 . We will ***b*** only about
Gal 6:14. . . . ***b*** about anything except
Eph 2:9 . . . . none of us can ***b*** about it.
Jas 1:9. . . . . . have something to ***b*** about,
Jas 4:16. . . . . ***b-ing*** about your own plans,

BOASTFUL (adj)
bragging, overproud, vainglorious
Ps 12:3 . . . . . and silence their ***b*** tongues.
1 Cor 13:4 . . Love is not jealous or ***b*** or proud

BOAT, BOATS (n)
a small vessel for travel on water; ship
Gen 6:14 . . . Build a large ***b*** from cypress
Luke 5:3. . . . Stepping into one of the ***b-s,***

BOAZ
1. Family redeemer and husband of the widow Ruth; ancestor of David in the family line of

Jesus (Ruth 2–4; especially 4:1-10, 18-21; see also 1 Chr 2:12-15; Matt 1:5; Luke 3:23).
2. Pillar's name at front of the Jerusalem Temple (1 Kgs 7:15-22).

BODILY (adj)
of or relating to the body
Col 2:23 . . . . and severe ***b*** discipline.

BODY, BODIES (n)
one's physical essence; a corpse; a group of people
see also FLESH
Job 19:26 . . . in my ***b*** I will see God!
Ps 49:14 . . . . Their ***b-ies*** will rot in the grave,
Isa 26:19. . . . their ***b-ies*** will rise again!
Matt 26:41 . . willing, but the ***b*** is weak!
Mark 14:22 . Take it, for this is my ***b.***
Rom 12:4. . . our ***b-ies*** have many parts
1 Cor 6:15 . . that your ***b-ies*** are actually
1 Cor 6:19 . . that your ***b*** is the temple
1 Cor 6:20 . . honor God with your ***b.***
1 Cor 11:24 . my ***b,*** which is given for
1 Cor 12:13 . into one ***b*** by one Spirit,
1 Cor 15:44 . be raised as spiritual ***b-ies.***
2 Cor 5:1 . . . eternal ***b*** made for us by God
2 Cor 5:2 . . . to put on our heavenly ***b-ies***
2 Cor 5:4 . . . so that these dying ***b-ies*** will
Eph 1:23 . . . the church is his ***b;***
Eph 3:6 . . . . Both are part of the same ***b,***
Eph 5:28 . . . love their own ***b-ies.***
Eph 5:30 . . . are members of his ***b.***
Col 1:24 . . . . for his ***b,*** the church.

BOLD (adj)
fearless before danger; self-assured, confident; prominent
2 Sam 7:27. . been ***b*** enough to pray
1 Chr 17:25 . been ***b*** enough to pray
Phil 1:20 . . . continue to be ***b*** for Christ,

BOLDLY (adv)
showing a fearless, daring spirit
Acts 26:26 . . I speak ***b,*** for I am sure
Eph 3:12 . . . ***b*** and confidently into God's
Heb 4:16 . . . let us come ***b*** to the throne
Heb 10:19 . . ***b*** enter heaven's Most Holy

BOLDNESS (n)
fearlessness before danger; self-assurance; confidence; prominence
Acts 4:13 . . . they saw the ***b*** of Peter
Acts 4:29 . . . give us, your servants, great ***b***

BONE, BONES (n)
one of the hard parts of the skeleton
Gen 2:23 . . . This one is ***b*** from my ***b,***
Ps 22:14 . . . . all my ***b-s*** are out of joint.
Ps 22:17 . . . . I can count all my ***b-s.***
Ezek 37:1. . . a valley filled with ***b-s.***
John 19:36 . . Not one of his ***b-s*** will be

BOOK, BOOKS (n)
a long written or printed literary composition; written records, register, or accounting
Josh 1:8 . . . . Study this ***B*** of Instruction
Ps 69:28 . . . . names from the ***B*** of Life;
Ps 139:16 . . . recorded in your ***b.***
Eccl 12:12 . . for writing ***b-s*** is endless,
Dan 7:10 . . . and the ***b-s*** were opened.
Dan 12:1 . . . name is written in the ***b***
John 21:25 . . could not contain the ***b-s***
Phil 4:3 . . . . are written in the ***B*** of Life.
Rev 3:5. . . . . names from the ***B*** of Life,
Rev 20:12. . . including the ***B*** of Life.
Rev 20:12. . . as recorded in the ***b-s.***
Rev 21:27. . . in the Lamb's ***B*** of Life.

BORN (v)
to give birth to or produce; to be productive; spiritually, to renew or confirm a commitment of faith
see also BEAR
Ps 51:5 . . . . . For I was ***b*** a sinner—
Eccl 3:2 . . . . time to be ***b*** and a time to die.
Isa 9:6. . . . . . For a child is ***b*** to us,
Luke 2:11. . . the Lord—has been ***b*** today
John 3:3 . . . . unless you are ***b*** again,
John 3:7 . . . . You must be ***b*** again.
1 Pet 1:3. . . . we have been ***b*** again,
1 Pet 1:23. . . you have been ***b*** again,

BORROWER, BORROWERS (n)
one who takes with the implied or expressed intention of returning the same; to borrow (money) with the intention of returning the same plus interest
Prov 22:7. . . the ***b*** is servant to the lender.
Isa 24:2. . . . . lenders and ***b-s,*** bankers and

BOSS (n)
one who directs or supervises workers
Eccl 10:4 . . . If your ***b*** is angry at you,
Luke 16:3. . . Now what? My ***b*** has fired me

BOTTOMLESS (adj)
unfathomable; boundless, unlimited
Luke 8:31. . . into the ***b*** pit.
Rev 9:1. . . . . shaft of the ***b*** pit.
Rev 9:11. . . . the angel from the ***b*** pit;

Rev 11:7. . . . up out of the ***b*** pit
Rev 17:8. . . . up out of the ***b*** pit
Rev 20:1. . . . the key to the ***b*** pit
Rev 20:3. . . . into the ***b*** pit,

BOUGHT (v)
to purchase; to obtain by way of sacrifice or expenditure
see also BUY
Job 28:15 . . . It cannot be ***b*** with gold.
1 Cor 6:20 . . God ***b*** you with a high price.
2 Pet 2:1. . . . the Master who ***b*** them.

BOUND (v)
to confine, restrain, or restrict as if with bonds; to put under an obligation
Acts 20:22 . . now I am ***b*** by the Spirit
Rev 20:2. . . . and ***b*** him in chains

BOUNDARY (n)
border, limit; dividing line
Num 34:3 . . The southern ***b*** will begin
Prov 22:28 . . moving the ancient ***b*** markers

BOUNTIFUL (adj)
given or provided abundantly; generous
Ps 65:11 . . . . year with a ***b*** harvest;
Ps 68:10 . . . . with a ***b*** harvest, O God,

BOUNTY (n)
crop yield; generosity
Deut 33:16. . gifts of the earth and its ***b,***

BOW, BOWED, BOWS (v)
to bend the head, body, or knee in reverence, submission, or shame
Gen 47:31 . . Jacob ***b-ed*** humbly
Deut 5:9. . . . You must not ***b*** down to them
1 Kgs 1:16 . . Bathsheba ***b-ed*** down before
1 Kgs 19:18 . never ***b-ed*** down to Baal
2 Chr 29:29 . everyone with him ***b-ed*** down
2 Chr 29:30 . and ***b-ed*** down in worship.
Esth 3:2 . . . . would ***b*** down before Haman
Ps 72:9 . . . . . nomads will ***b*** before him;
Ps 95:6 . . . . . let us worship and ***b*** down.
Isa 44:15. . . . an idol and ***b-s*** down in front
Mic 6:6. . . . . Should we ***b*** before God
Rom 11:4 . . . never ***b-ed*** down to Baal!
Phil 2:10 . . . every knee should ***b,*** in heaven

BOWL (n)
a concave vessel often used for holding food or liquids
Prov 15:17 . . A ***b*** of vegetables with
Luke 8:16. . . covers it with a ***b*** or hides

BOY, BOYS (n)
a male child from birth to puberty
Gen 21:17 . . God has heard the ***b*** crying
Gen 22:12 . . Don't lay a hand on the ***b!***
Exod 1:18 . . you allowed the ***b-s*** to live?
1 Sam 2:11. . the ***b*** served the LORD
1 Sam 3:8. . . who was calling the ***b.***
Matt 17:18. . rebuked the demon in the ***b,***

BRAG (v)
to talk boastfully
Prov 27:1. . . Don't ***b*** about tomorrow,
Amos 4:5. . . so you can ***b*** about it
2 Cor 5:12 . . you can answer those who ***b***

BRANCH, BRANCHES (n)
limb of a (family) tree; part of a complex body (of knowledge); figurative of offspring and of disciples (of Christ and his disciples)
Isa 4:2. . . . . . the ***b*** of the LORD will be beautiful
Dan 4:21 . . . nested in its ***b-es.***
Zech 3:8. . . . bring my servant, the ***B.***
Matt 13:32. . make nests in its ***b-es."***
John 15:2 . . . ***b*** of mine that doesn't
John 15:4 . . . a ***b*** cannot produce fruit if
John 15:5 . . . you are the ***b-es.***
Rom 11:20 . . those ***b-es*** were broken off
Rom 11:21 . . not spare the original ***b-es,***

BREAD (n)
basic staple in diet of ancient Israel, usually baked using flour or meal; signifies livelihood
see also FOOD
Exod 23:15 . Festival of Unleavened ***B.***
Prov 20:17. . Stolen ***b*** tastes sweet,
Mark 14:22 . Jesus took some ***b*** and
Luke 4:3. . . . stone to become a loaf of ***b.***
Luke 9:13. . . only five loaves of ***b***
John 6:48 . . . Yes, I am the ***b*** of life!
John 6:51 . . . I am the living ***b***
1 Cor 10:16 . when we break the ***b,***
1 Cor 11:23 . the Lord Jesus took some ***b***
1 Cor 11:26 . eat this ***b*** and drink

BREAK, BREAKING (v)
to fracture; to shatter; to violate or transgress; to burst forth; to separate into parts
see also BROKE
Lev 26:15. . . and if you ***b*** my covenant
Prov 25:15. . soft speech can ***b*** bones.
Matt 5:33. . . You must not ***b*** your vows;
1 Cor 10:16 . And when we ***b*** the bread,
1 Jn 3:4. . . . . who sins is ***b-ing*** God's law,

BREAKFAST (n)
first meal of the day, especially taken in the morning
Prov 31:15 . . to prepare *b* for her

BREATH (n)
air inhaled and exhaled in breathing; a spoken sound, utterance; a slight indication, suggestion
Gen 2:7 . . . . He breathed the *b* of life
Exod 15:8 . . At the blast of your *b,*
Ps 18:15 . . . . at the blast of your *b,*
Ps 144:4 . . . . we are like a *b* of air;

BREATHED (v)
to inhale and exhale freely; to blow softly
Gen 2:7 . . . . He *b* the breath of life
Mark 15:37 . and *b* his last.
John 20:22 . . Then he *b* on them

BREVITY (n)
shortness of duration
Ps 90:12 . . . . to realize the *b* of life,

BRIBE (n)
something that serves to induce or influence
Deut 16:19 . . Never accept a *b,*

BRIBERY (n)
the act or practice of giving or taking a bribe
Job 15:34 . . . homes, enriched through *b,*

BRICKS (n)
units for building or paving, made of mud and often a binding agent such as straw; in the ancient world bricks were baked or sun dried
Gen 11:3 . . . Let's make *b* and harden
Exod 5:7 . . . any more straw for making *b.*
Exod 5:13 . . Meet your daily quota of *b,*
Isa 9:10. . . . . the broken *b* of our ruins
Nah 3:14 . . . making *b* to repair the walls.

BRIDE (n)
a woman just married or about to be married
2 Cor 11:2 . . as a pure *b* to one husband—
Rev 19:7. . . . *b* has prepared herself.
Rev 21:2. . . . like a *b* beautifully dressed
Rev 21:9. . . . the *b,* the wife of the Lamb.
Rev 22:17. . . Spirit and the *b* say, "Come."

BRIDEGROOM (n)
a man just married or about to be married
Ps 19:5 . . . . . like a radiant *b* after
Matt 25:1 . . . and went to meet the *b.*
Matt 25:5 . . . When the *b* was delayed,

BRIDESMAIDS (n)
women attendants of a bride
Matt 25:1 . . . will be like ten *b* who

BRIDLE (n)
the headgear consisting of a bit and reigns with which a horse or other animal is governed
Prov 26:3. . . a donkey with a *b,* and a fool

BRIGHTNESS (n)
the quality or state of being bright; luminance; radiance
Ps 18:12 . . . . shielded the *b* around him
Isa 24:23. . . . the *b* of the sun will fade,

BRILLIANT (adj)
very bright, glittering; striking, distinctive
Hab 3:4 . . . . His coming is as *b* as
1 Tim 6:16 . . he lives in light so *b* that

BROAD (adj)
extending far and wide; spacious
Matt 7:13 . . . highway to hell is *b,*

BROKE, BROKEN (v)
see also BREAK
Josh 9:20 . . . if we *b* our oath.
1 Kgs 19:10 . have *b-n* their covenant
Ps 34:20 . . . . not one of them is *b-n!*
Ps 51:17 . . . . not reject a *b-n* and repentant
Eccl 4:12 . . . braided cord is not easily *b-n.*
Eccl 12:6 . . . the golden bowl is *b-n.*
Matt 26:26 . . Then he *b* it in pieces
Mark 14:22 . Then he *b* it in pieces
Luke 20:18. . stone will be *b-n* to pieces,
John 19:36 . . of his bones will be *b-n,*
Rom 11:20 . . those branches were *b-n* off
1 Cor 11:24 . Then he *b* it in pieces
2 Tim 1:10 . . He *b* the power of death
Jas 2:10. . . . . who has *b-n* all of God's laws.

BROKENHEARTED (n)
those who are overcome by grief or despair
Ps 34:18 . . . . The LORD is close to the *b;*
Ps 109:16 . . . he hounded the *b* to death.
Ps 147:3 . . . . He heals the *b* and

BROTHER, BROTHERS (n)
male family members with the same parents; kinsmen in the extended family, church, or nation; co-workers in ministry; fellow believers, followers, or friends in Christ
Ps 133:1 . . . . *b-s* live together in harmony!
Prov 18:24 . . friend sticks closer than a *b.*
Prov 27:10 . . to ask your *b* for assistance.
Mark 3:33 . . Who are my *b-s?*
Mark 10:29 . given up house or *b-s* or

John 7:5 . . . . even his ***b-s*** didn't believe
Heb 2:11 . . . ashamed to call them his ***b-s***
Heb 13:1 . . . each other as ***b-s*** and sisters.
Jas 2:15. . . . . you see a ***b*** or sister
Jas 4:11. . . . . against each other, dear ***b-s***
1 Pet 1:22. . . each other as ***b-s*** and sisters.
1 Pet 3:8. . . . Love each other as ***b-s*** and
1 Jn 2:9. . . . . a Christian ***b*** or sister,
1 Jn 3:16. . . . for our ***b-s*** and sisters.
1 Jn 3:17. . . . sees a ***b*** or sister in need
1 Jn 4:20. . . . hates a Christian ***b*** or sister,
1 Jn 4:21. . . . love their Christian ***b-s*** and
Rev 12:10. . . the accuser of our ***b-s*** and

BROTHERLY (adj)
natural or becoming to brothers; affectionate
2 Pet 1:7. . . . godliness with ***b*** affection,

BROUGHT (v)
to carry, lead, or otherwise cause something to move toward an end
Jer 40:2. . . . . has ***b*** this disaster on this land,
Rom 5:12. . . Adam's sin ***b*** death, so death
Eph 2:17 . . . He ***b*** this Good News

BUILD, BUILDING, BUILDS, BUILT (v)
to erect or construct; to edify or encourage; to increase, enlarge
Gen 6:14 . . . ***B*** a large boat from cypress
1 Kgs 6:14 . . Solomon finished ***b-ing*** the
Neh 4:17 . . . who were ***b-ing*** the wall.
Ps 127:1 . . . . Unless the LORD ***b-s*** a house,
Prov 14:1 . . . A wise woman ***b-s*** her home,
Prov 16:12. . his rule is ***b-t*** on justice.
Hag 1:9 . . . . ***b-ing*** your own fine houses.
Matt 7:24. . . who ***b-s*** a house on solid rock
Matt 16:18. . rock I will ***b*** my church,
Rom 14:19. . try to ***b*** each other up.
1 Cor 3:10 . . Now others are ***b-ing*** on it.
1 Cor 3:12 . . Anyone who ***b-s*** on that
2 Cor 10:8 . . But our authority ***b-s*** you up;
Eph 2:20 . . . ***b-t*** on the foundation of the
Eph 4:12 . . . work and ***b*** up the church,
Col 2:7. . . . . let your lives be ***b-t*** on him.
1 Thes 5:11 . and ***b*** each other up, just as
Heb 3:3 . . . . as a person who ***b-s*** a house
1 Pet 2:5. . . . God is ***b-ing*** into his spiritual
Jude 1:20 . . . friends, must ***b*** each other up

BUILDER, BUILDERS (n)
one who builds
Ps 118:22. . . The stone that the ***b-s*** rejected
Mark 12:10 . stone that the ***b-s*** rejected
Acts 4:11 . . . The stone that you ***b-s*** rejected
1 Cor 3:10 . . foundation like an expert ***b.***
1 Cor 3:14 . . that ***b*** will receive a reward.
Heb 3:4 . . . . For every house has a ***b,***
1 Pet 2:7. . . . The stone that the ***b-s*** rejected

BUILDING (n)
a walled structure built for permanent use; figurative of the Church
1 Cor 3:9 . . . You are God's ***b.***

BULL, BULLS (n)
a male, adult, uncastrated bovine
Lev 4:3. . . . . a young ***b*** with no defects.
Heb 10:4 . . . the blood of ***b-s*** and goats

BURDEN, BURDENS (n)
a (usually) heavy load to be borne – physically, emotionally, or spiritually
Ps 38:4 . . . . . a ***b*** too heavy to bear.
Matt 11:28. . weary and carry heavy ***b-s,***
Matt 11:30. . the ***b*** I give you is light.
Acts 15:28 . . to lay no greater ***b*** on you
2 Cor 11:9 . . a financial ***b*** to anyone.
2 Cor 11:28 . the daily ***b*** of my concern
2 Cor 12:14 . I will not be a ***b*** to you.
Gal 6:2. . . . . Share each other's ***b-s,***
1 Thes 2:9 . . so that we would not be a ***b***
2 Thes 3:8 . . so we would not be a ***b***

BURDENED (v)
to load; to oppress
Isa 43:23. . . . I have not ***b*** and wearied you
Isa 43:24. . . . Instead, you have ***b*** me
2 Tim 3:6 . . . are ***b*** with the guilt of sin

BURGLAR (n)
one who enters a building with the intent to commit a crime
Luke 12:39. . when a ***b*** was coming,

BURLAP (n)
a coarse, heavy, plain-woven fabric usually of jute or hemp used for bagging and wrapping
Dan 9:3 . . . . I also wore rough ***b***
Matt 11:21. . clothing themselves in ***b***

BURN, BURNED, BURNING (v)
to consume by fire; to be emotionally excited or agitated; to produce or undergo discomfort or pain
see also BURNING, BURNT
Exod 27:20 . keep the lamps ***b-ing***
Lev 6:9. . . . . must be kept ***b-ing*** all night.
Deut 7:5. . . . Asherah poles and ***b*** their idols.
Ps 79:5 . . . . . will your jealousy ***b*** like fire?
Isa 30:27. . . . far away, ***b-ing*** with anger,

Jer 23:29. . . . Does not my word ***b*** like fire?
Luke 24:32. . "Didn't our hearts ***b*** within us
Rom 1:27. . . ***b-ed*** with lust for each other.
1 Cor 7:9 . . . to marry than to ***b*** with lust.

BURNING (adj)
being on fire
see also BURN, BURNT
Prov 25:22. . heap ***b*** coals of shame
Rom 12:20. . heap ***b*** coals of shame
Rev 19:20. . . fiery lake of ***b*** sulfur.

BURNISHED (adj)
shiny or lustrous from rubbing; polished
1 Kgs 7:45 . . these things of ***b*** bronze
Ezek 1:7. . . . shone like ***b*** bronze.

BURNT (adj)
marked by alteration or destruction by fire
see also BURN
Gen 22:2 . . . sacrifice him as a ***b*** offering
Exod 18:12 . brought a ***b*** offering
Lev 1:3. . . . . present as a ***b*** offering
Josh 8:31 . . . they presented ***b*** offerings
Judg 6:26. . . Sacrifice the bull as a ***b***
Judg 13:16. . a ***b*** offering as a sacrifice
1 Kgs 3:4 . . . sacrificed 1,000 ***b*** offerings.
Ezra 3:2. . . . to sacrifice ***b*** offerings

BURY, BURIED (v)
to deposit in the earth or in a tomb; figurative of denying oneself and submitting to Christ
Deut 34:6. . . The LORD ***b-ied*** him
Ruth 1:17. . . and there I will be ***b-ied.***
Mark 6:29 . . get his body and ***b-ied*** it in
Luke 9:60. . . dead ***b*** their own dead!
Luke 23:30. . plead with the hills, '***B*** us.'
Rom 6:4. . . . and were ***b-ied*** with Christ
1 Cor 15:4 . . ***b-ied,*** and he was raised
Col 2:12. . . . For you were ***b-ied*** with Christ

BUSH (n)
a low, densely branched shrub
Exod 3:2 . . . fire from the middle of a ***b.***
Mark 12:26 . story of the burning ***b?***
Luke 20:37. . wrote about the burning ***b.***
Acts 7:35 . . . him in the burning ***b,***

BUSINESS (n)
economic dealings; affair or matter
Gen 40:8 . . . Interpreting dreams is God's ***b,***
Ps 112:5 . . . . conduct their ***b*** fairly.
1 Thes 4:11 . minding your own ***b*** and
2 Thes 3:11 . meddling in other people's ***b.***
1 Tim 5:13 . . meddling in other people's ***b***

BUSY (adj)
engaged in action; occupied
1 Kgs 20:40 . I was ***b*** doing something
Eccl 11:6 . . . keep ***b*** all afternoon,
Hag 1:9 . . . . ***b*** building your own fine houses.

BUY, BUYS (v)
to purchase; to redeem; to hire, bribe
see also BOUGHT
Prov 31:16. . to inspect a field and ***b-s*** it;
Gal 4:5. . . . . sent him to ***b*** freedom for us
Rev 13:17. . . no one could ***b*** or sell

CAESAR (n)
a title applied to several emperors of the Roman Empire
Matt 22:21 . . to *C* what belongs to *C,*

CALF (n)
the young of a domestic cow
Exod 32:4 . . it into the shape of a *c.*
Luke 15:23. . kill the *c* we have been
Acts 7:41 . . . made an idol shaped like a *c,*

CALL, CALLED, CALLING, CALLS (v)
to make a request or demand; to designate or name
see also CHOSE, CHOSEN
Gen 2:23 . . . She will be ***c-ed*** 'woman,'
1 Kgs 18:24 . *c* on the name of your god,
2 Kgs 5:11 . . leprosy and *c* on the name
2 Chr 7:14 . . who are ***c-ed*** by my name
Ps 147:4 . . . . stars and ***c-s*** them all by name.
Isa 40:26. . . . ***c-ing*** each by its name.
Isa 45:3. . . . . the one who ***c-s*** you by name.
Isa 56:7. . . . . Temple will be ***c-ed*** a house of
Hos 11:1 . . . I ***c-ed*** my son out of Egypt.
Joel 2:32. . . . everyone who ***c-s*** on the name
Matt 2:15. . . I ***c-ed*** my Son out of Egypt.
Matt 9:13. . . I have come to *c* not those
Matt 22:14. . many are ***c-ed,*** but few are
Matt 22:43. . *c* the Messiah 'my Lord'?
Mark 2:17 . . I have come to *c* not those
Mark 10:49 . Come on, he's ***c-ing*** you!
Luke 1:32. . . ***c-ed*** the Son of the Most High.
Luke 23:15. . this man has done ***c-s*** for
Acts 2:21 . . . everyone who ***c-s*** on the name
Acts 2:39 . . . have been ***c-ed*** by the Lord
Acts 9:14 . . . arrest everyone who ***c-s*** upon
Acts 22:16 . . sins washed away by ***c-ing*** on
Rom 1:6. . . . ***c-ed*** to belong to Jesus
Rom 8:28. . . ***c-ed*** according to his purpose
Rom 10:12. . to all who *c* on him.
Rom 10:13. . Everyone who ***c-s*** on the
Rom 11:29. . *c* can never be withdrawn.
1 Cor 1:2 . . . who have been ***c-ed*** by God
1 Cor 1:2 . . . *c* on the name of our Lord
1 Cor 1:24 . . ***c-ed*** by God to salvation,
1 Cor 7:17 . . when God first ***c-ed*** you.
Gal 1:6 . . . . . so soon from God, who ***c-ed***
Gal 5:13 . . . . been ***c-ed*** to live in freedom,
Eph 1:18 . . . to those he ***c-ed***—his holy
Col 3:15 . . . . you are ***c-ed*** to live in peace.
1 Thes 2:12 . ***c-ed*** you to share in his
1 Thes 4:7 . . God has ***c-ed*** us to live holy
1 Thes 5:24 . he who ***c-s*** you is faithful.
2 Tim 2:22 . . those who *c* on the Lord
Heb 9:15 . . . all who are ***c-ed*** can receive
1 Pet 2:9. . . . he ***c-ed*** you out of the darkness
1 Pet 3:9. . . . what God has ***c-ed*** you to do,
1 Pet 5:10. . . God ***c-ed*** you to share in his
2 Pet 1:10. . . are among those God has ***c-ed***

CALLING (n)
a strong inner impulse toward a particular course of action; an occupation or vocation
Eph 4:1 . . . . to lead a life worthy of your *c,*

CALM (v)
to make still; to free from agitation, excitement, or disturbance
Zeph 3:17 . . he will *c* all your fears.

CALVARY (KJV)
Luke 23:33. . place called ***The Skull,***

CAME (v)
to originate or proceed from
see also COME
John 1:17 . . . faithfulness *c* through Jesus
Heb 7:14 . . . our Lord *c* from the tribe of

CAMEL (n)
either of two large ruminant mammals used as draft and saddle animals in desert regions especially of Africa and Asia
Matt 19:24 . . easier for a *c* to go through
Matt 23:24 . . but you swallow a *c!*

CANAAN (n)
region along the Mediterranean Sea taken and settled by the Israelites
Num 33:51 . Jordan River into the land of *C,*
1 Chr 16:18 . *C* as your special possession.
Ps 105:11 . . . *C* as your special possession.
Acts 13:19 . . destroyed seven nations in *C*

CANCEL, CANCELED (v)
to destroy the force, effectiveness, or validty of; to annul
Deut 15:1 . . . year you must *c* the debts
Matt 15:6 . . . so you *c* the word of God
Col 2:14 . . . . *c-ed* the record of the charges

CANDLE (n)
a usually molded or dipped mass of wax or tallow containing a wick that may be burned
Isa 42:3. . . . . or put out a flickering *c.*
Matt 12:20 . . or put out a flickering *c.*

CANDLESTICK(S) (KJV)
Exod 25:31 . Make a ***lampstand*** of pure,
Dan 5:5 . . . . palace, near the ***lampstand.***
Matt 5:15 . . . a lamp is placed on a ***stand***
Heb 9:2 . . . . a ***lampstand,*** a table, and
Rev 1:12. . . . I saw seven gold ***lampstands***

CANOPY (n)
a cover (as of cloth) fixed or carried above a person of high rank or a sacred object; a protective covering
2 Kgs 16:18 . he also removed the *c* that
Isa 4:5. . . . . . He will provide a *c* of cloud
Isa 51:16. . . . stretched out the sky like a *c*
Jer 43:10. . . . spread his royal *c* over them.

CAPSTONE, HEADSTONE (KJV)
Ps 118:22 . . . become the ***cornerstone***
Zech 4:7. . . . the ***final stone*** of the Temple
Matt 21:42 . . now become the ***cornerstone.***
Luke 20:17. . now become the ***cornerstone.***

CAPTIVE (adj)
(people) taken and held against their will
Prov 5:22. . . is held *c* by his own sins;
Acts 8:23 . . . and are held *c* by sin.
2 Tim 2:26 . . they have been held *c*

CAPTIVES (n)
prisoners
Ps 68:18 . . . . you led a crowd of *c.*
Isa 60:11. . . . led as *c* in a victory
Isa 61:1. . . . . that *c* will be released
Luke 4:18. . . that *c* will be released,

CAPTIVITY (n)
imprisonment, exile; subjection or subservience
Deut 28:41. . they will be led away into *c.*

CAPTURE, CAPTURED (v)
an act of catching, winning, or gaining control by force, stratagem, or guile
1 Sam 4:11. . The Ark of God was ***c-ed,***
2 Sam 5:7. . . David ***c-ed*** the fortress of Zion,
Song 4:9. . . . You have ***c-ed*** my heart,
2 Cor 10:5 . . We *c* their rebellious
Col 2:8 . . . . . *c* you with empty philosophies

CARCASS (n)
a dead body; corpse
Judg 14:9. . . honey from the *c* of the lion.
Matt 24:28 . . vultures shows there is a *c*

CARE, CARED, CARES, CARING (v)
to feel interest or concern; to attend to or provide for the needs, operation, or treatment of
Deut 1:31. . . LORD your God ***c-d*** for you
Ps 8:4 . . . . . . human beings that you should *c*
Ps 37:17 . . . . LORD takes *c* of the godly.
Ps 65:9 . . . . . take *c* of the earth and
Ps 116:15 . . . ***c-s*** deeply when his loved
Ps 138:6 . . . . is great, he ***c-s*** for the humble,
Prov 12:10. . godly *c* for their animals,
Prov 27:23 . . into ***c-ing*** for your herds,
Isa 53:8. . . . . ***c-d*** that he died without
Jer 23:2. . . . . Instead of ***c-ing*** for my flock
Matt 6:30 . . . if God ***c-s*** so wonderfully for
Matt 25:36 . . sick, and you ***c-d*** for me.
Luke 10:34. . an inn, where he took *c* of
John 10:13 . . really *c* about the sheep.
John 12:25 . . who *c* nothing for their life
John 21:16 . . Then take *c* of my sheep,
Eph 5:29 . . . just as Christ ***c-s*** for the church.
Phil 2:21 . . . others *c* only for themselves
1 Thes 2:7 . . ***c-ing*** for her own children.
1 Tim 5:14 . . take *c* of their own homes.
1 Tim 5:16 . . she must take *c* of them and
Heb 2:6 . . . . that you should *c* for him?
1 Pet 5:2. . . . *C* for the flock that God
1 Pet 5:7. . . . and cares to God, for he ***c-s***

CAREFUL (adj)
marked by wary caution; meticulous
Exod 34:12 . *c* never to make a treaty
Lev 18:4. . . . and be *c* to obey my decrees,
Lev 22:2. . . . be very *c* with the sacred gifts
Lev 26:3. . . . are *c* to obey my commands,
Deut 4:9. . . . But watch out! Be *c* never to
Deut 6:3. . . . and be *c* to obey,
Deut 8:1. . . . Be *c* to obey all the commands
Deut 12:1. . . *c* to obey when you live in
Deut 12:28. . Be *c* to obey all my
Josh 1:7 . . . . and very courageous. Be *c*
Josh 23:11 . . be very *c* to love the LORD
2 Kgs 21:8 . . Israelites will be *c* to obey
1 Cor 8:9 . . . be *c* so that your freedom
1 Cor 10:12 . strong, be *c* not to fall.
Eph 5:15 . . . So be *c* how you live.

CAREFULLY (adv)
scrupulously attentive
Deut 11:13. . *c* obey all the commands
2 Kgs 18:6 . . he *c* obeyed all the commands
Prov 5:1. . . . to my wisdom; listen *c*
1 Cor 15:34 . *c* about what is right, and stop
Heb 2:1 . . . . must listen very *c* to the truth
Heb 3:1 . . . . think *c* about this Jesus

CARNAL(LY) (KJV)
Rom 7:14. . . ***all too human,*** a slave to sin
Rom 8:6. . . . letting your ***sinful nature*** control
1 Cor 3:3 . . . still controlled by your ***sinful nature***
2 Cor 10:4 . . not ***worldly*** weapons

CAROUSE, CAROUSING (v)
to drink liquor freely or excessively
Prov 23:20. . Do not *c* with drunkards
Luke 21:34. . your hearts be dulled by ***c-ing***

CARPENTER (n)
a worker who builds or repairs wooden structures or their structural parts
Matt 13:55. . He's just the *c*'s son,
Mark 6:3 . . . He's just a *c,* the son of Mary

CARRY, CARRIED, CARRIES (v)
to transport or convey; to sustain the weight of; to bring to a successful end
Exod 19:4 . . how I ***c-ied*** you on eagles'
Lev 16:22. . . will *c* all the people's sins
Deut 32:11. . to take them up and ***c-ied***
Ps 68:19 . . . . For each day he ***c-ies*** us in his
Ps 103:20 . . . ones who *c* out his plans,
Isa 40:11. . . . *c* the lambs in his arms,
Isa 53:4. . . . . it was our weaknesses he ***c-ied;***
Isa 63:9. . . . . He lifted them up and ***c-ied***
Luke 14:27. . do not *c* your own cross
Col 4:17 . . . . Be sure to *c* out the ministry
1 Pet 2:24. . . He personally ***c-ied*** our sins
2 Pet 3:17. . . not be ***c-ied*** away by the errors

CAST, CASTING (v)
to toss (dice); to drive out
Lev 16:8. . . . He is to *c* sacred lots to
Matt 10:1 . . . authority to *c* out evil spirits
Matt 12:26 . . if Satan is ***c-ing*** out Satan,

CATCH (v)
to entangle; to seize and hold firmly
see also CAUGHT
Luke 5:4. . . . let down your nets to *c* some fish.

CATTLE (n)
bovine animals on a farm or ranch
Ps 50:10 . . . . I own the *c* on a thousand

CAUGHT (v)
to get entangled; to seize and hold firmly
see also CATCH
Gen 22:13 . . saw a ram *c* by its horns
Prov 6:2. . . . and are *c* by what you said—
2 Cor 12:2 . . I was *c* up to the third heaven
1 Thes 4:17 . will be *c* up in the clouds

CAUTION (n)
prudent forethought to minimize risk; precaution; warning
Jude 1:23 . . . with great *c,* hating the sins

CEASE (v)
to come to an end; to discontinue
Lam 3:22 . . . His mercies never *c.*

CELEBRATE, CELEBRATED, CELEBRATING (v)
to perform (a sacrament or ceremony) publicly and with appropriate rites; to observe a notable occasion with festivities
Exod 10:9 . . together in ***c-ing*** a festival
Exod 12:47 . Israel must *c* this Passover
Exod 13:5 . . You must *c* this event in this
Exod 23:14 . *c* three festivals in my
Exod 34:18 . *c* the Festival of Unleavened
Exod 34:22 . *c* the Festival of the Final
Num 9:2 . . . *c* the Passover at the
Deut 16:1. . . your God, *c* the Passover
2 Sam 6:21. . so I *c* before the LORD.
2 Kgs 23:21 . *c* the Passover to the LORD
2 Chr 30:1 . . Jerusalem to *c* the Passover.
2 Chr 30:13 . *c* the Festival of Unleavened
2 Chr 30:23 . ***c-d*** joyfully for another

Neh 8:12 . . . to *c* with great joy
Esth 8:15 . . . people of Susa *c-d* the new
Esth 9:19 . . . villages *c* an annual festival
Esth 9:21 . . . to *c* an annual festival
Matt 25:21 . . Let's *c* together!
Luke 15:23. . We must *c* with a feast,
Luke 15:32. . We had to *c* this happy day.
John 18:28 . . to *c* the Passover.
Col 2:16 . . . . for not *c-ing* certain holy days
Rev 11:10. . . to *c* the death of the two prophets

CELEBRATION, CELEBRATIONS (n)
a party or festival in honor of a religious ceremony or holiday; the observation of a notable occasion with festivities
Num 9:3 . . . regulations concerning this *c.*
2 Sam 6:12. . City of David with a great *c.*
Esth 8:17 . . . had a great *c* and declared
Jer 31:13. . . . young—will join in the *c.*
Joel 1:16. . . . No joyful *c-s* are held in the
Zech 8:19. . . *c* for the people of Judah.
John 11:55 . . for the Jewish Passover *c,*

CENSUS (n)
count of population, sometimes including assessment of property value
2 Sam 24:1. . to harm them by taking a *c.*
Luke 2:1. . . . that a *c* should be taken

CENTURION (KJV)
Matt 8:5. . . . ***Roman officer*** came and
Luke 7:2. . . . slave of a ***Roman officer*** was sick
Acts 10:1 . . . ***Roman army officer*** named Cornelius

CEPHAS (n)
rock; Aramaic name of Simon Peter, given to him by Christ
John 1:42 . . . called *C"* (which means

CEREMONIAL (adj)
marked by, involved in, or belonging to ceremony; stressing careful attention to form and detail
Lev 14:2. . . . seeking *c* purification from a
John 2:6 . . . . used for Jewish *c* washing.
John 3:25 . . . Jew over *c* cleansing.
Heb 9:13 . . . bodies from *c* impurity.

CEREMONIALLY (adv)
in accordance with law and custom
Lev 4:12. . . . the camp that is *c* clean,
Lev 6:11. . . . to a place that is *c* clean.
Lev 10:14. . . in any place that is *c* clean.
Lev 12:2. . . . she will be *c* unclean for seven
Lev 13:3. . . . pronounce the person *c* unclean.
Lev 15:13. . . water, and he will be *c* clean.
Lev 15:33. . . intercourse with a woman who is *c* unclean."
Lev 21:1. . . . *c* unclean by touching
Lev 22:3. . . . any of your descendants is *c*
Num 5:2 . . . who has become *c* unclean by
Num 9:6 . . . the men had been *c* defiled
Num 18:11 . your family who is *c* clean
Num 19:7 . . *c* unclean until evening.
Num 19:18 . someone who is *c* clean must
Deut 12:22. . whether *c* clean or unclean,
Deut 14:7. . . so they are *c* unclean for you.
1 Sam 20:26. made David *c* unclean.

CEREMONY, CEREMONIES (n)
a formal act or series of acts prescribed by ritual, protocol, or convention
Exod 12:25 . continue to observe this *c.*
Exod 12:26 . ask, 'What does this *c* mean?'
Neh 12:27 . . to assist in the *c-ies.*
Acts 24:18 . . completing a purification *c.*
Heb 9:10 . . . and various cleansing *c-ies*—

CERTAIN (adj)
assured in mind or action; dependable, reliable; known or proved to be true, indisputable
Josh 23:13 . . know for *c* that the LORD
Eccl 7:14 . . . nothing is *c* in this life.
Luke 1:4. . . . so you can be *c* of the truth
Phil 1:6 . . . . *c* that God, who began the good work
Heb 6:11 . . . to make *c* that what you hope

CHAFF (n)
the seed coverings and other debris separated from the seed in threshing grain; something comparatively worthless
Ps 1:4 . . . . . . *c,* scattered by the wind.
Ps 35:5 . . . . . Blow them away like *c* in the
Dan 2:35 . . . like *c* on a threshing floor.
Matt 3:12. . . separate the *c* from the

CHAIN, CHAINS (n)
metal links or rings connected to one another and used for various purposes
Prov 1:9. . . . a *c* of honor around your neck.
Acts 26:29 . . as I am, except for these *c-s."*
Eph 6:20 . . . I am in *c-s* now, still preaching
Col 4:18 . . . . Remember my *c-s.*
2 Tim 1:16 . . because I was in *c-s.*

CHAINED (v)
to fasten, bind, or connect with or as with a chain; to obstruct

2 Tim 2:9 . . . the word of God cannot be *c.*
Jude 1:6 . . . . *c* in prisons of darkness,

CHALLENGE (v)
to put to a test or trial; to dispute with

Jer 49:19. . . . like me, and who can *c* me?

CHANCE (n)
something that happens unpredictably without discernible human intention or cause, luck; a situation favoring some purpose, opportunity

1 Sam 18:21. another *c* to see him killed
Eccl 9:11 . . . all decided by *c,* by being
Jer 15:6. . . . . giving you another *c.*
Phil 4:10 . . . didn't have the *c* to help

CHANGE, CHANGED, CHANGES (v)
to make different or transform; to shift, exchange, or transfer

Exod 32:14 . the LORD ***c-d*** his mind about
1 Sam 10:6. . be ***c-d*** into a different person.
1 Sam 15:29. human that he should *c*
Ps 93:5 . . . . . Your royal laws cannot be ***c-d.***
Isa 14:27. . . . who can *c* his plans?
Jer 33:25. . . . than I would *c* my laws
Jonah 3:9 . . . even yet God will *c* his mind
Mal 3:6. . . . . I am the LORD, and I do not *c.*
2 Cor 3:18 . . we are ***c-d*** into his glorious
Heb 6:17 . . . he would never *c* his mind.
Jas 1:17. . . . . never ***c-s*** or casts a shifting

CHARACTER (n)
moral excellence and firmness; main or essential nature

Rom 5:4. . . . develops strength of *c,*
1 Cor 15:33 . company corrupts good *c.*
Heb 1:3 . . . . expresses the very *c* of God,

CHARGE, CHARGES (n)
management, supervision; obligation, requirement; a formal assertion of illegality or statement of complaint

Deut 19:18. . brought false ***c-s*** against
Ps 8:6 . . . . . . gave them *c* of everything you
Prov 23:11. . bring their ***c-s*** against you.
Isa 50:8. . . . . dare to bring ***c-s*** against me
Mic 6:2. . . . . will bring ***c-s*** against Israel.
1 Cor 4:1 . . . in *c* of explaining God's
1 Cor 4:2 . . . in *c* as a manager must be

CHARGE, CHARGED, CHARGING (v)
to impose a financial burden on; to command, instruct, or exhort with authority

Ps 119:4 . . . . ***c-d*** us to keep your commandments
1 Cor 9:18 . . the Good News without ***c-ing***
Phlm 1:18 . . owes you anything, *c* it to me.

CHARIOT, CHARIOTS (n)
a two-wheeled horse-drawn battle car of ancient times used also in processions and races

2 Kgs 2:11 . . suddenly a *c* of fire appeared,
2 Kgs 6:17 . . with horses and ***c-s*** of fire.
Ps 20:7 . . . . . boast of their ***c-s*** and horses,
Ps 68:17 . . . . thousands of ***c-s,*** the LORD came
Ps 104:3 . . . . You make the clouds your *c;*

CHARITY (KJV)

1 Cor 8:1 . . . ***love*** that strengthens the church
1 Cor 13:1 . . but didn't ***love*** others, I would
Col 3:14 . . . . clothe yourselves with ***love,***
1 Tim 4:12 . . in your ***love,*** your faith, and
2 Pet 1:7. . . . with ***love*** for everyone

CHARM (n)
something worn about the person to ward off evil or ensure good fortune; a trait that fascinates, allures, or delights

Prov 17:8. . . A bribe is like a lucky *c;*
Prov 31:30. . *C* is deceptive, and beauty

CHASTE (KJV)

2 Cor 11:2 . . a ***pure*** bride to one husband—
Titus 2:5. . . . to live wisely and be ***pure***
1 Pet 3:2. . . . ***pure*** and reverent lives

CHASTEN(ED) (KJV)

Ps 6:1 . . . . . . or ***discipline*** me in your rage
Prov 19:18. . ***Discipline*** your children
1 Cor 11:32 . ***being disciplined*** so that we
Heb 12:11 . . No ***discipline*** is enjoyable
Rev 3:19. . . . I correct and ***discipline***

CHEAT, CHEATED, CHEATING, CHEATS (v)
to deprive of something valuable by deceit or fraud; to practice fraud or trickery

Gen 31:7 . . . he has ***c-ed*** me, changing my
1 Sam 12:3. . Have I ever ***c-ed*** any of you?
1 Sam 12:4. . have never ***c-ed*** or oppressed
Amos 8:5. . . get back to ***c-ing*** the helpless.
Mal 3:8. . . . . You have ***c-ed*** me of the tithes
Mark 10:19 . You must not *c* anyone.
Mark 12:40 . they shamelessly *c* widows

1 Cor 5:10 . . are greedy, or *c* people,
1 Cor 5:11 . . is a drunkard, or *c-s* people.
1 Cor 6:7 . . . not let yourselves be *c-ed?*
1 Cor 6:8 . . . who do wrong and *c* even
1 Cor 6:10 . . abusive, or *c* people—

CHEEK (n)
the fleshy side of the face below the eye and above and to the side of the mouth
Matt 5:39 . . . slaps you on the right *c,*
Luke 6:29. . . offer the other *c* also.

CHEERFUL (adj)
full of good spirits; merry, ungrudging
Prov 15:30 . . A *c* look brings joy
Prov 17:22 . . A *c* heart is good medicine,

CHEERFULLY (adv)
marked by or suggestive of lighthearted ease of mind and spirit; cheerily, gladly
2 Cor 9:7 . . . loves a person who gives *c.*
1 Pet 4:9. . . . *C* share your home with those

CHEERS (v)
to instill with hope, joy, hilarity, or comfort
Prov 12:25 . . encouraging word *c* a person

CHERISH (v)
to hold dear; to feel or show affection for
Ps 102:14 . . . *c* even the dust in her streets.
Prov 19:8 . . . people who *c* understanding

CHERUBIM (n)
winged angelic beings, often associated with worship and praise of God
Gen 3:24 . . . God stationed mighty *c* to the
Exod 25:19 . Mold the *c* on each end
1 Sam 4:4. . . enthroned between the *c.*
1 Kgs 6:23 . . He made two *c* of wild olive
Isa 37:16. . . . between the mighty *c!*
Ezek 10:1. . . over the heads of the *c.*

CHEST (n)
a wooden box or container; the trunk or rib cage of the human body
Exod 25:10 . a sacred *c* 45 inches long,
2 Kgs 12:9 . . a hole in the lid of a large *c*
Zech 13:6. . . those wounds on your *c?*
Rev 1:13. . . . with a gold sash across his *c.*

CHESTPIECE (n)
a breastplate attached to the front of an ephod worn by the high priest
Exod 28:15 . make a *c* to be worn for

CHILD, CHILDREN (n)
an unborn or recently born person; a young person between infancy and youth, not yet of age; offspring or descendants
see also SON(S)
Exod 20:5 . . family is affected—even *c-ren*
Deut 24:16. . sins of their *c-ren,* nor *c-ren*
Deut 32:46. . as a command to your *c-ren*
1 Kgs 3:26 . . Give her the *c*—please do
Job 1:5 . . . . . Perhaps my *c-ren* have sinned
Ps 8:2 . . . . . . have taught *c-ren* and infants
Prov 20:7. . . blessed are their *c-ren* who
Prov 23:13. . discipline your *c-ren.*
Prov 29:15. . To discipline a *c* produces
Prov 31:28. . Her *c-ren* stand and bless
Isa 7:14. . . . . The virgin will conceive a *c!*
Isa 9:6. . . . . . For a *c* is born to us,
Isa 54:13. . . . I will teach all your *c-ren,*
Mal 4:6. . . . . hearts of *c-ren* to their fathers.
Matt 1:23. . . The virgin will conceive a *c!*
Matt 5:9. . . . will be called the *c-ren* of God.
Matt 18:3. . . and become like little *c-ren,*
Mark 9:37 . . welcomes a little *c* like this
Mark 10:14 . Let the *c-ren* come to me.
Mark 10:16 . took the *c-ren* in his arms
Luke 1:42. . . and your *c* is blessed.
Luke 6:35. . . as *c-ren* of the Most High,
Luke 18:15. . their little *c-ren* to Jesus
John 1:12 . . . to become *c-ren* of God.
John 12:36 . . become *c-ren* of the light.
Acts 2:39 . . . to your *c-ren,* and even to the
Rom 9:26. . . called '*c-ren* of the living God.'
1 Cor 13:11 . and reasoned as a *c.*
Gal 3:26 . . . . you are all *c-ren* of God
Eph 3:6 . . . . riches inherited by God's *c-ren.*
Eph 6:1 . . . . *C-ren,* obey your parents
Eph 6:4 . . . . not provoke your *c-ren* to anger
Col 3:21 . . . . do not aggravate your *c-ren,*
1 Tim 3:4 . . . having *c-ren* who respect and
1 Tim 3:12 . . manage his *c-ren* and
1 Tim 5:10 . . brought up her *c-ren* well?
Heb 12:7 . . . treating you as his own *c-ren.*
1 Jn 4:7. . . . . who loves is a *c* of God
1 Jn 5:4. . . . . every *c* of God defeats this evil
1 Jn 5:18. . . . God's *c-ren* do not make a

CHILDISH (adj)
of, relating to, or befitting a child; marked by or suggestive of immaturity
1 Cor 13:11 . I put away *c* things.
1 Cor 14:20 . brothers and sisters, don't be *c*

CHILDLESS (adj)
a person characterized by lack of children; barren
Ps 113:9 . . . . He gives the *c* woman a family,

Isa 54:1. . . . . Sing, O *c* woman, you who
Gal 4:27 . . . . Rejoice, O *c* woman, you who

CHILDLIKE (adj)
resembling, suggesting, or appropriate to a child; marked by innocence, trust, and ingenuousness
Ps 116:6 . . . . protects those of *c* faith;
Matt 11:25 . . revealing them to the *c.*

CHOOSE, CHOOSES (v)
to decide; to have a preference for; to select freely and after consideration
see also CALL, CHOSE
Deut 30:19. . Oh, that you would *c* life, so
Josh 24:15 . . *c* today whom you will serve.
Eccl 10:2 . . . wise person *c-s* the right road;
Jer 27:5. . . . . things of mine to anyone I *c.*
Dan 4:25 . . . gives them to anyone he *c-s.*
John 15:16 . . You didn't *c* me. I chose you.
Rom 9:11 . . . God *c-s* people according to
Rom 9:18 . . . he *c-s* to harden the hearts of

CHOSE, CHOSEN (v)
to decide; to have a preference for
see also CALL, CHOOSE, CHOSEN
Matt 22:14 . . called, but few are *c-n.*
John 15:16 . . You didn't choose me. I *c* you.
Rom 1:1 . . . . *c-n* by God to be an apostle
Rom 8:29 . . . *c* them to become like his
1 Cor 1:1 . . . Paul, *c-n* by the will of God
1 Cor 1:27 . . *c* things that are powerless
Eph 1:4 . . . . loved us and *c* us in Christ
Eph 1:11 . . . God, for he *c* us in advance,
2 Thes 2:13 . thankful that God *c* you
1 Pet 1:15 . . . as God who *c* you is holy.
2 Pet 1:10 . . . God has called and *c-n.*

CHOSEN (adj)
selected or marked for special favor or privilege
see also CALLED
1 Chr 16:22 . Do not touch my *c* people,
Isa 41:8. . . . . my *c* one, descended from Abraham
Mark 13:20 . for the sake of his *c* ones
Luke 23:35. . God's Messiah, the *C* One.
John 1:34 . . . that he is the *C* One of God.
1 Pet 1:1. . . . writing to God's *c* people
1 Pet 2:9. . . . for you are a *c* people.

CHRIST (n)
Son of God, Messiah, Anointed One
see also JESUS, MESSIAH
John 1:17 . . . faithfulness came through Jesus *C.*
Rom 1:4. . . . He is Jesus *C* our Lord.
Rom 3:22. . . by placing our faith in Jesus *C.*
Rom 5:1 . . . . Jesus *C* our Lord has done
Rom 5:6 . . . . *C* came at just the right time
Rom 5:11 . . . *C* has made us friends of God.
Rom 6:4 . . . . as *C* was raised from the dead
Rom 6:23 . . . eternal life through *C* Jesus
Rom 7:4 . . . . when you died with *C.*
Rom 8:1 . . . . who belong to *C* Jesus.
Rom 8:34 . . . *C* Jesus died for us and
Rom 8:35 . . . separate us from *C*'s love?
Rom 14:9 . . . *C* died and rose again for this
Rom 15:5 . . . fitting for followers of *C* Jesus.
Rom 15:20 . . where the name of *C* has never
1 Cor 1:2 . . . the name of our Lord Jesus *C,*
1 Cor 1:13 . . Has *C* been divided into
1 Cor 1:17 . . cross of *C* would lose its power.
1 Cor 1:23 . . preach that *C* was crucified,
1 Cor 1:30 . . God has united you with *C*
1 Cor 5:7 . . . *C,* our Passover Lamb,
1 Cor 6:15 . . his body, which is part of *C,*
1 Cor 8:12 . . you are sinning against *C.*
1 Cor 9:19 . . to bring many to *C.*
1 Cor 10:4 . . that rock was *C.*
1 Cor 10:9 . . Nor should we put *C* to the test,
1 Cor 11:3 . . and the head of *C* is God.
1 Cor 12:27 . you together are *C*'s body,
1 Cor 15:3 . . *C* died for our sins,
2 Cor 1:5 . . . the more we suffer for *C,* the
2 Cor 3:3 . . . you are a letter from *C*
2 Cor 3:14 . . removed only by believing in *C.*
2 Cor 5:10 . . stand before *C* to be judged.
2 Cor 5:14 . . *C*'s love controls us.
2 Cor 5:20 . . we are *C*'s ambassadors;
Gal 1:7 . . . . . twist the truth concerning *C.*
Gal 2:4 . . . . . the freedom we have in *C* Jesus.
Gal 2:21 . . . . need for *C* to die.
Gal 3:13 . . . . But *C* has rescued us
Gal 4:19 . . . . continue until *C* is fully developed
Gal 5:4 . . . . . you have been cut off from *C!*
Gal 5:24 . . . . Those who belong to *C* Jesus
Eph 1:3 . . . . because we are united with *C.*
Eph 1:10 . . . under the authority of *C*—
Eph 1:20 . . . that raised *C* from the dead
Eph 2:10 . . . created us anew in *C* Jesus,
Eph 2:20 . . . the cornerstone is *C* Jesus
Eph 4:7 . . . . through the generosity of *C.*
Eph 4:32 . . . God through *C* has forgiven you.
Eph 5:21 . . . out of reverence for *C.*
Eph 5:23 . . . head of his wife as *C* is
Eph 5:25 . . . wives, just as *C* loved the

Phil 1:21 . . . living means living for **C**,
Phil 1:23 . . . with **C**, which would be far better
Phil 1:29 . . . the privilege of trusting in **C**
Phil 2:5 . . . . same attitude that **C** Jesus had.
Phil 3:18 . . . enemies of the cross of **C**.
Col 1:22 . . . . through the death of **C**
Col 2:2 . . . . . mysterious plan, which is **C**
Col 2:6 . . . . . accepted **C** Jesus as your Lord,
Col 2:13 . . . . God made you alive with **C**,
Col 3:1 . . . . . raised to new life with **C**,
Col 3:3 . . . . . life is hidden with **C** in God.
Col 3:15 . . . . peace that comes from **C**
1 Thes 5:9 . . through our Lord Jesus **C**,
1 Tim 1:15 . . **C** Jesus came into the world
1 Tim 2:5 . . . humanity—the man **C** Jesus.
2 Tim 1:10 . . by the appearing of **C** Jesus,
2 Tim 2:3 . . . as a good soldier of **C** Jesus.
2 Tim 2:10 . . eternal glory in **C** Jesus
2 Tim 3:12 . . a godly life in **C** Jesus will
2 Tim 3:15 . . by trusting in **C** Jesus.
2 Tim 4:1 . . . of God and **C** Jesus, who will
Titus 2:13 . . . and Savior, Jesus **C**, will be
Heb 3:14 . . . share in all that belongs to **C**.
Heb 6:1 . . . . teachings about **C** again and
Heb 9:14 . . . the blood of **C** will purify
Heb 9:28 . . . **C** died once for all time
Heb 10:10 . . body of Jesus **C**, once for all
Heb 13:8 . . . Jesus **C** is the same yesterday,
1 Pet 1:11 . . . the Spirit of **C** within them
1 Pet 1:19 . . . blood of **C**, the sinless,
1 Pet 2:21 . . . just as **C** suffered for you.
1 Pet 3:15 . . . you must worship **C** as Lord
1 Pet 4:13 . . . partners with **C** in his suffering,
2 Pet 1:16 . . . coming of our Lord Jesus **C**.
1 Jn 2:1 . . . . . He is Jesus **C**, the one who is
1 Jn 2:22 . . . . says that Jesus is not the **C**.
1 Jn 4:2 . . . . . that Jesus **C** came in a real
1 Jn 5:1 . . . . . Jesus is the **C** has become
1 Jn 5:20 . . . . fellowship with his Son, Jesus **C**.
Rev 1:1 . . . . . from Jesus **C**, which God gave
Rev 1:5 . . . . . his throne; and from Jesus **C**.
Rev 20:4 . . . . and they reigned with **C** for
Rev 20:6 . . . . God and of **C** and will reign

CHRISTIAN, CHRISTIANS (n)

one who professes belief in and follows the teachings of Jesus Christ; believer

Acts 11:26 . . believers were first called **C-s**.
Acts 26:28 . . persuade me to become a **C**
Gal 2:4 . . . . . some so-called **C-s**
1 Thes 4:12 . people who are not **C-s**
1 Pet 4:14 . . . insulted for being a **C**,
1 Pet 4:16 . . . to suffer for being a **C**.
1 Pet 5:9 . . . . your **C** brothers and sisters

CHURCH, CHURCHES (n)

"assembly" or "called ones"; the body of believers gathered to worship Jesus (not the building in which they meet)

Matt 16:18 . . this rock I will build my **c**,
Matt 18:17 . . take your case to the **c**.
Acts 16:5 . . . the **c-es** were strengthened
Acts 20:28 . . shepherd God's flock—his **c**,
1 Cor 15:9 . . way I persecuted God's **c**.
Gal 1:13 . . . . I violently persecuted God's **c**.
Eph 5:23 . . . Christ is the head of the **c**.
Col 1:18 . . . . head of the **c**, which is his
Col 1:24 . . . . continue for his body, the **c**.
2 Thes 1:4 . . tell God's other **c-es** about your
Rev 1:20 . . . . angels of the seven **c-es**,

CIRCUMCISE, CIRCUMCISED, CIRCUMCISING (v)

to cut off the foreskin of a male child

Gen 17:10 . . among you must be **c-d**.
Gen 17:12 . . **c-d** on the eighth day after his
Josh 5:3 . . . . made flint knives and **c-d**
John 7:23 . . . correct time for **c-ing** your son
Acts 21:21 . . not to **c** their children
Rom 4:11 . . . even before he was **c-d**.
1 Cor 7:19 . . or not a man has been **c-d**.

CIRCUMCISION (n)

the condition of being circumcised; the ceremony signifying Israel's covenant with God; act symbolic of cleansing

Rom 2:25 . . . **c** has value only if you obey
Rom 2:29 . . . true **c** is not merely
Gal 5:2 . . . . . you are counting on **c** to make

CIRCUMSTANCES (n)

conditions, facts, or events accompanying, conditioning, or determining another

1 Thes 5:18 . Be thankful in all **c**, for this

CITIZEN, CITIZENS (n)

a person owing allegiance to and deriving protection from a sovereign state

Acts 22:28 . . But I am a **c** by birth!
Eph 2:19 . . . You are **c-s** along with
Phil 3:20 . . . But we are **c-s** of heaven,

CITIZENSHIP (n)

the status of being a citizen; membership in a community

Eph 2:12 . . . excluded from **c** among

CLAIM, CLAIMS (v)
to assert in the face of possible contradiction; to take as the rightful owner
Eccl 8:17 . . . no matter what they *c.*
Song 7:10. . . and he *c-s* me as his own.
Isa 62:4. . . . . delights in you and will *c* you
Jas 1:26. . . . . *c* to be religious but don't
1 Jn 1:10. . . . If we *c* we have not sinned,
1 Jn 2:9. . . . . If anyone *c-s,* "I am living in

CLAP, CLAPPED (v)
to strike (the hands) together repeatedly, usually in applause
2 Kgs 11:12 . everyone ***c-ped*** their hands
Ps 47:1 . . . . . everyone! *C* your hands!
Ps 98:8 . . . . . Let the rivers *c* their hands
Isa 55:12. . . . trees of the field will *c*
Nah 3:19 . . . hear of your destruction will *c*

CLAY (n)
an earthy material that is pliable when moist but hard when fired and is used for brick, tile, and pottery
Isa 45:9. . . . . Does the *c* dispute with the one
Isa 64:8. . . . . *c,* and you are the potter.
Lam 4:2 . . . . are now treated like pots of *c*
Dan 2:33 . . . of iron and baked *c.*
Rom 9:21 . . . to use the same lump of *c*
2 Cor 4:7 . . . *c* jars containing this great
2 Tim 2:20 . . are made of wood and *c.*

CLEAN (adj)
unadulterated, pure; without guilt or moral corruption; without ceremonial defilement
see also PURE
Lev 10:10. . . unclean and what is *c.*
Ps 51:2 . . . . . Wash me *c* from my guilt.
Ps 51:7 . . . . . and I will be *c;* wash me,
Ps 51:10 . . . . Create in me a *c* heart, O God.
John 13:10 . . you disciples are *c,* but not all
Acts 10:15 . . if God has made it *c.*
2 Tim 2:21 . . Your life will be *c,*

CLEANSE, CLEANSED, CLEANSES (v)
to make clean, pure, holy
see also PURIFY, WASH
Ps 19:12 . . . . *C* me from these hidden
Prov 20:9 . . . Who can say, "I have ***c-d*** my
Jer 4:14. . . . . O Jerusalem, *c* your heart
Acts 15:9 . . . he ***c-d*** their hearts through
1 Cor 6:11 . . were ***c-d;*** you were made holy;
2 Cor 7:1 . . . let us *c* ourselves from
Titus 2:14. . . *c* us, and to make us his
Heb 1:3 . . . . he had ***c-d*** us from our sins,
Heb 9:13 . . . of a young cow could *c*
1 Pet 1:2. . . . and have been ***c-d*** by the blood
1 Pet 1:22. . . You were ***c-d*** from your sins
2 Pet 1:9. . . . that they have been ***c-d***
1 Jn 1:7. . . . . blood of Jesus, his Son, ***c-s*** us
1 Jn 1:9. . . . . to *c* us from all wickedness.

CLEAR, CLEARED (v)
to free from what obstructs or is unneeded
Ps 32:2 . . . . . whose record the LORD has ***c-ed***
John 1:23 . . . *C* the way for the Lord's coming!
Rom 4:8 . . . . whose record the LORD has ***c-ed***

CLEARHEADED (adj)
having or showing a clear understanding; able to think clearly
1 Thes 5:6 . . Stay alert and be *c.*

CLEVER (adj)
mentally quick and resourceful; marked by wit or ingenuity
Job 15:5 . . . . are based on *c* deception.
Isa 5:21. . . . . and think themselves so *c.*
Eph 4:14 . . . so *c* they sound like the truth.
2 Pet 1:16. . . we were not making up *c* stories

CLEVERNESS (n)
the state of being mentally quick and resourceful; showing wit or ingenuity
1 Cor 3:19 . . in the snare of their own *c.*

CLING (v)
to adhere as if glued firmly; to hold or hold on to tightly or tenaciously
Deut 10:20. . worship him and *c* to him.
Deut 13:4. . . listen to his voice, and *c* to
Matt 10:39. . If you *c* to your life,
Luke 8:15. . . who hear God's word, *c* to it,
John 20:17 . . "Don't *c* to me," Jesus
Phil 2:6 . . . . as something to *c* to.

CLOSE, CLOSED, CLOSES (v)
to draw near; to contract, fold, swing, or slide so as to leave no opening
Gen 7:16 . . . Then the LORD ***c-d*** the door
Prov 28:27 . . who *c* their eyes to poverty
Acts 28:27 . . and they have ***c-d*** their eyes—
Rev 3:7. . . . . what he ***c-s,*** no one can open:
Rev 21:25. . . Its gates will never be ***c-d***

CLOSE, CLOSER (adv)
being near in time, space, effect, or degree
Exod 3:5 . . . Do not come any *c,*
Ps 34:18 . . . . is *c* to the brokenhearted;
Ps 148:14 . . . of Israel who are *c* to him.
Prov 18:24 . . sticks *c* than a brother.
Isa 40:11. . . . in his arms, holding them *c*

CLOTHED (v)
to dress; to endow especially with power or a quality
Ps 30:11 . . . . mourning and *c* me with joy,
Prov 31:25 . . She is *c* with strength
Rev 7:9. . . . . They were *c* in white robes
Rev 7:13. . . . these who are *c* in white?

CLOTHES (n)
cloth articles of personal use that can be worn and washed
Deut 8:4. . . . years your *c* didn't wear out,
Isa 50:9. . . . . old *c* that have been eaten by
Matt 6:25 . . . food and drink, or enough *c*
Matt 27:35 . . soldiers gambled for his *c*
John 19:23 . . they divided his *c* among
Gal 3:27 . . . . like putting on new *c.*

CLOTHING (n)
garments in general; covering
Gen 3:21 . . . God made *c* from animal skins
Deut 22:5. . . must not put on men's *c,*
Ps 22:18 . . . . and throw dice for my *c.*
Matt 6:28. . . And why worry about your *c?*
1 Tim 6:8 . . . food and *c,* let us be content.

CLOUD, CLOUDS (n)
a visible mass of particles of condensed vapor suspended in the atmosphere
1 Kgs 18:44 . I saw a little *c* about the
Ps 68:4 . . . . . praises to him who rides the *c-s.*
Ps 108:4 . . . . faithfulness reaches to the *c-s.*
Isa 19:1. . . . . Egypt, riding on a swift *c.*
Dan 7:13 . . . coming with the *c-s* of heaven.
Mark 13:26 . coming on the *c-s* with great
Luke 21:27. . Son of Man coming on a *c*
1 Thes 4:17 . up in the *c-s* to meet the Lord
Rev 1:7. . . . . comes with the *c-s* of heaven.
Rev 14:14. . . I saw a white *c,* and seated on

COALS (n)
a piece of glowing carbon or charred wood; ember
Prov 25:22. . heap burning *c* of shame
Rom 12:20. . heap burning *c* of shame

COARSE (adj)
crude or unrefined in taste, manners, or language; harsh, raucous, or rough in tone
Eph 5:4 . . . . *c* jokes—these are not for you.

COAT (n)
an outer garment worn on the upper body
Matt 5:40. . . give your *c,* too.
Luke 6:29. . . your *c,* offer your shirt

COIN, COINS (n)
a usually flat piece of metal issued by governmental authority as money
Mark 12:15 . Show me a Roman *c,*
Mark 12:42 . dropped in two small *c-s.*
Luke 12:6. . . sparrows—two copper *c-s?*
Luke 15:8. . . woman has ten silver *c-s*

COLLAPSE (v)
to cave or fall in or give way
Matt 7:25 . . . it won't *c* because it is built
Luke 6:49. . . it will *c* into a heap of ruins.

COLLECTED (v)
to bring together into one body or place
Hos 13:12 . . Ephraim's guilt has been *c,*
1 Cor 16:1 . . about the money being *c*

COLT (n)
a young male animal of the horse family
Zech 9:9. . . . riding on a donkey's *c.*

COME, COMES, COMING (v)
to originate, arise; to move or journey to a vicinity with a specified purpose; to happen, occur
see also CAME
Ps 121:1 . . . . does my help *c* from there?
Prov 12:21. . No harm *c-s* to the godly,
1 Thes 3:13 . our Lord Jesus *c-s* again
Heb 9:28 . . . He will *c* again,
Heb 13:7 . . . good that has *c* from their
Jas 5:8. . . . . . for the *c-ing* of the Lord
Rev 7:10. . . . Salvation *c-s* from our God

COMFORT (n)
consolation in time of trouble or worry; solace
Gen 24:67 . . she was a special *c* to him
Job 10:20 . . . I may have a moment of *c*
Ps 94:19 . . . . your *c* gave me renewed hope
Zech 10:2. . . falsehoods that give no *c.*
2 Cor 1:5 . . . shower us with his *c*
2 Cor 1:7 . . . share in the *c* God gives us.
Col 4:11 . . . . And what a *c* they have been!

COMFORT, COMFORTED, COMFORTS (v)
to give strength and hope to; to console
Gen 37:35 . . he refused to be *c-ed.*
Ruth 2:13. . . You have *c-ed* me by speaking
Job 2:11 . . . . traveled from their homes to *c*
Job 42:11 . . . consoled him and *c-ed* him
Ps 69:20 . . . . one would turn and *c* me.
Ps 86:17 . . . . O LORD, help and *c* me.
Ps 119:50 . . . it *c-s* me in all my troubles.
Ps 119:52 . . . O LORD, they *c* me.

Isa 40:1. . . . . *C, c* my people,
Isa 49:13. . . . the LORD has ***c-ed*** his people
Isa 51:3. . . . . The LORD will ***c*** Israel again
Isa 51:12. . . . I, yes I, am the one who ***c-s*** you.
Isa 51:19. . . . Who is left to ***c*** you?
Isa 52:9. . . . . the LORD has ***c-ed*** his people.
Isa 61:1. . . . . to ***c*** the brokenhearted
Isa 66:13. . . . as a mother ***c-s*** her child.
Lam 1:2 . . . . there is no one left to ***c*** her.
Lam 1:17 . . . but no one ***c-s*** her.
Zech 1:17. . . the LORD will again ***c*** Zion
Matt 5:4. . . . mourn, for they will be ***c-ed.***
1 Cor 14:3 . . encourages them, and ***c-s***
2 Cor 1:4 . . . He ***c-s*** us in all our troubles
2 Cor 1:4 . . . so that we can ***c*** others.
2 Cor 1:6 . . . when we ourselves are ***c-ed,***
2 Cor 1:6 . . . we will certainly ***c*** you.
2 Cor 2:7 . . . forgive and ***c*** him.

COMFORTER (KJV)
John 14:16 . . another ***Advocate,*** who will
John 14:26 . . sends the ***Advocate*** as my
John 15:26 . . the ***Advocate***—the Spirit of
John 16:7 . . . if I don't, the ***Advocate*** won't

COMMAND, COMMANDS (n)
an order given; religious instruction
see also COMMANDMENT
Exod 20:6 . . who love me and obey my ***c-s.***
Exod 24:12 . the instructions and ***c-s***
Lev 22:31. . . keep all my ***c-s***
Num 15:39 . and obey all the ***c-s***
Deut 4:2. . . . or subtract from these ***c-s***
Deut 6:6. . . . wholeheartedly to these ***c-s***
Deut 7:9. . . . who love him and obey his ***c-s.***
Deut 8:1. . . . Be careful to obey all the ***c-s***
Deut 11:1. . . decrees, regulations, and ***c-s.***
Deut 11:27. . if you obey the ***c-s*** of the
Deut 28:1. . . keep all his ***c-s*** that I am giving
Deut 32:46. . as a ***c*** to your children
Josh 1:9 . . . . my ***c***—be strong and
1 Kgs 8:58 . . obey all the ***c-s,*** decrees,
1 Kgs 8:61 . . obey his decrees and ***c-s,***
1 Chr 28:7 . . if he continues to obey my ***c-s***
Neh 1:5 . . . . who love him and obey his ***c-s,***
Job 36:10 . . . ***c-s*** that they turn from evil.
Ps 33:9 . . . . . It appeared at his ***c.***
Ps 78:7 . . . . . and obeying his ***c-s.***
Ps 103:20 . . . listening for each of his ***c-s.***
Ps 112:1 . . . . and delight in obeying his ***c-s.***
Ps 119:32 . . . I will pursue your ***c-s,***
Ps 119:47 . . . How I delight in your ***c-s!***
Ps 119:73 . . . the sense to follow your ***c-s.***
Ps 119:96 . . . your ***c-s*** have no limit.
Ps 119:127 . . I love your ***c-s*** more than
Ps 119:143 . . I find joy in your ***c-s.***
Ps 119:172 . . all your ***c-s*** are right.
Ps 119:176 . . I have not forgotten your ***c-s.***
Prov 3:1 . . . . Store my ***c-s*** in your heart.
Prov 6:23 . . . For their ***c*** is a lamp
Eccl 12:13 . . Fear God and obey his ***c-s,***
Isa 48:18. . . . you had listened to my ***c-s!***
Dan 9:4 . . . . who love you and obey your ***c-s.***
Matt 28:20 . . disciples to obey all the ***c-s***
John 15:17 . . my ***c:*** Love each other.
Acts 17:30 . . he ***c-s*** everyone everywhere to
Rom 7:8. . . . sin used this ***c*** to arouse
Rom 7:9. . . . I learned the ***c*** not to covet,
Rom 7:12. . . law itself is holy, and its ***c-s*** are
1 Cor 14:37 . saying is a ***c*** from the Lord
Gal 5:14. . . . summed up in this one ***c:***
2 Thes 3:6 . . we give you this ***c***
2 Pet 2:21. . . reject the ***c*** they were given

COMMAND, COMMANDED, COMMANDING (v)
to issue a charge or directive
Gen 7:5 . . . . everything as the LORD ***c-ed***
Exod 7:6 . . . did just as the LORD had ***c-ed***
Exod 19:7 . . everything the LORD had ***c-ed***
Deut 6:1. . . . your God ***c-ed*** me to teach
Deut 6:24. . . our God ***c-ed*** us to obey
Deut 15:11. . why I am ***c-ing*** you to share
John 15:14 . . my friends if you do what I ***c.***
2 Tim 2:14 . . ***c*** them in God's presence
2 Pet 3:2. . . . Savior ***c-ed*** through your
1 Jn 3:23. . . . just as he ***c-ed*** us.
2 Jn 1:4. . . . . just as the Father ***c-ed.***

COMMANDER (n)
one in an official position of command or control
Eph 2:2 . . . . ***c*** of the powers in the unseen

COMMANDMENT, COMMANDMENTS (n)
a gracious provision of God's law or covenant, obeyed as an act of love and devotion
see also COMMAND
Exod 34:28 . Ten ***C-s***—on the stone
Deut 4:13. . . his covenant—the Ten ***C-s***
Deut 10:4. . . LORD wrote the Ten ***C-s*** on
Ps 103:18 . . . of those who obey his ***c-s!***
Ps 111:7 . . . . all his ***c-s*** are trustworthy.
Ps 111:10 . . . who obey his ***c-s*** will grow
Ps 119:93 . . . I will never forget your ***c-s,***
Prov 19:16 . . the ***c-s*** and keep your life;
Matt 5:19 . . . if you ignore the least ***c***
Matt 19:17 . . eternal life, keep the ***c-s.***
Matt 22:36 . . the most important ***c***
Matt 22:38 . . the first and greatest ***c.***

Mark 10:19 . you know the *c-s:*
Mark 12:28 . *c-s,* which is the most
Luke 18:20. . you know the *c-s:*
John 13:34 . . a new *c:* Love each other.
John 14:15 . . If you love me, obey my *c-s.*
Rom 13:9. . . in this one *c:* "Love your
1 Cor 7:19 . . is to keep God's *c-s.*
Eph 2:15 . . . law with its *c-s* and regulations.
Eph 6:2 . . . . the first *c* with a promise:
Heb 9:19 . . . had read each of God's *c-s*
1 Jn 2:3. . . . . know him if we obey his *c-s.*
1 Jn 3:24. . . . Those who obey God's *c-s*
1 Jn 5:3. . . . . God means keeping his *c-s,*
Rev 12:17. . . who keep God's *c-s* and

COMMEND, COMMENDING (v)
to entrust for care or preservation; to praise
Rom 16:1. . . I *c* to you our sister Phoebe,
2 Cor 5:12 . . Are we *c-ing* ourselves to you
2 Cor 10:18 . When people *c* themselves,

COMMENDATIONS (n)
a praiseworthy citation
2 Cor 12:11 . ought to be writing *c* for me,

COMMIT, COMMITS, COMMITTED, COMMITTING (v)
to carry into action deliberately, perpetrate; to obligate or pledge oneself
Deut 30:20. . *c-ting* yourself firmly to him.
2 Chr 16:9 . . hearts are fully *c-ted* to him.
2 Chr 17:6 . . deeply *c-ted* to the ways
Prov 6:32. . . the man who *c-s* adultery
Prov 29:22. . a hot-tempered person *c-s*
Matt 5:28. . . has already *c-ted* adultery
Matt 5:32. . . causes her to *c* adultery.
Matt 19:9. . . someone else *c-s* adultery—
Mark 10:11 . someone else *c-s* adultery
Mark 10:19 . You must not *c* adultery.
Luke 16:18. . her husband *c-s* adultery.
Rom 13:9. . . You must not *c* adultery.
Titus 2:14. . . totally *c-ted* to doing good
Jas 2:11. . . . . You must not *c* adultery,
Rev 18:3. . . . world have *c-ted* adultery with
Rev 18:9. . . . the world who *c-ted* adultery

COMMON (adj)
characterized by a lack of privilege or special status; belonging to or shared by two or more individuals or things or all members of a group
Lev 10:10. . . what is sacred and what is *c,*
1 Cor 9:22 . . I try to find *c* ground with

COMMUNITY (n)
a unified body of individuals
Num 20:1 . . whole *c* of Israel arrived

COMPANION , COMPANIONS (n)
a close friend or fellow participant
Ps 55:13 . . . . my *c* and close friend.
Ps 55:20 . . . . As for my *c,* he betrayed his
Prov 16:29. . mislead their *c-s,* leading

COMPANY (n)
association with another, fellowship; companions, associates
Prov 21:16. . end up in the *c* of the dead.
Prov 24:1. . . or desire their *c.*
Rom 12:16. . to enjoy the *c* of ordinary
1 Cor 15:33 . for "bad *c* corrupts good

COMPASSION (n)
sympathy, usually granted because of unusual or distressing circumstances
Exod 34:6 . . The God of *c* and mercy!
Ps 51:1 . . . . . Because of your great *c,*
Ps 86:15 . . . . a God of *c* and mercy, slow to
Ps 145:9 . . . . He showers *c* on all
Isa 49:13. . . . and will have *c* on them
Isa 63:15. . . . your mercy and *c* now?
Lam 3:32 . . . brings grief, he also shows *c*
Hos 2:19 . . . unfailing love and *c.*
Mic 7:19. . . . you will have *c* on us.
Zech 10:6. . . because of my *c.*
Mark 1:41 . . Moved with *c,* Jesus reached
Mark 6:34 . . and he had *c* on them
Luke 15:20. . with love and *c,* he ran to
Rom 9:15. . . show *c* to anyone I choose.

COMPASSIONATE (adj)
having or showing compassion; sympathetic
Ps 103:13 . . . tender and *c* to those who
Ps 112:4 . . . . They are generous, *c,*
Ps 145:8 . . . . is merciful and *c,* slow to
Joel 2:13. . . . he is merciful and *c,* slow to
Luke 6:36. . . You must be *c,* just as your
Phil 2:1 . . . . Are your hearts tender and *c?*

COMPELLED (v)
to drive or urge forcefully or irresistibly
1 Cor 9:16 . . I am *c* by God to do it.

COMPENSATION (n)
something that constitutes an equivalent or recompense
Prov 6:35. . . He will accept no *c,*

COMPLACENCY (n)
self-satisfaction especially when accompanied by unawareness of actual dangers or deficiencies
Prov 1:32. . . destroyed by their own *c.*
Isa 32:11. . . . throw off your *c.*

COMPLACENT (adj)
self-satisfied; unconcerned
Jer 49:31. . . . attack that *c* nation,
Zeph 1:12 . . who sit *c* in their sins.

COMPLAINED, COMPLAINING (v)
to express grief, pain, or discontent; to make a formal accusation or charge
Exod 15:24 . the people *c* and turned
Num 14:2 . . in the wilderness!" they *c.*
Num 14:29 . Because you *c* against me,
John 6:43 . . . Jesus replied, "Stop *c-ing*
Phil 2:14 . . . Do everything without *c-ing*

COMPLAINERS (n)
one who complains
Jude 1:16 . . . grumblers and *c,* living only

COMPLAINT (n)
a formal allegation against a party
Mic 6:2. . . . . listen to the LORD's *c!*

COMPLETE (adj)
having all necessary parts, elements, or steps
Eph 4:13 . . . full and *c* standard of Christ.
Jas 2:22. . . . . made his faith *c.*
2 Jn 1:12. . . . joy will be *c.*

COMPREHEND (v)
to grasp the nature, significance, or meaning of
Matt 13:14 . . I do, you will not *c.*

COMPREHENSION (n)
the act or action of grasping with the intellect; understanding
Ps 147:5 . . . . is beyond *c!*

CONCEAL, CONCEALED (v)
to prevent disclosure or recognition of; to place out of sight
Prov 25:2. . . God's privilege to *c*
Prov 28:13 . . People who *c* their sins will
Luke 8:17. . . everything that is *c-ed* will be

CONCEIT (n)
excessive appreciation of one's own worth or virtue
Ps 36:2 . . . . . In their blind *c,* they cannot

CONCEITED (adj)
having or showing an excessively high opinion of oneself
Gal 5:26 . . . . us not become *c,* or provoke

CONCEIVE, CONCEIVED (v)
to become pregnant; to devise or imagine
Gen 29:31 . . Rachel could not *c.*
Ps 7:14 . . . . . The wicked *c* evil; they are
Matt 1:20. . . was *c-d* by the Holy Spirit.
Luke 1:7. . . . Elizabeth was unable to *c,*
Luke 1:31. . . You will *c* and give birth

CONCERN, CONCERNS (n)
affair or business; an uneasy state of blended interest, uncertainty, and apprehension
Job 19:4 . . . . that is my *c,* not yours.
1 Cor 7:32 . . free from the *c-s* of this life.
2 Cor 7:11 . . such *c* to clear yourselves,
2 Cor 11:28 . the daily burden of my *c*

CONCERN, CONCERNED (v)
to involve; to be a care, trouble, or distress to
1 Sam 23:21. someone is *c-ed* about me!
Ps 131:1 . . . . I don't *c* myself with matters
1 Cor 10:24 . be *c-ed* for your own good
Phil 4:10 . . . have always been *c-ed* for me,

CONCUBINE, CONCUBINES (n)
a woman living in a man's household, though not married; of lower family status than the wife
Judg 19:1 . . . in Judah to be his *c.*
2 Sam 3:7. . . one of his father's *c-s,*
2 Sam 5:13. . David married more *c-s* and
2 Sam 16:22. sex with his father's *c-s.*
2 Sam 21:11. what Rizpah, Saul's *c,* had
1 Chr 1:32 . . Keturah, Abraham's *c,*
1 Chr 7:13 . . of Jacob's *c* Bilhah.

CONDEMN, CONDEMNED, CONDEMNING, CONDEMNS (v)
to declare guilty; to sentence or doom
Job 15:6 . . . . Your own mouth *c-s* you, not I.
Job 40:8 . . . . my justice and *c* me just to
Ps 37:33 . . . . or let the godly be *c-ed*
Ps 102:20 . . . to release those *c-ed* to die.
Prov 12:2. . . *c-s* those who plan wickedness.
Prov 17:15 . . guilty and *c-ing* the innocent—
Isa 53:8. . . . . Unjustly *c-ed,* he was led away.
Matt 12:7. . . not have *c-ed* my innocent
Matt 12:37 . . acquit you or *c* you.
Matt 12:41 . . on judgment day and *c* it,
Matt 27:3. . . Jesus had been *c-ed* to die,
Luke 11:31. . on judgment day and *c* it,
John 8:10 . . . even one of them *c* you?
Rom 2:1 . . . . think you can *c* such people,

Rom 2:1 . . . . you are *c-ing* yourself,
Rom 3:7 . . . . how can God *c* me as a sinner
Rom 3:8 . . . . deserve to be *c-ed.*
Rom 8:34 . . . Who then will *c* us? No one—
Rom 14:3 . . . foods must not *c* those who
Rom 14:13 . . So let's stop *c-ing* each other.
1 Cor 4:9 . . . a victor's parade, *c-ed* to die.
2 Cor 7:3 . . . saying this to *c* you.
Col 2:16 . . . . So don't let anyone *c* you
Jas 5:6. . . . . . You have *c-ed* and killed
Jas 5:12. . . . . not sin and be *c-ed.*

CONDEMNATION (n)
conviction of guilt; censure or blame
Rom 5:9 . . . . save us from God's *c.*
Rom 5:18 . . . Adam's one sin brings *c*
Rom 7:13 . . . bring about my *c* to death.
Rom 8:1 . . . . there is no *c* for those who
2 Cor 3:9 . . . which brings *c,* was glorious,

CONDUCT (n)
a mode or standard of personal behavior especially as based on moral principles
Prov 20:11 . . act, whether their *c* is pure,
Jer 32:19. . . . You see the *c* of all people,
Gal 6:5 . . . . . responsible for our own *c.*

CONDUCT, CONDUCTED, CONDUCTING (v)
to cause (oneself) to act or behave in a particular and controlled manner; to direct or take part in the management or operation of
Exod 18:20 . them how to *c* their lives.
2 Cor 1:12 . . how we have *c-ed* ourselves
Phil 1:27 . . . of heaven, *c-ing* yourselves in a
1 Tim 3:15 . . *c* themselves in the

CONFESS, CONFESSED, CONFESSES, CONFESSING (v)
to admit or acknowledge (sin or faith)
1 Sam 7:6. . . *c-ed* that they had sinned
Ezra 10:11 . . So now *c* your sin to
Ps 32:3 . . . . . I refused to *c* my sin,
Ps 32:5 . . . . . Finally, I *c-ed* all my sins
Ps 38:18 . . . . But I *c* my sins;
Ps 66:18 . . . . If I had not *c-ed* the sin in my
Dan 9:4 . . . . to the LORD my God and *c-ed:*
Dan 9:20 . . . praying and *c-ing* my sin
Matt 18:15 . . *c-es* it, you have won
Mark 1:5 . . . And when they *c-ed* their sins,
Rom 10:10 . . by *c-ing* with your mouth
Rom 14:11 . . every tongue will *c* and give
Phil 2:11 . . . and every tongue *c* that Jesus
1 Tim 6:12 . . which you have *c-ed* so well
Jas 5:16. . . . . *C* your sins to each other
1 Jn 1:9. . . . . But if we *c* our sins to him,

CONFESSION, CONFESSIONS (n)
a disclosure of one's sins; a formal statement of religious beliefs
Ezra 10:1 . . . and made this *c,* weeping
Hos 14:2 . . . your *c-s,* and return

CONFIDENCE (n)
faith or belief that one will act in a right, proper, or effective way; a feeling or consciousness of one's powers; a quality or state of being certain
Ps 146:3 . . . . Don't put your *c* in powerful
Isa 30:15. . . . In quietness and *c* is your
2 Cor 8:22 . . of his great *c* in you.
Phil 1:14 . . . believers here have gained *c*
Phil 2:24 . . . And I have *c* from the Lord
Phil 3:4 . . . . I could have *c* in my own
Col 2:2 . . . . . want them to have complete *c*
1 Thes 5:8 . . as our helmet the *c* of our
Titus 1:2. . . . This truth gives them *c*
Heb 11:1 . . . Faith is the *c* that what we
2 Pet 1:19. . . we have even greater *c*
1 Jn 4:17. . . . but we can face him with *c*

CONFIDENT (adj)
full of conviction, certain; trustful
Ps 27:13 . . . . Yet I am *c* I will see the
Ps 57:7 . . . . . My heart is *c* in you, O God;
2 Cor 3:4 . . . We are *c* of all this
Eph 1:18 . . . can understand the *c* hope
Col 1:5 . . . . . *c* hope of what God has reserved
Col 4:12 . . . . fully *c* that you are following
2 Thes 3:4 . . And we are *c* in the Lord
Heb 3:6 . . . . keep our courage and remain *c*

CONFIDENTLY (adv)
acting with confidence
Ps 112:7 . . . . they *c* trust the LORD
Rom 5:2. . . . we *c* and joyfully look forward
Eph 3:12 . . . boldly and *c* into God's

CONFIRM, CONFIRMED, CONFIRMING, CONFIRMS (v)
to strengthen; to remove doubt by authoritative statement or action
Gen 6:18 . . . I will *c* my covenant with you.
Gen 9:17 . . . sign of the covenant I am *c-ing*
Gen 17:21 . . will be *c-ed* with Isaac,
Heb 9:20 . . . This blood *c-s* the covenant

CONFLICT (n)
fight, battle, war
Prov 13:10 . . Pride leads to *c;*
Prov 17:1 . . . filled with feasting—and *c.*
Gal 3:21 . . . . Is there a *c,* then, between

CONFUSED (v)
to confound, stupify, perplex
Gen 11:9 . . . where the Lord *c* the people

CONFUSED (adj)
the state of being confounded, stupified, perplexed
Matt 9:36 . . . they were *c* and helpless,
Rom 1:21 . . . their minds became dark and *c.*

CONGRATULATE (v)
to express pleasure to (a person) on the occasion of success or good fortune
2 Sam 19:7 . . go out there and *c* your troops,

CONGREGATION (n)
an assembly or gathering (not church)
Ps 107:32 . . . exalt him publicly before the *c*

CONQUER, CONQUERED, CONQUERING (v)
to gain or acquire by force of arms
see also OVERCOME
Gen 22:17 . . descendants will *c* the cities
Num 13:30 . We can certainly *c* it!
Prov 16:32 . . than to *c* a city.
Dan 2:44 . . . never be destroyed or ***c-ed.***
Matt 16:18 . . of hell will not *c* it.
Rom 12:21 . . Don't let evil *c* you,
Col 2:23 . . . . no help in ***c-ing*** a person's evil

CONQUEROR (n)
one who subdues, defeats, or vanquishes
Mic 1:15. . . . I will bring a *c* to capture

CONSCIENCE, CONSCIENCES (n)
one's moral sensitivity or scruples
2 Sam 24:10. census, David's *c* began to
Acts 24:16 . . maintain a clear *c* before God
Rom 14:2 . . . with a sensitive *c* will eat
1 Cor 8:7 . . . their weak ***c-s*** are violated.
1 Cor 8:10 . . to violate their *c* by eating
1 Cor 10:25 . raising questions of *c.*
1 Tim 1:5 . . . a clear *c,* and genuine faith.
1 Tim 1:19 . . and keep your *c* clear.
Titus 1:15. . . minds and ***c-s*** are corrupted.
Heb 9:9 . . . . are not able to cleanse the ***c-s***
Heb 9:14 . . . will purify our ***c-s*** from sinful
Heb 10:22 . . guilty ***c-s*** have been sprinkled
Heb 13:18 . . for our *c* is clear
1 Pet 3:16. . . Keep your *c* clear.
1 Pet 3:21. . . to God from a clean *c.*

CONSCIENTIOUS (adj)
scrupulous, meticulous, careful
2 Chr 29:34 . been more *c* about purifying

CONSECRATE, CONSECRATED (v)
to devote irrevocably to God by a solemn ceremony; to make or declare sacred
see also DEDICATE, DEVOTE, ORDAINED
Exod 40:9 . . all its furnishings to *c* them
Lev 19:24. . . the entire crop must be ***c-d***
2 Chr 29:31 . you have ***c-d*** yourselves

CONSIDER (v)
to think about carefully; to come to judge or classify; to regard
Job 37:14 . . . Stop and *c* the wonderful
Rom 6:11 . . . *c* yourselves to be dead
Jas 1:2. . . . . . troubles come your way, *c* it

CONSIDERATE (adj)
thoughtful of the rights and feelings of others
Phil 4:5 . . . . see that you are *c* in all you

CONSOLE, CONSOLING (v)
to alleviate the grief or sense of loss; to offer just reward
John 11:19 . . come to *c* Martha and Mary
John 11:31 . . at the house ***c-ing*** Mary

CONSTANT (adj)
marked by steadfast faithfulness; continually occurring or recurring
Ps 119:98 . . . they are my *c* guide.
Prov 27:15 . . is as annoying as *c* dripping
Luke 18:5. . . with her *c* requests!

CONSTRUCT (v)
to build
1 Kgs 6:1 . . . he began to *c* the Temple

CONSULT (v)
to ask the advice or opinion of; to confer
Gal 1:16 . . . . rush out to *c* with any human

CONSUME, CONSUMED (v)
to engage fully, engross
Ps 69:9 . . . . . Passion for your house has ***c-d***
John 2:17 . . . Passion for God's house will *c*

CONTAIN (v)
to keep within limits; to restrain or control
1 Kgs 8:27 . . heavens cannot *c* you.
John 21:25 . . world could not *c* the books

CONTAMINATE (v)
to soil, corrupt, or infect
Jude 1:23 . . . the sins that *c* their lives.

CONTEMPT (n)
the state of despising; displaying disgust, scorn, or disdain
Gen 25:34 . . showed *c* for his rights
Ps 119:51 . . . The proud hold me in utter *c,*
Prov 18:3. . . scandalous behavior brings *c.*
Mal 1:6. . . . . ever shown *c* for your name?

CONTENT, CONTENTED (adj)
feeling or showing satisfaction with one's possessions, status, or situation; pleased
Josh 7:7 . . . . If only we had been *c*
1 Kgs 4:20 . . They were very *c-ed,*
Prov 13:25. . godly eat to their hearts' *c,*
Luke 3:14. . . And be *c* with your pay.
Phil 4:11 . . . I have learned how to be *c*
1 Tim 6:8 . . . food and clothing, let us be *c.*

CONTENTMENT (n)
the quality or state of being contented
1 Tim 6:6 . . . godliness with *c* is

CONTINUAL (adj)
continuing indefinitely in time
Prov 15:15. . life is a *c* feast.

CONTINUALLY (adv)
in continual or steadily recurring manner
1 Chr 16:11 . *c* seek him.

CONTINUE, CONTINUED, CONTINUES (v)
to maintain without interruption a condition, course, or action
Ps 100:5 . . . . unfailing love *c-s* forever,
Jer 32:20. . . . have *c-d* to do
Acts 13:43 . . *c* to rely on
Acts 14:22 . . encouraged them to *c*
Rom 11:22. . if you *c* to trust in
Col 1:23 . . . . But you must *c* to believe
Col 2:6 . . . . . you must *c* to follow
1 Tim 2:15 . . assuming they *c* to live in
1 Jn 3:6. . . . . who *c-s* to live in him
Rev 22:11. . . *c* to be holy.

CONTRACT (n)
a binding agreement between two or more persons or parties
Exod 21:8 . . who broke the *c* with her.

CONTRIBUTIONS (n)
a payment imposed by authorities for a special purpose; the act of giving to a common fund or store
Mark 12:43 . who are making *c.*

CONTRITE (adj)
feeling or showing sorrow or remorse for a sin
see also HUMBLE, REPENTANT
Isa 66:2. . . . . have humble and *c* hearts,

CONTROL, CONTROLS (v)
to exercise restraining or directing influence over; to rule
Job 37:15 . . . know how God *c-s* the storm
Rom 6:12. . . Do not let sin *c*
Rom 8:6 . . . . letting the Spirit *c* your mind
Rom 8:8 . . . . still under the *c* of
1 Cor 7:9 . . . they can't *c* themselves,
1 Cor 7:37 . . and he can *c* his passion,
2 Cor 5:14 . . Christ's love *c-s* us.
Jas 1:26. . . . . but don't *c* your tongue,
Jas 3:2. . . . . . could also *c* ourselves
2 Pet 2:19. . . a slave to whatever *c-s* you.

CONTROVERSY, CONTROVERSIES (n)
a dispute or quarrel
Acts 26:3 . . . customs and *c-ies.*
1 Tim 2:8 . . . from anger and *c.*

CONVERTED (v)
to bring over from one belief, view, or party to another
Acts 6:7 . . . . priests were *c,* too.
Acts 15:3 . . . the Gentiles, too, were being *c.*

CONVICT, CONVICTED (v)
to find or prove guilty of an offense
Prov 24:25. . for those who *c* the guilty;
John 7:51 . . . Is it legal to *c* a man
John 16:8 . . . he will *c* the world of
1 Cor 14:24 . they will be *c-ed* of sin
Jude 1:15 . . . He will *c* every person

CONVICTIONS (n)
strongly held beliefs or principles
Rom 14:23. . you are not following your *c.*

CONVINCE, CONVINCED, CONVINCING (v)
to persuade to a belief, consent, or course of action
Exod 4:31 . . people of Israel were *c-d*
Acts 18:4 . . . to *c* the Jews and Greeks
Rom 2:19. . . are *c-d* that you are a guide
Rom 8:38. . . I am *c-d* that nothing
Rom 14:14. . I know and am *c-d*
Rom 15:14. . I am fully *c-d,*
Phil 1:25 . . . I am *c-d* that I will

COPY (n)
an imitation or reproduction of an original work; a duplicate
Heb 8:5 . . . . that is only a *c*,
Heb 9:24 . . . was only a *c* of

COPY (v)
to duplicate; to model oneself on
Deut 17:18. . he must *c* for himself
Rom 12:2. . . Don't *c* the behavior and

CORD (n)
a long, slender, flexible material usually consisting of several strands woven together
Eccl 4:12 . . . for a triple-braided *c*

CORNERSTONE (n)
a stone forming a corner or angle in a wall; foundation
Ps 118:22. . . now become the *c*.
Mark 12:10 . now become the *c*.
Acts 4:11 . . . now become the *c*.
Eph 2:20 . . . And the *c* is Christ
1 Pet 2:7. . . . now become the *c*.

CORRECT, CORRECTED, CORRECTING, CORRECTS (v)
to set right with remedies, revisions, or reforms
Job 5:17 . . . . joy of those ***c-ed*** by God!
Ps 141:5 . . . . If they *c* me,
Prov 3:12. . . For the LORD ***c-s*** those
Prov 9:8. . . . don't bother ***c-ing*** mockers;
Prov 19:25. . if you *c* the wise,
Jer 5:3. . . . . . refused to be ***c-ed***.
Jer 10:24. . . . Do not *c* me in anger,
2 Tim 3:16 . . It ***c-s*** us when we
2 Tim 4:2 . . . Patiently *c*, rebuke,
Titus 2:15. . . the authority to *c* them
Heb 12:5 . . . give up when he ***c-s*** you.

CORRECTION (n)
a rebuke or punishment; the action of making right
Prov 10:17. . those who ignore *c*
Prov 12:1. . . it is stupid to hate *c*.
Prov 15:5. . . learns from *c* is wise.
Prov 15:10. . whoever hates *c* will die.
Prov 15:32. . if you listen to *c*,

CORRUPT (adj)
morally degenerate and perverted; depraved
Gen 6:11 . . . the earth had become *c*
Ps 14:1 . . . . . They are *c*,
Ps 14:3 . . . . . all have become *c*.
Prov 19:28. . A *c* witness
Luke 9:41. . . faithless and *c* people!

CORRUPT, CORRUPTED, CORRUPTS (v)
to change from good to bad, physically or morally
Eccl 7:7 . . . . and bribes *c* the heart.
1 Cor 15:33 . bad company ***c-s*** good
Titus 1:15. . . and consciences are ***c-ed***.
Jas 1:27. . . . . let the world *c* you.

CORRUPTION (n)
impairment of integrity, virtue, or moral principle; depravity, decay
2 Pet 1:4. . . . the world's *c* caused
2 Pet 2:19. . . slaves of sin and *c*.

CORRUPTLY (adv)
marked by moral perversion and degeneracy
Deut 32:5. . . they have acted *c*

COST (n)
loss or penalty incurred especially in gaining something; price
Num 16:38 . sinned at the *c* of their lives,
Luke 14:28. . calculating the *c*

COST (v)
to require effort, suffering, or loss
Prov 7:23. . . it would *c* him his life.
Rev 6:6. . . . . barley will *c* a day's pay.

COUNCIL (n)
a group elected or appointed as an advisory or legislative body
Acts 17:19 . . to the high *c* of the city.
Acts 17:22 . . standing before the *c*,
Acts 17:34 . . a member of the *c*,

COUNSEL (n)
advice; policy, plan, or action
Ps 37:30 . . . . godly offer good *c*;
Ps 73:24 . . . . guide me with your *c*,
Ps 107:11 . . . scorning the *c* of the
Prov 27:9. . . The heartfelt *c* of a friend
1 Cor 7:40 . . I am giving you *c*

COUNSEL (v)
to advise
Col 3:16 . . . . Teach and *c* each other

COUNSELOR (n)
one who gives advice or wisdom
see also ADVOCATE, HOLY SPIRIT
Isa 9:6. . . . . . Wonderful ***C***, Mighty God,

COUNT, COUNTED, COUNTING, COUNTS (v)

to number; to consider

Gen 15:6 . . . and the LORD ***c-ed*** him as
Ps 22:17 . . . . I can ***c*** all my bones.
Ps 130:5 . . . . yes, I am ***c-ing*** on him.
Ps 147:4 . . . . He ***c-s*** the stars
Prov 20:25 . . and only later ***c-ing*** the cost.
Acts 5:41 . . . ***c-ed*** them worthy to suffer
Rom 4:9 . . . . Abraham was ***c-ed*** as righteous
Rom 4:24 . . . that God will also ***c*** us
Rom 5:13 . . . it was not ***c-ed*** as sin
2 Cor 5:19 . . no longer ***c-ing*** people's sins
Gal 3:6 . . . . . and God ***c-ed*** him as righteous
Jas 2:23. . . . . and God ***c-ed*** him as righteous

COUNTENANCE (KJV)

Gen 4:6 . . . . Why do you ***look*** so dejected
Num 6:26 . . LORD ***show you his favor***
1 Sam 16:7 . . Don't judge by his ***appearance***
Prov 15:13 . . glad heart makes a happy ***face***
Luke 9:29. . . ***appearance of his face*** was transformed

COURAGE (n)

mental or moral strength

Judg 5:21 . . . March on with ***c***, my soul!
2 Chr 15:8 . . he took ***c*** and removed
Dan 11:25 . . stir up his ***c*** and raise a
Mark 6:50 . . Take ***c***! I am here!
Acts 27:22 . . But take ***c***!
Heb 3:6 . . . . if we keep our ***c***
Jas 5:8. . . . . . Take ***c***, for the coming
1 Jn 2:28 . . . . be full of ***c*** and not shrink

COURAGEOUS (adj)

having or characterized by courage; brave

Deut 31:6. . . So be strong and ***c***!
Josh 1:6 . . . . Be strong and ***c***,
2 Sam 10:12. Be ***c***! Let us fight
2 Chr 32:7 . . Be strong and ***c***!
Ps 31:24 . . . . be strong and ***c***,
1 Cor 16:13 . Be ***c***. Be strong.

COURT, COURTS (n)

a place for the administration of justice; an open space enclosed by buildings

Ps 82:1 . . . . . presides over heaven's ***c***;
Ps 84:10 . . . . single day in your ***c-s***
Ps 96:8 . . . . . come into his ***c-s***.
Ps 100:4 . . . . go into his ***c-s***
Prov 22:22 . . exploit the needy in ***c***.
Isa 3:13. . . . . takes his place in ***c***
Amos 5:15 . . ***c-s*** into true halls of justice.
Zech 8:16. . . verdicts in your ***c-s***
Matt 5:25 . . . are on the way to ***c***

COURTROOM (n)

a room in which a court of law is held

Eccl 3:16 . . . evil in the ***c***.

COURTYARD (n)

enclosed area adjacent to a building

Exod 27:9 . . make the ***c*** for the Tabernacle,
Exod 27:18 . the entire ***c*** will be 150 feet long
Matt 26:69 . . sitting outside in the ***c***.

COVENANT, COVENANTS (n)

a mutual agreement or contract (between persons, between nations, or between God and humanity) with conditions and consequences spelled out

see also PROMISE, VOW

Gen 9:9 . . . . hereby confirm my ***c***
Gen 17:2 . . . I will make a ***c*** with you,
Exod 19:5 . . and keep my ***c***,
Deut 4:13. . . He proclaimed his ***c***—
Judg 2:1 . . . . never break my ***c***
1 Kgs 8:21 . . which contains the ***c***
2 Kgs 23:2 . . Book of the ***C*** that had been
2 Chr 6:14 . . You keep your ***c***
Neh 1:5 . . . . keeps his ***c*** of unfailing love
Ps 105:8 . . . . stands by his ***c***—
Prov 2:17. . . and ignores the ***c***
Isa 61:8. . . . . an everlasting ***c*** with them.
Jer 31:31. . . . make a new ***c*** with the people
Hos 10:4 . . . make ***c-s*** they don't intend
Mal 3:1. . . . . messenger of the ***c***,
Mark 14:24 . confirms the ***c*** between God
Luke 22:20. . new ***c*** between God and his
Rom 9:4 . . . . He made ***c-s*** with them
1 Cor 11:25 . new ***c*** between God and his
2 Cor 3:6 . . . under the new ***c***,
Heb 8:6 . . . . a far better ***c*** with God,
Heb 9:15 . . . mediates a new ***c*** between
Heb 12:24 . . the new ***c*** between God and

COVER (n)

something that is placed over or about another thing; lid or top piece

Exod 25:17 . make the Ark's ***c***—
Exod 25:21 . put the atonement ***c***
Lev 16:2. . . . the atonement ***c***.

COVER, COVERED, COVERS (v)

to hide from sight or knowledge; to lay or spread something over; to lie over

Gen 3:7 . . . . to ***c*** themselves.
Exod 33:22 . and ***c*** you with my hand
Job 29:14 . . . Righteousness ***c-ed*** me
Ps 85:2 . . . . . you ***c-ed*** all their sins.
Ps 91:4 . . . . . He will ***c*** you with
Isa 6:2. . . . . . they ***c-ed*** their faces,

Matt 10:26 . . everything that is *c-ed*
1 Cor 11:4 . . if he *c-s* his head while
2 Cor 3:15 . . their hearts are *c-ed*
Jas 3:14. . . . . don't *c* up the truth
1 Pet 4:8. . . . love *c-s* a multitude of sins.

COVERING (n)
something that covers or conceals
1 Cor 11:5 . . without a *c* on her head,
1 Cor 11:15 . given to her as a *c.*

COVET, COVETED, COVETING (v)
to inordinately desire unjust gain or another's property
see also DESIRE
Exod 20:17 . not *c* your neighbor's wife,
Exod 34:24 . so no one will *c* and conquer
Deut 7:25. . . must not *c* the silver or gold
Acts 20:33 . . *c-ed* anyone's silver or gold
Rom 7:7. . . . known that *c-ing* is wrong
Rom 13:9. . . You must not *c.*

COWARDS (n)
one who shows disgraceful fear or timidity
Rev 21:8. . . . But *c,* unbelievers, the

COWS (n)
the mature female of cattle
Gen 41:2 . . . he saw seven fat, healthy *c*

CRAFTSMAN, CRAFTSMEN (n)
a worker who practices a trade or handicraft
Isa 45:16. . . . All *c-en* who make idols
Jer 10:3. . . . . and a *c* carves an idol.

CRAFTSMANSHIP (n)
the product of a craftsman that demonstrates his skill
Ps 19:1 . . . . . the skies display his *c.*

CRAVE, CRAVED, CRAVES (v)
to want greatly; to yearn for
Num 11:4 . . began to *c* the good things
Num 11:34 . people who had *c-d* meat
Ps 78:18 . . . . the foods they *c-d.*
Ps 78:29 . . . . gave them what they *c-d.*
Prov 31:4. . . should not *c* alcohol.
Gal 5:16 . . . . your sinful nature *c-s.*
1 Pet 2:2. . . . *c* pure spiritual milk
1 Jn 2:17. . . . everything that people *c.*

CRAVING (n)
an intense, urgent, or abnormal desire or longing
Ps 78:30 . . . . they satisfied their *c,*
Prov 10:3. . . satisfy the *c* of the wicked.
1 Jn 2:16. . . . world offers only a *c*

CREATE, CREATED, CREATING (v)
to bring into being; to form, make, or produce
see also FORMED, MADE, MAKE
Gen 1:1 . . . . God *c-d* the heavens
Gen 1:27 . . . male and female he *c-d* them;
Gen 6:7 . . . . human race I have *c-d* from
Ps 51:10 . . . . *C* in me a clean heart
Ps 104:30 . . . life is *c-d,* and you renew
Prov 8:22. . . before he *c-d* anything else.
Isa 43:1. . . . . the LORD who *c-d* you.
Isa 43:7. . . . . I who *c-d* them.
Isa 45:8. . . . . I, the LORD, *c-d* them.
Isa 54:16. . . . I have *c-d* the blacksmith
Isa 65:17. . . . I am *c-ing* new heavens and
John 1:3 . . . . *c-d* everything through him,
Rom 1:20. . . since the world was *c-d,*
Rom 1:25. . . served the things God *c-d*
Rom 9:20. . . the thing that was *c-d* say
Eph 2:10 . . . He has *c-d* us anew
Eph 2:15 . . . by *c-ing* in himself
Eph 4:24 . . . *c-d* to be like God—
Col 1:16 . . . . Everything was *c-d* through
1 Tim 4:3 . . . But God *c-d* those foods
Heb 1:2 . . . . through the Son he *c-d*
1 Pet 4:19. . . to the God who *c-d* you,
Rev 4:11. . . . For you *c-d* all things,
Rev 10:6. . . . who *c-d* the heavens

CREATION (n)
something that is created; the world; the act of bringing the world into existence
Gen 2:3 . . . . from all his work of *c.*
Mark 10:6 . . from the beginning of *c.*
Rom 8:19. . . For all *c* is waiting
Rom 8:39. . . nothing in all *c* will ever
Gal 6:15 . . . . into a new *c.*
Col 1:17 . . . . holds all *c* together.
Heb 12:27 . . all of *c* will be shaken
Jas 1:18. . . . . we, out of all *c,*
Rev 3:14. . . . of God's new *c:*

CREATOR (n)
maker; one who creates
see also MAKER
Gen 14:19 . . God Most High, *C* of heaven
Job 40:19 . . . only its *C* can threaten
Eccl 12:1 . . . to forget your *C.*
Isa 40:28. . . . the *C* of all the earth.
Isa 45:9. . . . . argue with their *C.*
Isa 51:13. . . . the LORD, your *C,*
Jer 51:19. . . . He is the *C* of everything
Rom 1:25. . . instead of the *C* himself,
Eph 3:9 . . . . the *C* of all things,
Eph 3:15 . . . the *C* of everything

CREATURE, CREATURES (n)
something created either animate or inanimate
Lev 17:14. . . the life of any *c* is in
Ps 104:24 . . . full of your *c-s.*

CREDIT (n)
honor, recognition, or acknowledgment
Luke 6:33. . . should you get *c?*
1 Pet 2:20. . . no *c* for being patient

CRETE (n)
an island in the Mediterranean Sea
Acts 27:12 . . up the coast of *C,*
Titus 1:12. . . "The people of *C* are all liars,

CRIME, CRIMES (n)
a grave offense; criminal activity
Deut 22:26. . no *c* worthy of death
Judg 19:30. . Such a horrible *c* has
1 Sam 20:1. . What is my *c?* How have I
Job 31:11 . . . lust is a shameful sin, a *c*
Ps 52:1 . . . . . about your *c-s,* great warrior?
Luke 11:48. . join in their *c* by
Luke 23:41. . deserve to die for our *c-s,*

CRIMINAL, CRIMINALS (n)
one who has broken the law
Ps 59:2 . . . . . Rescue me from these *c-s;*
Isa 53:9. . . . . he was buried like a *c;*
Luke 23:32. . Two others, both *c-s,*

CRIMSON (n)
any of several deep purplish reds
Isa 1:18. . . . . Though they are red like *c,*

CRIPPLED (adj)
lame, physically disabled
2 Sam 9:3. . . He is *c* in both feet.
Luke 14:13. . invite the poor, the *c,* the lame,
Acts 14:8 . . . came upon a man with *c* feet.

CRITIC (n)
one who expresses an opinion on a matter involving a judgment of its value, truth, righteousness, beauty, or technique
Job 40:2 . . . . You are God's *c,* but do you

CRITICISM (n)
a critical observation or remark; critique
Prov 15:31. . listen to constructive *c,*
Prov 25:12. . valid *c* is like a gold
Prov 28:23. . people appreciate honest *c*
Prov 29:1. . . refuses to accept *c*
2 Cor 8:20 . . guard against any *c*

CRITICIZE, CRITICIZED, CRITICIZING (v)
to find fault with; to point out the faults of
Job 34:29 . . . who can *c* him?
Eccl 7:5 . . . . be *c-d* by a wise person
Rom 14:16. . not be *c-d* for doing
Phil 2:15 . . . no one can *c* you.
Titus 2:8. . . . teaching can't be *c-d.*
Jas 4:11. . . . . *c-ing* and judging God's law.

CROOKED (adj)
not straight, twisted; dishonest, evil
Ps 125:5 . . . . those who turn to *c* ways,
Prov 5:6. . . . staggers down a *c* trail
Prov 8:8. . . . nothing devious or *c* in it.
Prov 10:9. . . those who follow *c* paths
Prov 21:8. . . The guilty walk a *c* path;
Eccl 7:13 . . . what he has made *c?*
Isa 59:8. . . . . have mapped out *c* roads,

CROP, CROPS (n)
the product or yield after a harvest
Exod 23:16 . bring me the first *c-s*
Prov 28:3. . . that destroys the *c-s.*
Hos 10:12 . . harvest a *c* of love.
Matt 13:8. . . they produced a *c* that was
Matt 21:41. . his share of the *c*

CROSS (n)
an upright post used as an instrument of death in ancient times; the means by which atonement was made between God and humanity
Mark 8:34 . . take up your *c,*
Luke 9:23. . . take up your *c* daily,
Acts 2:23 . . . you nailed him to a *c*
Acts 5:30 . . . hanging him on a *c.*
1 Cor 1:18 . . message of the *c* is
Gal 3:1 . . . . . death on the *c.*
Gal 6:12. . . . that the *c* of Christ alone
Phil 2:8 . . . . criminal's death on a *c.*
Col 1:20. . . . Christ's blood on the *c.*
Heb 12:2 . . . he endured the *c,*
1 Pet 2:24. . . his body on the *c*

CROSSED (v)
to fold one (arm) over the other
Gen 48:14 . . But Jacob *c* his arms

CROSSROADS (n)
the place of intersection of two or more roads
Jer 6:16. . . . . Stop at the *c* and look

CROUCHING (v)
to lie close to the ground with the legs bent
Gen 4:7 . . . . Sin is *c* at the door,

CROW, CROWED, CROWS (v)
to make the loud shrill sound characteristic of a rooster
Matt 26:34 . . before the rooster ***c-s,***
Matt 26:74 . . the rooster ***c-ed.***

CROWD, CROWDS (n)
a large number of persons especially when collected together
Exod 23:2 . . by the ***c*** to twist justice.
Matt 9:36 . . . When he saw the ***c-s,***
Heb 12:1 . . . such a huge ***c*** of witnesses
Rev 19:1. . . . like a vast ***c*** in heaven

CROWDED (v)
to push or force
Mark 4:19 . . the message is ***c*** out

CROWN, CROWNS (n)
top of the head; a cap or headdress worn by victors, priests, or royalty
Prov 16:31 . . Gray hair is a ***c*** of glory;
Song 3:11. . . He wears the ***c*** his mother
Isa 61:3. . . . . will give a ***c*** of beauty
Isa 62:3. . . . . a splendid ***c*** in the hand
Zech 9:16. . . like jewels in a ***c.***
Matt 27:29 . . thorn branches into a ***c***
Mark 15:17 . thorn branches into a ***c***
John 19:2 . . . wove a ***c*** of thorns
John 19:5 . . . wearing the ***c*** of thorns
Phil 4:1 . . . . and the ***c*** I receive
1 Thes 2:19 . our proud reward and ***c***
Jas 1:12. . . . . will receive the ***c*** of life
Rev 2:10. . . . will give you the ***c*** of life.
Rev 3:11. . . . take away your ***c.***
Rev 4:4. . . . . had gold ***c-s*** on their heads.
Rev 4:10. . . . lay their ***c-s*** before the throne
Rev 12:3. . . . with seven ***c-s*** on his heads.
Rev 14:14. . . He had a gold ***c*** on his head
Rev 19:12. . . on his head were many ***c-s.***

CROWNED, CROWNS (v)
to place a crown on the head of; to bless or adorn
Ps 8:5 . . . . . . and ***c-ed*** them with
Ps 149:4 . . . . he ***c-s*** the humble
Prov 14:18 . . are ***c-ed*** with knowledge.
Isa 51:11. . . . ***c-ed*** with everlasting joy.
Heb 2:7 . . . . and ***c-ed*** them with
Heb 2:9 . . . . ***c-ed*** with glory and honor.

CRUCIFIXION (n)
the execution or death of a person on a cross
Matt 23:34 . . you will kill some by ***c,***
John 19:41 . . The place of ***c*** was near

CRUCIFY, CRUCIFIED (v)
to execute or nail to the cross; to put to death
Matt 26:2. . . handed over to be ***c-ied.***
Matt 27:22 . . "***C*** him!"
Matt 27:44 . . who were ***c-ied*** with him
Mark 15:13 . "***C*** him!"
Mark 15:27 . revolutionaries were ***c-ied***
Mark 15:32 . who were ***c-ied*** with Jesus
Mark 16:6 . . who was ***c-ied.***
Luke 23:21. . "***C*** him! ***C*** him!"
Luke 23:23. . that Jesus be ***c-ied,***
Luke 23:33. . criminals were also ***c-ied*** –
Luke 24:20. . and they ***c-ied*** him.
John 19:6 . . . "***C*** him! ***C*** him!"
John 19:10 . . to release you or ***c*** you?
John 19:20 . . where Jesus was ***c-ied***
John 19:32 . . the two men ***c-ied*** with Jesus.
Acts 4:10 . . . the man you ***c-ied***
Rom 6:6 . . . . were ***c-ied*** with Christ
1 Cor 1:13 . . Was I, Paul, ***c-ied*** for you?
1 Cor 1:23 . . preach that Christ was ***c-ied,***
1 Cor 2:8 . . . would not have ***c-ied***
2 Cor 13:4 . . he was ***c-ied*** in weakness,
Gal 5:24 . . . . and ***c-ied*** them there.
Rev 11:8. . . . where their Lord was ***c-ied.***

CRUEL (adj)
disposed to inflict pain or suffering; devoid of human feelings
2 Tim 3:3 . . . They will be ***c*** and hate
1 Pet 2:18. . . even if they are ***c.***

CRUELTY (n)
the quality or state of being cruel; inhuman treatment
Prov 11:17 . . your ***c*** will destroy you.

CRUSH, CRUSHED (v)
to squeeze or force by pressure so as to alter or destroy; to oppress or burden grievously
Ps 34:18 . . . . whose spirits are ***c-ed.***
Prov 31:8. . . justice for those being ***c-ed.***
Isa 42:3. . . . . will not ***c*** the weakest reed
Isa 42:13. . . . and ***c*** all his enemies.
Isa 53:5. . . . . ***c-ed*** for our sins.
Matt 26:38 . . My soul is ***c-ed*** with grief
Luke 10:19. . scorpions and ***c*** them.
Rom 16:20 . . will soon ***c*** Satan
2 Cor 1:8 . . . were ***c-ed*** and overwhelmed
2 Cor 4:8 . . . but we are not ***c-ed.***

CRY, CRIES (n)
entreaty, appeal; an inarticulate utterance of distress, rage, or pain
Exod 2:23 . . their ***c*** rose up to God.

Ps 5:2 . . . . . . Listen to my *c* for help,
Ps 34:15 . . . . open to their *c-ies* for help.
Ps 142:6 . . . . Hear my *c,* for I am
Prov 21:13 . . to the *c-ies* of the poor

CRY, CRIED (v)
to shout; to beg or beseech; to shed tears often noisily
Exod 14:10 . They *c-ied* out to the LORD,
Josh 24:7 . . . When your ancestors *c-ied* out
Judg 3:9 . . . . people of Israel *c-ied* out
Judg 4:3 . . . . people of Israel *c-ied* out
Judg 6:6 . . . . Then the Israelites *c-ied* out
Judg 10:12 . . you *c-ied* out to me
Ps 18:6 . . . . . in my distress I *c-ied* out
Eccl 3:4 . . . . A time to *c* and a time
Lam 2:18 . . . *C* aloud before the LORD,
Hab 2:11 . . . walls *c* out against you,

CULTIVATE (v)
to foster the growth of; to encourage
Job 4:8 . . . . . plant trouble and *c* evil

CUP (n)
a drinking vessel; figurative of human vessel; token of tangible consolation, salvation of Christ, wrath of God, drunkenness, or fate
Ps 23:5 . . . . . My *c* overflows
Matt 26:39 . . let this *c* of suffering
Matt 26:42 . . If this *c* cannot be
Mark 10:39 . drink from my bitter *c*
Mark 14:23 . And he took a *c* of wine
Mark 14:36 . take this *c* of suffering
Luke 22:20 . . This *c* is the new covenant
John 18:11 . . from the *c* of suffering
1 Cor 10:16 . When we bless the *c*
1 Cor 10:21 . from the *c* of the Lord
1 Cor 11:25 . took the *c* of wine after
1 Cor 11:25 . This *c* is the new covenant

CUP-BEARER (n)
one who tasted and served wine to a king
Gen 40:1 . . . Pharaoh's chief *c*
Neh 1:11 . . . I was the king's *c.*

CURE (n)
recovery or relief from a disease; a complete or permanent solution
Jer 30:15. . . . wound that has no *c?*
Luke 8:43. . . she could find no *c.*

CURE, CURED (v)
to restore to health, soundness, or normality
Isa 30:26. . . . and *c* the wounds
Matt 11:5 . . . the lepers are *c-d,*
John 5:10 . . . said to the man who was *c-d,*

CURSE, CURSES, CURSING (n)
a condemnation or judgment
Num 5:23 . . priest will write these *c-s*
Josh 8:34 . . . blessings and *c-s* Moses had
Rom 8:20 . . . was subjected to God's *c.*
Gal 3:10 . . . . right with God are under his *c,*
Gal 3:13 . . . . the *c* for our wrongdoing.
Rom 3:14 . . . full of *c-ing* and bitterness.
Jas 3:10. . . . . and *c-ing* come pouring out
Rev 22:3. . . . No longer will there be a *c*

CURSE, CURSES (v)
to pronounce a sentence; to afflict; to call upon a supernatural power to bring injury upon; to utter profane language against
Gen 8:21 . . . will never again *c* the ground
Gen 12:3 . . . *c* those who treat you
Prov 3:33 . . . *c-s* the house of the wicked,
Matt 5:22 . . . And if you *c* someone,
Rom 12:14 . . Don't *c* them;
1 Cor 12:3 . . will *c* Jesus, and no one
Jas 3:9. . . . . . and sometimes it *c-s* those who

CURSED (adj)
being under or deserving a curse
Gen 3:17 . . . the ground is *c* because
Deut 21:23 . . anyone who is hung is *c*
Deut 27:16 . . *C* is anyone who dishonors
Deut 27:18 . . *C* is anyone who leads
Deut 27:20 . . *C* is anyone who has sexual
Deut 27:24 . . *C* is anyone who attacks a
Deut 27:26 . . *C* is anyone who does not
Prov 28:27 . . poverty will be *c.*
Gal 3:10 . . . . *C* is everyone who does not
Gal 3:13 . . . . *C* is everyone who is hung

CURTAIN (n)
a hanging screen usually capable of being drawn back or up
Isa 40:22. . . . the heavens like a *c*
Mark 15:38 . And the *c* in the sanctuary

CUT OFF (v)
separated; isolated
Gen 17:14 . . fails to be circumcised will be *c*
Ps 31:22 . . . . "I am *c* from the Lord!"
Prov 21:28 . . false witness will be *c,* but a
Ezek 21:4. . . will *c* both the righteous
Hos 10:7 . . . Samaria and its king will be *c*
Zech 13:8. . . in the land will be *c* and die
Rom 9:3 . . . . *c* from Christ!—if that
Gal 5:4 . . . . . the law, you have been *c*

DAILY (adv)
every day
Deut 17:19. . read it ***d*** as long as he
Acts 17:17 . . spoke ***d*** in the public square

DAN
1. First son of Jacob and Bilhah (Gen 30:3-6), who gave his name to a tribe of Israel; his tribe was blessed (Gen 49:16-17; Deut 33:22), numbered (Num 1:39), allotted land and cities (Josh 19:40-47); took the town of Laish and renamed it Dan (Judg 18).
2. Town at the northern boundary of Israel (Judg 20:1), earlier known as Laish; captured and renamed by Danites (Josh 19:47); became a center for idolatry (1 Kgs 12:28-30); attacked by Ben-hadad (1 Kgs 15:20).

DANCE, DANCING (n)
a series of rhythmic bodily movements usually performed to music
Ps 30:11 . . . . into joyful ***d-ing.***
Mark 6:22 . . a ***d*** that greatly pleased

DANCE, DANCED (v)
to move in a rhythmic manner, usually to music
2 Sam 6:14. . David ***d-d*** before the LORD
Eccl 3:4 . . . . and a time to ***d.***
Matt 11:17. . and you didn't ***d,***

DANGER (n)
harm or damage
Ps 57:1 . . . . . until the ***d*** passes by.
Prov 22:3. . . prudent person foresees ***d***
Matt 5:22. . . in ***d*** of being brought
Rom 8:35. . . or in ***d,*** or threatened
2 Cor 1:10 . . did rescue us from mortal ***d,***
2 Cor 11:26 . I have faced ***d*** from rivers

DANGEROUS (adj)
able or likely to inflict injury or harm
Prov 29:25. . Fearing people is a ***d*** trap,

DANIEL
1. Prophet of Judah (southern kingdom), exiled to Babylon; also called "Belteshazzar" (Dan 1:6-7); refused food of the Babylonian court (Dan 1:8-17); interpreted dreams (Dan 2) and writing on a wall (Dan 5:12-29); survived in lion's den (Dan 6:1-23); recorded visions (Dan 7–12); identified as a hero of renown (Ezek 14:14, 20; 28:3).
2. Son of David (1 Chr 3:1), also called "Kileab" (2 Sam 3:3).

DARK, DARKEST (adj)
devoid or partially devoid of light; wholly or partially black
Exod 20:21 . approached the ***d*** cloud
Ps 23:4 . . . . . walk through the ***d-est*** valley,
Song 1:6. . . . because I am ***d***—
Song 5:10. . . My lover is ***d*** and dazzling,
Joel 2:31. . . . The sun will become ***d,***
Acts 2:20 . . . The sun will become ***d,***
2 Pet 1:19. . . lamp shining in a ***d*** place—

DARKENED (v)
to make dark
Matt 24:29. . the sun will be ***d,***

DARKNESS (n)
the state of being devoid of light; nightfall; in spiritual terms, secret, closed, blinded, or evil; place of punishment (hell)
Gen 1:2 . . . . and ***d*** covered the deep waters.
Gen 1:4 . . . . the light from the ***d.***
Ps 18:28 . . . . my God, lights up my ***d.***
Matt 4:16. . . people who sat in ***d***
Luke 23:44. . it was about noon, and ***d*** fell
John 1:5 . . . . light shines in the ***d,***

John 3:19 . . . people loved the ***d*** more
John 12:35 . . the ***d*** will not overtake
2 Cor 4:6 . . . Let there be light in the ***d,***
2 Cor 6:14 . . can light live with ***d?***
Eph 5:8 . . . . once you were full of ***d,***
Eph 5:11 . . . deeds of evil and ***d;***
1 Pet 2:9. . . . called you out of the ***d***
1 Jn 1:5. . . . . there is no ***d*** in him at all.
1 Jn 2:9. . . . . is still living in ***d.***
Jude 1:6 . . . . chained in prisons of ***d,***

DARLING (n)
a dearly loved person
Song 2:10. . . Rise up, my ***d!***
Jer 31:20. . . . my son, my ***d*** child?" says

DAUGHTER, DAUGHTERS (n)
the female offspring or adopted offspring of parents
Gen 19:36 . . Lot's ***d-s*** became pregnant
Num 36:10 . The ***d-s*** of Zelophehad
Judg 11:40 . . the fate of Jephthah's ***d.***
Esth 2:7 . . . . raised her as his own ***d.***
Joel 2:28. . . . sons and ***d-s*** will prophesy.
Mark 5:34 . . said to her, "***D,*** your faith
Mark 7:29 . . the demon has left your ***d."***

DAVID
King of Israel (united kingdom); son of Jesse, in the family line of Jesus (Ruth 4:17-22; Matt 1:1; Luke 3:31); anointed king (1 Sam 16:1-13); skillful musician to Saul (1 Sam 16:14-23; 18:10); David and Goliath (1 Sam 17); faithful friendship with Jonathan (1 Sam 18:1-4); envied by Saul; loved by the people (1 Sam 18:5-16); married Michal (1 Sam 18:17-30); wives and children (2 Sam 3:2-5; 5:13-16; 1 Chr 3:1-9); fled from Saul (1 Sam 19–23); ate used "Bread of the Presence" (1 Sam 21:1-6; Matt 12:3-4); dealings with the Philistines (1 Sam 21:10-14; 27–30); spared Saul twice (1 Sam 22–24; 26); married widow Abigail (1 Sam 25:2-42); lamented death of Saul and Jonathan (2 Sam 1); contended with Saul's dynasty (2 Sam 2–4); anointed king of Judah (2 Sam 2:1-7); lamented Abner's death (2 Sam 3:31-39); made king over all Israel (2 Sam 5:1-5); victories over the Philistines (2 Sam 5:17-25; 21:15-22; 1 Chr 14:8-17; 20:4-8); made Jerusalem the royal city (2 Sam 5:6-16); moved Ark to Jerusalem (2 Sam 6); eternal covenant with God (2 Sam 7; 1 Chr 17); showed loyal love to Mephibosheth (2 Sam 9); committed adultery with Bathsheba (2 Sam 11–12; Pss 32; 51); plotted Uriah's death (2 Sam 11:14-25); rebuked by Nathan (2 Sam 12:1-12); repented of affair and intrigue (2 Sam 12:13); rebellion and death of Absalom (2 Sam 14–18); lamented Absalom's death (2 Sam 18:33–19:8); rebellion and death of Sheba (2 Sam 20); judged for taking census (2 Sam 24:1-25); made Solomon next king (1 Kgs 1:28–2:9); final words to Solomon (1 Kgs 2:1-9); died (1 Kgs 2:10-12); preparations for the Temple (1 Chr 22–29).

DAWN (n)
first appearance of light in the morning followed by sunrise
Exod 14:24 . But just before ***d*** the LORD
Ps 37:6 . . . . . radiate like the ***d,*** and the
Prov 4:18. . . gleam of ***d,*** which shines ever
Prov 31:15. . gets up before ***d*** to prepare
Amos 4:13. . the light of ***d*** into darkness
Acts 20:11 . . talking to them until ***d,***

DAWNS (v)
to begin to grow light as the sun rises
Hos 10:15 . . day of judgment ***d,*** the king
2 Pet 1:19. . . until the Day ***d,*** and Christ

DAY, DAYS (n)
the time of light between one night and the next; a specified time or period; a 24-hour time period
Gen 1:5 . . . . called the light "***d"*** and the
Gen 2:2 . . . . On the seventh ***d*** God had
Exod 16:30 . any food on the seventh ***d.***
Lev 23:28. . . it is the ***D*** of Atonement,
Josh 1:8 . . . . Meditate on it ***d*** and night so
2 Kgs 7:9 . . . This is a ***d*** of good news,
Ps 23:6 . . . . . all the ***d-s*** of my life,
Ps 84:10 . . . . A single ***d*** in your
Ps 118:24 . . . This is the ***d*** the LORD has
Isa 13:9. . . . . coming—the terrible ***d*** of his
Jer 46:10. . . . this is the ***d*** of the LORD,
Jer 50:31. . . . Your ***d*** of reckoning
Hos 3:5 . . . . In the last ***d-s,*** they will
Joel 1:15. . . . How terrible that ***d*** will be!
Joel 2:31. . . . great and terrible ***d*** of the
Amos 5:20. . Yes, the ***d*** of the LORD
Zeph 1:14 . . That terrible ***d*** of the
Zech 14:1. . . Watch, for the ***d*** of the LORD
Zech 14:7. . . there will be continuous ***d!***
Mal 4:5. . . . . great and dreadful ***d*** of the
Matt 24:38. . In those ***d-s*** before the
Luke 11:3. . . Give us each ***d*** the food we
Acts 2:17 . . . 'In the last ***d-s,'*** God says,
Rom 14:5. . . some think one ***d*** is more holy
1 Cor 5:5 . . . be saved on the ***d*** the Lord
2 Cor 4:16 . . renewed every ***d.***
1 Thes 5:2 . . the ***d*** of the Lord's return
1 Thes 5:4 . . surprised when the ***d*** of the
2 Thes 2:2 . . say that the ***d*** of the Lord
2 Tim 3:1 . . . in the last ***d-s*** there will be

Heb 1:2 . . . . now in these final ***d-s,*** he has
2 Pet 3:3. . . . in the last ***d-s*** scoffers will
2 Pet 3:10. . . But the ***d*** of the Lord
Rev 16:14. . . that great judgment ***d*** of God

DAZZLING (adj)
characterized by shining brilliantly or arousing admiration
Job 37:22 . . . is clothed in ***d*** splendor.
Song 5:10. . . My lover is dark and ***d,***
Mark 9:3 . . . his clothes became ***d*** white,

DEACON, DEACONS (n)
a servant; an officer of the church
see also ELDERS
Phil 1:1 . . . . the elders and ***d-s.***
1 Tim 3:8 . . . ***d-s*** must be well respected
1 Tim 3:10 . . they are appointed as ***d-s,***
1 Tim 3:12 . . A ***d*** must be faithful
1 Tim 3:13 . . Those who do well as ***d-s***

DEAD (n)
those who have died (physically or spiritually)
Matt 8:22. . . the spiritually ***d*** bury their
Luke 24:46. . rise from the ***d*** on the third
1 Cor 15:29 . If the ***d*** will not be raised
Rev 20:12. . . I saw the ***d,*** both great and

DEAD (adj)
without (physical or spiritual) life; fatal; useless; unresponsive
Rom 6:11 . . . be ***d*** to the power of sin
Eph 2:1 . . . . Once you were ***d*** because of
Jas 2:17. . . . . good deeds, it is ***d*** and useless.
1 Pet 2:24. . . that we can be ***d*** to sin and
Rev 2:8. . . . . Last, who was ***d*** but is now

DEAF (adj)
lacking or deficient in the sense of hearing
Ps 94:9 . . . . . Is he ***d***—the one who made

DEAR (adj)
highly valued; precious
1 Cor 10:14 . my ***d*** friends, flee from
2 Cor 7:1 . . . these promises, ***d*** friends,
Eph 5:1 . . . . you are his ***d*** children.
2 Tim 1:2. . . to Timothy, my ***d*** son.
Jas 1:16. . . . . don't be misled, my ***d*** brothers
1 Jn 4:4. . . . . to God, my ***d*** children.
3 Jn 1:1. . . . . to Gaius, my ***d*** friend, whom I
Jude 1:20 . . . But you, ***d*** friends, must

DEATH (n)
the cessation of (physical or spiritual) life; personification and consequence of evil
Exod 21:12 . must be put to ***d.***
Ruth 1:17. . . anything but ***d*** to separate
Prov 11:19. . evil people find ***d.***
Prov 14:12. . it ends in ***d.***
Prov 23:14. . save them from ***d.***
Song 8:6. . . . love is as strong as ***d,***
Isa 38:17. . . . have rescued me from ***d***
Acts 2:24 . . . for ***d*** could not keep him
Rom 5:12. . . brought ***d,*** so ***d*** spread to
Rom 6:23. . . the wages of sin is ***d,***
Rom 7:24. . . dominated by sin and ***d?***
1 Cor 15:21 . see, just as ***d*** came into the
1 Cor 15:26 . enemy to be destroyed is ***d.***
2 Cor 3:6 . . . written covenant ends in ***d;***
Gal 3:1 . . . . . the meaning of Jesus Christ's ***d***
2 Tim 1:10 . . power of ***d*** and illuminated
Heb 2:14 . . . who had the power of ***d.***
Heb 9:17 . . . after the person's ***d.***
1 Jn 5:16. . . . there is a sin that leads to ***d,***
Rev 2:11. . . . by the second ***d.***
Rev 20:6. . . . them the second ***d*** holds no
Rev 20:14. . . of fire is the second ***d.***
Rev 21:4. . . . be no more ***d*** or sorrow or
Rev 21:8. . . . This is the second ***d.***

DEBATERS (n)
one who contends or argues
1 Cor 1:20 . . world's brilliant ***d?***

DEBAUCHERY (KJV)
Rom 13:13 . . promiscuity and ***immoral living***
2 Cor 12:21 . ***eagerness for lustful pleasure***
Gal 5:19 . . . . impurity, ***lustful pleasures***
1 Pet 4:3. . . . their ***immorality*** and lust, their

DEBT, DEBTS (n)
what is owing; sense of obligation
Deut 15:1. . . cancel the ***d-s*** of everyone
Deut 15:3. . . This release from ***d,*** however,
Deut 15:9. . . year for canceling ***d-s*** is close
1 Sam 22:2. . trouble or in ***d*** or who were
2 Kgs 4:7 . . . pay your ***d-s,*** and
Prov 22:26. . another person's ***d*** or put up
Neh 10:31 . . will cancel all ***d-s*** owed to us.
Matt 18:25. . to pay the ***d.***
Matt 18:27. . and forgave his ***d.***
Matt 18:30. . in prison until the ***d*** could
Matt 18:32. . you that tremendous ***d***
Luke 7:42. . . canceling their ***d-s.***
Luke 7:43. . . canceled the larger ***d.***

DEBTORS (n)
those who owe a debt
Hab 2:7 . . . . Suddenly, your ***d*** will take

DECAY (n)
a wasting or wearing away
Rom 8:21 . . . freedom from death and ***d.***
1 Pet 1:4 . . . . the reach of change and ***d.***

DECAY, DECAYED (v)
to undergo decomposition
Job 19:26 . . . my body has ***d-ed,*** yet in my
Acts 13:37 . . whose body did not ***d.***

DECEIT (n)
fraud; trickery; lying
Mark 7:22 . . greed, wickedness, ***d,*** lustful
Acts 13:10 . . of every sort of ***d*** and fraud,
1 Pet 2:1 . . . . done with all ***d,*** hypocrisy,

DECEITFUL (adj)
not honest; misleading, deceptive
Isa 59:13 . . . . planning our ***d*** lies.
2 Cor 11:13 . They are ***d*** workers who

DECEIVE, DECEIVED, DECEIVES, DECEIVING (v)
to lead astray; to cause to accept as true what is false
Gen 3:13 . . . "The serpent ***d-d*** me," she
Prov 10:31 . . the tongue that ***d-s*** will be
Prov 14:8 . . . but fools ***d*** themselves.
Prov 26:24 . . but they're ***d-ing*** you.
Matt 24:24 . . so as to ***d,*** if possible, even
Mark 13:6 . . They will ***d*** many.
Rom 7:11 . . . those commands and ***d-d*** me;
Rom 16:18 . . they ***d*** innocent people.
1 Cor 3:18 . . Stop ***d-ing*** yourselves.
2 Cor 11:3 . . as Eve was ***d-d*** by the cunning
Col 2:4 . . . . . so no one will ***d*** you with
1 Tim 2:14 . . The woman was ***d-d,*** and sin
2 Tim 3:13 . . They will ***d*** others and will
2 Tim 3:13 . . will themselves be ***d-d.***
Heb 3:13 . . . you will be ***d-d*** by sin
Rev 20:3 . . . . Satan could not ***d*** the nations
Rev 20:10 . . . devil, who had ***d-d*** them, was

DECEIVER, DECEIVERS (n)
one who leads astray; one who causes another to accept as true what is false
Ps 101:7 . . . . will not allow ***d-s*** to serve in
Matt 27:63 . . remember what that ***d*** once said
2 Jn 1:7 . . . . . because many ***d-s*** have gone
2 Jn 1:7 . . . . . Such a person is a ***d*** and an

DECENT (adj)
conforming to the standards of propriety or morality; modest
1 Tim 2:9 . . . should wear ***d*** and appropriate

DECEPTION (n)
something that deceives; trick; the act of deceiving
Isa 28:15 . . . . refuge made of lies and ***d.***
Dan 8:25 . . . He will be a master of ***d***
Rom 1:29 . . . quarreling, ***d,*** malicious
Eph 4:22 . . . corrupted by lust and ***d.***
2 Thes 2:10 . kind of evil ***d*** to fool those
1 Jn 4:6 . . . . . truth or spirit of ***d.***

DECEPTIVE (adj)
tending or having power to deceive; misleading
Prov 31:30 . . Charm is ***d,*** and beauty
1 Tim 4:1 . . . will follow ***d*** spirits and

DECIDE, DECIDED, DECIDES (v)
to make a final choice or judgment about; to select as a course of action
1 Sam 14:7 . . whatever you ***d.***
Job 14:5 . . . . You have ***d-d*** the length of
Ps 75:7 . . . . . he ***d-s*** who will rise and
Rom 14:13 . . ***D*** instead to live
Rom 14:22 . . they have ***d-d*** is right.
1 Cor 2:2 . . . For I ***d-d*** that while I
1 Cor 6:2 . . . can't you ***d*** even these
1 Cor 12:11 . He alone ***d-s*** which gift
2 Cor 9:7 . . . You must each ***d*** in your heart

DECISION, DECISIONS (n)
a determination arrived at after consideration; conclusion
Joel 3:14 . . . . waiting in the valley of ***d.***
Mic 3:11 . . . . You rulers make ***d-s*** based on
Rom 11:33 . . to understand his ***d-s*** and his

DECLARE, DECLARED, DECLARING (v)
to make known formally, officially, or explicitly; to state emphatically, affirm; to make evident, show
Deut 25:1 . . . and the judges ***d*** that one is
Ps 71:8 . . . . . praising you; I ***d*** your glory
Ps 92:15 . . . . They will ***d,*** "The LORD
Prov 31:31 . . deeds publicly ***d*** her praise.
Dan 4:24 . . . what the Most High has ***d-d***
Mark 7:19 . . saying this, he ***d-d*** that every
Acts 20:27 . . didn't shrink from ***d-ing*** all
Rom 4:6 . . . . who are ***d-d*** righteous without
Heb 3:1 . . . . Jesus whom we ***d*** to be God's

DECREE, DECREES (n)
an order usually having the force of law; a foreordaining will
Exod 15:25 . them the following ***d***
Exod 15:26 . and keeping all his ***d-s,*** then I
Exod 18:20 . Teach them God's ***d-s,***

Lev 18:4. . . . to obey my ***d-s,*** for I am the
Num 15:15 . to the same ***d-s.***
Deut 4:1. . . . to these ***d-s*** and regulations
1 Kgs 3:3 . . . and followed all the ***d-s*** of his
1 Chr 16:17 . it to Jacob as a ***d,***
Ps 2:7. . . . . . proclaims the LORD's ***d:***
Ps 119:12 . . . LORD; teach me your ***d-s.***
Ps 119:54 . . . Your ***d-s*** have
Ps 148:6 . . . . His ***d*** will never be

DECREED (v)

to determine or order judicially; to command by or as if by decree
Dan 9:24 . . . sets of seven has been ***d***
Luke 2:1. . . . Augustus, ***d*** that a census

DEDICATE, DEDICATED (v)

to devote to the worship of a divine being; to set apart to a definite use
see also CONSECRATE, DEVOTE, ORDAINED
Exod 13:2 . . ***D*** to me every firstborn
Num 6:9 . . . the hair they have ***d-d*** will be
Num 6:18 . . the hair that had been ***d-d***
Num 18:6 . . a gift to you, ***d-d*** to the LORD
1 Kgs 8:63 . . Israel ***d-d*** the Temple
Neh 3:1 . . . . which they ***d-d,*** and the Tower
Luke 2:23. . . he must be ***d-d*** to the LORD.

DEDICATION (n)

an act or rite of dedicating to a diving being or to sacred use
John 10:22 . . the Festival of ***D.***

DEED, DEEDS (n)

a signed instrument containing some legal transfer, bargain, or contract; a usually illustrious act or action; feat, exploit
see also WORKS
Ps 45:4 . . . . . perform awe-inspiring ***d-s!***
Ps 66:3 . . . . . awesome are your ***d-s!***
Ps 71:24 . . . . your righteous ***d-s*** all day
Ps 88:12 . . . . your wonderful ***d-s?***
Ps 96:3 . . . . . his glorious ***d-s*** among the
Ps 105:2 . . . . his wonderful ***d-s.***
Prov 31:31 . . Let her ***d-s*** publicly declare
Isa 64:6. . . . . our righteous ***d-s,*** they are
Jer 32:10. . . . and sealed the ***d*** of purchase
Matt 5:16 . . . let your good ***d-s*** shine out for
Rom 4:2. . . . If his good ***d-s*** had made him
2 Cor 9:9 . . . Their good ***d-s*** will be
Col 3:9 . . . . . all its wicked ***d-s.***
Jas 2:18. . . . . my faith by my good ***d-s.***
Jas 2:20. . . . . without good ***d-s*** is useless?

DEEP, DEEPER (adj)

extending far downward from some surface or area; situated well within the boundaries; difficult to penetrate or comprehend
Gen 1:2 . . . . covered the ***d*** waters.
Rom 6:19 . . . which led ever ***d-er*** into sin.
1 Cor 2:10 . . shows us God's ***d*** secrets.

DEEPLY (adv)

in an intense, profound manner
Ps 116:15 . . . The LORD cares ***d***
Isa 66:11. . . . Drink ***d*** of her glory

DEER (n)

a mammal with usually brownish fur and antlers borne by the males
Ps 42:1 . . . . . As the ***d*** longs for streams of

DEFEAT (n)

an overthrow especially of an army in battle; loss, destruction
Ps 25:2 . . . . . enemies rejoice in my ***d.***
1 Cor 6:7 . . . with one another is a ***d***

DEFEAT, DEFEATED, DEFEATS (v)

to destroy; to win victory over
Ps 129:2 . . . . they have never ***d-d*** me.
1 Jn 5:4. . . . . child of God ***d-s*** this evil
Rev 12:11. . . And they have ***d-d*** him by the
Rev 17:14. . . the Lamb will ***d*** them

DEFEND, DEFENDING, DEFENDS (v)

to maintain or support in the face of argument or hostile criticism; to drive danger or attack away from
Deut 33:7. . . strength to ***d*** their cause;
Ps 10:14 . . . . You ***d*** the orphans.
Ps 34:7 . . . . . he surrounds and ***d-s*** all who
Ps 72:4 . . . . . Help him to ***d*** the poor,
Ps 106:8 . . . . saved them—to ***d*** the honor of
Phil 1:7 . . . . and in ***d-ing*** and confirming
Phil 1:16 . . . been appointed to ***d*** the Good
Jude 1:3 . . . . urging you to ***d*** the faith

DEFENDER (n)

one who guards and protects
Ps 68:5 . . . . . the fatherless, ***d*** of widows—
Prov 22:23 . . the LORD is their ***d.***
Isa 51:22. . . . your God and ***D,*** says:

DEFENSE (n)

the act of defending
Ps 35:23 . . . . Rise to my ***d!***

DEFILE, DEFILED, DEFILING (v)
to make unclean – either physically, sexually, ethically, or ceremonially
Num 6:7 . . . must not ***d*** themselves,
Num 15:39 . desires and ***d-ing*** yourselves,
Ezek 23:7. . . idols and ***d-ing*** herself.
Ezek 44:7. . . this way, you ***d-d*** my Temple
Matt 15:11 . . you are ***d-d*** by the words
Mark 7:23 . . they are what ***d*** you.
Acts 21:28 . . even ***d-s*** this holy place
2 Cor 7:1 . . . that can ***d*** our body or

DEFLECTS (v)
to turn aside; deviate
Prov 15:1 . . . A gentle answer ***d*** anger,

DEFY, DEFIED, DEFYING (v)
to challenge to combat, dare; to disregard
1 Sam 17:10 . I ***d*** the armies of Israel
1 Sam 17:45 . whom you have ***d-ied.***
Isa 37:23. . . . Whom have you been ***d-ing***

DELAY (n)
the state of being delayed; putting off; wait
Rev 10:6. . . . There will be no more ***d.***

DELAY, DELAYED (v)
to put off; to postpone
Eccl 5:4 . . . . don't ***d*** in following through,
Matt 25:5 . . . the bridegroom was ***d-ed,***
Heb 10:37 . . will come and not ***d.***

DELIBERATE (adj)
characterized by awareness of the consequences
Ps 19:13 . . . . servant from ***d*** sins!

DELICACIES (n)
indulgences; something pleasing to eat that is considered rare or luxurious
Ps 141:4 . . . . share in the ***d*** of those who
Prov 23:6 . . . don't desire their ***d.***

DELIGHT, DELIGHTS (n)
source of great pleasure; joy
Ps 36:8 . . . . . your river of ***d-s.***
Ps 40:6 . . . . . You take no ***d*** in sacrifices
Ps 119:111 . . they are my heart's ***d.***
Prov 8:30 . . . I was his constant ***d,***
Isa 58:13. . . . and speak of it with ***d***
Jer 15:16. . . . my joy and my heart's ***d,***
Mal 3:12. . . . your land will be such a ***d,***
Mark 12:37 . to him with great ***d.***

DELIGHT, DELIGHTED, DELIGHTING, DELIGHTS (v)
to enjoy
Exod 4:14 . . He will be ***d-ed*** to see you.
2 Sam 22:20 . because he ***d-s*** in me.
Ps 1:2 . . . . . . But they ***d*** in the law of
Ps 18:19 . . . . he rescued me because he ***d-s***
Ps 27:4 . . . . . ***d-ing*** in the LORD's
Ps 37:4 . . . . . Take ***d*** in the LORD,
Ps 119:70 . . . I ***d*** in your instructions.
Prov 3:12 . . . a child in whom he ***d-s.***
Prov 11:1 . . . he ***d-s*** in accurate weights.
Prov 11:20 . . he ***d-s*** in those with integrity.
Song 8:10. . . he is ***d-ed*** with what he sees.
Isa 11:3. . . . . He will ***d*** in obeying
Isa 65:19. . . . and ***d*** in my people.
Isa 66:3. . . . . ***d-ing*** in their detestable sins –
Jer 9:24. . . . . I ***d*** in these things.

DELIGHTFUL (adj)
highly pleasing
Prov 3:17 . . . guide you down ***d*** paths;
Song 2:3. . . . sit in his ***d*** shade and taste

DELIVER (v)
to save, liberate, set free from
Ps 82:4 . . . . . ***d*** them from the grasp of evil
2 Tim 4:18 . . ***d*** me from every evil attack

DELIVERANCE (n)
freedom from harm, salvation
Esth 4:14 . . . ***d*** and relief for the Jews will arise
Isa 51:1. . . . . "Listen to me, all who hope for ***d***
Phil 1:19 . . . this will lead to my ***d.***

DEMON-POSSESSED (adj)
characterized by the possession or control of demons
Matt 4:24 . . . if they were ***d*** or epileptic
Matt 8:16 . . . That evening many ***d*** people
Matt 8:33 . . . happened to the ***d*** men.
Matt 9:32 . . . When they left, a ***d*** man who
Matt 12:22 . . Then a ***d*** man, who was
Mark 1:32 . . many sick and ***d*** people were
Mark 5:16 . . about the ***d*** man and
Luke 8:36. . . others how the ***d*** man had

DEMON, DEMONS (n)
an agent of the Devil; an evil spirit
Deut 32:17 . . They offered sacrifices to ***d-s,***
Matt 8:31 . . . So the ***d-s*** begged, "If you cast
Matt 9:34 . . . by the prince of ***d-s.***
Matt 11:18 . . He's possessed by a ***d.***
Matt 12:24 . . he can cast out ***d-s.***
Matt 12:28 . . if I am casting out ***d-s*** by the
Matt 17:18 . . Jesus rebuked the ***d***
Mark 1:34 . . But because the ***d-s*** knew who
Mark 5:15 . . by the legion of ***d-s.***

Mark 5:18 . . been ***d*** possessed begged
Mark 7:29 . . the ***d*** has left your daughter."
Mark 9:38 . . to cast out ***d-s,*** but we told
Mark 16:9 . . cast out seven ***d-s.***
Mark 16:17 . will cast out ***d-s*** in my name,
Luke 4:33. . . possessed by a ***d***—an evil
Luke 7:33. . . 'He's possessed by a ***d.'***
Luke 8:2. . . . he had cast out seven ***d-s;***
Luke 8:30. . . with many ***d-s.***
Luke 8:33. . . Then the ***d-s*** came out of the
Luke 8:38. . . freed from the ***d-s*** begged
Luke 9:49. . . to cast out ***d-s,*** but we told
Luke 10:17. . "Lord, even the ***d-s*** obey us
Luke 11:14. . Jesus cast out a ***d*** from
Luke 11:19. . They cast out ***d-s,*** too, so they
Luke 11:20. . casting out ***d-s*** by the power
John 8:49 . . . Jesus said, "I have no ***d*** in me.
John 10:21 . . possessed by a ***d!***
Rom 8:38. . . neither angels nor ***d-s,***
1 Cor 10:20 . to participate with ***d-s.***
1 Cor 10:21 . the cup of ***d-s,*** too.
1 Cor 10:21 . the table of ***d-s,*** too.
1 Tim 4:1 . . . teachings that come from ***d-s.***
Rev 9:20. . . . to worship ***d-s*** and idols made
Rev 18:2. . . . become a home for ***d-s.***

DEMONIC (adj)
of, relating to, or suggestive of a demon
Jas 3:15. . . . . unspiritual, and ***d.***
Rev 16:14. . . They are ***d*** spirits who work

DEMONSTRATE (v)
to show clearly
Ezek 39:21. . ***d*** my glory to the nations.
Rom 3:26 . . . to ***d*** his righteousness,

DEN (n)
the lair of a wild, usually predatory, animal; a center of secret activity
Dan 6:16 . . . thrown into the ***d*** of lions.
Matt 21:13. . into a ***d*** of thieves!

DENY, DENIED, DENIES (v)
to disavow or refuse to accept as true; to refuse to grant
Exod 23:6 . . you must not ***d*** justice to the
Deut 27:19. . is anyone who ***d-ies*** justice
Prov 30:9. . . I may ***d*** you and say,
Matt 10:33. . everyone who ***d-ies*** me
Matt 26:35. . I will never ***d*** you!
Matt 26:70. . But Peter ***d-ied*** it
Luke 12:9. . . anyone who ***d-ies*** me
Luke 22:34. . you will ***d*** three times
John 18:25. . He ***d-ied*** it, saying,
Acts 4:16 . . . We can't ***d*** that they
1 Tim 5:8 . . . have ***d-ied*** the true faith.
2 Tim 2:12. . ***d*** him, he will ***d*** us.
Titus 1:16. . . ***d*** him by the way they live.
2 Pet 2:1. . . . and even ***d*** the Master who
1 Jn 2:22. . . . Anyone who ***d-ies*** the Father
1 Jn 2:23. . . . Anyone who ***d-ies*** the Son
Jude 1:4 . . . . they have ***d-ied*** our only Master
Rev 3:8. . . . . and did not ***d*** me.

DEPEND (v)
to place reliance or trust
Prov 3:5 . . . . do not ***d*** on your own
Jer 49:11. . . . widows, too, can ***d*** on me
Gal 3:10 . . . . But those who ***d*** on the law

DEPOSIT (v)
to place especially for safekeeping
Matt 25:27. . why didn't you ***d*** my money in

DEPRAVED (adj)
characterized by moral corruption or evil; perverted
2 Tim 3:8 . . . They have ***d*** minds and

DEPRESSION (n)
a state of feeling sad; dejection
Ps 143:7 . . . . answer me, for my ***d*** deepens.

DEPRIVE (v)
to withhold something from; to remove
Isa 10:2. . . . . They ***d*** the poor
1 Cor 7:5 . . . Do not ***d*** each other of

DEPTHS (n)
a deep place in a body of water; the quality of being deep
Ps 130:1 . . . . From the ***d*** of despair,
Mic 7:19. . . . them into the ***d*** of the ocean!

DESCENDANT, DESCENDANTS (n)
those who came or originated from; offspring, children
see also OFFSPRING, SON(S)
Gen 12:7 . . . give this land to your ***d-s.***
Gen 13:16 . . will give you so many ***d-s*** that,
Gen 17:9 . . . You and all your ***d-s*** have this
Deut 30:19. . you and your ***d-s*** might live!
Isa 53:8. . . . . he died without ***d-s,*** that his
Isa 53:10. . . . he will have many ***d-s.***
Jer 23:5. . . . . I will raise up a righteous ***d***
Matt 1:1. . . . the Messiah, a ***d*** of David and
Acts 3:25 . . . Through your ***d-s*** all the
Rom 4:18. . . That's how many ***d-s*** you will
Rom 9:8. . . . Abraham's physical ***d-s*** are not

DESCEND, DESCENDED, DESCENDING (v)
to pass from a higher place or level to a lower one
Matt 3:16 . . . Spirit of God ***d-ing*** like a dove
Mark 1:10 . . the Holy Spirit ***d-ing*** on him
Eph 4:9 . . . . that Christ also ***d-ed*** to our

DESECRATE, DESECRATED (v)
to profane something holy or treat it with contempt
Neh 13:18 . . Sabbath to be ***d-d*** in this way!
Isa 56:6. . . . . and do not ***d*** the Sabbath day

DESECRATION (n)
violation of something sacred; profanation; blasphemy
Dan 11:31 . . object that causes ***d.***
Dan 12:11 . . object that causes ***d*** is set
Matt 24:15 . . causes ***d*** standing in the

DESERT, DESERTS (n)
arid land with usually sparse vegetation
see also WILDERNESS
Prov 21:19 . . better to live alone in the ***d***
Isa 32:2. . . . . like streams of water in the ***d***
Isa 43:20. . . . giving them water in the ***d.***
2 Cor 11:26 . cities, in the ***d-s,*** and on the

DESERTED (v)
to abandon
Matt 26:56 . . all the disciples ***d*** him and
2 Tim 1:15 . . of Asia has ***d*** me—even

DESERVE, DESERVED, DESERVES (v)
to be worthy, fit, or suitable for some reward or requital; to merit
Judg 9:16 . . . the honor he ***d-s*** for all he
2 Sam 12:5 . . do such a thing ***d-s*** to die!
Neh 9:33 . . . gave us only what we ***d-d.***
Ps 103:10 . . . with us, as we ***d.***
Prov 14:14 . . Backsliders get what they ***d;***
Dan 9:18 . . . not because we ***d*** help,
Zech 1:6. . . . received what we ***d-d*** from the
Luke 7:4. . . . If anyone ***d-s*** your help,
Acts 26:31 . . done anything to ***d*** death or
Rom 3:8 . . . . who say such things ***d*** to be
Rom 11:9 . . . get what they ***d.***
2 Cor 11:15 . their wicked deeds ***d.***
1 Tim 5:18 . . Those who work ***d*** their pay!
Heb 3:3 . . . . But Jesus ***d-s*** far more

DESIRABLE (adj)
attractive; worth seeking or doing
Ps 19:10 . . . . They are more ***d*** than gold,

DESIRE, DESIRES (n)
conscious impulse toward something that promises enjoyment or satisfaction in its attainment; longing, craving
Job 17:11 . . . My heart's ***d-s*** are broken.
Ps 10:3 . . . . . brag about their evil ***d-s;***
Ps 37:4 . . . . . give you your heart's ***d-s.***
Ps 145:19 . . . He grants the ***d-s*** of those who
Song 6:12. . . my strong ***d-s*** had taken me
Mark 4:19 . . wealth, and the ***d*** for other
Rom 1:26 . . . to their shameful ***d-s.***
Rom 6:12 . . . not give in to sinful ***d-s.***
Rom 7:5 . . . . sinful ***d-s*** were at work
Rom 13:14 . . indulge your evil ***d-s.***
Gal 5:24 . . . . the passions and ***d-s*** of their
Phil 2:13 . . . you the ***d*** and the power
Col 2:23 . . . . a person's evil ***d-s.***
Col 3:5 . . . . . lust, and evil ***d-s.***
1 Tim 6:9 . . . and harmful ***d-s*** that plunge
2 Tim 4:3 . . . follow their own ***d-s*** and will
Jas 1:14. . . . . from our own ***d-s,*** which entice
Jas 4:1. . . . . . from the evil ***d-s*** at war within
1 Pet 2:11 . . . from worldly ***d-s*** that wage
1 Pet 4:2. . . . chasing your own ***d-s,***
2 Pet 2:10 . . . their own twisted sexual ***d,***
2 Pet 2:18 . . . twisted sexual ***d-s,*** they lure
2 Pet 3:3. . . . following their own ***d-s.***
Jude 1:18 . . . their ungodly ***d-s.***

DESIRE, DESIRED, DESIRES (v)
to long or hope for; to wish or request
see also COVET
Gen 3:16 . . . And you will ***d*** to control
Ps 51:6 . . . . . But you ***d*** honesty from
Ps 51:16 . . . . You do not ***d*** a sacrifice,
Prov 8:11 . . . Nothing you ***d*** can compare
Prov 21:10 . . Evil people ***d*** evil;
Rom 1:24 . . . things their hearts ***d-d.***
1 Cor 12:31 . earnestly ***d*** the most
1 Cor 14:1 . . you should also ***d*** the special
1 Tim 3:1 . . . an elder, he ***d-s*** an honorable
Jas 1:20. . . . . righteousness God ***d-s.***
Rev 22:17. . . Let anyone who ***d-s*** drink

DESOLATE (adj)
deserted; joyless; alone; barren
Isa 54:1. . . . . For the ***d*** woman now has
Gal 4:27 . . . . For the ***d*** woman now has

DESPAIR (n)
utter loss of hope
Ps 40:2 . . . . . out of the pit of ***d,***
Ps 79:8 . . . . . on the brink of ***d.***
Ps 130:1 . . . . the depths of ***d,*** O LORD,
Isa 61:3. . . . . praise instead of ***d.***
2 Cor 4:8 . . . but not driven to ***d.***

DESPISE, DESPISED, DESPISES (n)
to scorn or regard as unworthy, sometimes with malice or outrage
2 Sam 12:9. . you ***d-d*** the word of the LORD
Job 5:17 . . . . Do not ***d*** the discipline
Job 9:21 . . . . to me—I ***d*** my life.
Ps 22:6 . . . . . I am scorned and ***d-d*** by all!
Prov 1:7. . . . but fools ***d*** wisdom and
Prov 12:8. . . a warped mind is ***d-d.***
Prov 15:5. . . Only a fool ***d-s*** a parent's
Prov 15:20. . foolish children ***d*** their
Prov 29:27. . The righteous ***d*** the unjust;
Prov 30:17. . and ***d-s*** a mother's
Isa 53:3. . . . . He was ***d-d,*** and we did not
Mic 7:6. . . . . For the son ***d-s*** his father.
Luke 16:13. . to one and ***d*** the other.
Gal 4:14 . . . . you did not ***d*** me or
2 Pet 2:10. . . and who ***d*** authority.

DESTINED (v)
to decree beforehand; to predetermine
Luke 2:34. . . This child is ***d*** to cause
Heb 9:27 . . . each person is ***d*** to die once

DESTINY (n)
a predetermined course of events; fate or fortune
Ps 73:17 . . . . understood the ***d*** of the
Eccl 9:2 . . . . The same ***d*** ultimately awaits

DESTITUTE (adj)
lacking possessions and resources; suffering extreme poverty
Ps 82:3 . . . . . of the oppressed and the ***d.***
Ps 102:17 . . . prayers of the ***d.***
Rom 8:35. . . or hungry, or ***d,*** or in
Heb 11:37 . . ***d*** and oppressed

DESTROY, DESTROYED, DESTROYING, DESTROYS (v)
to kill; to cause devastation or ruin
see also PERISH
Gen 6:17 . . . that will ***d*** every living
Gen 9:11 . . . will a flood ***d*** the earth.
Num 32:15 . responsible for ***d-ing*** this
Deut 28:63. . find pleasure in ***d-ing*** you.
Josh 10:40 . . He completely ***d-ed*** everyone
Prov 6:32. . . fool, for he ***d-s*** himself.
Prov 10:21. . fools are ***d-ed*** by their lack
Prov 10:29. . but it ***d-s*** the wicked.
Prov 11:3. . . dishonesty ***d-s*** treacherous
Prov 11:9. . . the godless ***d*** their friends,
Prov 18:9. . . as someone who ***d-s*** things.
Prov 18:24. . "friends" who ***d*** each other,
Prov 29:1. . . will suddenly be ***d-ed*** beyond
Isa 11:4. . . . . his mouth will ***d*** the wicked.
Dan 2:44 . . . never be ***d-ed*** or conquered.
Jonah 3:9 . . . fierce anger from ***d-ing*** us.
Jonah 4:2. . . turn back from ***d-ing*** people.
Matt 10:28. . God, who can ***d*** both soul
Luke 9:25. . . but are yourself lost or ***d-ed?***
John 10:10 . . and kill and ***d.***
Rom 2:12. . . they will be ***d-ed,*** even though
1 Cor 3:17 . . anyone who ***d-s*** this temple.
1 Cor 5:5 . . . nature will be ***d-ed*** and he
1 Cor 8:11 . . died will be ***d-ed.***
1 Cor 15:24 . ***d-ed*** every ruler and
1 Cor 15:26 . enemy to be ***d-ed*** is death.
2 Cor 4:9 . . . are not ***d-ed.***
Gal 5:15. . . . Beware of ***d-ing*** one another.
Heb 7:16 . . . that cannot be ***d-ed.***
2 Pet 2:12. . . be caught and ***d-ed.***
2 Pet 3:7. . . . people will be ***d-ed.***
Jude 1:5 . . . . but later he ***d-ed*** those who did
Rev 11:18. . . It is time to ***d*** all who have

DESTRUCTION (n)
the state or fact of being destroyed, ruin; place of punishment (hell)
Ps 1:6 . . . . . . of the wicked leads to ***d.***
Prov 16:18. . Pride goes before ***d,***
1 Cor 1:18 . . are headed for ***d!***
2 Thes 1:9 . . punished with eternal ***d,***
2 Thes 2:3 . . the one who brings ***d.***
1 Tim 6:9. . . into ruin and ***d.***
2 Pet 2:3. . . . their ***d*** will not be delayed.
Rev 17:8. . . . and go to eternal ***d.***

DESTRUCTIVE (adj)
designed or tending to hurt or destroy; ruinous
1 Pet 4:4. . . . and ***d*** things they do.
2 Pet 2:1. . . . cleverly teach ***d*** heresies and

DETERMINE, DETERMINED, DETERMINES (v)
to decide; to resolve
Exod 28:30 . objects used to ***d*** the LORD's
Ezra 7:10 . . . because Ezra had ***d-d*** to study
Ps 17:3 . . . . . I am ***d-d*** not to sin in
Ps 119:30 . . . I have ***d-d*** to live by
Ps 119:112 . . I am ***d-d*** to keep your
Prov 4:23. . . it ***d-s*** the course of your life.
Prov 16:9. . . but the LORD ***d-s*** our steps.
Dan 1:8 . . . . But Daniel was ***d-d*** not to
Dan 11:36 . . what has been ***d-d*** will surely
Matt 12:34. . heart ***d-s*** what you say.
Luke 22:22. . it has been ***d-d*** that the Son
Acts 4:28 . . . was ***d-d*** beforehand according

DETEST, DETESTS (v)
to loathe; to denounce
Prov 8:7. . . . the truth and ***d*** every kind of
Prov 12:22. . The LORD ***d-s*** lying lips,

Prov 15:8 . . . The LORD ***d-s*** the sacrifice
Prov 15:26 . . The LORD ***d-s*** evil plans,
Prov 16:5 . . . The LORD ***d-s*** the proud;
Prov 20:10 . . the LORD ***d-s*** double
Prov 24:9 . . . everyone ***d-s*** a mocker.

DETESTABLE(adj)
arousing or meriting intense dislike; abominable
Lev 11:10 . . . They are ***d*** to you.
Prov 3:32 . . . wicked people are ***d*** to the
Prov 17:15 . . both are ***d*** to the LORD.
Prov 21:27 . . an evil person is ***d,***
Luke 16:15 . . What this world honors is ***d***

DEVIL (n)
Satan; enemy of God and of everything good; destroyer, tempter, adversary
see also SATAN
Matt 4:1 . . . . tempted there by the ***d.***
Matt 4:11 . . . Then the ***d*** went away,
Matt 13:39 . . among the wheat is the ***d.***
Matt 25:41 . . prepared for the ***d*** and his
Luke 4:2. . . . tempted by the ***d*** for forty
Luke 4:13. . . When the ***d*** had finished
Luke 8:12. . . to have the ***d*** come and take
John 6:70 . . . twelve of you, but one is a ***d.***
John 13:2 . . . ***d*** had already prompted
Eph 4:27 . . . foothold to the ***d.***
Eph 6:11 . . . strategies of the ***d.***
Eph 6:16 . . . fiery arrows of the ***d.***
2 Tim 2:26 . . escape from the ***d***'s trap.
Jas 4:7. . . . . Resist the ***d,*** and he
1 Jn 3:8. . . . . the works of the ***d.***
1 Jn 3:10. . . . children of the ***d.***
Jude 1:9 . . . . accuse the ***d*** of blasphemy,
Rev 12:9. . . . called the ***d,*** or Satan,

DEVOTE, DEVOTED (v)
to commit by a solemn act
see also CONSECRATE, DEDICATE
2 Chr 31:4 . . could ***d*** themselves fully
Acts 2:42 . . . the believers ***d-d*** themselves to
Col 4:2 . . . . . ***D*** yourselves to prayer

DEVOTED (adj)
characterized by loyalty and devotion
1 Kgs 18:3 . . (Obadiah was a ***d*** follower of
Ps 86:2 . . . . . for I am ***d*** to you.
Matt 6:24 . . . you will be ***d*** to one and
1 Tim 2:10 . . claim to be ***d*** to God should

DEVOTION (n)
religious fervor; being ardently dedicated and loyal
1 Chr 29:3 . . of my ***d*** to the Temple
2 Chr 32:32 . his acts of ***d*** are recorded
2 Chr 35:26 . his acts of ***d*** (carried out
1 Cor 16:16 . serve with such ***d.***
2 Cor 11:3 . . and undivided ***d*** to Christ
Col 2:23 . . . . they require strong ***d,*** pious
1 Tim 5:11 . . overpower their ***d*** to Christ

DEVOUR, DEVOURED, DEVOURING, DEVOURS (v)
to consume by eating; to destroy (as if by eating); to enjoy avidly
2 Sam 11:25. The sword ***d-s*** this one
Isa 66:24. . . . the worms that ***d*** them will
Jer 15:16. . . . your words, I ***d-ed*** them.
Jer 30:16. . . . you will be ***d-ed,*** and all your
Gal 5:15 . . . . biting and ***d-ing*** one another,
1 Pet 5:8. . . . for someone to ***d.***

DEVOURING (adj)
characterized by consuming or destroying ravenously
Deut 4:24. . . your God is a ***d*** fire; he is a
Heb 12:29 . . our God is a ***d*** fire.

DEVOUT (adj)
very religious; devoted
Luke 2:25. . . was righteous and ***d*** and was
Acts 2:5 . . . . time there were ***d*** Jews from
Acts 10:2 . . . He was a ***d,*** God-fearing man,
Acts 10:7 . . . servants and a ***d*** soldier,
Acts 13:43 . . Many Jews and ***d*** converts to
Titus 1:8. . . . must live a ***d*** and disciplined

DEW (n)
moisture condensed upon cool surfaces especially at night
Judg 6:37 . . . is wet with ***d*** in the morning

DICE (n)
small cubes marked on each face with numbers and used usually for games and gambling by being shaken and thrown
Ps 22:18 . . . . throw ***d*** for my clothing
Matt 27:35 . . his clothes by throwing ***d.***

DIE, DIED, DIES (v)
to pass from physical life; to cease from existence
see also DYING, PERISH
Gen 2:17 . . . you are sure to ***d.***
Gen 3:3 . . . . if you do, you will ***d.***
Esth 4:16 . . . If I must ***d,*** I must ***d.***
Job 2:9 . . . . . Curse God and ***d.***
Prov 5:23 . . . He will ***d*** for lack of
Prov 11:7 . . . When the wicked ***d,*** their
Prov 11:10 . . when the wicked ***d.***
Prov 23:13 . . They won't ***d*** if you
Eccl 7:2 . . . . After all, everyone ***d-s***—

Isa 22:13. . . . drink, for tomorrow we ***d!***
Isa 66:24. . . . that devour them will never ***d,***
Jer 31:30. . . . All people will ***d*** for their
Matt 26:52. . will ***d*** by the sword.
Mark 9:48 . . the maggots never ***d*** and the
Luke 16:22. . The rich man also ***d-d*** and
John 13:37 . . I'm ready to ***d*** for you.
Rom 4:25. . . handed over to ***d*** because of
Rom 5:6. . . . the right time and ***d-d*** for us
Rom 5:7. . . . be willing to ***d*** for a person
Rom 5:8. . . . by sending Christ to ***d*** for us
Rom 5:14. . . Still, everyone ***d-d***—from the
Rom 6:7. . . . when we ***d-d*** with Christ we
Rom 6:10. . . When he ***d-d,*** he ***d-d*** once
Rom 7:2. . . . But if he ***d-s,*** the laws of
Rom 7:6. . . . the law, for we ***d-d*** to it and
Rom 14:8. . . whether we live or ***d,*** we
1 Cor 7:39 . . If her husband ***d-s,*** she is free
1 Cor 9:15 . . I would rather ***d*** than lose
1 Cor 15:6 . . though some have ***d-d.***
1 Cor 15:18 . all who have ***d-d*** believing in
1 Cor 15:22 . Just as everyone ***d-s*** because
1 Cor 15:32 . for tomorrow we ***d!***
1 Cor 15:36 . plant unless it ***d-s*** first.
1 Cor 15:42 . in the ground when we ***d,***
1 Cor 15:51 . will not all ***d,*** but we will
2 Cor 5:15 . . for Christ, who ***d-d*** and was
Col 2:20. . . . You have ***d-d*** with Christ,
1 Thes 4:16 . who have ***d-d*** will rise from
1 Thes 5:10 . Christ ***d-d*** for us so
1 Tim 6:16 . . He alone can never ***d,***
2 Tim 2:11 . . saying: If we ***d*** with him,
Heb 9:27 . . . is destined to ***d*** once and
1 Pet 3:18. . . sinned, but he ***d-d*** for sinners

DIFFERENCE (n)
the quality or state of being different; a significant change in or affect on a situation
2 Chr 12:8 . . know the ***d*** between serving
Ezek 22:26. . teach my people the ***d***
Gal 2:6 . . . . . leaders made no ***d*** to me,

DIFFERENT (adj)
not the same as; dissimilar; another
Lev 19:19. . . woven from two ***d*** kinds of
1 Sam 10:6. . into a ***d*** person.
Dan 7:24 . . . king will arise, ***d*** from the
Rom 12:6. . . God has given us ***d*** gifts for
1 Cor 12:4 . . There are ***d*** kinds of
1 Cor 12:6 . . God works in ***d*** ways, but it
2 Cor 11:4 . . if they preach a ***d*** Jesus than
Gal 1:8 . . . . . who preaches a ***d*** kind of Good

DIFFICULT (adj)
hard to understand; hard to do or carry out; hard to manage or overcome
Deut 30:11. . ***d*** for you to understand,
2 Kgs 2:10 . . have asked a ***d*** thing," Elijah
Acts 15:19 . . should not make it ***d*** for the
2 Tim 3:1 . . . will be very ***d*** times.

DIFFICULTY (n)
the quality or state of being difficult; trouble
Phil 4:14 . . . in my present ***d.***

DIGNITY (n)
the quality or state of being worthy, honored, or esteemed
Prov 31:25. . with strength and ***d,*** and she

DILIGENT (adj)
characterized by steady, earnest, and energetic effort; painstaking
Ezra 4:22 . . . Be ***d,*** and don't
Prov 12:27. . but the ***d*** make use of

DILIGENTLY (adv)
in a diligent manner
Deut 6:17. . . You must ***d*** obey the

DINING (v)
to take or give a dinner
Prov 23:1. . . While ***d*** with a ruler,

DINNER (n)
the principal meal of the day
1 Cor 10:27 . believer asks you home for ***d,***

DIRECT, DIRECTED, DIRECTS (v)
to regulate the activities or course of
Gen 18:19 . . that he will ***d*** his sons and
Gen 24:51 . . as the LORD has ***d-ed.***
Job 38:31 . . . Can you ***d*** the movement of
Prov 20:24. . The LORD ***d-s*** our steps,
Jer 13:2. . . . . as the LORD ***d-ed*** me, and I put
Gal 5:18 . . . . you are ***d-ed*** by the Spirit,

DISAPPEAR, DISAPPEARED, DISAPPEARING (v)
to pass from view; to cease to be
1 Kgs 20:40 . the prisoner ***d-ed***!
Job 17:11 . . . My hopes have ***d-ed.***
Ps 37:20 . . . . they will ***d*** like smoke.
Prov 26:20. . and quarrels ***d*** when gossip
Isa 29:14. . . . of the intelligent will ***d.***
Isa 51:6. . . . . the skies will ***d*** like smoke,
Matt 5:18. . . until heaven and earth ***d,***
Matt 24:35. . Heaven and earth will ***d,***
Mark 13:31 . Heaven and earth will ***d,***
Luke 16:17. . and earth to ***d*** than for the

John 5:13 . . . for Jesus had ***d-ed*** into the
Heb 8:13 . . . and will soon ***d.***
1 Jn 2:8. . . . . the darkness is ***d-ing,*** and the

DISAPPOINTED (v)
to fail to meet the expectation or hope of; to frustrate
Prov 23:18 . . hope will not be ***d.***

DISAPPOINTMENT (n)
the state or emotion of being frustrated, failed, or let down
Rom 5:5 . . . . this hope will not lead to ***d.***

DISARMED (v)
to make harmless
Col 2:15 . . . . this way, he ***d*** the spiritual

DISASTER, DISASTERS (n)
a sudden calamitous event bringing great damage, loss, or destruction; a sudden or great misfortune or failure
Exod 32:12 . this terrible ***d*** you have
Deut 31:17. . will say, 'These ***d-s*** have come
Deut 31:21. . when great ***d-s*** come down
Ps 91:6 . . . . . nor the ***d*** that strikes at
Prov 3:25. . . not be afraid of sudden ***d***
Prov 27:10. . When ***d*** strikes,
Jer 17:17. . . . my hope in the day of ***d.***
Jer 29:11. . . . plans for good and not for ***d,***
1 Thes 5:3 . . then ***d*** will fall on them

DISCERNMENT (n)
the quality of being able to grasp and comprehend what is obscure
Ps 119:125 . . Give ***d*** to me,
Prov 1:4. . . . knowledge and ***d*** to the young.
Prov 5:2. . . . you will show ***d,*** and your
Prov 8:12. . . knowledge and ***d.***
Prov 28:11. . a poor person with ***d*** can see

DISCIPLE, DISCIPLES (n)
student or follower of some doctrine or teacher
Matt 28:19. . go and make ***d-s*** of all the
Mark 16:20 . the ***d-s*** went everywhere and
Luke 6:13. . . all of his ***d-s*** and chose twelve
Luke 14:26. . you cannot be my ***d.***
Luke 14:33. . become my ***d*** without
John 6:66 . . . many of his ***d-s*** turned away
John 8:31 . . . are truly my ***d-s*** if you remain
John 13:5 . . . to wash the ***d-s'*** feet, drying
John 13:23 . . The ***d*** Jesus loved
John 15:8 . . . fruit, you are my true ***d-s.***
John 19:26 . . there beside the ***d*** he loved,
John 21:7 . . . Then the ***d*** Jesus loved
John 21:20 . . the ***d*** Jesus loved—

DISCIPLINE (n)
punishment; instruction
Deut 11:2. . . the ***d*** of the LORD
Prov 10:17. . People who accept ***d*** are on
Prov 13:1. . . child accepts a parent's ***d;***
Prov 13:24. . spare the rod of ***d*** hate their
Prov 15:32. . If you reject ***d,*** you only
Heb 12:5 . . . of the LORD's ***d,*** and don't
Heb 12:11 . . No ***d*** is enjoyable

DISCIPLINE, DISCIPLINED, DISCIPLINES (v)
to punish or correct with love; to exercise self-control
Deut 8:5. . . . as a parent ***d-s*** a child,
Deut 8:5. . . . your God ***d-s*** you for your
Ps 38:1 . . . . . in your anger or ***d*** me in your
Ps 39:11 . . . . When you ***d*** us for our
Ps 119:67 . . . wander off until you ***d-d*** me;
Ps 119:75 . . . you ***d-d*** me because I needed
Prov 15:10. . right path will be severely ***d-d;***
Jer 30:11. . . . I will ***d*** you, but with
Jer 31:18. . . . saying, 'You ***d-d*** me severely,
1 Cor 9:25 . . All athletes are ***d-d*** in their
1 Cor 9:27 . . I ***d*** my body like an athlete
1 Cor 11:32 . we are being ***d-d*** so that we
Heb 12:6 . . . For the LORD ***d-s*** those he
Heb 12:7 . . . who is never ***d-d*** by its father?
Heb 12:9 . . . fathers who ***d-d*** us, shouldn't
1 Pet 4:7. . . . be earnest and ***d-d*** in your

DISCOURAGED (v)
to dissuade or hinder; to deprive of courage or confidence
Deut 31:8. . . be afraid or ***d,*** for the LORD
2 Sam 11:25. not to be ***d,"*** David said.
1 Chr 28:20 . afraid or ***d,*** for the LORD
Isa 41:10. . . . Don't be ***d,*** for I am
2 Cor 7:6 . . . who are ***d,*** encouraged us by
Col 3:21 . . . . will become ***d.***

DISCOURAGEMENT (n)
the state of being discouraged
2 Cor 2:7 . . . may be overcome by ***d.***

DISCRETION (n)
cautious reserve in speech; prudent or modest in behavior and dress
Prov 11:22. . woman who lacks ***d*** is like a

DISCRIMINATION (n)
prejudiced outlook, action, or treatment
see also FAVORITISM, PARTIALITY
Jas 2:4. . . . . . doesn't this ***d*** show that your

DISEASE, DISEASES (n)
sickness, malady
Exod 4:6 . . . a severe skin ***d.***
2 Chr 16:12 . a serious foot ***d.***
Ps 91:6 . . . . . not dread the ***d*** that stalks
Ps 103:3 . . . . heals all my ***d-s.***
Matt 9:35 . . . every kind of ***d*** and illness.
Matt 10:1 . . . every kind of ***d*** and illness.
Luke 4:40. . . matter what their ***d-s*** were,

DISGRACE (n)
loss of grace, favor, or honor; source of shame
Prov 11:2. . . Pride leads to ***d,*** but with
Prov 14:34 . . but sin is a ***d*** to any people.
Acts 5:41 . . . worthy to suffer ***d*** for the
Heb 13:13 . . and bear the ***d*** he bore.

DISGRACE, DISGRACED (v)
to cause to lose favor or standing; to be a source of shame to
Ps 25:3 . . . . . trusts in you will ever be ***d-d,***
Ps 37:19 . . . . will not be ***d-d*** in hard times;
Prov 29:15 . . but a mother is ***d-d*** by an
Matt 1:19 . . . did not want to ***d*** her
Rom 9:33 . . . in him will never be ***d-d.***
Rom 10:11 . . in him will never be ***d-d.***
1 Tim 3:7 . . . will not be ***d-d*** and fall into

DISGRACEFUL (adj)
bringing or involving disgrace
Prov 12:4 . . . a ***d*** woman is like cancer
Prov 17:2. . . over the master's ***d*** son and
1 Cor 11:14 . it's ***d*** for a man to have

DISGUISES (v)
to mask the identity of; to use pretense or deception
2 Cor 11:14 . Even Satan ***d*** himself as an

DISGUSTS (v)
to provoke loathing, repugnance, or aversion
Isa 1:13. . . . . of your offerings ***d*** me!

DISHONEST (adj)
characterized by lack of truth, honesty, or trustworthiness
Lev 19:35 . . . Do not use ***d*** standards when
Prov 20:23 . . not pleased by ***d*** scales.
Luke 16:8. . . to admire the ***d*** rascal for
Luke 16:10. . But if you are ***d*** in little

DISHONESTLY (adv)
in a shameful, unfair, or deceptive manner
Hab 2:9 . . . . houses with money gained ***d!***

DISHONESTY (n)
lack of honesty or integrity
Jer 22:17. . . . eyes only for greed and ***d!***
Jer 23:14. . . . commit adultery and love ***d.***
Rom 3:7. . . . sinner if my ***d*** highlights his
Rev 21:27. . . idolatry and ***d***—but only

DISHONOR, DISHONORED, DISHONORING, DISHONORS (v)
to degrade or bring shame upon
Exod 21:17 . Anyone who ***d-s*** father or
Exod 22:28 . You must not ***d*** God or
Lev 20:19. . . This would ***d*** a close
Deut 27:16. . is anyone who ***d-s*** father or
Ezra 4:14 . . . see the king ***d-ed*** in this way,
Lam 2:2 . . . . ***d-ing*** the kingdom and its
John 8:49 . . . my Father—and you ***d*** me.
Rom 2:23 . . . the law, but you ***d*** God by
1 Cor 11:4 . . A man ***d-s*** his head if
1 Cor 11:5 . . a woman ***d-s*** her head if
Jas 2:6. . . . . . But you ***d*** the poor!

DISMAYED (v)
to cause to lose courage or resolution; to be upset or perturbed
Ps 49:16 . . . . So don't be ***d*** when the wicked

DISOBEDIENCE (n)
refusal or neglect to obey
Ps 32:1 . . . . . those whose ***d*** is forgiven,
Rom 11:32 . . imprisoned everyone in ***d***

DISOBEDIENT (adj)
refusing or neglecting to obey
Neh 9:26 . . . they were ***d*** and rebelled
2 Cor 10:6 . . everyone who remains ***d.***
Titus 1:16. . . detestable and ***d,*** worthless

DISOBEY, DISOBEYED, DISOBEYING (v)
to fail to obey
Judg 2:2. . . . But you ***d-ed*** my command.
1 Kgs 13:26 . man of God who ***d-ed*** the
2 Chr 24:20 . says: Why do you ***d*** the
Neh 9:29 . . . and obstinate and ***d-ed*** your
Esth 3:3 . . . . Why are you ***d-ing*** the king's
Dan 9:11 . . . Israel has ***d-ed*** your instruction
Acts 7:53 . . . You deliberately ***d-ed*** God's
Rom 1:30. . . and they ***d*** their parents.
Rom 5:19. . . Because one person ***d-ed*** God,
Eph 5:6 . . . . fall on all who ***d*** him.
Heb 3:18 . . . the people who ***d-ed*** him?
Heb 4:6 . . . . enter because they ***d-ed*** God.
Heb 4:11 . . . But if we ***d*** God, as the
1 Pet 3:20. . . those who ***d-ed*** God long ago

DISORDER (n)
lack of order; confusion
1 Cor 14:33 . not a God of ***d*** but of peace,
Jas 3:16. . . . . you will find ***d*** and evil of

DISORDERLY (adj)
in a manner that lacks order; turbulent
2 Cor 12:20 . arrogance, and ***d*** behavior.

DISPLAY (n)
a presentation of something in open view; exhibition
1 Cor 4:9 . . . apostles on ***d,*** like prisoners

DISPLAYED, DISPLAYING (v)
to put or spread before the view; to make evident
Neh 9:10 . . . You ***d*** miraculous signs
Isa 5:16. . . . . The holiness of God will be ***d***
Isa 63:12. . . . power was ***d*** when Moses
Rom 9:17 . . . purpose of ***d-ing*** my power

DISPLEASED (v)
to incur the disapproval or dislike of
2 Sam 11:27. But the LORD was ***d*** with
Prov 24:18. . LORD will be ***d*** with you and

DISPUTE, DISPUTES (n)
verbal controversy; quarrel or debate
Prov 18:18. . it settles ***d-s*** between
1 Cor 6:1 . . . you has a ***d*** with another

DISSENSION (n)
disagreement; discord
Gal 5:20 . . . . selfish ambition, ***d,*** division,

DISTINCTION (n)
the distinguishing of a difference; division
Acts 15:9 . . . He made no ***d*** between us and

DISTORT (v)
to twist out of the true meaning or proportion
Acts 20:30 . . rise up and ***d*** the truth in

DISTRACTED (v)
to divert one's attention
Luke 10:40. . But Martha was ***d*** by the big

DISTRACTIONS (n)
something that distracts
1 Cor 7:35 . . with as few ***d*** as possible.

DISTRESS (n)
a troubling or painful situation; a state of danger or desperate need
Exod 3:7 . . . their cries of ***d*** because of
Job 36:16 . . . to a place free from ***d.***
Ps 18:6 . . . . . But in my ***d*** I cried out
Ps 118:5 . . . . In my ***d*** I prayed to
Ps 143:11 . . . bring me out of this ***d.***
Jas 1:27. . . . . and widows in their ***d***

DISTRESSED (v)
to subject one to grief or misery
Rom 14:15 . . another believer is ***d*** by

DISTURB (v)
to interfere with; to interrupt
Ezra 6:7 . . . . Do not ***d*** the construction of

DIVIDE, DIVIDED (v)
to separate into parts; to distribute; to make distinctions
Ps 22:18 . . . . They ***d*** my garments
Luke 12:51. . have come to ***d*** people
1 Cor 1:13 . . Has Christ been ***d-d*** into
Jas 4:8. . . . . . loyalty is ***d-d*** between God

DIVINATION (n)
the attempt through ritual means to know the future or other hidden knowledge
Num 24:1 . . he did not resort to ***d*** as before.
2 Kgs 21:6 . . He practiced sorcery and ***d,***

DIVINE (adj)
of, relating to, or preceding directly from God or a god
Prov 29:18. . not accept ***d*** guidance,
Rom 1:20. . . power and ***d*** nature.
2 Pet 1:4. . . . to share his ***d*** nature

DIVISION, DIVISIONS (n)
act or process of dividing, separating, distributing; a portion, part, grouping, or distinction
1 Cor 1:10 . . there be no ***d-s*** in the church.
1 Cor 11:18 . that there are ***d-s*** among
Gal 5:20 . . . . selfish ambition, dissension, ***d,***
Titus 3:10. . . are causing ***d-s*** among you,

DIVORCE (n)
the action or an instance of legally dissolving a marriage
Deut 24:1. . . a letter of ***d,*** hands it to
Mal 2:16. . . . "For I hate ***d!"*** says the
Matt 19:8 . . . Moses permitted ***d*** only as a

DIVORCE, DIVORCED, DIVORCES (v)
to dissolve a marriage; to end a relationship
Lev 21:7. . . . a woman who is ***d-d*** from her
Lev 21:14. . . who is ***d-d,*** or a woman
Lev 22:13. . . a widow or is ***d-d*** and has no
Num 30:9 . . is a widow or is ***d-d,*** she must
Deut 22:19. . and he may never ***d*** her.
1 Chr 8:8 . . . After Shaharaim ***d-d*** his wives

Jer 3:1. . . . . . If a man ***d-s*** a woman and
Jer 3:8. . . . . . saw that I ***d-d*** faithless Israel
Matt 5:31 . . . A man can ***d*** his wife by
Matt 5:32. . . a man who ***d-s*** his wife, unless
Matt 5:32. . . who marries a ***d-d*** woman also
Mark 10:2 . . be allowed to ***d*** his wife?
Mark 10:11 . Whoever ***d-s*** his wife and
Mark 10:12 . if a woman ***d-s*** her husband
Luke 16:18. . a man who ***d-s*** his wife and
Luke 16:18. . marries a woman ***d-d*** from

DOCTOR, DOCTORS (n)
a person skilled or specializing in healing arts
Matt 9:12. . . don't need a ***d***—sick people
Mark 5:26 . . great deal from many ***d-s,***

DOG, DOGS (n)
a carnivorous (usually domestic) mammal similar to wolves and coyotes
Prov 26:11. . As a ***d*** returns to its
Eccl 9:4 . . . . to be a live ***d*** than a dead
Matt 15:26. . throw it to the ***d-s."***
Phil 3:2 . . . . Watch out for those ***d-s,***
2 Pet 2:22. . . this proverb: "A ***d*** returns to

DONKEY (n)
a domestic mammal smaller than the horse and having long ears
Num 22:30 . same ***d*** you have ridden
Matt 21:5. . . riding on a ***d***—riding on a
2 Pet 2:16. . . when his ***d*** rebuked him

DOOMED (adj)
condemned; certain to be destroyed
Isa 6:5 I am ***d,*** for I am

DOOR, DOORS (n)
a barrier by which an entry is closed and opened; a means of access or participation
Ps 24:7 . . . . . Open up, ancient ***d-s,*** and let
Matt 7:7. . . . the ***d*** will be opened to you.
Luke 13:24. . enter the narrow ***d*** to God's
Acts 14:27 . . had opened the ***d*** of faith to
1 Cor 16:9 . . is a wide-open ***d*** for a great
2 Cor 2:12 . . opened a ***d*** of opportunity
Rev 3:20. . . . stand at the ***d*** and knock.

DOORPOSTS (n)
the two sides of a doorway, similar to a door frame
Deut 6:9. . . . Write them on the ***d*** of

DOUBLE-EDGED (adj)
having two cutting edges
Prov 5:4. . . . dangerous as a ***d*** sword.

DOUBT, DOUBTS (n)
uncertainty of belief or opinion; lack of confidence; distrust
Mark 11:23 . have no ***d*** in your heart.
Luke 24:38. . hearts filled with ***d?***
Rom 14:23. . if you have ***d-s*** about whether

DOUBT (v)
to distrust; to be uncertain
Matt 14:31. . Why did you ***d*** me?
Matt 21:21. . faith and don't ***d,*** you

DOVE, DOVES (n)
a small wild pigeon, often symbolic of gentleness
Gen 8:8 . . . . also released a ***d*** to see if
Matt 3:16. . . like a ***d*** and settling on him.
Matt 10:16. . snakes and harmless as ***d-s.***

DOWNTRODDEN (adj)
suffering oppression
Ps 74:21 . . . . Don't let the ***d*** be humiliated

DRAGON (n)
a huge serpent
Rev 12:7. . . . fought against the ***d*** and his
Rev 20:2. . . . He seized the ***d***—that old

DRAW, DRAWING, DRAWS (v)
to pull; to bring in or gather; to come steadily or gradually
John 6:44. . . who sent me ***d-s*** them to me,
John 12:32. . I will ***d*** everyone to myself.
Heb 10:25 . . day of his return is ***d-ing*** near.

DREAD (n)
great fear; extreme uneasiness in the face of a disagreeable prospect
Isa 51:13. . . . remain in constant ***d*** of human

DREADFUL (adj)
causing great and oppressive fear; inspiring awe or reverence
Job 25:2 . . . . powerful and ***d.***

DREAM, DREAMS (n)
a strongly desired goal or purpose; a series of thoughts, images, or emotions occurring during sleep
Prov 13:12. . sick, but a ***d*** fulfilled is a
Prov 13:19. . pleasant to see ***d-s*** come true,
Eccl 5:3 . . . . gives you restless ***d-s;***

DREAM (v)
to have a dream
Joel 2:28. . . . old men will ***d*** dreams,
Acts 2:17 . . . old men will ***d*** dreams.

DRESSED (v)
to put on clothing
Exod 12:11 . Be fully ***d,*** wear your
Ps 104:2 . . . . You are ***d*** in a robe
Isa 61:10. . . . For he has ***d*** me with the

DRINK, DRINKING, DRINKS (v)
to swallow; to partake of alcoholic beverages
1 Sam 1:13 . . she had been ***d-ing.***
Isa 5:22. . . . . who are heroes at ***d-ing*** wine
Isa 12:3. . . . . you will ***d*** deeply from
Matt 26:27 . . Each of you ***d*** from it,
Mark 16:18 . ***d*** anything poisonous,
John 4:13 . . . Anyone who ***d-s*** this water
John 6:54 . . . my flesh and ***d-s*** my blood has
Rom 14:17 . . we eat or ***d,*** but of living a
1 Cor 11:27 . this bread or ***d-s*** this cup of
Rev 14:10. . . ***d*** the wine of God's anger.
Rev 22:17. . . who desires ***d*** freely from

DRINKER, DRINKERS (n)
a person who drinks alcoholic beverages
1 Tim 3:3 . . . not be a heavy ***d*** or be violent.
1 Tim 3:8 . . . not be heavy ***d-s*** or dishonest
Titus 2:3. . . . or be heavy ***d-s.***

DRIVE (v)
to exert inescapable or coercive pressure on; to force
Exod 23:30 . I will ***d*** them out a little
Num 33:52 . you must ***d*** out all the people
Josh 13:13 . . failed to ***d*** out the people of
Josh 23:13 . . will no longer ***d*** them out of

DROUGHT (n)
a period of prolonged dryness
1 Kgs 18:1 . . in the third year of the ***d,***
Jer 17:8. . . . . by long months of ***d.***

DROWNED (v)
to suffocate by submersion especially in water
Exod 15:4 . . officers are ***d*** in the Red
Matt 18:6 . . . neck and be ***d*** in the depths
Heb 11:29 . . they were all ***d.***

DRUNK (adj)
having the faculties impaired by alcohol; intoxicated
Acts 2:15 . . . These people are not ***d,*** as

DRUNKARD, DRUNKARDS (n)
one who is habitually drunk
Prov 23:20 . . not carouse with ***d-s*** or feast
Matt 11:19 . . glutton and a ***d,*** and a friend
1 Cor 5:11 . . or is a ***d,*** or cheats people.
1 Cor 6:10 . . greedy people, or ***d-s,*** or are

DRUNKENNESS
Ezek 23:33 . . ***D*** and anguish will fill you,
Rom 13:13 . . darkness of wild parties and ***d***

DRY (adj)
free or relatively free from a liquid, especially water
Gen 1:9 . . . . so ***d*** ground may appear.
Exod 14:16 . of the sea on ***d*** ground.
Josh 3:17 . . . Covenant stood on ***d*** ground
Isa 53:2. . . . . a root in ***d*** ground.

DULL (adj)
slow in action, sluggish; slow in perception or sensibility
Heb 6:12 . . . not become spiritually ***d*** and

DUST (n)
specks or clumps of earthy matter; ground or earth
Gen 2:7 . . . . man from the ***d*** of the ground.
Gen 3:19 . . . were made from ***d,*** and to ***d***
Ps 22:15 . . . . laid me in the ***d*** and left me
Eccl 3:20 . . . they return to ***d.***
Matt 10:14 . . shake its ***d*** from your feet
1 Cor 15:47 . from the ***d*** of the earth,

DUTY, DUTIES (n)
moral or legal obligation; assigned service or task
Eccl 8:3 . . . . to avoid doing your ***d,***
Eccl 12:13 . . is everyone's ***d.***
Dan 8:27 . . . performed my ***d-ies*** for the

DWELLING (n)
a shelter (as a house) in which one lives; residence
see also HOME, HOUSE
Exod 15:17 . your own ***d,*** the sanctuary,
Eph 2:22 . . . made part of this ***d*** where God

DWELLS (v)
to stay for a time; to live as a resident
see also LIVE(S)
Ps 26:8 . . . . . glorious presence ***d.***

DYING (v)
see also DIE
John 11:25 . . even after ***d.***
2 Cor 4:16 . . our bodies are ***d,*** our spirits
Phil 1:21 . . . for Christ, and ***d*** is even

DYNASTY (n)
a succession of rulers of the same line of descent
see also HOUSE
2 Sam 3:1. . . Saul's ***d*** became weaker and
1 Chr 17:17 . your servant a lasting ***d!***

EAGER (adj)
marked by enthusiastic or impatient desire or interest
Rom 15:23 . . I am ***e*** to visit you.
1 Cor 14:39 . sisters, be ***e*** to prophesy,
1 Pet 5:2. . . . because you are ***e*** to serve

EAGERLY (adv)
in an enthusiastic or impatient manner
Rom 8:19. . . creation is waiting ***e*** for that

EAGERNESS (n)
the state or quality of enthusiasm for a desire or interest
Ps 119:36 . . . Give me an ***e*** for your laws

EAGLE, EAGLES (n)
any of various large diurnal birds of prey noted for their strength, size, keenness of vision, and powers of flight
Deut 32:11. . Like an ***e*** that rouses her chicks
Isa 40:31. . . . soar high on wings like ***e-s.***
Rev 4:7. . . . . was like an ***e*** in flight.
Rev 12:14. . . wings like those of a great ***e***

EARN, EARNED (v)
to receive as return for effort or work done
2 Thes 3:12 . ***e*** their own living.
Heb 11:2 . . . ***e-ed*** a good reputation.

EARNEST (adj)
characterized by or proceeding from an intense and serious state of mind; ardent or fervent
Jas 5:16. . . . . The ***e*** prayer of a righteous
1 Pet 4:7. . . . be ***e*** and disciplined

EARNESTLY (adv)
in a manner that is intense and serious; fervently
2 Chr 15:15 . they ***e*** sought after God,
Col 4:12. . . . He always prays ***e*** for you,

EARNINGS (n)
pay; wages
Prov 31:16. . with her ***e*** she plants a vineyard.

EARRING, EARRINGS (n)
an ornament for the ear and especially the earlobe
Exod 35:22 . gold—brooches, ***e-s,*** rings
Prov 25:12. . valid criticism is like a gold ***e***

EARS (n)
the external organ for hearing, expressing the entire faculty of understanding
Prov 2:2. . . . Tune your ***e*** to wisdom,
Eccl 5:1 . . . . ***e*** open and your mouth shut.
2 Tim 4:3 . . . whatever their itching ***e*** want

EARTH (n)
the ground; the planet on which we live
Gen 1:1 . . . . created the heavens and the ***e.***
Gen 7:24 . . . floodwaters covered the ***e***
Gen 14:19 . . Creator of heaven and ***e.***
Job 26:7 . . . . and hangs the ***e*** on nothing.
Job 38:4 . . . . I laid the foundations of the ***e?***
Ps 24:1 . . . . . The ***e*** is the LORD's, and
Ps 108:5 . . . . your glory shine over all the ***e.***
Prov 8:23. . . first, before the ***e*** began.
Prov 8:26. . . had made the ***e*** and fields
Isa 6:3. . . . . . whole ***e*** is filled with his glory!
Isa 40:22. . . . God sits above the circle of the ***e.***
Isa 44:23. . . . O depths of the ***e!***
Isa 55:9. . . . . higher than the ***e,*** so my ways
Isa 65:17. . . . new heavens and a new ***e,***
Isa 66:1. . . . . and the ***e*** is my footstool.
Jer 23:24. . . . in all the heavens and ***e?***
Hab 2:20 . . . Let all the ***e*** be silent
Matt 5:18. . . until heaven and ***e*** disappear,
Matt 5:35. . . do not say, 'By the ***e!'***

Matt 6:10 . . . your will be done on *e,*
Matt 16:19 . . Whatever you forbid on *e*
Matt 28:18 . . in heaven and on *e.*
Luke 2:14. . . and peace on *e*
Acts 4:24 . . . Creator of heaven and *e,*
Acts 7:49 . . . the *e* is my footstool.
Rom 8:39. . . or in the *e* below—
1 Cor 10:26 . the *e* is the Lord's,
Eph 3:15 . . . in heaven and on *e.*
Phil 2:10 . . . in heaven and on *e* and under
Col 3:2 . . . . . not the things of *e.*
Heb 1:10 . . . laid the foundation of the *e*
2 Pet 3:13. . . and new *e* he has promised,
Rev 20:11. . . The *e* and sky fled
Rev 21:1. . . . a new heaven and a new *e,*
Rev 21:1. . . . the old *e* had disappeared.

EARTHLY (adj)
belonging to the earth; mundane or worldly; temporal or temporary; human
Rom 1:3 . . . . In his *e* life he was born
Col 3:5 . . . . . put to death the sinful, *e* things

EARTHQUAKE, EARTHQUAKES (n)
a shaking or trembling of the earth
Matt 24:7. . . There will be famines and *e-s*
Matt 28:2. . . there was a great *e!*
Rev 6:12. . . . there was a great *e.*

EAST (n)
the general direction of the sunrise
Gen 2:8 . . . . a garden in Eden in the *e,*
Ps 103:12. . . far from us as the *e* is from

EASTERN (adj)
coming from the east
Matt 2:1. . . . wise men from *e* lands arrived

EASY (adj)
causing or involving little difficulty or discomfort
Matt 11:30. . For my yoke is *e* to bear,

EAT, EATEN, EATING, EATS (v)
to ingest, chew, and swallow in turn
see also ATE
Gen 2:16 . . . You may freely *e* the fruit
Gen 3:11 . . . Have you *e-en* from the tree
Deut 14:4. . . the animals you may *e:*
Isa 65:25. . . . The lion will *e* hay
Jer 31:29. . . . parents have *e-en* sour grapes,
Matt 26:26. . Take this and *e* it,
Luke 15:2. . . sinful people—even *e-ing* with
John 6:52 . . . give us his flesh to *e?*
John 6:54 . . . anyone who *e-s* my flesh and
Acts 10:13 . . "Get up, Peter; kill and *e* them."
Acts 10:14 . . I have never *e-en* anything
Rom 14:15. . Don't let your *e-ing* ruin
1 Cor 8:4 . . . So, what about *e-ing* meat that
1 Cor 8:10 . . *e-ing* in the temple of an idol,
1 Cor 10:31 . So whether you *e* or drink,
1 Cor 11:26 . every time you *e* this bread
1 Cor 11:27 . anyone who *e-s* this bread or

EDEN (n)
the garden where Adam and Eve first lived
Gen 2:8 . . . . a garden in *E* in the east,
Ezek 28:13. . in *E,* the garden of God.

EDIFY, EDIFYING (KJV)
1 Cor 10:23 . but not everything is ***beneficial***
1 Cor 14:5 . . will be ***strengthened***
1 Cor 14:17 . won't ***strengthen*** the people
Eph 4:12 . . . work and ***build up*** the church,

EFFORT, EFFORTS (n)
conscious exertion of power; hard work; a serious attempt
2 Chr 31:21 . *e-s* to follow God's laws
Ps 90:17 . . . . make our *e-s* successful.
Gal 3:3 . . . . . by your own human *e?*
Eph 4:3 . . . . Make every *e* to keep
2 Pet 1:5. . . . make every *e* to respond
2 Pet 3:14. . . make every *e* to be found

EGYPT (n)
the country in the northeast corner of Africa that extended from the Mediterranean Sea on the north to the Nile River on the south
Gen 46:6 . . . his entire family went to *E*—
Exod 3:11 . . people of Israel out of *E?*
Exod 12:40 . Israel had lived in *E*
Hos 11:1 . . . I called my son out of *E.*
Matt 2:15. . . I called my Son out of *E.*
Heb 11:27 . . Moses left the land of *E,*

ELDER, ELDERS (n)
older, wise man; ruling body of decision makers invested with authority by virtue of their age, character, or experience
see also DEACONS
Acts 14:23 . . appointed *e-s* in every church.
Acts 15:2 . . . talk to the apostles and *e-s*
Acts 20:17 . . a message to the *e-s* of the
Acts 20:28 . . appointed you as *e-s.*
Phil 1:1 . . . . including the *e-s* and deacons.
1 Tim 3:1 . . . aspires to be an *e,* he desires
1 Tim 3:2 . . . *e* must be a man whose life is
1 Tim 4:14 . . *e-s* of the church laid their
1 Tim 5:19 . . against an *e* unless it is
Titus 1:6. . . . An *e* must live a blameless life.
Titus 1:7. . . . An *e* is a manager of God's

Jas 5:14. . . . . call for the ***e-s*** of the church
1 Pet 5:1. . . . a word to you who are ***e-s***
1 Pet 5:1. . . . I, too, am an ***e*** and a witness
1 Pet 5:5. . . . the authority of the ***e-s.***
2 Jn 1:1. . . . . letter is from John, the ***e.***
3 Jn 1:1. . . . . letter is from John, the ***e.***
Rev 4:10. . . . the twenty-four ***e-s*** fall down

ELDERLY (n)
people of advanced age
Lev 19:32. . . the ***e,*** and show respect

ELECT (KJV)
Isa 42:1. . . . . ***chosen one,*** who pleases me
Matt 24:31 . . gather his ***chosen ones*** from all
Rom 8:33. . . ***us whom God has chosen*** for
Col 3:12. . . . ***chose*** you to be the holy people
2 Tim 2:10 . . Jesus to ***those God has chosen***

ELEMENTS (n)
any of four substances air, water, fire, and earth
2 Pet 3:10. . . the very ***e*** themselves
2 Pet 3:12. . . the ***e*** will melt away

ELIJAH
Powerful prophet in Israel (northern kingdom); proclaimed drought (1 Kgs 17:1; Jas 5:17); hid and was fed by ravens (1 Kgs 17:2-6); performed miracles for widow (1 Kgs 17:8-24; Luke 4:25); proclaimed truth to King Ahab (1 Kgs 18:1-15); defeated Baal and his prophets on Mount Carmel (1 Kgs 18:16-40); brought rain (1 Kgs 18:41-46; Jas 5:17); ran for his life (1 Kgs 19:3); served by angels (1 Kgs 19:1-9); given assurance by God (1 Kgs 19:9-18); put mantle on Elisha (1 Kgs 19:19-21); condemned by Ahab (1 Kgs 21:17-29); whirlwind and fire took him into heaven (2 Kgs 2:11); return prophesied and expected (Mal 4:5-6; Matt 11:14; Luke 1:17; John 1:25); compared to John the Baptist (Matt 17:9-13; Mark 9:9-13; Luke 1:17); appeared at Jesus' Transfiguration (Matt 17:1-8; Mark 9:1-8).

ELISHA
Powerful prophet in Israel (northern kingdom) who replaced Elijah (1 Kgs 19:16-21); inherited Elijah's cloak (2 Kgs 2:1-18); asked for double measure of spirit (2 Kgs 2:9); witnessed Elijah's departure (2 Kgs 2:11-12); healed bad water (2 Kgs 2:19-22); cursed 42 mockers (2 Kgs 2:23-25); prophesied victory over Moab (2 Kgs 3:11-27); provided abundant oil for widow (2 Kgs 4:1-7); raised child to life (2 Kgs 4:32-37); made stew edible (2 Kgs 4:38-41); fed a multitude with few loaves (2 Kgs 4:42-44); healed Naaman's leprosy (2 Kgs 5:14-15); made an ax head float (2 Kgs 6:1-7); prophesied the availability of food (2 Kgs 7:1); prophesied death of Ben-hadad (2 Kgs 8:7-15); died (2 Kgs 13:20); bones produced miracle after death (2 Kgs 13:21).

ELIZABETH
Mother of John the Baptist, cousin of Mary the mother of Jesus (Luke 1:5-66).

EMBARRASSED (v)
to become anxiously self-conscious
Luke 14:9. . . you will be ***e,*** and you will

EMBARRASSMENT (n)
the state of being anxiously self-conscious
2 Cor 9:4 . . . not to mention your own ***e***—

EMPLOYER (n)
one who provides with a job that pays wages
Luke 16:5. . . owed money to his ***e*** to come

EMPOWER, EMPOWERED (v)
to give official authority or legal power to; to enable
Luke 11:18. . You say I am ***e-ed*** by Satan.
Eph 3:16 . . . resources he will ***e*** you with

EMPTINESS (n)
a void; containing nothing
Job 15:31 . . . for ***e*** will be their only
Isa 40:17. . . . nothing—mere ***e*** and froth

EMPTY (adj)
containing nothing; having no purpose or result; destitute of effect or force
Gen 1:2 . . . . formless and ***e,*** and darkness
Deut 32:47. . not ***e*** words—they are your life!
Job 26:7 . . . . the northern sky over ***e*** space
Isa 45:18. . . . not to be a place of ***e*** chaos.
Jer 4:23. . . . . and it was ***e*** and formless.
Luke 1:53. . . the rich away with ***e*** hands.
1 Cor 14:9 . . be talking into ***e*** space.
1 Pet 1:18. . . to save you from the ***e*** life
2 Pet 2:18. . . with ***e,*** foolish boasting.

EMPTY-HANDED (adj)
having, bringing, or gaining nothing
Eccl 5:15 . . . as naked and ***e*** as on the day

ENABLE, ENABLED (v)
to make possible, provide an opportunity for
2 Cor 3:6 . . . ***e-ed*** us to be ministers of his
2 Thes 1:11 . to ***e*** you to live a life worthy
2 Pet 1:4. . . . ***e*** you to share his divine

ENCOURAGE, ENCOURAGED, ENCOURAGES, ENCOURAGING (v)
to inspire with courage or hope; to spur on
Isa 41:7. . . . . The carver ***e-s*** the goldsmith,
Acts 11:23 . . and he ***e-d*** the believers
Acts 15:32 . . length to the believers, ***e-ing***
Acts 20:1 . . . sent for the believers and ***e-d***
Acts 28:15 . . he was ***e-d*** and thanked God.
Rom 1:12. . . I also want to be ***e-d*** by yours.
Rom 12:8. . . your gift is to ***e*** others,
1 Cor 8:12 . . other believers by ***e-ing***
1 Cor 14:3 . . strengthens others, ***e-s*** them,
2 Cor 7:6 . . . who ***e-s*** those who are
2 Cor 7:6 . . . ***e-d*** us by the arrival of Titus.
2 Cor 7:13 . . have been greatly ***e-d*** by this.
Eph 6:22 . . . how we are doing and to ***e***
Col 4:8 . . . . . how we are doing and to ***e*** you.
1 Thes 2:12 . pleaded with you, ***e-d*** you,
1 Thes 3:2 . . to strengthen you, to ***e*** you
1 Thes 3:7 . . we have been greatly ***e-d*** in
1 Thes 5:11 . So ***e*** each other and build
1 Thes 5:14 . ***E*** those who are timid.
Titus 1:9. . . . he will be able to ***e*** others
Heb 12:5 . . . you forgotten the ***e-ing*** words
1 Pet 5:12. . . purpose in writing is to ***e*** you
2 Jn 1:11. . . . Anyone who ***e-s*** such people

ENCOURAGEMENT (n)
the act of encouraging; the state of being encouraged
Rom 15:5. . . who gives this patience and ***e,***
1 Cor 16:18 . a wonderful ***e*** to me,
2 Cor 7:13 . . In addition to our own ***e,***
Eph 4:29 . . . an ***e*** to those who hear them.
Phil 2:1 . . . . any ***e*** from belonging to Christ?
Phlm 1:20 . . Give me this ***e*** in Christ.

END, ENDS (n)
the point where something ceases to exist; death and destruction; the goal or result toward which some action or agent is heading
Ps 65:8 . . . . . live at the ***e-s*** of the earth stand
Eccl 3:11 . . . work from beginning to ***e.***
Isa 30:8. . . . . stand until the ***e*** of time
Isa 49:6. . . . . bring my salvation to the ***e-s***
Matt 24:13. . the one who endures to the ***e***
Matt 24:14. . and then the ***e*** will come.
Matt 24:31. . farthest ***e-s*** of the earth
1 Cor 15:24 . After that the ***e*** will come,
Phil 3:14 . . . press on to reach the ***e*** of
Rev 21:6. . . . the Beginning and the ***E.***
Rev 22:13. . . the Beginning and the ***E.***

END, ENDING, ENDS (v)
to come to an end; to die
1 Sam 12:23. sin against the LORD by ***e-ing***
Prov 14:12. . but it ***e-s*** in death.
Prov 14:13. . the laughter ***e-s,*** the grief
Prov 29:23. . Pride ***e-s*** in humiliation,
Isa 9:7. . . . . . its peace will never ***e.***
Eph 2:15 . . . by ***e-ing*** the system of law

ENDANGER (v)
to bring into danger or peril
Prov 22:25. . be like them and ***e*** your soul.

ENDLESS (adj)
being or seeming to be without end
Eccl 12:12 . . writing books is ***e,***
Amos 5:24. . an ***e*** river of righteous
Eph 3:8 . . . . the ***e*** treasures available

ENDURANCE (n)
the ability to withstand hardship or adversity
see also PERSEVERANCE
Rom 5:3. . . . they help us develop ***e.***
Col 1:11 . . . . have all the ***e*** and patience
2 Thes 1:4 . . your ***e*** and faithfulness
Heb 12:1 . . . let us run with ***e*** the race
Jas 1:3. . . . . . your faith is tested, your ***e***
2 Pet 1:6. . . . self-control with patient ***e,***
Rev 1:9. . . . . in the patient ***e*** to which Jesus

ENDURE, ENDURED, ENDURES, ENDURING (v)
to withstand, suffer, or persevere
see also PERSEVERE
Ps 89:2 . . . . . Your faithfulness is as ***e-ing*** as
Ps 136:1 . . . . faithful love ***e-s*** forever.
Matt 10:22. . everyone who ***e-s*** to the end
Mark 13:13 . one who ***e-s*** to the end
1 Cor 13:7 . . ***e-s*** through every
2 Cor 1:6 . . . Then you can patiently ***e***
2 Cor 6:4 . . . patiently ***e*** troubles and
2 Tim 2:3 . . . ***E*** suffering along with me,
2 Tim 2:12. . If we ***e*** hardship,
2 Tim 3:11. . suffering I have ***e-d.***
Heb 12:2 . . . he ***e-d*** the cross,
Heb 12:3 . . . hostility he ***e-d*** from sinful
Heb 12:7 . . . As you ***e*** this divine discipline,
Jas 1:12. . . . . who patiently ***e*** testing and
Jas 5:11. . . . . those who ***e*** under suffering.
1 Pet 2:19. . . patiently ***e*** unfair treatment.
Rev 13:10. . . must ***e*** persecution patiently

ENEMY, ENEMIES (n)
foe – personal, national, or spiritual
Ps 23:5 . . . . . the presence of my ***e-ies.***
Ps 62:7 . . . . . rock where no ***e*** can reach me.
Prov 16:7. . . even their ***e-ies*** are at peace
Prov 24:17. . rejoice when your ***e-ies*** fall;
Prov 25:21. . If your ***e-ies*** are hungry,

Prov 27:6. . . than many kisses from an ***e.***
Isa 59:18. . . . repay his ***e-ies*** for their evil
Matt 5:44. . . love your ***e-ies!*** Pray for those
Luke 6:35. . . Love your ***e-ies!*** Do good to
Luke 10:19. . over all the power of the ***e,***
Rom 5:10. . . while we were still his ***e-ies,***
Rom 12:20. . If your ***e-ies*** are hungry,
1 Cor 15:25 . until he humbles all his ***e-ies***
1 Cor 15:26 . the last ***e*** to be destroyed
Phil 3:18 . . . they are really ***e-ies*** of the cross
Jas 4:4. . . . . . makes you an ***e*** of God?
1 Pet 5:8. . . . Watch out for your great ***e,***

ENERGY (n)
vigorous exertion of power; effort
Ezra 5:8 . . . . with great ***e*** and success.
John 6:27. . . your ***e*** seeking the eternal

ENGAGED (adj)
pledged to be married; betrothed
Matt 1:18. . . His mother, Mary, was ***e*** to

ENGAGEMENT (n)
a pledge to marry; betrothal
Matt 1:19. . . to break the ***e*** quietly.

ENJOY, ENJOYED, ENJOYING (v)
to have a good time; to experience; to take pleasure in
see also HAPPY, JOY
Deut 6:2. . . . you will ***e*** a long life.
Neh 9:25 . . . grew fat and ***e-ed*** themselves
Eccl 5:19 . . . good health to ***e*** it.
Eccl 5:20 . . . so busy ***e-ing*** life that
Eccl 8:15 . . . eat, drink, and ***e*** life.
2 Tim 2:6. . . the first to ***e*** the fruit
Heb 11:25 . . ***e-ing*** the fleeting pleasures
1 Pet 3:10. . . If you want to ***e*** life

ENJOYABLE (adj)
of or relating to having a good time; pleasurable
Heb 12:11 . . No discipline is ***e*** while

ENJOYMENT (n)
an attitude, circumstance, or favorable response to a stimulus that tends to make one gratified or happy; delight; joy
1 Tim 6:17. . all we need for our ***e.***

ENQUIRE (KJV)
1 Sam 28:7. . a medium, so I can go and ***ask***
2 Kgs 1:2 . . . the god of Ekron, to ***ask***

ENRICH, ENRICHED (v)
to make rich or richer; to enhance
Prov 31:11. . she will greatly ***e*** his life.
2 Cor 9:11 . . you will be ***e-ed*** in every way

ENSLAVE, ENSLAVED (v)
to reduce to slavery; to subjugate
Gal 2:4 . . . . . wanted to ***e*** us and force us
2 Pet 2:20. . . get tangled up and ***e-d*** by sin

ENSURE (v)
to make sure, certain, or safe; to guarantee
Prov 31:8. . . ***e*** justice for those being crushed.

ENTER, ENTERED, ENTERING, ENTERS (v)
to go or come in
Ps 100:4 . . . . ***E*** his gates with thanksgiving
Matt 5:20. . . you will never ***e*** the Kingdom
Matt 7:13. . . ***e*** God's Kingdom only
Matt 19:23. . rich person to ***e*** the
Mark 9:43 . . ***e*** eternal life with only
Mark 10:23 . for the rich to ***e*** the
Luke 11:52. . prevent others from ***e-ing.***
Luke 13:24. . Work hard to ***e*** the narrow
Luke 18:17. . like a child will never ***e*** it.
John 3:5 . . . . no one can ***e*** the Kingdom
John 10:2. . . who ***e-s*** through the gate
Rom 5:12. . . When Adam sinned, sin ***e-ed***
Heb 3:11 . . . will never ***e*** my place of rest.
Heb 4:1 . . . . God's promise of ***e-ing*** his rest
Heb 4:11 . . . do our best to ***e*** that rest.
Heb 9:12 . . . of goats and calves—he ***e-ed***

ENTERTAIN, ENTERTAINS (v)
to provide entertainment for; to amuse
Ps 45:8 . . . . . music of strings ***e-s*** you.
Hos 7:3 . . . . The people ***e*** the king

ENTERTAINMENT (n)
amusement or diversion provided especially by performers
Dan 6:18 . . . refused his usual ***e***

ENTHRONED (v)
to seat ceremonially on a throne or in a place associated with power and authority
1 Sam 4:4. . . ***e*** between the cherubim.
2 Kgs 19:15 . ***e*** between the mighty
1 Chr 13:6 . . ***e*** between the cherubim.
Ps 22:3 . . . . . you are holy, ***e*** on the praises
Ps 113:5 . . . . God, who is ***e*** on high?
Isa 37:16. . . . God of Israel, you are ***e***

ENTHUSIASM (n)
strong excitement of feeling; zeal, fervor, passion
Neh 4:6 . . . . the people had worked with ***e.***
Prov 19:2. . . ***E*** without knowledge
Rom 10:2. . . I know what ***e*** they have
2 Cor 8:7 . . . your ***e,*** and your love

2 Cor 8:16 . . Titus the same *e* for you
2 Cor 9:2 . . . your *e* that stirred up
Eph 6:7 . . . . Work with *e,* as though

ENTHUSIASTIC (adj)
filled with or marked by zeal, fervor, or passion
Ps 45:15 . . . . a joyful and *e* procession
Acts 18:25 . . about Jesus with an *e* spirit
Rom 15:17 . . I have reason to be *e* about

ENTICE, ENTICED, ENTICES (v)
to tempt; to lure
Deut 13:6. . . someone secretly *e-s* you—
Job 31:27 . . . secretly *e-d* in my heart
Prov 1:10. . . if sinners *e* you, turn your back
Prov 7:21. . . and *e-d* him with her flattery.
Jas 1:14. . . . . our own desires, which *e* us

ENTRUST, ENTRUSTED (v)
to commit to another with confidence
Ps 31:5 . . . . . I *e* my spirit into your hand.
Luke 12:48. . has been *e-ed* with much,
Luke 23:46. . I *e* my spirit into your
Acts 15:40 . . left, the believers *e-ed* him
Acts 20:32 . . And now I *e* you to God
Rom 3:2. . . . Jews were *e-ed* with the whole
1 Thes 2:4 . . to be *e-ed* with the Good News.
1 Tim 1:11 . . Good News *e-ed* to me
2 Tim 1:14 . . truth that has been *e-ed* to you.
1 Pet 5:2. . . . flock that God has *e-ed* to you.

ENVY (n)
discontent or resentment because of another's success, advantages, or superiority
see also JEALOUSY
Mark 7:22 . . lustful desires, *e,* slander,
Rom 1:29. . . sin, greed, hate, *e,* murder,
Gal 5:21 . . . . *e,* drunkenness, wild parties,
Titus 3:3. . . . full of evil and *e,* and we hated
Jas 4:5. . . . . . within us is filled with *e?*

ENVY (v)
to feel or show envy; to begrudge
Prov 3:31 . . . Don't *e* violent people
Prov 24:1. . . Don't *e* evil people

EPILEPTIC (adj)
relating to, affected with, or having characteristics of epilepsy
Matt 4:24. . . were demon-possessed or *e* or

EQUAL (adj)
like in quantity, quality, nature, or status
John 5:18 . . . making himself *e* with God.
2 Cor 8:14 . . In this way, things will be *e.*

EQUIP (v)
to prepare; to furnish for service or action
Eph 4:12 . . . to *e* God's people to do
2 Tim 3:17 . . to prepare and *e* his people
Heb 13:21 . . *e* you with all you need

ERASE (v)
to blot out, cause to disappear
Ps 34:16 . . . . *e* their memory from the earth.
Rev 3:5. . . . . *e* their names from the Book

ESCAPE (n)
evasion of something undesirable
1 Thes 5:3 . . there will be no *e.*

ESCAPE, ESCAPED, ESCAPING (v)
to avoid; to get free of or break away from
Ps 89:48 . . . . can *e* the power of the grave.
Ps 139:7 . . . . I can never *e* from your Spirit!
Matt 23:33. . will you *e* the judgment
1 Cor 3:15 . . barely *e-ing* through a wall of
Heb 2:3 . . . . think we can *e* if we ignore
Heb 12:25 . . we will certainly not *e* if we
2 Pet 2:18. . . those who have barely *e-d*
2 Pet 2:20. . . *e* from the wickedness

ESTABLISH, ESTABLISHED (v)
to institute permanently; to set up; to bring into existence
1 Kgs 9:5 . . . *e* the throne of your dynasty
Ps 89:4 . . . . . I will *e* your descendants as kings
Prov 8:28. . . when he *e-ed* springs
Isa 16:5. . . . . God will *e* one of David's

ESTEEM (n)
the regard in which one is held; worth; value
2 Chr 18:1 . . great riches and high *e,*
Prov 22:1. . . being held in high *e* is better

ESTHER
Jewish exile who became queen of Persia, also known as "Hadassah" (Esth 1:1); cousin of Mordecai (Esth 2:7); brought into king's harem (Esth 2:8-9); crowned queen (Esth 2:17); agreed to help Jews (Esth 4:14-17); invited king to a banquet (Esth 5:1-8); revealed Haman's plan (Esth 7:3-6); rescued the Jews (Esth 8:8); established Festival of Purim (Esth 9:18-32).

ETERNAL (adj)
having infinite duration; valid or existing at all times
see also EVERLASTING, FOREVER
Gen 9:16 . . . will remember the *e* covenant
Exod 3:15 . . my *e* name, my name to
Lev 24:8. . . . a requirement of the *e*

Num 18:19 . an *e* and unbreakable
Ps 119:142 . . Your justice is *e,*
Jer 50:5. . . . . with an *e* covenant
Dan 4:34 . . . and his kingdom is *e.*
Dan 7:14 . . . His rule is *e*—
Matt 18:8. . . better to enter *e* life with
Matt 19:16. . must I do to have *e* life?
Matt 25:41. . into the *e* fire prepared
Matt 25:46. . away into *e* punishment,
Mark 3:29 . . a sin with *e* consequences.
Luke 10:25. . should I do to inherit *e* life?
Luke 18:18. . should I do to inherit *e* life?
John 3:15 . . . in him will have *e* life.
John 3:16 . . . not perish but have *e* life.
John 3:36 . . . believes in God's Son has *e*
John 5:29 . . . will rise to experience *e* life,
John 5:39 . . . you think they give you *e* life.
John 6:68 . . . the words that give *e* life.
John 12:50 . . his commands lead to *e* life;
John 17:2. . . He gives *e* life prepared for
Rom 1:20. . . *e* power and divine nature
Rom 5:21 . . . resulting in *e* life through
Rom 6:23. . . free gift of God is *e* life
Rom 9:5. . . . is worthy of *e* praise! Amen.
Rom 16:26. . the *e* God has commanded,
Eph 3:11 . . . This was his *e* plan,
2 Thes 1:9 . . punished with *e* destruction,
1 Tim 6:12. . Hold tightly to the *e* life
Titus 3:7. . . . we will inherit *e* life.
Heb 5:9 . . . . source of *e* salvation
Heb 9:15 . . . *e* inheritance God has
Heb 13:20 . . an *e* covenant with his blood—
1 Pet 1:23. . . from the *e,* living word
1 Pet 5:10. . . to share in his *e* glory
1 Jn 1:2. . . . . he is the one who is *e* life.
1 Jn 2:25. . . . we enjoy the *e* life he
1 Jn 5:20. . . . and he is *e* life.
Jude 1:7. . . . the *e* fire of God's judgment.
Jude 1:21 . . . who will bring you *e* life.

ETERNALLY (adv)
in an endless, infinite manner
Eph 6:24 . . . May God's grace be *e* upon all

ETERNITY (n)
immortality; infinite time
Eccl 3:11 . . . has planted *e* in the human
Isa 57:15. . . . who lives in *e,* the Holy One,
John 12:25 . . will keep it for *e.*

EUNUCH, EUNUCHS (n)
male attendant, often castrated, implying singular devotion to a master
Isa 56:4. . . . . I will bless those *e-s* who keep
Matt 19:12. . some have been made *e-s* by
Acts 8:27 . . . The *e* had gone to Jerusalem

EVALUATE, EVALUATED (v)
to determine the significance, worth, or value of
1 Cor 2:15 . . Those who are spiritual can *e*
1 Cor 2:15 . . cannot be *e-d* by others.
1 Cor 4:3 . . . *e-d* by you or by any human
1 Cor 14:29 . let the others *e* what is said.

EVALUATION (n)
the determination of the significance, worth, or value of
Rom 12:3. . . in your *e* of yourselves,

EVANGELIST, EVANGELISTS (n)
preacher of the gospel
Acts 21:8 . . . Philip the *E,* one of the seven
Eph 4:11 . . . apostles, the prophets, the *e-s,*

EVE
First woman and mother of all people; created from Adam's rib (Gen 2:21-23; 1 Tim 2:13); deceived by the serpent (Gen 3:1-13; 2 Cor 11:3); named "Eve" by Adam (Gen 3:20); cursed with painful childbirth (Gen 3:16; 4:1); descendants of (Gen 5).

EVENING (n)
the latter part and close of the day
Gen 1:5 . . . . *e* passed and morning came,

EVER-LIVING (adj)
eternal; immortal
Rom 1:23. . . the glorious, *e* God,

EVER (adv)
always; at any time
Exod 15:18 . will reign forever and *e!*
Ps 145:1 . . . . praise your name forever and *e.*
Dan 7:18 . . . they will rule forever and *e.*
John 1:18 . . . No one has *e* seen God.
Phil 4:20 . . . forever and *e!* Amen.
2 Tim 4:18 . . glory to God forever and *e!*
Heb 1:8 . . . . endures forever and *e.*
1 Pet 4:11. . . to him forever and *e!* Amen.
1 Jn 4:12. . . . No one has *e* seen God.
Rev 1:6. . . . . to him forever and *e!* Amen.
Rev 1:18. . . . I am alive forever and *e!*
Rev 22:5. . . . they will reign forever and *e.*

EVERLASTING (adj)
continuing indefinitely
see also ETERNAL, FOREVER
Gen 17:7 . . . This is the *e* covenant:
Gen 48:4 . . . as an *e* possession.
2 Sam 23:5. . made an *e* covenant with
Ps 139:24 . . . lead me along the path of *e* life.
Isa 9:6. . . . . . God, *E* Father, Prince of Peace.

Isa 35:10. . . . crowned with *e* joy.
Isa 40:28. . . . The LORD is the *e* God,
Isa 54:8. . . . . But with *e* love
Isa 55:3. . . . . an *e* covenant with you.
Isa 60:19. . . . God will be your *e* light,
Isa 60:20. . . . the LORD will be your *e* light.
Isa 61:7. . . . . and *e* joy will be yours.
Isa 61:8. . . . . an *e* covenant with them.
Jer 10:10. . . . the living God and the *e* King!
Jer 31:3. . . . . with an *e* love.
Ezek 16:60 . . establish an *e* covenant with
Dan 4:34 . . . His rule is *e*,
Dan 9:24 . . . to bring in *e* righteousness,
Dan 12:2 . . . to *e* life and some to shame
Gal 6:8 . . . . . will harvest *e* life from the

EVERYTHING (n)

all that exists; all that relates to the subject

Ps 145:17 . . . is righteous in *e* he does;
Matt 6:6. . . . your Father, who sees *e*,
Mark 12:44 . has given *e* she had to live on.
Acts 2:44 . . . and shared *e* they had.
2 Cor 1:22 . . *e* he has promised
2 Cor 6:10 . . and yet we have *e*.
Heb 13:18 . . to live honorably in *e* we do.

EVIDENCE (n)

an outward sign; proof

Acts 11:23 . . *e* of God's blessing,
Heb 11:4 . . . *e* that he was a righteous man,

EVIL-MINDED (adj)

having an evil disposition or evil thoughts

Ps 119:115 . . out of my life, you *e* people,

EVIL (adj)

bad, sinful, or morally reprehensible; of the devil

Gen 6:5 . . . . was consistently and totally *e*.
Exod 32:22 . know how *e* these people
Ps 51:4 . . . . . what is *e* in your sight.
Ps 140:8 . . . . not let *e* people have their way.
Prov 15:26 . . The LORD detests *e* plans,
Matt 6:13 . . . rescue us from the *e* one.
Matt 12:45 . . spirits more *e* than itself,
Matt 15:19 . . from the heart come *e*
Mark 7:21 . . heart, come *e* thoughts,
Luke 11:24. . When an *e* spirit leaves
John 17:15 . . them safe from the *e* one.
Acts 19:13 . . casting out *e* spirits.
Rom 2:9. . . . keeps on doing what is *e*—
Rom 13:14 . . to indulge your *e* desires.
1 Cor 5:13 . . remove the *e* person from
Eph 5:16 . . . in these *e* days.
Col 3:5 . . . . . lust, and *e* desires.
2 Thes 3:3 . . guard you from the *e* one.
1 Tim 6:4 . . . slander, and *e* suspicions.
2 Tim 3:13 . . *e* people and impostors
1 Jn 2:13. . . . your battle with the *e* one.
1 Jn 3:12. . . . who belonged to the *e* one
1 Jn 5:18. . . . the *e* one cannot touch

EVIL (n)

something that brings sorrow, distress, or misfortune

Gen 2:9 . . . . the knowledge of good and *e*.
Gen 3:5 . . . . knowing both good and *e*.
Judg 6:1 . . . . The Israelites did *e*
Ps 5:5 . . . . . . for you hate all who do *e*.
Ps 14:4 . . . . . those who do *e* never learn?
Ps 34:13 . . . . tongue from speaking *e*
Ps 37:27 . . . . Turn from *e* and do good,
Ps 45:7 . . . . . You love justice and hate *e*.
Ps 53:4 . . . . . those who do *e* never learn?
Ps 92:15 . . . . There is no *e* in him!
Ps 101:4 . . . . and stay away from every *e*.
Ps 125:5 . . . . with those who do *e*.
Prov 6:18. . . a heart that plots *e*,
Prov 8:13. . . fear the LORD will hate *e*.
Prov 11:27. . search for *e*, it will find you!
Prov 13:6. . . but the *e* are misled by sin.
Prov 17:13. . repay good with *e*, *e* will
Prov 20:30. . cleanses away *e*; such
Isa 5:20. . . . . those who say that *e* is good
Isa 13:11. . . . punish the world for its *e*
Jer 23:14. . . . who are doing *e* so that
Hab 1:13 . . . cannot stand the sight of *e*.
Mal 3:15. . . . those who do *e* get rich,
Matt 5:45. . . to both the *e* and the good,
Luke 13:27. . all you who do *e*.
John 3:20 . . . All who do *e* hate the light
Rom 12:21 . . Don't let *e* conquer you,
1 Cor 14:20 . babies when it comes to *e*,
1 Thes 5:15 . no one pays back *e* for *e*,
1 Thes 5:22 . away from every kind of *e*.
1 Tim 6:10 . . the root of all kinds of *e*.
2 Tim 2:19 . . must turn away from *e*.
Heb 1:9 . . . . You love justice and hate *e*.
Jas 1:21. . . . . get rid of all the filth and *e*
Jas 3:8. . . . . . It is restless and *e*,
1 Pet 2:16. . . as an excuse to do *e*.
1 Pet 3:9. . . . Don't repay *e* for *e*.
1 Pet 3:11. . . Turn away from *e* and do
3 Jn 1:11. . . . those who do *e* prove that they

EVILDOERS (n)

one who does evil

Ps 92:7 . . . . . like weeds and *e* flourish,
Ps 92:9 . . . . . perish; all *e* will be scattered.
Ps 94:16 . . . . will stand up for me against *e*?
Prov 21:15 . . it terrifies *e*.
Prov 24:19 . . Don't fret because of *e*;

EXALT, EXALTED, EXALTING, EXALTS (v)
to elevate; to glorify; to raise in rank or power
see also GLORIFY, HONOR
Exod 15:2 . . and I will *e* him!
2 Sam 22:47 . of my salvation, be *e-ed!*
Neh 9:5 . . . . be *e-ed* above all blessing
Job 36:7 . . . . kings and *e-s* them forever.
Ps 18:46 . . . . God of my salvation be *e-ed!*
Ps 30:1 . . . . . I will *e* you, LORD,
Ps 92:8 . . . . . O LORD, will be *e-ed* forever.
Ps 97:9 . . . . . you are *e-ed* far above all gods.
Ps 107:32 . . . Let them *e* him publicly
Ps 145:1 . . . . I will *e* you, my God and King,
Dan 11:36 . . as he pleases, *e-ing* himself
Luke 14:11 . . those who *e* themselves will
Acts 2:33 . . . is *e-ed* to the place of highest
2 Thes 2:4 . . He will *e* himself

EXAMINE, EXAMINED, EXAMINES, EXAMINING (v)
to test the condition of; to inspect closely
1 Chr 29:17 . you *e* our hearts
Ps 11:4 . . . . . *e-ing* every person on earth.
Ps 11:5 . . . . . The LORD *e-s* both
Ps 17:3 . . . . . *e-d* my heart in the night.
Ps 139:1 . . . . LORD, you have *e-d* my heart
Prov 5:21 . . . *e-ing* every path he takes.
Prov 21:2 . . . the LORD *e-s* their heart.
Jer 11:20 . . . . you *e* the deepest thoughts
Jer 17:10 . . . . and *e* secret motives.
Lam 3:40 . . . let us test and *e* our ways.
1 Cor 4:4 . . . Lord himself who will *e*
1 Cor 11:28 . you should *e* yourself
2 Cor 13:5 . . *E* yourselves to see
1 Thes 2:4 . . He alone *e-s* the motives

EXAMPLE, EXAMPLES (n)
one that serves as a pattern to be or not to be imitated
John 13:15 . . given you an *e* to
1 Cor 10:11 . happened to them as *e-s* for
2 Thes 3:9 . . give you an *e* to follow.
Titus 2:7 . . . . *e* to them by doing good
Heb 13:7 . . . and follow the *e* of their faith.
Jas 5:10 . . . . . For *e-s* of patience in suffering,
1 Pet 2:21 . . . He is your *e,* and you must

EXCEEDS (v)
to be greater than or superior to
Phil 4:7 . . . . *e* anything we can understand.

EXCEL (v)
to surpass in accomplishment or achievement
2 Cor 8:7 . . . *e* also in this gracious act of

EXCELLENCE (n)
something that gives especial worth or value
2 Pet 1:5 . . . . generous provision of moral *e,*

EXCELLENT (adj)
very good of its kind; superior
Phil 4:8 . . . . Think about things that are *e*

EXCHANGE (n)
the act of giving or taking one thing for another
Lev 17:11 . . . blood, given in *e* for a life,

EXCHANGED (v)
to part with for a substitute
Jer 2:11 . . . . . have *e* their glorious God
Hos 4:7 . . . . They have *e* the glory of God

EXCUSE (n)
the apology or justification offered
John 15:22 . . they have no *e* for their sin.
Rom 1:20 . . . no *e* for not knowing God.
Rom 2:1 . . . . and you have no *e!*
1 Pet 2:16 . . . your freedom as an *e*

EXCUSE (v)
to overlook, justify, or make an apology for
Exod 34:7 . . But I do not *e* the guilty.
Eph 5:6 . . . . those who try to *e* these sins,

EXECUTED (v)
to put to death
Num 35:16 . the murderer must be *e.*
Deut 21:22 . . and is *e* and hung on a tree,

EXECUTION (n)
a putting to death especially as a legal penalty
Num 35:31 . murder and subject to *e;*

EXHAUST (v)
to consume entirely
Isa 7:13 . . . . . you *e* the patience of my God

EXHAUSTION (n)
fatigue, tiredness, collapse
2 Cor 6:5 . . . worked to *e,* endured

EXHORT(ATION) (KJV)
Rom 12:8 . . . If your gift is to ***encourage***
1 Thes 2:3 . . not ***preaching*** with any deceit
Heb 3:13 . . . You must ***warn*** each other

EXILE, EXILES (n)
the state of forced absence from one's country or home; a person who is in exile
2 Kgs 25:11 . took as *e-s* the rest of
2 Kgs 25:21 . sent into *e* from their land.
Ezra 2:1 . . . . the Jewish *e-s* of the provinces
Jer 52:27 . . . . sent into *e* from their land.

EXILED (v)
to banish or expel
2 Kgs 17:6 . . of Israel were *e* to Assyria.
2 Kgs 17:23 . So Israel was *e* from their land

EXISTS (v)
to have real being whether material or spiritual
Heb 11:6 . . . must believe that God *e*

EXORCISTS (n)
one who expels evil spirits
Luke 11:19. . what about your own *e?*

EXPELLED, EXPELS (v)
to force to leave
Ezek 28:16. . I *e* you, O mighty guardian,
1 Jn 4:18. . . . perfect love ***e-s*** all fear.

EXPENSES (n)
financial costs
1 Cor 9:7 . . . has to pay his own *e?*

EXPENSIVE (adj)
involving high cost
Mark 14:3 . . alabaster jar of *e* perfume
Luke 7:25. . . a man dressed in *e* clothes?
John 12:3 . . . a twelve-ounce jar of *e* perfume
1 Tim 2:9 . . . gold or pearls or *e* clothes.

EXPERIENCE (v)
to learn by or have direct observation or participation
Deut 28:2. . . You will *e* all these blessings
Eph 3:19 . . . May you *e* the love of Christ,

EXPLAIN, EXPLAINED, EXPLAINS (v)
to make plain or understandable; to give the reason or cause
Gen 2:24 . . . This ***e-s*** why a man leaves his
Neh 8:8 . . . . and clearly ***e-ed*** the meaning
Matt 19:5. . . This ***e-s*** why a man leaves his
Acts 17:3 . . . He ***e-ed*** the prophecies
Acts 18:28 . . ***e-ed*** to them that Jesus was
Eph 6:19 . . . *e* God's mysterious plan
2 Tim 2:15 . . correctly ***e-s*** the word of
1 Pet 3:15. . . always be ready to *e* it.

EXPLOIT (v)
to make use of meanly or unfairly for one's own advantage
Exod 22:22 . not *e* a widow or an orphan.
Prov 22:22. . or *e* the needy in court.

EXPLOITED (n)
one unfairly used for another's advantage
Isa 11:4. . . . . fair decisions for the *e.*

EXPLORE (v)
to investigate, study, or analyze
Num 13:2 . . Send out men to *e* the land
Num 32:8 . . to *e* the land.

EXPOSE, EXPOSED, EXPOSES, EXPOSING (v)
to make known; to display
Prov 20:27. . ***e-ing*** every hidden motive.
Lam 4:22 . . . your many sins will be ***e-d.***
John 3:20 . . . fear their sins will be ***e-d.***
Eph 5:11 . . . instead, *e* them.
Heb 4:12 . . . It ***e-s*** our innermost thoughts
Heb 4:13 . . . naked and ***e-d*** before his eyes,

EXTENDS (v)
to stretch out to the fullest length; to proffer
Ps 119:90 . . . faithfulness *e* to every
Prov 31:20. . She *e* a helping hand

EXTINGUISH (v)
to cause to cease burning
John 1:5 . . . . the darkness can never *e* it.

EXTOL(LED) (KJV)
Ps 66:17 . . . . to him for help, ***praising*** him
Ps 68:4 . . . . . ***Sing loud praises*** to him who
Isa 52:13. . . . he will be ***highly exalted***

EXTORTION (n)
the act or practice of obtaining money or property by illegal power
Lev 6:4. . . . . or the money you took by *e,*

EXTREME
Josh 15:21 . . of Edom in the *e* south
Ezek 46:19. . a place at the *e* west end
Ezek 48:1. . . Dan is in the *e* north

EXTREMES (n)
something situated at or marking one end or the other of a range
Eccl 7:18 . . . will avoid both *e.*

EXULT (v)
to be extremely joyful; to rejoice
Ps 89:16 . . . . They *e* in your righteousness.

EYE, EYES (n)
organ of (physical and spiritual) sight
Exod 21:24 . an *e* for an *e,*
Deut 16:19. . bribes blind the ***e-s*** of
Job 36:7 . . . . never takes his ***e-s*** off the
Ps 119:37 . . . Turn my ***e-s*** from worthless
Ps 123:1 . . . . I lift my ***e-s*** to you,
Prov 4:25. . . and fix your ***e-s*** on what
Matt 5:29. . . *e*—causes you to lust,

Matt 5:38. . . An ***e*** for an ***e,***
Matt 6:22. . . When your ***e*** is good,
1 Cor 2:9 . . . when they say, "No ***e*** has seen,
Heb 12:2 . . . by keeping our ***e-s*** on Jesus,
Rev 21:4. . . . wipe every tear from their ***e-s,***

EYELIDS (n)

the movable fold of skin and muscle that closes over the eyeball

2 Kgs 9:30 . . painted her ***e*** and fixed her hair

EYEWITNESS (n)

one who sees an occurrence or object

Luke 1:2. . . . They used the ***e*** reports

EZEKIEL

Prophet of Judah (southern kingdom) and priest (Ezek 1:3); exiled to Babylon near the Kebar River (Ezek 3:15).

EZRA

Postexilic priestly reformer in time of Artaxerxes (Ezra 7; 10; Neh 8; 12); descendant of Seraiah (Ezra 7:1); skillful, learned teacher of the Law (Ezra 7:6); determined to study and obey the Law (Ezra 7:10); served as priest (Ezra 7:11); restored Temple and its worship (Ezra 7–8); corrected pagan intermarriage (Ezra 9–10); dedicated Jerusalem's repaired walls (Neh 12).

FACE (n)

in or into direct contact or confrontation (as in "face to face"); countenance; presence; the front part of the head

Gen 32:30 . . I have seen God *f* to *f*,
Exod 33:11 . speak to Moses *f* to *f*,
Exod 34:29 . his *f* had become radiant
Num 12:8 . . I speak to him *f* to *f*,
Deut 31:17. . hiding my *f* from them,
Judg 6:22. . . angel of the LORD *f* to *f*!
2 Chr 7:14 . . and seek my *f* and turn from
Ps 4:6 . . . . . . Let your *f* smile on us,
Ps 17:15 . . . . I will see you *f* to *f*
Ps 67:1 . . . . . May his *f* smile with favor
Luke 9:29. . . appearance of his *f* was
2 Cor 3:7 . . . For his *f* shone with the glory
Rev 1:16. . . . And his *f* was like the sun
Rev 22:4. . . . they will see his *f*,

FACE, FACED, FACING (v)

to confront; to be confronted by

Ps 112:8 . . . . *f* their foes triumphantly.
Ps 116:6 . . . . I was ***f-ing*** death, and he saved
2 Cor 6:5 . . . ***f-d*** angry mobs,

FADE, FADING (v)

to lose freshness, strength, or vitality

Isa 40:7. . . . . and the flowers *f*
1 Cor 9:25 . . to win a prize that will *f*
2 Cor 3:7 . . . brightness was already ***f-ing***
2 Cor 3:13 . . it was destined to *f* away.
Jas 1:11. . . . . the rich will *f* away
1 Jn 2:17. . . . this world is ***f-ing*** away,

FAIL, FAILED, FAILS (v)

to disappoint; to fall short; to weaken; to miss performing an expected service; to be unsuccessful

Num 23:19 . spoken and ***f-ed*** to act?
Deut 31:6. . . He will neither *f* you
Josh 23:14 . . Not a single one has ***f-ed!***
1 Kgs 8:56 . . Not one word has ***f-ed***
Ps 77:8 . . . . . his promises permanently ***f-ed?***
Luke 13:24. . try to enter but will *f*.
Luke 22:32. . faith should not *f*.
Rom 9:6 . . . . has God ***f-ed*** to fulfill his promise
2 Cor 13:5 . . if not, you have ***f-ed*** the test
2 Cor 13:6 . . we have not ***f-ed*** the test
Heb 12:15 . . none of you ***f-s*** to receive
Heb 13:5 . . . I will never *f* you.
1 Pet 4:19. . . he will never *f* you.

FAINT (adj)

lacking strength or vigor

Jonah 4:8 . . . grew *f* and wished to die.

FAINT (v)

to become weak or lose courage in body or spirit

Isa 40:31. . . . will walk and not *f*.

FAIR (adj)

free from self-interest, prejudice, or favoritism; beautiful

Prov 1:3. . . . do what is right, just, and *f*.
Song 2:13. . . away with me, my *f* one!
Isa 11:4. . . . . make *f* decisions for the
Rom 3:25. . . God was being *f* when he
Rom 3:26. . . he himself is *f* and just,
Col 4:1 . . . . . be just and *f* to your slaves.

FAIRNESS (n)

the quality of being free from self-interest, prejudice, or favoritism

Ps 9:8 . . . . . . rule the nations with *f*.
Ps 98:9 . . . . . and the nations with *f*.
Ps 99:4 . . . . . you have established *f*.
Isa 9:7. . . . . . will rule with *f* and justice

FAITH (n)

reliance, loyalty, or complete trust in God; a system of religious beliefs

see also BELIEVE, TRUST

Exod 14:31 . They put their *f* in the LORD
Isa 7:9. . . . . . Unless your *f* is firm,
Matt 9:2. . . . Seeing their *f*, Jesus said
Matt 9:29. . . Because of your *f*, it will
Matt 15:28. . your *f* is great.
Matt 17:20. . *f* even as small as a mustard
Matt 21:22. . if you have *f*, you will receive
Mark 10:52 . for your *f* has healed you.
Luke 5:20. . . Seeing their *f*, Jesus said
Luke 7:50. . . Your *f* has saved you;
Luke 8:48. . . your *f* has made you well.
Luke 12:28. . Why do you have so little *f*?
Luke 17:6. . . *f* even as small as a mustard
Luke 18:8. . . find on the earth who have *f*?
John 16:1 . . . won't abandon your *f*.
Acts 6:5 . . . . full of *f* and the Holy Spirit
Acts 14:9 . . . he had *f* to be healed.
Acts 14:27 . . opened the door of *f* to the
Acts 16:5 . . . strengthened in their *f* and
Acts 24:24 . . told them about *f* in Christ
Rom 1:8 . . . . *f* in him is being talked about
Rom 1:12. . . to encourage you in your *f*,
Rom 1:17. . . from start to finish by *f*.
Rom 1:17. . . through *f* that a righteous
Rom 3:28. . . right with God through *f*
Rom 3:30. . . right with himself only by *f*,
Rom 3:31. . . only when we have *f*
Rom 4:5. . . . because of their *f* in God
Rom 4:9. . . . righteous because of his *f*.
Rom 4:12. . . same kind of *f* Abraham had
Rom 4:13. . . with God that comes by *f*.
Rom 4:14. . . then *f* is not necessary
Rom 4:16. . . the promise is received by *f*.
Rom 4:16. . . if we have *f* like Abraham's.
Rom 4:19. . . Abraham's *f* did not weaken,
Rom 4:20. . . In fact, his *f* grew stronger,
Rom 5:1. . . . made right in God's sight by *f*,
Rom 5:2. . . . Because of our *f*, Christ has
Rom 10:8. . . message about *f* that we preach:
Rom 10:17. . So *f* comes from hearing,
Rom 12:6. . . speak out with as much *f* as
Rom 14:1. . . believers who are weak in *f*,
1 Cor 12:9 . . gives great *f* to another,
1 Cor 13:13 . *f*, hope, and love—
1 Cor 15:14 . and your *f* is useless.
1 Cor 16:13 . Stand firm in the *f*.
2 Cor 1:24 . . put your *f* into practice.
2 Cor 13:5 . . failed the test of genuine *f*.
Gal 1:23 . . . . the very *f* he tried to destroy!
Gal 3:9 . . . . . all who put their *f* in Christ
Gal 3:11 . . . . *f* that a righteous person
Gal 3:12 . . . . This way of *f* is very different
Gal 3:14 . . . . Holy Spirit through *f*.
Gal 3:23 . . . . way of *f* in Christ was available
Gal 3:24 . . . . made right with God through *f*.
Gal 3:25 . . . . the way of *f* has come,
Gal 3:26 . . . . of God through *f* in Christ
Gal 5:5 . . . . . eagerly wait to receive by *f*
Eph 1:15 . . . . of your strong *f* in the Lord
Eph 4:5 . . . . one Lord, one *f*, one baptism,
Eph 6:16 . . . hold up the shield of *f*
Phil 1:25 . . . experience the joy of your *f*.
Phil 3:9 . . . . righteous through *f* in Christ.
Col 1:4 . . . . . have heard of your *f* in Christ
1 Thes 1:8 . . telling us about your *f* in God.
1 Thes 3:5 . . your *f* was still strong.
1 Thes 3:10 . fill the gaps in your *f*.
2 Thes 1:3 . . because your *f* is flourishing
1 Tim 1:4 . . . live a life of *f* in God.
1 Tim 1:19 . . Cling to your *f* in Christ,
1 Tim 3:9 . . . mystery of the *f* now
1 Tim 4:1 . . . will turn away from the true *f*;
1 Tim 6:10 . . have wandered from the true *f*
1 Tim 6:12 . . good fight for the true *f*.
2 Tim 1:5 . . . remember your genuine *f*,
2 Tim 2:18 . . away from the *f*.
2 Tim 3:10 . . You know my *f*, my patience,
Titus 1:1. . . . have been sent to proclaim *f*
Titus 1:13. . . make them strong in the *f*.
Titus 2:2. . . . must have sound *f* and be filled
Phlm 1:5 . . . about your *f* in the Lord
Phlm 1:6 . . . that comes from your *f*
Heb 4:2 . . . . they didn't share the *f*
Heb 6:1 . . . . and placing our *f* in God.
Heb 6:12 . . . their *f* and endurance.
Heb 10:38 . . righteous ones will live by *f*.
Heb 11:5 . . . It was by *f* that Enoch
Heb 11:7 . . . It was by *f* that Noah
Heb 11:8 . . . It was by *f* that Abraham
Heb 11:23 . . It was by *f* that Moses' parents
Heb 11:29 . . It was by *f* that the people
Heb 12:2 . . . initiates and perfects our *f*.
Jas 1:3. . . . . . when your *f* is tested,
Jas 2:5. . . . . . this world to be rich in *f*?
Jas 2:14. . . . . Can that kind of *f* save anyone?
Jas 2:17. . . . . *f* by itself isn't enough.
Jas 2:18. . . . . Some people have *f*;
Jas 2:20. . . . . *f* without good deeds
Jas 2:22. . . . . made his *f* complete.
Jas 2:24. . . . . what we do, not by *f* alone.
Jas 2:26. . . . . so also *f* is dead without good
Jas 5:15. . . . . prayer offered in *f* will heal
1 Pet 1:21. . . have placed your *f* and hope
2 Pet 1:1. . . . the same precious *f* we have.
Jude 1:3 . . . . defend the *f* that God
Jude 1:20 . . . in your most holy *f*,

FAITHFUL (adj)
firm in adherence, utterly loyal
see also LOYAL, TRUSTWORTHY, UNFAILING
Deut 7:9. . . . He is the *f* God who keeps his
1 Sam 2:9. . . will protect his *f* ones,
1 Sam 20:14. me with the *f* love of the
2 Sam 22:26. you show yourself *f;* to those
1 Kgs 8:61 . . you be completely *f* to the
1 Kgs 15:14 . remained completely *f* to
2 Kgs 20:3 . . have always been *f* to you
Ps 18:25 . . . . you show yourself *f;*
Ps 71:22 . . . . because you are *f* to your
Ps 89:8 . . . . . You are entirely *f.*
Ps 89:49 . . . . to David with a *f* pledge.
Ps 143:1 . . . . you are *f* and righteous.
Isa 38:3. . . . . have always been *f* to you and
Hos 11:12 . . God and is *f* to the Holy One.
Zech 8:3. . . . be called the *F* City;
Zech 8:8. . . . I will be *f* and just toward
Matt 24:45 . . A *f,* sensible servant is one
Matt 25:21 . . You have been *f* in handling
Matt 25:23 . . my good and *f* servant.
Luke 12:42. . Lord replied, "A *f,* sensible
Luke 16:10. . If you are *f* in little things,
1 Cor 4:17 . . my beloved and *f* child in the
2 Cor 1:18 . . as God is *f,* our word to you
Eph 1:1 . . . . who are *f* followers of Christ
Phil 2:17 . . . just like your *f* service is
Col 4:7. . . . . brother and *f* helper who
Col 4:9 . . . . . Onesimus, a *f* and beloved
1 Thes 1:3 . . we think of your *f* work,
1 Thes 5:24 . for he who calls you is *f.*
2 Thes 3:3 . . But the Lord is *f;* he will
1 Tim 3:2. . . He must be *f* to his wife.
1 Tim 3:11 . . and be *f* in everything they
1 Tim 5:9. . . old and was *f* to her husband.
2 Tim 4:7. . . I have remained *f.*
Heb 2:17 . . . merciful and *f* High Priest
Heb 3:2 . . . . For he was *f* to God, who
Heb 8:9 . . . . They did not remain *f* to my
Heb 13:4 . . . marriage, and remain *f* to one
1 Jn 1:9. . . . . to him, he is *f* and just to
Rev 1:5. . . . . He is the *f* witness to these
Rev 2:10. . . . But if you remain *f* even when
Rev 3:14. . . . is the Amen—the *f* and true
Rev 17:14. . . chosen and *f* ones will be

FAITHFUL (n)
those who practice faith
Ps 149:1 . . . . assembly of the *f.*
Ps 149:5 . . . . Let the *f* rejoice that he

FAITHFULLY (adv)
in a manner that is firm, regular, and steady
Deut 7:12. . . regulations and *f* obey them,
1 Kgs 8:25 . . and *f* follow me
2 Chr 32:1 . . Hezekiah had *f* carried out
Neh 13:14 . . all that I have *f* done for
Isa 61:8. . . . . I will *f* reward my people for

FAITHFULNESS (n)
the quality of steadfast loyalty or firm adherence to promises
Exod 34:6 . . unfailing love and *f.*
Ps 25:10 . . . . with unfailing love and *f*
Ps 36:5 . . . . . your *f* reaches beyond
Ps 57:10 . . . . Your *f* reaches to the clouds.
Ps 92:2 . . . . . your *f* in the evening,
Ps 100:5 . . . . *f* continues to each
Prov 14:22. . unfailing love and *f.*
Prov 16:6. . . love and *f* make atonement
Prov 20:28 . . love and *f* protect the king;
Isa 38:18. . . . no longer hope in your *f.*
Lam 3:23 . . . Great is his *f;*
Gal 5:22. . . . kindness, goodness, *f,*
Eph 6:23 . . . give you love with *f.*
2 Thes 1:4 . . your endurance and *f*
2 Tim 2:22 . . pursue righteous living, *f,*

FAITHLESS (adj)
disloyal; lacking trust
Ps 78:57 . . . . and were as *f* as their parents.
Jer 3:8. . . . . . I divorced *f* Israel because
Jer 3:11. . . . . Even *f* Israel is less guilty than
Jer 3:12. . . . . Israel, my *f* people, come home
Matt 17:17 . . You *f* and corrupt people!
Mark 9:19 . . You *f* people!
John 20:27 . . Don't be *f* any longer.

FALL, FALLEN, FALLING (v)
to collapse; to drop down (wounded or dead); to become lower in degree or level; to come by assignment or inheritance; to descend; to stumble or stray (morally)
2 Sam 1:19. . the mighty heroes have ***f-en!***
Ps 37:24 . . . . they will never *f,*
Ps 69:9 . . . . . who insult you have ***f-en*** on
Prov 10:8. . . babbling fools *f* flat on their
Prov 24:17. . when your enemies *f;*
Isa 14:12. . . . How you are ***f-en*** from heaven,
Matt 13:21 . . They *f* away as soon as
Luke 10:18. . I saw Satan *f* from heaven
Rom 3:23. . . we all *f* short of God's glorious
Rom 14:13 . . believer to stumble and *f.*
Gal 5:4 . . . . . ***f-en*** away from God's grace.
2 Pet 1:10. . . and you will never *f* away.
Jude 1:24 . . . to keep you from ***f-ing*** away

FALSE (adj)
intentionally untrue; dishonest; misleading; unwise; faithless
Prov 12:17 . . a *f* witness tells lies.
Isa 44:25. . . . I expose the *f* prophets as
Matt 24:11 . . And many *f* prophets will
Mark 13:22 . For *f* messiahs and *f* prophets
2 Cor 11:13 . These people are *f* apostles.
Titus 1:11. . . by their *f* teaching.
2 Pet 2:1. . . . were also *f* prophets in Israel,
1 Jn 4:1. . . . . many *f* prophets in the world.
Rev 16:13. . . and the *f* prophet.
Rev 19:20. . . beast and his *f* prophet were
Rev 20:10. . . the beast and the *f* prophet.

FALSEHOOD (n)
a lie; the practice of lying
Ps 119:163 . . hate and abhor all *f*,

FALSELY (adv)
in an untrue, deceptive, or misleading manner
Exod 20:16 . must not testify *f* against
Mark 10:19 . You must not testify *f*.

FAME (n)
popular acclaim
Exod 9:16 . . spread my *f* throughout the earth.
Ps 49:12 . . . . but their *f* will not last.
Ps 102:12 . . . Your *f* will endure
Isa 66:19. . . . heard of my *f* or seen my glory.

FAMILY, FAMILIES (n)
a household unit of related people, as in a clan
see also HOUSEHOLD
Josh 24:15 . . my *f*, we will serve the LORD.
Ps 68:6 . . . . . God places the lonely in ***f-ies;***
Mark 3:25 . . a *f* splintered by feuding
Luke 9:61. . . let me say good-bye to my *f*.
Luke 12:52. . ***f-ies*** will be split apart,
Gal 6:10 . . . . to those in the *f* of faith.
Eph 2:19 . . . members of God's *f*.
1 Tim 3:4 . . . manage his own *f* well,
Titus 1:11. . . whole ***f-ies*** away from the truth
1 Jn 3:9. . . . . have been born into God's *f*

FAMINE (n)
extreme scarcity of food
Gen 12:10 . . a severe *f* struck the land
Gen 26:1 . . . A severe *f* now struck the
Gen 41:30 . . seven years of *f* so great
Ruth 1:1. . . . a severe *f* came upon the land.
1 Kgs 18:2 . . the *f* had become very
Amos 8:11 . . I will send a *f* on the land—

FAMOUS (adj)
widely known; honored for achievement
Gen 11:4 . . . This will make us *f*
Gen 12:2 . . . bless you and make you *f*,
Isa 63:12. . . . making himself *f* forever?

FANCY (adj)
not plain; ornamental
1 Pet 3:3. . . . outward beauty of *f* hairstyles,

FANTASIES (n)
unrealistic or improbable mental images
Prov 12:11 . . who chases *f* has no sense.

FAR (adv)
at a considerable distance in space or degree
Ps 22:19 . . . . Lord, do not stay *f* away!
Ezek 11:15 . . are *f* away from the Lord
Eph 2:13 . . . you were *f* away from God,
Col 1:21 . . . . were once *f* away from God

FARMER (n)
one who cultivates crops or raises animals for food
Isa 28:24. . . . Does a *f* always plow and
Isa 55:10. . . . producing seed for the *f*
Matt 13:18 . . the parable about the *f* planting
2 Cor 9:6 . . . a *f* who plants only a few seeds
2 Cor 9:10 . . seed for the *f* and then bread

FARTHEST (adj)
most distant, especially in space or time
Acts 13:47 . . bring salvation to the *f* corners

FAST, FASTING (v)
to abstain from food
Ps 35:13 . . . . denied myself by ***f-ing*** for
Matt 6:16 . . . when you *f*, don't make it
Acts 13:2 . . . worshiping the Lord and ***f-ing,***

FATE (n)
an inevitable and often adverse outcome or end
Prov 1:19 . . . the *f* of all who are greedy
Eccl 9:3 . . . . suffers the same *f*.
1 Pet 2:8. . . . the *f* that was planned for them.

FATHER, FATHERS (n)
male parent; ancestor(s); characteristic of a mentor or provider relationship; name and role for God in relation to the children he fosters/adopts; originator or creator
see also PARENT
Gen 2:24 . . . a man leaves his *f* and mother
Gen 17:4 . . . make you the *f* of a multitude
Exod 20:12 . Honor your *f* and mother.
Exod 21:15 . Anyone who strikes *f* or
Deut 32:6. . . he your **F** who created you?

2 Sam 7:14. . I will be his *f,* and he
Ps 2:7 . . . . . . Today I have become your **F.**
Ps 89:26 . . . . You are my **F,** my God,
Prov 10:1 . . . wise child brings joy to a *f;*
Prov 23:22. . Listen to your *f,* who gave you
Isa 9:6. . . . . . Everlasting **F,** Prince of Peace.
Isa 63:16. . . . you would still be our **F.**
Jer 3:19. . . . . forward to your calling me '**F,**'
Ezek 22:10. . sleep with their *f-s'* wives
Mal 2:10. . . . children of the same **F?**
Mal 4:6. . . . . will turn the hearts of *f-s*
Matt 5:16 . . . will praise your heavenly **F.**
Matt 6:9. . . . Our **F** in heaven, may your
Matt 6:14 . . . heavenly **F** will forgive
Matt 10:37. . If you love your *f* or mother
Matt 11:27. . no one truly knows the **F**
Matt 15:4 . . . Honor your *f* and mother,
Matt 16:27. . in the glory of his **F**
Matt 19:5 . . . a man leaves his *f* and mother
Matt 19:29. . or *f* or mother or children
Matt 23:9 . . . is your spiritual **F.**
Luke 1:17. . . hearts of the *f-s* to their
Luke 9:59. . . return home and bury my *f.*"
John 4:21 . . . you worship the **F** on this
John 5:17 . . . My **F** is always working,
John 5:20 . . . For the **F** loves the Son
John 6:44 . . . come to me unless the **F**
John 6:65 . . . unless the **F** gives them
John 8:19 . . . you don't know who my **F** is.
John 8:41 . . . God himself is our true **F.**
John 10:38. . understand that the **F** is in me,
John 14:6 . . . come to the **F** except through
John 14:21. . love me, my **F** will love
John 15:8 . . . brings great glory to my **F.**
John 15:23. . also hates my **F.**
John 20:17. . ascending to my **F** and
Acts 13:33. . Today I have become your **F.**
Rom 4:11. . . Abraham is the spiritual *f*
Rom 4:16. . . Abraham is the *f* of all who
Rom 8:15. . . we call him, "Abba, **F.**"
2 Cor 6:18 . . I will be your **F,** and you
Eph 5:31 . . . man leaves his *f* and mother
Eph 6:2 . . . . Honor your *f* and mother.
Eph 6:4 . . . . ***F-s,*** do not provoke
Phil 2:11 . . . to the glory of God the **F.**
Col 3:21 . . . . ***F-s,*** do not aggravate
Heb 12:7 . . . is never disciplined by its *f?*
Heb 12:9 . . . earthly *f-s* who disciplined
1 Jn 1:3. . . . . fellowship is with the **F** and
1 Jn 2:15. . . . the love of the **F** in you.
1 Jn 2:22. . . . who denies the **F** and the Son
1 Jn 3:1. . . . . See how very much our **F** loves
Rev 3:21. . . . sat with my **F** on his throne.

FATHERLESS (adj)
without a father; orphaned
see also ORPHAN
Ps 68:5 . . . . . Father to the *f,* defender of

FATTENING (v)
to feed (as a stock animal) and make fat for slaughter
Luke 15:23. . calf we have been *f.*

FAULT (n)
lack or error; moral weakness less serious than a vice
1 Sam 29:3. . never found a single *f* in
Prov 17:9 . . . when a *f* is forgiven,
Acts 20:26 . . eternal death, it's not my *f,*
2 Cor 6:3 . . . no one will find *f* with our
Eph 5:27 . . . she will be holy and without *f.*
Jude 1:24 . . . without a single *f.*

FAULTLESS (adj)
having no fault; irreproachable
1 Thes 2:10 . honest and *f* toward all of you

FAVOR, FAVORS (n)
gracious kindness; approval from a superior; a special privilege or right granted or conceded
see also GRACE
Gen 6:8 . . . . Noah found *f* with the LORD.
Exod 34:9 . . if it is true that I have found *f*
1 Sam 2:26. . and grew in *f* with the LORD
Prov 3:4. . . . you will find *f* with both God
Prov 18:22. . receives *f* from the LORD.
Prov 19:6 . . . Many seek *f-s* from a ruler;
Zech 11:7. . . named one **F** and the other
Luke 1:30. . . you have found *f* with God!
Luke 2:40. . . and God's *f* was on him.
Luke 2:52. . . and in *f* with God
Luke 4:19. . . the time of the LORD's *f*
Rom 11:7. . . have not found the *f* of God
Phil 1:7 . . . . with me the special *f* of God,

FAVOR, FAVORING (v)
to show partiality toward
Lev 19:15. . . justice in legal matters by *f-ing*
Jas 2:9. . . . . . But if you *f* some people over

FAVORITE (adj)
specially favored or liked
Gen 27:4 . . . Prepare my *f* dish,

FAVORITES (n)
persons specially loved, trusted, or provided with favors
see also PARTIALITY
Job 32:21 . . . I won't play *f*
Matt 22:16. . and don't play *f.*

Gal 2:6 . . . . . for God has no *f.*
Eph 6:9 . . . . he has no *f.*
Col 3:25 . . . . For God has no *f.*

FAVORITISM (n)
the showing of special favor; partiality
see also DISCRIMINATION, PARTIALITY
Prov 24:23 . . *f* when passing judgment.
Mal 2:9. . . . . *f* in the way you carry out
Acts 10:34 . . that God shows no *f.*
Rom 2:11 . . . God does not show *f.*
Jas 3:17. . . . . It shows no *f* and is always

FEAR, FEARS (n)
dread or alarm in facing danger; profound reverence and awe
2 Sam 23:3 . . who rules in the *f* of God,
Ps 2:11 . . . . . Serve the LORD with reverent *f,*
Ps 34:4 . . . . . freed me from all my *f-s.*
Prov 1:33 . . . untroubled by *f* of harm.
Heb 13:6 . . . will have no *f.*

FEAR, FEARED, FEARING, FEARS (v)
to have reverential awe of God; to be afraid or apphrehensive
Deut 6:13. . . You must *f* the LORD your
Deut 8:6. . . . walking in his ways and ***f-ing***
Deut 13:4. . . your God and *f* him alone.
Deut 31:12. . learn to *f* the LORD your God
Josh 4:24 . . . might *f* the LORD your God
1 Sam 12:14. if you *f* and worship
2 Chr 26:5 . . taught him to *f* God.
Neh 5:15 . . . But because I ***f-ed*** God,
Neh 7:2 . . . . a faithful man who ***f-ed*** God
Job 1:1 . . . . . He ***f-ed*** God and stayed
Job 1:8 . . . . . ***f-s*** God and stays away from
Ps 34:7 . . . . . and defends all who *f* him.
Ps 46:2. . . . . not *f* when earthquakes come
Ps 61:5 . . . . . for those who *f* your name.
Ps 76:7 . . . . . you are greatly ***f-ed!***
Ps 103:17 . . . with those who *f* him.
Ps 128:1 . . . . joyful are those who *f* the
Prov 8:13. . . All who *f* the LORD will
Prov 28:14. . those who *f* to do wrong,
Prov 31:30. . a woman who ***f-s*** the LORD
Isa 25:3. . . . . nations will *f* you.
Jer 2:19. . . . . your God and not to *f* him.
Mal 3:16. . . . those who ***f-ed*** the LORD spoke
Mal 4:2. . . . . for you who *f* my name,
2 Cor 7:1 . . . because we *f* God.
Rev 11:18. . . and all who *f* your name,

FEARFUL (adj)
very great – used as an intensive
2 Cor 5:11 . . our *f* responsibility to the Lord,

FEAST (n)
an elaborate meal; banquet
Ps 23:5 . . . . . You prepare a *f* for me
Prov 15:15. . life is a continual *f.*
Luke 15:29. . goat for a *f* with my friends.

FEAST, FEASTING (v)
to enjoy a good meal
Esth 9:17 . . . a day of ***f-ing*** and gladness.
Prov 17:1. . . a house filled with ***f-ing*** – and
Prov 23:20. . or *f* with gluttons,
Isa 22:13. . . . You *f* on meat and drink wine.

FED (v)
to give food to
see also FEED
Deut 8:16. . . He *f* you with manna
Ezek 3:2. . . . mouth, and he *f* me the scroll.
John 6:26 . . . want to be with me because I *f*

FEED, FEEDS (v)
to give food to; to eat; to provide something essential to the development, sustenance, maintenance, or operation of
see also FED
Prov 15:14. . while the fool ***f-s*** on trash.
Prov 22:9. . . because they *f* the poor.
Jer 50:19. . . . own land, to *f* in the fields
Matt 6:26. . . your heavenly Father ***f-s*** them.
Matt 14:16. . necessary – you *f* them."
Matt 25:42. . and you didn't *f* me.
John 6:57 . . . anyone who ***f-s*** on me will live
John 21:15. . "Then *f* my lambs,"
John 21:17. . "Then *f* my sheep."
Rom 12:20. . enemies are hungry, *f* them.

FEEL (v)
to perceive by physical sensation
Ps 115:7 . . . . have hands but cannot *f,*

FEET (n)
see also FOOT
Ps 22:16 . . . . pierced my hands and *f.*
Ps 40:2. . . . . He set my *f* on solid ground
Ps 73:2 . . . . . My *f* were slipping,
Ps 119:105 . . a lamp to guide my *f*
Isa 52:7. . . . . are the *f* of the messenger
Matt 10:14. . shake its dust from your *f*
Luke 24:39. . Look at my *f.*
John 13:5 . . . began to wash the disciples' *f,*
John 13:14. . wash each other's *f.*
Rom 10:15. . beautiful are the *f* of
Rom 16:20. . crush Satan under your *f.*
1 Cor 15:25 . his enemies beneath his *f.*
Heb 1:13 . . . a footstool under your *f.*
Heb 12:13 . . a straight path for your *f*

FELLOWSHIP (n)
friendship; association; company; partnership
Gen 5:24 . . . walking in close *f* with God.
1 Cor 5:2 . . . remove this man from your *f.*
2 Cor 13:14 . and the *f* of the Holy Spirit
1 Jn 1:3. . . . . you may have *f* with us.
1 Jn 1:3. . . . . our *f* is with the Father and
1 Jn 1:6. . . . . we say we have *f* with God but
1 Jn 2:27. . . . remain in *f* with Christ.

FEMALE (adj)
of, relating to, or being a woman
Gen 1:27 . . . male and *f* he created them.
Gen 5:2 . . . . He created them male and *f,*
Mark 10:6 . . God made them male and *f*
Gal 3:28 . . . . slave or free, male and *f.*

FERTILE (adj)
capable of sustaining abundant growth; productive
Mark 4:8 . . . other seeds fell on *f* soil,

FESTIVAL, FESTIVALS (n)
a time of celebration marked by special observances
Lev 23:2. . . . the LORD's appointed ***f-s,***
Isa 30:29. . . . at the holy ***f-s.***
Amos 5:21 . . religious ***f-s*** and solemn
Zech 14:18. . of Egypt refuse to attend the *f,*
1 Cor 5:8 . . . let us celebrate the *f,*

FESTIVE (adj)
joyful, happy
Isa 61:3. . . . . *f* praise instead of despair.

FEVER (n)
a rise of body temperature above the normal
Job 30:30 . . . my bones burn with *f.*
Matt 8:14. . . sick in bed with a high *f.*
Luke 4:38. . . very sick with a high *f.*
John 4:52 . . . his *f* suddenly disappeared!
Acts 28:8 . . . was ill with *f* and dysentery.

FEW (adj)
not many; a low number of
Prov 17:27 . . wise person uses *f* words;
Matt 9:37. . . is great, but the workers are *f.*
Matt 22:14. . many are called, but *f* are

FIANCÉE (n)
a woman engaged to be married
1 Cor 7:36 . . treating his *f* improperly

FIELD, FIELDS (n)
an open land area free of woods and buildings; an area of cleared land used for cultivation
Lev 19:9. . . . along the edges of your ***f-s,***
Ruth 2:2. . . . into the harvest ***f-s*** to pick
Isa 40:6. . . . . the flowers in a *f.*
Matt 6:28 . . . Look at the lilies of the *f*
Matt 13:44 . . discovered hidden in a *f.*
Luke 2:8. . . . staying in the ***f-s*** nearby,
John 4:35 . . . The ***f-s*** are already ripe
1 Cor 3:9 . . . And you are God's *f.*
1 Pet 1:24. . . like a flower in the *f.*

FIERY (adj)
consisting of fire
Eph 6:16 . . . stop the *f* arrows of the devil.

FIG, FIGS (n)
an oblong or pear-shaped syconium fruit of a tree of the mulberry family; a fruit-producing plant which could be either a tall tree or a low-spreading shrub
Gen 3:7 . . . . they sewed *f* leaves together
Judg 9:10. . . they said to the *f* tree,
Prov 27:18. . workers who tend a *f* tree
Mic 4:4. . . . . grapevines and *f* trees,
Zech 3:10. . . grapevine and *f* tree.
Matt 21:19. . a *f* tree beside the road.
Luke 13:6. . . man planted a *f* tree in his
Jas 3:12. . . . . Does a *f* tree produce olives,
Jas 3:12. . . . . or a grapevine produce ***f-s?***

FIGHT, FIGHTS (n)
a hostile encounter; a struggle for a goal or an objective
Prov 15:18. . hot-tempered person starts ***f-s;***
Prov 20:3. . . Avoiding a *f* is a mark of
Prov 29:22. . An angry person starts ***f-s;***
2 Tim 4:7 . . . fought the good *f,*
Jas 4:1. . . . . . causing the quarrels and ***f-s***

FIGHT, FIGHTING, FIGHTS (v)
to actively oppose or combat, as with weapons; to gain by struggle
see also FOUGHT
Exod 14:14 . LORD himself will *f* for you.
Josh 23:10 . . LORD your God ***f-s*** for you,
1 Sam 17:32. I'll go *f* him!
1 Sam 25:28. are ***f-ing*** the LORD's battles.
Neh 4:20 . . . our God will *f* for us!
Prov 28:25. . Greed causes ***f-ing;***
Ps 35:1 . . . . . ***F*** those who *f* against me.
Isa 49:25. . . . I will *f* those who *f* you,
1 Cor 15:32 . value was there in ***f-ing*** wild
Phil 1:27 . . . one purpose, ***f-ing*** together for
1 Tim 6:12. . ***F*** the good fight
Jas 4:2. . . . . . so you *f* and wage war

FILL, FILLED, FILLS (v)
to occupy the whole of; to supply fully; to spread through
Gen 1:28 . . . ***F*** the earth and govern it.
Exod 34:6 . . ***f-ed*** with unfailing love
1 Kgs 8:11 . . presence of the LORD ***f-ed***
Ps 81:10 . . . . and I will ***f*** it with good things.
Ps 107:9 . . . . the thirsty and ***f-s*** the hungry
Ps 119:64 . . . unfailing love ***f-s*** the earth;
Ps 123:3 . . . . have had our ***f*** of contempt.
Isa 6:3. . . . . . earth is ***f-ed*** with his glory!
Joel 2:13. . . . and ***f-ed*** with unfailing love.
Jonah 4:2 . . . and ***f-ed*** with unfailing love.
Hag 2:7 . . . . I will ***f*** this place with glory,
Luke 1:15. . . be ***f-ed*** with the Holy Spirit,
Luke 1:41. . . was ***f-ed*** with the Holy Spirit.
Luke 1:67. . . ***f-ed*** with the Holy Spirit
Luke 2:40. . . He was ***f-ed*** with wisdom,
Luke 24:49. . Holy Spirit comes and ***f-s***
Acts 2:4 . . . . was ***f-ed*** with the Holy Spirit
Acts 2:28 . . . you will ***f*** me with the joy
Acts 4:8 . . . . ***f-ed*** with the Holy Spirit,
Acts 4:31 . . . all ***f-ed*** with the Holy Spirit.
Acts 9:17 . . . be ***f-ed*** with the Holy Spirit.
Acts 13:9 . . . was ***f-ed*** with the Holy Spirit,
Rom 5:5. . . . Holy Spirit to ***f*** our hearts
Rom 15:13 . . ***f*** you completely with joy
Eph 1:23 . . . by Christ, who ***f-s*** all things
Eph 5:18 . . . be ***f-ed*** with the Holy Spirit,
Col 3:16 . . . . in all its richness, ***f*** your lives.

FILTH (n)
moral corruption or defilement
Isa 4:4. . . . . . wash the ***f*** from beautiful Zion

FILTHY (adj)
covered with, containing, or characterized by foul or putrid matter or moral corruption
Isa 6:5. . . . . . I have ***f*** lips, and I live
Isa 64:6. . . . . they are nothing but ***f*** rags.
Zech 3:4. . . . Take off his ***f*** clothes.
2 Cor 6:17 . . Don't touch their ***f*** things,

FINANCIAL (adj)
relating to money
2 Cor 11:9 . . did not become a ***f*** burden

FIND, FINDS (v)
to attain or reach (a goal or conclusion); to discover by searching or effort; to experience
see also FOUND
1 Chr 28:9 . . seek him, you will ***f*** him.
Job 23:3 . . . . knew where to ***f*** God,
Prov 3:13. . . the person who ***f-s*** wisdom,
Prov 8:17. . . who search will surely ***f*** me.
Prov 8:35. . . For whoever ***f-s*** me ***f-s*** life
Prov 11:27. . you will ***f*** favor;
Prov 31:10. . Who can ***f*** a virtuous and
Isa 55:6. . . . . while you can ***f*** him.
Jer 6:16. . . . . will ***f*** rest for your souls.
Matt 7:7. . . . seeking, and you will ***f***.
Matt 7:8. . . . Everyone who seeks, ***f-s***.
Matt 10:39 . . your life for me, you will ***f*** it.
Luke 11:9. . . and you will ***f***.
Luke 11:10. . Everyone who seeks, ***f-s***.
Luke 15:4. . . that is lost until he ***f-s*** it?
Luke 15:8. . . search carefully until she ***f-s*** it?

FINEST (adj)
superior in kind, quality, or appearance
Isa 55:2. . . . . will enjoy the ***f*** food.
Jer 3:19. . . . . the ***f*** possession in the world.

FINGER, FINGERS (n)
any of the five terminating members of the hand; figurative for the power of God
Exod 8:19 . . This is the ***f*** of God!
Exod 31:18 . written by the ***f*** of God.
Deut 9:10. . . had written with his own ***f***
Luke 16:24. . dip the tip of his ***f*** in water
John 8:6 . . . . wrote in the dust with his ***f***.
John 20:25 . . in his hands, put my ***f-s*** into

FINISH (n)
the end
Rom 1:17 . . . from start to ***f*** by faith.

FINISH, FINISHED, FINISHING (v)
to bring to completion; to bring to an end
Gen 2:2 . . . . had ***f-ed*** his work of creation,
John 4:34 . . . and from ***f-ing*** his work.
John 19:30 . . he said, "It is ***f-ed!***"
Acts 20:24 . . I use it for ***f-ing*** the work
2 Cor 8:11 . . Now you should ***f*** what you
2 Tim 4:7 . . . I have ***f-ed*** the race,
Rev 20:3. . . . the thousand years were ***f-ed***.

FIRE, FIRES (n)
hot flame and burning light; symbolic of hell; severe trial or ordeal
Exod 3:2 . . . ***f*** from the middle of a bush.
Exod 13:21 . at night with a pillar of ***f***.
Dan 3:25 . . . walking around in the ***f***
Matt 3:11. . . the Holy Spirit and with ***f***.
Matt 5:22. . . are in danger of the ***f-s*** of hell.
Matt 18:8. . . be thrown into eternal ***f***
Mark 9:43 . . the unquenchable ***f-s*** of hell
Mark 9:49 . . be tested with ***f***.
Luke 3:16. . . with the Holy Spirit and with ***f***.
Acts 2:3 . . . . tongues of ***f*** appeared and
Heb 12:29 . . God is a devouring ***f***.
Jas 3:6. . . . . . it is set on ***f*** by hell itself.

FIRM (adj)
securely or solidly fixed in place; not weak or uncertain
Isa 7:9. . . . . . Unless your faith is *f,*
2 Cor 1:21 . . to stand *f* for Christ.
2 Cor 1:24 . . own faith that you stand *f.*
Eph 6:13 . . . will still be standing *f.*
1 Thes 3:8 . . you are standing *f* in the Lord.
2 Thes 2:15 . brothers and sisters, stand *f*
1 Pet 5:9. . . . Stand *f* against him,

FIRMAMENT (KJV)
Gen 1:7 . . . . ***space*** to separate the waters
Ps 19:1 . . . . . ***skies*** display his craftsmanship
Ezek 1:22. . . surface like the ***sky,*** glittering
Dan 12:3 . . . will shine as bright as the ***sky***

FIRST (adj)
preceding all others in time, order, or importance
Gen 1:5 . . . . came, marking the *f* day.
Isa 44:6. . . . . I am the ***F*** and the Last;
Isa 48:12. . . . God, the **F** and the Last.
Matt 22:38 . . the *f* and greatest
Mark 9:35 . . wants to be *f* must take last
Mark 13:10 . Good News must *f* be
Rom 1:16. . . Jew *f* and also the Gentile.
Rom 2:9. . . . Jew *f* and also for the Gentile.
1 Cor 15:45 . The *f* man, Adam,
Eph 6:2 . . . . the *f* commandment with a
1 Tim 2:13 . . God made Adam *f,*
Heb 10:9 . . . He cancels the *f* covenant
1 Jn 4:19. . . . because he loved us *f.*
Rev 1:17. . . . I am the ***F*** and the Last.
Rev 22:13. . . and the Omega, the ***F*** and the

FIRSTBEGOTTEN (KJV)
Heb 1:6 . . . . his ***supreme Son*** into the world

FIRSTBORN (adj)
eldest; the most prominent; the rightful heir
Exod 11:5 . . All the *f* sons will die
Exod 34:20 . buy back every *f* son.
Ps 89:27 . . . . I will make him my *f* son,
Mic 6:7. . . . . sacrifice our *f* children to pay
Heb 12:23 . . assembly of God's *f* children

FIRSTBORN (n)
the eldest offspring; one possessing special rights of inheritance
Gen 25:34 . . for his rights as the *f.*
Exod 13:2 . . every *f* among the Israelites.
Exod 34:19 . The *f* of every animal

FIRSTFRUITS (KJV)
Exod 23:16 . the ***first crops*** of your harvest
Exod 23:19 . bring the ***very best*** of
Lev 2:14. . . . ***first portion*** of your harvest
Lev 23:10. . . you harvest its ***first crops,***
Num 28:26 . the ***first*** of your new grain
Rev 14:4. . . . as a ***special offering*** to God

FISH (n)
any of numerous cold-blooded aquatic vertebrates
Jonah 1:17 . . had arranged for a great *f*
Matt 12:40 . . in the belly of the great *f*
Luke 9:13. . . loaves of bread and two *f,*
John 6:9 . . . . five barley loaves and two *f.*

FISH, FISHED, FISHING (v)
to attempt to catch fish
Mark 1:16 . . for they ***f-ed*** for a living.
Mark 1:17 . . how to *f* for people!
Luke 5:10. . . you'll be ***f-ing*** for people!

FISHERMEN (n)
those who fish for a living
Ezek 26:5. . . a rock in the sea, a place for *f*
Luke 5:2. . . . for the *f* had left them

FISHERS (KJV)
Isa 19:8. . . . . ***fishermen*** will lament for lack of work
Jer 16:16. . . . ***fishermen*** who will catch
Matt 4:19. . . ***how to fish*** for people

FLAME, FLAMES (n)
a state of blazing combustion; burning zeal or passion
Isa 5:24. . . . . and dry grass shrivels in the *f,*
1 Cor 3:15 . . escaping through a wall of ***f-s.***
2 Tim 1:6 . . . fan into ***f-s*** the spiritual gift
Rev 1:14. . . . his eyes were like ***f-s*** of fire.

FLAMING (adj)
blazing; intense
Isa 4:5. . . . . . and smoke and *f* fire at night,
2 Thes 1:8 . . in *f* fire, bringing judgment on
Heb 12:18 . . to a place of *f* fire, darkness,

FLASHED (v)
to break forth in or like a sudden flame; to give off light suddenly
1 Kgs 18:38 . the fire of the LORD *f* down
Dan 10:6 . . . His face *f* like lightning,

FLATTER (v)
to praise excessively out of self-interest
Job 32:21 . . . or try to *f* anyone.
Prov 29:5. . . To *f* friends is
Dan 11:32 . . He will *f* and win over those
Jude 1:16 . . . *f* others to get what they want.

FLATTERING (adj)
characterized by excessive praise out of self-interest
Ps 12:2. . . . . speaking with *f* lips
Ps 12:3. . . . . cut off their *f* lips
Prov 26:28. . and *f* words cause ruin.

FLATTERY (n)
insincere or excessive praise
Job 32:22 . . . For if I tried *f,* my Creator
Ps 5:9. . . . . . tongues are filled with *f.*
Prov 28:23. . criticism far more than *f.*
1 Thes 2:5 . . try to win you with *f,*

FLEE (v)
to run away; to shun
1 Cor 10:14 . *f* from the worship of idols.
Jas 4:7. . . . . . and he will *f* from you.

FLEECE (n)
the wool obtained from a sheep at one shearing
Judg 6:37. . . If the *f* is wet with dew

FLEETING (adj)
passing swiftly
Ps 39:4. . . . . how *f* my life is.

FLESH (n)
the meaty part of animal and human bodies
see also BODY, HUMAN
Gen 2:23 . . . and *f* from my *f!*
John 6:51. . . so the world may live, is my *f.*
1 Cor 15:39 . different kinds of *f—*

FLIGHT (n)
an act or instance of running away
Deut 32:30. . put ten thousand to *f,*

FLIRTING (v)
to behave amorously without serious intent
Isa 3:16. . . . . *f* with her eyes,

FLOCK, FLOCKS (n)
a group of animals assembled or herded together; a group under the guidance of a leader
Isa 40:11. . . . feed his *f* like a shepherd.
Jer 10:21. . . . and their *f-s* are scattered.
Jer 31:10. . . . as a shepherd does his *f.*
Zech 11:17. . who abandons the *f!*
Matt 26:31. . the *f* will be scattered.
Luke 2:8. . . . guarding their *f-s* of sheep.
Luke 12:32. . don't be afraid, little *f.*
John 10:16. . one *f* with one shepherd.
Acts 20:28. . shepherd God's *f—*

FLOGGED (v)
to beat with a rod or whip
Deut 25:2. . . is sentenced to be *f,*
John 19:1. . . Pilate had Jesus *f*
Acts 5:40 . . . and had them *f.*

FLOOD, FLOODS (n)
a rising and overflowing of a body of water; the destruction of the world by water during the time of Noah
Gen 7:7 . . . . the boat to escape the *f—*
Prov 27:4. . . cruel, and wrath is like a *f,*
Matt 24:38. . In those days before the *f,*
Luke 6:49. . . the *f-s* sweep down against
2 Pet 2:5. . . . ungodly people with a vast *f.*

FLOUR (n)
a product consisting of finely milled wheat
Lev 2:1. . . . . must consist of choice *f.*
Num 7:13 . . *f* moistened with olive oil.
Luke 17:35. . grinding *f* together at the mill;

FLOURISH, FLOURISHING (v)
to grow luxuriantly; to prosper or thrive
Ps 72:7. . . . . all the godly *f* during his reign.
Ps 92:7. . . . . and evildoers *f,* they will be
Ps 92:12. . . . the godly will *f* like palm trees
Prov 14:11. . the tent of the godly will *f.*
Prov 28:28. . meet disaster, the godly *f.*
Isa 35:7. . . . . reeds and rushes will *f*
2 Thes 1:3 . . your faith is *f-ing*

FLOW, FLOWING, FLOWS (v)
to proceed smoothly and readily; to abound
Exod 3:8 . . . *f-ing* with milk and honey—
Exod 33:3 . . land that *f-s* with milk and
Num 13:27 . *f-ing* with milk and honey.
Josh 5:6 . . . . *f-ing* with milk and honey.
Ps 119:171 . . Let praise *f* from my lips,
Jer 32:22. . . . *f-ing* with milk and honey.
Lam 1:16 . . . tears *f* down my cheeks.
John 7:38. . . living water will *f* from his
Rev 22:1. . . . *f-ing* from the throne of God

FLOWER, FLOWERS (n)
the blossom of a plant
Job 14:2 . . . . We blossom like a *f* and then
Isa 40:6. . . . . as quickly as the *f-s* in a field.
Isa 40:7. . . . . *f-s* fade beneath the breath
Jas 1:10. . . . . like a little *f* in the field.

FOCUS (v)
to concentrate attention or effort
1 Tim 4:13 . . *f* on reading the Scriptures

FOES (n)
adversary, opponent, or enemy
Ps 112:8 . . . . face their *f* triumphantly.

FOLLOW, FOLLOWED, FOLLOWING, FOLLOWS (v)
to pursue or run after; to imitate; to obey
Deut 1:36. . . because he has ***f-ed*** the LORD
Deut 5:32. . . ***f-ing*** his instructions
Josh 14:14 . . he wholeheartedly ***f-ed*** the
1 Kgs 3:3 . . . loved the LORD and ***f-ed***
Prov 4:27. . . feet from ***f-ing*** evil.
Prov 10:9. . . those who *f* crooked paths
Isa 57:2. . . . . For those who *f* godly paths
Isa 65:2. . . . . But they *f* their own evil paths
Matt 4:20 . . . at once and ***f-ed*** him.
Matt 7:24. . . listens to my teaching and ***f-s***
Matt 8:19. . . I will *f* you wherever you go.
Matt 8:22. . . ***F*** me now. Let the
Matt 9:9. . . . got up and ***f-ed*** him.
Matt 16:24 . . take up your cross, and *f*
Matt 19:27 . . given up everything to *f* you.
Matt 26:58 . . Meanwhile, Peter ***f-ed*** him
Mark 1:17 . . Come, *f* me, and I will show
Luke 9:23. . . your cross daily, and *f* me.
Luke 17:23. . go out and *f* them.
Luke 18:43. . ***f-ed*** Jesus, praising God.
John 8:12 . . . If you *f* me, you won't have to
John 10:4 . . . they *f* him because they know
John 10:27 . . know them, and they *f* me.
John 12:26 . . to be my disciple must *f* me,
John 21:19 . . Jesus told him, "***F*** me."
1 Cor 1:12 . . or "I *f* only Christ."
1 Cor 4:17 . . of how I *f* Christ Jesus,
Gal 5:7 . . . . . you back from ***f-ing*** the truth?
Gal 5:25 . . . . *f* the Spirit's leading
Phil 2:12 . . . always ***f-ed*** my instructions
Phil 3:17 . . . those who *f* our example.
2 Thes 3:6 . . and don't *f* the tradition
1 Pet 2:21. . . must *f* in his steps.
Rev 14:4. . . . as virgins, ***f-ing*** the Lamb

FOLLOWER, FOLLOWERS (n)
one who follows the teachings of another; a disciple
1 Kgs 18:3 . . was a devoted *f* of the LORD.
Matt 10:42 . . one of the least of my ***f-s,***
Matt 18:20 . . together as my ***f-s,*** I am there
Acts 9:21 . . . Jesus' ***f-s*** in Jerusalem?

FOLLY (KJV)
Prov 14:18 . . clothed with ***foolishness***
Prov 26:11 . . a fool repeats his ***foolishness***
Eccl 2:13 . . . is better than ***foolishness***
Isa 9:17. . . . . they all speak ***foolishness***
2 Tim 3:9 . . . recognize what ***fools*** they are

FOOD (n)
something that nourishes, sustains, or supplies energy and vitality
see also BREAD
Lev 11:2. . . . the ones you may use for *f.*
Prov 25:21 . . hungry, give them *f* to eat.
Isa 58:7. . . . . Share your *f* with the hungry,
Dan 1:8 . . . . defile himself by eating the *f*
Matt 6:11 . . . today the *f* we need,
Matt 6:25 . . . Isn't life more than *f,*
Mark 7:19 . . every kind of *f* is acceptable
John 6:55 . . . my flesh is true *f,* and my
John 13:18 . . eats my *f* has turned against
Acts 15:20 . . abstain from eating *f*
Rom 14:6 . . . kind of *f* do so to honor
1 Tim 6:8 . . . have enough *f* and clothing,
Jas 2:15. . . . . who has no *f* or clothing,

FOOL, FOOLS (n)
one deficient in intellectual, practical, or moral sense
1 Sam 25:25. He is a *f,* just as his name
Ps 14:1 . . . . . Only ***f-s*** say in their hearts,
Prov 6:32. . . commits adultery is an utter *f,*
Prov 10:8. . . babbling ***f-s*** fall flat on
Prov 10:23 . . wrong is fun for a *f,*
Prov 17:7. . . are not fitting for a *f;*
Prov 17:16 . . to pay tuition to educate a *f,*
Prov 26:1. . . associated with ***f-s*** than snow
Prov 26:7. . . A proverb in the mouth of a *f*
Prov 29:11 . . ***F-s*** vent their anger,
Prov 29:20 . . more hope for a *f* than for
Rom 1:22. . . became utter ***f-s.***
1 Cor 3:18 . . need to become a *f* to be
2 Cor 11:21 . I'm talking like a *f* again—
Eph 5:15 . . . Don't live like ***f-s,***
2 Tim 3:9 . . . recognize what ***f-s*** they are,

FOOL, FOOLED, FOOLING (v)
to trick or deceive
Ps 119:118 . . are only ***f-ing*** themselves.
Jer 7:4. . . . . . don't be ***f-ed*** by those who
1 Cor 15:33 . Don't be ***f-ed*** by those who
Gal 6:3 . . . . . you are only ***f-ing*** yourself.
Eph 5:6 . . . . Don't be ***f-ed*** by those who try
2 Thes 2:3 . . Don't be ***f-ed*** by what they say.
Jas 1:22. . . . . are only ***f-ing*** yourselves.
Jas 1:26. . . . . you are ***f-ing*** yourself,
1 Jn 1:8. . . . . we are only ***f-ing*** ourselves

FOOLISH (adj)
lacking in sense, judgment, or discretion; irreverent
Prov 26:4. . . the *f* arguments of fools,
Rom 1:28. . . abandoned them to their *f*
1 Cor 1:18 . . the cross is *f* to those who

1 Cor 1:27 . . world considers *f* in order to
1 Cor 2:14 . . It all sounds *f* to them
Eph 5:4 . . . . Obscene stories, *f* talk,
1 Tim 6:20 . . Avoid godless, *f* discussions
Titus 3:9. . . . not get involved in *f* discussions

FOOLISHNESS (n)
aimless behavior befitting a fool
Prov 19:3. . . ruin their lives by their own *f*
Prov 22:15 . . heart is filled with *f*,
Eccl 10:1 . . . so a little *f* spoils great
Mark 7:22 . . envy, slander, pride, and *f*.

FOOT (n)
the end of the leg upon which an individual stands
see also FEET
Josh 1:3 . . . . Wherever you set *f*,
Matt 18:8. . . with only one hand or one *f*
Luke 4:11. . . won't even hurt your *f*
1 Cor 12:15 . If the *f* says,
Rev 10:2. . . . and his left *f* on the land.

FOOTHOLD (n)
a strategic position enabling further advance or advantage
Eph 4:27 . . . anger gives a *f* to the devil.

FOOTSTOOL (n)
a low stool used to support the feet
Ps 110:1 . . . . making them a *f* under
Isa 66:1. . . . . throne, and the earth is my *f*.
Matt 5:35. . . the earth is his *f*.
Acts 7:49 . . . the earth is my *f*.
Heb 1:13 . . . making them a *f* under
Heb 10:13 . . and made a *f* under

FORBID, FORBIDDEN (v)
to command against
Matt 16:19 . . Whatever you *f* on earth
Matt 16:19 . . will be ***f-den*** in heaven,
Matt 18:18 . . whatever you *f* on earth
1 Cor 14:39 . don't *f* speaking in

FORCE (n)
violence, compulsion, or constraint exerted upon or against a person or thing
Zech 4:6. . . . is not by *f* nor by strength,

FORCE, FORCED (v)
to compel by physical, moral, or intellectual means
Matt 27:32 . . soldiers ***f-d*** him to carry
John 6:15 . . . were ready to *f* him to be

FORCEFUL (adj)
possessing or filled with force; effective
2 Cor 10:10 . letters are demanding and *f*,

(FORE)FATHERS (KJV)
Exod 10:6 . . ***ancestors*** seen a plague like
Num 11:12 . swore to give their ***ancestors***
Jer 11:10. . . . the sins of their ***forefathers***
Matt 23:32 . . what your ***ancestors*** started

FOREHEAD, FOREHEADS (n)
the part of the face above the eyes
Exod 13:9 . . on your hand or your *f*.
Deut 6:8. . . . wear them on your *f*
1 Sam 17:49. hit the Philistine in the *f*.
Rev 9:4. . . . . seal of God on their ***f-s***.
Rev 13:16. . . right hand or on the *f*.
Rev 14:1. . . . written on their ***f-s***.

FOREIGN (adj)
related to or dealing with other nations; pagan
see also STRANGE
2 Chr 14:3 . . He removed the *f* altars and
2 Chr 33:15 . also removed the *f* gods and
Isa 28:11. . . . through *f* oppressors

FOREIGNER, FOREIGNERS (n)
nonresident, alien, or sojourner
see also STRANGER
Exod 22:21 . not mistreat or oppress ***f-s***
Exod 23:9 . . must not oppress ***f-s***.
Lev 24:22. . . to the ***f-s*** living among you.
Neh 9:2 . . . . separated themselves from all ***f-s***
Ps 119:19 . . . I am only a *f* in the land
Hos 7:8 . . . . mingle with godless ***f-s***,
Luke 17:18. . glory to God except this *f*?
1 Cor 14:11 . I will be a *f* to someone
Eph 2:19 . . . no longer strangers and ***f-s***.
1 Pet 1:1. . . . living as ***f-s*** in the provinces
1 Pet 2:11. . . temporary residents and ***f-s***

FOREKNOW, FOREKNEW, FOREKNOWLEDGE (KJV)
Acts 2:23 . . . God ***knew what would happen***
Rom 8:29. . . God ***knew*** his people ***in advance***
Rom 11:2. . . whom he ***chose from the very beginning***
1 Pet 1:2. . . . Father ***knew you and chose you***

FOREORDAINED (KJV)
1 Pet 1:20. . . ***chose*** him ***as*** your ransom

FORESKIN (n)
flap of skin covering the tip of the penis
Gen 17:11 . . cut off the flesh of your *f* as

Exod 4:25 . . touched his feet with the *f* and
Lev 12:3. . . . boy's *f* must be circumcised.

FORETASTE (n)
a small anticipatory sample
Rom 8:23 . . . as a *f* of future glory,

FORETOLD (v)
to tell beforehand; to predict
Rom 16:26 . . as the prophets *f*

FOREVER (adv)
for a limitless time; continually
see also ETERNAL, EVERLASTING
Gen 3:22 . . . they will live *f*!
Gen 17:8 . . . be their possession *f*,
2 Sam 7:26. . name be honored *f*
1 Chr 17:24 . be established and honored *f*
1 Chr 29:10 . be praised *f* and ever!
Ezra 9:12 . . . prosperity to your children *f*.
Ps 9:7 . . . . . . the LORD reigns *f*,
Ps 21:4 . . . . . of his life stretch on *f*.
Ps 28:9 . . . . . in your arms *f*.
Ps 37:28 . . . . keep them safe *f*,
Ps 61:8 . . . . . sing praises to your name *f*
Ps 73:26 . . . . he is mine *f*.
Ps 79:13 . . . . will thank you *f* and ever,
Ps 86:12 . . . . glory to your name *f*,
Ps 92:8 . . . . . will be exalted *f*.
Ps 100:5 . . . . unfailing love continues *f*,
Ps 103:17 . . . the LORD remains *f* with
Ps 107:1 . . . . faithful love endures *f*.
Ps 110:4 . . . . are a priest *f*
Ps 111:8 . . . . They are *f* true,
Ps 112:9 . . . . be remembered *f*.
Ps 119:152 . . laws will last *f*.
Ps 146:6 . . . . every promise *f*.
Isa 32:17. . . . and confidence *f*.
Isa 51:6. . . . . but my salvation lasts *f*.
Isa 60:15. . . . make you beautiful *f*,
Isa 63:12. . . . making himself famous *f*?
Jer 25:5. . . . . you and your ancestors *f*.
Dan 2:44 . . . and it will stand *f*.
Dan 4:3 . . . . kingdom will last *f*, his rule
Dan 7:27 . . . kingdom will last *f*,
John 6:51 . . . eats this bread will live *f*;
1 Cor 13:8 . . But love will last *f*!
1 Cor 13:13 . Three things will last *f*—
1 Cor 15:42 . will be raised to live *f*.
1 Cor 15:50 . inherit what will last *f*.
2 Cor 4:17 . . and will last *f*!
2 Cor 4:18 . . cannot see will last *f*.
1 Thes 4:17 . will be with the Lord *f*.
2 Thes 1:9 . . destruction, *f* separated
Heb 5:6 . . . . a priest *f* in the order
Heb 7:17 . . . a priest *f* in the order
Heb 7:24 . . . Jesus lives *f*,
Heb 9:12 . . . secured our redemption *f*.
Heb 13:8 . . . yesterday, today, and *f*.
1 Pet 1:25. . . word of the Lord remains *f*.
1 Jn 2:17. . . . will live *f*.
Rev 22:5. . . . they will reign *f* and ever.

FORGAVE (v)
to pardon or acquit of guilt
see also FORGIVE
Ps 78:38 . . . . was merciful and *f* their sins
Luke 7:42. . . so he kindly *f* them both,
Eph 1:7 . . . . his Son and *f* our sins.
Col 1:14 . . . . our freedom and *f* our sins.
Col 2:13 . . . . with Christ, for he *f* all our

FORGET, FORGETTING (v)
to slip from remembrance; to disregard intentionally; to cease from remembering
see also FORGOT
Deut 4:9. . . . careful never to *f*
Ps 78:7 . . . . . hope anew on God, not ***f-ting***
Ps 119:16 . . . and not *f* your word.
Prov 3:1 . . . . My child, never *f*
Eccl 12:1 . . . cause you to *f* your Creator.
Jer 2:32. . . . . a young woman *f* her jewelry?
Luke 12:6. . . God does not *f* a single one
Rom 3:31 . . . we can *f* about the law?
Phil 3:13 . . . ***F-ting*** the past and looking
Heb 13:16 . . And don't *f* to do good
Jas 1:24. . . . . walk away, and *f*
Jas 1:25. . . . . and don't *f* what you heard,
2 Pet 1:9. . . . ***f-ting*** that they have been
2 Pet 3:8. . . . must not *f* this one thing,

FORGIVE, FORGIVEN, FORGIVES, FORGIVING (v)
to pardon or acquit of sins
see also ATONE, FORGAVE
Gen 50:17 . . Please *f* your brothers
Exod 23:21 . he will not *f* your rebellion.
Exod 34:7 . . I *f* iniquity, rebellion,
Exod 34:9 . . but please *f* our iniquity and
Num 14:18 . ***f-ing*** every kind of sin
Num 14:19 . just as you have ***f-n*** them
1 Sam 3:14. . never be ***f-n*** by sacrifices
1 Kgs 8:34 . . hear from heaven and *f*
Ps 65:3 . . . . . by our sins, you *f* them all.
Ps 79:9 . . . . . Save us and *f* our sins
Ps 86:5 . . . . . so good, so ready to *f*,
Ps 103:3 . . . . He ***f-s*** all my sins
Prov 17:9 . . . when a fault is ***f-n***,
Isa 22:14. . . . you will never be ***f-n*** for this
Isa 38:17. . . . and ***f-n*** all my sins.
Isa 55:7. . . . . for he will *f* generously.
Jer 31:34. . . . I will *f* their wickedness,

Dan 9:19 . . . O Lord, hear. O Lord, *f.*
Hos 14:2 . . . ***F*** all our sins and
Matt 6:12. . . and *f* us our sins,
Matt 6:14. . . If you *f* those who sin
Matt 6:15. . . if you refuse to *f* others,
Matt 9:6. . . . authority on earth to *f* sins.
Matt 18:21 . . how often should I *f*
Matt 26:28 . . to *f* the sins of many.
Mark 2:7 . . . Only God can *f* sins!
Mark 2:10 . . authority on earth to *f* sins.
Mark 3:29 . . will never be ***f-n.***
Mark 11:25 . first *f* anyone you are
Mark 11:25 . will *f* your sins,
Luke 5:21. . . Only God can *f* sins!
Luke 5:24. . . authority on earth to *f* sins.
Luke 6:37. . . ***F*** others, and you will be
Luke 7:47. . . a person who is ***f-n*** little
Luke 7:49. . . he goes around ***f-ing*** sins?
Luke 11:4. . . *f* us our sins, as we
Luke 17:3. . . if there is repentance, *f.*
Luke 17:4. . . asks forgiveness, you must *f.*
Luke 23:34. . Father, *f* them,
John 20:23 . . If you *f* anyone's sins,
Acts 5:31 . . . repent of their sins and be ***f-n.***
Acts 8:22 . . . Perhaps he will *f* your evil
Rom 4:5. . . . faith in God who ***f-s*** sinners.
Rom 4:7. . . . whose disobedience is ***f-n,***
2 Cor 2:7 . . . time to *f* and comfort
2 Cor 2:10 . . When you *f* this man,
Col 3:13. . . . so you must *f* others.
Heb 8:12 . . . I will *f* their wickedness,
1 Jn 1:9. . . . . is faithful and just to *f* us

FORGIVENESS (n)
aquittal or pardon of sins
see also ATONEMENT, MERCY
Neh 9:17 . . . you are a God of *f,*
Luke 24:47. . There is *f* of sins for all
Acts 13:38 . . this man Jesus there is *f*
Rom 5:15. . . his gift of *f* to many
Heb 9:22 . . . of blood, there is no *f.*
Jas 5:20. . . . . bring about the *f* of many sins.

FORGOT, FORGOTTEN (v)
see also FORGET
Deut 32:18. . *f* the God who had given
Ps 44:20 . . . . If we had ***f-ten*** the name
Ps 78:11 . . . . They *f* what he had done—
Ps 106:13 . . . how quickly they *f*
Ps 119:176 . . not ***f-ten*** your commands.
Isa 17:10. . . . You have ***f-ten*** the Rock
Isa 51:13. . . . Yet you have ***f-ten*** the LORD,
Hos 8:14 . . . Israel has ***f-ten*** its Maker

FORMED (v)
to create, fashion, or give shape to something
see also CREATE(D), MADE, MAKE
Gen 2:7 . . . . the LORD God *f* the man
Gen 2:19 . . . LORD God *f* from the ground
Ps 94:9 . . . . . the one who *f* your eyes?
Jer 1:5. . . . . . knew you before I *f* you
Heb 11:3 . . . universe was *f* at God's

FORMLESS (adj)
lacking order or arrangement; having no physical existence
Gen 1:2 . . . . The earth was *f* and empty,
Jer 4:23. . . . . and it was empty and *f.*

FORNICATION (KJV)
Isa 23:17. . . . ***be a prostitute*** to all kingdoms
Matt 19:9. . . wife has been ***unfaithful***
1 Cor 5:1 . . . ***sexual immorality*** going on
1 Cor 6:18 . . ***sexual immorality*** is a sin
Jude 1:7. . . . were filled with ***immorality***

FORSAKE (v)
to renounce or turn away from entirely
1 Chr 28:9 . . But if you *f* him, he will
Job 28:28 . . . to *f* evil is real understanding.

FORTRESS (n)
a fortified place; a place of security or survival
see also REFUGE
2 Sam 22:2. . my *f,* and my savior;
Ps 27:1 . . . . . The LORD is my *f,*
Ps 71:3 . . . . . my rock and my *f.*
Ps 144:2 . . . . and my *f,* my tower of safety,
Prov 18:10. . LORD is a strong *f;*
Zeph 3:6 . . . devastating their *f* walls and

FORTUNE-TELLER, FORTUNE-TELLERS (n)
one who professes to foretell future events
Jer 29:8. . . . . your prophets and ***f-s*** who are
Acts 16:16 . . She was a *f* who earned a lot

FORTUNE-TELLING (n)
the act of one foretelling future events by occultic means
Lev 19:26. . . not practice *f* or witchcraft.

FORTY (adj)
the number 40
Gen 7:4 . . . . for *f* days and *f* nights,
Exod 16:35 . Israel ate manna for *f* years
Exod 24:18 . *f* days and *f* nights.
Num 14:34 . wilderness for *f* years—
Matt 4:2. . . . For *f* days and *f* nights
Acts 1:3 . . . . the *f* days after his crucifixion,
Acts 13:18 . . *f* years of wandering

FOUGHT (v)
see also FIGHT
Gen 32:28 . . because you have *f* with God
Josh 10:14 . . Surely the LORD *f* for Israel
2 Tim 4:7 . . . I have *f* the good fight,

FOUND (v)
see also FIND
2 Kgs 22:8 . . I have *f* the Book of the Law
2 Kgs 23:24 . Hilkiah the priest had *f*
2 Chr 15:15 . after God, and they *f*
Luke 15:6. . . I have *f* my lost sheep.'
Luke 15:9. . . because I have *f* my lost coin.'
Luke 15:24. . but now he is *f*.'
Jas 2:8. . . . . . the royal law as *f* in the
Rev 5:4. . . . . because no one was *f* worthy

FOUNDATION (n)
basis upon which something is built, supported, or added to; substructure
Prov 1:7. . . . Fear of the LORD is the *f*
Prov 9:10. . . the LORD is the *f* of wisdom.
Isa 28:16. . . . placing a *f* stone in Jerusalem,
Luke 6:49. . . a house without a *f*.
Eph 2:20 . . . built on the *f* of the apostles
1 Tim 3:15 . . pillar and *f* of the truth.
2 Tim 2:19 . . stands firm like a *f* stone
Heb 1:10 . . . you laid the *f* of the earth

FOUNTAIN (n)
source; spring of water
Isa 12:3. . . . . from the *f* of salvation!
Zech 13:1. . . a *f* to cleanse them

FOXES (n)
any of various carnivorous mammals of the dog family with shorter legs, pointed muzzles, and long bushy tails
Song 2:15. . . Catch all the *f*, those little *f*,
Luke 9:58. . . *F* have dens to live in,

FRAGRANCE (n)
a sweet or delicate odor
see also PERFUME
2 Cor 2:15 . . are a Christ-like *f* rising up

FRANKINCENSE (n)
an aromatic gum resin obtained from the Boswellia tree
Matt 2:11 . . . gifts of gold, *f*, and myrrh.

FRAUD (n)
an act of deceiving or misrepresenting; trickery
Lev 6:2. . . . . you steal or commit *f*,
Acts 13:10 . . every sort of deceit and *f*,

FREE (adj)
not bound, confined, or detained by force; without restraint, inhibition, or cost; possessing the rights of citizenship
John 8:32 . . . the truth will set you *f*.
John 8:36 . . . sets you *f*, you are truly *f*.
Rom 6:7. . . . we were set *f* from the power
Rom 6:18 . . . you are *f* from your slavery
Gal 3:28 . . . . slave or *f*, male and female.
Jas 1:25. . . . . the perfect law that sets you *f*,
1 Pet 2:16. . . For you are *f*, yet

FREED, FREES (v)
to relieve or rid of what restrains, confines, restricts, or embarrasses
Ps 116:16 . . . ***f-d*** me from my chains.
Ps 146:7 . . . . The LORD ***f-s*** the prisoners.
Isa 61:1. . . . . prisoners will be ***f-d***.
Rom 3:24 . . . he ***f-d*** us from the penalty
1 Cor 1:30 . . and he ***f-d*** us from sin.
Rev 1:5. . . . . and has ***f-d*** us from our sins

FREEDOM (n)
liberation from slavery, restraint, or the power of another
Ps 119:45 . . . I will walk in *f*, for I have
2 Cor 3:17 . . the Lord is, there is *f*.
Gal 2:4 . . . . . the *f* we have in Christ
Gal 4:5 . . . . . sent him to buy *f* for us
Gal 5:13 . . . . don't use your *f* to satisfy
Eph 1:7 . . . . purchased our *f* with the blood
1 Pet 2:16. . . don't use your *f* as an excuse

FRIEND, FRIENDS (n)
intimate associate; a favored companion
Prov 16:28 . . separates the best of ***f-s***.
Prov 17:9 . . . on it separates close ***f-s***.
Prov 20:6 . . . will say they are loyal ***f-s***,
Prov 27:6 . . . Wounds from a sincere *f* are
Prov 29:5 . . . To flatter ***f-s*** is to lay a trap
Isa 41:8. . . . . from Abraham my *f*,
Zech 13:6. . . was wounded at my ***f-s'*** house!
John 11:3 . . . Lord, your dear *f* is very sick.
John 15:13 . . one's life for one's ***f-s***.
John 15:14 . . You are my ***f-s*** if you do
John 15:15 . . Now you are my ***f-s***,
John 19:12 . . you are no '*f* of Caesar.'
Jas 2:23. . . . . even called the *f* of God.
Jas 4:4. . . . . . want to be a *f* of the world,

FRIENDSHIP (n)
association of familiarity and companionship
Prov 3:32. . . he offers his *f* to the godly.
Rom 5:10. . . since our *f* with God was
Jas 4:4. . . . . . you realize that *f* with the world

FRIGHTENED (v)
to terrify; to make afraid
Heb 12:21 . . was so *f* at the sight

FRINGE (n)
the edge; the threads hanging from cut or raveled edges
Matt 9:20 . . . touched the *f* of his robe,

FROGS (n)
a leaping aquatic amphibian with smooth moist skin, long hind legs, and webbed feet
Exod 8:2 . . . I will send a plague of *f*
Rev 16:13. . . spirits that looked like *f*

FRUIT (n)
a product of plant growth; product or result
Ps 1:3 . . . . . bearing *f* each season.
Isa 11:1. . . . . new Branch bearing *f* from
Dan 4:12 . . . loaded with *f* for all to eat.
Matt 3:10 . . . not produce good *f* will be
Matt 7:20 . . . can identify a tree by its *f*,
Matt 12:33 . . is bad, its *f* will be bad.
John 15:2 . . . that doesn't produce *f*,
John 15:16 . . go and produce lasting *f*,
Gal 5:22. . . . produces this kind of *f*
Phil 1:11 . . . the *f* of your salvation—
2 Tim 2:6 . . . first to enjoy the *f*
Rev 22:2. . . . bearing twelve crops of *f*,

FRUITFUL (adj)
bearing fruit (product of a tree or plant); abundant (at producing work or in bearing children)
Gen 1:22 . . . Be *f* and multiply.
Gen 9:1 . . . . Be *f* and multiply.
Gen 35:11 . . Be *f* and multiply.
Ps 128:3 . . . . will be like a *f* grapevine,
Jer 2:7. . . . . . brought you into a *f* land
Phil 1:22 . . . do more *f* work for Christ.

FRUSTRATES (v)
to impede or obstruct; to make invalid or with no effect
Ps 33:10 . . . . The LORD *f* the plans

FULFILL, FULFILLED, FULFILLS (v)
to complete or perform as promised; to measure up or satisfy
Ps 57:2. . . . . to God who will *f* his purpose
Dan 9:4 . . . . You always *f* your covenant
Matt 2:15 . . . This ***f-ed*** what the Lord had
Matt 2:23 . . . This ***f-ed*** what the prophets
Matt 13:35 . . ***f-ed*** what God had spoken
Matt 27:9 . . . This ***f-ed*** the prophecy of
Luke 4:21. . . has been ***f-ed*** this very day!
Luke 24:44. . Psalms must be ***f-ed***.
John 18:9 . . . this to *f* his own statement:
John 19:28 . . and to *f* Scripture he said,
Acts 1:16 . . . Scriptures had to be ***f-ed***
Rom 3:31 . . . do we truly *f* the law.
Rom 13:8 . . . you will *f* the requirements
Rom 13:10 . . love ***f-s*** the requirements
Eph 1:9 . . . . to *f* his own good pleasure.

FULFILLMENT (n)
the act of bringing to completion as promised
John 19:36 . . happened in *f* of the Scriptures

FULL (adj)
possessing or containing a great amount
Deut 34:9. . . was *f* of the spirit of wisdom,
Luke 4:1. . . . Then Jesus, *f* of the Holy Spirit,
Acts 6:3 . . . . *f* of the Spirit and wisdom.
Acts 6:5 . . . . Stephen (a man *f* of faith and
Acts 7:55 . . . Stephen, *f* of the Holy Spirit,
Acts 11:24 . . man, *f* of the Holy Spirit

FULLNESS (n)
the quality or state of containing all that is wanted, needed, or possible
Eph 3:19 . . . with all the *f* of life and
Col 1:19 . . . . God in all his *f* was pleased
Col 2:9 . . . . . lives all the *f* of God

FUN (n)
providing entertainment, amusement, or enjoyment
Prov 10:23 . . Doing wrong is *f* for a fool,
Prov 14:9. . . Fools make *f* of guilt,

FUNDAMENTAL (adj)
primary; basic; central
Heb 6:1 . . . . the *f* importance of repenting

FUNERAL (adj)
of, relating to, or constituting the observances held for a dead person
2 Sam 1:17. . David composed a *f* song
Luke 7:32. . . so we played *f* songs,

FUNERALS (n)
the observances held for a dead person
Eccl 7:2 . . . . Better to spend your time at *f*

FURIOUS (adj)
exhibiting or goaded by anger
Judg 14:19. . But Samson was *f*
2 Sam 12:5. . David was *f*.
Jer 21:5. . . . . You have made me *f*!

FURNACE (n)
an enclosed structure in which heat is produced
Dan 3:6 . . . . be thrown into a blazing *f.*
Matt 13:42 . . throw them into the fiery *f,*

FURY (n)
wrath; fierceness; rage
Exod 15:7 . . You unleash your blazing *f;*
Deut 29:28 . . In great anger and *f*
Ps 7:6 . . . . . . against the *f* of my enemies!
Jer 32:37 . . . . will scatter them in my *f.*
Zeph 2:2 . . . the fierce *f* of the LORD.

FUTILITY
the state of having no hope of success
Job 7:3 . . . . . months of *f,* long and weary

FUTURE (adj)
existing or occurring at a later time
Deut 29:15 . . also with the *f* generations
Rom 8:19 . . . waiting eagerly for that *f* day
Eph 2:7 . . . . can point to us in all *f* ages
Heb 2:5 . . . . will control the *f* world

FUTURE (n)
time that is to come; what is going to happen
Num 24:14 . do to your people in the *f.*
Ps 31:15 . . . . My *f* is in your hands.
Ps 37:37 . . . . a wonderful *f* awaits those
Isa 42:9. . . . . tell you the *f* before it happens.
Isa 46:10. . . . can tell you the *f* before it
Jer 29:11. . . . to give you a *f* and a hope.
Jer 31:17. . . . There is hope for your *f,*

GABRIEL
Angel who stands in God's presence; seen in Daniel's visions (Dan 8:16-18; 9:21); announced birth of John the Baptist (Luke 1:11-20); announced birth of Jesus (Luke 1:26-28).

GAIN (n)
winnings or profits
Isa 56:11. . . . intent on personal *g.*

GAIN, GAINED, GAINS (v)
to acquire or win; to profit or increase
Prov 3:13 . . . one who ***g-s*** understanding.
Prov 11:16 . . gracious woman ***g-s*** respect,
Mark 8:36 . . *g* the whole world but lose
Luke 9:25. . . *g* the whole world but are
1 Cor 13:3 . . I would have ***g-ed*** nothing.

GALILEE (n)
a Roman province of Palestine during the time of Jesus
Isa 9:1. . . . . . a time in the future when *G*
Matt 4:15 . . . beyond the Jordan River, in *G*
Matt 26:32 . . I will go ahead of you to *G*
Matt 28:10 . . my brothers to leave for *G,*

GARBAGE (n)
food waste; discarded or useless material
1 Cor 4:13 . . treated like the world's *g,*
Phil 3:8 . . . . counting it all as *g,*

GARDEN (n)
a planted area where fruits, vegetables, and flowers are cultivated
Gen 2:8 . . . . God planted a *g* in Eden
Gen 2:15 . . . God placed the man in the *G*
1 Kgs 4:25 . . had its own home and *g.*
Song 4:12. . . my private *g,* my treasure,
Isa 58:11. . . . will be like a well-watered *g,*
Jer 31:12. . . . life will be like a watered *g,*
Ezek 28:13 . . in Eden, the *g* of God.

GARDENER (n)
one who takes care of a garden
John 15:1 . . . my Father is the *g.*
John 20:15 . . She thought he was the *g.*

GARMENT, GARMENTS (n)
an article of clothing
Exod 28:2 . . Make sacred ***g-s*** for Aaron
Lev 16:23. . . he must take off the linen ***g-s***
Lev 16:24. . . put on his regular ***g-s,*** and go
Ps 102:26 . . . You will change them like a *g*
John 19:24 . . divided my ***g-s*** among

GATE, GATES (n)
opening in a (city) wall or fence, consisting of a door and protected by defensive structures (as towers); the place of judicial decisions, town criers, and marketplace trade; entrance
Esth 6:10 . . . sits at the *g* of the palace.
Ps 24:7. . . . . Open up, ancient ***g-s!***
Ps 100:4 . . . . his ***g-s*** with thanksgiving;
Isa 62:10. . . . Go out through the ***g-s!***
Matt 7:13 . . . only through the narrow *g.*
John 10:1 . . . going through the *g,*
John 10:2 . . . who enters through the *g*
John 10:7 . . . I am the *g* for the sheep.
Heb 13:12 . . died outside the city ***g-s***
Rev 21:21. . . ***g-s*** were made of pearls—
Rev 21:21. . . each *g* from a single pearl!

GATEKEEPER (n)
one who guards or tends a gate
Ps 84:10 . . . . a *g* in the house of my God

GATHER, GATHERED, GATHERING (v)
to bring together; to reap or harvest; to assemble
Exod 16:18 . Those who ***g-ed*** a lot
Jer 23:3. . . . . will *g* together the remnant
Zech 14:2. . . I will *g* all the nations

Matt 24:31 . . they will *g* his chosen ones
Matt 25:26 . . ***g-ed*** crops I didn't cultivate,
Matt 25:32 . . the nations will be ***g-ed*** in his
Mark 13:27 . to *g* his chosen ones
Luke 3:17 . . . ***g-ing*** the wheat into his barn
Luke 13:34 . . wanted to *g* your children
2 Cor 8:15 . . say, "Those who ***g-ed*** a lot
2 Thes 2:1 . . we will be ***g-ed*** to meet him.
Rev 16:16 . . . demonic spirits ***g-ed*** all

GAVE (v)
to suffer the loss of
see also GIVE
John 3:16 . . . he *g* his one and only Son,
Rom 8:32 . . . *g* him up for us all,
Gal 2:20 . . . . loved me and *g* himself for me.
1 Tim 2:6 . . . He *g* his life to purchase

GENERATION, GENERATIONS (n)
the whole body of individuals born about the same time (nation or racial group); the period of time during which those individuals lived (also, age or era); offspring
Gen 17:7 . . . after you, from *g* to *g*.
Exod 20:6 . . love for a thousand ***g-s***
Num 32:13 . the entire *g* that sinned
Judg 2:10 . . . After that *g* died,
1 Chr 16:15 . to a thousand ***g-s***.
Ps 71:18 . . . . your power to this new *g*,
Ps 100:5 . . . . continues to each *g*.
Ps 102:12 . . . endure to every *g*.
Ps 102:18 . . . recorded for future ***g-s***,
Ps 105:8 . . . . to a thousand ***g-s***.
Ps 119:90 . . . extends to every *g*,
Ps 145:4 . . . . Let each *g* tell its children
Ps 146:10 . . . throughout the ***g-s***.
Prov 27:24 . . not be passed to the next *g*.
Isa 41:4 . . . . . summoning each new *g*
Lam 5:19 . . . continues from *g* to *g*.
Joel 1:3 . . . . . the story down from *g* to *g*.
Matt 12:39 . . Only an evil, adulterous *g*
Mark 13:30 . this *g* will not pass
Luke 1:48 . . . all ***g-s*** will call me blessed.
Luke 11:29 . . This evil *g* keeps asking me
Acts 2:40 . . . from this crooked *g!*
Eph 3:5 . . . . not reveal it to previous ***g-s***,
Eph 3:21 . . . all ***g-s*** forever and ever!

GENEROSITY (n)
the quality or fact of being magnanimous, kindly, or openhanded; abundance
Acts 2:46 . . . meals with great joy and *g*—
2 Cor 9:10 . . a great harvest of *g* in you.
Eph 4:7 . . . . through the *g* of Christ.
Phlm 1:6 . . . put into action the *g* that

GENEROUS (adj)
magnanimous, kindly; liberal in giving; abundant
Deut 15:8 . . . Instead, be *g* and lend
Ps 37:26 . . . . godly always give *g* loans to
2 Cor 9:6 . . . will get a *g* crop.
1 Tim 6:18 . . *g* to those in need,

GENTILE, GENTILES (n)
non-Jewish individuals or nations, often connoting heathens or pagans
see also NATION(S)
Isa 49:6 . . . . . make you a light to the ***G-s***,
Luke 21:24 . . period of the ***G-s*** comes
Acts 10:45 . . out on the ***G-s***, too.
Acts 14:27 . . faith to the ***G-s***, too.
Acts 15:14 . . God first visited the ***G-s***
Acts 21:25 . . As for the ***G*** believers,
Acts 28:28 . . also been offered to the ***G-s***,
Rom 1:16 . . . Jews first and also the ***G***.
Rom 2:9 . . . . Jews first and also for the ***G***.
Rom 3:9 . . . . people, whether Jews or ***G-s***,
Rom 3:29 . . . God of the ***G-s?***
Rom 10:12 . . Jew and ***G*** are the same
Rom 11:11 . . available to the ***G-s***.
Rom 15:9 . . . the ***G-s*** might give glory
Rom 15:27 . . ***G-s*** received the spiritual
Gal 2:2 . . . . . preaching to the ***G-s***.
Gal 2:8 . . . . . apostle to the ***G-s***.
Gal 2:9 . . . . . keep preaching to the ***G-s***,
Gal 3:8 . . . . . God would declare the ***G-s***
Gal 3:14 . . . . blessed the ***G-s*** with the same
Gal 3:28 . . . . no longer Jew or ***G***, slave or
Eph 3:8 . . . . the privilege of telling the ***G-s***
Col 3:11 . . . . a Jew or a ***G***, circumcised or

GENTLE (adj)
kind; mild-mannered; soft
1 Kgs 19:12 . sound of a *g* whisper.
Prov 15:1 . . . A *g* answer deflects anger,
Prov 15:4 . . . *G* words are a tree of life;
Matt 11:29 . . am humble and *g* at heart,
1 Cor 4:21 . . love and a *g* spirit?
Eph 4:2 . . . . be humble and *g*. Be patient
1 Tim 3:3 . . . must be *g*, not quarrelsome,
Titus 3:2 . . . . be *g* and show true humility
Jas 3:17 . . . . . *g* at all times,

GENTLENESS (n)
mildness of manners or disposition
Gal 5:23 . . . . *g*, and self-control.
Col 3:12 . . . . kindness, humility, *g*, and
1 Tim 6:11 . . perseverance, and *g*.

GENUINE (adj)

actual, true, authentic, sincere

John 1:47 . . . here is a *g* son of Israel—
2 Cor 8:8 . . . I am testing how *g* your love
Phil 1:18 . . . motives are false or *g*,
2 Tim 1:5 . . . I remember your *g* faith,

GETHSEMANE (n)

the garden where Jesus often went for prayer, rest, or fellowship; the site where Judas betrayed Jesus before the crucifixion

Matt 26:36 . . to the olive grove called ***G***,
Mark 14:32 . to the olive grove called ***G***,

GHOST, GHOSTS (n)

the soul of a dead person believed to appear to the living in bodily likeness

Luke 24:39. . I am not a *g*, because ***g-s***

GIDEON

Judge of Israel, also called "Jerub-baal" (Judg 6–8; 7:1; Heb 11:32); called by angel of the LORD *(Judg 6:11-16); cut down Baal's altar (Judg 6:25-32); used fleece for guidance (Judg 6:36-40); led Israel against Midianite oppressors (Judg 7:1–8:21); refused kingship (Judg 8:22-23); made an ephod (Judg 8:24-28); died (Judg 8:29-35).*

GIFT, GIFTS (n)

a present from people to people (often a bribe); a sacrifice from people to God; anything given voluntarily or at no cost; that which is given from God, enabling or empowering his people

Prov 18:16 . . Giving a *g* can open doors;
Matt 2:11 . . . and gave him ***g-s*** of gold,
Luke 11:13. . how to give good ***g-s*** to your
Rom 4:16 . . . given as a free *g*.
Rom 5:15 . . . and God's gracious *g*.
Rom 6:23 . . . free *g* of God is eternal
Rom 11:29 . . For God's ***g-s*** and his call
1 Cor 12:4 . . kinds of spiritual ***g-s***,
1 Cor 12:7 . . A spiritual *g* is given
1 Cor 12:31 . the most helpful ***g-s***.
2 Cor 9:5 . . . I want it to be a willing *g*,
2 Cor 9:15 . . Thank God for this *g*
Gal 2:9 . . . . . recognized the *g* God had
Eph 2:8 . . . . it is a *g* from God.
Eph 4:8 . . . . and gave ***g-s*** to his people.
2 Tim 1:6 . . . the spiritual *g* God gave you
Heb 2:4 . . . . ***g-s*** of the Holy Spirit
1 Pet 3:7. . . . equal partner in God's *g*
1 Pet 4:10. . . of spiritual ***g-s***.

GIRL (n)

a female child from birth to adulthood

2 Kgs 5:2 . . . was a young *g* who had been
Mark 5:41 . . which means "Little *g*, get up!"

GIVE, GIVEN, GIVES, GIVING (v)

to grant, bestow, convey, offer, provide, or designate; to yield or produce; to suffer the loss of (life)

Exod 30:15 . poor must not *g* less.
1 Sam 1:28. . ***g-ing*** him to the LORD,
Ps 112:9 . . . . share freely and *g* generously
Ps 119:130 . . your word ***g-s*** light,
Prov 21:26. . the godly love to *g!*
Prov 23:26. . O my son, *g* me your heart.
Isa 9:6. . . . . . a son is ***g-n*** to us.
Matt 7:11. . . heavenly Father *g* good gifts
Matt 16:19. . And I will *g* you the keys
Matt 22:30. . marry nor be ***g-n*** in marriage.
Mark 6:7 . . . by two, ***g-ing*** them authority
Luke 11:13. . know how to *g* good gifts to
Luke 14:33. . my disciple without ***g-ing*** up
Luke 22:19. . body, which is ***g-n*** for you.
John 1:17. . . the law was ***g-n*** through Moses,
John 5:21 . . . so the Son ***g-s*** life to anyone
John 13:34 . . So now I am ***g-ing*** you a new
John 14:27 . . And the peace I *g* is a gift
Acts 5:32 . . . Spirit, who is ***g-n*** by God
Acts 14:3 . . . was true by ***g-ing*** them power
Acts 15:8 . . . by ***g-ing*** them the Holy Spirit
Acts 20:35 . . is more blessed to *g* than to
Rom 2:7. . . . He will *g* eternal life
Rom 5:5. . . . because he has ***g-n*** us the Holy
Rom 8:32. . . won't he also *g* us everything
Rom 10:12. . Lord, who ***g-s*** generously
Rom 12:8. . . is giving, *g* generously.
Rom 14:12. . each of us will *g* a personal
1 Cor 9:17 . . God has ***g-n*** me this sacred
1 Cor 11:24 . body, which is ***g-n*** for you.
1 Cor 15:57 . thank God! He ***g-s*** us victory
2 Cor 3:6 . . . the Spirit ***g-s*** life.
2 Cor 8:6 . . . this ministry of ***g-ing***.
2 Cor 9:7 . . . how much to *g*.
Eph 4:7 . . . . he has ***g-n*** each one of us
Eph 4:28 . . . and then *g* generously to
1 Thes 4:8 . . rejecting God, who ***g-s***
1 Tim 6:17. . God, who richly ***g-s*** us all we
1 Jn 4:13. . . . And God has ***g-n*** us his Spirit

GLAD (adj)

joyful or happy, often with shouts

Ps 16:9 . . . . . my heart is *g*, and I rejoice.
Ps 32:11 . . . . LORD and be *g*, all you who
Ps 69:32 . . . . at work and be *g*.

Ps 97:1 . . . . . coastlands be *g.*
Ps 104:15 . . . wine to make them *g,*
Ps 118:24 . . . will rejoice and be *g* in it.
Prov 10:8 . . . The wise are *g* to be
Prov 27:11 . . make my heart *g.*
Isa 35:1. . . . . and desert will be *g*
Zeph 3:14 . . O Israel! Be *g* and rejoice
Matt 5:12 . . . Be very *g!*
John 11:15 . . for your sakes, I'm *g* I wasn't
Acts 13:48 . . they were very *g*
1 Cor 12:26 . the parts are *g.*
2 Cor 2:2 . . . will make me *g?*
Rev 19:7. . . . Let us be *g* and rejoice,

GLADNESS (n)

the quality or state of joy or delight; happiness
Ps 40:16 . . . . with joy and *g* in you.
Ps 90:15 . . . . Give us *g* in proportion to
Isa 35:10. . . . filled with joy and *g.*
Jer 48:33. . . . Joy and *g* are gone
Zeph 3:17 . . in you with *g.*

GLEAMING (adj)

shining with or as if with moderate brightness
Ezek 1:27 . . . he looked like *g* amber,

GLORIFY, GLORIFIED, GLORIFIES, GLORIFYING (v)

to bestow honor or praise (as in worship); to magnify
see also EXALT, HONOR
Ps 147:12 . . . *G* the LORD, O Jerusalem!
Isa 26:8. . . . . desire is to *g* your name.
Isa 42:12. . . . the whole world *g* the LORD;
Dan 4:37 . . . praise and *g* and honor the
Luke 2:20. . . flocks, *g-ing* and praising
John 8:50 . . . no wish to *g* myself, God is
John 13:31 . . God will be ***g-ied***
John 17:1 . . . *G* your Son so
John 21:19 . . of death he would *g* God.
2 Cor 8:19 . . a service that ***g-ies*** the Lord
Eph 1:14 . . . would praise and *g* him.
Rev 15:4. . . . you, Lord, and *g* your name?

GLORIOUS (adj)

possessing or deserving special honor; splendid or magnificent
Exod 15:6 . . O LORD, is *g* in power.
Exod 33:18 . show me your *g* presence.
Deut 32:3. . . the LORD; how *g* is our God!
1 Chr 16:28 . the LORD is *g* and strong.
Neh 9:5 . . . . prayed: "May your *g* name be
Job 37:5 . . . . God's voice is *g* in the
Ps 45:3 . . . . . You are so *g,* so majestic!
Ps 76:4 . . . . . You are *g* and more majestic
Ps 96:3 . . . . . Publish his *g* deeds among the
Ps 149:9 . . . . This is the *g* privilege of
Isa 55:5. . . . . of Israel, have made you *g.*
Isa 63:15. . . . from your holy, *g* home,
Dan 8:9 . . . . east and toward the *g* land of
Dan 11:45 . . between the *g* holy mountain
Matt 19:28 . . sits upon his *g* throne,
Acts 2:20 . . . that great and *g* day of the
Acts 7:2 . . . . Our *g* God appeared to
Rom 1:23 . . . worshiping the *g,* ever-living
Rom 3:23 . . . of God's *g* standard.
Rom 8:21 . . . children in *g* freedom from
2 Cor 3:9 . . . how much more *g* is the new
2 Cor 3:10 . . first glory was not *g* at all
2 Cor 3:18 . . into his *g* image.
Eph 1:6 . . . . God for the *g* grace he has
Eph 1:17 . . . asking God, the *g* Father of
Eph 3:16 . . . that from his *g,* unlimited
Eph 5:27 . . . himself as a *g* church without
Phil 3:21 . . . them into *g* bodies like his
Phil 4:19 . . . from his *g* riches, which have
Col 1:11 . . . . with all his *g* power so you
Jas 2:1. . . . . . faith in our *g* Lord Jesus
1 Pet 1:8. . . . with a *g,* inexpressible joy.
1 Pet 4:14. . . for then the *g* Spirit of God
Jude 1:24 . . . into his *g* presence without a

GLORY (n)

honor bestowed; splendor or magnificence; a distinguishing quality, asset, or attribute
Exod 16:10 . awesome *g* of the LORD
Num 14:21 . filled with the LORD's *g,*
Josh 7:19 . . . My son, give *g* to the LORD,
1 Sam 4:21 . . said, "Israel's *g* is gone."
Ps 8:5 . . . . . . them with *g* and honor.
Ps 19:1 . . . . . proclaim the *g* of God.
Ps 29:1 . . . . . LORD for his *g* and strength.
Ps 44:8 . . . . . O God, we give *g* to you
Ps 57:11 . . . . May your *g* shine over all the
Ps 71:8 . . . . . I declare your *g* all day
Ps 86:12 . . . . I will give *g* to your name
Ps 108:5 . . . . May your *g* shine over all the
Ps 145:12 . . . the majesty and *g* of your
Prov 16:31 . . is a crown of *g;* it is gained
Isa 6:3. . . . . . earth is filled with his *g!*
Isa 24:16. . . . songs that give *g* to the
Isa 35:2. . . . . display his *g,* the splendor
Isa 42:8. . . . . not give my *g* to anyone else,
Isa 48:11. . . . not share my *g* with idols!
Isa 66:11. . . . Drink deeply of her *g* even
Isa 66:19. . . . they will declare my *g* to the
Ezek 44:4. . . saw that the *g* of the LORD
Matt 16:27 . . angels in the *g* of his Father
Matt 25:31 . . comes in his *g,* and all the
Mark 13:26 . great power and *g.*
Luke 2:14. . . *G* to God in highest heaven,

Luke 9:26. . . and in the *g* of the Father
Luke 9:32. . . they saw Jesus' *g* and the two
Luke 21:27. . power and great *g*.
John 1:14 . . . have seen his *g*, the *g* of
John 7:39 . . . not yet entered into his *g*.
John 11:40 . . you would see God's *g* if
John 12:23 . . enter into his *g*.
John 12:41 . . the Messiah's *g*.
John 14:13 . . the Son can bring *g* to the
John 16:14 . . will bring me *g* by telling
John 17:22 . . given them the *g* you gave
Acts 3:13 . . . who has brought *g* to his
Rom 2:7. . . . seeking after the *g* and honor
Rom 2:10. . . there will be *g* and honor and
Rom 3:7. . . . and brings him more *g?*
Rom 4:20. . . in this he brought *g* to God.
Rom 8:17. . . heirs of God's *g*.
Rom 8:18. . . compared to the *g* he will
Rom 8:30. . . gave them his *g*.
Rom 9:4. . . . God revealed his *g* to them.
Rom 9:23. . . riches of his *g* shine even
Rom 9:23. . . in advance for *g*.
Rom 15:6. . . giving praise and *g* to God,
Rom 15:9. . . Gentiles might give *g* to God
Rom 16:27. . All *g* to the only wise God
1 Cor 2:7 . . . for our ultimate *g* before the
1 Cor 10:31 . all for the *g* of God.
1 Cor 15:43 . will be raised in *g*.
2 Cor 1:20 . . to God for his *g*.
2 Cor 3:7 . . . shone with the *g* of God, even
2 Cor 3:10 . . In fact, that first *g* was not
2 Cor 4:4 . . . about the *g* of Christ, who is
2 Cor 4:17 . . for us a *g* that vastly
Eph 1:12 . . . bring praise and *g* to God.
Phil 1:11 . . . will bring much *g* and praise
Phil 2:11 . . . is Lord, to the *g* of God the
Phil 4:20 . . . Now all *g* to God our
1 Thes 2:12 . Kingdom and *g*.
2 Thes 2:14 . share in the *g* of our Lord
1 Tim 1:17. . All honor and *g* to God
1 Tim 3:16. . to heaven in *g*.
2 Tim 4:18. . All *g* to God forever
Titus 2:13. . . when the *g* of our great God
Heb 1:3 . . . . God's own *g* and expresses the
Heb 2:9 . . . . crowned with *g* and honor.
Heb 3:3 . . . . far more *g* than Moses, just
1 Pet 1:7. . . . much praise and *g* and honor
1 Pet 1:21. . . gave him great *g*.
1 Pet 5:4. . . . of never-ending *g* and honor.
2 Pet 1:3. . . . means of his marvelous *g* and
2 Pet 1:17. . . from the majestic *g* of God
Jude 1:25. . . All *g*, majesty, power,
Rev 4:9. . . . . beings give *g* and honor and
Rev 4:11. . . . God, to receive *g* and honor
Rev 5:12. . . . honor and *g* and blessing.
Rev 5:13. . . . and honor and *g* and power
Rev 11:13. . . terrified and gave *g* to the
Rev 16:9. . . . God and give him *g*.
Rev 21:11. . . shone with the *g* of God and
Rev 21:23. . . for the *g* of God
Rev 21:26. . . will bring their *g* and honor

GLUTTON, GLUTTONS (n)

one given habitually to greedy and voracious eating and drinking
Prov 23:20. . or feast with ***g-s***,
Matt 11:19. . He's a *g* and a drunkard,
Titus 1:12. . . cruel animals, and lazy ***g-s***.

GNASHING (v)

to grate or grind one's teeth together as an expression of hatred, scorn, or utter despair
Matt 8:12. . . be weeping and *g* of teeth.

GNAT, GNATS (n)

any of various small usually biting dipteran flies
Exod 8:16 . . swarms of ***g-s*** throughout the
Matt 23:24. . swallow a *g*, but you swallow

GOAL (n)

the end toward which effort is directed; aim
1 Cor 14:1 . . be your highest *g!*
2 Cor 5:9 . . . our *g* is to please him.
1 Thes 4:11 . Make it your *g* to live a

GOAT, GOATS (n)

any of various hollow-horned ruminant mammals with backwardly arching horns, a short tail, and usually straight hair
Gen 15:9 . . . a three-year-old female *g*,
Gen 30:32 . . all the sheep and ***g-s*** that are
Gen 37:31 . . killed a young *g* and dipped
Lev 16:9. . . . sin offering the *g* chosen by
Num 7:16 . . and a male *g* for a sin
Num 7:17 . . rams, five male ***g-s***, and five
Isa 11:6. . . . . with the baby *g*.
Dan 8:5 . . . . a male *g* appeared from the
Matt 25:32. . the sheep from the ***g-s***.
Heb 10:4 . . . blood of bulls and ***g-s***

GOD, GODS (n)

eternal, infinite Spirit; Creator, Redeemer, sovereign Lord; impotent pagan diety; image of pagan diety (made of wood, metal, or stone)
see also IDOL(S)
Gen 1:1 . . . . In the beginning ***G*** created
Gen 1:27 . . . In the image of ***G*** he created
Gen 3:1 . . . . Did ***G*** really say you must not
Gen 6:2 . . . . The sons of ***G*** saw the
Gen 14:18 . . a priest of ***G*** Most High,
Gen 17:1 . . . El-Shaddai—'***G*** Almighty.'

Gen 22:12 . . I know that you truly fear *G.*
Gen 50:20 . . *G* intended it all for good.
Exod 20:5 . . am a jealous *G* who will not
Exod 22:28 . must not dishonor *G* or curse
Exod 32:4 . . these are the *g-s* who brought
Exod 34:6 . . The *G* of compassion
Deut 6:4. . . . LORD is our *G,* the LORD
Deut 23:5. . . LORD your *G* loves you.
Deut 32:16. . by worshiping foreign *g-s;* they
Deut 32:39. . There is no other *g* but me!
Deut 33:27. . The eternal *G* is
Josh 24:19 . . a holy and jealous *G.*
1 Kgs 8:23 . . there is no *G* like you
1 Kgs 18:21 . if Baal is *G,* then follow
2 Kgs 19:15 . You alone are *G* of all
Ezra 9:9 . . . . unfailing love our *G* did not
Neh 1:5 . . . . awesome *G* who keeps
Ps 19:1 . . . . . proclaim the glory of *G.*
Ps 22:1 . . . . . My *G,* my *G,* why have
Ps 42:2 . . . . . I thirst for *G,* the living *G.*
Ps 42:8 . . . . . praying to *G* who gives
Ps 51:10 . . . . a clean heart, O *G.*
Ps 82:6 . . . . . say, 'You are *g-s;* you are all
Ps 100:3 . . . . the LORD is *G!*
Ps 139:23 . . . Search me, O *G,* and know
Prov 24:12. . For *G* understands all
Eccl 12:13 . . conclusion: Fear *G* and obey
Isa 9:6. . . . . . Mighty *G,* Everlasting Father,
Isa 43:10. . . . I alone am *G.*
Dan 6:16 . . . May your *G,* whom you
Jonah 4:2 . . . compassionate *G,* slow to
Mic 6:8. . . . . walk humbly with your *G.*
Mic 7:18. . . . Where is another *G* like you,
Nah 1:2 . . . . a jealous *G,* filled with
Mark 2:7 . . . Only *G* can forgive
Mark 3:35 . . Anyone who does *G's* will is
Mark 15:34 . My *G,* my *G,* why
Luke 2:14. . . Glory to *G* in highest
Luke 10:9. . . The Kingdom of *G* is near
Luke 16:13. . cannot serve both *G* and
Luke 20:38. . So he is the *G* of the living,
John 1:1 . . . . Word was with *G*
John 1:18 . . . One, who is himself *G,* is near
John 1:29 . . . The Lamb of *G* who
John 3:16 . . . For *G* loved the world so
John 10:34 . . I say, you are *g-s!*
John 14:1 . . . Trust in *G,* and trust also
Acts 5:29 . . . We must obey *G* rather than
Acts 12:24 . . word of *G* continued to
Acts 19:26 . . aren't really *g-s* at all.
Rom 1:16 . . . the power of *G* at work,
Rom 3:23 . . . short of *G's* glorious
Rom 5:1 . . . . have peace with *G* because
Rom 5:5. . . . know how dearly *G* loves us,
Rom 6:23 . . . free gift of *G* is eternal
Rom 8:17 . . . are heirs of *G's* glory.
Rom 12:2. . . learn to know *G's* will for you,
1 Cor 1:18 . . the very power of *G.*
1 Cor 1:25 . . foolish plan of *G* is wiser
1 Cor 6:20 . . you must honor *G* with your
1 Cor 14:33 . not a *G* of disorder but
2 Cor 10:4 . . We use *G's* mighty weapons,
Gal 3:6 . . . . . believed *G,* and *G* counted him
Eph 2:10 . . . For we are *G's* masterpiece.
Eph 5:1 . . . . Imitate *G,* therefore, in
Phil 2:6 . . . . equality with *G* as something
Phil 4:7 . . . . you will experience *G's* peace,
Col 2:9 . . . . . the fullness of *G* in a human
1 Thes 5:18 . for this is *G's* will
1 Tim 2:5 . . . is only one *G* and one
Titus 1:2. . . . *G*—who does not lie—
Heb 6:18 . . . is impossible for *G* to lie.
Heb 7:19 . . . we draw near to *G.*
Heb 11:6 . . . believe that *G* exists
Jas 2:19. . . . . there is one *G.*
Jas 2:23. . . . . Abraham believed *G,* and *G*
Jas 4:8. . . . . . Come close to *G,* and *G*
1 Pet 2:15. . . It is *G's* will that your
1 Pet 5:5. . . . for "*G* opposes the proud
1 Jn 1:5. . . . . declare to you: *G* is light,
1 Jn 4:21. . . . Those who love *G* must also
Rev 19:6. . . . the Lord our *G,* the Almighty,
Rev 21:23. . . glory of *G* illuminates the

GOD-BREATHED (KJV)
2 Tim 3:16 . . Scripture is ***inspired by God***

GOD-FEARING (adj)
having a reverent feeling toward God; devout
Acts 10:2 . . . was a devout, *G* man,
Acts 10:22 . . is a devout and *G* man,
Acts 13:26 . . and also you *G* Gentiles—this
Acts 17:4 . . . along with many *G* Greek men
Acts 17:17 . . Jews and the *G* Gentiles,

GODDESS (n)
a female god
Acts 19:27 . . of the great *g* Artemis will

GODLESS (adj)
not acknowledging a deity or divine law
see also UNGODLY
Job 20:5 . . . . joy of the *g* has been only
Hos 7:8 . . . . mingle with *g* foreigners,
1 Tim 6:20 . . Avoid *g,* foolish
2 Tim 2:16 . . to more *g* behavior.
Titus 2:12. . . to turn from *g* living and
1 Pet 4:3. . . . things that *g* people enjoy—
1 Pet 4:18. . . will happen to *g* sinners?

GODLINESS (n)
devotion to God; piety
see also RIGHTEOUSNESS
Prov 16:8 . . . Better to have little, with *g*,
1 Tim 4:8 . . . but training for *g* is much
1 Tim 5:4 . . . to show *g* at home
1 Tim 6:6 . . . Yet true *g* with contentment

GODLY (adj)
marked by or showing reverence for God and devotion to worship
see also RIGHTEOUS, UPRIGHT
Ps 31:23 . . . . LORD, all you *g* ones!
Ps 34:9 . . . . . LORD, you his *g* people,
Prov 16:31 . . by living a *g* life.
Prov 23:24 . . The father of *g* children has
Acts 22:12 . . He was a *g* man, deeply
Gal 6:1 . . . . . you who are *g* should gently
1 Tim 6:3 . . . promote a *g* life.
2 Tim 3:12 . . to live a *g* life in Christ
Titus 1:1. . . . how to live *g* lives.
2 Pet 2:9. . . . how to rescue *g* people from
2 Pet 3:11. . . what holy and *g* lives you

GODLY (n)
people who are righteous or devout
Ps 1:5 . . . . . . no place among the *g*.
Ps 37:21 . . . . but the *g* are generous givers.
Ps 37:30 . . . . The *g* offer good counsel;
Ps 68:3 . . . . . But let the *g* rejoice.
Ps 118:20 . . . LORD, and the *g* enter there.
Prov 3:32. . . friendship to the *g*.
Prov 10:11 . . The words of the *g* are a
Prov 10:20 . . The words of the *g* are like
Prov 10:28 . . The hopes of the *g* result in
Prov 11:5 . . . The *g* are directed by
Prov 11:28 . . But the *g* flourish like
Prov 13:9 . . . The life of the *g* is full of
Prov 20:7 . . . The *g* walk with
Prov 21:15 . . Justice is a joy to the *g*,
Prov 28:1 . . . the *g* are as bold as lions.

GOLD (n)
a valuable yellow malleable metal especially used in coins and jewelry
1 Kgs 20:3 . . Your silver and *g* are mine,
Ps 19:10 . . . . more desirable than *g*,
Ps 119:127 . . even the finest *g*.
Prov 3:14 . . . are better than *g*.
Matt 2:11 . . . gifts of *g*, frankincense,
Rev 3:18. . . . advise you to buy *g* from me—

GOLGOTHA (n)
a hill just outside Jerusalem; the place where Jesus was crucified
Matt 27:33 . . a place called *G*
Mark 15:22 . a place called *G*
John 19:17 . . (in Hebrew, *G*).

GOLIATH
Great Philistine warrior killed by David (1 Sam 17:4, 8, 23; 21:9; 22:10; 2 Sam 21:19; 1 Chr 20:5).

GOMORRAH (n)
one of the five "cities of the plain" located in the Valley of Siddim; God destroyed this city by fire for its extreme wickedness
Gen 19:24 . . on Sodom and *G*.
Matt 10:15 . . and *G* will be better
2 Pet 2:6. . . . of Sodom and *G* and turned
Jude 1:7 . . . . forget Sodom and *G* and their

GOOD (adj)
kind; profitable; excellent; fitting or appropriate; morally right
Gen 1:4 . . . . that the light was *g*.
Gen 1:31 . . . it was very *g!*
Gen 2:18 . . . It is not *g* for the man to
2 Chr 7:3 . . . He is *g!* His faithful
2 Chr 31:20 . was pleasing and *g* in the
Ps 34:8 . . . . . see that the LORD is *g*.
Ps 119:68 . . . You are *g* and do only
Eccl 7:20 . . . earth is always *g* and never
Isa 5:20. . . . . that evil is *g* and *g* is
Isa 45:7. . . . . I send *g* times and
Mic 6:8. . . . . told you what is *g*, and this is
Matt 5:29. . . eye—even your *g* eye—causes
Matt 19:17 . . is only One who is *g*.
Matt 22:10 . . they could find, *g* and bad
Matt 25:21 . . Well done, my *g* and
Mark 3:4 . . . the law permit *g* deeds on the
Mark 10:18 . God is truly *g*.
Luke 6:45. . . person produces *g* things from
Luke 6:45. . . treasury of a *g* heart,
Luke 8:15. . . seeds that fell on the *g* soil
Luke 14:34. . Salt is *g* for seasoning.
Luke 18:19. . God is truly *g*.
Luke 19:17. . You are a *g* servant.
John 10:11 . . I am the *g* shepherd.
Rom 7:12. . . and right and *g*.
Rom 7:16. . . that the law is *g*.
Rom 7:18. . . know that nothing *g* lives in
Rom 7:19. . . do what is *g*, but I don't.
Rom 12:2. . . you, which is *g* and pleasing
Rom 12:9. . . Hold tightly to what is *g*.
1 Cor 6:12 . . not everything is *g* for you.
1 Cor 7:1 . . . Yes, it is *g* to abstain
1 Cor 15:33 . corrupts *g* character.
Gal 6:9 . . . . . doing what is *g*.
Eph 2:10 . . . so we can do the *g* things he
Phil 1:6 . . . . who began the *g* work within

1 Thes 5:21 . Hold on to what is *g*.
1 Tim 4:4 . . . everything God created is *g*,
1 Tim 6:12 . . Fight the *g* fight
2 Tim 3:17 . . people to do every *g* work.
2 Tim 4:7 . . . I have fought the *g* fight,
Titus 3:8. . . . These teachings are *g*
Heb 10:24 . . of love and *g* works.
Heb 12:10 . . is always *g* for us,
Jas 2:8. . . . . indeed, it is *g* when you obey

GOOD (n)
something that is excellent, profitable, or morally right; advancement of prosperity or well-being; something useful or beneficial
Gen 2:9 . . . . the knowledge of *g* and evil.
Gen 3:22 . . . knowing both *g* and evil.
Gen 50:20 . . God intended it all for *g*.
1 Sam 26:23. reward for doing *g* and for
Ps 14:1 . . . . . not one of them does *g!*
Ps 53:3 . . . . . No one does *g*, not a single
Prov 3:27. . . Do not withhold *g* from those
Prov 11:27. . If you search for *g*, you will
Prov 31:12. . She brings him *g*, not harm,
Isa 55:2. . . . . does you no *g?*
Jer 13:23. . . . you start doing *g*, for you
Jer 32:39. . . . for their own *g* and for the
Matt 5:45. . . evil and the *g*, and he sends
Rom 3:12. . . No one does *g*, not a single
Rom 8:28. . . together for the *g* of those
Rom 13:4. . . sent for your *g*.
1 Cor 10:24 . but for the *g* of others.
Gal 6:10. . . . we should do *g* to everyone—
Eph 6:8 . . . . each one of us for the *g* we do,
1 Tim 5:10 . . because of the *g* she has
Heb 13:16 . . forget to do *g* and to share
1 Pet 2:20. . . suffer for doing *g* and endure
1 Pet 3:17. . . suffer for doing *g*, if that

GOODNESS (n)
the beneficial quality of something; kindness
Ps 145:7 . . . . the story of your wonderful *g*;
Isa 63:7. . . . . in his great *g* to Israel,
Rom 14:17. . a life of *g* and peace and joy
Rom 15:14. . that you are full of *g*.

GOSPEL (KJV)
Mark 1:1 . . . the *Good News* about Jesus
Luke 4:18. . . anointed me to bring *Good News*
Rom 1:16. . . not ashamed of this *Good News*
Rom 10:15. . feet of messengers who bring *good news*
Gal 3:8 . . . . . proclaimed this *good news*

GOSSIP (n)
rumor or report revealing personal or sensational facts about others
Prov 16:28. . of strife; *g* separates the
Prov 26:20. . disappear when *g* stops.
2 Cor 12:20 . slander, *g*, arrogance,

GOSSIP, GOSSIPING (v)
to relate rumors or reports about others
Ps 15:3 . . . . . who refuse to *g* or harm their
1 Tim 5:13 . . spend their time ***g-ing***

GOVERN (v)
to exercise continuous sovereign authority over; to control or rule
Gen 1:16 . . . larger one to *g* the day,
Gen 1:28 . . . the earth and *g* it.
Gen 49:16 . . Dan will *g* his people, like
Job 34:17 . . . Could God *g* if he hated
Ps 67:4 . . . . . because you *g* the nations

GOVERNMENT (n)
the organization or agency through which a political unit exercises authority
Isa 9:6. . . . . . The *g* will rest on his
Rom 13:6. . . For *g* workers need
Titus 3:1. . . . to submit to the *g* and its

GRACE (n)
God's free and unmerited favor toward sinful humanity
see also FAVOR
Acts 6:8 . . . . full of God's *g* and power,
Acts 14:3 . . . about the *g* of the Lord.
Acts 15:11 . . by the undeserved *g* of the
Acts 20:32 . . message of his *g* that is able
Rom 5:15. . . is God's wonderful *g* and his
Rom 5:21. . . now God's wonderful *g* rules
Rom 6:1. . . . of his wonderful *g?*
Rom 11:5. . . of God's *g*—his undeserved
Rom 12:6. . . In his *g*, God has given us
1 Cor 3:10 . . Because of God's *g* to me,
1 Cor 16:23 . May the *g* of the Lord
2 Cor 4:15 . . And as God's *g* reaches more
2 Cor 9:14 . . of the overflowing *g* God has
Gal 1:15. . . . by his marvelous *g*.
Gal 2:21. . . . do not treat the *g* of God as
Gal 5:4. . . . . away from God's *g*.
Eph 1:7 . . . . in kindness and *g* that he
Eph 2:5 . . . . only by God's *g* that you have
Eph 2:7 . . . . wealth of his *g* and kindness
Eph 2:8 . . . . saved you by his *g* when you
Eph 3:2 . . . . of extending his *g* to you
Eph 3:7 . . . . By God's *g* and mighty
Phil 4:23 . . . May the *g* of the Lord
2 Thes 1:12 . because of the *g* of our God

2 Thes 2:16 . and by his *g* gave us eternal
1 Tim 1:2 . . . Lord give you *g*, mercy,
2 Tim 1:9 . . . show us his *g* through Christ
2 Tim 2:1 . . . strong through the *g* that God
2 Tim 4:22 . . And may his *g* be with all of
Titus 2:11 . . . For the *g* of God has
Titus 3:7. . . . Because of his *g* he declared
Titus 3:15. . . May God's *g* be with you
Heb 4:16 . . . and we will find *g* to help us
Heb 12:15 . . to receive the *g* of God.
Heb 13:9 . . . comes from God's *g*, not from
Heb 13:25 . . May God's *g* be with you all.
Jas 4:6. . . . . gives us even more *g* to stand
1 Pet 5:12. . . Stand firm in this *g*.
2 Pet 3:18. . . grow in the *g* and knowledge
Rev 22:21. . . May the *g* of the Lord

GRACIOUS (adj)
abounding in grace and kindness; merciful, compassionate
2 Kgs 13:23 . the LORD was *g* and merciful
Ps 145:13 . . . he is *g* in all he
Prov 11:16 . . A *g* woman gains
John 1:16 . . . received one *g* blessing after
2 Cor 8:7 . . . also in this *g* act of giving.
Col 4:6 . . . . . your conversation be *g* and
1 Tim 1:14 . . generous and *g* our Lord was!
1 Pet 1:10. . . about this *g* salvation
1 Pet 1:13. . . to the *g* salvation that will

GRAFTED (v)
to unite a shoot or bud with a growing plant so they grow as one
Rom 11:18 . . not brag about being *g* in to

GRANDCHILDREN (n)
the child of one's son or daughter
1 Tim 5:4 . . . children or *g*, their first

GRANDMOTHER (n)
the mother of one's father or mother
2 Tim 1:5 . . . first filled your *g* Lois and

GRANT (n)
property transferred by deed or writing
Josh 14:3 . . . already given a *g* of land to

GRANT, GRANTED (v)
to permit as a right, privilege, or favor; to consent to carry out for a person
Prov 10:24 . . of the godly will be ***g-ed***.
Isa 26:12. . . . LORD, you will *g* us peace;
Matt 15:28 . . Your request is ***g-ed***." And her
John 15:7 . . . and it will be ***g-ed***!

GRAPES (n)
a smooth-skinned juicy greenish-white to deep red or purple berry
Gen 40:10 . . it produced clusters of ripe *g*
Lev 19:10. . . not pick up the *g* that fall
Num 6:3 . . . not eat *g* or raisins
Num 13:23 . single cluster of *g* so large
Deut 32:32. . Their *g* are poison
Job 15:33 . . . a vine whose *g* are harvested
Isa 5:4. . . . . . expected sweet *g*, why did
Isa 63:3. . . . . my enemies as if they were *g*
Matt 7:16 . . . *g* from thornbushes, or figs
Rev 14:19. . . *g* into the great winepress

GRAPEVINE (n)
the vine on which grapes grow
Ps 128:3 . . . . a fruitful *g*, flourishing
Isa 36:16. . . . from your own *g* and fig tree
John 15:1 . . . am the true *g*, and my Father

GRASS (n)
green plants that grow from the ground and are suitable for grazing animals
Isa 40:6. . . . . people are like the *g*.
1 Pet 1:24. . . The *g* withers and

GRAVE, GRAVES (n)
burial place; euphemism for Hades, hell, or Sheol
Ps 5:9 . . . . . . from an open *g*.
Ps 49:15 . . . . power of the *g*.
John 5:28 . . . dead in their ***g-s*** will hear the
Acts 2:27 . . . rot in the *g*.
Rom 3:13 . . . from an open *g*.
Rev 20:13. . . death and the *g* gave up their

GRAVECLOTHES (n)
strips of cloth wrapped around a corpse in preparation for burial
John 11:44 . . and feet bound in *g*, his face

GREAT, GREATER, GREATEST (adj)
huge; remarkable in magnitude, degree, or effectiveness
Deut 10:17 . . He is the *g* God, the mighty
2 Sam 24:14. his mercy is *g*.
Ps 107:8 . . . . LORD for his *g* love and for
Ps 147:5 . . . . How *g* is our LORD!
Dan 9:4 . . . . you are a *g* and awesome God!
Matt 12:41 . . someone ***g-er*** than Jonah is
Matt 12:42 . . ***g-er*** than Solomon
Matt 19:30 . . who are the ***g-est*** now will be
Matt 22:38 . . first and ***g-est*** commandment.
John 3:30 . . . He must become ***g-er***
John 15:13 . . There is no ***g-er*** love than to
1 Cor 13:13 . and the ***g-est*** of these is love.
Rev 20:11. . . I saw a *g* white throne and

GREED (n)
a selfish and excessive desire for more of something (as money) than is needed
Prov 15:27 . . *G* brings grief
Rom 1:29 . . . of wickedness, sin, *g,* hate,
2 Pet 2:3 . . . . In their *g* they will make up
2 Pet 2:14 . . . well trained in *g.*

GREEDY (adj)
having or showing a selfish desire for wealth and possessions
1 Sam 8:3 . . . for they were *g* for money.
Prov 1:19 . . . all who are *g* for money;
Prov 21:26 . . people are always *g*
1 Cor 6:10 . . are thieves, or *g* people,
Eph 5:5 . . . . For a *g* person is an
Col 3:5 . . . . . Don't be *g,* for a *g*

GREEKS (n)
natives or inhabitants of Greece
1 Cor 1:22 . . And it is foolish to the *G,*

GREEN (adj)
of the color green; pleasantly alluring
Ps 23:2 . . . . . lets me rest in *g* meadows;

GREET (v)
to address with expressions of kind wishes upon meeting or arrival
Rom 16:16 . . *G* each other in Christian
1 Cor 16:20 . *G* each other with
2 Cor 13:12 . *G* each other with
1 Thes 5:26 . *G* all the brothers
1 Pet 5:14 . . . *G* each other with

GREW (v)
to increase; to develop in maturity
see also GROW
Luke 1:80 . . . John *g* up and became
Luke 2:52 . . . Jesus *g* in wisdom
Acts 9:31 . . . Spirit, it also *g* in numbers.
Acts 16:5 . . . faith and *g* larger every day.

GRIEF (n)
deep and poignant distress due to bereavement; a cause of suffering
Job 16:5 . . . . take away your *g.*
Ps 10:14 . . . . the trouble and *g* they cause.
Prov 10:1 . . . a foolish child brings *g* to a
Prov 15:27 . . Greed brings *g* to the
John 16:20 . . your *g* will suddenly turn
Rom 9:2 . . . . sorrow and unending *g*

GRIEVE, GRIEVED (v)
to feel, show, or cause distress, vexation, sorrow, or regret
Eccl 3:4 . . . . A time to *g* and a time
Isa 63:10 . . . . rebelled against him and ***g-d***
Lam 3:20 . . . time, as I *g* over my loss.
1 Thes 4:13 . so you will not *g* like people

GROAN, GROANINGS, GROANINGS (n)
a deep moan indicative of pain, grief, or annoyance
Exod 2:24 . . God heard their ***g-ing,*** and he
Ps 90:9 . . . . . ending our years with a *g.*
Rom 8:26 . . . for us with ***g-ings*** that cannot

GROAN, GROANING (v)
to utter a deep moan indicative of pain, grief, or annoyance
Job 35:9 . . . . They *g* beneath the power
Rom 8:22 . . . creation has been ***g-ing*** as
Rom 8:23 . . . believers also *g,* even though
2 Cor 5:4 . . . bodies, we *g* and sigh,

GROUND (n)
soil, earth, or territory
Gen 1:10 . . . called the dry *g* "land" and
Gen 3:17 . . . the *g* is cursed because of you.
Gen 4:2 . . . . Cain cultivated the *g.*
Gen 4:10 . . . cries out to me from the *g!*
Exod 3:5 . . . standing on holy *g.*
Exod 15:19 . sea on dry *g!*
Isa 53:2 . . . . . like a root in dry *g.*
Matt 10:29 . . fall to the *g* without your

GROW, GROWING, GROWS (v)
to become; to spring up and develop to maturity
see also GREW
Isa 40:31 . . . . run and not *g* weary.
1 Cor 3:6 . . . God who made it *g.*
Eph 4:16 . . . is healthy and ***g-ing*** and full of
Phil 1:25 . . . all of you *g* and experience
Col 2:19 . . . . it ***g-s*** as God nourishes it.
2 Thes 1:3 . . one another is ***g-ing.***
Jas 1:15 . . . . . when sin is allowed to *g,*
2 Pet 3:18 . . . Rather, you must *g* in the

GRUDGE (n)
a feeling of deep-seated resentment or ill will
Mark 11:25 . you are holding a *g* against,

GRUMBLE (v)
to mutter in discontent
1 Cor 10:10 . And don't *g* as some
Jas 5:9 . . . . . . Don't *g* about each other

GRUMBLERS (n)
those who mutter in discontent
Jude 1:16 . . . people are *g* and complainers,

GUARANTEE (n)
an assurance for the fulfillment of a condition
2 Cor 5:5 . . . and as a *g* he has given us

GUARANTEED, GUARANTEEING, GUARANTEES (v)
to assure that some agreement or condition will be fulfilled; to give security for
Ps 111:9 . . . . He has *g* his covenant
2 Cor 1:22 . . first installment that ***g-s***
Eph 4:30 . . . ***g-ing*** that you will be saved
Heb 7:22 . . . is the one who ***g-s*** this better

GUARD (adj)
defensively watchful; alert
2 Pet 3:17. . . Be on *g* so that you

GUARD, GUARDING, GUARDS (v)
to protect by watchful attention; to watch over
see also KEEP
Prov 4:23. . . *G* your heart
Prov 7:2. . . . as you *g* your own eyes.
Prov 24:12. . He who ***g-s*** your soul knows
Luke 2:8. . . . fields nearby, ***g-ing*** their flocks
Phil 4:7 . . . . His peace will *g* your hearts
2 Thes 3:3 . . and *g* you from

GUARDIAN (n)
one caring for the person or property of another
Gen 4:9 . . . . Am I my brother's *g*?
Gal 3:25 . . . . the law as our *g*.
1 Pet 2:25. . . your Shepherd, the *G* of your

GUIDANCE (n)
direction or counsel provided by another person
2 Chr 26:5 . . as the king sought *g* from
Prov 24:6. . . go to war without wise *g*;
Prov 29:18. . do not accept divine *g*,

GUIDE, GUIDED, GUIDES, GUIDING (v)
to direct, supervise, or influence usually to a particular end
Exod 13:21 . He ***g-d*** them during the
Exod 15:13 . In your might, you *g* them
Deut 1:33. . . ***g-ing*** you with a pillar of fire
Job 10:10 . . . ***g-d*** my conception and formed
Ps 16:7 . . . . . bless the LORD who ***g-s*** me;
Ps 23:3 . . . . . He ***g-s*** me along
Ps 32:8 . . . . . I will *g* you along
Ps 139:10 . . . your hand will *g* me,
John 16:13 . . he will *g* you into all
Gal 5:16 . . . . let the Holy Spirit *g* your lives.
Jas 2:4. . . . . . are ***g-d*** by evil motives?

GUIDES (n)
those who lead or direct another's way
Matt 23:16 . . Blind *g*! What sorrow
Matt 23:24 . . Blind *g*! You strain

GUILT (n)
the state or feeling of one who has committed an offense
Job 6:29 . . . . Stop assuming my *g*, for I
Ps 32:2 . . . . . the LORD has cleared of *g*,
Ps 38:4 . . . . . My *g* overwhelms me—
Ps 51:2 . . . . . Wash me clean from my *g*.
Isa 6:7. . . . . . Now your *g* is removed,
Dan 9:24 . . . atone for their *g*, to bring

GUILTY (adj)
justly chargeable with wrongdoing
Lev 19:17. . . not be held *g* for their sin.
Rom 3:19 . . . entire world is *g* before God.
1 Cor 11:27 . *g* of sinning against
1 Jn 3:20. . . . if we feel *g*, God is greater
1 Jn 3:21. . . . we don't feel *g*, we can come

HAGAR
Sarah's Egyptian servant and rival, mother of Ishmael (Gen 16); sent away by Abraham, son's cries heard by God (Gen 21:9-21); Paul's analogy using Hagar and Sarah (Gal 4:24-25).

HAIL (n)
precipitation in the form of small balls of ice and snow
Exod 9:19 . . die when the ***h*** falls.
Ps 18:12 . . . . rained down ***h*** and
Rev 8:7. . . . . his trumpet, and ***h*** and fire

HAIR, HAIRS (n)
a slender threadlike outgrowth of the skin of an animal or human
Lev 19:27. . . Do not trim off the ***h*** on your
2 Sam 18:9. . his ***h*** got caught in the tree.
Matt 10:30. . And the very ***h-s*** on your head
1 Cor 11:6 . . to have her ***h*** cut or her head
1 Cor 11:14 . man to have long ***h?***
1 Cor 11:15 . And isn't long ***h*** a woman's
Rev 1:14. . . . His head and his ***h*** were white

HAIRSTYLES (n)
a way of wearing the hair
1 Pet 3:3. . . . outward beauty of fancy ***h,***

HAIRY (adj)
covered with hair
Gen 27:11. . . Esau, is a ***h*** man, and my skin

HALF, HALVES (n)
either of two equal parts that compose something
Gen 15:17 . . the ***h-ves*** of the carcasses.
1 Kgs 3:25 . . to one woman and ***h*** to the
1 Kgs 10:7 . . not heard the ***h*** of it!
Esth 5:3 . . . . if it is ***h*** the kingdom!
Dan 7:25 . . . a time, times, and ***h*** a time.
Jer 34:18. . . . between its ***h-ves*** to solemnize
Mark 6:23 . . ask, up to ***h*** my kingdom!

HALLELUJAH (KJV)
Rev 19:1. . . . shouting, ***"Praise the Lord!***
Rev 19:3. . . . rang out: ***"Praise the Lord!***
Rev 19:4. . . . "Amen! ***Praise the Lord!"***
Rev 19:6. . . . ***"Praise the Lord!*** For the Lord

HALLOW(ED) (KJV)
Exod 20:11 . Sabbath day and ***set*** it ***apart as holy***
Lev 25:10. . . ***Set*** this year ***apart as holy***
1 Kgs 9:3 . . . ***set*** this Temple ***apart to be holy***
Matt 6:9. . . . ***may*** your name ***be kept holy***

HAND, HANDS (n)
the end of the arm that serves as a grasping and handling tool for humans; symbolic of power
Gen 47:29 . . Put your ***h*** under my
Exod 15:6 . . Your right ***h,*** O Lord,
Exod 29:10 . will lay their ***h-s*** on its head.
Exod 33:22 . cover you with my ***h*** until
1 Kgs 13:4 . . king's ***h*** became paralyzed
Ps 22:16 . . . . have pierced my ***h-s*** and feet.
Ps 24:4 . . . . . those whose ***h-s*** and hearts
Ps 32:4 . . . . . your ***h*** of discipline
Ps 44:3 . . . . . It was your right ***h*** and
Ps 63:4 . . . . . my ***h-s*** to you in prayer.
Ps 75:8 . . . . . a cup in his ***h*** that is full
Ps 110:1 . . . . at my right ***h*** until I humble
Ps 137:5 . . . . let my right ***h*** forget how to
Ps 145:16 . . . you open your ***h,*** you satisfy
Isa 40:12. . . . the oceans in his ***h?***
Isa 41:13. . . . by your right ***h***—I, the Lord
Isa 55:12. . . . will clap their ***h-s!***
Isa 64:8. . . . . formed by your ***h.***
Dan 10:10 . . Just then a ***h*** touched me
Matt 5:30. . . And if your ***h***—even your
Matt 6:3. . . . don't let your left ***h*** know what
Matt 18:8. . . with only one ***h*** or one foot
Matt 26:64. . at God's right ***h*** and coming

Mark 12:36 . at my right ***h*** until I humble
Acts 6:6 . . . . they laid their ***h-s*** on them.
Acts 7:55 . . . at God's right ***h.***
Acts 8:18 . . . laid their ***h-s*** on people,
Acts 13:3 . . . men laid their ***h-s*** on them
Acts 19:6 . . . Paul laid his ***h-s*** on them,
Acts 28:8 . . . and laying his ***h-s*** on him,
1 Thes 4:11 . working with your ***h-s,***
1 Tim 2:8 . . . pray with holy ***h-s*** lifted up
1 Tim 4:14 . . church laid their ***h-s*** on you.
2 Tim 1:6 . . . when I laid my ***h-s*** on you.
Heb 1:13 . . . at my right ***h*** until I humble
Rev 13:16. . . mark on the right ***h*** or on the

HANDED (v)
to yield control of
Rom 4:25 . . . He was ***h*** over to die
1 Tim 1:20 . . them out and ***h*** them over

HANDFUL (n)
a small quantity or number
Eccl 4:6 . . . . to have one ***h*** with quietness

HANDSOME (adj)
having a pleasing and unusually impressive appearance; beautiful
Gen 39:6 . . . Joseph was a very ***h*** and
1 Sam 16:12. dark and ***h,*** with beautiful
2 Sam 14:25. as the most ***h*** man in all Israel.
1 Kgs 1:6 . . . he was very ***h.***
Ezek 23:6. . . commanders dressed in ***h*** blue,

HANGED, HANGING, HANGS (v)
to suspend; to execute (on a tree or gallows)
see also HUNG
Job 26:7 . . . . ***h-s*** the earth on nothing.
Matt 27:5. . . went out and ***h-ed*** himself.
Acts 10:39 . . death by ***h-ing*** him on a cross,

HAPPINESS (n)
a state of well-being and contentment; joy
Deut 24:5. . . ***h*** to the wife he has married.
Job 7:7 . . . . . never again feel ***h.***
Job 9:25 . . . . a glimpse of ***h.***
Ps 86:4 . . . . . Give me ***h,*** O LORD,
Ps 119:35 . . . that is where my ***h*** is found.
Eccl 8:15 . . . ***h*** along with all the hard work
Isa 65:18. . . . Jerusalem as a place of ***h.***
Luke 6:24. . . you have your only ***h*** now.

HAPPY (adj)
expressing, reflecting, or suggestive of happiness
see also BLESSED
Deut 16:14. . festival will be a ***h*** time
Ps 113:9 . . . . making her a ***h*** mother.
Prov 15:13 . . A glad heart makes a ***h*** face;
Prov 15:15 . . for the ***h*** heart, life is
Eccl 9:7 . . . . drink your wine with a ***h*** heart,
Zech 10:7. . . will be made ***h*** as if by wine.
Rom 12:15 . . Be ***h*** with those who are ***h,***
Phil 2:2 . . . . make me truly ***h*** by agreeing
Jas 5:13. . . . . Are any of you ***h?***

HARBOR (n)
a part of a body of water where ships dock; a place of security and comfort
Ps 107:30 . . . brought them safely into ***h!***

HARD (adj)
lacking in responsiveness, unfeeling; demanding the exertion of energy
Rom 11:25 . . of Israel have ***h*** hearts,
Rev 2:2. . . . . I have seen your ***h*** work and

HARD, HARDER (adv)
with great or utmost effort or energy
Prov 13:4 . . . those who work ***h***
Acts 20:35 . . in need by working ***h.***
Rom 16:12 . . has worked so ***h***
1 Cor 15:10 . worked ***h-er*** than any of
2 Cor 11:23 . worked ***h-er,*** been put in
1 Thes 5:12 . They work ***h*** among you
2 Thes 3:8 . . We worked ***h*** day and night

HARD-HEARTED (adj)
lacking in sympathetic understanding; unfeeling
Deut 15:7. . . do not be ***h*** or tightfisted

HARDEN, HARDENED (v)
to make callous or unfeeling
Exod 4:21 . . But I will ***h*** his heart
Exod 10:20 . LORD ***h-ed*** Pharaoh's heart
Ps 95:8 . . . . . Don't ***h*** your hearts as Israel did
Isa 6:10. . . . . ***H*** the hearts of these people.
Matt 13:15 . . hearts of these people are ***h-ed,***
John 12:40 . . and ***h-ed*** their hearts—
Eph 4:18 . . . minds and ***h-ed*** their hearts
Heb 3:8 . . . . don't ***h*** your hearts as Israel did

HARDSHIPS (n)
things that cause or entail suffering or privation
Acts 14:22 . . must suffer many ***h*** to enter
2 Cor 6:4 . . . troubles and ***h*** and calamities
2 Thes 1:4 . . and ***h*** you are suffering.
Jas 5:13. . . . . Are any of you suffering ***h?***

HARLOT (KJV)
Gen 38:15 . . thought she was a ***prostitute***
Josh 2:1 . . . . a ***prostitute*** named Rahab
Hos 4:15 . . . you, Israel, are a ***prostitute***
Matt 21:31 . . ***prostitutes*** will get into the Kingdom
Rev 17:5. . . . Mother of All ***Prostitutes*** and

HARM (n)
physical or mental damage; injury, hurt
Ps 37:8 . . . . . it only leads to ***h.***
Prov 3:29 . . . Don't plot ***h*** against your
Prov 19:23 . . and protection from ***h.***
Prov 31:12 . . brings him good, not ***h,*** all
1 Cor 11:17 . more ***h*** than good is done

HARM, HARMED, HARMS (v)
to injure or hurt
Ps 121:6 . . . . sun will not ***h*** you by day,
Jer 10:5. . . . . they can neither ***h*** you nor do
Zech 2:8. . . . who ***h-s*** you ***h-s*** my most
Rev 2:11. . . . will not be ***h-ed*** by the second

HARMLESS (adj)
lacking capacity or intent to injure
Matt 10:16 . . shrewd as snakes and ***h*** as

HARMONY (n)
tranquility; agreement; unity
Zech 6:13. . . will be perfect ***h*** between his
Rom 12:16 . . Live in ***h*** with each other.
Rom 14:19 . . aim for ***h*** in the church
Rom 15:5 . . . live in complete ***h*** with each
1 Cor 12:25 . This makes for ***h***
2 Cor 6:15 . . What ***h*** can there be
2 Cor 13:11 . Live in ***h*** and peace.
Col 3:14 . . . . together in perfect ***h.***

HARP, HARPS (n)
a plucked stringed instrument
Gen 4:21 . . . all who play the ***h*** and flute.
1 Sam 16:23. would play the ***h.***
Ps 33:2 . . . . . on the ten-stringed ***h.***
Ps 98:5 . . . . . with the ***h*** and melodious song,
Ps 137:2 . . . . our ***h-s,*** hanging them
Ps 144:9 . . . . a ten-stringed ***h.***
Ps 147:7 . . . . praises to our God with a ***h.***
Ps 150:3 . . . . praise him with the lyre and ***h!***
Rev 5:8. . . . . Each one had a ***h,*** and they

HARSH (adj)
causing a disagreeable reaction; unduly exacting
Prov 15:1 . . . ***h*** words make tempers flare.
Eph 4:31 . . . rage, anger, ***h*** words,

HARVEST, HARVESTS (n)
the time or fruit of reaping or gathering in a crop – physically or spiritually
Deut 16:15. . blesses you with bountiful ***h-s***
Matt 9:37 . . . The ***h*** is great, but
John 4:35 . . . fields are already ripe for ***h.***
1 Cor 15:23 . raised as the first of the ***h;***
2 Cor 9:10 . . great ***h*** of generosity
Gal 6:9 . . . . . we will reap a ***h*** of blessing
Heb 12:11 . . peaceful ***h*** of right living
Jas 3:18. . . . . reap a ***h*** of righteousness.
Rev 14:15. . . the time of ***h*** has come;

HARVEST, HARVESTS (v)
to gather in (a crop); to reap
Gen 8:22 . . . there will be planting and ***h,***
Job 4:8 . . . . . and cultivate evil will ***h***
Prov 10:5. . . wise youth ***h-s*** in the summer,
Gal 6:8 . . . . . sinful nature will ***h*** decay and

HARVESTER, HARVESTERS (n)
one who gathers in (a crop)
Ruth 2:3. . . . to gather grain behind the ***h-s.***
John 4:36 . . . planter and the ***h*** alike!

HASTE (n)
rash or headlong action; swiftness
Prov 19:2. . . ***h*** makes mistakes.

HASTY (adj)
done or made in a hurry; impatient; speedy
Prov 21:5. . . ***h*** shortcuts lead to poverty.
Eccl 5:2 . . . . don't be ***h*** in bringing matters

HATE, HATED, HATES, HATING (v)
to feel extreme enmity toward; to have a strong aversion to
Ps 45:7 . . . . . love justice and ***h*** evil.
Prov 1:22. . . you fools ***h*** knowledge?
Prov 6:16. . . six things the LORD ***h-s*** –
Prov 13:5. . . The godly ***h*** lies;
Prov 15:27. . those who ***h*** bribes will live.
Prov 26:28. . A lying tongue ***h-s*** its victims,
Prov 28:16. . but one who ***h-s*** corruption
Mal 2:16. . . . "For I ***h*** divorce!"
Matt 5:43. . . and ***h*** your enemy.
Matt 24:9. . . be ***h-d*** all over the world
Luke 6:22. . . when people ***h*** you
John 3:20 . . . All who do evil ***h*** the light
John 15:18 . . remember that it ***h-d*** me
2 Tim 3:3 . . . be cruel and ***h*** what is good.
Heb 1:9 . . . . You love justice and ***h*** evil.
1 Jn 2:9. . . . . ***h-s*** a Christian brother or
1 Jn 4:20. . . . ***h-s*** a Christian brother or
Jude 1:23 . . . ***h-ing*** the sins that contaminate

HATERS (n)
one who feels or expresses enmity or aversion
Rom 1:30 . . . are backstabbers, ***h*** of God,

HATRED (n)
strong emotional aversion
Lev 19:17. . . Do not nurse ***h*** in your heart
Prov 26:24. . People may cover their ***h***

HAUGHTY (adj)
blatantly and disdainfully proud
Prov 6:17 . . . ***h*** eyes, a lying tongue,
Prov 21:24 . . are proud and ***h;*** they act

HAY (n)
herbage and especially grass mowed and cured for fodder
1 Cor 3:12 . . jewels, wood, ***h,*** or straw.

HEAD, HEADS (n)
top part of the body that contains the brain; one in charge; person, individual
Gen 3:15 . . . He will strike your ***h,*** and
Lev 26:13 . . . walk with your ***h-s*** held high.
Ps 22:7 . . . . . shake their ***h-s,*** saying,
Ps 23:5 . . . . . by anointing my ***h*** with oil.
Ps 133:2 . . . . over Aaron's ***h,*** that ran
Prov 25:22 . . coals of shame on their ***h-s,***
Matt 27:39 . . shaking their ***h-s*** in mockery.
John 19:2 . . . thorns and put it on his ***h,***
Acts 18:6 . . . your own ***h-s***—I am innocent.
Rom 12:20 . . coals of shame on their ***h-s.***
Eph 1:22 . . . and has made him ***h*** over all
Eph 5:23 . . . as Christ is the ***h*** of the
Rev 4:4 . . . . . crowns on their ***h-s.***
Rev 14:14 . . . He had a gold crown on his ***h***
Rev 19:12 . . . on his ***h*** were many crowns.

HEADCLOTH (n)
portion of burial garb covering the head and face
John 11:44 . . wrapped in a ***h.***

HEAL, HEALED, HEALING, HEALS (v)
to mend, cure, make whole; to restore to health
Gen 20:17 . . and God ***h-ed*** Abimelech,
Exod 15:26 . I am the LORD who ***h-s*** you.
Num 12:13 . I beg you, please ***h*** her!
Deut 32:39 . . one who wounds and ***h-s;***
2 Chr 30:20 . prayer and ***h-ed*** the people.
Job 5:18 . . . . his hands also ***h.***
Ps 6:2 . . . . . . ***H*** me, LORD,
Ps 103:3 . . . . and ***h-s*** all my diseases.
Ps 107:20 . . . his word and ***h-ed*** them,
Prov 3:8 . . . . will have ***h-ing*** for your body
Prov 13:17 . . messenger brings ***h-ing.***
Isa 6:10 . . . . . and turn to me for ***h-ing.***
Isa 30:26 . . . . LORD begins to ***h*** his people
Isa 57:18 . . . . but I will ***h*** them anyway!
Isa 57:19 . . . . the LORD, who ***h-s*** them.
Jer 8:18 . . . . . My grief is beyond ***h-ing;***
Jer 17:14 . . . . O LORD, if you ***h*** me, I will
Jer 17:14 . . . . I will be truly ***h-ed;***
Jer 30:13 . . . . No medicine can ***h*** you.
Hos 6:1 . . . . now he will ***h*** us.
Hos 7:1 . . . . I want to ***h*** Israel, but its
Hos 14:4 . . . Then I will ***h*** you of your
Zech 11:16 . . nor ***h*** the injured,
Mal 4:2 . . . . . with ***h-ing*** in his wings.
Matt 4:23 . . . And he ***h-ed*** every kind
Matt 8:7 . . . . will come and ***h*** him.
Matt 8:16 . . . and he ***h-ed*** all the sick.
Matt 9:35 . . . he ***h-ed*** every kind of disease
Matt 10:8 . . . ***H*** the sick, raise the
Matt 15:30 . . Jesus, and he ***h-ed*** them all.
Matt 17:16 . . they couldn't ***h*** him.
Mark 1:34 . . So Jesus ***h-ed*** many people
Mark 3:2 . . . If he ***h-ed*** the man's
Mark 3:10 . . He had ***h-ed*** many people
Mark 5:28 . . touch his robe, I will be ***h-ed.***
Mark 6:5 . . . sick people and ***h*** them.
Mark 6:13 . . and ***h-ed*** many sick
Mark 6:56 . . who touched him were ***h-ed.***
Mark 10:52 . your faith has ***h-ed*** you.
Luke 4:23 . . . Physician, ***h*** yourself
Luke 4:40 . . . his hand ***h-ed*** every one.
Luke 6:7 . . . . If he ***h-ed*** the man's
Luke 8:50 . . . faith, and she will be ***h-ed.***
Luke 10:9 . . . ***H*** the sick, and tell them
Luke 13:14 . . indignant that Jesus had ***h-ed***
Luke 14:3 . . . ***h*** people on the Sabbath
Luke 14:4 . . . the sick man and ***h-ed*** him
Luke 17:19 . . Your faith has ***h-ed*** you.
Luke 18:42 . . Your faith has ***h-ed*** you.
Luke 22:51 . . man's ear and ***h-ed*** him.
John 4:47 . . . to Capernaum to ***h*** his son,
John 7:23 . . . angry with me for ***h-ing*** a man
John 12:40 . . and have me ***h*** them.
Acts 3:16 . . . this man was ***h-ed***—
Acts 4:9 . . . . to know how he was ***h-ed?***
Acts 4:14 . . . see the man who had been ***h-ed***
Acts 4:22 . . . sign—the ***h-ing*** of a man
Acts 8:7 . . . . or lame were ***h-ed.***
Acts 9:34 . . . Jesus Christ ***h-s*** you! Get up,
Acts 10:38 . . and ***h-ing*** all who were
Acts 28:8 . . . his hands on him, he ***h-ed***
Acts 28:27 . . turn to me and let me ***h***
1 Cor 12:28 . the gift of ***h-ing,***
1 Cor 12:30 . have the gift of ***h-ing?***
Jas 5:16 . . . . . so that you may be ***h-ed.***
1 Pet 2:24 . . . By his wounds you are ***h-ed.***
Rev 13:3 . . . . fatal wound was ***h-ed!***
Rev 13:12 . . . wound had been ***h-ed.***

HEALING (adj)
marked by restoring to original purity or integrity
Luke 6:19 . . . ***h*** power went out from him,
Acts 4:30 . . . your hand with ***h*** power;

HEALTH (n)
the general condition of the body
Ps 38:3 . . . . . my ***h*** is broken because of
Ps 38:7 . . . . . and my ***h*** is broken.
Prov 15:30 . . makes for good ***h.***
Isa 38:16. . . . You restore my ***h***
Jer 30:17. . . . I will give you back your ***h***

HEALTHY, HEALTHIER (adj)
enjoying good health and vigor of body, mind, or spirit
Ps 73:4 . . . . . bodies are so ***h*** and strong.
Prov 16:24 . . the soul and ***h*** for the body.
Dan 1:15 . . . friends looked ***h-ier*** and better
Zech 11:16. . nor feed the ***h.*** Instead,
Matt 9:12. . . he said, "***H*** people don't need
Mark 2:17 . . "***H*** people don't need
Luke 5:31. . . answered them, "***H*** people
Eph 4:16 . . . whole body is ***h*** and growing
3 Jn 1:2. . . . . that you are as ***h*** in body as

HEAP (v)
to pile in great quantity; to load heavily
Prov 25:22. . You will ***h*** burning coals of
Rom 12:20. . you will ***h*** burning coals of

HEAR, HEARD, HEARING (v)
to perceive sound; to listen with attention; to be informed of; to take testimony from and make a legal decision
see also LISTEN
Gen 3:8 . . . . and his wife ***h-d*** the LORD God
Exod 2:24 . . God ***h-d*** their groaning,
Deut 1:16. . . judges, 'You must ***h*** the cases
Josh 7:9 . . . . people living in the land ***h***
1 Kgs 8:30 . . May you ***h*** the humble
2 Chr 7:14 . . I will ***h*** from heaven and will
Neh 1:11 . . . O LORD, please ***h*** my prayer!
Ps 5:1 . . . . . . O LORD, ***h*** me as I pray;
Ps 89:1 . . . . . Young and old will ***h*** of your
Isa 29:18. . . . the deaf will ***h*** words read
Isa 30:21. . . . own ears will ***h*** him.
Isa 40:28. . . . Have you never ***h-d***?
Isa 59:1. . . . . too deaf to ***h*** you call.
Dan 10:12 . . has been ***h-d*** in heaven.
Matt 5:21 . . . have ***h-d*** that our ancestors
Matt 5:43 . . . You have ***h-d*** the law
Matt 11:5. . . cured, the deaf ***h,*** the dead
Matt 13:14. . When you ***h*** what I say,
Mark 4:12 . . When they ***h*** what I say,
Luke 7:22. . . cured, the deaf ***h,*** the dead
John 8:26 . . . what I have ***h-d*** from the one
Acts 2:6 . . . . When they ***h-d*** the loud noise,
Acts 13:7 . . . he wanted to ***h*** the word of
Rom 10:14. . how can they ***h*** about him
Rom 10:17. . faith comes from ***h-ing,***
1 Cor 2:9 . . . no ear has ***h-d,*** and no mind
1 Cor 12:17 . how would you ***h?***
Heb 3:7 . . . . Today when you ***h*** his voice,
2 Jn 1:6. . . . . just as you ***h-d*** from the
Rev 3:20. . . . If you ***h*** my voice and
Rev 22:8. . . . I, John, am the one who ***h-d***

HEART, HEARTS (n)
figuratively, the seat of emotions, thoughts, and intentions; personality, disposition; courage; love, affection; central or most vital part of something
Gen 6:6 . . . . It broke his ***h.***
Exod 4:21 . . will harden his ***h*** so he
Exod 35:21 . All whose ***h-s*** were stirred
Deut 6:5. . . . LORD your God with all your ***h,***
Deut 9:10. . . from the ***h*** of the fire
Deut 20:3. . . Do not lose ***h*** or panic
Deut 28:65. . will cause your ***h*** to tremble,
Josh 22:5 . . . with all your ***h*** and all your
Josh 23:14 . . Deep in your ***h-s*** you know
1 Sam 1:15. . pouring out my ***h***
1 Sam 10:9. . God gave him a new ***h,***
1 Sam 12:20. the LORD with all your ***h,***
1 Sam 13:14. a man after his own ***h.***
1 Sam 16:7. . but the LORD looks at the ***h.***
1 Kgs 8:48 . . with their whole ***h*** and soul
1 Kgs 11:2 . . turn your ***h-s*** to their gods.
1 Kgs 11:3 . . turn his ***h*** away from the LORD.
1 Kgs 14:8 . . followed me with all his ***h***
2 Kgs 23:3 . . with all his ***h*** and soul.
1 Chr 22:19 . God with all your ***h*** and soul.
2 Chr 6:38 . . with their whole ***h*** and soul
2 Chr 22:9 . . sought the LORD with all his ***h.***
2 Chr 34:31 . with all his ***h*** and soul.
Ezra 1:5 . . . . stirred the ***h-s*** of the priests
Job 4:5 . . . . . trouble strikes, you lose ***h.***
Ps 9:1 . . . . . . praise you, LORD, with all my ***h;***
Ps 14:1 . . . . . say in their ***h-s,*** "There is no
Ps 19:14 . . . . meditation of my ***h***
Ps 24:4 . . . . . whose hands and ***h-s*** are pure,
Ps 27:8 . . . . . my ***h*** responds, "LORD,
Ps 36:1 . . . . . within their ***h-s.*** They have no
Ps 42:11 . . . . Why is my ***h*** so sad?
Ps 45:1 . . . . . Beautiful words stir my ***h.***
Ps 51:10 . . . . Create in me a clean ***h,*** O God.
Ps 57:7 . . . . . my ***h*** is confident.
Ps 73:7 . . . . . everything their ***h-s*** could ever
Ps 73:26 . . . . the strength of my ***h;***
Ps 108:1 . . . . with all my ***h!***
Ps 111:1 . . . . thank the LORD with all my ***h***
Ps 119:2 . . . . with all their ***h-s.***
Ps 119:11 . . . hidden your word in my ***h,***
Ps 119:58 . . . With all my ***h*** I want your
Ps 119:145 . . I pray with all my ***h;***

Ps 139:23 . . . and know my *h;* test me and
Prov 3:3. . . . deep within your *h.*
Prov 4:23. . . Guard your *h* above all else,
Prov 13:12. . deferred makes the *h* sick,
Prov 14:30. . A peaceful *h* leads to a
Prov 15:13. . a broken *h* crushes the
Prov 15:30. . look brings joy to the *h;*
Prov 17:22. . A cheerful *h* is good
Prov 20:9. . . have cleansed my *h;* I am pure
Prov 23:15. . wise, my own *h* will rejoice!
Prov 27:23. . and put your *h* into caring
Song 4:9. . . . captured my *h,* my treasure,
Song 5:2. . . . I slept, but my *h* was awake,
Song 5:4. . . . and my *h* thrilled within me.
Song 8:6. . . . like a seal over your *h,*
Isa 1:5. . . . . . and your *h* is sick.
Isa 6:10. . . . . Harden the *h-s* of these people.
Isa 42:4. . . . . or lose *h* until justice
Jer 3:15. . . . . shepherds after my own *h,*
Jer 3:22. . . . . your wayward *h-s.*
Jer 9:26. . . . . have uncircumcised *h-s.*
Jer 20:9. . . . . burns in my *h* like a fire.
Jer 32:39. . . . will give them one *h* and one
Ezek 44:7. . . who have no *h* for God.
Joel 2:12. . . . Give me your *h-s.* Come with
Matt 5:8. . . . those whose *h-s* are pure,
Matt 5:28. . . adultery with her in his *h.*
Matt 11:29. . I am humble and gentle at *h,*
Matt 12:34. . whatever is in your *h*
Matt 15:19. . For from the *h* come evil
Matt 18:35. . and sisters from your *h.*
Matt 22:37. . God with all your *h,* all your
Mark 11:23 . have no doubt in your *h.*
Mark 12:30 . God with all your *h,* all your
Mark 12:33 . love him with all my *h* and
Luke 6:45. . . treasury of a good *h,*
Luke 10:27. . God with all your *h,* all your
Luke 12:34. . desires of your *h* will also
Luke 24:38. . Why are your *h-s* filled with
John 5:38 . . . your *h-s,* because you do not
Acts 1:24 . . . you know every *h.* Show us
Acts 4:32 . . . were united in *h* and mind.
Acts 8:21 . . . this, for your *h* is not right
Acts 15:8 . . . God knows people's *h-s,* and
Acts 16:14 . . Lord opened her *h,* and she
Acts 28:27 . . hear, and their *h-s* cannot
Rom 1:9. . . . with all my *h* by spreading
Rom 2:15. . . written in their *h-s,* for their
Rom 2:29. . . changed *h* seeks praise
Rom 10:9. . . believe in your *h* that God
2 Cor 2:4 . . . with a troubled *h* and many
2 Cor 7:2 . . . Please open your *h-s* to us.
2 Cor 9:7 . . . decide in your *h* how much to
Eph 1:18 . . . I pray that your *h-s* will be
Eph 3:13 . . . don't lose *h* because of my
Eph 5:19 . . . music to the Lord in your *h-s.*
Eph 6:6 . . . . of God with all your *h.*
Phil 1:7 . . . . place in my *h.* You share with
1 Tim 1:5 . . . comes from a pure *h,* a clear

HEARTLESS (adj)
lacking feeling; cruel
Rom 1:31 . . . promises, are *h,* and have no

HEATHEN, HEATHENS (n)
one who does not worship the true God; uncivilized; without religion
Acts 7:51 . . . You are *h* at heart and deaf to
Eph 2:11 . . . called "uncircumcised *h-s*" by

HEAVEN, HEAVENS (n)
sky and stars above; God's dwelling place; abode of eternal bliss
Deut 30:12. . is not kept in *h,* so distant
Job 41:11 . . . Everything under *h* is mine.
Ps 18:16 . . . . down from *h* and rescued me;
Ps 71:19 . . . . to the highest *h-s.* You have
Ps 108:4 . . . . than the *h-s.* Your faithfulness
Matt 11:25 . . Father, Lord of *h* and earth,
Matt 24:30 . . appear in the *h-s,* and there
Rom 10:6 . . . go up to *h?'* (to bring Christ
2 Cor 12:2 . . to the third *h* fourteen years
Heb 9:24 . . . He entered into *h* itself to

HEAVENLY (adj)
celestial; of or pertaining to God in the highest
Ps 29:1 . . . . . the LORD, you *h* beings;

HEIR, HEIRS (n)
one who succeeds to a hereditary title; one who inherits
see also INHERIT(ANCE)
Isa 11:10. . . . In that day the *h* to David's
Rom 8:17 . . . with Christ we are *h-s* of God's

HELL (n)
abode of the dead; place of punishment; personification of evil; lowest place one can go
see also UNDERWORLD
Matt 5:22. . . of the fires of *h.*
Matt 16:18 . . all the powers of *h* will not
Matt 23:33 . . judgment of *h?*
Mark 9:43 . . fires of *h* with two hands.
Luke 12:5. . . throw you into *h.*
Jas 3:6. . . . . . on fire by *h* itself.
2 Pet 2:4. . . . threw them into *h,* in gloomy

HELMET (n)
any of various protective head coverings usually made of hard metal
Isa 59:17. . . . and placed the *h* of salvation
Eph 6:17 . . . salvation as your *h,* and take

HELP (n)
aid, assistance
2 Sam 22:36. your ***h*** has made me great.
Ps 30:2 . . . . . I cried to you for ***h,*** and you
Ps 33:20 . . . . He is our ***h*** and our shield.
Ps 108:12 . . . for all human ***h*** is useless.
Isa 30:18. . . . wait for his ***h.***
Isa 38:14. . . . looking to heaven for ***h.*** I am
Phil 4:16 . . . you sent ***h*** more than once.

HELP, HELPED, HELPING, HELPS (v)
to give assistance or support; to rescue or save
Exod 23:5 . . Instead, stop and ***h.***
Deut 2:36. . . our God also ***h-ed*** us conquer
1 Sam 7:12. . the LORD has ***h-ed*** us!
Ps 46:1 . . . . . always ready to ***h*** in times of
Ps 72:12 . . . . he will ***h*** the oppressed,
Ps 145:14 . . . The LORD ***h-s*** the fallen
Prov 11:4. . . Riches won't ***h*** on the
Prov 14:31. . their Maker, but ***h-ing*** the poor
Prov 19:17. . If you ***h*** the poor,
Isa 41:10. . . . strengthen you and ***h*** you.
Isa 44:10. . . . that cannot ***h*** him one bit?
Jer 51:9. . . . . We would have ***h-ed*** her if we
Lam 4:16 . . . he no longer ***h-s*** them.
Mark 9:24 . . but ***h*** me overcome
Acts 9:36 . . . for others and ***h-ing*** the poor.
Acts 16:9 . . . to Macedonia and ***h*** us!
Rom 12:13. . be ready to ***h*** them.
1 Cor 12:28 . those who can ***h*** others,
2 Cor 6:2 . . . salvation, I ***h-ed*** you.
Gal 6:1 . . . . . and humbly ***h*** that person back
1 Tim 5:10 . . Has she ***h-ed*** those who
2 Tim 2:7 . . . Lord will ***h*** you understand
Heb 10:33 . . you ***h-ed*** others who
1 Pet 4:11. . . the gift of ***h-ing*** others?

HELPER (n)
one who gives aid; co-worker
Gen 2:18 . . . I will make a ***h*** who is just
Ps 70:5 . . . . . You are my ***h*** and my savior;
Ps 115:9 . . . . He is your ***h*** and your shield.
Heb 13:6 . . . The LORD is my ***h,*** so I will

HELPFUL (adj)
of service or assistance; useful
Job 22:2 . . . . Can even a wise person be ***h***
Prov 10:32. . the godly speak ***h*** words,
1 Cor 12:31 . desire the most ***h*** gifts.
Eph 4:29 . . . be good and ***h,*** so that your

HELPLESS (adj)
without any aid, comfort, protection, or chance of success
Ps 9:12 . . . . . cares for the ***h.*** He does not
Ps 10:12 . . . . not ignore the ***h!***
Ps 34:2 . . . . . let all who are ***h*** take heart.
Ps 35:10 . . . . Who else protects the ***h***
Amos 2:7. . . They trample ***h*** people in the
Matt 9:36 . . . confused and ***h,*** like sheep
Rom 5:6 . . . . were utterly ***h,*** Christ came

HEN (n)
a female chicken especially over a year old
Matt 23:37 . . together as a ***h*** protects her
Luke 13:34. . together as a ***h*** protects her

HEROD
1. Herod the Great, ruler of Palestine at birth of John the Baptist and Jesus (Luke 1:5); tried to kill baby Jesus (Matt 2:1-18); died (Matt 2:19).
2. Herod Antipas, tetrarch of Galilee (Luke 3:1), son of Herod the Great; arrested and beheaded John the Baptist (Matt 14:1-12; Mark 1:14; 6:14-29; Luke 3:19-20; 9:7-9); tried Jesus (Luke 23:7-15).
3. Herod Agrippa I, grandson of Herod the Great; killed the apostle James (Acts 12:1-2); arrested Peter (Acts 12:3-19); died (Acts 12:21-23).
4. Herod Agrippa II, great-grandson of Herod the Great; spoke at Paul's trial (Acts 25–26).

HEROES (n)
greatly admired persons
Ps 16:3 . . . . . in the land are my true ***h!***

HEZEKIAH
King of Judah (southern kingdom) (2 Kgs 18–20; 2 Chr 29–32); reformed the Temple and its worship (2 Chr 29:20-36); offered effective prayer during war against Assyria (2 Kgs 19:14-19; 2 Chr 32:1-23; Isa 36:14-20); became sick but was healed (2 Kgs 20:1-11; 2 Chr 32:24-26; Isa 38:1-22); showed kingdom's treasures to Babylonians (2 Kgs 20:12-19; 2 Chr 32:31; Isa 39); died (2 Kgs 20:20-21; 2 Chr 32:32-33).

HID, HIDDEN (v)
to remain out of sight; unrevealed
see also HIDE
Ps 119:11 . . . I have ***h-den*** your word
Matt 13:35. . explain things ***h-den*** since the
Matt 13:44. . discovered ***h-den*** in a field.
Matt 13:44. . he ***h*** it again and
Matt 25:25. . your money, so I ***h*** it in the
Mark 4:22 . . that is ***h-den*** will eventually be
1 Cor 2:7 . . . was previously ***h-den,*** even
Col 3:3 . . . . . real life is ***h-den*** with Christ in
Heb 11:23 . . that Moses' parents ***h*** him

HIDE, HIDING (v)
to shield; to seek protection; to put or remain out of sight
see also HID
Deut 31:17. . abandon them, ***h-ing*** my face
1 Sam 10:22. "He is ***h-ing*** among the
Ps 27:5 . . . . . he will ***h*** me in his
Ps 57:1 . . . . . I will ***h*** beneath the shadow
Ps 143:9 . . . . run to you to ***h*** me.
Jer 16:17. . . . cannot hope to ***h*** from me.
Matt 11:25 . . thank you for ***h-ing*** these

HIGH, HIGHER, HIGHEST (adj)
foremost in rank, dignity, or standing; having large extension upward; of greater degree or value than average, usual, or expected
Gen 14:18 . . of God Most ***H,*** brought Abram
Gen 14:22 . . LORD, God Most ***H,*** Creator of
Ps 113:4 . . . . glory is ***h-er*** than the heavens.
Isa 14:14. . . . be like the Most ***H.***
Dan 4:17 . . . that the Most ***H*** rules over
Mark 5:7 . . . Son of the Most ***H*** God?
Phil 2:9 . . . . the place of ***h-est*** honor and
Heb 7:1 . . . . a priest of God Most ***H.***

HIGHLIGHTS (v)
to throw a strong light on
Rom 3:7. . . . sinner if my dishonesty ***h*** his

HIGHWAY (n)
a main direct road
Isa 40:3. . . . . Make a straight ***h*** through the
Matt 7:13. . . The ***h*** to hell is broad

HILLS (n)
a usually rounded natural elevation of land lower than a mountain
1 Kgs 20:23 . are gods of the ***h;***
Ps 50:10 . . . . the cattle on a thousand ***h.***
Isa 40:4. . . . . mountains and ***h.*** Straighten
Hos 10:8 . . . plead with the ***h,*** "Fall on
Matt 24:16. . Judea must flee to the ***h.***
Luke 3:5. . . . mountains and ***h*** made level.
Luke 23:30. . plead with the ***h,*** 'Bury us.'
Rev 17:9. . . . the seven ***h*** where the woman

HILLTOP (n)
the highest part of a hill
Matt 5:14. . . a city on a ***h*** that cannot be

HINDER, HINDERED (v)
to delay, impede, or prevent action
1 Sam 14:6. . for nothing can ***h*** the LORD.
1 Pet 3:7. . . . will not be ***h-ed.***

HIRE (v)
to engage the personal services of for pay
Luke 15:15. . a local farmer to ***h*** him,

HOARD, HOARDING (v)
to keep something to oneself
Prov 11:26. . those who ***h*** their grain,
Eccl 5:13 . . . ***H-ing*** riches harms

HOLD, HOLDING, HOLDS (v)
to keep under restraint; to have or maintain in the grasp; to keep from falling or moving; to have in the mind or express as a judgment, opinion, or belief; to maintain control of
2 Kgs 4:16 . . you will be ***h-ing*** a son in
Ps 3:3 . . . . . . the one who ***h-s*** my head high.
Ps 37:24 . . . . for the LORD ***h-s*** them by the
Ps 39:1 . . . . . I will ***h*** my tongue when
Ps 63:8 . . . . . right hand ***h-s*** me securely.
Prov 27:16. . ***h*** something with greased
Isa 40:11. . . . ***h-ing*** them close to his heart.
Isa 48:9. . . . . name, I will ***h*** back my anger
Matt 4:6. . . . And they will ***h*** you up with
Mark 11:25 . forgive anyone you are ***h-ing***
Col 1:17 . . . . and he ***h-s*** all creation
Col 2:19 . . . . For he ***h-s*** the whole body
Heb 4:14 . . . God, let us ***h*** firmly to what
Heb 10:23 . . Let us ***h*** tightly without

HOLINESS (n)
sanctity or purity
Exod 15:11 . glorious in ***h,*** awesome in
Deut 32:51. . to demonstrate my ***h*** to the
Ps 29:2 . . . . . the splendor of his ***h.***
Luke 1:75. . . in ***h*** and righteousness for
1 Cor 7:14 . . wife brings ***h*** to her
2 Cor 1:12 . . a God-given ***h*** and sincerity
1 Thes 4:4 . . and live in ***h*** and honor—
1 Tim 2:15 . . faith, love, ***h,*** and modesty.
Heb 12:10 . . share in his ***h.***

HOLY (adj)
consecrated or set aside for sacred use (as opposed to pagan or common use); standing apart from sin and evil; characteristic of God, especially the third person of the Trinity
see also PURE
Gen 2:3 . . . . and declared it ***h,*** because it
Exod 3:5 . . . are standing on ***h*** ground.
Exod 19:6 . . priests, my ***h*** nation.
Exod 26:33 . separate the ***H*** Place
Exod 29:37 . be absolutely ***h,***
Exod 30:10 . LORD's most ***h*** altar.
Exod 31:13 . the LORD, who makes you ***h.***
Lev 11:45. . . you must be ***h*** because I am
Lev 19:8. . . . for defiling what is ***h*** to the

Lev 20:7. . . . set yourselves apart to be ***h,***
Lev 20:26. . . You must be ***h*** because I,
Lev 21:12. . . for he has been made ***h*** by the
Lev 22:32. . . the LORD who makes you ***h.***
Lev 27:9. . . . LORD will be considered ***h.***
Deut 5:12. . . by keeping it ***h,*** as the LORD
Josh 5:15 . . . where you are standing is ***h.***
Josh 24:19 . . he is a ***h*** and jealous God.
1 Chr 16:35 . we can thank your ***h*** name
Neh 11:1 . . . in Jerusalem, the ***h*** city.
Ps 22:3 . . . . . Yet you are ***h,*** enthroned on
Ps 30:4 . . . . . Praise his ***h*** name.
Ps 99:3 . . . . . Your name is ***h!***
Ps 105:3 . . . . Exult in his ***h*** name; rejoice,
Ps 111:9 . . . . What a ***h,*** awe-inspiring name
Prov 9:10. . . of the ***H*** One results in good
Isa 6:3. . . . . . to each other, "***H, h, h***
Isa 40:25. . . . my equal?" asks the ***H*** One.
Isa 54:5. . . . . your Redeemer, the ***H*** One of
Isa 66:20. . . . them to my ***h*** mountain in
Dan 7:18 . . . But in the end, the ***h*** people
Dan 9:24 . . . anoint the Most ***H*** Place.
Zech 14:5. . . and all his ***h*** ones with him.
Matt 24:15. . standing in the ***H*** Place.
Mark 1:24 . . you are—the ***H*** One of God!"
Luke 1:35. . . baby to be born will be ***h,***
Luke 1:49. . . Mighty One is ***h,*** and he has
Luke 4:34. . . you are—the ***H*** One of God
Luke 11:2. . . may your name be kept ***h.***
John 6:69 . . . you are the ***H*** One of God!"
John 17:17 . . Make them ***h*** by your
Acts 13:35 . . not allow your ***H*** One to rot
Rom 7:12. . . the law itself is ***h,*** and its
Rom 14:5. . . day is more ***h*** than another
Rom 15:16 . . made ***h*** by the ***H*** Spirit.
1 Cor 1:2 . . . be his own ***h*** people.
1 Cor 1:30 . . made us pure and ***h,***
1 Cor 3:17 . . God's temple is ***h,*** and you
1 Cor 6:11 . . you were made ***h;*** you were
1 Cor 7:14 . . children would not be ***h,*** but
Eph 1:4 . . . . in Christ to be ***h*** and without
Eph 2:21 . . . becoming a ***h*** temple for
Eph 4:24 . . . righteous and ***h.***
Eph 5:26 . . . to make her ***h*** and clean,
Col 1:22. . . . and you are ***h*** and blameless
1 Thes 3:13 . blameless, and ***h*** as you
1 Thes 4:7 . . called us to live ***h*** lives,
1 Thes 5:23 . make you ***h*** in every
2 Thes 1:10 . from his ***h*** people—praise
1 Tim 2:8 . . . to pray with ***h*** hands lifted
2 Tim 1:9 . . . called us to live a ***h*** life.
2 Tim 3:15 . . taught the ***h*** Scriptures from
Heb 2:11 . . . ones he makes ***h*** have the same
Heb 10:14 . . those who are being made ***h.***
Heb 10:19 . . heaven's Most ***H*** Place
Heb 10:29 . . which made us ***h,*** as if it
Heb 13:12 . . make his people ***h*** by means
1 Pet 1:16. . . You must be ***h*** because I am
1 Pet 2:5. . . . you are his ***h*** priests.
1 Pet 2:9. . . . priests, a ***h*** nation, God's
1 Pet 3:5. . . . is how the ***h*** women of old
2 Pet 1:18. . . on the ***h*** mountain.
2 Pet 2:21. . . to live a ***h*** life.
2 Pet 3:11. . . like this, what ***h*** and godly
Rev 3:7. . . . . one who is ***h*** and true,
Rev 4:8. . . . . on saying, "***H, h, h*** is
Rev 15:4. . . . you alone are ***h.*** All nations
Rev 20:6. . . . Blessed and ***h*** are those who
Rev 22:11. . . continue to be ***h.***

HOLY GHOST (KJV)

Matt 1:18 . . . the power of the ***Holy Spirit***
Matt 3:11 . . . baptize you with the ***Holy Spirit***
Matt 28:19 . . the Son and the ***Holy Spirit***
Luke 3:22. . . ***Holy Spirit,*** in bodily form,
1 Jn 5:7-8 . . . three witnesses—the ***Spirit***

HOLY SPIRIT

the third person of the Holy Trinity
see ADVOCATE, COUNSELOR

Luke 11:13. . give the ***H*** to those
2 Cor 5:5 . . . he has given us his ***H.***
Eph 1:13 . . . ***H,*** whom he promised
Eph 4:30 . . . sorrow to God's ***H***
1 Thes 4:8 . . gives his ***H*** to you

HOME (n)

one's place of residence; place of origin, destiny, or comfort; family-style social unit
see also DWELLING, HOUSE

Deut 11:19. . when you are at ***h*** and
1 Chr 16:43 . turned and went ***h*** to bless
Ps 46:4 . . . . . God, the sacred ***h*** of the Most
Prov 3:33. . . but he blesses the ***h*** of the
Prov 27:8. . . person who strays from ***h***
Matt 10:11 . . stay in his ***h*** until you leave
Luke 10:7. . . move around from ***h***
Luke 19:9. . . has come to this ***h*** today,
John 14:2 . . . in my Father's ***h.*** If this
John 14:23 . . make our ***h*** with each
Acts 16:15 . . come and stay at my ***h."***
Rom 16:5. . . meets in their ***h.*** Greet my
Eph 3:17 . . . will make his ***h*** in your
1 Tim 5:4 . . . show godliness at ***h***
Heb 13:14 . . not our permanent ***h;*** we are
1 Pet 4:9. . . . share your ***h*** with those who

HOMELAND (n)
area set aside to be a state for a people of a particular national, cultural, or racial origin
2 Sam 7:10 . . And I will provide a ***h*** for my

HOMETOWN (n)
the city or town where one was born or grew up
Matt 13:57 . . in his own ***h*** and among his
Luke 4:24. . . is accepted in his own ***h.***
John 4:44 . . . is not honored in his own ***h.***

HOMOSEXUALITY (n)
erotic activity with another of the same sex
1 Cor 6:9 . . . prostitutes, or practice ***h,***
1 Tim 1:10 . . or who practice ***h,*** or are

HONEST (adj)
truthful; genuine; reputable; marked by integrity
Exod 18:21 . some capable, ***h*** men
2 Kgs 12:15 . were ***h*** and trustworthy
Ps 37:37 . . . . those who are ***h*** and good,
Prov 12:17 . . An ***h*** witness tells
Prov 28:6. . . Better to be poor and ***h*** than
Jer 5:1. . . . . . even one just and ***h*** person,
Matt 22:16 . . we know how ***h*** you are.
1 Thes 2:10 . devout and ***h*** and faultless

HONESTY (n)
fairness and straightforwardness of conduct; sincerity
Ps 51:6 . . . . . But you desire ***h*** from the
Prov 11:5. . . are directed by ***h;*** the wicked
Jer 5:3. . . . . . searching for ***h.*** You struck

HONEY (n)
a sweet liquid substance produced by bees; symbolic of abundance or delight in God's word
Exod 3:8 . . . with milk and ***h***—the land
1 Sam 14:26. They didn't dare touch the ***h***
Ps 19:10 . . . . sweeter than ***h,*** even ***h***
Ps 119:103 . . they are sweeter than ***h.***
Isa 7:15. . . . . eating yogurt and ***h.***
Rev 10:9. . . . be sweet as ***h*** in your mouth,

HONEYCOMB (n)
a mass of hexagonal wax cells in a honeybee nest that stores honey
Song 5:1. . . . and eat ***h*** with my honey.

HONOR, HONORS (n)
having a renowned reputation or social standing; physical or spiritual blessing (from God); a showing of merited respect
Ps 8:5 . . . . . . crowned them with glory and ***h.***
Ps 104:1 . . . . are robed with ***h*** and majesty.
Prov 3:35. . . The wise inherit ***h,*** but fools
Prov 15:33. . humility precedes ***h.***
Prov 25:27. . not good to seek ***h-s***
Isa 53:12. . . . I will give him the ***h-s*** of a
Isa 55:13. . . . will bring great ***h*** to the
Luke 14:8. . . don't sit in the seat of ***h.***
Eph 1:20 . . . the place of ***h*** at God's right
Heb 13:4 . . . Give ***h*** to marriage,
1 Pet 2:6. . . . chosen for great ***h,*** and
1 Pet 2:12. . . they will give ***h*** to God when
1 Pet 3:7. . . . husbands must give ***h*** to
2 Pet 1:17. . . when he received ***h*** and glory
Rev 4:9. . . . . give glory and ***h*** and thanks
Rev 19:7. . . . and let us give ***h*** to him.

HONOR, HONORED, HONORING, HONORS (v)
of God, to reverence his majesty; of man, to respect or esteem; to confer honor upon
Exod 20:12 . ***H*** your father and mother.
1 Kgs 8:43 . . Temple I have built ***h-s***
Neh 1:11 . . . who delight in ***h-ing*** you.
Ps 29:1 . . . . . ***H*** the Lord, you
Ps 45:11 . . . . ***h*** him, for he is your Lord.
Ps 46:10 . . . . I will be ***h-ed*** by every nation.
Ps 47:9 . . . . . He is highly ***h-ed*** everywhere.
Prov 14:31 . . helping the poor ***h-s*** him.
Isa 66:5. . . . . the Lord be ***h-ed!***
Matt 15:4. . . God says, '***H*** your father and
Mark 6:4 . . . A prophet is ***h-ed*** everywhere
Luke 16:15. . What this world ***h-s***
John 5:23 . . . that everyone will ***h*** the Son,
John 12:26 . . the Father will ***h*** anyone who
Rom 12:10. . delight in ***h-ing*** each other.
Rom 13:3. . . and they will ***h*** you.
1 Cor 6:20 . . So you must ***h*** God with your
1 Cor 12:26 . if one part is ***h-ed,*** all the
Eph 6:2 . . . . ***H*** your father and mother
Col 1:10 . . . . the way you live will always ***h***
1 Thes 5:12 . and sisters, ***h*** those who are
2 Thes 1:12 . be ***h-ed*** along with him.
Titus 2:3. . . . a way that ***h-s*** God.

HONORABLE (adj)
characterized by integrity; upright
Rom 12:17 . . everyone can see you are ***h.***
2 Cor 8:21 . . to see that we are ***h.***
Phil 4:8 . . . . is true, and ***h,*** and right,
1 Pet 2:12. . . will see your ***h*** behavior,

HOOKS (n)
a pole bearing a curved blade for pruning plants
Isa 2:4. . . . . . into pruning ***h.*** Nation will
Joel 3:10. . . . your pruning ***h*** into spears.
Mic 4:3. . . . . into pruning ***h.*** Nation will

HOPE, HOPES (n)
confident trust with the expectation of fulfillment
1 Sam 9:20. . focus of all Israel's ***h-s.***
Job 31:16 . . . crushed the ***h-s*** of widows?
Ps 10:17. . . . LORD, you know the ***h-s*** of the
Ps 42:5. . . . . I will put my ***h*** in God!
Ps 112:10 . . . slink away, their ***h-s*** thwarted.
Ps 119:49 . . . to me; it is my only ***h.***
Ps 119:74 . . . I have put my ***h*** in your word.
Prov 10:24. . the ***h-s*** of the godly will be
Prov 13:12. . ***H*** deferred makes the heart
Zech 9:12. . . prisoners who still have ***h!***
Rom 5:4. . . . our confident ***h*** of salvation.
Rom 8:20. . . curse. But with eager ***h,***
Rom 12:12. . Rejoice in our confident ***h.***
Rom 15:4. . . give us ***h*** and encouragement
Rom 15:13. . God, the source of ***h,*** will
1 Cor 13:13 . faith, ***h,*** and love—
1 Cor 15:19 . And if our ***h*** in Christ is
Eph 2:12 . . . without God and without ***h.***
1 Thes 1:3 . . and the enduring ***h*** you have
1 Tim 4:10. . struggle, for our ***h*** is in the
Heb 10:23 . . wavering to the ***h*** we affirm,
1 Pet 3:15. . . about your Christian ***h,***

HOPE (v)
to desire with expectation of obtainment
Rom 8:24. . . don't need to ***h*** for it.

HOPEFUL (adj)
full of or inclined to hope
1 Cor 13:7 . . is always ***h,*** and endures

HORN, HORNS (n)
a bony material arising from the head of many animals; a projection on the four corners of the altar in the tabernacle and Temple; a symbol of power and might
Exod 19:13 . when the ram's ***h*** sounds a
Exod 27:2 . . so that the ***h-s*** and altar are
Judg 7:19. . . blew the rams' ***h-s*** and broke
Dan 7:8 . . . . This little ***h*** had eyes
Dan 7:24 . . . Its ten ***h-s*** are ten kings
Amos 2:2. . . and the ram's ***h*** sounds.
Zech 9:14. . . sound the ram's ***h*** and attack
Rev 5:6. . . . . He had seven ***h-s*** and seven
Rev 12:3. . . . heads and ten ***h-s,*** with seven
Rev 13:1. . . . heads and ten ***h-s,*** with ten
Rev 17:3. . . . and ten ***h-s,*** and blasphemies

HORROR (n)
painful and intense fear, dread, or aversion
Jer 2:12. . . . . shrink back in ***h*** and dismay,

HORSE (n)
a large solid-hoofed herbivorous mammal often used for working or riding
Ps 147:10 . . . strength of a ***h*** or in human
Prov 26:3. . . Guide a ***h*** with a
Zech 1:8. . . . on a red ***h*** that was standing
Rev 6:2. . . . . saw a white ***h*** standing there.
Rev 6:4. . . . . Then another ***h*** appeared,
Rev 6:5. . . . . saw a black ***h,*** and its rider
Rev 6:8. . . . . and saw a ***h*** whose color was
Rev 19:11. . . and a white ***h*** was standing

HOSANNA (KJV)
Matt 21:9. . . ***Praise God*** in highest heaven!
Matt 21:15. . ***Praise God*** for the Son of David
Mark 11:9 . . ***Praise God!*** Blessings on the
Mark 11:10 . ***Praise God*** in highest heaven
John 12:13. . ***Praise God!*** Blessings on the

HOSPITALITY (n)
generous and cordial treatment, reception, or disposition
Matt 25:38. . and show you ***h?***
Luke 10:7. . . Don't hesitate to accept ***h,***
Rom 12:13. . be eager to practice ***h.***

HOSTILE (adj)
openly opposed or resisting
Rom 8:7. . . . nature is always ***h*** to God.

HOSTILITY (n)
deep-seated ill will; enmity
Gen 3:15 . . . I will cause ***h*** between you
Lev 26:28. . . I will give full vent to my ***h.***
Gal 5:20. . . . sorcery, ***h,*** quarreling,
Eph 2:14 . . . the wall of ***h*** that separated
Eph 2:16 . . . our ***h*** toward each other was
Heb 12:3 . . . of all the ***h*** he endured from

HOUR (n)
a (short) unit or passage of time; moment
John 12:27. . save me from this ***h'?***
John 13:1 . . . knew that his ***h*** had come
John 17:1 . . . Father, the ***h*** has come.

HOUSE, HOUSES (n)
living quarters; a family including ancestors, descendants, and kindred extended family unit, including ancestors and descendants
see also DWELLING, DYNASTY, HOME, TEMPLE
Exod 12:22 . doorframes of your ***h-s.***
Exod 12:27 . he passed over the ***h-s*** of the
Exod 20:17 . your neighbor's ***h.***
2 Sam 7:11. . he will make a ***h*** for you—

Ps 23:6 . . . . . live in the ***h*** of the LORD
Ps 27:4 . . . . . to live in the ***h*** of the LORD
Ps 69:9 . . . . . for your ***h*** has consumed me,
Ps 127:1 . . . . Unless the LORD builds a ***h,***
Isa 54:2. . . . . Enlarge your ***h;*** build an
Amos 5:11 . . beautiful stone ***h-s,*** you will
Matt 7:24 . . . who builds a ***h*** on solid rock.
Matt 19:29 . . given up ***h-s*** or brothers or
Mark 11:17 . be called a ***h*** of prayer for
John 2:17 . . . for God's ***h*** will consume me.

HOUSEHOLD (n)
a social unit composed of those living together in the same dwelling; family
see also FAMILY
Exod 12:3 . . one animal for each ***h.***
Acts 16:31 . . everyone in your ***h.***
1 Tim 3:5 . . . manage his own ***h,***
1 Tim 3:12 . . children and ***h*** well.
1 Tim 3:15 . . themselves in the ***h*** of God.
1 Pet 4:17 . . . begin with God's ***h.***

HOUSETOPS (n)
roofs
Matt 10:27 . . shout from the ***h*** for all to

HUMAN (adj)
of, relating to, or characteristic of men and women collectively; mortal; finite
see also FLESH
Gen 1:26 . . . Let us make ***h*** beings in our
Gen 3:22 . . . Look, the ***h*** beings have
Gen 9:6 . . . . If anyone takes a ***h*** life,
Ps 9:20 . . . . . they are merely ***h.***
Ps 33:13 . . . . sees the whole ***h*** race.
Ps 89:47 . . . . futile this ***h*** existence!
John 1:14 . . . So the Word became ***h***
John 2:24 . . . because he knew ***h*** nature.
John 8:15 . . . judge me by ***h*** standards,
Rom 6:19 . . . weakness of your ***h*** nature,
1 Cor 2:5 . . . trust not in ***h*** wisdom but in
1 Cor 2:13 . . come from ***h*** wisdom.
2 Cor 3:3 . . . of stone, but on ***h*** hearts.
2 Cor 10:3 . . We are ***h,*** but we
Gal 3:3 . . . . . by your own ***h*** effort?
Col 2:9 . . . . . of God in a ***h*** body.
1 Thes 2:13 . words as mere ***h*** ideas.
Heb 7:28 . . . limited by ***h*** weakness.
2 Pet 1:21 . . . or from ***h*** initiative.

HUMAN, HUMANS (n)
a homo sapien; mankind
Gen 6:3 . . . . Spirit will not put up with ***h-s***
Isa 2:22. . . . . trust in mere ***h-s.*** They are as
Jer 17:5. . . . . trust in mere ***h-s,*** who rely on

HUMANITY (n)
the quality or state of being human; the human race
Job 14:1 . . . . How frail is ***h!*** How short
Zech 2:13 . . . Be silent before the LORD, all ***h,***

HUMBLE (adj)
not proud or haughty; can imply lower social or economic status; meek or gentle
Num 12:3 . . Moses was very ***h***—
Ps 138:6 . . . . cares for the ***h,*** but he keeps
Ps 149:4 . . . . he crowns the ***h*** with victory.
Zech 9:9. . . . yet he is ***h,*** riding on a
Matt 5:5. . . . those who are ***h,***
Matt 11:29 . . I am ***h*** and gentle at
Matt 21:5 . . . He is ***h,*** riding on a
Eph 4:2 . . . . Always be ***h*** and gentle.
Phil 2:3 . . . . Be ***h,*** thinking of
Jas 4:6. . . . . . but favors the ***h.***
1 Pet 3:8. . . . and keep a ***h*** attitude.

HUMBLE, HUMBLED, HUMBLES (v)
to not think too highly of oneself; to bring low or prostrate
Isa 26:5. . . . . He ***h-s*** the proud and
Luke 14:11 . . themselves will be ***h-d,***
Luke 18:14 . . will be ***h-d,*** and those who
2 Cor 11:7 . . wrong when I ***h-d*** myself
Phil 2:8 . . . . he ***h-d*** himself in obedience
Jas 1:10. . . . . that God has ***h-d*** them.
Jas 4:10. . . . . ***H*** yourselves before the Lord,
1 Pet 5:6. . . . So ***h*** yourselves under

HUMBLY (adv)
in an unhaughty, unproud manner; in an insignificant or unpretentious manner
Zeph 2:3 . . . and to live ***h.*** Perhaps even
Acts 20:19 . . I have done the Lord's work ***h***
1 Tim 5:10 . . served other believers ***h?***

HUMILIATE, HUMILIATED (v)
to shame or mortify
Deut 21:14 . . for you have ***h-ed*** her.
2 Sam 22:28 . watch the proud and ***h***
Ps 18:27 . . . . but you ***h*** the proud

HUMILIATION (n)
shame, mortification, disgrace, dishonor
Job 19:5 . . . . using my ***h*** as evidence
Ps 44:15 . . . . the constant ***h;*** shame is
Prov 29:23 . . ends in ***h,*** while humility

HUMILITY (n)
show of meekness; quality of being humble
Prov 11:2. . . but with ***h*** comes wisdom.
Prov 15:33 . . ***h*** precedes honor.

Prov 22:4 . . . True *h* and fear
Col 3:12 . . . . kindness, *h,* gentleness,
Jas 3:13. . . . . works with the *h* that comes
1 Pet 5:5. . . . each other in *h,* for "God

HUNDRED (n)
the number 100
Matt 13:8 . . . and even a *h* times as much as
Luke 8:8. . . . that was a *h* times as much as

HUNG (v)
to suspend
see also HANG
Deut 21:23. . anyone who is *h* is cursed
Luke 19:48. . all the people *h* on every word
Gal 3:13 . . . . When he was *h* on the cross,

HUNGER (n)
a craving or urgent need for food
Ps 145:16 . . . you satisfy the *h* and thirst

HUNGRY (adj)
feeling a strong desire for food; a craving for anything
Prov 25:21 . . If your enemies are *h,*
Matt 15:32. . to send them away *h,*
Matt 25:35. . For I was *h,* and you fed me.
Luke 1:53. . . He has filled the *h* with good
Luke 6:21. . . you who are *h* now, for you
John 6:35 . . . never be *h* again.
Rom 8:35 . . . or are persecuted, or *h,* or
Rom 12:20 . . enemies are *h,* feed them.
Rev 7:16. . . . never again be *h* or thirsty;

HUNT, HUNTED (v)
to pursue with intent to capture
Ps 119:86 . . . from those who *h* me
2 Cor 4:9 . . . We are *h-ed* down,

HURT, HURTING, HURTS (v)
to wound, injure, or damage
1 Chr 16:22 . and do not *h* my prophets.
Ps 15:4 . . . . . promises even when it *h-s.*
Eccl 8:9 . . . . the power to *h* each other.
Lam 3:33 . . . he does not enjoy *h-ing* people
Matt 4:6. . . . you won't even *h* your foot on

HUSBAND, HUSBANDS (n)
male partner in a marriage; head of family; protector and provider; figurative of Christ
Esth 1:8 . . . . kindness to your *h* and to me.
Prov 12:4. . . is a crown for her *h,*
Prov 31:28 . . Her *h* praises her:
Rom 7:2. . . . binds her to her *h* as long as
1 Cor 7:3 . . . The *h* should fulfill
1 Cor 7:10 . . not leave her *h.*
1 Cor 7:39 . . is bound to her *h* as long as
2 Cor 11:2 . . bride to one *h*—Christ.
Gal 4:27. . . . lives with her *h!*
Eph 5:22 . . . submit to your *h-s* as to the
Eph 5:23 . . . For a *h* is the head
Eph 5:25 . . . For *h-s,* this means
Eph 5:28 . . . same way, *h-s* ought to love
Col 3:18. . . . submit to your *h-s,* as is
Col 3:19. . . . *H-s,* love your
1 Tim 5:9 . . . faithful to her *h.*
Titus 2:4. . . . to love their *h-s* and their
1 Pet 3:1. . . . the authority of your *h-s.*
1 Pet 3:7. . . . same way, you *h-s* must give

HYMN, HYMNS (n)
a song of praise to God
Ps 40:3 . . . . . to sing, a *h* of praise to our
Matt 26:30. . they sang a *h* and went out
Mark 14:26 . they sang a *h* and went out
Acts 16:25 . . praying and singing *h-s*
Eph 5:19 . . . psalms and *h-s* and spiritual
Col 3:16. . . . psalms and *h-s* and spiritual

HYPOCRISY (n)
feigning to be what one is not; pretense of piety
Matt 23:28. . your hearts are filled with *h*
Mark 12:15 . saw through their *h*
Gal 2:13 . . . . followed Peter's *h,* and even
Gal 2:13 . . . . led astray by their *h.*
1 Pet 2:1. . . . all deceit, *h,* jealousy,

HYPOCRITE, HYPOCRITES (n)
a person who portrays a false appearance of religion; a pretender
Matt 6:16 . . . make it obvious, as the *h-s*
Matt 7:5. . . . *H!* First get rid of the log
Matt 23:13. . and you Pharisees. *H-s!*
Luke 6:42. . . the log in your own eye? *H!*
Luke 13:15. . Lord replied, "You *h-s!*
1 Tim 4:2 . . . These people are *h-s* and liars,

HYSSOP (n)
an aromatic shrub of the species of marjoram and a member of the mint family that has clusters of yellow flowers
Exod 12:22 . Brush the *h* across the
John 19:29. . put it on a *h* branch, and held it

I

IDEAS (n)
formulated thoughts or opinions; notions or concepts
Ps 73:20 . . . . you will laugh at their silly *i*
Ps 81:12 . . . . living according to their own *i.*

IDENTIFY, IDENTIFIED (v)
to establish the distinguishing character or personality of; to relate to in solidarity
Matt 7:16 . . . You can *i* them by their fruit,
Matt 12:33 . . A tree is ***i-ied*** by its fruit.
Eph 1:13 . . . believed in Christ, he ***i-ied*** you

IDLE (adj)
not employed or useful for work; inactive, lazy
2 Thes 3:6 . . believers who live *i* lives
2 Thes 3:7 . . not *i* when we were with you.
2 Thes 3:11 . you are living *i* lives,

IDLENESS (n)
a state of unemployment, inactivity, or laziness
Prov 19:15 . . but *i* leaves them hungry.
Eccl 10:18 . . *i* leads to a leaky house.

IDOL, IDOLS (n)
a representation or symbol of a false god
Exod 20:4 . . make for yourself an *i*
Deut 27:15 . . who carves or casts an *i*
1 Sam 15:23 . as bad as worshiping ***i-s.***
Isa 40:19 . . . . Can he be compared to an *i*
Isa 44:9 . . . . . who worship ***i-s*** don't know
Isa 44:15 . . . . makes an *i* and bows down
Isa 44:17 . . . . and makes his god: a carved *i!*
Isa 44:19 . . . . who made the *i* never stops to
Hab 2:18 . . . What good is an *i* carved
Acts 15:20 . . eating food offered to ***i-s,***
Rom 1:23 . . . worshiped ***i-s*** made to look
1 Cor 6:9 . . . or who worship ***i-s,*** or commit
1 Cor 8:1 . . . has been offered to ***i-s.***
1 Cor 8:4 . . . an *i* is not really a god
Rev 2:14 . . . . sin by eating food offered to ***i-s***

IDOLATER (n)
worshiper of idols; one who worships an undeserving object blindly
Eph 5:5 . . . . a greedy person is an *i,*
Col 3:5 . . . . . a greedy person is an *i,*

IDOLATRY (n)
the worship of a physical object as a god; immoderate attachment or devotion to something
Gal 5:20 . . . . pleasures, *i,* sorcery,

IGNORANT (adj)
resulting from or showing lack of knowledge, comprehension, or intelligence; unaware, uninformed
Job 38:2 . . . . questions my wisdom with such *i*
Heb 5:2 . . . . with *i* and wayward people
1 Pet 2:15 . . . lives should silence those *i*
2 Pet 3:16 . . . are *i* and unstable have twisted

IGNORE (v)
to refuse to take notice of
Ps 9:12 . . . . . He does not *i* the cries of
Ps 9:17 . . . . . all the nations who *i* God.
Ps 10:12 . . . . Do not *i* the helpless!
Prov 13:18 . . If you *i* criticism,
Heb 2:3 . . . . if we *i* this great salvation

ILL-TEMPERED (adj)
having a cross or surly disposition; quarrelsome
1 Sam 25:17 . He's so *i* that no

ILLEGITIMATE (adj)
not recognized as lawful offspring
Heb 12:8 . . . means that you are *i* and

ILLUMINATES (v)
to supply or brighten with light
Rev 21:23 . . . the glory of God *i* the city,

IMAGE (n)
a God-given likeness or reflection; a tangible or visible representation
Gen 1:26 . . . make human beings in our ***i,***
Gen 1:27 . . . human beings in his own ***i.***
Gen 9:6 . . . . made human beings in his own ***i.***
Col 1:15 . . . . Christ is the visible ***i*** of the
Jas 3:9. . . . . . made in the ***i*** of God.

IMAGINE, IMAGINED (v)
to form a mental image of; to suppose or guess
Gen 6:5 . . . . ***i-d*** was consistently and totally
Job 37:5 . . . . can't even ***i*** the greatness
1 Cor 2:9 . . . no mind has ***i-ed*** what God has

IMITATE, IMITATED (v)
to follow as a pattern, model, or example; to resemble; to mimic
1 Cor 4:16 . . I urge you to ***i*** me.
1 Cor 11:1 . . should ***i*** me, just as I ***i***
1 Thes 1:6 . . you ***i-d*** both us and the Lord
1 Thes 2:14 . you ***i-d*** the believers
2 Thes 3:7 . . that you ought to ***i*** us.

IMMANUEL
Hebrew name meaning "God is with us"
Isa 7:14. . . . . to a son and will call him ***I***
Isa 8:8. . . . . . one end to the other, O ***I.***
Matt 1:23 . . . a son, and they will call him ***I,***

IMMATURE (adj)
lacking complete growth, development, or maturity
Eph 4:14 . . . no longer be ***i*** like children.

IMMORAL (adj)
characterized by conflicting with traditionally (biblically) held moral principles; sinful or impure
Prov 2:16. . . save you from the ***i*** woman,
Prov 6:24. . . keep you from the ***i*** woman,
Prov 22:14. . an ***i*** woman is a dangerous
Luke 7:37. . . a certain ***i*** woman from
Rom 13:13 . . promiscuity and ***i*** living,
Eph 5:5 . . . . be sure that no ***i,*** impure,
1 Tim 1:10 . . people who are sexually ***i,***
Jude 1:4 . . . . grace allows us to live ***i*** lives.
Rev 22:15. . . the sorcerers, the sexually ***i,***

IMMORALITY (n)
the quality or state of being immoral; an immoral act or practice
Matt 15:19 . . all sexual ***i,*** theft, lying,
Acts 15:29 . . animals, and from sexual ***i.***
1 Cor 6:13 . . made for sexual ***i.***
1 Cor 6:18 . . ***i*** is a sin against
1 Cor 7:2 . . . there is so much sexual ***i,***
Gal 5:19 . . . . very clear: sexual ***i,*** impurity,
2 Pet 2:7. . . . who was sick of the shameful ***i***
Jude 1:7 . . . . towns, which were filled with ***i***

IMMORTAL (adj)
exempt from death; imperishable
1 Cor 15:53 . transformed into ***i*** bodies.

IMMORTALITY (n)
unending existence; lasting fame
Rom 2:7 . . . . and honor and ***i***
2 Tim 1:10 . . the way to life and ***i***

IMMOVABLE (adj)
incapable of being moved; steadfast, unyielding
1 Cor 15:58 . be strong and ***i.*** Always work

IMPALED (v)
to torture or kill by fixing on a sharp stake
Esth 7:10 . . . they ***i*** Haman on the pole

IMPARTIAL (adj)
not partial or biased; treating all equally
Deut 1:17. . . and ***i*** in your judgments.
Matt 22:16 . . ***i*** and don't play favorites.

IMPATIENT (adj)
restless or short of temper especially under irritation, delay, or opposition
Zech 11:8. . . I became ***i*** with these sheep,

IMPORTANT (adj)
marked by or indicative of significant worth or consequence
Matt 23:23 . . ignore the more ***i*** aspects of
Matt 23:23 . . do not neglect the more ***i***
Mark 12:29 . The most ***i*** commandment
Mark 12:33 . I know it is ***i*** to love him
1 Cor 7:19 . . The ***i*** thing is to keep God's
1 Cor 15:3 . . what was most ***i*** and what
Gal 5:6 . . . . . What is ***i*** is faith expressing

IMPOSSIBLE (adj)
incapable of being or occurring
Zech 8:6. . . . this may seem ***i*** to you now,
Luke 1:37. . . For nothing is ***i*** with God.
Heb 6:4 . . . . it is ***i*** to bring back
Heb 11:6 . . . it is ***i*** to please God

IMPOSTORS (n)
those who assume false identity or title for the purpose of deception
2 Cor 6:8 . . . are honest, but they call us ***i.***
2 Tim 3:13 . . evil people and ***i*** will flourish.

IMPRESS, IMPRESSED (v)
to gain the admiration or interest of
Dan 1:19 . . . ***i-ed*** him as much as Daniel,
Phil 2:3 . . . . don't try to ***i*** others. Be humble

IMPRESSION (n)
an often indistinct or imprecise notion or remembrance
Luke 19:11. . correct the ***i*** that the Kingdom

IMPRESSIVE (adj)
having the power to excite attention, awe, or admiration
Ps 107:24 . . . his ***i*** works on the deepest seas.

IMPURE (adj)
ritually unclean; lewd, unchaste
Acts 11:8 . . . have declared ***i*** or unclean.
Eph 5:5 . . . . no immoral, ***i,*** or greedy person
1 Thes 2:3 . . with any deceit or ***i*** motives
1 Thes 4:7 . . live holy lives, not ***i*** lives.

IMPURITY, IMPURITIES (n)
something that is impure or makes something else impure; the quality or state of being impure
Prov 25:4. . . Remove the ***i-ies*** from silver,
Gal 5:19 . . . . clear: sexual immorality, ***i,***
Col 3:5 . . . . . to do with sexual immorality, ***i,***

INCENSE (n)
material used to produce a fragrant odor when burned
Exod 30:1 . . acacia wood for burning ***i.***
Exod 30:38 . Anyone who makes ***i***
Exod 40:5 . . Place the gold ***i*** altar
Ps 141:2 . . . . Accept my prayer as ***i*** offered
Heb 9:4 . . . . In that room were a gold ***i*** altar
Rev 5:8. . . . . held gold bowls filled with ***i,***
Rev 8:3. . . . . great amount of ***i*** was given
Rev 8:4. . . . . smoke of the ***i,*** mixed with the

INCORRUPTIBLE (KJV)
1 Cor 15:52 . will be raised ***to live forever.***
1 Pet 1:4. . . . ***beyond the reach of*** change and ***decay.***

INCREASE, INCREASED, INCREASES (v)
to become progressively greater (as in size, amount, number, or intensity)
1 Sam 2:10. . he ***i-s*** the strength of his anointed
Ps 62:10 . . . . if your wealth ***i-s,*** don't
Luke 17:5. . . Show us how to ***i*** our faith.
Acts 6:7 . . . . number of believers greatly ***i-d***

INCREDIBLE (adj)
too extraordinary and improbable to be believed; amazing, extraordinary
Acts 26:8 . . . does it seem ***i*** to any of you
Eph 2:7 . . . . examples of the ***i*** wealth of

INCURABLE (adj)
unlikely to be changed or corrected
Jer 30:12. . . . Your injury is ***i***—a terrible

INDEPENDENT (adj)
not requiring or relying on others; not subject to control by others
1 Cor 11:11 . women are not ***i*** of men,
1 Cor 11:11 . men are not ***i*** of women.

INDULGE, INDULGED, INDULGES (v)
to take unrestrained pleasure in
Rom 1:26. . . ***i-d*** in sex with each other.
Rom 13:14. . ways to ***i*** your evil desires.
1 Cor 5:9 . . . people who ***i*** in sexual sin.
1 Cor 5:11 . . claims to be a believer yet ***i-s***

INEXPRESSIBLE (adj)
not capable of being expressed; indescribable
1 Pet 1:8. . . . rejoice with a glorious, ***i*** joy.

INFANTS (n)
a child in the first period of (physical or spiritual) life
Ps 8:2 . . . . . . and ***i*** to tell of your strength,
Matt 21:16. . and ***i*** to give you praise.
1 Cor 3:1 . . . were ***i*** in the Christian life.

INFINITE (adj)
subject to no limitation or external determination
Phil 3:8 . . . . compared with the ***i*** value

INFLUENCE, INFLUENCED (v)
to sway; to affect or modify
Luke 20:21. . ***i-d*** by what others think.
3 Jn 1:11. . . . bad example ***i*** you.

INFLUENTIAL (adj)
exerting or possessing the power or capacity of causing an effect in indirect ways
Ruth 2:1. . . . there was a wealthy and ***i*** man

INHERIT, INHERITED (v)
to receive as a legacy or promise; to take possession as a rightful heir
Matt 5:5 . . . . they will ***i*** the whole earth.
Matt 25:34. . ***i*** the Kingdom prepared
Mark 10:17 . I do to ***i*** eternal life?
1 Cor 6:9 . . . will not ***i*** the Kingdom

Eph 3:6 . . . . share equally in the riches ***i-ed***
Eph 5:5 . . . . impure, or greedy person will ***i***
Rev 21:7. . . . All who are victorious will ***i***

INHERITANCE (n)
the acquisition of a possession, condition, or trait from past generations; something that is or may be inherited
Ps 16:6 . . . . . What a wonderful ***i!***
Ps 33:12 . . . . people he has chosen as his ***i.***
Ps 61:5 . . . . . an ***i*** reserved for those who
Gal 4:30 . . . . will not share the ***i***
Eph 1:14 . . . give us the ***i*** he promised
Col 3:24 . . . . give you an ***i*** as your reward,
Heb 9:15 . . . receive the eternal ***i*** God has

INIQUITY, INIQUITIES (KJV)
Ps 51:9 . . . . . Remove the stain of my ***guilt***
Isa 6:7. . . . . . your ***guilt*** is removed,
Isa 53:6. . . . . laid on him the ***sins*** of us all.
1 Cor 13:6 . . not rejoice about ***injustice***
Rev 18:5. . . . God remembers her ***evil deeds***

INJURE, INJURED (v)
to do an injustice to; to harm or impair
Prov 8:36. . . who miss me ***i*** themselves.
Ezek 34:16. . I will bandage the ***i-ed*** and
Zech 11:16. . nor heal the ***i-ed,*** nor feed

INJUSTICE (n)
unfairness; wrongs
1 Cor 6:7 . . . accept the ***i*** and leave it
1 Cor 13:6 . . It does not rejoice about ***i***

INK (n)
a colored, usually liquid, material for writing and printing
2 Cor 3:3 . . . is written not with pen and ***i,***

INNOCENCE (n)
freedom from guilt or sin through being unacquainted with evil; blamelessness
Gen 20:5 . . . I acted in complete ***i!***
2 Sam 22:25. He has seen my ***i.***
Hos 8:5 . . . . will you be incapable of ***i?***

INNOCENT (adj)
regarded as righteous; free from guilt or sin; unaware or ignorant
Job 13:18 . . . I will be proved ***i.***
Job 34:5 . . . . Job also said, 'I am ***i,***
Ps 7:8 . . . . . . for I am ***i,*** O Most High!
Ps 26:1 . . . . . Declare me ***i,*** O LORD, for I
Ps 143:2 . . . . no one is ***i*** before you.
Matt 27:4. . . I have betrayed an ***i*** man.
Matt 27:24. . I am ***i*** of this man's blood.
Rom 16:18. . they deceive ***i*** people.

INQUIRE (v)
to ask about or look into
Deut 12:30. . Do not ***i*** about their gods,
Deut 32:7. . . ***I*** of your elders
1 Chr 21:30 . to go there to ***i*** of God

INSIGHT (n)
the power or act of seeing into a situation; discernment
Ps 19:8 . . . . . are clear, giving ***i*** for living.
Prov 7:4. . . . make ***i*** a beloved member
Eph 1:17 . . . and ***i*** so that you might grow

INSOLENCE (n)
the quality or state of being overbearing or impudent
1 Tim 1:13 . . In my ***i,*** I persecuted his people.

INSPECT (v)
to view closely in critical appraisal
Prov 31:16. . She goes to ***i*** a field

INSPIRATION (n)
guidance by divine influence
Matt 22:43. . under the ***i*** of the Spirit

INSPIRED (adj)
influenced, moved; guided or created by divine influence
2 Tim 3:16 . . All Scripture is ***i*** by God

INSTINCT, INSTINCTS (n)
a natural or inherent aptitude, impulse, or capacity
2 Pet 2:12. . . creatures of ***i,*** born to be caught
Jude 1:10 . . . whatever their ***i-s*** tell them,
Jude 1:19 . . . They follow their natural ***i-s***

INSTITUTED (v)
to originate and get established; to set going
Rom 13:2. . . against what God has ***i,***

INSTRUCT, INSTRUCTED, INSTRUCTS (v)
to provide with authoritative information or advice; to teach, train, or direct
Exod 4:12 . . I will ***i*** you in what to say.
Deut 2:1. . . . just as the LORD had ***i-ed*** me,
Deut 4:36. . . so he could ***i*** you.
Josh 11:9 . . . chariots, as the LORD had ***i-ed.***
Josh 11:23 . . as the LORD had ***i-ed*** Moses.
Ps 105:22 . . . He could ***i*** the king's aides
Prov 9:9. . . . ***I*** the wise, and they will be
Prov 10:8 . . . The wise are glad to be ***i-ed,***
Prov 21:11. . if you ***i*** the wise,

Acts 8:31 . . . unless someone ***i-s*** me?
2 Tim 2:25 . . Gently ***i*** those who oppose
Titus 2:12. . . ***i-ed*** to turn from godless living

INSTRUCTION, INSTRUCTIONS (n)
a command or principle intended especially as a general rule of action; an order; directions; the action, practice, or profession of teaching
see also COMMANDMENT(S), LAW(S)
Exod 34:32 . Moses gave them all the ***i-s***
Deut 31:11. . you must read this Book of ***I***
Josh 1:7 . . . . Be careful to obey all the ***i-s***
Josh 1:8 . . . . Study this Book of ***I***
Ps 19:7. . . . . The ***i-s*** of the LORD are perfect,
Ps 40:8 . . . . . ***i-s*** are written on my heart.
Ps 119:97 . . . Oh, how I love your ***i-s!***
Prov 4:13. . . Take hold of my ***i-s;***
Prov 7:2. . . . Guard my ***i-s*** as you guard
Prov 8:33. . . Listen to my ***i*** and be wise.
Prov 23:12. . Commit yourself to ***i;***
Isa 40:14. . . . need ***i*** about what is good?
Jer 31:33. . . . put my ***i-s*** deep within
Zech 7:12. . . they could not hear the ***i-s***
1 Tim 1:5 . . . purpose of my ***i*** is that all
1 Tim 1:18 . . here are my ***i-s*** for you,

INSTRUMENT, INSTRUMENTS (n)
a device used to produce music; one used by another as a means or aid; a means whereby something is achieved, performed, or furthered
Dan 3:7 . . . . at the sound of the musical ***i-s,***
Hab 3:19 . . . accompanied by stringed ***i-s.***)
Acts 9:15 . . . Saul is my chosen ***i***
Rom 6:13. . . part of your body become an ***i***

INSULT, INSULTS (n)
a gross indignity
Job 20:3 . . . . I've had to endure your ***i-s,***
Ps 69:7 . . . . . For I endure ***i-s*** for your sake;
Ps 69:9 . . . . . the ***i-s*** of those who insult you
Ps 69:20 . . . . Their ***i-s*** have broken my heart,
Prov 9:7. . . . will get an ***i*** in return.
Prov 22:10. . and ***i-s*** will disappear.
Rom 15:3. . . The ***i-s*** of those who insult you,
2 Cor 12:10 . and in the ***i-s,*** hardships,
Jude 1:15 . . . all the ***i-s*** that ungodly sinners

INSULT, INSULTED (v)
to treat with insolence, indignity, or contempt
Prov 12:16 . . stays calm when ***i-ed.***
Prov 20:20 . . ***i*** your father or mother,
Prov 30:9. . . and thus ***i*** God's holy name.
Heb 10:29 . . have ***i-ed*** and disdained
1 Pet 2:23. . . not retaliate when he was ***i-ed,***
1 Pet 3:9. . . . insults when people ***i*** you.
1 Pet 4:14. . . be happy when you are ***i-ed***

INTEGRITY (n)
honesty; without compromise or corruption
Job 2:3 . . . . . a man of complete ***i.***
Job 2:9 . . . . . still trying to maintain your ***i?***
Job 27:5 . . . . I will defend my ***i*** until I die.
Ps 25:21 . . . . May ***i*** and honesty protect me,
Ps 26:11 . . . . I live with ***i.*** So redeem
Ps 111:8 . . . . faithfully and with ***i.***
Ps 119:1 . . . . Joyful are people of ***i,***
Prov 2:7. . . . shield to those who walk with ***i.***
Prov 10:9. . . People with ***i*** walk safely,
Titus 2:7. . . . you do reflect the ***i***

INTELLIGENCE (n)
the ability to learn or understand; mental acuteness
Isa 29:14. . . . the ***i*** of the intelligent will
1 Cor 1:19 . . the ***i*** of the intelligent.

INTELLIGENT (adj)
having or indicating a high or satisfactory degree of mental capacity
Job 32:8 . . . . that makes them ***i.***
Prov 17:28. . mouths shut, they seem ***i.***

INTERCEDE, INTERCEDED (v)
to mediate or plead another's case for justice or mercy
Isa 53:12. . . . of many and ***i-d*** for rebels.
1 Tim 2:1 . . . ***i*** on their behalf, and
Heb 7:25 . . . lives forever to ***i*** with God

INTEREST, INTERESTS (n)
a charge for borrowed money; the profit in goods or money that is made on invested capital; a feeling that accompanies or causes special attention to an object
Lev 25:36. . . Do not charge ***i*** or make a profit
Deut 23:20. . You may charge ***i*** to foreigners,
Deut 23:20. . not charge ***i*** to Israelites,
Neh 5:10 . . . stop this business of charging ***i.***
Ps 15:5 . . . . . lend money without charging ***i,***
Prov 28:8. . . Income from charging high ***i***
Matt 25:27. . I could have gotten some ***i***
1 Cor 7:34 . . His ***i-s*** are divided.
Phil 2:4 . . . . look out only for your own ***i-s,***

INTERMARRY, INTERMARRYING (v)
to marry across group boundaries
Deut 7:3. . . . You must not ***i*** with them.
Ezra 9:14 . . . ***i-ing*** with people who

INTERPRET, INTERPRETS (v)
to explain; to translate
Gen 41:15 . . a dream you can ***i*** it.

Matt 16:3 . . . how to *i* the weather
1 Cor 12:30 . to *i* unknown languages?
1 Cor 14:5 . . unless someone ***i-s*** what you
1 Cor 14:13 . *i* what has been said.
1 Cor 14:26 . another will *i* what is said.
1 Cor 14:27 . must *i* what they say.
1 Cor 14:28 . is present who can *i,*

INTIMIDATED (v)
to make timid or fearful
Phil 1:28 . . . Don't be *i* in any way

INVADED (v)
to enter for conquest or plunder
2 Kgs 17:5 . . king of Assyria *i* the entire
2 Kgs 24:1 . . Nebuchadnezzar of Babylon *i*

INVENT (v)
to devise by thinking; to find or discover
Rom 1:30 . . . They *i* new ways of sinning,

INVISIBLE (adj)
hidden; imperceptible
Rom 1:20 . . . see his *i* qualities—
Col 1:15 . . . . visible image of the *i* God.
Heb 11:27 . . his eyes on the one who is *i.*

INVITATION (n)
an often formal request to be present or participate
1 Cor 10:27 . accept the *i* if you want to.

INVITE, INVITED (v)
to request the presence or participation of; to welcome
Matt 25:35 . . a stranger, and you ***i-d*** me
Luke 14:12 . . For they will *i* you back,
Rev 19:9 . . . . Blessed are those who are ***i-d***

IRON (n)
metal used in instruments of war, farming, and building; symbolic of strength for both security and destruction
Ps 2:9 . . . . . . break them with an *i* rod
Prov 27:17 . . As *i* sharpens *i,* so
Dan 2:33 . . . its legs were *i,* and its feet
Rev 2:27 . . . . rule the nations with an *i* rod
Rev 12:5 . . . . nations with an *i* rod.
Rev 19:15 . . . rule them with an *i* rod.

IRRITABLE (adj)
easily exasperated or excited
1 Cor 13:5 . . It is not *i,* and it keeps

ISAAC
Patriarch, son of Abraham; promised by God (Gen 17:16-22; 18:14); born (Gen 21:1-7; 1 Chr 1:28; Acts 7:8); recipient of divine covenant (Gen 17:21; 26:2-5); offered to God by Abraham (Gen 22:1-19; Heb 11:17-19); took Rebekah as wife (Gen 24:67); inherited wealth (Gen 25:5); prayed for wife to have children (Gen 25:20-21); father of twins, Esau and Jacob (Gen 25:24; 1 Chr 1:34); preferred Esau (Gen 25:28); dealings with Abimelech (Gen 26:1-31); tricked into blessing Jacob (Gen 27:1-29); died (Gen 35:27-29); father of a nation (Deut 29:13; Rom 9:7, 10); often mentioned in NT (Luke 3:34; Gal 4:28; Heb 11:9, 17-20; Jas 2:21).

ISAIAH
Prophet of Judah (southern kingdom) who prophesied during the reigns of four consecutive kings (Isa 1:1); called by God in a vision (Isa 6); prophesied Immanuel's coming (Isa 7–11); prophesied to Hezekiah (2 Kgs 19–20; Isa 36–38); recorded history of kings (2 Chr 26:22; 32:32); often quoted in NT (Matt 3:3; 4:14; 8:17; 12:17; 13:14; 15:7; Luke 4:17; John 12:38; Acts 8:28; 28:25; Rom 9:27; 10:16, 20).

ISLAND (n)
small tract of land surrounded by water
Rev 1:9 . . . . . I was exiled to the *i* of Patmos
Rev 16:20 . . . And every *i* disappeared,

ISRAEL
1. Another name for Jacob (Gen 32:28)
2. The united kingdom of Israel, including all twelve tribes, as ruled by Saul, David, and Solomon.
3. The northern kingdom of Israel, including the ten northern tribes, in contrast to Judah (southern kingdom) (see 2 Sam 19:41-43).
Exod 3:9 . . . cry of the people of ***I*** has
Exod 12:37 . ***I*** left Rameses and started
Exod 16:1 . . ***I*** set out from Elim
Exod 28:29 . ***I*** on the sacred chestpiece
Exod 31:16 . ***I*** must keep the Sabbath day
Exod 39:42 . ***I*** followed all of the LORD's
Lev 25:55 . . . the people of ***I*** belong to me.
Num 6:23 . . ***I*** with this special blessing:
Num 9:17 . . ***I*** would break camp and follow
Num 20:22 . community of ***I*** left Kadesh
Num 27:12 . I have given the people of ***I.***
Num 35:10 . instructions to the people of ***I.***
Deut 10:12 . . ***I,*** what does the LORD your
Josh 21:3 . . . ***I*** gave the Levites the following
Judg 17:6 . . . In those days ***I*** had no king;
1 Sam 3:20 . . And all ***I,*** from Dan
1 Sam 4:21 . . said, "***I***'s glory is gone."
1 Sam 15:26 . rejected you as king of ***I.***
1 Sam 18:16 . all ***I*** and Judah loved David

2 Sam 14:25 . handsome man in all ***I.***
1 Kgs 1:35 . . him to be ruler over ***I***
1 Kgs 12:1 . . ***I*** had gathered to make him king.
1 Kgs 19:18 . preserve 7,000 others in ***I***
2 Kgs 17:24 . replacing the people of ***I.***
1 Chr 11:4 . . and all ***I*** went to Jerusalem
1 Chr 21:1 . . Satan rose up against ***I***
2 Chr 9:8 . . . Because God loves ***I***
Ps 73:1 . . . . . Truly God is good to ***I,***
Ps 98:3 . . . . . to love and be faithful to ***I.***
Isa 44:6. . . . . says—***I***'s King and Redeemer,
Isa 44:21. . . . you are my servant, O ***I.***
Jer 2:3. . . . . . In those days ***I*** was holy
Jer 31:2. . . . . give rest to the people of ***I.***
Jer 31:9. . . . . For I am ***I***'s father,
Jer 31:31. . . . covenant with the people of ***I***
Ezek 3:17. . . as a watchman for ***I.***
Hos 1:10 . . . ***I***'s people will be like the sands
Hos 3:1 . . . . LORD still loves ***I,*** even though
Amos 4:12. . in judgment, you people of ***I!***
Amos 8:2. . . Like this fruit, ***I*** is ripe
Mic 5:2. . . . . a ruler of ***I*** will come from you,
Mal 1:5. . . . . far beyond ***I***'s borders!
Matt 2:6. . . . the shepherd for my people ***I.***
Matt 10:6. . . people of ***I***—God's lost sheep.
Matt 15:24. . lost sheep—the people of ***I.***
Mark 12:29 . Listen, O ***I!***
Acts 1:6 . . . . time come for you to free ***I***
Acts 9:15 . . . as well as to the people of ***I.***
Rom 9:4. . . . ***I,*** chosen to be God's adopted
Rom 9:6. . . . ***I*** are truly members of God's
Rom 9:27. . . ***I*** are as numerous as the sand
Rom 9:31. . . ***I,*** who tried so hard to get
Rom 10:1. . . the people of ***I*** to be saved.
Rom 11:7. . . ***I*** have not found the favor
Rom 11:26. . And so all ***I*** will be saved.
Eph 2:12 . . . citizenship among the people of ***I,***
Phil 3:5 . . . . a pure-blooded citizen of ***I*** and
Heb 8:8 . . . . covenant with the people of ***I***
Rev 7:4. . . . . sealed from all the tribes of ***I:***
Rev 21:12. . . ***I*** were written on the gates.

ISRAELITE, ISRAELITES (n)
members of the nation of Israel
see also JEW(S)
Exod 1:7 . . . the ***I-s,*** had many children
Exod 16:12 . heard the ***I-s'*** complaints.
Num 10:12 . ***I-s*** set out from the wilderness
Josh 1:2 . . . . lead these people, the ***I-s,***
Josh 7:1 . . . . was very angry with the ***I-s.***
Judg 2:7. . . . ***I-s*** served the LORD throughout
Judg 3:12. . . ***I-s*** did evil in the LORD's sight,
Judg 6:1. . . . ***I-s*** did evil in the LORD's sight.
Judg 10:16. . ***I-s*** put aside their foreign
Rom 11:1. . . I myself am an ***I,*** a descendant
2 Cor 11:22 . Are they ***I-s?*** So am I.

ITALY (n)
a long boot-shaped country that juts into the Mediterranean Sea
Acts 27:1 . . . we set sail for ***I.***
Heb 13:24 . . believers from ***I*** send

J

JACOB

Patriarch, son of Isaac, grandson of Abraham; younger twin son of Issac and Rebekah (Gen 25:23–35:26; 48–49); also known as "Israel" (Gen 32:28); favored by Rebekah (Gen 25:28); bought Esau's birthright for a meal (Gen 25:29-34); deceived Isaac to receive his blessing (Gen 27:1-29); fled from Esau (Gen 27:41-45); married inside of clan (Gen 28:1-5); Jacob's ladder (Gen 28:12); covenant extended to Jacob in a dream (Gen 28:13-15); wives and concubines, Rachel favored (Gen 29:1-30); children (Gen 29:31–30:24; 35:16-26); prospered at his uncle Laban's expense (Gen 30:25-43); fled from Laban (Gen 31); name changed to "Israel" (Gen 32:22-32); reconciled with Esau (Gen 33); favored Rachel's oldest son Joseph (Gen 37:3); overwhelmed by loss of Joseph (Gen 37:33-35); migrated to Egypt (Gen 46:5-7); blessed Joseph's sons (Gen 48); blessed his own sons (Gen 49:1-28); died (Gen 49:33); buried (Gen 50:1-14); often mentioned in NT (John 4:5-6, 12; Acts 7:8-15; Rom 9:13; Heb 11:20-21).

see ISRAEL

JAMES

1. One of the 12 disciples, brother of John, son of Zebedee (Matt 10:2; Mark 3:17); called by Jesus (Matt 4:21; Luke 5:10); zealous for the Lord (Luke 9:54); wanted honor (Mark 10:35-45); witnessed the Transfiguration (Matt 17:1-9; Mark 9:2-8; Luke 9:28-36); killed by Herod Agrippa I (Acts 12:2).

2. One of the 12 disciples, son of Alphaeus (Matt 10:3; Mark 3:18; Luke 6:15); called "the younger" (Mark 15:40).

3. Half-brother of Jesus (Matt 13:55; Mark 6:3; Luke 24:10; 1 Cor 15:7; Gal 1:19; 2:9, 12), brother of Jude (Jude 1:1); leader of Jerusalem Council (Acts 15:13; 21:18); with select group before Pentecost (Acts 1:13); wrote letter (Jas 1:1).

4. Father of the apostle Judas, not Iscariot (Luke 6:16).

5. Son of a certain Mary, perhaps the same as the "son of Alphaeus" (Matt 27:56).

JAR, JARS (n)

an open container, typically made of clay in the ancient world

John 12:3 . . . *j* of expensive perfume
John 19:29 . . A *j* of sour wine was
2 Cor 4:7 . . . like fragile clay ***j-s*** containing

JAVELIN (n)

a light spear thrown as a weapon of war or in hunting

1 Sam 17:45. sword, spear, and ***j***, but I

JAWBONE (n)

either of two bony structures that border the mouth

Judg 15:15 . . *j* of a recently killed donkey.

JEALOUS (adj)

intolerant of rivalry or unfaithfulness; hostile toward a rival

Exod 20:5 . . am a *j* God who will not
Exod 34:14 . whose very name is ***J***,
Prov 6:34 . . . *j* husband will be furious,
Nah 1:2 . . . . a *j* God, filled with vengeance
Rom 11:14 . . *j* of what you Gentiles have,
1 Cor 13:4 . . Love is not *j* or boastful
Gal 5:26 . . . . provoke one another, or be *j*
Jas 3:14. . . . . if you are bitterly *j* and there is

JEALOUSY (n)

a jealous feeling, disposition, or attitude

Prov 27:4. . . but *j* is even more dangerous.
Rom 10:19. . I will rouse your *j*

Rom 13:13 . . or in quarreling and *j.*
1 Cor 10:22 . dare to rouse the Lord's *j?*
2 Cor 11:2 . . you with the *j* of God
Gal 5:20 . . . . *j,* outbursts of anger,
1 Tim 6:4 . . . arguments ending in *j,*
1 Pet 2:1. . . . with all deceit, hypocrisy, *j,*

JEERED, JEERS (v)

to scoff; to taunt
Job 27:23 . . . ***j-s*** at them and mocks them.
Heb 11:36 . . Some were ***j-ed*** at,

JEHOVAH (KJV)

Exod 6:3 . . . I did not reveal my name, ***Yahweh,*** to them
Ps 83:18 . . . . you alone are called ***the Lord***
Isa 12:2. . . . . The Lord ***God*** is my strength
Isa 26:4. . . . . the Lord ***God*** is the eternal

JEREMIAH

Prophet of Judah (southern kingdom) from Anathoth (Jer 11:18-23); never married (Jer 16:2); put in stocks (Jer 20:1-6); threatened by priests and prophets (Jer 26:8); brought death to false prophet (Jer 28:16-17); writings burned (Jer 36); imprisoned in dungeon (Jer 37:15); removed from the dungeon by King Zedekiah (Jer 37:21); lowered into cistern (Jer 38:1-6); set free by invaders (Jer 39:11–40:6); taken to Egypt (Jer 43); mentioned in NT (Matt 2:17; 27:9).

JERICHO (n)

a city in the plain of the Jordan Valley at the foot of the ascent to the Judean mountains
Num 22:1 . . across from *J.*
Josh 3:16 . . . near the town of *J.*
Josh 5:10 . . . at Gilgal on the plains of *J,*
Luke 10:30. . from Jerusalem down to *J,*
Heb 11:30 . . around *J* for seven days,

JERUSALEM (n)

sacred city and well-known capital of Palestine during Bible times
Josh 10:1 . . . Adoni-zedek, king of *J,* heard
Josh 15:8 . . . where the city of *J* is located.
Judg 1:8. . . . attacked *J* and captured it,
2 Sam 5:5. . . *J* he reigned over all Israel
2 Sam 11:1. . David stayed behind in *J.*
1 Kgs 9:15 . . terraces, the wall of *J,*
1 Kgs 10:26 . and some near him in *J.*
1 Kgs 14:25 . came up and attacked *J.*
2 Kgs 8:17 . . he reigned in *J* eight years.
2 Kgs 12:1 . . He reigned in *J* forty years.
2 Kgs 14:2 . . reigned in *J* twenty-nine years.
2 Kgs 15:2 . . he reigned in *J* fifty-two years.
2 Kgs 16:2 . . he reigned in *J* sixteen years.
2 Kgs 18:2 . . reigned in *J* twenty-nine years.
2 Kgs 19:31 . will spread out from *J,*
2 Kgs 21:12 . I will bring such disaster on *J*
2 Kgs 22:1 . . reigned in *J* thirty-one years.
2 Kgs 23:31 . he reigned in *J* three months.
2 Kgs 24:8 . . he reigned in *J* three months.
2 Kgs 24:14 . Nebuchadnezzar took all of *J*
2 Kgs 24:20 . anger against the people of *J*
2 Kgs 25:9 . . and all the houses of *J.*
1 Chr 21:16 . reaching out over *J.*
2 Chr 3:1 . . . the Temple of the Lord in *J*
2 Chr 9:1 . . . she came to *J* to test him
2 Chr 20:15 . all you people of Judah and *J!*
2 Chr 29:8 . . has fallen upon Judah and *J.*
2 Chr 36:19 . tore down the walls of *J,*
Ezra 2:1 . . . . but now they returned to *J*
Ezra 4:12 . . . came here to *J* from Babylon
Ezra 6:12 . . . who has chosen the city of *J*
Ezra 9:9 . . . . a protective wall in Judah and *J.*
Neh 1:3 . . . . The wall of *J* has been torn
Neh 3:8 . . . . They left out a section of *J*
Neh 11:1 . . . of the people were living in *J,*
Neh 12:43 . . joy of the people of *J* could be
Ps 9:11 . . . . . the Lord who reigns in *J.*
Ps 51:18 . . . . rebuild the walls of *J.*
Ps 74:2 . . . . . remember *J,* your home here
Ps 79:1 . . . . . made *J* a heap of ruins.
Ps 87:2 . . . . . He loves the city of *J* more than
Ps 102:13 . . . arise and have mercy on *J*—
Ps 122:2 . . . . standing inside your gates, O *J.*
Ps 122:6 . . . . Pray for peace in *J.*
Ps 125:2 . . . . *J,* so the Lord surrounds
Ps 128:5 . . . . May you see *J* prosper
Ps 137:3 . . . . Sing us one of those songs of *J!*
Ps 137:5 . . . . If I forget you, O *J,*
Ps 147:2 . . . . The Lord is rebuilding *J*
Ps 147:12 . . . Glorify the Lord, O *J!*
Isa 1:1. . . . . . saw concerning Judah and *J.*
Isa 3:1. . . . . . take away from *J* and Judah
Isa 4:3. . . . . . who survive the destruction of *J*
Isa 27:13. . . . return to *J* to worship the Lord
Isa 31:5. . . . . will hover over *J* and protect it
Isa 40:2. . . . . Speak tenderly to *J.*
Isa 51:11. . . . They will enter *J* singing,
Isa 52:1. . . . . clothes, O holy city of *J,*
Isa 52:8. . . . . see the Lord returning to *J.*
Isa 62:7. . . . . makes *J* the pride of the earth.
Jer 2:2. . . . . . Go and shout this message to *J.*
Jer 4:5. . . . . . to Judah, and broadcast to *J!*
Jer 6:6. . . . . . ramps against the walls of *J.*
Jer 9:11. . . . . will make *J* into a heap of ruins,
Jer 23:14. . . . prophets of *J* are even worse!
Jer 26:18. . . . *J* will be reduced to ruins!
Jer 39:1. . . . . came with his army to besiege *J.*
Jer 51:50. . . . think about your home in *J.*

Lam 1:7 . . . . *J* remembers her ancient splendor.
Dan 6:10 . . . windows open toward *J.*
Dan 9:2 . . . . *J* must lie desolate for seventy
Dan 9:12 . . . a disaster as happened in *J.*
Dan 9:25 . . . command is given to rebuild *J*
Joel 3:16. . . . from Zion and thunder from *J,*
Amos 2:5. . . fortresses of *J* will be destroyed.
Obad 1:11 . . and cast lots to divide up *J,*
Mic 4:2. . . . . his word will go out from *J.*
Zeph 3:16 . . the announcement to *J* will be,
Zech 1:17. . . Zion and choose *J* as his own.
Zech 2:4. . . . *J* will someday be so full
Zech 8:8. . . . home again to live safely in *J.*
Zech 8:22. . . nations will come to *J* to seek
Zech 9:10. . . and the warhorses from *J.*
Zech 12:10. . and on the people of *J.*
Zech 14:8. . . waters will flow out from *J,*
Matt 20:18 . . going up to *J,* where the Son
Matt 21:10 . . city of *J* was in an uproar
Matt 23:37 . . *J,* the city that kills the
Mark 10:33 . going up to *J,* where the Son
Luke 2:22. . . parents took him to *J*
Luke 2:41. . . Jesus' parents went to *J*
Luke 4:9. . . . Then the devil took him to *J,*
Luke 9:31. . . about to be fulfilled in *J.*
Luke 13:34. . O *J, J,* the city that kills
Luke 18:31. . to *J,* where all the predictions
Luke 21:20. . you see *J* surrounded
Luke 24:47. . nations, beginning in *J:*
Acts 1:8 . . . . about me everywhere—in *J,*
Acts 6:7 . . . . believers greatly increased in *J,*
Acts 20:22 . . bound by the Spirit to go to *J.*
Acts 23:11 . . a witness to me here in *J,*
Rom 9:33. . . I am placing a stone in *J*
Rom 11:26. . rescues will come from *J,*
Rom 15:19. . from *J* all the way to Illyricum.
Gal 4:25 . . . . *J* is just like Mount Sinai
Gal 4:26 . . . . represents the heavenly *J.*
Heb 12:22 . . living God, the heavenly *J,*
Rev 21:10. . . he showed me the holy city, *J,*

JESUS

see also CHRIST, MESSIAH

Family line (Matt 1:1-17; Luke 3:23-38); birth announced (Matt 1:18-25; Luke 1:26-38); born in Bethlehem (Luke 2:1-20); circumcised, officially named, and presented at Temple (Luke 2:21-40); visited by Magi (Matt 2:1-12); escape to and return from Egypt (Matt 2:13-23); amazed the Temple scholars (Luke 2:41-50); summary of youth (Luke 2:51-52); baptized by John (Matt 3:13-17; Mark 1:9-11; Luke 3:21-22; John 1:32-34); tempted by Satan (Matt 4:1-11; Mark 1:12-13; Luke 4:1-13); ministered in Galilee (Matt 4:12–18:35; Mark 1:14–9:50); transfigured on a mountain (Matt 17:1-13; Mark 9:2-13; Luke 9:28-36; 2 Pet 1:16-18); triumphal entry (Matt 21:1-11; Mark 11:1-11; Luke 19:28-44; John 12:12-19); the Last Supper (Matt 26:17-35; Mark 14:12-31; Luke 22:7-38; John 13–17); betrayed and tried (Matt 26:36–27:31; Mark 14:32–15:20; Luke 22:39–23:25; John 18:1–19:16); crucified, died, and was buried (Matt 27:32-66; Mark 15:21-47; Luke 23:26-56; John 19:17-42); rose again and appeared to followers (Matt 28; Mark 16; Luke 24; John 20–21; Acts 1:1-11; 7:55-56; 9:3-6; 1 Cor 15:1-8; Rev 1:1-20); ascended to heaven (Mark 16:19; Luke 24:50-53; John 1:51; Acts 1:9; Eph 4:8).

JEW, JEWS (n)

a name applied first to the people living in the southern kingdom of Judah; broadly, a descendant of Abraham

see also ISRAELITE(S)

Esth 3:13 . . . property of the ***J-s*** would be
Zech 8:23. . . clutch at the sleeve of one *J.*
Matt 2:2. . . . the newborn king of the ***J-s?***
John 19:3 . . . Hail! King of the ***J-s!***
Acts 20:21 . . message for ***J-s*** and Greeks
Acts 21:39 . . I am a *J* and a citizen of
Rom 1:16. . . everyone who believes—the *J*
Rom 2:28. . . you are not a true *J*
Rom 9:24. . . from the ***J-s*** and from
Rom 10:12. . *J* and Gentile are the same
1 Cor 9:20 . . with the ***J-s,*** I lived like a *J*
1 Cor 12:13 . ***J-s,*** some are Gentiles,
Gal 2:8 . . . . . Peter as the apostle to the ***J-s***
Gal 2:14 . . . . *J* by birth, have discarded
Gal 3:28 . . . . There is no longer *J* or Gentile,
Eph 3:6 . . . . Gentiles and ***J-s*** who believe
Col 3:11 . . . . *J* or a Gentile, circumcised or

JEWEL, JEWELS (n)

a precious stone; gem

Prov 3:22. . . They are like ***j-s*** on a necklace.
Song 4:9. . . . with a single *j* of your necklace.
Isa 61:10. . . . or a bride with her ***j-s.***
Zech 9:16. . . in his land like ***j-s*** in a crown.
1 Cor 3:12 . . gold, silver, ***j-s,*** wood, hay,

JEWELRY (n)

objects of precious metal worn for personal adornment

Prov 25:12. . earring or other gold *j.*
Jer 2:32. . . . . a young woman forget her *j?*
Ezek 16:11. . I gave you lovely *j,* bracelets,

JEWISH (adj)
of, relating to, or characteristic of the Jews
Esth 2:5 . . . . a *J* man in the fortress of Susa
John 3:10 . . . You are a respected *J* teacher,

JEZEBEL
Queen of Israel (northern kingdom), daughter of Ethbaal, king of Sidon; evil, influential wife of King Ahab (1 Kgs 21:25); Baal worshiper (1 Kgs 16:31-33); tried to kill all the Lord's prophets (1 Kgs 18:4, 13); vowed to kill Elijah (1 Kgs 19:1-2); arranged murder to get vineyard for Ahab (1 Kgs 21:1-16); death foretold and fulfilled (1 Kgs 21:23; 2 Kgs 9:10, 30-37).

JOB
Man who feared God and had integrity (Job 1:1-5); slandered and attacked by Satan (Job 1:6–2:10); debated suffering with his "friends" (Job 3–37); enlightened by vision of the Lord (Job 38–41); restored to peace and prosperity (Job 42); example of righteousness (Ezek 14:14, 20); example of endurance in suffering (Jas 5:11).

JOHN
1. The Baptist, son of Zechariah and Elizabeth (Luke 1:5-25, 57-80); called to prepare the way for the Messiah (Isa 40:3-5; Luke 3:1-6; John 1:19-28); called to preach and baptize (Matt 3:1-12; Mark 1:1-8); preached repentance (Luke 3:7-20); baptized Jesus (Matt 3:13-17; Luke 3:21-22); confirmed Jesus' ministry (Matt 3:11-12; Mark 1:7-8; Luke 3:15-18; John 3:22-36; 5:33); ministry compared to Elijah (Mal 4:5; Matt 11:11-19; Mark 9:11-13; Luke 7:24-35); arrested and beheaded by Herod Antipas (Matt 14:1-12; Mark 6:14-29; Luke 9:7-9).
2. One of the 12 disciples, brother of James, son of Zebedee (Matt 10:2; Mark 3:17); witnessed the Transfiguration (Matt 17:1-9; Mark 9:2-8; Luke 9:28-36); inner circle of Jesus' followers (Matt 17:1; Mark 5:37; 9:2; 13:3; Luke 8:51; 9:28; Gal 2:9); with Peter, healed a man and was arrested (Acts 3–4); with Peter, rebuked sorcerer (Acts 8:14-25); wrote fourth Gospel (John 13:23-25; see also 20:2; 21:20-25), letters of John (the "elder," 2 Jn 1:1; 3 Jn 1:1), and Revelation (the "servant," Rev 1:1, 9; 22:8).
3. See MARK, *also known as John Mark.*

JOIN, JOINED, JOINS (v)
to put or bring into close association or relationship; to take part in a collective activity
Ps 26:5 . . . . . I refuse to *j* in with the wicked.
Dan 11:34 . . who *j* them will not be sincere.
Zech 2:11 . . . will *j* themselves to the LORD
Matt 19:6 . . . what God has ***j-ed*** together.
Mark 10:9 . . what God has ***j-ed*** together.
Rom 6:3 . . . . ***j-ed*** with Christ Jesus in baptism,
Rom 8:16 . . . his Spirit ***j-s*** with our spirit
Rom 15:30 . . *j* in my struggle by praying
1 Cor 6:16 . . if a man ***j-s*** himself to
Eph 2:21 . . . carefully ***j-ed*** together in him,

JOINT (n)
the point of contact between bone and the parts surrounding and supporting it
Ps 22:14 . . . . all my bones are out of *j.*
Heb 4:12 . . . between *j* and marrow.

JOKE, JOKES (n)
something said or done to provoke laughter
Ps 44:14 . . . . made us the butt of their ***j-s;***
Ps 89:41 . . . . he has become a *j* to his
Eph 5:4 . . . . coarse ***j-s*** — these are not

JOKING (v)
to jest; to kid
Gen 19:14 . . men thought he was only *j.*
Prov 26:19 . . and then says, "I was only *j.*"

JONAH
Prophet of Israel (northern kingdom) in the days of Jeroboam II (2 Kgs 14:25); swallowed by great fish (Jonah 1:17); survived and then preached to Nineveh (Jonah 3); mentioned by Jesus as a sign (Matt 12:39-41; 16:4; Luke 11:29-32).

JORDAN (n)
the longest and most important river in Palestine
Josh 4:22 . . . crossed the *J* on dry ground.
Matt 3:6 . . . . them in the *J* River.
Matt 4:15 . . . sea, beyond the *J* River, in
Mark 1:9 . . . him in the *J* River.

JOSEPH
1. Oldest son of Jacob and Rachel (Gen 30:24); loved by Jacob – hated by brothers (Gen 37:3-4); dreamer of dreams (Gen 37:5-11); captured to be killed, but sold into slavery (Gen 37:20, 27-28); faithfully served Egyptian master (Gen 39:3); wrongfully accused and imprisoned (Gen 39); interpreted dreams of royal staff (Gen 40); interpreted dreams of Pharaoh, then ruled Egypt (Gen 41:4-44); prepared Egypt for famine (Gen 41:46-57); tested brothers, revealed identity, and reconciled with them (Gen 42–45); brought his father Jacob and family to Egypt (Gen 46–47); sons, Ephraim and Manasseh, blessed by Jacob (Gen 48); Joseph blessed by Jacob (Gen 49:22-26;

Deut 33:13-17); reassured his brothers (Gen 50:15-21); died (Gen 50:22-26; Heb 11:22); remembered as one chosen and helped by God (Acts 7:9-18); 12,000 descendants will be marked by God (Rev 7:8).
2. Husband of Mary the mother of Jesus; accepted supernatural pregnancy of Mary (Matt 1:16-25); had no relations with Mary until birth of Jesus (Matt 1:25); was present at birth and dedication of Jesus (Luke 2:4-38); fled to Egypt, then Nazareth (Matt 2:13-22); ancestor of David in the family line of Jesus (Luke 3:23); Jesus called his son (Luke 4:22; John 1:45; 6:42).

JOSHUA
Son of Nun, who led Israel into Promised Land (Acts 7:45; Heb 4:8); commanded by Moses to fight Amalek (Exod 17:8-16); assistant to Moses (Exod 24:13); explored Canaan (Num 13:8); demonstrated faith in his report (Num 14:6-9); allowed to enter Promised Land (Num 14:30; Deut 1:38); became Israel's leader after Moses (Num 27:18-23; Deut 31:1-18); went with Moses up the mountain of God (Exod 24:13); assumed command (Josh 1); sent spies to Jericho (Josh 2); led Israel across the Jordan (Josh 3–4); established memorial stones (Josh 4); circumcised the people (Josh 5:2-9); conquered Jericho (Josh 6) and Ai (Josh 7–8); uncovered Achan's sin (Josh 7:10-26); made pact with the Gibeonites (Josh 9); sun stood still (Josh 10:1-15); conquered southern Canaan (Josh 10:28-43); conquered northern Canaan (Josh 11–12); divided the land (Josh 13–22); gave final words to Israel (Josh 23); made covenant at Shechem (Josh 8:30-35; 24:1-28); died (Josh 24:29-30).

JOURNEY (n)
an act or instance of traveling from one place to another

Judg 18:6 . . . LORD is watching over your *j*.
Ezra 8:21 . . . give us a safe *j*
Rom 15:24 . . provide for my *j*.

JOY, JOYS (n)
the emotion evoked by well-being, success, or good fortune

Deut 16:15. . be a time of great *j* for all.
1 Sam 18:6. . danced for *j* with tambourines
1 Chr 16:27 . and *j* fill his dwelling.
1 Chr 29:22 . with great *j* that day.
Ezra 3:12 . . . however, were shouting for *j*.
Neh 8:10 . . . *j* of the LORD is your strength!
Neh 8:17 . . . they were all filled with great *j!*
Esth 9:22 . . . and their mourning into *j*.
Job 3:22 . . . . with *j* when they finally die,
Job 8:21 . . . . your lips with shouts of *j*.
Ps 1:1 . . . . . . *j-s* of those who do not follow
Ps 2:12 . . . . . *j* for all who take refuge in him!
Ps 9:2 . . . . . . filled with *j* because of you.
Ps 19:8 . . . . . bringing *j* to the heart.
Ps 21:1 . . . . . He shouts with *j*
Ps 28:7 . . . . . my heart is filled with *j*.
Ps 30:11 . . . . and clothed me with *j*,
Ps 32:2 . . . . . what *j* for those whose record
Ps 33:12 . . . . *j* for the nation whose God
Ps 41:1 . . . . . *j-s* of those who are kind
Ps 42:4 . . . . . singing for *j* and giving thanks
Ps 45:7 . . . . . pouring out the oil of *j* on you
Ps 46:4 . . . . . A river brings *j* to the city
Ps 51:12 . . . . to me the *j* of your salvation,
Ps 65:8 . . . . . you inspire shouts of *j*.
Ps 65:13 . . . . They all shout and sing for *j!*
Ps 71:23 . . . . I will shout for *j* and sing
Ps 92:4 . . . . . I sing for *j* because of what
Ps 98:4 . . . . . in praise and sing for *j!*
Ps 105:43 . . . his people out of Egypt with *j*,
Ps 106:5 . . . . Let me rejoice in the *j*
Ps 119:92 . . . hadn't sustained me with *j*,
Ps 126:2 . . . . laughter, and we sang for *j*.
Ps 132:9 . . . . loyal servants sing for *j*.
Ps 132:16 . . . servants will sing for *j*.
Ps 145:7 . . . . *j* about your righteousness.
Prov 10:1 . . . A wise child brings *j*
Prov 11:10. . *j* when the wicked die.
Prov 14:10. . no one else can fully share its *j*.
Prov 15:20. . Sensible children bring *j* to
Prov 21:15. . Justice is a *j* to the godly,
Prov 23:25. . your father and mother *j!*
Prov 29:6 . . . righteous escape, shouting for *j*.
Isa 12:6. . . . . shout his praise with *j!*
Isa 16:9. . . . . no more shouts of *j* over your
Isa 16:10. . . . gone the *j* of harvest.
Isa 26:19. . . . will rise up and sing for *j!*
Isa 35:10. . . . crowned with everlasting *j*.
Isa 42:11. . . . Let the people of Sela sing for *j;*
Isa 49:13. . . . Sing for *j*, O heavens!
Isa 51:11. . . . filled with *j* and gladness.
Isa 52:8. . . . . watchmen shout and sing with *j*,
Isa 56:7. . . . . fill them with *j* in my house
Isa 60:15. . . . beautiful forever, a *j* to all
Isa 61:7. . . . . everlasting *j* will be yours.
Isa 65:14. . . . My servants will sing for *j*, but
Jer 31:13. . . . young women will dance for *j*,
Jer 31:13. . . . turn their mourning into *j*.
Jer 33:11. . . . the sounds of *j* and laughter.
Jer 48:33. . . . treads the grapes with shouts of *j*.
Jer 49:25. . . . a city of *j*, will be forsaken!
Joel 1:12. . . . the people's *j* has dried up

Matt 2:10 . . . they were filled with *j!*
Matt 28:8 . . . but also filled with great *j,*
Mark 1:11 . . Son, and you bring me great *j.*
Mark 4:16 . . receive it with *j.*
Luke 1:14. . . have great *j* and gladness,
Luke 1:44. . . in my womb jumped for *j.*
Luke 2:10. . . bring great *j* to all people.
Luke 6:23. . . be happy! Yes, leap for *j!*
Luke 10:21. . with the *j* of the Holy Spirit,
Luke 24:41. . filled with *j* and wonder.
John 15:11 . . you will be filled with my *j.*
John 16:20 . . turn to wonderful *j.*
John 16:24 . . and you will have abundant *j.*
John 20:20 . . *j* when they saw the Lord!
Acts 2:28 . . . you will fill me with the *j*
Acts 2:46 . . . their meals with great *j*
Acts 11:23 . . he was filled with *j,*
Acts 13:52 . . believers were filled with *j*
Acts 15:3 . . . much to everyone's *j*—
Rom 14:17 . . and *j* in the Holy Spirit.
Rom 15:13 . . with *j* and peace because
2 Cor 1:24 . . so you will be full of *j,*
2 Cor 2:3 . . . ought to give me the greatest *j.*
2 Cor 2:3 . . . *j* comes from your being joyful.
2 Cor 6:10 . . but we always have *j.*
2 Cor 7:7 . . . I was filled with *j!*
Gal 5:22. . . . fruit in our lives: love, *j,* peace,
Phil 1:4 . . . . requests for all of you with *j,*
Phil 1:25 . . . experience the *j* of your faith.
Phil 4:1 . . . . you are my *j* and the crown
1 Thes 1:6 . . received the message with *j*
1 Thes 2:19 . what gives us hope and *j,*
1 Thes 2:20 . Yes, you are our pride and *j.*
1 Thes 3:9 . . we have great *j*
2 Tim 1:4. . . with *j* when we are together
Heb 10:34 . . you accepted it with *j.*
Heb 12:2 . . . Because of the *j* awaiting him,
Heb 13:17 . . reason to do this with *j*
Jas 1:2. . . . . . it an opportunity for great *j.*
1 Pet 1:8. . . . a glorious, inexpressible *j.*
1 Pet 4:13. . . the wonderful *j* of seeing his
1 Jn 1:4. . . . . you may fully share our *j.*

JOYFUL (adj)
characterized by gladness or delight
Ps 30:11 . . . . my mourning into *j* dancing.
Ps 66:1 . . . . . Shout *j* praises to God, all the
Ps 98:6 . . . . . a *j* symphony before the LORD,
Ps 137:3 . . . . insisted on a *j* hymn:
Rom 15:32. . come to you with a *j* heart,
Gal 4:15 . . . . that *j* and grateful spirit
Gal 4:27. . . . Break into a *j* shout, you who
1 Thes 5:16 . Always be *j.*
Heb 12:22 . . angels in a *j* gathering.

JOYOUS (adj)
characterized by gladness or delight
2 Chr 29:30 . offered *j* praise and bowed
Neh 12:43 . . were offered on that *j* day,
Isa 61:3. . . . . for ashes, a *j* blessing instead
Jer 33:11. . . . with the *j* songs of people

JUBILEE (n)
a year of celebration, emancipation, and restoration
Lev 25:11. . . fiftieth year will be a *j*

JUDAH
1. Fourth son of Jacob and Leah (Gen 29:35), who gave his name to a tribe of Israel; interceded for Joseph (Gen 37:26-27); failed to uphold daughter-in-law Tamar's rights (Gen 38:1-30); offered himself as slave and ransom (Gen 44:18-34); given the family birthright by Jacob (Gen 49:3-10); his tribe was numbered (Num 1:26-27), allotted land and cities (Josh 15:1-63), led the conquest of Canaan (Judg 1:2); 12,000 will be marked by God (Rev 7:7).
2. The southern kingdom of Judah, including the tribes of Judah and Benjamin, in contrast to Israel (northern kingdom) (see 2 Sam 12:8).

JUDAISM (n)
the cultural, social, and religious beliefs and practices of the Jews
Acts 13:43 . . converts to *J* followed Paul

JUDAS
1. One of the 12 disciples, also known as "Iscariot" (Mark 3:19; Luke 6:16); criticized Mary (John 12:3-6); foretold as betrayer (John 6:70-71; 13:21-30); made deal for 30 pieces of silver (Matt 26:14-15; see also Mark 14:10); identified as a thief (John 12:6); entered by Satan (Luke 22:3; John 13:27); betrayed Jesus with kiss (Mark 14:43-45); had remorse and committed suicide (Matt 27:3-10; Acts 1:18); his position refilled (Acts 1:20-26).
2. Brother of James and half-brother of Jesus, also known as "Jude" (Matt 13:55; Mark 6:3; Jude 1:1).
3. One of the 12 disciples, son of James, likely also called Thaddaeus (Matt 10:3; Mark 3:18), not Iscariot (John 14:22); see also Luke 6:16; Acts 1:13.

JUDEA (n)
the Greco-Roman name for the land of Judah
Matt 2:1 . . . . was born in Bethlehem in *J,*
Matt 24:16 . . in *J* must flee to the hills.
Luke 3:1. . . . Pilate was governor over *J;*

Acts 1:8 . . . . throughout *J,* in Samaria,
Acts 9:31 . . . had peace throughout *J,*
1 Thes 2:14 . in God's churches in *J*

JUDGE, JUDGES (n)

a public official authorized to decide issues brought before a court; one of a cycle of charismatic deliverers of ancient Israel

Deut 17:12. . to reject the verdict of the *j*
Judg 2:16. . . LORD raised up *j-s* to rescue
Judg 2:18. . . the LORD raised up a *j*
1 Sam 7:6. . . Samuel became Israel's *j.*)
1 Sam 7:15. . continued as Israel's *j*
Ps 50:6 . . . . . God himself will be the *j.*
Isa 33:22. . . . the LORD is our *j,* our lawgiver,
Acts 7:35 . . . you a ruler and *j* over us?
Acts 10:42 . . *j* of all—the living and
Rev 14:7. . . . he will sit as *j.*

JUDGE, JUDGED, JUDGES, JUDGING (v)

to form an evaluation of; to decide as a judge; to govern or rule; to punish or condemn; to form a negative opinion about

1 Sam 16:7. . Don't *j* by his appearance or
1 Sam 24:12. the LORD *j* between us.
2 Chr 19:7 . . *j* with integrity, for the LORD
Ps 7:8 . . . . . . The LORD *j-s* the nations.
Ps 9:4 . . . . . . For you have *j-d* in my favor;
Ps 9:8 . . . . . . He will *j* the world
Ps 82:8 . . . . . Rise up, O God, and *j* the earth,
Ps 96:10 . . . . He will *j* all peoples fairly.
Ps 96:13 . . . . will *j* the world with justice,
Prov 16:10. . he must never *j* unfairly.
Prov 29:14. . If a king *j-s* the poor fairly,
Isa 11:3. . . . . He will not *j* by appearance
Isa 66:16. . . . He will *j* the earth,
Matt 7:1. . . . Do not *j* others, and you
Matt 16:27. . will *j* all people according
Matt 19:28. . thrones, *j-ing* the twelve
John 3:18 . . . been *j-d* for not believing
John 5:22. . . the Father *j-s* no one.
John 5:22. . . absolute authority to *j,*
John 5:27. . . authority to *j* everyone
John 5:30 . . . I *j* as God tells me.
John 12:31 . . time for *j-ing* this world
John 12:47 . . not *j* those who hear me
Acts 17:31 . . he has set a day for *j-ing*
Rom 2:16. . . Jesus, will *j* everyone's secret
Rom 3:6. . . . be qualified to *j* the world?
1 Cor 6:2 . . . we believers will *j* the world?
1 Cor 11:31 . we would not be *j-d*
2 Cor 5:10 . . stand before Christ to be *j-d.*
2 Tim 4:1 . . . Jesus, who will someday *j*
Heb 10:30 . . The LORD will *j* his own
Heb 13:4 . . . *j* people who are immoral
Jas 2:13. . . . . will be merciful when he *j-s*
Jas 3:1. . . . . . we who teach will be *j-d* more
Jas 4:11. . . . . criticizing and *j-ing* God's law.
Jas 4:12. . . . . So what right do you have to *j*
1 Pet 1:17. . . He will *j* or reward you
1 Pet 2:23. . . God, who always *j-s* fairly.
Rev 19:11. . . *j-s* fairly and wages a righteous
Rev 20:4. . . . given the authority to *j.*
Rev 20:12. . . the dead were *j-d* according to

JUDGMENT, JUDGMENTS (n)

a ruling or decision by a ruler, a judge, or an individual; the process of forming an opinion or evalution by discerning and comparing

see also JUSTICE

Deut 1:17. . . impartial in your *j-s.*
1 Sam 3:13. . warned him that *j* is coming
Ps 1:5 . . . . . . be condemned at the time of *j.*
Ps 37:13 . . . . he sees their day of *j* coming.
Ps 51:4 . . . . . your *j* against me is just.
Prov 4:1. . . . Pay attention and learn good *j,*
Prov 4:7. . . . else you do, develop good *j.*
Prov 9:10. . . results in good *j.*
Isa 3:14. . . . . comes forward to pronounce *j*
Jer 11:20. . . . you make righteous *j-s,*
Jer 25:31. . . . His cry of *j* will reach
Dan 9:11 . . . curses and *j-s* written in
Hos 6:5 . . . . with *j-s* as inescapable as light.
Joel 3:12. . . . LORD, will sit to pronounce *j*
Matt 5:21 . . . murder, you are subject to *j.*
Matt 11:24. . will be better off on *j* day
Matt 12:36. . on *j* day for every idle word
Matt 12:41. . this generation on *j* day
John 5:30 . . . *j* is just, because I carry out
John 8:16 . . . if I did, my *j* would be correct
John 16:8 . . . and of the coming *j.*
Acts 24:25 . . coming day of *j,*
1 Cor 4:3 . . . I don't even trust my own *j*
1 Cor 4:5 . . . don't make *j-s* about anyone
1 Cor 11:29 . eating and drinking God's *j*
2 Thes 1:8 . . *j* on those who don't know
Heb 9:27 . . . and after that comes *j,*
1 Pet 4:17. . . And if *j* begins with us,
2 Pet 2:9. . . . until the day of final *j.*
2 Pet 3:7. . . . being kept for the day of *j,*
Jude 1:6 . . . . waiting for the great day of *j.*
Rev 16:7. . . . your *j-s* are true and just.

JUST (adj)

conforming to a standard of correctness; faithful to the original design; honest, fair, upright

see also RIGHT, RIGHTEOUS

Gen 18:19 . . by doing what is right and *j.*
Deut 32:4. . . Everything he does is *j*

2 Sam 8:15 . . did what was *j* and right
Neh 9:13 . . . and instructions that were *j,*
Job 37:23 . . . he is *j* and righteous,
Ps 33:5 . . . . . loves whatever is *j* and good;
Ps 92:15 . . . . The LORD is *j!* He is
Ps 119:121 . . I have done what is *j*
Prov 1:3 . . . . do what is right, *j,* and fair.
Prov 2:9 . . . . understand what is right, *j,*
Prov 12:5 . . . The plans of the godly are *j;*
Isa 16:5. . . . . He will always do what is *j*
Isa 59:8. . . . . or what it means to be *j*
Jer 22:3. . . . . Be fair-minded and *j.*
Ezek 18:5 . . . and does what is *j* and right.
Dan 4:37 . . . All his acts are *j* and true,
Matt 5:45 . . . rain on the *j* and the unjust
1 Jn 1:9. . . . . he is faithful and *j* to forgive
Rev 15:3. . . . *J* and true are your ways,
Rev 16:5. . . . You are *j,* O Holy One,
Rev 16:7. . . . your judgments are true and *j.*
Rev 19:2. . . . His judgments are true and *j.*

JUSTICE (n)

the administration of law that determines what is right, based on principles of equity and correctness, and rewards accordingly; the quality of being just, impartial, or fair

see also JUDGMENT, RIGHTEOUSNESS

Exod 23:2 . . by the crowd to twist *j.*
Lev 19:15 . . . Do not twist *j* in legal matters
Deut 16:19 . . never twist *j* or show partiality
Deut 32:36 . . LORD will give *j* to his
1 Sam 8:3 . . . bribes and perverted *j.*
1 Kgs 3:11 . . governing my people with *j*
1 Kgs 7:7 . . . Hall of *J,* where he sat to hear
2 Chr 9:8 . . . so you can rule with *j*
Job 8:3 . . . . . Does God twist *j?*
Job 19:7 . . . . I protest, but there is no *j.*
Job 31:6 . . . . weigh me on the scales of *j,*
Job 34:17 . . . God govern if he hated *j?*
Ps 9:8 . . . . . . He will judge the world with *j*
Ps 10:18 . . . . You will bring *j* to the orphans
Ps 36:6 . . . . . your *j* like the ocean depths.
Ps 45:4 . . . . . defending truth, humility, and *j.*
Ps 45:7 . . . . . You love *j* and hate evil.
Ps 72:1 . . . . . Give your love of *j* to the king,
Ps 82:3 . . . . . Give *j* to the poor
Ps 96:13 . . . . He will judge the world with *j,*
Ps 98:9 . . . . . *j,* and the nations with fairness.
Ps 99:4 . . . . . You have acted with *j*
Ps 103:6 . . . . *j* to all who are treated
Ps 146:7 . . . . He gives *j* to the oppressed
Prov 16:12 . . his rule is built on *j.*
Prov 19:28 . . makes a mockery of *j;*
Prov 29:26 . . but *j* comes from the LORD.
Prov 31:9 . . . and see that they get *j.*
Isa 1:17. . . . . Seek *j.* Help the oppressed.
Isa 1:27. . . . . Zion will be restored by *j;*
Isa 5:16. . . . . will be exalted by his *j.*
Isa 10:2. . . . . They deprive the poor of *j*
Isa 28:17. . . . with the measuring line of *j*
Isa 33:5. . . . . make Jerusalem his home of *j*
Isa 42:1. . . . . He will bring *j* to the nations.
Isa 51:4. . . . . my *j* will become a light
Isa 59:9. . . . . there is no *j* among us,
Isa 59:14. . . . *j* is nowhere to be found.
Isa 61:8. . . . . I, the LORD, love *j.*
Jer 4:2. . . . . . you could do so with truth, *j,*
Jer 9:24. . . . . who brings *j* and righteousness
Jer 21:12. . . . Give *j* each morning
Jer 30:11. . . . discipline you, but with *j;*
Lam 3:36 . . . if they twist *j* in the courts—
Hos 2:19 . . . righteousness and *j,*
Amos 5:7. . . You twist *j,* making it a bitter
Amos 5:15 . . courts into true halls of *j.*
Amos 6:12 . . when you turn *j* into poison
Mic 3:8. . . . . I am filled with *j* and strength
Hab 1:4 . . . . there is no *j* in the courts.
Zeph 3:5 . . . Day by day he hands down *j,*
Mal 2:17. . . . Where is the God of *j?*
Matt 5:6. . . . who hunger and thirst for *j,*
Matt 12:18 . . proclaim *j* to the nations.
Matt 23:23 . . aspects of the law—*j,*
Luke 11:42 . . ignore *j* and the love of God.
Luke 18:3. . . Give me *j* in this dispute
Acts 8:33 . . . humiliated and received no *j.*
Acts 17:31 . . *j* by the man he has appointed
Rom 2:2. . . . God, in his *j,* will punish
2 Thes 1:5 . . persecution to show his *j*
2 Thes 1:6 . . In his *j* he will pay back
Heb 1:8 . . . . You rule with a scepter of *j.*
Heb 7:2 . . . . Melchizedek means "king of *j,*"
Heb 11:33 . . ruled with *j,* and received

JUSTIFY, JUSTIFIED (v)

to prove to be just, right, or reasonable; to acquit or absolve

see also RIGHT, RIGHTEOUS

Luke 10:29 . . wanted to *j* his actions,
Luke 18:14 . . returned home ***j-ied***
2 Cor 8:24 . . boasting about you is ***j-ied.***

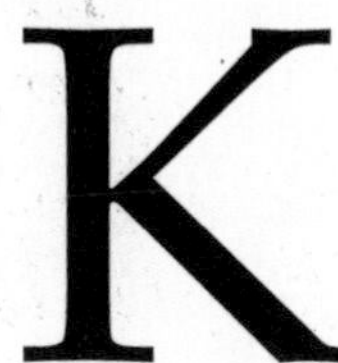

KEEP, KEEPING, KEEPS, KEPT (v)
to be faithful to; to have in control; to refrain from granting, giving, or allowing; to cause to remain in a given place, situation, or condition; to refrain from revealing; to maintain or preserve
see also GUARD, OBEY, PROTECT
Exod 12:42 . the LORD ***k-pt*** his promise
Exod 20:8 . . Sabbath day by ***k-ing*** it holy.
Exod 31:13 . Be careful to ***k*** my Sabbath
Deut 5:12. . . Sabbath day by ***k-ing*** it holy,
Deut 7:8. . . . ***k-ing*** the oath he had sworn
Deut 7:9. . . . God who ***k-s*** his covenant for a
Deut 7:12. . . your God will ***k*** his covenant
2 Chr 6:14 . . You ***k*** your covenant
2 Chr 34:31 . to obey the LORD by ***k-ing***
Neh 1:5 . . . . God who ***k-s*** his covenant of
Ps 15:4 . . . . . ***k*** their promises even when
Ps 116:14 . . . I will ***k*** my promises to
Ps 119:100 . . ***k-pt*** your commandments.
Ps 121:7 . . . . The LORD ***k-s*** you from
Ps 130:3 . . . . LORD, if you ***k-pt*** a record of
Ps 146:6 . . . . He ***k-s*** every promise
Prov 10:19 . . and ***k*** your mouth
Prov 15:3. . . ***k-ing*** his eye on
Prov 21:23 . . your tongue and ***k***
Eccl 3:6 . . . . A time to ***k*** and a time to
John 17:6 . . . and they have ***k-pt*** your word.
Acts 2:24 . . . death could not ***k*** him in its
Rom 10:3. . . by trying to ***k*** the law.
Rom 14:22 . . ***k*** it between yourself
1 Cor 1:8 . . . He will ***k*** you strong
1 Cor 7:19 . . ***k*** God's commandments.
1 Cor 13:5 . . it ***k-s*** no record
Eph 4:3 . . . . effort to ***k*** yourselves united
1 Tim 5:22 . . ***K*** yourself pure.
2 Tim 4:5 . . . But you should ***k*** a clear mind
Heb 11:27 . . going because he ***k-pt*** his eyes
Jas 2:10. . . . . the person who ***k-s*** all of the
1 Pet 1:4. . . . ***k-pt*** in heaven for you, pure
1 Jn 5:3. . . . . ***k-ing*** his commandments,
Jude 1:21 . . . ***k*** yourselves safe in God's love.
Rev 12:17. . . ***k*** God's commandments

KEY, KEYS (n)
instrument that opens (or locks) doors or gates; symbolic of authority, power, and control
Matt 16:19 . . the ***k-s*** of the Kingdom
Rev 1:18. . . . And I hold the ***k-s*** of death and
Rev 20:1. . . . with the ***k*** to the bottomless

KILL, KILLED, KILLING, KILLS (v)
to take or deprive of life
Gen 4:8 . . . . Abel, and ***k-ed*** him.
Exod 2:12 . . Moses ***k-ed*** the Egyptian
Exod 21:12 . assaults and ***k-s*** another
Lev 24:21. . . whoever ***k-s*** another person
2 Sam 2:26 . . always be ***k-ing*** each other?
Neh 9:26 . . . they ***k-ed*** your prophets
Job 13:15 . . . God might ***k*** me, but I
Ps 44:22 . . . . for your sake we are ***k-ed***
Prov 6:17. . . hands that ***k*** the innocent,
Eccl 3:3 . . . . A time to ***k*** and a time to
Matt 10:28 . . who want to ***k*** your body;
Matt 16:21 . . He would be ***k-ed,***
Mark 10:34 . flog him with a whip, and ***k***
Luke 11:48. . They ***k-ed*** the prophets,
Acts 3:15 . . . You ***k-ed*** the author
Rom 8:36. . . For your sake we are ***k-ed***
1 Tim 1:9 . . . who ***k*** their father or mother
1 Jn 3:12. . . . evil one and ***k-ed*** his brother.

KIND (adj)
affectionate, loving; of a sympathetic or helping nature; gentle
Luke 6:35. . . for he is ***k*** to those who are
1 Cor 13:4 . . is patient and ***k.*** Love is not
Eph 4:32 . . . Instead, be ***k*** to each other,
2 Tim 2:24 . . but must be ***k*** to everyone,

KIND, KINDS (n)
nature, family, type, or category
Gen 1:12 . . . and trees of the same ***k***.
1 Cor 12:4 . . different ***k-s*** of spiritual gifts,
1 Tim 6:10 . . root of all ***k-s*** of evil.

KINDNESS (n)
a kind deed; affection; the quality or state of being kind
Ps 106:7 . . . . his many acts of ***k*** to them.
Rom 2:4 . . . . his ***k*** is intended to turn you
Rom 3:24 . . . with undeserved ***k***, declares
Rom 12:8 . . . gift for showing ***k*** to others,
2 Cor 6:1 . . . marvelous gift of God's ***k***
2 Cor 8:1 . . . God in his ***k*** has done through
2 Cor 10:1 . . gentleness and ***k*** of Christ—
Gal 5:22 . . . . peace, patience, ***k***, goodness,
Eph 2:7 . . . . his grace and ***k*** toward us,
Col 3:12 . . . . mercy, ***k***, humility,
Titus 3:4. . . . revealed his ***k*** and love,
1 Pet 2:3. . . . a taste of the Lord's ***k***.

KING, KINGS (n)
a sovereign ruler (often God); chief among competitors
Deut 17:14. . We should select a ***k*** to rule
Judg 17:6 . . . In those days Israel had no ***k***;
1 Sam 8:5. . . Give us a ***k*** to judge us
1 Sam 11:15. they made Saul ***k***.
2 Sam 2:4. . . and anointed him ***k*** over the
2 Kgs 19:15 . of all the ***k-s*** of the earth.
Ps 44:4 . . . . . You are my ***K*** and my God.
Ps 68:32 . . . . to God, you ***k-s*** of the earth.
Ps 72:11 . . . . All ***k-s*** will bow
Ps 97:1 . . . . . The Lord is ***k***!
Isa 32:1. . . . . a righteous ***k*** is coming!
Isa 37:16. . . . of all the ***k-s*** of the earth.
Dan 2:21 . . . he removes ***k-s*** and sets
Dan 4:17 . . . Most High rules over the ***k-s***
Dan 4:37 . . . and honor the ***K*** of heaven.
Dan 7:24 . . . Its ten horns are ten ***k-s***
Zeph 3:8 . . . to gather the ***k-s*** of the earth
Zech 9:9. . . . Look, your ***k*** is coming to you.
Matt 27:11 . . Are you the ***k*** of the Jews?
John 1:49 . . . Son of God—the ***K*** of Israel!
John 12:13 . . Hail to the ***K*** of Israel!
Acts 17:7 . . . to another ***k***, named Jesus.
1 Tim 1:17 . . is the eternal ***K***, the unseen
1 Tim 6:15 . . the ***K*** of all ***k-s*** and
1 Pet 2:13. . . the ***k*** as head of state,
Rev 1:5. . . . . of all the ***k-s*** of the world.
Rev 17:14. . . all lords and ***K*** of all ***k-s***.
Rev 19:16. . . ***K*** of all ***k-s*** and Lord

KINGDOM (n)
rule or realm; dominion of a king
Exod 19:6 . . will be my ***k*** of priests,
1 Kgs 11:31 . to tear the ***k*** from the hand
1 Chr 28:7 . . make his ***k*** last forever.
Ps 145:11 . . . glory of your ***k***;
Matt 3:2. . . . for the ***K*** of Heaven is near.
Matt 4:23 . . . Good News about the ***K***.
Matt 5:10 . . . right, for the ***K*** of Heaven is
Matt 5:19 . . . great in the ***K*** of Heaven.
Matt 6:10 . . . May your ***K*** come soon.
Matt 7:21 . . . will enter the ***K*** of Heaven.
Matt 8:12 . . . for whom the ***K*** was prepared—
Matt 10:7 . . . them that the ***K*** of Heaven is
Matt 11:12. . until now, the ***K*** of Heaven
Matt 12:26 . . His own ***k*** will not
Matt 13:11 . . secrets of the ***K*** of Heaven,
Matt 13:38 . . represents the people of the ***K***.
Matt 13:43 . . their Father's ***K***. Anyone with
Matt 13:45 . . Again, the ***K*** of Heaven is
Matt 13:52 . . a disciple in the ***K*** of Heaven
Matt 16:28 . . Son of Man coming in his ***K***.
Matt 18:4 . . . greatest in the ***K*** of Heaven.
Matt 19:12 . . sake of the ***K*** of Heaven.
Matt 19:23 . . to enter the ***K*** of Heaven.
Matt 20:1 . . . For the ***K*** of Heaven is
Matt 21:43 . . I tell you, the ***K*** of God will
Matt 23:13 . . shut the door of the ***K*** of Heaven
Matt 24:14 . . Good News about the ***K*** will be
Matt 25:34 . . inherit the ***K*** prepared for
Mark 3:24 . . A ***k*** divided by
Mark 4:11 . . secret of the ***K*** of God.
Mark 4:30 . . I describe the ***K*** of God?
Mark 9:1 . . . they see the ***K*** of God arrive
Mark 10:15 . doesn't receive the ***K*** of God
Mark 10:24 . to enter the ***K*** of God.
Mark 11:10 . on the coming ***K*** of our
Mark 13:8 . . and ***k*** against ***k***.
Mark 15:43 . waiting for the ***K*** of God to
Luke 4:43. . . Good News of the ***K*** of God in
Luke 7:28. . . least person in the ***K*** of God
Luke 8:10. . . secrets of the ***K*** of God.
Luke 9:11. . . taught them about the ***K*** of God,
Luke 9:60. . . preach about the ***K*** of God.
Luke 10:9. . . tell them, 'The ***K*** of God is
Luke 10:11. . know this—the ***K*** of God is
Luke 11:17. . he said, "Any ***k*** divided
Luke 11:20. . the ***K*** of God has arrived
Luke 12:31. . Seek the ***K*** of God
Luke 13:18. . What is the ***K*** of God like?
Luke 14:15. . a banquet in the ***K*** of God!
Luke 17:20. . When will the ***K*** of God
Luke 17:21. . For the ***K*** of God is

Luke 18:24. . to enter the ***K*** of God!
Luke 18:29. . for the sake of the ***K*** of God,
Luke 21:10. . and ***k*** against ***k.***
Luke 22:16. . fulfilled in the ***K*** of God.
Luke 22:29. . granted me a ***K,*** I now grant
Luke 23:42. . come into your ***K.***
John 3:3 . . . . you cannot see the ***K*** of God.
John 3:5 . . . . no one can enter the ***K*** of God
John 18:36 . . But my ***K*** is not of
Acts 1:3 . . . . talked to them about the ***K*** of God.
Acts 1:6 . . . . restore our ***k?***
Acts 8:12 . . . News concerning the ***K*** of God
Acts 19:8 . . . about the ***K*** of God.
Acts 28:23 . . testified about the ***K*** of God
Rom 14:17. . For the ***K*** of God is
1 Cor 4:20 . . For the ***K*** of God is
1 Cor 6:10 . . will inherit the ***K*** of God.
1 Cor 15:24 . will turn the ***K*** over to God
1 Cor 15:50 . cannot inherit the ***K*** of God.
Gal 5:21 . . . . will not inherit the ***K*** of God.
Eph 5:5 . . . . will inherit the ***K*** of Christ
Col 4:11 . . . . with me here for the ***K*** of God.
1 Thes 2:12 . to share in his ***K*** and glory.
2 Thes 1:5 . . worthy of his ***K,*** for which
2 Tim 4:18 . . his heavenly ***K.*** All glory to
Heb 12:28 . . we are receiving a ***K*** that is
Jas 2:5. . . . . . inherit the ***K*** he promised to
2 Pet 1:11. . . into the eternal ***K*** of our
Rev 1:6. . . . . made us a ***K*** of priests for
Rev 5:10. . . . to become a ***K*** of priests for
Rev 11:15. . . now become the ***K*** of our Lord
Rev 12:10. . . power and the ***K*** of our God,
Rev 16:10. . . ***k*** was plunged into darkness.

KINSMAN-REDEEMER (KJV)
Ruth 3:9. . . . my ***family redeemer***
Ruth 3:12. . . of your ***family redeemers***
Ruth 4:1. . . . the ***family redeemer*** he had

KISS, KISSES (n)
a greeting or caress with the lips; an expression of affection
Prov 27:6. . . better than many ***k-es*** from an
Song 7:9. . . . May your ***k-es*** be as
Mark 14:45 . and gave him the ***k.***
Luke 22:48. . the Son of Man with a ***k?"***

KISS, KISSING (v)
to caress with the lips
Song 1:2. . . . ***K*** me and ***k*** me again,
Song 8:1. . . . Then I could ***k*** you no matter
Luke 7:38. . Then she kept ***k-ing*** his feet

KNEE, KNEES (n)
the joint in the middle part of the leg; when bent, symbolic of submission or defeat
Isa 35:3. . . . . those who have weak ***k-s.***
Isa 45:23. . . . Every ***k*** will bend to me,
Luke 5:8. . . . he fell to his ***k-s*** before Jesus
Rom 14:11 . . every ***k*** will bend to me,
Eph 3:14 . . . I fall to my ***k-s*** and pray to
Phil 2:10 . . . at the name of Jesus every ***k***
Heb 12:12 . . strengthen your weak ***k-s.***

KNEEL, KNELT (v)
to bend the knee; to fall or rest on the knees; usually a gesture of submission, defeat, or reverence
2 Chr 6:13 . . then he ***k-lt*** in front of
Ps 95:6 . . . . . Let us ***k*** before the LORD
Dan 6:10 . . . went home and ***k-lt*** down
Matt 8:2. . . . approached him and ***k-lt***
Matt 9:18. . . came and ***k-lt*** before him.
Matt 17:14. . came and ***k-lt*** before Jesus
Matt 27:29. . ***k-lt*** before him in mockery
Luke 22:41. . stone's throw, and ***k-lt*** down
Acts 20:36 . . speaking, he ***k-lt*** and prayed
Acts 21:5 . . . There we ***k-lt,*** prayed,

KNEW (v)
to be familiar with
see also KNOW
Matt 7:23. . . reply, 'I never ***k*** you.
John 2:24 . . . because he ***k*** human nature.
John 19:28 . . Jesus ***k*** that his mission
Acts 2:23 . . . But God ***k*** what would
Rom 1:21 . . . Yes, they ***k*** God,
Rom 8:29. . . God ***k*** his people in advance,
1 Pet 1:2. . . . God the Father ***k*** you and

KNIT (v)
to link firmly or closely
Ps 139:13 . . . ***k*** me together in my mother's
Col 2:2. . . . . encouraged and ***k*** together by

KNOCK, KNOCKING, KNOCKS (v)
to strike sharply
Matt 7:7. . . . Keep on ***k-ing,*** and the door
Matt 7:8. . . . to everyone who ***k-s,*** the door
Rev 3:20. . . . I stand at the door and ***k.***

KNOW, KNOWING, KNOWN, KNOWS (v)
to be intimately familiar with; to discern, recognize, regard, acknowledge, pay heed to, approve, learn
see also KNEW
Gen 3:5 . . . . like God, ***k-ing*** both good and
Gen 3:22 . . . like us, ***k-ing*** both good and

Gen 22:12 . . for now I ***k*** that you truly
Exod 6:7 . . . Then you will ***k*** that I am the
Deut 18:21. . How will we ***k*** whether or not
Deut 29:29. . God has secrets ***k-n*** to no
Josh 23:14 . . Deep in your hearts you ***k*** that
Job 19:25 . . . for me, I ***k*** that my Redeemer
Ps 9:10 . . . . . Those who ***k*** your name trust
Ps 19:2 . . . . . after night they make him ***k-n.***
Ps 44:21 . . . . for he ***k-s*** the secrets of
Ps 46:10 . . . . Be still, and ***k*** that I am
Ps 94:10 . . . . doesn't he also ***k*** what you
Ps 94:11 . . . . The LORD ***k-s*** people's thoughts;
Ps 103:14 . . . For he ***k-s*** how weak we are;
Ps 119:168 . . you ***k*** everything I do.
Ps 139:2 . . . . You ***k*** when I sit
Ps 139:23 . . . O God, and ***k*** my heart;
Isa 12:4. . . . . Let them ***k*** how mighty
Jer 9:24. . . . . that they truly ***k*** me and
Jer 31:34. . . . will ***k*** me already,
Dan 11:32 . . the people who ***k*** their God
Matt 6:3. . . . don't let your left hand ***k*** what
Matt 10:29. . without your Father ***k-ing*** it.
Matt 11:27. . no one truly ***k-s*** the Father
Mark 12:24 . you don't ***k*** the Scriptures,
Luke 11:13. . if you sinful people ***k*** how to
Luke 13:25. . will reply, 'I don't ***k*** you
Luke 16:15. . but God ***k-s*** your hearts.
Luke 23:34. . they don't ***k*** what they are
John 3:11 . . . you what we ***k*** and have seen,
John 4:42 . . . Now we ***k*** that he
John 6:69 . . . we ***k*** you are the Holy One
John 7:28 . . . Yes, you ***k*** me, and you
John 8:14 . . . For I ***k*** where I came
John 8:32 . . . And you will ***k*** the truth,
John 10:4 . . . because they ***k*** his voice.
John 10:27 . . I ***k*** them, and they follow
John 13:17 . . Now that you ***k*** these things,
John 14:7 . . . If you had really ***k-n*** me,
John 16:30 . . we understand that you ***k***
John 17:23 . . the world will ***k*** that you sent
John 21:15 . . Peter replied, "you ***k*** I love
Acts 1:24 . . . O Lord, you ***k*** every heart.
Rom 1:19 . . . They ***k*** the truth
Rom 7:18 . . . And I ***k*** that nothing good
Rom 8:26 . . . we don't ***k*** what God wants us
Rom 8:27 . . . the Father who ***k-s*** all hearts
Rom 11:34 . . For who can ***k*** the LORD's
Rom 12:16 . . And don't think you ***k*** it all!
Rom 16:26 . . message is made ***k-n*** to all
1 Cor 2:11 . . no one can ***k*** God's thoughts
1 Cor 13:12 . All that I ***k*** now is partial
2 Cor 4:6 . . . so we could ***k*** the glory of
Gal 4:9 . . . . . now that you ***k*** God (or should
Phil 3:10 . . . I want to ***k*** Christ and
Col 1:10 . . . . you learn to ***k*** God better and
1 Thes 3:3 . . But you ***k*** that we
1 Thes 5:2 . . For you ***k*** quite well
2 Thes 1:8 . . on those who don't ***k*** God
1 Tim 1:7 . . . but they don't ***k*** what they
1 Tim 3:15 . . you will ***k*** how people must
2 Tim 1:12 . . I ***k*** the one in whom I trust,
2 Tim 2:19 . . The LORD ***k-s*** those who are
Heb 8:11 . . . greatest, will ***k*** me already.
Heb 11:8 . . . without ***k-ing*** where he
Jas 1:3. . . . . . For you ***k*** that when your faith
Jas 4:14. . . . . How do you ***k*** what your life
Jas 4:17. . . . . it is sin to ***k*** what you ought
1 Pet 2:19. . . do what you ***k*** is right and
2 Pet 2:21. . . they had never ***k-n*** the way to
1 Jn 2:3. . . . . we can be sure that we ***k*** him
1 Jn 2:4. . . . . claims, "I ***k*** God," but
1 Jn 2:5. . . . . is how we ***k*** we are living in
1 Jn 2:11. . . . person does not ***k*** the way to
1 Jn 2:29. . . . Since we ***k*** that Christ
1 Jn 3:2. . . . . But we do ***k*** that we will be
1 Jn 3:24. . . . And we ***k*** he lives in us
1 Jn 4:6. . . . . is how we ***k*** if someone has
1 Jn 4:7. . . . . is a child of God and ***k-s*** God.
1 Jn 4:8. . . . . does not ***k*** God, for God
1 Jn 5:13. . . . you may ***k*** you have eternal
1 Jn 5:15. . . . And since we ***k*** he hears us
1 Jn 5:20. . . . And we ***k*** that the Son of
Rev 3:15. . . . I ***k*** all the things you do,

KNOWLEDGE (n)

the fact or condition of being aware of something, of having information, or of being learned; information, wisdom

Gen 2:9 . . . . the tree of the ***k*** of good and
Gen 2:17 . . . the tree of the ***k*** of good and
Prov 1:7. . . . foundation of true ***k,*** but fools
Prov 2:6. . . . From his mouth come ***k*** and
Prov 3:20. . . By his ***k*** the deep
Prov 8:10. . . ***k*** rather than pure gold.
Prov 14:6. . . ***k*** comes easily to those with
Prov 18:15. . Their ears are open for ***k.***
Isa 11:2. . . . . the Spirit of ***k*** and the fear
Luke 11:52. . remove the key to ***k*** from
Rom 2:20. . . gives you complete ***k***
1 Cor 12:8 . . gives a message of special ***k.***
1 Cor 13:2 . . and possessed all ***k,***
1 Cor 13:9 . . Now our ***k*** is partial
2 Cor 2:14 . . to spread the ***k*** of Christ
Eph 1:17 . . . grow in your ***k*** of God.
Eph 4:13 . . . our faith and ***k*** of God's Son
Phil 1:9 . . . . will keep on growing in ***k*** and
Col 1:9. . . . . to give you complete ***k*** of his
Col 2:3 . . . . . treasures of wisdom and ***k.***
Heb 10:26 . . we have received ***k*** of the
2 Pet 1:5. . . . and moral excellence with ***k,***
2 Pet 1:8. . . . ***k*** of our Lord Jesus Christ.
2 Pet 3:18. . . the grace and ***k*** of our Lord

LABOR (adj)
of or relating to manual labor; of or relating to the physical activities of giving birth
1 Kgs 12:4 . . Lighten the harsh *l* demands
Gal 4:19 . . . . I'm going through *l* pains for

LABOR (n)
work that produces goods and services; the physical activities of giving birth
Ps 128:2 . . . . enjoy the fruit of your *l.*
Isa 54:1. . . . . you who have never been in *l.*
Gal 4:27 . . . . have never been in *l!*

LACK (n)
the fact or state of being wanting or deficient; absence
Prov 5:23 . . . die for *l* of self-control;
Prov 15:22 . . go wrong for *l* of advice;
1 Cor 7:5 . . . because of your *l* of self-control.

LACK, LACKED, LACKING (v)
to be deficient, missing, or short; to have need of something
Deut 2:7. . . . and you have ***l-ed*** nothing.
Deut 28:48. . naked, and ***l-ing*** in everything.
Neh 9:21 . . . and they ***l-ed*** nothing.
Prov 28:27 . . the poor will *l* nothing,

LAID (v)
to place or set down
see also LAY
Isa 53:6. . . . . Yet the LORD *l* on him the
Acts 6:6 . . . . as they *l* their hands on them.
Acts 8:18 . . . the apostles *l* their hands on
1 Tim 4:14 . . elders of the church *l* their
2 Tim 1:6 . . . when I *l* my hands on

LAKE (n)
a considerable inland body of standing water
Matt 8:24. . . a fierce storm struck the *l,*
Luke 8:33. . . into the *l* and drowned.
John 6:25 . . . on the other side of the *l*
Rev 19:20. . . into the fiery *l* of burning
Rev 20:14. . . This *l* of fire is

LAKESHORE (n)
the land bordering a lake
Mark 4:1 . . . Jesus began teaching by the *l.*

LAMB, LAMBS (n)
a young sheep that is less than one year old
Exod 12:21 . pick out a *l* or young goat
Isa 53:7. . . . . He was led like a *l* to the
Mark 14:12 . the Passover *l* is sacrificed,
Luke 10:3. . . out as ***l-s*** among wolves.
John 1:29 . . . and said, "Look! The *L* of God
John 21:15 . . "Then feed my ***l-s,"*** Jesus
Acts 8:32 . . . And as a *l* is silent before
1 Pet 1:19. . . sinless, spotless *L* of God.
Rev 5:6. . . . . Then I saw a *L* that looked as
Rev 5:12. . . . Worthy is the *L* who was
Rev 7:14. . . . robes in the blood of the *L*
Rev 15:3. . . . the song of the *L:*
Rev 17:14. . . to war against the *L,* but the
Rev 19:9. . . . to the wedding feast of the *L.*
Rev 21:23. . . and the *L* is its light.

LAME (adj)
having a disabled body part as to impair freedom of movement
Isa 33:23. . . . Even the *l* will take
Isa 35:6. . . . . The *l* will leap like a
Matt 11:5 . . . blind see, the *l* walk,
Matt 15:31 . . the *l* were walking,
Luke 14:21. . the blind, and the *l.*
Heb 12:13 . . weak and *l* will not fall

LAMP, LAMPS (n)
a source of intellectual or spiritual illumination; any of various devices for producing light
2 Sam 22:29. O LORD, you are my *l.*

Ps 18:28 . . . . You light a *l* for me.
Ps 119:105 . . Your word is a *l* to guide my
Prov 6:23 . . . For their command is a *l*
Prov 31:18 . . her *l* burns late
Matt 6:22 . . . Your eye is a *l* that
Matt 25:1 . . . who took their ***l-s***
Matt 25:7 . . . got up and prepared their ***l-s.***
Luke 8:16 . . . No one lights a *l* and then
Luke 12:35 . . and keep your ***l-s*** burning,
Rev 22:5 . . . . no need for ***l-s*** or sun—for the

LAMPSTAND, LAMPSTANDS (n)

a support that holds a lamp
Exod 25:31 . Make the entire *l* and its
2 Chr 4:7 . . . cast ten gold ***l-s*** according to
Zech 4:2 . . . . a solid gold *l* with a bowl of
Zech 4:11 . . . on each side of the *l,*
Heb 9:2 . . . . In the first room were a *l,*
Rev 1:12 . . . . I saw seven gold ***l-s.***
Rev 1:20 . . . . the seven gold ***l-s:***
Rev 2:5 . . . . . and remove your *l* from its

LAND (n)

the solid part of the surface of the earth; a portion of the earth's solid surface distinguishable by boundaries or ownership
Gen 1:10 . . . the dry ground "*l*" and the
Gen 15:18 . . I have given this *l* to your
Exod 6:8 . . . you into the *l* I swore to
Deut 8:7 . . . . you into a good *l* of flowing
Ps 37:11 . . . . will possess the *l* and will

LANGUAGE, LANGUAGES (n)

means of communication peculiar to a certain people; a special language gift given by the Holy Spirit
see also TONGUE(S)
Gen 11:9 . . . the people with different ***l-s.***
Isa 28:11 . . . . speak a strange *l!*
Mark 16:17 . they will speak in new ***l-s.***
Acts 2:4 . . . . speaking in other ***l-s,*** as the
1 Cor 12:28 . speak in unknown ***l-s.***
1 Cor 12:30 . to interpret unknown ***l-s?***
1 Cor 13:8 . . in unknown ***l-s*** and special
1 Cor 14:19 . in an unknown *l.*
Eph 4:29 . . . or abusive *l.* Let everything
Col 3:8 . . . . . slander, and dirty *l.*
Rev 5:9 . . . . . every tribe and *l* and people
Rev 7:9 . . . . . and tribe and people and *l,*
Rev 14:6 . . . . nation, tribe, *l,* and people.

LAP (v)

to take in food or drink with the tongue
Judg 7:5 . . . . and *l* it up with their tongues

LASCIVIOUSNESS (KJV)
Mark 7:22 . . deceit, ***lustful desires,*** envy,
2 Cor 12:21 . and ***eagerness for lustful pleasure***
Gal 5:19 . . . . impurity, ***lustful pleasures***
Eph 4:19 . . . They live for ***lustful pleasure***
1 Pet 4:3 . . . . their ***immorality*** and lust,

LAST, LASTING (adj)

following all the rest; being the only remaining; belonging to the final stage; of or relating to being continuous in time; existing or continuing a long while
Prov 10:25 . . have a ***l-ing*** foundation.
Matt 20:16 . . who are *l* now will be first
John 15:16 . . to go and produce ***l-ing*** fruit,
Acts 2:17 . . . 'In the *l* days,' God says,
1 Cor 15:26 . And the *l* enemy to be
1 Cor 15:52 . *l* trumpet is blown.
2 Tim 3:1 . . . that in the *l* days there will
2 Pet 3:3 . . . . that in the *l* days scoffers
Jude 1:18 . . . you that in the *l* times there

LAST (n)

the one who is at or endures to the end
Isa 41:4 . . . . . First and the **L.** I alone
Isa 44:6 . . . . . First and the ***L;*** there is no
Isa 48:12 . . . . God, the First and the **L.**
Rev 1:17 . . . . I am the First and the **L.**
Rev 22:13 . . . the Omega, the First and the ***L,***

LAST, LASTS (v)

to continue in time
Ps 30:5 . . . . . For his anger *l* only a moment,
1 Cor 13:13 . *l* forever—faith, hope, and

LAUGH, LAUGHED, LAUGHS (v)

to show mirth or joy or to despise or mock something with a chuckle or explosive vocal sound
Gen 17:17 . . ***l-ed*** to himself in disbelief.
Gen 18:12 . . So she ***l-ed*** silently to herself
Ps 2:4 . . . . . . one who rules in heaven ***l-s.***
Ps 37:13 . . . . the LORD just ***l-s,*** for he sees
Ps 59:8 . . . . . But LORD, you *l* at them.
Prov 31:25 . . and she ***l-s*** without fear of
Eccl 3:4 . . . . and a time to *l.* A time to
Luke 6:21 . . . for in due time you will *l.*
Luke 6:25 . . . awaits you who *l* now,

LAUGHTER (n)

a chuckle or explosive vocal sound; cause for merriment
Gen 21:6 . . . God has brought me *l.*
Ps 126:2 . . . . We were filled with *l,* and we
Eccl 2:2 . . . . So I said, "***L*** is silly.

Jer 7:34. . . . . happy singing and *l* in the
Jas 4:9. . . . . . instead of *l,* and gloom

LAVER(S) (KJV)
Exod 30:18 . Make a bronze ***washbasin***
Lev 8:11. . . . ***washbasin*** and its stand,
1 Kgs 7:38 . . ten smaller bronze ***basins***
2 Chr 4:14 . . carts holding the ***basins***

LAVISH (v)
to expend or bestow with profusion
Exod 34:7 . . I *l* unfailing love

LAW, LAWS (n)
words of Moses; a binding decree; a universal principle; governing authority
see also COMMANDMENT(S), INSTRUCTION(S), REGULATIONS, TEACHING(S)
2 Chr 17:9 . . the Book of the *L*
Ps 1:2. . . . . . delight in the *l* of the LORD,
Ps 93:5. . . . . Your royal ***l-s*** cannot be
Ps 119:14 . . . rejoiced in your ***l-s*** as much as
Ps 119:36 . . . for your ***l-s*** rather than a love
Ps 119:125 . . I will understand your ***l-s.***
Ps 119:152 . . days that your ***l-s*** will last
Matt 5:17 . . . to abolish the *l* of Moses or
Matt 5:19 . . . who obeys God's ***l-s***
Matt 22:40 . . The entire *l* and all the
Matt 23:23 . . of the *l*—justice, mercy,
Mark 7:8 . . . ignore God's *l* and substitute
Luke 11:52. . experts in religious *l!*
Luke 23:56. . rested as required by the *l.*
Luke 24:44. . written about me in the *l*
John 1:17 . . . For the *l* was given
Rom 2:12 . . . be judged by that *l* when they
Rom 2:15 . . . that God's *l* is written in
Rom 2:20 . . . that God's *l* gives you
Rom 2:25 . . . if you don't obey God's *l,*
Rom 3:19 . . . Obviously, the *l* applies to
Rom 3:21 . . . requirements of the *l,* as was
Rom 3:28 . . . not by obeying the *l.*
Rom 4:13 . . . his obedience to God's *l,*
Rom 4:16 . . . according to the *l* of Moses,
Rom 5:13 . . . was not yet any *l* to break.
Rom 6:15 . . . has set us free from the *l,*
Rom 7:4. . . . power of the *l* when you died
Rom 7:5. . . . the *l* aroused these evil desires
Rom 7:8. . . . If there were no *l,* sin would
Rom 7:12 . . . But still, the *l* itself is
Rom 7:22 . . . I love God's *l* with all my
Rom 7:25 . . . I really want to obey God's *l,*
Rom 8:3. . . . did what the *l* could not do.
Rom 8:4. . . . requirement of the *l* would be
Rom 8:7. . . . did obey God's ***l-s,*** and it
Rom 9:4. . . . gave them his *l.* He gave them
Rom 9:31 . . . with God by keeping the *l,*
Rom 10:4 . . . for which the *l* was given.
Rom 13:10 . . requirements of God's *l.*
1 Cor 9:9 . . . For the *l* of Moses
1 Cor 9:21 . . I obey the *l* of Christ.
2 Cor 3:6 . . . not of written ***l-s,*** but of the
Gal 2:16 . . . . by obeying the *l.* And we have
Gal 2:19 . . . . So I died to the *l*—I stopped
Gal 3:2. . . . . by obeying the *l* of Moses?
Gal 3:5. . . . . because you obey the *l?*
Gal 3:11 . . . . by trying to keep the *l.*
Gal 3:19 . . . . But the *l* was designed
Gal 3:21 . . . . If the *l* could give us
Gal 3:23 . . . . placed under guard by the *l.*
Gal 4:21 . . . . live under the *l,* do you know
Gal 5:3. . . . . in the whole *l* of Moses.
Gal 5:14 . . . . the whole *l* can be summed
Gal 6:2. . . . . this way obey the *l* of Christ.
Eph 2:15 . . . the system of *l* with its
Phil 3:6 . . . . I obeyed the *l* without fault.
1 Tim 1:8 . . . know that the *l* is good when
Heb 10:1 . . . under the *l* of Moses
Jas 1:25. . . . . into the perfect *l* that sets
Jas 2:8. . . . . . obey the royal *l* as found in
Jas 2:10. . . . . all of the ***l-s*** except one is as

LAWGIVER (n)
one who gives a code of laws to a people
Isa 33:22. . . . is our judge, our *l,* and our

LAWLESS (adj)
not regulated by law; not restrained or controlled by law; unruly
Acts 2:23 . . . the help of *l* Gentiles,
Heb 10:17 . . their sins and *l* deeds.

LAWLESSNESS (n)
the quality or state of not being restrained or controlled by law
2 Thes 2:3 . . the man of *l* is revealed—
2 Thes 2:7 . . For this *l* is already
2 Thes 2:8 . . Then the man of *l* will be

LAWSUITS (n)
an act or instance of suing
1 Cor 6:7 . . . Even to have such *l* with one

LAY, LAYING (v)
to put or set down
see also LAID
Exod 29:10 . his sons will *l* their hands
Lev 1:4. . . . . *L* your hand on
Lev 4:15. . . . must then *l* their hands on
Num 8:10 . . of Israel must *l* their hands
Num 27:18 . in him, and *l* your hands on
Acts 8:19 . . . so that when I *l* my hands on

Heb 6:2 . . . . the *l-ing* on of hands,
Rev 4:10. . . . And they *l* their crowns

LAZINESS (n)
a disinclination to activity or exertion
Prov 31:27. . suffers nothing from *l.*
Ezek 16:49. . gluttony, and *l,* while the

LAZY (adj)
disinclined to activity or exertion; not energetic or vigorous
Prov 12:27. . *L* people don't
Prov 20:4. . . Those too *l* to plow in the
Rom 12:11. . Never be *l,* but work
1 Tim 5:13 . . they will learn to be *l*
Titus 1:12. . . animals, and *l* gluttons.

LAZYBONES (n)
a lazy person
Prov 6:6 . . . . from the ants, you *l.*

LEAD, LEADING, LEADS (v)
to guide by direction or example; to go at the head of; to result in
see also LED
Deut 27:18. . anyone who *l-s* a blind
Deut 31:2. . . no longer able to *l* you.
Josh 1:6 . . . . one who will *l* these people
2 Chr 1:10 . . knowledge to *l* them
Ps 25:9 . . . . . He *l-s* the humble in
Ps 73:24 . . . . with your counsel, *l-ing* me to
Prov 6:22. . . counsel will *l* you.
Prov 14:30. . A peaceful heart *l-s* to a
Prov 19:23. . Fear of the LORD *l-s* to life,
Isa 11:6. . . . . little child will *l* them all.
Matt 15:14. . blind guides *l-ing* the blind,
John 10:3 . . . by name and *l-s* them out.
Rom 6:16. . . to sin, which *l-s* to death,
Rom 6:22. . . things that *l* to holiness and
1 Tim 5:24 . . *l-ing* them to certain judgment.
Rev 7:17. . . . He will *l* them to

LEADER, LEADERS (n)
a person who has commanding authority or influence; chief among others
1 Sam 13:14. to be the *l* of his people,
Prov 17:26. . to flog *l-s* for being honest.
Jer 51:46. . . . *l-s* fight against each other.
Matt 20:26 . . a *l* among you must be
Mark 10:43 . a *l* among you must be
Luke 22:26. . *l* should be like a servant.
Acts 13:27 . . Jerusalem and their *l-s* did not
1 Thes 5:12 . who are your *l-s* in the Lord's
Heb 13:7 . . . Remember your *l-s* who taught
Heb 13:17 . . Obey your spiritual *l-s,* and do
3 Jn 1:9. . . . . to be the *l,* refuses to have

LEADERSHIP (n)
the office or position of a leader; capacity to lead
Num 33:1 . . under the *l* of Moses
1 Cor 12:28 . those who have the gift of *l,*

LEAP, LEAPED (v)
to spring from (or as if from) the ground
Isa 35:6. . . . . The lame will *l* like a deer,
Luke 1:41. . . Elizabeth's child *l-ed* within

LEARN, LEARNED, LEARNS (v)
to come to know or realize; to acquire knowledge, skill, or behavioral tendency
Deut 4:10. . . Then they will *l* to fear me
Deut 5:1. . . . so you may *l* them and obey
Prov 9:9 . . . . and they will *l* even more.
Prov 18:15. . are always ready to *l.*
Isa 1:17. . . . . *L* to do good.
Isa 26:9. . . . . will people *l* what is right.
Isa 29:13. . . . man-made rules *l-ed* by rote.
Matt 2:7. . . . and he *l-ed* from them the time
John 6:45 . . . listens to the Father and *l-s*
Phil 4:9 . . . . all you *l-ed* and received from
Phil 4:11 . . . have *l-ed* how to be content
Col 1:10 . . . . grow as you *l* to know God
1 Tim 2:11 . . Women should *l* quietly and
2 Tim 1:13 . . teaching you *l-ed* from me—
Heb 5:8 . . . . he *l-ed* obedience from the

LEAST (adj)
lowest in importance or position
Matt 19:30. . will be *l* important then,
Mark 10:31 . will be *l* important then,

LEATHER (adj)
of or relating to animal skin dressed for use
2 Kgs 1:8 . . . he wore a *l* belt around his
Matt 3:4. . . . he wore a *l* belt around his

LEAVEN (KJV)
Exod 12:20 . anything made with ***yeast***
Exod 13:7 . . any ***yeast*** at all found within
Matt 13:33. . of Heaven is like the ***yeast***
Matt 16:6. . . the ***yeast*** of the Pharisees
1 Cor 5:6 . . . this sin is like a little ***yeast***

LED (v)
to guide by direction or example
see also LEAD
Ps 68:18 . . . . the heights, you *l* a crowd of
Isa 53:7. . . . . He was *l* like a lamb
Jer 11:19. . . . like a lamb being *l* to the
Luke 4:1. . . . He was *l* by the Spirit
Acts 8:32 . . . He was *l* like a sheep
Rom 8:14. . . all who are *l* by the Spirit
Eph 4:8 . . . . the heights, he *l* a crowd of

LEFT (adj)
of, relating to, situated on, or being the side of the body in which the heart is mostly located
Matt 6:3. . . . don't let your *l* hand know

LEFT (n)
the location or direction of the left side
Josh 1:7 . . . . or to the *l*. Then you will be
Josh 23:6 . . . either to the right or to the *l*.
Isa 30:21. . . . to the right or to the *l*.
Matt 25:33 . . and the goats at his *l*.
Matt 25:41 . . those on the *l* and say, 'Away

LEFT (v)
to depart from; to allow to remain
Isa 53:6. . . . . We have *l* God's paths
Ezek 34:8. . . and *l* the sheep to starve.

LEFTOVERS (n)
something that remains unused or unconsumed
Matt 14:20 . . picked up twelve baskets of *l*.

LEGION (n)
a very large number; multitude
Mark 5:9 . . . My name is *L*, because there

LEND, LENDING (v)
to give for temporary use on condition that the same or its equivalent be returned
Lev 25:37. . . interest on money you *l*
Deut 15:8. . . and *l* them whatever
Ps 15:5 . . . . . Those who *l* money without
Prov 19:17 . . you are ***l-ing*** to the LORD—
Luke 6:34. . . Even sinners will *l* to other

LENDER, LENDERS (n)
one who loans to another
Exod 22:25 . as a money *l* would.
Prov 22:7. . . borrower is servant to the *l*.
Isa 24:2. . . . . and sellers, ***l-s*** and borrowers,

LENGTHENS (v)
to make longer; to extend
Prov 10:27 . . of the LORD *l* one's life,

LEPERS (n)
one who suffers from a severe contagious skin and nerve disease
Matt 11:5. . . lame walk, the *l* are cured,
Luke 17:12. . ten *l* stood at a distance,

LEPROSY (n)
a chronic infectious disease affecting the skin and peripheral nerves which causes loss of sensation, paralysis, and deformities
Num 12:10 . as white as snow from *l*.
2 Kgs 5:1 . . . he suffered from *l*.
2 Kgs 7:3 . . . four men with *l* sitting at
2 Chr 26:21 . King Uzziah had *l* until the

LESSON (n)
something learned by study or experience; an instructive example
Lev 26:23. . . to learn the *l* and continue
Prov 6:6. . . . Take a *l* from the ants,

LETTER, LETTERS (n)
a piece of written communication
Deut 24:1. . . he writes her a *l* of divorce,
2 Cor 3:2 . . . Your lives are a *l* written in
2 Cor 10:10 . Paul's ***l-s*** are demanding
2 Thes 3:14 . obey what we say in this *l*.
2 Pet 3:16. . . have twisted his ***l-s*** to mean

LEVEL (v)
to make flat
Isa 40:4. . . . . valleys, and *l* the mountains

LEVI
1. Third son of Jacob and Leah (Gen 29:34), who gave his name to a tribe of Israel; violently avenged his sister Dinah (Gen 34); cursed for his violent temper (Gen 49:5-7); his tribe was blessed (Deut 33:8-11), chosen for priestly service (Num 3–4), numbered (Num 3:39; 26:62), allotted cities, but not land (Josh 13:14; see also Num 18:21-32); 12,000 will be marked by God (Rev 7:7).
2. See MATTHEW, *also known as Levi.*

LEVIATHAN (n)
a sea monster represented as a cruel enemy defeated by God
Job 41:1 . . . . Can you catch **L** with a hook
Ps 74:14 . . . . crushed the heads of **L** and
Isa 27:1. . . . . and punish ***L***, the swiftly

LEWDNESS
that which lacks legal or moral restraints; sexual obscenity or vulgarity
Ezek 23:27. . stop to the *l* and prostitution
Ezek 24:13. . impurity is your *l* and

LIAR, LIARS (n)
a person who deceives by telling untruths or falsehoods
Ps 63:11 . . . . while ***l-s*** will be silenced.
Ps 116:11 . . . These people are all ***l-s!***
Prov 17:4. . . ***l-s*** pay close attention to
Prov 29:12. . pays attention to ***l-s***, all his
Prov 30:6. . . expose you as a *l*.
Isa 57:4. . . . . of sinners and ***l-s!***
John 8:44. . . a *l* and the father of lies.
Rom 3:4. . . . else is a *l*, God is true.

1 Tim 1:10 . . are slave traders, ***l-s,*** promise
Titus 1:12. . . are all ***l-s,*** cruel animals,
1 Jn 1:10. . . . calling God a ***l*** and showing
1 Jn 2:4. . . . . that person is a ***l*** and is not
1 Jn 4:20. . . . that person is a ***l;*** for if we
1 Jn 5:10. . . . calling God a ***l*** because they
Rev 3:9. . . . . synagogue—those ***l-s*** who say
Rev 21:8. . . . and all ***l-s***—their fate is in

LIBERATORS (n)
one who frees or sets at liberty
Neh 9:27 . . . you sent them ***l*** who rescued

LICK (v)
to draw the tongue over
Isa 49:23. . . . before you and ***l*** the dust

LIE, LIES (n)
an untrue or inaccurate statement; something that misleads or deceives
Ps 7:14 . . . . . give birth to ***l-s.***
Ps 24:4 . . . . . and never tell ***l-s.***
Ps 34:13 . . . . lips from telling ***l-s!***
Prov 12:17. . a false witness tells ***l-s.***
Prov 30:8. . . never to tell a ***l.***
John 8:44 . . . the father of ***l-s.***
Rom 1:25. . . about God for a ***l.***
Rom 3:13. . . filled with ***l-s.***
Eph 4:14 . . . to trick us with ***l-s*** so clever
Eph 4:25 . . . So stop telling ***l-s.***
2 Thes 2:11 . they will believe these ***l-s.***
1 Pet 3:10. . . and your lips from telling ***l-s.***
2 Pet 2:3. . . . make up clever ***l-s*** to get hold
1 Jn 2:21. . . . between truth and ***l-s.***
Rev 14:5. . . . They have told no ***l-s;***

LIE, LIED, LIES (v)
to make an untrue statement with intent to deceive; to create a false or misleading impression
see also LYING
Lev 6:3. . . . . lost property and ***l*** about it,
Job 31:5 . . . . Have I ***l-d*** to anyone or
Ps 58:3 . . . . . even from birth they have ***l-d***
Ps 89:35 . . . . in my holiness I cannot ***l:***
Prov 24:28. . don't ***l*** about them.
Prov 26:19. . who ***l-s*** to a friend
Jer 7:9. . . . . . commit adultery, ***l,*** and burn
Matt 5:11. . . persecute you and ***l***
Col 3:9 . . . . . Don't ***l*** to each other,
Titus 1:2. . . . God—who does not ***l***

LIFE (n)
the quality that distinguishes a vital and functional being from a dead body; period from birth to death; a way or manner of living; spiritual existence transcending death; salvation
see also LIVES
Gen 1:30 . . . everything that has ***l.***
Gen 2:7 . . . . He breathed the breath of ***l***
Gen 2:9 . . . . the tree of ***l*** and the tree of
Gen 9:5 . . . . who takes another person's ***l.***
Gen 9:6 . . . . a human ***l,*** that person's ***l***
Exod 21:23 . the injury: a ***l*** for a ***l,***
Num 35:31 . payment for the ***l*** of someone
Deut 19:21. . be ***l*** for ***l,*** eye for eye,
Deut 30:19. . choice between ***l*** and death,
Deut 32:39. . kills and gives ***l;*** I am the
1 Sam 2:6. . . both death and ***l;*** he brings
Ps 23:6 . . . . . the days of my ***l,*** and I will
Ps 69:28 . . . . the Book of ***L;*** don't let them
Ps 91:16 . . . . with a long ***l*** and give them
Ps 139:24 . . . the path of everlasting ***l.***
Prov 3:2. . . . your ***l*** will be satisfying.
Prov 6:26. . . will cost you your ***l.***
Prov 13:3. . . have a long ***l;*** opening your
Prov 15:4. . . Gentle words are a tree of ***l;***
Prov 21:21. . will find ***l,*** righteousness,
Prov 28:16. . will have a long ***l.***
Isa 53:8. . . . . that his ***l*** was cut short in
Isa 55:3. . . . . you will find ***l.*** I will make
Lam 3:58 . . . you have redeemed my ***l.***
Dan 12:2 . . . to everlasting ***l*** and some to
Matt 7:14. . . But the gateway to ***l*** is very
Matt 18:8. . . to enter eternal ***l*** with only
Matt 20:28. . and to give his ***l*** as a ransom
Mark 8:35 . . to hang on to your ***l,***
Mark 10:45 . and to give his ***l*** as a ransom
Luke 6:9. . . . a day to save ***l*** or to destroy
Luke 9:24. . . give up your ***l*** for my sake,
Luke 12:25. . single moment to your ***l?***
John 1:4 . . . . The Word gave ***l*** to everything
John 3:15 . . . will have eternal ***l.***
John 4:14 . . . giving them eternal ***l.***
John 5:24 . . . passed from death into ***l.***
John 5:39 . . . they give you eternal ***l.***
John 6:27 . . . the eternal ***l*** that the Son of
John 6:35 . . . I am the bread of ***l.***
John 6:47 . . . who believes has eternal ***l.***
John 6:53 . . . have eternal ***l*** within you.
John 6:68 . . . the words that give eternal ***l.***
John 10:10 . . a rich and satisfying ***l.***
John 10:15 . . So I sacrifice my ***l*** for the
John 10:28 . . give them eternal ***l,*** and they
John 12:25 . . nothing for their ***l*** in this
John 14:6 . . . the truth, and the ***l.***
John 17:2 . . . He gives eternal ***l*** to each
John 20:31 . . you will have ***l*** by the power
Acts 3:15 . . . You killed the author of ***l,***
Rom 1:17. . . a righteous person has ***l.***

Rom 2:7. . . . will give eternal *l* to those
Rom 4:25. . . he was raised to *l* to make us
Rom 5:10. . . be saved through the *l* of his
Rom 5:18. . . God and new *l* for everyone.
Rom 5:21. . . in eternal *l* through Jesus
Rom 6:13. . . now you have new *l.*
Rom 6:22. . . result in eternal *l.*
Rom 6:23. . . is eternal *l* through Christ
Rom 8:6. . . . mind leads to *l* and peace.
Rom 8:11. . . he will give *l* to your mortal
Rom 8:38. . . death nor *l,* neither angels
2 Cor 3:6 . . . the Spirit gives *l.*
2 Cor 4:10 . . so that the *l* of Jesus may
Gal 3:11 . . . . a righteous person has *l.*
Gal 3:21 . . . . give us new *l,* we could be
Gal 6:8 . . . . . harvest everlasting *l* from
Eph 2:5 . . . . he gave us *l* when he raised
Eph 4:1 . . . . to lead a *l* worthy of your
Phil 2:16 . . . Hold firmly to the word of *l;*
Phil 4:3 . . . . written in the Book of *L.*
Col 3:3 . . . . . and your real *l* is hidden
1 Tim 1:16 . . and receive eternal *l.*
1 Tim 4:8 . . . and in the *l* to come.
1 Tim 6:19 . . may experience true *l.*
2 Tim 1:9 . . . called us to live a holy *l.*
2 Tim 3:12 . . to live a godly *l* in Christ
Titus 3:5. . . . new *l* through the Holy Spirit.
Heb 7:16 . . . power of a *l* that cannot be
Jas 1:12. . . . . the crown of *l* that God has
1 Pet 3:7. . . . God's gift of new *l.*
1 Pet 3:10. . . want to enjoy *l* and see many
1 Pet 3:16. . . see what a good *l* you live
2 Pet 1:3. . . . for living a godly *l.*
1 Jn 1:1. . . . . He is the Word of *l.*
1 Jn 3:14. . . . have passed from death to *l.*
1 Jn 3:16. . . . gave up his *l* for us.
1 Jn 5:20. . . . God, and he is eternal *l.*
Jude 1:21 . . . bring you eternal *l.*
Rev 3:5. . . . . names from the Book of *L,*
Rev 13:8. . . . in the Book of *L* before the
Rev 17:8. . . . in the Book of *L* before the
Rev 20:12. . . the Book of *L.* And the dead
Rev 21:27. . . in the Lamb's Book of *L.*
Rev 22:1. . . . with the water of *l,* clear as
Rev 22:2. . . . a tree of *l,* bearing twelve
Rev 22:14. . . eat the fruit from the tree of *l.*
Rev 22:17. . . from the water of *l.*
Rev 22:19. . . in the tree of *l* and in the

LIFE-GIVING (adj)

giving or having power to give life and spirit; invigorating

Prov 10:11 . . the godly are a *l* fountain;
Prov 16:22 . . Discretion is a *l* fountain to
Rom 8:2. . . . the power of the *l* Spirit has
1 Cor 15:45 . Christ—is a *l* Spirit.
2 Cor 2:16 . . we are a *l* perfume.
Rev 7:17. . . . to springs of *l* water.

LIFETIME (n)

the duration of the existence of a living being or thing

Ps 30:5 . . . . . his favor lasts a *l!*
Ps 39:5 . . . . . My entire *l* is just a
Luke 16:25. . that during your *l* you had

LIFT, LIFTED, LIFTING, LIFTS (v)

to raise from a lower to a higher position; to raise in rank or condition

Lev 23:11. . . the priest will *l* it up
1 Sam 2:7. . . some down and *l-s* others up.
Neh 8:6 . . . . as they *l-ed* their hands.
Ps 28:2 . . . . . I *l* my hands toward your holy
Ps 63:4 . . . . . *l-ing* up my hands to you in prayer.
Ps 89:13 . . . . Your right hand is *l-ed* high in
Ps 113:7 . . . . He *l-s* the poor from the dust
Ps 123:1 . . . . I *l* my eyes to you, O God
Ps 134:2 . . . . *L* up holy hands
Lam 1:9 . . . . no one to *l* her out.
Lam 3:41 . . . Let us *l* our hearts and
John 3:14 . . . Son of Man must be *l-ed* up,
John 8:28 . . . When you have *l-ed* up the Son
John 12:32 . . And when I am *l-ed* up
1 Tim 2:8 . . . holy hands *l-ed* up to God,
Jas 4:10. . . . . he will *l* you up in honor.
1 Pet 5:6. . . . he will *l* you up in honor.

LIGHT, LIGHTS (n)

daylight; brightness; illumination; celestial body; spiritual enlightenment; exposure to the truth and justice

Gen 1:3 . . . . "Let there be *l,*" and there
Gen 1:14 . . . said, "Let *l-s* appear in the sky
Exod 13:21 . and he provided *l* at night
Job 38:19 . . . Where does *l* come from,
Ps 27:1 . . . . . The LORD is my *l* and my
Ps 56:13 . . . . in your life-giving *l.*
Ps 119:105 . . my feet and a *l* for my path.
Ps 132:17 . . . will be a *l* for my people.
Ps 139:12 . . . Darkness and *l* are the
Isa 2:5. . . . . . us walk in the *l* of the LORD!
Isa 42:6. . . . . you will be a *l* to guide the
Isa 45:7. . . . . I create the *l* and make the
Isa 49:6. . . . . make you a *l* to the Gentiles,
Matt 5:14 . . . You are the *l* of the world—
Luke 2:32. . . He is a *l* to reveal God to
Luke 11:33. . its *l* can be seen by all
John 1:4 . . . . life brought *l* to everyone.
John 1:9 . . . . who is the true *l,* who gives
John 3:20 . . . All who do evil hate the *l*

John 3:21 . . . come to the *l* so others can
John 8:12 . . . I am the *l* of the world.
John 9:5 . . . . I am the *l* of the world.
John 12:46 . . I have come as a *l* to shine
Acts 13:47 . . made you a *l* to the Gentiles,
2 Cor 4:6 . . . said, "Let there be *l* in the
2 Cor 6:14 . . can *l* live with darkness?
2 Cor 11:14 . as an angel of *l*.
Eph 1:18 . . . be flooded with *l* so that you
Eph 5:8 . . . . live as people of *l*!
Phil 2:15 . . . like bright *l-s* in a world
1 Thes 5:5 . . children of the *l* and of the
1 Tim 6:16 . . he lives in *l* so brilliant
1 Pet 2:9. . . . into his wonderful *l*.
1 Jn 1:5. . . . . God is *l*, and there is
1 Jn 1:7. . . . . living in the *l*, as God is in
1 Jn 2:9. . . . . I am living in the *l*,
Rev 21:23. . . city, and the Lamb is its *l*.

LIGHT, LIGHTS (v)

to brighten; to ignite something

Ps 18:28 . . . . The LORD, my God, *l-s* up my
Luke 8:16. . . No one *l-s* a lamp and

LIGHTNING (n)

the flashing of light produced by a discharge of atmospheric electricity

Exod 9:23 . . *l* flashed toward the earth.
Exod 20:18 . saw the flashes of *l* and the
Dan 10:6 . . . face flashed like *l*, and his
Matt 24:27. . For as the *l* flashes in the
Matt 28:3. . . face shone like *l*, and his
Luke 10:18. . from heaven like *l*!
Rev 4:5. . . . . came flashes of *l* and the

LIKE (prep)

similar in appearance, character, quality

Gen 1:26 . . . to be *l* us. They will
Ps 86:8 . . . . . No pagan god is *l* you, O LORD.
Isa 14:14. . . . and be *l* the Most High.
Luke 13:18. . Kingdom of God *l*?
Rom 8:3. . . . Son in a body *l* the bodies we
Rom 8:29. . . to become *l* his Son,

LIKENESS (n)

copy; resemblance; appearance

2 Cor 4:4 . . . is the exact *l* of God.

LINEN (adj)

made of flax

Lev 16:4. . . . *l* undergarments worn next to
Prov 31:24. . makes belted *l* garments
Mark 15:46 . a long sheet of *l* cloth.
John 20:6 . . . noticed the *l* wrappings lying

LINEN (n)

cloth made of flax and noted for its strength, coolness, and luster

Prov 31:22. . dresses in fine *l* and purple
Rev 15:6. . . . in spotless white *l* with gold
Rev 19:8. . . . of pure white *l* to wear.

LION, LIONS (n)

a wild beast with a threatening roar; symbolic of a strong and fierce enemy

Isa 11:7. . . . . The *l* will eat hay like a cow.
Isa 65:25. . . . The *l* will eat hay like a cow.
Dan 6:7 . . . . thrown into the den of *l-s*.
Dan 7:4 . . . . was like a *l* with eagles'
1 Pet 5:8. . . . like a roaring *l*, looking for
Rev 5:5. . . . . Look, the *L* of the tribe of

LIPS (n)

the fleshy, muscular folds that surround the mouth; symbolic of speech

Ps 140:3 . . . . drips from their *l*.
Prov 12:22. . The LORD detests lying *l*,
Isa 6:5. . . . . . I have filthy *l*, and I live
Matt 15:8 . . . honor me with their *l*,
Rom 3:13. . . venom drips from their *l*.
1 Pet 3:10. . . evil and your *l* from telling

LISTEN, LISTENED, LISTENING (v)

to hear something with thoughtful attention

see also HEAR

Deut 6:4. . . . *L*, O Israel! The LORD
Deut 18:15. . You must *l* to him.
1 Sam 3:9. . . LORD, your servant is *l-ing*.
Neh 8:3 . . . . All the people *l-ed* closely to
Ps 95:7 . . . . . If only you would *l* to his voice
Prov 12:15. . but the wise *l* to others.
Prov 18:13. . Spouting off before *l-ing* to
Isa 6:9. . . . . . to this people, '*L* carefully,
Dan 9:6 . . . . We have refused to *l* to your
Mark 9:7 . . . dearly loved Son. *L* to him.
Luke 10:39. . the Lord's feet, *l-ing* to
Luke 16:31. . If they won't *l* to Moses and
John 10:27. . My sheep *l* to my
John 15:20. . And if they had *l-ed* to me,
Rom 2:13. . . For merely *l-ing* to the law
1 Tim 2:12. . Let them *l* quietly.
Jas 1:19. . . . . be quick to *l*, slow to speak,
1 Jn 4:6. . . . . they do not *l* to us.
Rev 1:3. . . . . he blesses all who *l* to its
Rev 2:7. . . . . to hear must *l* to the Spirit

LIVE, LIVED, LIVES, LIVING (v)

to be alive or come to life; to endure a period of time (a life span); to attain eternal life; to dwell;

to subsist; to continue alive; to conduct or pass one's life
see also DWELLS
Gen 3:22 . . . Then they will *l* forever!
Exod 20:12 . Then you will *l* a long, full
Lev 26:11. . . I will *l* among you,
Deut 6:2. . . . as long as you *l.*
Deut 8:3. . . . that people do not *l* by bread
Job 14:14 . . . Can the dead *l* again?
Job 19:25 . . . that my Redeemer ***l-s,*** and he
Ps 23:6 . . . . . and I will *l* in the house of
Ps 37:3 . . . . . Then you will *l* safely in the
Ps 61:4 . . . . . Let me *l* forever in your
Ps 104:33 . . . as long as I *l.* I will praise
Prov 21:19. . It's better to *l* alone in the
Isa 33:14. . . . Who can *l* with this
Isa 45:18. . . . He made the world to be ***l-d*** in,
Amos 5:6. . . to the LORD and *l!*
Hab 2:4 . . . . the righteous will *l* by their
Zech 2:11. . . I will *l* among you,
Matt 4:4. . . . People do not *l* by bread
John 14:19 . . Since I *l,* you also will *l.*
Acts 17:28 . . For in him we *l* and move
Rom 2:8. . . . on those who *l* for themselves,
Rom 6:10. . . he ***l-s,*** he ***l-s*** for the glory
Rom 8:11. . . same Spirit ***l-ing*** within you.
Rom 13:13. . we must *l* decent lives
Rom 14:7. . . For we don't *l* for ourselves
1 Cor 3:16 . . Spirit of God ***l-s*** in you?
2 Cor 5:7 . . . For we *l* by believing
2 Cor 6:16 . . said: "I will *l* in them and
Gal 2:20 . . . . no longer I who *l,* but Christ
Gal 5:25. . . . Since we are ***l-ing*** by the Spirit,
Col 1:19 . . . . was pleased to *l* in Christ,
Col 2:5 . . . . . you are ***l-ing*** as you should
1 Thes 4:11 . your goal to *l* a quiet life,
1 Thes 5:13 . And *l* peacefully with
1 Tim 2:2. . . so that we can *l* peaceful and
1 Tim 4:16. . close watch on how you *l*
2 Tim 3:12. . who wants to *l* a godly life
Heb 10:38 . . righteous ones will *l* by faith.
Heb 12:14 . . and work at ***l-ing*** a holy life,
1 Pet 1:17. . . So you must *l* in reverent
1 Jn 1:7. . . . . But if we are ***l-ing*** in the light,
1 Jn 4:16. . . . God, and God ***l-s*** in them.

LIVES (n)
way or manner of living
see also LIFE
Exod 23:26 . I will give you long, full *l.*
1 Thes 2:8 . . but our own *l,* too.
1 Tim 2:2. . . and quiet *l* marked by
1 Pet 3:2. . . . pure and reverent *l.*
1 Pet 4:2. . . . rest of your *l* chasing your

LIVING (adj)
having life; active, functioning
Gen 2:7 . . . . man became a *l* person.
Gen 6:17 . . . destroy every *l* thing that
Jer 2:13. . . . . the fountain of *l* water.
Matt 22:32. . God of the *l,* not the dead.
John 4:10. . . would give you *l* water.
John 6:51 . . . I am the *l* bread that came
Rom 12:1. . . Let them be a *l* and holy
Heb 10:31 . . the hands of the *l* God.
Rev 1:18. . . . I am the *l* one.

LIVING (n)
conduct or manner of life
Phil 1:21 . . . to me, *l* means living for
2 Tim 2:22. . righteous *l,* faithfulness,

LOAF, LOAVES (n)
a shaped or molded mass of bread
Mark 6:41 . . took the five ***l-ves*** and two fish,
Mark 8:6 . . . the seven ***l-ves,*** thanked God
Luke 11:5. . . to borrow three ***l-ves*** of bread.
1 Cor 10:17 . all eat from one *l* of bread,

LOAN, LOANS (n)
money lent at interest
Deut 15:2. . . must cancel the ***l-s*** they have
Deut 15:9. . . refuse someone a *l*
Deut 24:6. . . as security for a *l,* for the
Ps 37:26 . . . . give generous ***l-s*** to others,

LOANED (v)
to give for temporary use
Luke 7:41. . . A man *l* money to two

LOCKED (v)
to fasten in or out or to make secure or inaccessible by means of locks
Job 38:10 . . . For I *l* it behind barred
John 20:26 . . doors were *l;* but suddenly,

LOCUSTS (n)
a short-horned grasshopper
Exod 10:4 . . a swarm of *l* on your country.
Joel 2:25. . . . and the cutting *l.* It was I
Matt 3:4. . . . he ate *l* and wild honey.
Rev 9:3. . . . . Then *l* came from

LODGING (n)
a temporary place to stay
Luke 2:7. . . . there was no *l* available for

LOFTY (adj)
elevated in character, spirit, and status; rising to a great height
Isa 6:1. . . . . sitting on a *l* throne,
Isa 57:15. . . The high and *l* one who lives

LOG (n)
a usually bulky piece or length of a tree
Matt 7:3. . . . you have a *l* in your own?
Luke 6:41. . . you have a *l* in your own?

LONG (adj)
extending over a considerable time or space
Deut 5:33. . . will live *l* and prosperous
1 Cor 11:14 . man to have *l* hair?
Eph 3:18 . . . how wide, how *l,* how high,

LONG, LONGING, LONGS (v)
to feel a strong desire or craving; to yearn
Job 7:2 . . . . . a worker who ***l-s*** for the shade,
Ps 42:1 . . . . . As the deer ***l-s*** for streams of
Ps 119:131 . . ***l-ing*** for your commands.
Luke 16:21. . lay there ***l-ing*** for scraps from
Phil 1:8 . . . . I love you and ***l*** for you with
Phil 2:26 . . . he has been ***l-ing*** to see you,

LONGING (n)
a strong desire, especially for something unattainable; craving
Rom 10:1 . . . the ***l*** of my heart and
2 Cor 7:11 . . such alarm, such ***l*** to see me,
1 Thes 2:17 . of our intense ***l*** to see you

LONGSUFFERING (KJV)
Exod 34:6 . . I am ***slow to anger*** and filled
Num 14:18 . LORD is ***slow to anger***
Ps 86:15 . . . . mercy, ***slow to get angry***
Gal 5:22. . . . love, joy, peace, ***patience,***
Eph 4:2 . . . . Be ***patient*** with each other

LOOK (n)
glance
Prov 15:30. . A cheerful ***l*** brings joy to

LOOK, LOOKED, LOOKING, LOOKS (v)
to direct the eyes; to examine; to see; to make sure or take care (that something is done); to regard with contempt; to seem; to search
Gen 19:17 . . And don't ***l*** back or
Gen 19:26 . . But Lot's wife ***l-ed*** back as she
Exod 3:6 . . . was afraid to ***l*** at God.
1 Sam 6:19. . they ***l-ed*** into the Ark
1 Sam 16:7. . LORD ***l-s*** at the heart.
Ps 34:5 . . . . . Those who ***l*** to him for
Ps 113:6 . . . . He stoops to ***l*** down on heaven
Ps 123:2 . . . . We keep ***l-ing*** to the LORD
Isa 65:1. . . . . but no one was ***l-ing*** for me.
Dan 10:5 . . . I ***l-ed*** up and saw a man
Hab 3:6 . . . . When he ***l-s,*** the nations
Zech 12:10. . They will ***l*** on me
Matt 5:28. . . who even ***l-s*** at a woman
Mark 16:6 . . You are ***l-ing*** for Jesus
Luke 9:62. . . plow and then ***l-s*** back is not
Luke 22:61. . turned and ***l-ed*** at Peter.
John 4:23 . . . The Father is ***l-ing*** for those
John 17:1 . . . Jesus ***l-ed*** up to heaven
Rom 14:10. . Why do you ***l*** down
Phil 2:4 . . . . Don't ***l*** out only
Heb 11:16 . . they were ***l-ing*** for a better
Jas 1:25. . . . . But if you ***l*** carefully into
2 Pet 3:12. . . ***l-ing*** forward to the day
Rev 5:6. . . . . I saw a Lamb that ***l-ed*** as if it

LOOSE (adv)
in an unrigidly fastened or unsecure manner
Isa 33:23. . . . sails hang ***l*** on broken masts

LORD
traditionally rendered Jehovah (Hebrew, Yahweh); *the sovereign God Almighty*
see also YAHWEH
Gen 2:4 . . . . When the ***L*** God made
Gen 4:4 . . . . The ***L*** accepted Abel
Gen 15:6 . . . Abram believed the ***L,*** and
Gen 22:14 . . the ***L*** will provide
Gen 31:49 . . May the ***L*** keep watch
Exod 6:2 . . . I am Yahweh—'the ***L.***'
Exod 15:26 . I am the ***L*** who heals you.
Exod 40:34 . the glory of the ***L*** filled
Lev 20:26. . . because I, the ***L,*** am holy.
Lev 23:4. . . . these are the ***L***'s appointed
Num 6:24 . . May the ***L*** bless you and
Num 14:18 . The ***L*** is slow to anger
Num 14:21 . filled with the ***L***'s glory,
Num 14:41 . disobeying the ***L***'s orders
Deut 5:9. . . . I, the ***L*** your God, am a jealous
Deut 6:5. . . . love the ***L*** your God with all
Deut 6:18. . . good in the ***L***'s sight,
Deut 10:13. . obey the ***L***'s commands
Deut 10:20. . must fear the ***L*** your God
Deut 11:1. . . must love the ***L*** your God
Deut 29:29. . The ***L*** our God has secrets
Deut 30:20. . obey the ***L,*** you will live
Josh 23:11 . . to love the ***L*** your God.
2 Sam 22:2. . sang: "The ***L*** is my rock,
2 Sam 22:31. All the ***L***'s promises prove
2 Kgs 22:2 . . pleasing in the ***L***'s sight
2 Kgs 22:8 . . Law in the ***L***'s Temple!
1 Chr 17:1 . . Ark of the ***L***'s Covenant is
2 Chr 16:9 . . The eyes of the ***L*** search
Neh 9:6 . . . . You alone are the ***L.***
Job 38:1 . . . . Then the ***L*** answered Job
Ps 1:6 . . . . . . For the ***L*** watches over
Ps 12:6 . . . . . The ***L***'s promises are pure,
Ps 18:30 . . . . All the ***L***'s promises prove
Ps 23:1 . . . . . The ***L*** is my shepherd;

Ps 24:1 . . . . . The earth is the ***L***'s,
Ps 34:3 . . . . . tell of the ***L***'s greatness;
Ps 34:8 . . . . . see that the **L** is good.
Ps 89:1 . . . . . sing of the ***L***'s unfailing love
Ps 92:13 . . . . to the ***L***'s own house.
Ps 95:6 . . . . . kneel before the **L** our maker,
Ps 97:1 . . . . . The **L** is king!
Ps 99:5 . . . . . Exalt the **L** our God!
Ps 100:5 . . . . For the **L** is good.
Ps 107:1 . . . . thanks to the **L**, for he is
Ps 118:8 . . . . better to take refuge in the **L**
Ps 118:23 . . . This is the ***L***'s doing,
Ps 121:2 . . . . help comes from the **L**, who
Ps 145:17 . . . The **L** is righteous
Ps 146:7 . . . . The **L** frees the prisoners.
Ps 147:11 . . . No, the ***L***'s delight is
Prov 3:5 . . . . Trust in the **L** with all your
Prov 3:9 . . . . Honor the **L** with your
Prov 3:11 . . . reject the ***L***'s discipline,
Prov 12:22 . . The **L** detests lying
Prov 15:33 . . Fear of the **L**
Prov 19:21 . . the ***L***'s purpose will prevail.
Prov 21:2 . . . the **L** examines their heart.
Prov 31:30 . . a woman who fears the **L** will
Isa 6:3. . . . . . holy is the **L** of Heaven's
Isa 24:14. . . . praise the ***L***'s majesty.
Isa 30:9. . . . . to the ***L***'s instructions.
Isa 42:8. . . . . I am the **L**; that is my name!
Isa 43:11. . . . I, am the **L**, and there is
Isa 49:4. . . . . leave it all in the ***L***'s hand;
Isa 53:6. . . . . Yet the **L** laid on him
Isa 53:10. . . . was the ***L***'s good plan
Isa 55:13. . . . honor to the ***L***'s name;
Isa 61:2. . . . . time of the ***L***'s favor
Isa 66:15. . . . See, the **L** is coming
Jer 8:7. . . . . . do not know the ***L***'s laws.
Jer 17:10. . . . But I, the **L**, search all
Jer 31:11. . . . For the **L** has redeemed
Jer 48:10. . . . to do the ***L***'s work,
Jer 51:7. . . . . cup in the ***L***'s hands,
Ezek 7:19. . . day of the ***L***'s anger.
Ezek 44:4. . . the glory of the **L** filled
Joel 1:15. . . . The day of the **L** is near,
Joel 3:18. . . . from the ***L***'s Temple, watering
Jonah 2:9 . . . salvation comes from the **L**
Mic 4:1. . . . . mountain of the ***L***'s house
Mic 6:2. . . . . listen to the ***L***'s complaint!
Nah 1:2 . . . . The **L** is a jealous God,
Nah 1:7 . . . . The **L** is good, a strong
Hab 2:16 . . . cup of the ***L***'s judgment,
Zeph 2:3 . . . yet the **L** will protect
Matt 3:3. . . . way for the ***L***'s coming!
Matt 4:7. . . . not test the **L** your God.
Matt 4:10. . . must worship the **L** your God
Matt 22:37. . must love the **L** your God
Mark 1:3 . . . way for the ***L***'s coming!
Mark 12:11 . This is the ***L***'s doing,
John 1:23 . . . way for the ***L***'s coming!
Acts 2:21 . . . name of the **L** will be saved.
Rom 10:13. . name of the **L** will be saved.
Rom 11:34. . can know the ***L***'s thoughts?
1 Cor 10:26 . the earth is the ***L***'s,
Heb 12:5 . . . of the ***L***'s discipline,

LORD, LORDS (n)

honored one or a superior; master (to a slave); king or ruler; God or Jesus
see also LORD
Deut 10:17. . of gods and **L** of ***l-s***.
Neh 4:14 . . . Remember the **L**, who is
Isa 6:1. . . . . . I saw the **L**. He was sitting
Dan 9:19 . . . O **L**, listen and act!
Matt 12:8. . . Son of Man is **L**, even
Luke 1:38. . . I am the ***L***'s servant.
Acts 10:36 . . Christ, who is **L** of all.
Acts 16:31 . . Believe in the **L** Jesus
Rom 10:9. . . that Jesus is **L** and believe
1 Cor 8:6 . . . only one **L**, Jesus Christ,
1 Cor 11:26 . announcing the ***L***'s death
1 Cor 12:3 . . say Jesus is **L**, except
Eph 4:5 . . . . There is one **L**, one faith,
Phil 2:11 . . . Jesus Christ is **L**,
Col 2:6 . . . . . Jesus as your **L**, you must
1 Thes 5:2 . . day of the ***L***'s return
1 Tim 6:15 . . kings and **L** of all ***l-s***.
Jas 5:8. . . . . . the coming of the **L** is near.
1 Pet 2:3. . . . taste of the ***L***'s kindness.
1 Pet 3:15. . . worship Christ as **L** of
Rev 4:8. . . . . holy, holy is the **L** God,
Rev 4:11. . . . are worthy, O **L** our God,
Rev 19:16. . . kings and **L** of all ***l-s***.
Rev 22:20. . . Amen! Come, **L** Jesus!

LOSE, LOSES (v)

to fail to keep, sustain, or maintain; to damn
Matt 10:39 . . cling to your life, you will ***l***
Mark 8:36 . . whole world but ***l*** your own
Luke 15:8. . . silver coins and ***l-s*** one.
Luke 17:33. . cling to your life, you will ***l***
John 6:39 . . . I should not ***l*** even one of
2 Jn 1:8. . . . . you do not ***l*** what we have

LOSS (n)

the act of losing possession; deprivation
1 Cor 3:15 . . the builder will suffer great ***l***.

LOST (adj)

no longer possessed or known; lacking assurance of eternal salvation
Jer 50:6. . . . . have been ***l*** sheep.
Ezek 34:16. . will search for my ***l*** ones

Luke 15:4. . . and one of them gets *l*,
Luke 15:6. . . I have found my *l* sheep.
Luke 15:9. . . have found my *l* coin
Luke 15:24. . He was *l*, but now he

LOTS (n)

small stones or other devices used for making choices, much like throwing dice or drawing straws

Josh 18:10 . . Joshua cast sacred *l* in the
Obad 1:11 . . wealth and cast *l* to divide
Acts 1:26 . . . they cast *l*, and Matthias was

LOUD (adj)

marked by intensity or volume of sound

Isa 54:1. . . . . Break into *l* and joyful song,

LOVE (n)

the ultimate expression of God's loyalty, purity, and mercy extended toward his people – to be reflected in human relationships of brotherly concern, marital fidelity, and adoration of God; a beloved person

Gen 24:12 . . unfailing *l* to my master,
Gen 32:10 . . unfailing *l* and faithfulness
Gen 34:3 . . . he fell in *l* with her, and he
Gen 39:21 . . showed him his faithful *l*.
Exod 20:6 . . unfailing *l* for a thousand
Exod 34:6 . . filled with unfailing *l* and
Num 14:18 . with unfailing *l*, forgiving
Num 14:19 . unfailing *l*, please pardon
Deut 5:10. . . unfailing *l* for a thousand
Deut 7:9. . . . his unfailing *l* on those who
Deut 10:15. . the objects of his *l*.
Deut 10:18. . He shows *l* to the
Deut 10:19. . must show *l* to foreigners,
Judg 16:4. . . Samson fell in *l* with a woman
1 Sam 18:20. had fallen in *l* with David,
1 Kgs 8:23 . . and show unfailing *l* to all
1 Kgs 10:9 . . LORD's eternal *l* for Israel,
1 Chr 16:41 . for "his faithful *l* endures
1 Chr 29:18 . See to it that their *l*
2 Chr 5:13 . . His faithful *l* endures
2 Chr 20:21 . faithful *l* endures forever!
Ezra 3:11 . . . His faithful *l* for Israel
Job 37:13 . . . to show his unfailing *l*.
Ps 6:4 . . . . . . because of your unfailing *l*.
Ps 13:5 . . . . . I trust in your unfailing *l*.
Ps 18:50 . . . . you show unfailing *l* to your
Ps 21:7 . . . . . The unfailing *l* of the
Ps 23:6 . . . . . and unfailing *l* will pursue
Ps 25:6 . . . . . and unfailing *l*, which you
Ps 25:10 . . . . leads with unfailing *l* and
Ps 26:3 . . . . . of your unfailing *l*, and I
Ps 31:7 . . . . . in your unfailing *l*, for you
Ps 31:16 . . . . your unfailing *l*, rescue me.
Ps 32:10 . . . . but unfailing *l* surrounds
Ps 33:5 . . . . . the unfailing *l* of the
Ps 33:18 . . . . who rely on his unfailing *l*.
Ps 33:22 . . . . your unfailing *l* surround us,
Ps 36:5 . . . . . Your unfailing *l*, O LORD, is
Ps 36:10 . . . . Pour out your unfailing *l* on
Ps 40:10 . . . . of your unfailing *l* and
Ps 40:11 . . . . Let your unfailing *l* and
Ps 42:8 . . . . . his unfailing *l* upon me,
Ps 48:9 . . . . . on your unfailing *l* as we
Ps 51:1 . . . . . your unfailing *l*. Because of
Ps 57:3 . . . . . send forth his unfailing *l* and
Ps 57:10 . . . . For your unfailing *l* is as
Ps 59:10 . . . . In his unfailing *l*, my God
Ps 59:16 . . . . your unfailing *l*. For you
Ps 59:17 . . . . shows me unfailing *l*.
Ps 62:12 . . . . unfailing *l*, O LORD, is yours.
Ps 66:20 . . . . his unfailing *l* from me.
Ps 69:16 . . . . LORD, for your unfailing *l* is
Ps 77:8 . . . . . his unfailing *l* gone forever?
Ps 85:7 . . . . . us your unfailing *l*, O LORD,
Ps 86:5 . . . . . full of unfailing *l* for all
Ps 86:15 . . . . filled with unfailing *l* and
Ps 88:11 . . . . your unfailing *l*?
Ps 89:1 . . . . . LORD's unfailing *l* forever!
Ps 89:14 . . . . Unfailing *l* and truth
Ps 89:49 . . . . is your unfailing *l*?
Ps 90:14 . . . . with your unfailing *l*, so we
Ps 92:2 . . . . . your unfailing *l* in the
Ps 100:5 . . . . His unfailing *l* continues
Ps 101:1 . . . . sing of your *l* and justice,
Ps 103:4 . . . . crowns me with *l* and tender
Ps 103:11 . . . his unfailing *l* toward those
Ps 103:17 . . . But the *l* of the LORD
Ps 106:1 . . . . His faithful *l* endures
Ps 106:45 . . . because of his unfailing *l*.
Ps 107:31 . . . for his great *l* and for the
Ps 107:43 . . . the faithful *l* of the LORD.
Ps 108:4 . . . . your unfailing *l* is higher
Ps 109:26 . . . because of your unfailing *l*.
Ps 115:1 . . . . for your unfailing *l* and
Ps 118:1 . . . . His faithful *l* endures
Ps 119:41 . . . give me your unfailing *l*,
Ps 119:76 . . . let your unfailing *l* comfort
Ps 119:124 . . deal with me in unfailing *l*,
Ps 130:7 . . . . LORD there is unfailing *l*.
Ps 138:2 . . . . unfailing *l* and faithfulness;
Ps 143:12 . . . your unfailing *l*, silence all
Ps 147:11 . . . hope in his unfailing *l*.
Prov 5:19. . . be captivated by her *l*.
Prov 14:22. . will receive unfailing *l* and
Prov 16:6. . . Unfailing *l* and
Prov 20:28. . is made secure through *l*.
Prov 21:21. . and unfailing *l* will find
Prov 27:5. . . better than hidden *l*!

Song 1:4. . . . We praise your *l* even more
Song 1:7. . . . Tell me, my *l,* where are you
Song 1:16. . . so handsome, my *l,* pleasing
Song 2:7. . . . not to awaken *l* until the
Song 2:17. . . to me, my *l,* like a gazelle
Song 3:4. . . . I found my *l!*
Song 4:10. . . Your *l* delights me,
Song 4:16. . . your garden, my *l;* taste its
Song 5:5. . . . door for my *l,* and my hands
Song 5:8. . . . tell him I am weak with *l.*
Song 7:6. . . . How pleasing, my *l,* how full
Song 7:12. . . will give you my *l.*
Song 8:4. . . . not to awaken *l* until the
Song 8:6. . . . for *l* is as strong as death
Song 8:7. . . . cannot quench *l,* nor can
Song 8:14. . . Come away, my *l!*
Isa 55:3. . . . . the unfailing *l* I promised to
Isa 63:7. . . . . LORD's unfailing *l.*
Isa 63:9. . . . . In his *l* and mercy he
Jer 2:25. . . . . I'm in *l* with these
Jer 9:24. . . . . demonstrates unfailing *l* and
Jer 16:5. . . . . taken away my unfailing *l*
Jer 31:3. . . . . with an everlasting *l.*
Jer 33:11. . . . His faithful *l* endures
Lam 3:22 . . . The faithful *l* of the
Lam 3:32 . . . the greatness of his unfailing *l.*
Dan 9:4 . . . . of unfailing *l* to those who
Hos 1:7 . . . . I will show *l* to the people
Hos 2:19 . . . and justice, unfailing *l* and
Hos 2:23 . . . I will show *l* to those I
Hos 6:4 . . . . For your *l* vanishes like the
Hos 6:6 . . . . want you to show *l,* not offer
Hos 11:4 . . . my ropes of kindness and *l.*
Hos 12:6 . . . Act with *l* and justice,
Joel 2:13. . . . filled with unfailing *l.*
Jonah 4:2 . . . filled with unfailing *l.*
Zeph 3:17 . . With his *l,* he will
Zech 8:17. . . Stop your *l* of telling
Mark 10:21 . Jesus felt genuine *l* for him.
John 5:42 . . . have God's *l* within you.
John 15:9 . . . Remain in my *l.*
John 15:10 . . remain in his *l.*
John 15:13 . . is no greater *l* than to lay
John 17:26 . . Then your *l* for me will
Rom 5:5 . . . . fill our hearts with his *l.*
Rom 5:8 . . . . showed his great *l* for us by
Rom 8:35 . . . us from Christ's *l?*
Rom 8:39 . . . us from the *l* of God that is
Rom 13:10 . . *L* does no wrong
Rom 13:10 . . to others, so *l* fulfills the
Rom 14:15 . . not acting in *l* if you eat
Rom 15:30 . . because of your *l* for me,
1 Cor 4:21 . . I come with *l* and a gentle
1 Cor 8:1 . . . it is *l* that strengthens the
1 Cor 13:13 . faith, hope, and *l*—and the
1 Cor 13:13 . the greatest of these is *l.*
2 Cor 2:4 . . . know how much *l* I have for
2 Cor 2:8 . . . to reaffirm your *l* for him.
2 Cor 5:14 . . Either way, Christ's *l* controls
2 Cor 8:7 . . . and your *l* from us—I want
2 Cor 8:24 . . show them your *l,* and prove
Gal 5:22. . . . *l,* joy, peace, patience,
Eph 1:15 . . . Jesus and your *l* for God's
Eph 3:17 . . . down into God's *l* and keep
Eph 3:18 . . . how deep his *l* is.
Eph 4:15 . . . the truth in *l,* growing in
Eph 5:2 . . . . filled with *l,* following the
Eph 6:23 . . . give you *l* with faithfulness.
Phil 1:9 . . . . that your *l* will overflow
Col 1:4 . . . . . Jesus and your *l* for all of
Col 1:8 . . . . . told us about the *l* for others
Col 2:2 . . . . . strong ties of *l.*
1 Thes 3:6 . . your faith and *l.*
1 Thes 3:12 . the Lord make your *l* for one
1 Thes 5:13 . and wholehearted *l* because of
2 Thes 3:5 . . expression of the *l* of God
1 Tim 1:5 . . . be filled with *l* that comes
1 Tim 2:15 . . in faith, *l,* holiness,
1 Tim 4:12 . . live, in your *l,* your faith,
1 Tim 6:10 . . For the *l* of money is the
1 Tim 6:11 . . with faith, *l,* perseverance,
2 Tim 1:7 . . . but of power, *l,* and
2 Tim 1:13 . . the faith and *l* that you have
2 Tim 2:22 . . living, faithfulness, *l,* and
2 Tim 3:10 . . my patience, my *l,* and my
Titus 2:2. . . . filled with *l* and patience.
Titus 3:4. . . . revealed his kindness and *l,*
Heb 10:24 . . to acts of *l* and good works.
1 Pet 4:8. . . . for *l* covers a multitude
1 Pet 5:14. . . with Christian *l.*
1 Jn 3:14. . . . who has no *l* is still dead.
1 Jn 3:16. . . . know what real *l* is because
1 Jn 4:7. . . . . for *l* comes from God.
1 Jn 4:8. . . . . for God is *l.*
1 Jn 4:10. . . . This is real *l*—not that we
1 Jn 4:16. . . . put our trust in his *l.*
1 Jn 4:16. . . . God is *l,* and all who
1 Jn 4:17. . . . live in God, our *l* grows more
1 Jn 4:18. . . . because perfect *l* expels all
Jude 1:12 . . . commemorating the Lord's *l,*
Jude 1:21 . . . safe in God's *l.*
Rev 2:19. . . . have seen your *l,* your faith,

LOVE, LOVED, LOVES, LOVING (v)
to hold dear; to feel a lover's passion, devotion, or tenderness for; to feel affection or experience desire; to like or desire actively

Gen 22:2 . . . Isaac, whom you *l* so much—
Gen 29:32 . . my husband will *l* me.
Exod 21:5 . . may declare, 'I *l* my master,

Lev 19:34. . . as you *l* yourself.
Deut 4:37. . . Because he ***l-d*** your ancestors,
Deut 6:5. . . . And you must *l* the LORD your
Deut 7:8. . . . that the LORD ***l-s*** you, and he
Deut 7:13. . . He will *l* you and
Deut 11:13. . and if you *l* the LORD your
Deut 13:3. . . if you truly *l* him with all
Deut 15:16. . because he ***l-s*** you and
Deut 21:15. . son of the wife he does not *l.*
Deut 23:5. . . LORD your God ***l-s*** you.
Deut 30:6. . . that you will *l* him with all
Deut 30:16. . to *l* the LORD
Deut 30:20. . this choice by ***l-ing*** the LORD
Deut 30:20. . And if you *l* and obey the
Deut 33:3. . . Indeed, he ***l-s*** his people;
Josh 23:11 . . be very careful to *l* the LORD
Judg 14:16. . said, "You don't *l* me;
Judg 16:15. . tell me, 'I *l* you,' when you
1 Sam 18:1. . for Jonathan ***l-d*** David.
2 Sam 12:24. The LORD ***l-d*** the child
2 Sam 19:6. . You seem to *l* those who hate
1 Kgs 3:3 . . . Solomon ***l-d*** the LORD and
1 Kgs 11:1 . . Solomon ***l-d*** many foreign
2 Chr 2:11 . . the LORD ***l-s*** his people
2 Chr 19:2 . . the wicked and *l* those who
Neh 1:5 . . . . with those who *l* him and obey
Neh 13:26 . . ***l-d*** him and made him king
Ps 11:5 . . . . . those who *l* violence.
Ps 11:7 . . . . . righteous LORD ***l-s*** justice.
Ps 18:1 . . . . . I *l* you, LORD;
Ps 26:8 . . . . . I *l* your sanctuary,
Ps 36:10 . . . . on those who *l* you;
Ps 40:16 . . . . those who *l* your salvation
Ps 44:3 . . . . . helped them, for you ***l-d*** them.
Ps 45:7 . . . . . You *l* justice and
Ps 52:3 . . . . . You *l* evil more
Ps 52:4 . . . . . You *l* to destroy
Ps 70:4 . . . . . those who *l* your salvation
Ps 78:68 . . . . Mount Zion, which he ***l-d.***
Ps 89:28 . . . . I will *l* him and be
Ps 89:33 . . . . I will never stop ***l-ing*** him nor
Ps 91:14 . . . . rescue those who *l* me.
Ps 97:10 . . . . You who *l* the LORD,
Ps 98:3 . . . . . his promise to *l* and be
Ps 119:48 . . . I honor and *l* your commands.
Ps 119:97 . . . how I *l* your instructions!
Ps 119:113 . . but I *l* your instructions.
Ps 119:119 . . no wonder I *l* to obey your
Ps 119:127 . . I *l* your commands more
Ps 119:140 . . that is why I *l* them so much.
Ps 122:6 . . . . May all who *l* this city
Ps 145:20 . . . all those who *l* him, but he
Ps 146:8 . . . . The LORD ***l-s*** the godly.
Prov 3:12. . . corrects those he ***l-s,*** just as
Prov 8:17. . . *l* all who *l* me.
Prov 8:21. . . Those who *l* me inherit
Prov 8:36. . . All who hate me *l* death.
Prov 9:8. . . . and they will *l* you.
Prov 12:1. . . you must *l* discipline; it is
Prov 15:17. . with someone you *l* is better
Prov 17:19. . Anyone who ***l-s*** to quarrel
Prov 18:21. . those who *l* to talk
Prov 19:8. . . wisdom is to *l* oneself;
Prov 21:17. . Those who *l* pleasure
Prov 22:11. . Whoever ***l-s*** a pure
Prov 30:19. . how a man ***l-s*** a woman.
Eccl 3:8 . . . . A time to *l* and a time
Eccl 9:9 . . . . the woman you *l* through all
Song 1:3. . . . the young women *l* you!
Song 3:2. . . . search for the one I *l.*
Song 3:3. . . . Have you seen the one I *l?*
Isa 1:23. . . . . All of them *l* bribes and
Isa 56:6. . . . . serve him and *l* his name, who
Isa 61:8. . . . . I, the LORD, *l* justice.
Jer 2:2. . . . . . long ago, how you ***l-d*** me and
Jer 8:2. . . . . . my people have ***l-d,*** served,
Jer 31:20. . . . to punish him, but I still *l* him,
Hos 2:1 . . . . Ruhamah—'The ones I *l.*'
Hos 2:4 . . . . I will not *l* her children,
Hos 2:23 . . . to those I called 'Not ***l-d.***'
Hos 9:15 . . . I will *l* them no
Hos 11:1 . . . was a child, I ***l-d*** him, and I
Hos 12:7 . . . scales—they *l* to cheat.
Amos 4:5. . . you Israelites *l* to do," says
Amos 5:15. . Hate evil and *l* what is good;
Mic 6:8. . . . . is right, to *l* mercy, and to
Mal 1:2. . . . . "I have always ***l-d*** you," says
Matt 5:43. . . that says, '***L*** your neighbor'
Matt 5:44. . . But I say, *l* your enemies!
Matt 5:46. . . If you *l* only those
Matt 6:24. . . hate one and *l* the other;
Matt 10:37. . If you *l* your father or
Matt 19:19. . ***L*** your neighbor
Matt 22:37. . You must *l* the LORD your
Mark 12:6 . . his son whom he ***l-d*** dearly.
Mark 12:30 . you must *l* the LORD your
Mark 12:33 . it is important to *l* him with
Mark 12:33 . and to *l* my neighbor as
Luke 6:27. . . I say, *l* your enemies!
Luke 6:32. . . If you *l* only those who
Luke 6:35. . . ***L*** your enemies!
Luke 10:27. . You must *l* the LORD your
Luke 10:27. . And, '***L*** your neighbor
Luke 16:13. . hate one and *l* the other;
John 3:16 . . . For God ***l-d*** the world so
John 3:35 . . . The Father ***l-s*** his Son
John 5:20 . . . For the Father ***l-s*** the Son and
John 8:42 . . . you would *l* me, because I
John 10:17 . . The Father ***l-s*** me because I
John 11:36 . . See how much he ***l-d*** him!

John 12:25 . . Those who *l* their life
John 12:43 . . For they ***l-d*** human praise more
John 13:1 . . . He had ***l-d*** his disciples during
John 13:34 . . *L* each other. Just as I have
John 14:21 . . are the ones who *l* me.
John 14:28 . . If you really ***l-d*** me, you
John 14:31 . . know that I *l* the Father.
John 17:23 . . and that you *l* them as much
John 17:24 . . gave me because you ***l-d*** me
John 19:26 . . beside the disciple he ***l-d,***
John 20:2 . . . one whom Jesus ***l-d.***
John 21:15 . . do you *l* me more than
John 21:16 . . son of John, do you *l* me?
John 21:20 . . the disciple Jesus ***l-d***—the one
Rom 8:28 . . . of those who *l* God and are
Rom 8:37 . . . through Christ, who ***l-d*** us.
Rom 9:13 . . . Scriptures, "I ***l-d*** Jacob, but I
Rom 9:25 . . . And I will *l* those whom I did
Rom 12:10 . . *L* each other with genuine
1 Cor 2:9 . . . for those who *l* him.
1 Cor 13:2 . . but didn't *l* others, I would
1 Cor 16:22 . anyone does not *l* the Lord,
2 Cor 9:7 . . . For God ***l-s*** a person
2 Cor 12:15 . the more I *l* you, the less
Gal 2:20 . . . . of God, who ***l-d*** me and gave
Eph 1:4 . . . . God ***l-d*** us and chose us
Eph 2:4 . . . . mercy, and he ***l-d*** us so much,
Eph 5:25 . . . this means *l* your wives, just
Eph 5:25 . . . just as Christ ***l-d*** the church.
Eph 5:28 . . . a man who ***l-s*** his wife actually
Eph 5:33 . . . love his wife as he ***l-s*** himself,
Phil 1:16 . . . preach because they *l* me,
Phil 2:2 . . . . each other, ***l-ing*** one another,
1 Thes 1:4 . . God ***l-s*** you and has chosen
1 Thes 4:10 . urge you to *l* them even
2 Thes 2:10 . they refuse to *l* and accept
2 Thes 2:16 . our Father, who ***l-d*** us and
1 Tim 3:3 . . . and not *l* money.
1 Tim 6:2 . . . believers who are well ***l-d.***
2 Tim 3:2 . . . people will *l* only themselves
Titus 1:8. . . . and he must *l* what is good.
Titus 2:4. . . . women to *l* their husbands
Titus 3:15. . . believers—all who *l* us.
Heb 12:6 . . . disciplines those he ***l-s,***
Heb 13:1 . . . Keep on ***l-ing*** each other as
Heb 13:5 . . . Don't *l* money;
Jas 2:5. . . . . . to those who *l* him?
1 Pet 1:8. . . . You *l* him even though
1 Pet 2:17. . . Respect everyone, and *l* your
1 Pet 3:8. . . . *L* each other as brothers
2 Pet 2:15. . . ***l-d*** to earn money by doing
1 Jn 2:5. . . . . how completely they *l* him.
1 Jn 2:10. . . . Anyone who ***l-s*** another
1 Jn 3:1. . . . . very much our Father ***l-s*** us,
1 Jn 3:14. . . . If we *l* our Christian
1 Jn 4:9. . . . . how much he ***l-d*** us by sending
1 Jn 4:10. . . . not that we ***l-d*** God, but that
1 Jn 4:11. . . . since God ***l-d*** us that much,
1 Jn 4:11. . . . surely ought to *l* each other.
1 Jn 4:19. . . . We *l* each other because he ***l-d***
1 Jn 4:20. . . . someone says, "I *l* God," but
1 Jn 5:1. . . . . everyone who ***l-s*** the Father
Jude 1:1 . . . . God the Father, who ***l-s*** you
Rev 1:5. . . . . glory to him who ***l-s*** us and
Rev 2:4. . . . . You don't *l* me or each other
Rev 3:9. . . . . you are the ones I *l.*
Rev 3:19. . . . discipline everyone I *l.*
Rev 12:11. . . they did not *l* their lives so
Rev 22:15. . . and all who *l* to live a lie.

LOVE, LOVED, LOVING (adj)

of or relating to a strong affection for another; affectionate, painstaking

Ps 88:18 . . . . my companions and ***l-d*** ones.
Ps 127:2 . . . . gives rest to his ***l-d*** ones.
Ezek 33:32. . who sings *l* songs with a
Mark 1:11 . . are my dearly ***l-d*** Son, and you
Mark 9:7 . . . is my dearly ***l-d*** Son.
1 Thes 1:3 . . work, your ***l-ing*** deeds, and the

LOVELY (adj)

eliciting love by moral or ideal worth; beautiful

Phil 4:8 . . . . pure, and *l,* and admirable.

LOVER, LOVERS (n)

one who loves; two persons in love with each other; a person with whom one has sexual relations

Ps 99:4 . . . . . Mighty King, *l* of justice,
Song 2:9. . . . My *l* is like a
Song 5:2. . . . I heard my *l* knocking and
Ezek 16:33. . gifts to your ***l-s,*** bribing them
Ezek 16:39. . who are your ***l-s,*** and they will
Hos 2:5 . . . . run after other ***l-s*** and sell

LOVINGKINDNESS (KJV)

Ps 25:6 . . . . . ***unfailing love,*** which you have
Ps 40:11 . . . . Let your ***unfailing love*** and
Ps 63:3 . . . . . ***unfailing love*** is better than life
Ps 143:8 . . . . ***unfailing love*** each morning
Isa 63:7. . . . . according to his ***mercy and love***

LOWER, LOWEST (adj)

of lesser position, rank, or order

Ps 8:5 . . . . . . only a little *l* than God and
Luke 14:10. . Instead, take the ***l-est*** place at
Heb 2:7 . . . . them only a little *l* than the

LOWLY (adj)
humble in manner or spirit; of or relating to a low social or economic rank
Ps 37:11 . . . . The ***l*** will possess
Ezek 21:26 . . Now the ***l*** will be

LOYAL (adj)
unswerving in allegiance; faithful
2 Sam 2:6 . . . May the LORD be ***l*** to you in
1 Chr 12:33 . and completely ***l*** to David.
Ps 31:23 . . . . those who are ***l*** to him,
Ps 51:10 . . . . Renew a ***l*** spirit within
Prov 17:17 . . A friend is always ***l***, and a

LOYALTY, LOYALTIES (n)
the quality or state or an instance of being loyal
Judg 8:35 . . . Nor did they show any ***l*** to
Ps 119:113 . . I hate those with divided ***l-ies***,
Prov 19:22 . . ***L*** makes a person

LUKE
The beloved doctor (Col 4:14); faithful co-worker of Paul (2 Tim 4:11; Phlm 1:23-24); noted fact-gatherer and writer of the third Gospel and the book of Acts.

LURE (n)
enticement, appeal, attraction
Mark 4:19 . . the ***l*** of wealth,

LURE (v)
to draw with a hint of pleasure or gain
2 Pet 2:18 . . . they ***l*** back into sin those

LUST, LUSTS (n)
unbridled sexual desire; an intense longing
1 Cor 7:9 . . . than to burn with ***l***.
Eph 4:22 . . . corrupted by ***l*** and deception.
Col 3:5 . . . . . immorality, impurity, ***l***, and
2 Tim 2:22 . . stimulates youthful ***l-s***.
Titus 3:3. . . . to many ***l-s*** and pleasures.

LUST, LUSTED (v)
to have an intense (sexual) desire
Prov 6:25 . . . Don't ***l*** for her
Ezek 23:5 . . . Then Oholah ***l-ed*** after other

LUSTFUL (adj)
excited by lust; lecherous
Mark 7:22 . . deceit, ***l*** desires, envy,
Gal 5:19 . . . . impurity, ***l*** pleasures,
Eph 4:19 . . . They live for ***l*** pleasure and

LUXURY (n)
a condition of abundance or great ease and comfort
Prov 21:17 . . those who love wine and ***l***
Jas 5:5. . . . . . your years on earth in ***l***,

LYING (adj)
marked by or containing falsehoods; false
Prov 6:17 . . . haughty eyes, a ***l*** tongue,
Prov 12:22 . . The LORD detests ***l*** lips,
Prov 21:6 . . . Wealth created by a ***l*** tongue
Prov 26:28 . . A ***l*** tongue hates

LYING (v)
to make an untrue statement with the intent to deceive
see also LIE
Mic 6:12. . . . are so used to ***l*** that their
Matt 15:19 . . immorality, theft, ***l***, and
Acts 5:4 . . . . You weren't ***l*** to us but
1 Cor 15:15 . would all be ***l*** about God—

MACEDONIA (n)
a mountainous country north of Greece in the Balkan Peninsula
Acts 16:9 . . . A man from ***M*** in northern

MAD (adj)
insane; carried away by intense anger
Deut 28:34. . You will go ***m*** because of

MADE (v)
to create, prepare, or fashion; to bring about
see also CREATE(D), FORMED, MAKE
Gen 1:7 . . . . God ***m*** this space to separate
Gen 1:16 . . . He also ***m*** the stars.
Gen 1:25 . . . ***m*** all sorts of wild animals,
Gen 1:31 . . . God looked over all he had ***m,***
Gen 2:4 . . . . LORD God ***m*** the earth and
Gen 2:22 . . . LORD God ***m*** a woman
Gen 6:6 . . . . LORD was sorry he had ever ***m***
Gen 9:6 . . . . God ***m*** human beings in his
Exod 20:11 . the LORD ***m*** the heavens,
2 Chr 2:12 . . ***m*** the heavens and
Job 10:9 . . . . that you ***m*** me from dust—
Ps 95:5 . . . . . sea belongs to him, for he ***m*** it.
Ps 115:15 . . . who ***m*** heaven and earth.
Prov 22:2. . . The LORD ***m*** them both.
Eccl 3:11 . . . God has ***m*** everything
Isa 27:11. . . . the one who ***m*** them will
Isa 43:7. . . . . I have ***m*** them for my glory.
Isa 57:16. . . . all the souls I have ***m.***
Jer 51:15. . . . The LORD ***m*** the earth
Jonah 1:9 . . . God of heaven, who ***m*** the sea
Matt 19:4. . . ***m*** them male and female.
Matt 19:28 . . when the world is ***m*** new
1 Cor 11:9 . . man was not ***m*** for woman,
2 Cor 5:1 . . . an eternal body ***m*** for us by
1 Tim 2:13 . . For God ***m*** Adam first,
Heb 4:3 . . . . since he ***m*** the world.
Rev 13:8. . . . before the world was ***m***—
Rev 14:7. . . . him who ***m*** the heavens,

MAGIC (adj)
having seemingly supernatural qualities or powers
Ezek 13:20. . all your ***m*** charms,

MAGICIANS (n)
ones skilled in extraordinary power or influence seemingly from a supernatural source; sorcerers
Exod 7:11 . . Egyptian ***m*** did the same
Dan 2:2 . . . . called in his ***m,*** enchanters,

MAGNIFICENT (adj)
grand or lavish; strikingly beautiful or impressive
Num 14:19 . In keeping with your ***m,***
1 Chr 22:5 . . must be a ***m*** structure,
Ps 48:2 . . . . . It is high and ***m;***
Isa 63:14. . . . and gained a ***m*** reputation.

MAJESTIC (adj)
having or exhibiting majesty; grand, stately
Ps 8:1 . . . . . . your ***m*** name fills the earth!
Ps 29:4 . . . . . the voice of the LORD is ***m.***
Ps 145:5 . . . . I will meditate on your ***m,***
Isa 53:2. . . . . nothing beautiful or ***m*** about
Heb 1:3 . . . . hand of the ***m*** God in heaven.
Heb 8:1 . . . . the throne of the ***m*** God
2 Pet 1:16. . . saw his ***m*** splendor with our
2 Pet 1:17. . . from the ***m*** glory of God

MAJESTY (n)
greatness or splendor of quality or character; sovereign power, authority, or dignity
Exod 15:7 . . In the greatness of your ***m,***
1 Chr 16:27 . and ***m*** surround him;
Job 40:10 . . . splendor, your honor and ***m.***
Ps 21:5 . . . . . with splendor and ***m.***
Ps 68:34 . . . . His ***m*** shines down on Israel;
Ps 93:1 . . . . . is king! He is robed in ***m.***
Ps 145:12 . . . about the ***m*** and glory of
Isa 2:10. . . . . and the glory of his ***m.***

Isa 26:10. . . . no notice of the LORD's ***m.***
Jude 1:25 . . . All glory, ***m,*** power, and

MAKE, MAKES, MAKING (v)
to create, prepare, or fashion; to force; to bring about; to render
see also CREATE(D), FORMED, MADE
Gen 1:26 . . . Let us ***m*** human beings in our
Gen 2:18 . . . will ***m*** a helper who is just
Exod 4:11 . . Who ***m-s*** a person's mouth?
Exod 25:40 . you ***m*** everything
Lev 16:34. . . ***m-ing*** them right with the
Ps 19:7 . . . . . ***m-ing*** wise the simple.
Ps 139:14 . . . ***m-ing*** me so wonderfully
Prov 13:12. . Hope deferred ***m-s*** the heart
Isa 8:14. . . . . stone that ***m-s*** people stumble,
Isa 29:16. . . . "He didn't ***m*** me"?
Isa 44:10. . . . fool would ***m*** his own god—
Jer 18:4. . . . . he was ***m-ing*** did not turn out
Jer 23:16. . . . ***m-ing*** up everything they say.
Jer 31:31. . . . when I will ***m*** a new covenant
Matt 28:19 . . ***m*** disciples of all
John 5:18 . . . ***m-ing*** himself equal with God.
Rom 14:20 . . it ***m-s*** another person stumble.
1 Cor 3:7 . . . that God ***m-s*** the seed grow.
Heb 8:5 . . . . you ***m*** everything according to
1 Pet 2:8. . . . stone that ***m-s*** people stumble,

MAKER (n)
one who makes; God
see also CREATOR
Ps 95:6 . . . . . before the LORD our ***m,***
Ps 149:2 . . . . Israel, rejoice in your ***M.***
Prov 17:5. . . mock the poor insult their ***M;***
Isa 45:9. . . . . clay pot argue with its ***m?***
Hos 8:14 . . . Israel has forgotten its ***M***

MALE (adj)
of, relating to, or being of the masculine sex
Gen 1:27 . . . ***m*** and female he created them.
Matt 19:4. . . God made them ***m*** and female.
Gal 3:28 . . . . slave or free, ***m*** and female.

MALICIOUS (adj)
given to, marked by, or arising from a desire to cause pain, injury, or distress to another
Rom 1:29. . . deception, ***m*** behavior,
Col 3:8 . . . . . of anger, rage, ***m*** behavior,

MAMMON (KJV)
Matt 6:24. . . serve both God and ***money***
Luke 16:9. . . ***worldly resources*** to benefit
Luke 16:11. . untrustworthy about ***worldly wealth,***

MAN (n)
an adult male human; individual, person
Gen 2:7 . . . . the ***m*** from the dust
Gen 2:15 . . . the ***m*** in the Garden
Gen 2:18 . . . for the ***m*** to be alone.
Gen 2:23 . . . she was taken from '***m.***'
Gen 2:25 . . . ***m*** and his wife were both
Gen 3:9 . . . . God called to the ***m,*** "Where
Isa 53:3. . . . . rejected—a ***m*** of sorrows,
1 Cor 11:3 . . of every ***m*** is Christ,
1 Cor 11:3 . . the head of woman is ***m,***
1 Cor 15:45 . The first ***m,*** Adam,
Eph 5:31 . . . A ***m*** leaves his father and
1 Tim 2:5 . . . the ***m*** Christ Jesus.

MAN-MADE (adj)
manufactured, created, or constructed by human beings
Matt 15:9. . . teach ***m*** ideas as commands

MANAGE, MANAGING (v)
to handle or direct with a degree of skill
Luke 12:42. . of ***m-ing*** his other household
1 Tim 3:4 . . . ***m*** his own family well,
1 Tim 3:12 . . he must ***m*** his children

MANAGER (n)
a person who conducts business or household affairs
Luke 16:1. . . a ***m*** handling his affairs.
1 Cor 4:2 . . . as a ***m*** must be faithful.
Titus 1:7. . . . a ***m*** of God's household,

MANGER (n)
a trough or open box in a stable designed to hold feed for livestock
Luke 2:7. . . . cloth and laid him in a ***m,***
Luke 2:12. . . strips of cloth, lying in a ***m.***

MANNA (n)
miraculous supply of food given to Israel in the wilderness; symbolic of spiritual nourishment
Exod 16:31 . Israelites called the food ***m.***
Deut 8:16. . . He fed you with ***m*** in the
John 6:49 . . . Your ancestors ate ***m*** in the
Rev 2:17. . . . some of the ***m*** that has been

MANNER (n)
a mode of procedure or way of acting
Phil 1:27 . . . a ***m*** worthy of the Good News

MANSIONS (n)
very large houses
Isa 5:9. . . . . . beautiful ***m*** will be empty.
Amos 3:15 . . their winter ***m*** and their

MARANATHA (KJV)
1 Cor 16:22 . ***Our Lord, come!***

MARCH (v)
to move along steadily usually with a rhythmic stride and in step with others; to advance or proceed
Josh 6:4 . . . . you are to ***m*** around the town
Isa 42:13. . . . The LORD will ***m*** forth

MARK
Son of Mary of Jerusalem (Acts 12:12); traveled with Barnabas and Paul (Acts 12:25; 13:5); returned to Jerusalem (Acts 13:13); went to Cyprus with Barnabas (Acts 15:37-39); in Paul's greetings (Col 4:10; 2 Tim 4:11; Phlm 1:24); Peter's "son" (1 Pet 5:13).

MARK (n)
an impression (as a scratch, scar, or stain) made on something; a distinguishing trait or quality
Gen 4:15 . . . LORD put a ***m*** on Cain
Rev 13:16. . . given a ***m*** on the right hand or

MARKETPLACE, MARKETPLACES (n)
an open square or place in town where markets or public sales are held
Matt 23:7 . . . as they walk in the ***m-s,***
John 2:16 . . . my Father's house into a ***m!***

MARRIAGE (adj)
of or relating to marriage
Gen 49:4 . . . you defiled my ***m*** couch.
Mal 2:14. . . . the wife of your ***m*** vows.

MARRIAGE (n)
the state of being lawfully united to a person of the opposite sex as husband or wife; an act of marrying
Matt 22:30 . . marry nor be given in ***m.***
Rom 7:2 . . . . laws of ***m*** no longer apply
1 Cor 7:14 . . brings holiness to her ***m,***
1 Cor 7:27 . . do not seek to end the ***m.***
Heb 13:4 . . . Give honor to ***m,*** and remain

MARRY, MARRIED, MARRIES, MARRYING (v)
to take a spouse according to law or custom
Exod 21:10 . who has ***m-ied*** a slave wife
Deut 24:4. . . first husband may not ***m*** her
Deut 24:5. . . newly ***m-ied*** man must not be
Deut 25:5. . . husband's brother should ***m***
Ezra 10:10 . . By ***m-ing*** pagan women,
Hos 1:2 . . . . Go and ***m*** a prostitute, so that
Matt 1:18 . . . to be ***m-ied*** to Joseph.
Matt 19:9 . . . divorces his wife and ***m-ies***
Matt 22:30 . . will neither ***m*** nor be given
Mark 12:23 . all seven were ***m-ied*** to her.
Luke 16:18. . his wife and ***m-ies*** someone
Rom 7:2. . . . when a woman ***m-ies,*** the law
1 Cor 7:9 . . . better to ***m*** than to burn
1 Cor 7:28 . . if you do get ***m-ied,*** it is not
1 Cor 7:33 . . a ***m-ied*** man has to think
1 Tim 5:14 . . these younger widows to ***m***

MARTYRED (v)
to put to death for adhering to a belief, faith, or profession
Rev 6:9. . . . . who had been ***m*** for the word

MARVELING (v)
to become filled with surprise, wonder, or amazed curiosity
Luke 9:43. . . everyone was ***m*** at

MARVELOUS (adj)
astonishing; miraculous, supernatural
Ps 9:1 . . . . . . tell of all the ***m*** things
Rev 15:1. . . . heaven another ***m*** event
Rev 15:3. . . . Great and ***m*** are your works,

MARY
1. Mother of Jesus, the foretold virgin (Matt 1:16-25; Luke 1:26-38); psalmist of the Magnificat (Luke 1:46-56); gave birth in Bethlehem (Luke 2:5-20); at first sign (miracle) of Jesus (John 2:1-5); at the cross (John 19:25-27); Jesus assigned her care to John (John 19:25-27); in upper room after the ascension (Acts 1:14).
2. Mary Magdalene, former demoniac, supporter of Jesus (Luke 8:1-3); at the cross and Jesus' burial (Matt 27:55-61; Mark 15:40-47; John 19:25); saw angel after resurrection (Matt 28:1-10; Mark 16:1-9; Luke 24:10); saw Jesus after resurrection (John 20:1-18).
3. Sister of Martha and Lazarus (Luke 10:38-42; John 11; 12:1-8).
4. Mother of James and Joseph (Matt 27:56; Mark 15:40, 47; 16:1).
5. Mother of John Mark (Acts 12:12).
6. A woman in Rome greeted by Paul (Rom 16:6).

MASTER, MASTERS (n)
one in authority or leadership; employer; teacher; lord or Lord
Jer 3:14. . . . . the LORD, "for I am your ***m.***
Matt 10:24 . . are not greater than their ***m.***
Luke 16:13. . No one can serve two ***m-s.***
Rom 6:14 . . . Sin is no longer your ***m,***
Eph 6:5 . . . . obey your earthly ***m-s*** with
Col 3:22 . . . . Slaves, obey your earthly ***m-s***

1 Tim 6:1 . . . full respect for their ***m-s***
1 Tim 6:2 . . . If the ***m-s*** are believers,
2 Tim 2:21 . . ready for the ***M*** to use you
Titus 2:9. . . . always obey their ***m-s*** and do
1 Pet 2:18. . . the authority of your ***m-s***
2 Pet 2:1. . . . deny the ***M*** who bought them.
Jude 1:4 . . . . denied our only ***M*** and Lord,

MAT (n)
a large thick pad or cushion
Mark 2:9 . . . pick up your ***m,*** and walk'?
Acts 9:34 . . . and roll up your sleeping ***m!***

MATTHEW
One of the 12 disciples (Matt 10:3; Mark 3:18; Luke 6:15; Acts 1:13); former tax collector who followed Jesus (Matt 9:9-10); also known as "Levi" (Mark 2:14).

MATURE (adj)
of or relating to a condition of full development or to attaining a desired or final state
1 Cor 2:6 . . . I am among ***m*** believers,
1 Cor 14:20 . but be ***m*** in understanding
2 Cor 13:9 . . that you will become ***m.***
Eph 4:13 . . . we will be ***m*** in the Lord,
Phil 3:15 . . . all who are spiritually ***m*** agree
Heb 6:1 . . . . ***m*** in our understanding.
1 Jn 2:13. . . . who are ***m*** in the faith

MATURITY (n)
the quality or state of being fully developed
Luke 8:14. . . so they never grow into ***m.***
2 Cor 13:11 . Grow to ***m.*** Encourage each

MEADOWS (n)
a grassy land area
Ps 23:2 . . . . . He lets me rest in green ***m;***

MEAL, MEALS (n)
a portion of food eaten usually at designated times in the day to satisfy appetite; an act or time of eating
Matt 26:18 . . I will eat the Passover ***m***
Heb 12:16 . . firstborn son for a single ***m.***
Jude 1:12 . . . in your fellowship ***m-s***

MEAN-SPIRITED (adj)
exhibiting or characterized by meanness of spirit
Deut 15:9. . . not be ***m*** and refuse someone

MEAN, MEANS (v)
to serve or intend to convey, show, or indicate
Gen 41:16 . . God can tell you what it ***m-s***
Rom 3:3. . . . that ***m*** God will be unfaithful?

MEANING (n)
the thing that is conveyed especially by language
Neh 8:8 . . . . and clearly explained the ***m***

MEANINGLESS (adj)
having no meaning; lacking any significance
Eccl 1:2 . . . . ***m,"*** says the Teacher,
Eccl 8:14 . . . not all that is ***m*** in our world.
1 Tim 1:6 . . . their time in ***m*** discussions.

MEASURE, MEASURED, MEASURING (v)
to gauge or regulate the specific dimensions of; to have a specified measurement; to regulate by a standard
Ps 145:3 . . . . No one can ***m*** his greatness.
Isa 40:28. . . . No one can ***m*** the depths
Jer 31:37. . . . heavens cannot be ***m-d*** and
Ezek 45:3. . . area, ***m*** out a portion of land
Dan 5:27 . . . balances and have not ***m-d*** up.
Zech 2:2. . . . I am going to ***m*** Jerusalem,
Luke 12:15. . Life is not ***m-d*** by how much
Eph 4:13 . . . mature in the Lord, ***m-ing*** up
Rev 11:1. . . . Go and ***m*** the Temple

MEASURES (n)
instruments or utensils for measuring; a system of standard units of measure
Deut 25:14. . must use full and honest ***m.***
Prov 20:10. . unequal ***m*** — the LORD detests

MEAT (n)
animal tissue considered especially as food
Rom 14:21. . better not to eat ***m*** or drink
1 Cor 8:13 . . sin, I will never eat ***m*** again
1 Cor 10:25 . may eat any ***m*** that is sold

MEDDLING (v)
to interest oneself in what is not one's concern; to interfere without right or propriety
2 Thes 3:11 . refusing to work and ***m*** in
1 Tim 5:13 . . ***m*** in other people's

MEDIATE, MEDIATES (v)
to act as an intermediary agent in bringing, effecting, or communicating; to interpose
Job 16:21 . . . to ***m*** between God and me,
Isa 2:4. . . . . . LORD will ***m*** between nations
Heb 8:6 . . . . the one who ***m-s*** for us a far
Heb 9:15 . . . who ***m-s*** a new covenant
Heb 12:24 . . Jesus, the one who ***m-s***

MEDIATOR (n)
one who mediates
Job 9:33 . . . . If only there were a ***m*** between
1 Tim 2:5 . . . one God and one ***M*** who can

MEDICINE (n)
a substance or preparation used in treating disease; something that affects well-being
Prov 17:22 . . A cheerful heart is good ***m,***
Jer 8:22. . . . . Is there no ***m*** in Gilead?
Rev 22:2. . . . The leaves were used for ***m***

MEDITATE, MEDITATING (v)
to contemplate, reflect, or ponder
see also PONDER, THINK
Gen 24:63 . . ***m-ing*** in the fields,
Ps 1:2 . . . . . . ***m-ing*** on it day and night.
Ps 48:9 . . . . . O God, we ***m*** on your unfailing
Ps 63:6 . . . . . ***m-ing*** on you through the night.
Ps 119:23 . . . but I will ***m*** on your decrees.
Ps 119:27 . . . ***m*** on your wonderful deeds.
Ps 119:48 . . . I ***m*** on your decrees.
Ps 145:5 . . . . I will ***m*** on your majestic,

MEDITATION (n)
the act or process of meditating
Ps 19:14 . . . . words of my mouth and the ***m***

MEDIUMS (n)
psychics; those through whom it is thought the dead communicate with the living
Lev 20:27 . . . who act as ***m*** or who consult

MELCHIZEDEK
King of Salem, priest of God Most High (Gen 14:18); blessed Abram and accepted his tithe (Gen 14:19-20); associated with mysterious priesthood (Ps 110:4; Heb 7:11).

MELODIOUS (adj)
having a pleasant melody
Ps 98:5 . . . . . the harp and ***m*** song,

MELODY (n)
a sweet succession or arrangement of sounds
Ps 92:3 . . . . . harp and the ***m*** of the lyre.

MELT, MELTS (v)
to dissolve or disintegrate; to disappear as if by dissolving
Jer 9:7. . . . . . ***m*** them down in a crucible
Amos 9:5 . . . touches the land and it ***m-s,***

MEMBERS (n)
the individuals composing a group; parts of a whole
see also PARTS
Eph 5:30 . . . And we are ***m*** of his body.
Col 3:15 . . . . For as ***m*** of one body

MERCIFUL (adj)
compassionate; forgiving
Deut 4:31. . . your God is a ***m*** God;
Ps 78:38 . . . . Yet he was ***m*** and forgave
Dan 4:27 . . . and be ***m*** to the poor.
Dan 9:9 . . . . our God is ***m*** and forgiving,
Matt 5:7. . . . God blesses those who are ***m,***
Luke 1:54. . . and remembered to be ***m.***
Heb 2:17 . . . ***m*** and faithful High Priest
Jas 2:13. . . . . God will be ***m*** when he judges

MERCY, MERCIES (n)
a blessing that is an act of divine favor or compassion; withholding of the punishment or judgment our sins deserve
see also COMPASSION, FORGIVENESS
Exod 34:6 . . God of compassion and ***m!***
2 Sam 24:14. for his ***m*** is great.
Neh 9:27 . . . In your great ***m,*** you sent
Job 41:3 . . . . beg you for ***m*** or implore
Ps 28:6 . . . . . he has heard my cry for ***m.***
Ps 103:4 . . . . me with love and tender ***m-ies.***
Ps 119:77 . . . with your tender ***m-ies*** so I
Ps 119:156 . . how great is your ***m;***
Isa 14:1. . . . . LORD will have ***m*** on
Isa 49:10. . . . LORD in his ***m*** will lead
Isa 60:10. . . . I will now have ***m*** on you
Lam 3:22 . . . His ***m-ies*** never cease.
Lam 3:23 . . . ***m-ies*** begin afresh each morning.
Dan 9:18 . . . because of your ***m.***
Jonah 2:8 . . . their backs on all God's ***m-ies.***
Mic 6:8. . . . . do what is right, to love ***m,***
Matt 5:7. . . . for they will be shown ***m.***
Matt 9:13 . . . I want you to show ***m,***
Matt 18:33 . . just as I had ***m*** on you?
Matt 23:23 . . law—justice, ***m,*** and faith.
Rom 9:15 . . . I will show ***m*** to anyone
Rom 9:18 . . . God chooses to show ***m***
Rom 11:32 . . have ***m*** on everyone.
2 Cor 4:1 . . . God in his ***m*** has given us
Gal 1:6 . . . . . through the loving ***m*** of Christ.
Eph 2:4 . . . . But God is so rich in ***m,*** and
1 Tim 1:13 . . But God had ***m*** on me
Titus 3:5. . . . but because of his ***m.***
Heb 4:16 . . . we will receive his ***m,***
Heb 10:29 . . who brings God's ***m*** to us.
Jas 2:13. . . . . will be no ***m*** for those
Jas 3:17. . . . . It is full of ***m*** and good
1 Pet 1:3. . . . by his great ***m*** that we
Jude 1:22 . . . show ***m*** to those whose faith

MERCYSEAT (KJV)
Heb 9:5 . . . . the ***Ark's cover, the place of atonement.***

MESSAGE (n)
a communication in writing, in speech, or by signals; an underlying theme or idea
Isa 53:1. . . . . Who has believed our ***m?***
Isa 62:11. . . . LORD has sent this ***m***
John 12:38 . . who has believed our ***m?***
Acts 5:20 . . . give the people this ***m*** of life!
Acts 10:36 . . This is the ***m*** of Good News
Rom 10:16 . . who has believed our ***m?***
1 Cor 1:18 . . The ***m*** of the cross
2 Cor 5:19 . . wonderful ***m*** of reconciliation.
Titus 1:9. . . . belief in the trustworthy ***m***
2 Pet 1:19. . . confidence in the ***m*** proclaimed

MESSENGER, MESSENGERS (n)
one who bears a message or does an errand
Prov 13:17 . . a reliable ***m*** brings healing.
Prov 25:13 . . Trustworthy ***m-s*** refresh like
Isa 52:7. . . . . feet of the ***m*** who brings good
Isa 66:19. . . . who survive to be ***m-s*** to the
Mal 3:1. . . . . my ***m,*** and he will prepare
Matt 11:10 . . am sending my ***m*** ahead
Rom 10:15 . . feet of ***m-s*** who bring good
Rom 15:16 . . a special ***m*** from Christ
2 Cor 12:7 . . ***m*** from Satan to torment
Phil 2:25 . . . he was your ***m*** to help me
1 Thes 2:4 . . speak as ***m-s*** approved by God
Heb 3:1 . . . . to be God's ***m*** and High Priest.

MESSIAH, MESSIAHS (n)
the one anointed by God to deliver His people and establish His kingdom
see also CHRIST, JESUS
Matt 24:24 . . false ***m-s*** and false
Mark 13:22 . false ***m-s*** and false
John 1:41 . . . him, "We have found the ***M***"
John 4:25 . . . I know the ***M*** is coming—

METHUSELAH
The oldest man, who lived 969 years; the son of Enoch, who never died (Gen 5:21-24); the father of Lamech (Gen 5:25-27).

MICHAEL
Ruling angel (Jude 1:9; Rev 12:7); great defender-prince in the visions of Daniel (Dan 10:13, 21; 11:1; 12:1).

MIDNIGHT (n)
the middle of the night
Exod 12:29 . at ***m,*** the Lord struck down
Acts 16:25 . . Around ***m*** Paul and Silas were

MIDWIVES (n)
those who assist women in childbirth
Exod 1:17 . . because the ***m*** feared God,

MIGHT (n)
the power, energy, or intensity of which one is capable
Josh 9:9 . . . . heard of the ***m*** of the LORD
2 Sam 6:14 . . the LORD with all his ***m,***
Ps 54:1 . . . . . Defend me with your ***m.***
Isa 11:2. . . . . the Spirit of counsel and ***m,***
Isa 63:15. . . . and the ***m*** you used to show

MIGHTY, MIGHTIER, MIGHTIEST (adj)
powerful; great or imposing in size or extent
Gen 49:24 . . hands of the ***M*** One of Jacob,
Deut 10:17 . . God, the ***m*** and awesome
Deut 34:12 . . With ***m*** power, Moses
2 Sam 23:8 . . David's ***m-iest*** warriors.
2 Chr 20:6 . . You are powerful and ***m;***
Neh 9:32 . . . and ***m*** and awesome God,
Job 9:4 . . . . . For God is so wise and so ***m.***
Job 36:5 . . . . He is ***m*** in both power and
Ps 24:8 . . . . . LORD, strong and ***m;***
Ps 47:5 . . . . . ascended with a ***m*** shout.
Ps 50:1 . . . . . LORD, the ***M*** One, is God,
Ps 71:16 . . . . I will praise your ***m*** deeds,
Ps 77:12 . . . . thinking about your ***m*** works.
Ps 89:27 . . . . son, the ***m-iest*** king on earth.
Ps 93:4 . . . . . ***m-ier*** than the violent raging
Ps 93:4 . . . . . LORD above is ***m-ier*** than these!
Ps 95:4 . . . . . and the ***m-iest*** mountains.
Ps 145:4 . . . . children of your ***m*** acts;
Ps 145:12 . . . will tell about your ***m*** deeds
Ps 150:2 . . . . Praise him for his ***m*** works;
Prov 24:5 . . . wise are ***m-ier*** than the strong,
Isa 9:6. . . . . . Wonderful Counselor, ***M*** God,
Isa 60:16. . . . your Redeemer, the ***M*** One of
Zeph 3:17 . . He is a ***m*** savior.
Eph 1:19 . . . This is the same ***m*** power
Eph 6:10 . . . in the Lord and in his ***m***
Heb 1:3 . . . . sustains everything by the ***m***
1 Pet 5:6. . . . yourselves under the ***m***
Jude 1:9 . . . . Michael, one of the ***m-iest*** of the angels,

MILE (n)
in the Roman Empire, a unit of distance equal to 4,854 feet
Matt 5:41 . . . gear for a ***m,*** carry it two

MILK (n)
from goats, cows, or sheep, used for food and drink; figurative of abundant produce, prosperity, spiritual food, or salvation
Exod 3:8 . . . flowing with ***m*** and honey—
1 Cor 3:2 . . . feed you with ***m,*** not with
1 Pet 2:2. . . . must crave pure spiritual ***m***

MILLSTONE (n)
either of two circular stones used for grinding
Luke 17:2. . . into the sea with a ***m*** hung

MIND, MINDS (n)
the part of humans that engages in conscious thinking, feeling, and decision making; in the Bible, mind is akin to the heart, not the brain
Num 23:19 . he does not change his ***m.***
1 Sam 15:29. nor will he change his ***m,***
Mark 12:30 . all your soul, all your ***m,***
Luke 24:45. . opened their ***m-s***
Acts 4:32 . . . were united in heart and ***m.***
Rom 8:6. . . . Spirit control your ***m***
1 Cor 1:10 . . be of one ***m,*** united in
1 Cor 2:9 . . . heard, and no ***m*** has imagined
2 Cor 4:4 . . . has blinded the ***m-s*** of those
Col 2:18 . . . . sinful ***m-s*** have made them
2 Tim 4:5 . . . clear ***m*** in every situation.
Heb 8:10 . . . I will put my laws in their ***m-s,***
Heb 10:16 . . I will write them on their ***m-s.***

MINDING (v)
to be concerned about
1 Thes 4:11 . live a quiet life, ***m*** your own

MINISTERS (n)
agent; one who serves or assists another of higher rank
2 Cor 3:6 . . . to be ***m*** of his new covenant.

MINISTRY (n)
exercise of one's gifts and resources
2 Cor 9:12 . . from this ***m*** of giving—
2 Cor 9:13 . . As a result of your ***m,*** they
Heb 8:6 . . . . a ***m*** that is far superior to

MIRACLE, MIRACLES (n)
an extraordinary event manifesting divine intervention in human affairs
Exod 3:20 . . performing all kinds of ***m-s***
Exod 7:9 . . . demand, 'Show me a ***m.'***
Deut 13:1. . . they promise you signs or ***m-s,***
Job 9:10 . . . . He performs countless ***m-s.***
Ps 105:5 . . . . he has performed, his ***m-s,***
Ps 106:2 . . . . the glorious ***m-s*** of the LORD?
Jer 32:19. . . . and do great and mighty ***m-s.***
Matt 7:22. . . and performed many ***m-s***
Matt 13:54. . and the power to do ***m-s?***
Mark 6:2 . . . power to perform such ***m-s?***
Mark 9:39 . . No one who performs a ***m***
Luke 19:37. . wonderful ***m-s*** they had
Luke 23:8. . . to see him perform a ***m.***
John 7:21 . . . I did one ***m*** on the Sabbath,
Acts 2:22 . . . by doing powerful ***m-s,***
Acts 8:13 . . . ***m-s*** Philip performed.
Acts 19:11 . . to perform unusual ***m-s.***
1 Cor 12:28 . those who do ***m-s,*** those
2 Cor 12:12 . and ***m-s*** among you.
Gal 3:5 . . . . . and work ***m-s*** among you
Heb 2:4 . . . . and various ***m-s*** and gifts of

MIRACULOUS (adj)
working or able to work miracles; supernatural
Ps 106:7 . . . . the LORD's ***m*** deeds.
Matt 12:39. . would demand a ***m***
John 9:16 . . . sinner do such ***m*** signs?
John 12:37 . . despite all the ***m*** signs Jesus
John 20:30 . . do many other ***m*** signs
Acts 2:43 . . . performed many ***m*** signs
Acts 4:16 . . . have performed a ***m*** sign,
Rom 15:19. . of ***m*** signs and wonders

MIRROR (n)
a polished or smooth surface (as of glass) that forms images by reflection
1 Cor 13:12 . puzzling reflections in a ***m,***
Jas 1:23. . . . . glancing at your face in a ***m.***

MISERABLE (adj)
being in a pitiable state of distress or unhappiness
Rom 7:24. . . Oh, what a ***m*** person I am!

MISERY (n)
a state of suffering or discomfort; a state of great unhappiness and emotional distress
Judg 10:16. . And he was grieved by their ***m.***
Rom 3:16. . . Destruction and ***m*** always

MISFORTUNE (n)
bad luck; a distressing or unfortunate incident or event
Prov 17:5. . . who rejoice at the ***m*** of others
Obad 1:12 . . Judah suffered such ***m.***

MISLEAD, MISLED (v)
to lead astray; to deceive
Prov 13:6. . . the evil are ***m-ed*** by sin.
Prov 16:29. . ***m*** their companions,
Matt 24:4. . . Don't let anyone ***m*** you,
Gal 6:7 . . . . . Don't be ***m-ed***—you cannot
Jas 1:16. . . . . So don't be ***m-ed,*** my dear

MISTREAT, MISTREATED (v)
to treat badly; to abuse
Exod 22:21 . You must not ***m*** or oppress
Prov 19:26. . Children who ***m*** their father
Heb 13:3 . . . those being ***m-ed,*** as if you

MISUSE (v)
to use incorrectly; to mistreat or abuse
Exod 20:7 . . must not ***m*** the name of

Deut 5:11 . . . must not ***m*** the name of
Ps 139:20 . . . your enemies ***m*** your name.

MOCK, MOCKED, MOCKS (v)

to treat with contempt or ridicule; to mimic in sport or derision

Job 11:3 . . . . When you ***m*** God, shouldn't
Ps 22:7 . . . . . Everyone who sees me ***m-s*** me.
Ps 89:51 . . . . Your enemies have ***m-ed*** me,
Prov 3:34 . . . The LORD ***m-s*** the mockers
Prov 30:17 . . The eye that ***m-s*** a father and
Mic 6:16 . . . . with contempt, ***m-ed*** by all
Matt 5:11 . . . blesses you when people ***m***
Matt 27:41 . . the elders also ***m-ed*** Jesus.
Mark 10:34 . They will ***m*** him, spit on
Luke 6:22 . . . and exclude you and ***m*** you
Gal 6:7 . . . . . cannot ***m*** the justice of God.

MOCKER, MOCKERS (n)

one who mocks

Ps 1:1 . . . . . . sinners, or join in with ***m-s.***
Prov 3:34 . . . The LORD mocks the ***m-s***
Prov 9:7 . . . . Anyone who rebukes a ***m*** will
Prov 20:1 . . . Wine produces ***m-s;*** alcohol

MOCKERY (n)

a subject of laughter, derision, or sport; insulting or contemptuous action or speech

1 Kgs 9:7 . . . object of ***m*** and ridicule
Isa 50:6 . . . . . not hide my face from ***m*** and
Joel 2:17 . . . . become an object of ***m.***
Matt 27:29 . . in ***m*** and taunted,

MODEL (n)

an example for imitation or emulation

Ezek 28:12 . . were the ***m*** of perfection,

MODESTY (n)

propriety in dress, speech, or conduct; freedom from conceit or vanity

1 Tim 2:15 . . faith, love, holiness, and ***m.***

MOLTEN (adj)

made by melting and casting

Exod 34:17 . not make any gods of ***m*** metal

MOMENT (n)

a comparatively brief period of time; instant

Ps 30:5 . . . . . lasts only a ***m,*** but his favor
Prov 11:18 . . get rich for the ***m,***
Isa 54:7 . . . . . For a brief ***m*** I abandoned you,
Isa 66:8 . . . . . come forth in a mere ***m?***
Matt 6:27 . . . your worries add a single ***m***
Gal 2:5 . . . . . give in to them for a single ***m.***

MONEY (n)

officially coined currency

see also POSSESSIONS, RICHES, TREASURE(S), WEALTH

2 Chr 24:10 . gladly brought their ***m*** and
Eccl 5:10 . . . who love ***m*** will never have
Matt 6:24 . . . serve both God and ***m.***
Luke 3:14 . . Don't extort ***m*** or make false
1 Tim 3:3 . . . and not love ***m.***
1 Tim 6:10 . . love of ***m*** is the root of all
1 Tim 6:17 . . and not to trust in their ***m,***
1 Jn 3:17 . . . . If someone has enough ***m***

MONTH, MONTHS (n)

a measure of time corresponding nearly to the period of the moon's revolution and amounting to approximately 4 weeks or 30 days

Ezek 47:12 . . will be a new crop every ***m,***
Gal 4:10 . . . . certain days or ***m-s*** or seasons
Rev 11:2 . . . . trample the holy city for 42 ***m-s.***
Rev 13:5 . . . . he wanted for forty-two ***m-s.***
Rev 22:2 . . . . fruit, with a fresh crop each ***m.***

MOON (n)

a celestial body that orbits the earth

Josh 10:13 . . and the ***m*** stayed in place
Ps 121:6 . . . . harm you by day, nor the ***m*** at
Ps 148:3 . . . . Praise him, sun and ***m!***
Joel 2:31 . . . . the ***m*** will turn blood red
Hab 3:11 . . . The sun and ***m*** stood still
Matt 24:29 . . the ***m*** will give no light,
Acts 2:20 . . . the ***m*** will turn blood red
Col 2:16 . . . . or new ***m*** ceremonies
Rev 21:23 . . . city has no need of sun or ***m,***

MORE (adv)

to a greater or higher degree

Ps 73:25 . . . . I desire you ***m*** than anything
1 Pet 1:2 . . . . give you ***m*** and ***m*** grace

MORNING (n)

the time from sunrise to noon

Gen 1:5 . . . . evening passed and ***m*** came,
Ps 5:3 . . . . . . Listen to my voice in the ***m,***
Lam 3:23 . . . mercies begin afresh each ***m.***

MORNING STAR (n)

a bright planet (Venus) seen in the eastern sky before or at sunrise

2 Pet 1:19 . . . and Christ the ***M*** shines
Rev 2:28 . . . . give them the ***m!***
Rev 22:16 . . . I am the bright ***m.***

MORTAL (adj)

subject to death

Gen 6:3 . . . . for they are only ***m*** flesh.

Rom 8:11 . . . will give life to your ***m*** bodies
1 Cor 15:53 . our ***m*** bodies must be

MORTALS (n)
human beings
Ps 8:4 . . . . . . mere ***m*** that you should think
Ps 144:3 . . . . mere ***m*** that you should think

MOSES
Deliverer of Israel from Egypt, lawgiver, servant of God; "drawn out" of the Nile, raised in Pharaoh's house (Exod 2:1-10); killed an Egyptian and fled to Midian (Exod 2:11-15; Acts 7:24); married Zipporah and had a child (Exod 2:16-22); saw the L*ORD at the burning bush (Exod 3:1–4:17); returned to Egypt (Exod 4:18-31); conflict with Pharaoh and the ten plagues (Exod 5–11); brother of Aaron and Miriam (1 Chr 6:3); Passover and the Exodus (Exod 12–14; 1 Cor 10:2); song of salvation and praise (Exod 15:1-21; Rev 15:3); heavenly provisions (Exod 15:22–17:7); raised arms to defeat enemies (Exod 17:8-16); delegated judgeships (Exod 18); received the law at Sinai (Exod 19–23; John 1:17; Heb 12:21); received Tabernacle plans (Exod 25–31); broke tablets at gold calf incident (Exod 32); received new tablets (Exod 33–34); face glowed with the* L*ORD's glory (Exod 34:29-35; 2 Cor 3:13-15); directed the building of the Tabernacle (Exod 35–40); anointed Tabernacle and Aaronic priesthood (Lev 8–9); opposed by Aaron and Miriam, interceded for sister (Num 12); interceded for Israel when they refused to enter Canaan (Num 14:11-25); Korah's rebellion (Num 16); water at Meribah (Num 20:1-13); denied entrance to Promised Land (Num 20:12; Deut 1:37; 3:23-28); bronze snake healed (Num 21:4-9; John 3:14); succeeded by Joshua (Num 27:12-23; Deut 31:1-8); received additional laws (Num 28–30); gave concluding messages to Israel (Deut 1–33); gave final blessings to the tribes (Deut 33; see also Gen 49); died and was exalted (Deut 34; Heb 3:2); wrote a psalm (Ps 90); recorded book of the law (Ezra 3:2; Neh 13:1; Luke 24:44); appeared with Elijah at the Transfiguration (Luke 9:30).*

MOTHER (n)
a female parent; a woman in authority
see also PARENT
Gen 2:24 . . . a man leaves his father and ***m***
Gen 3:20 . . . she would be the ***m*** of all who
Exod 20:12 . Honor your father and ***m.***
Deut 21:18. . not obey his father or ***m,***
Judg 5:7. . . . Deborah arose as a ***m***
Prov 10:1 . . . brings grief to a ***m.***
Prov 23:22. . don't despise your ***m***
Isa 66:13. . . . as a ***m*** comforts her child.
Matt 10:35. . a daughter against her ***m,***
Matt 10:37. . father or ***m*** more than you
Matt 12:48. . Who is my ***m?***
Mark 10:19 . Honor your father and ***m.***
John 19:27. . disciple, "Here is your ***m.***"
Eph 5:31 . . . A man leaves his father and ***m***
Eph 6:2 . . . . Honor your father and ***m.***

MOTHER-IN-LAW (n)
the mother of one's spouse
Ruth 2:19. . . Ruth told her ***m*** about the man
Matt 10:35. . daughter-in-law against her ***m.***

MOTHS (n)
insects whose larvae eat wool, fur, or feathers
Matt 6:19. . . on earth, where ***m*** eat them

MOTIVES (n)
something (as a need or desire) that causes a person to act
1 Chr 29:17 . all this with good ***m,***
Ps 26:2. . . . . Test my ***m*** and my heart.
Prov 16:2. . . LORD examines their ***m.***
Jer 17:10. . . . hearts and examine secret ***m.***
1 Cor 4:5 . . . will reveal our private ***m.***
Phil 1:18 . . . Whether their ***m*** are false or
1 Thes 2:3 . . with any deceit or impure ***m***
1 Thes 2:4 . . He alone examines the ***m*** of
Jas 4:3. . . . . your ***m*** are all wrong—

MOUNT (n)
a high hill; mountain
Exod 17:6 . . on the rock at ***M*** Sinai
Exod 19:18 . ***M*** Sinai was covered with smoke
Zech 14:4. . . the ***M*** of Olives will split
Matt 24:3. . . Jesus sat on the ***M*** of Olives
Luke 22:39. . as usual to the ***M*** of Olives

MOUNTAIN, MOUNTAINS (n)
a landmass that projects conspicuously above its surroundings and is higher than a hill
Exod 24:18 . on the ***m*** forty days
Deut 5:4. . . . At the ***m*** the LORD
Ps 36:6 . . . . . is like the mighty ***m-s,***
Ps 121:1 . . . . I look up to the ***m-s***—
Isa 14:13. . . . preside on the ***m*** of the gods
Matt 17:20. . say to this ***m,*** 'Move
Mark 9:2 . . . led them up a high ***m***
Mark 9:9 . . . went back down the ***m,***
Luke 23:30. . beg the ***m-s,*** 'Fall on us,'
1 Cor 13:2 . . faith that I could move ***m-s,***
2 Pet 1:18. . . with him on the holy ***m.***
Rev 6:16. . . . they cried to the ***m-s*** and

MOUNTAINTOPS (n)
the summits of mountains
Isa 42:11. . . . shout praises from the ***m!***

MOURN (v)
to feel or express grief or sorrow
Gen 50:11 . . watched them ***m***
Zech 12:10. . have pierced and ***m*** for him
Matt 5:4. . . . God blesses those who ***m,***

MOURNING (n)
the act of sorrowing; a period of time during which signs of grief are shown
Ps 30:11 . . . . my clothes of ***m*** and clothed
Isa 60:20. . . . Your days of ***m*** will come to
Isa 61:3. . . . . instead of ***m,*** festive praise
Jer 31:13. . . . I will turn their ***m*** into joy.
Zech 8:19. . . times of ***m*** you have kept

MOUTH, MOUTHS (n)
the natural opening through which food passes into the body of an animal; voice, speech
Ps 10:7 . . . . . Their ***m-s*** are full of cursing,
Ps 19:14 . . . . words of my ***m*** and
Prov 13:3. . . opening your ***m*** can ruin
Isa 51:16. . . . have put my words in your ***m***
Isa 53:7. . . . . he did not open his ***m.***
Isa 59:3. . . . . and your ***m*** spews corruption.
Jer 31:29. . . . their children's ***m-s*** pucker
Matt 4:4. . . . word that comes from the ***m***
Rom 3:14. . . Their ***m-s*** are full of cursing
Rom 10:9. . . ***m*** that Jesus is Lord
Rev 2:16. . . . with the sword of my ***m.***

MOVE, MOVED, MOVES, MOVING (v)
to change the place or position of; to go from one place to another in continuous motion; to carry on one's life or activities in a specified environment; to stir the emotions or passions of; to prompt to the doing of something
Exod 35:21 . and whose spirits were ***m-d***
Deut 19:14. . steal anyone's land by ***m-ing***
Deut 23:14. . LORD your God ***m-s*** around
Prov 4:15. . . Turn away and keep ***m-ing.***
Prov 23:10. . cheat your neighbor by ***m-ing***
Isa 54:10. . . . For the mountains may ***m***
Acts 17:28 . . For in him we live and ***m***
1 Cor 13:2 . . faith that I could ***m***
2 Pet 1:21. . . were ***m-d*** by the Holy Spirit,

MUD (n)
soft, wet earth
Ps 40:2. . . . . pit of despair, out of the ***m***
John 9:6 . . . . spread the ***m*** over the blind

MUDDYING (v)
to soil or stain with or as if with mud
Prov 25:26. . a fountain or ***m*** a spring.

MULTIPLY, MULTIPLIED (v)
to increase greatly in extent or number
Gen 1:22 . . . Be fruitful and ***m.***
Acts 6:1 . . . . the believers rapidly ***m-ied,***

MULTITUDE (n)
a great number
1 Pet 4:8. . . . love covers a ***m*** of sins.

MURDER (n)
the personal, intentional killing of another person
Matt 5:21. . . If you commit ***m,***
Rom 1:29. . . hate, envy, ***m,*** quarreling,

MURDER, MURDERED, MURDERS (v)
to kill (a human being) unlawfully and with premeditated malice
Gen 9:5 . . . . ***m-s*** a fellow human must die.
Exod 20:13 . You must not ***m.***
Deut 5:17. . . You must not ***m.***
Matt 23:31. . who ***m-ed*** the prophets.
Acts 7:52 . . . whom you betrayed and ***m-ed.***
Rom 13:9. . . You must not ***m.***
Jas 2:11. . . . . You must not ***m.***

MURDERER, MURDERERS (n)
one who commits the crime of murder
Num 35:16 . ***m*** must be executed.
Ps 5:6 . . . . . . LORD detests ***m-s*** and deceivers.
Ps 26:9 . . . . . condemn me along with ***m-s.***
Ps 59:2 . . . . . save me from these ***m-s.***
Ezek 18:10. . a robber or ***m*** and refuses
1 Jn 3:15. . . . brother or sister is really a ***m***
Rev 21:8. . . . the corrupt, ***m-s,*** the immoral,
Rev 22:15. . . the sexually immoral, the ***m-s,***

MUSIC (n)
vocal, instrumental, or mechanical sounds having rhythm, melody, or harmony
Judg 5:3. . . . I will make ***m*** to the LORD,
1 Chr 6:31 . . lead the ***m*** at the house of
Neh 12:27 . . and with the ***m*** of cymbals,
Ps 45:8 . . . . . the ***m*** of strings entertains
Amos 5:23. . to the ***m*** of your harps.
Eph 5:19 . . . and making ***m*** to the Lord

MUSICAL (adj)
of or relating to music
1 Chr 23:5 . . praise the LORD with the ***m***
2 Chr 23:13 . with ***m*** instruments
Neh 12:36 . . the ***m*** instruments

Dan 3:5 . . . . and other ***m*** instruments,
Dan 3:15 . . . of the ***m*** instruments.

MUSICIAN, MUSICIANS (n)
a composer, conductor, or performer of music; instrumentalist
1 Chr 6:33 . . Heman the ***m*** was from
1 Chr 9:33 . . ***m-s,*** all prominent Levites,
1 Chr 15:16 . were singers and ***m-s*** to sing
1 Chr 15:19 . The ***m-s*** Heman, Asaph,
2 Chr 9:11 . . lyres and harps for the ***m-s.***
2 Chr 35:15 . ***m-s,*** descendants of

MUSTARD (n)
a plant whose seeds are used as a condiment and for oil; in Jesus' time, the smallest seed known
Matt 13:31 . . is like a ***m*** seed planted
Matt 17:20 . . as small as a ***m*** seed,
Mark 4:31 . . is like a ***m*** seed planted

MUTILATORS (n)
those who cripple or maim
Phil 3:2 . . . . ***m*** who say you must be

MUZZLE (v)
to fit with a fastening or covering for the mouth of an animal to prevent eating or biting
Deut 25:4. . . You must not ***m*** an ox
1 Tim 5:18 . . You must not ***m*** an ox

MYRRH (n)
an aromatic extract from a stiff-branched tree with white flowers and plum-like fruit
Song 1:13. . . My lover is like a sachet of ***m***
Matt 2:11 . . . gold, frankincense, and ***m.***
Mark 15:23 . wine drugged with ***m,***
John 19:39 . . ointment made from ***m*** and
Rev 18:13. . . incense, ***m,*** frankincense,

MYSTERIOUS (adj)
exciting wonder, curiosity, or surprise while baffling efforts to comprehend or identify; of, relating to, or constituting mystery
1 Cor 14:2 . . Spirit, but it will all be ***m.***
Eph 1:9 . . . . now revealed to us his ***m*** plan
Eph 3:3 . . . . revealed his ***m*** plan to me.
Eph 6:19 . . . explain God's ***m*** plan that the
Col 2:2. . . . . they understand God's ***m*** plan,
Col 4:3. . . . . about his ***m*** plan concerning
Rev 10:7. . . . God's ***m*** plan will be fulfilled.

MYSTERY, MYSTERIES (n)
something not understood or beyond understanding; a religious truth that one can know only by revelation and cannot fully understand
see also SECRET(S)
Dan 4:9 . . . . and that no ***m*** is too great
Rom 11:25. . to understand this ***m,***
1 Cor 2:7 . . . speak of is the ***m*** of God—
1 Cor 4:1 . . . explaining God's ***m-ies.***
1 Tim 3:9 . . . to the ***m*** of the faith
1 Tim 3:16 . . the great ***m*** of our faith:
Rev 1:20. . . . the ***m*** of the seven stars
Rev 17:7. . . . tell you the ***m*** of this woman

MYTHS (n)
a popular belief or tradition that has grown up around something or someone
1 Tim 1:4 . . . in endless discussion of ***m***
Titus 1:14. . . listening to Jewish ***m***

NAILED, NAILING (v)

to fasten with or as if with a nail

Matt 27:35 . . had ***n*** him to the cross,
Mark 15:24 . soldiers ***n*** him to the
Acts 2:23 . . . you ***n*** him to a cross
Col 2:14 . . . . away by ***n-ing*** it to the cross.
Heb 6:6 . . . . are ***n-ing*** him to the cross

NAKED (adj)

not covered by clothing; nude

Gen 2:25 . . . man and his wife were both ***n,***
Job 1:21 . . . . and I will be ***n*** when I leave.
Eccl 5:15 . . . the end of our lives as ***n***

NAME, NAMES (n)

a word or phrase that constitutes the distinctive designation of a person or thing; reputation

see also REPUTATION

Gen 2:19 . . . the man chose a ***n*** for each
Exod 3:15 . . my ***n*** to remember
Exod 28:9 . . on them the ***n-s*** of the tribes
Exod 34:14 . whose very ***n*** is Jealous,
Lev 24:11. . . blasphemed the ***N***
Deut 18:5. . . minister in the LORD's ***n***
Deut 28:58. . awesome ***n*** of the LORD
1 Chr 17:8 . . will make your ***n*** as famous
2 Chr 7:14 . . called by my ***n*** will humble
Ps 8:1 . . . . . . your majestic ***n*** fills the earth!
Ps 23:3 . . . . . paths, bringing honor to his ***n.***
Ps 34:3 . . . . . let us exalt his ***n*** together.
Ps 66:2 . . . . . Sing about the glory of his ***n!***
Ps 103:1 . . . . I will praise his holy ***n.***
Ps 138:2 . . . . I praise your ***n*** for your
Ps 147:4 . . . . stars and calls them all by ***n.***
Isa 40:26. . . . calling each by its ***n.***
Isa 42:8. . . . . I am the LORD; that is my ***n!***
Jer 15:16. . . . I bear your ***n,*** O LORD
Dan 12:1 . . . people whose ***n*** is written in
Joel 2:32. . . . calls on the ***n*** of the LORD
Mic 5:4. . . . . majesty of the ***n*** of the LORD
Zech 14:9. . . one LORD—his ***n*** alone
Mal 1:6. . . . . shown contempt for my ***n!***
Matt 24:5 . . . come in my ***n,*** claiming, 'I am
Matt 28:19 . . baptizing them in the ***n*** of
Luke 10:20. . your ***n-s*** are registered
Luke 11:2. . . may your ***n*** be kept holy.
John 16:24 . . Ask, using my ***n,*** and you
Acts 2:21 . . . calls on the ***n*** of the LORD
Acts 4:12 . . . no other ***n*** under heaven
Rom 10:13 . . calls on the ***n*** of the LORD
Phil 2:9 . . . . gave him the ***n*** above all
Phil 2:10 . . . that at the ***n*** of Jesus every
Phil 4:3 . . . . whose ***n-s*** are written in the Book of Life.
Heb 12:23 . . ***n-s*** are written in heaven.
Jas 5:14. . . . . with oil in the ***n*** of the Lord.
Rev 2:17. . . . stone will be engraved a new ***n***
Rev 3:5. . . . . erase their ***n-s*** from the Book
Rev 3:12. . . . write on them the ***n***
Rev 20:15. . . whose ***n*** was not found
Rev 21:27. . . ***n-s*** are written in the Lamb's

NAME (v)

to give a name to; to call

Matt 1:21 . . . you are to ***n*** him Jesus,

NARROW (adj)

of slender width

Matt 7:13 . . . only through the ***n*** gate.
Matt 7:14 . . . the gateway to life is very ***n***

NATION, NATIONS (n)

group of people defined by geography or ethnicity

see also GENTILE(S), PEOPLE(S)

Gen 12:2 . . . I will make you into a great ***n.***
Gen 17:4 . . . father of a multitude of ***n-s!***
Gen 17:16 . . the mother of many ***n-s.***
Gen 25:23 . . will become two ***n-s.***
Gen 28:3 . . . and become many ***n-s!***

Exod 19:6 . . of priests, my holy ***n.***
Deut 15:6. . . You will rule many ***n-s,*** but
Deut 28:10. . the ***n-s*** of the world will see
Ps 2:8 . . . . . . you the ***n-s*** as your inheritance,
Ps 22:28 . . . . He rules all the ***n-s.***
Ps 46:10 . . . . I will be honored by every ***n.***
Ps 66:7 . . . . . every movement of the ***n-s;***
Ps 68:30 . . . . Scatter the ***n-s*** that delight in
Ps 87:6 . . . . . the LORD registers the ***n-s,***
Ps 99:2 . . . . . exalted above all the ***n-s.***
Ps 113:4 . . . . LORD is high above the ***n-s;***
Prov 14:34. . Godliness makes a ***n*** great,
Isa 11:10. . . . The ***n-s*** will rally to him,
Isa 34:1. . . . . listen, O ***n-s*** of the earth.
Isa 40:15. . . . for all the ***n-s*** of the world
Isa 42:1. . . . . He will bring justice to the ***n-s.***
Isa 52:15. . . . And he will startle many ***n-s.***
Isa 56:7. . . . . a house of prayer for all ***n-s.***
Isa 60:12. . . . the ***n-s*** that refuse to serve
Isa 66:8. . . . . Has a ***n*** ever been born in a
Ezek 37:22. . divided into two ***n-s*** or into
Joel 3:2. . . . . my people among the ***n-s,***
Amos 9:12. . . ***n-s*** I have called to be mine.
Mic 4:3. . . . . disputes between strong ***n-s***
Mic 5:7. . . . . take their place among the ***n-s.***
Zeph 3:8 . . . stand and accuse these evil ***n-s.***
Hag 2:7 . . . . I will shake all the ***n-s,***
Zech 8:13. . . Among the other ***n-s,*** Judah
Zech 12:2. . . makes the nearby ***n-s*** stagger
Matt 12:18. . proclaim justice to the ***n-s.***
Matt 24:14. . so that all ***n-s*** will hear it;
Matt 28:19. . make disciples of all the ***n-s,***
Mark 11:17 . house of prayer for all ***n-s,***
Acts 4:25 . . . Why were the ***n-s*** so angry?
Gal 3:8 . . . . . All ***n-s*** will be blessed through
1 Pet 2:9. . . . royal priests, a holy ***n,***
Rev 5:9. . . . . language and people and ***n.***
Rev 14:6. . . . to every ***n,*** tribe, language,
Rev 21:24. . . The ***n-s*** will walk in its light,
Rev 22:2. . . . for medicine to heal the ***n-s.***

NATIVITY (KJV)
Gen 11:28 . . the land of his ***birth***
Jer 46:16. . . . to the land of our ***birth.***

NATURAL (adj)
having a physical existence as contrasted with one that is spiritual
1 Cor 15:44 . as there are ***n*** bodies,

NATURE (n)
inherent character or essence
Rom 1:20 . . . eternal power and divine ***n.***
Rom 8:4 . . . . follow our sinful ***n***
Rom 8:7 . . . . For the sinful ***n*** is always
Gal 5:19 . . . . the desires of your sinful ***n,***
Gal 5:24. . . . desires of their sinful ***n*** to
2 Pet 1:4. . . . share his divine ***n*** and escape

NAZARENE, NAZARENES (n)
a native or resident of Nazareth; an early name given to followers of Jesus
Matt 2:23 . . . He will be called a ***N.***
Acts 24:5 . . . of the cult known as the ***N-s.***
Acts 26:9 . . . the very name of Jesus the ***N.***

NAZARETH (n)
a town of lower Galilee where Jesus spent his boyhood years
Matt 4:13 . . . He went first to ***N,***
Mark 14:67 . those with Jesus of ***N.***
Mark 16:6 . . looking for Jesus of ***N,*** who
John 1:46 . . . anything good come from ***N?***

NAZIRITE (n)
a person consecrated to God by a vow to avoid drinking wine, cutting the hair, and being defiled by the presence of a corpse
Num 6:2 . . . take the special vow of a ***N,***
Judg 13:7 . . . be dedicated to God as a ***N***

NECK (n)
the part of the body that connects the head and the torso
Prov 6:21 . . . Tie them around your ***n.***
Matt 18:6 . . . millstone tied around your ***n***

NECKLACE (n)
an ornament worn around the neck
Prov 3:22. . . They are like jewels on a ***n.***

NEED, NEEDS (n)
a condition requiring supply or relief; poverty; obligation; a lack of something requisite, desirable, or useful
1 Kgs 8:59 . . according to each day's ***n-s.***
Ps 79:8 . . . . . quickly meet our ***n-s,***
Ps 112:9 . . . . give generously to those in ***n.***
Prov 11:26 . . who sells in time of ***n.***
Prov 30:8 . . . just enough to satisfy my ***n-s.***
Matt 6:2. . . . give to someone in ***n,***
Acts 2:45 . . . the money with those in ***n.***
Acts 20:35 . . you can help those in ***n*** by
Rom 12:13. . God's people are in ***n,***
1 Cor 7:3 . . . fulfill his wife's sexual ***n-s,***
Eph 4:28 . . . give generously to others in ***n.***
Phil 4:19 . . . supply all your ***n-s*** from his
Titus 3:14. . . by meeting the urgent ***n-s***

NEED, NEEDED, NEEDING (v)
to require; to be necessary; to be in want
Ps 34:9 . . . . . fear him will have all they ***n.***
Ps 119:75 . . . disciplined me because I ***n-ed***

Phil 4:6 . . . . Tell God what you ***n,*** and
Heb 4:16 . . . grace to help us when we ***n*** it
Jas 1:4. . . . . . complete, ***n-ing*** nothing.
Jas 1:5. . . . . . If you ***n*** wisdom, ask our

NEEDLE (n)
a small slender instrument that has an eye for thread at one end and is used for sewing
Matt 19:24 . . go through the eye of a ***n***

NEEDY (adj)
poverty-stricken; marked by want of affection, attention, or emotional support
1 Sam 2:8. . . ***n*** from the garbage dump.
Ps 9:18 . . . . . the ***n*** will not be ignored
Ps 68:10 . . . . you provided for your ***n***
Ps 69:33 . . . . LORD hears the cries of the ***n;***
Prov 22:22. . or exploit the ***n*** in court.
Prov 31:20. . opens her arms to the ***n.***

NEGLECT (v)
to disregard; to overlook; to ignore
Deut 12:19. . careful never to ***n*** the Levites
Deut 14:27. . And do not ***n*** the Levites
Ezra 4:22 . . . and don't ***n*** this matter,
Neh 10:39 . . together not to ***n*** the Temple
Luke 11:42. . do not ***n*** the more important
1 Tim 4:14 . . Do not ***n*** the spiritual

NEHEMIAH
Cupbearer of the Persian king Artaxerxes (Neh 1:11); governor of Israel (Neh 5:14; 8:9); prayed for restoration (1:4); king commissioned him to rebuild Jerusalem's walls (Neh 2:8); rebuilt walls over opposition (Neh 2:9–6:19); reestablished worship (Neh 8:1-18); prayer of praise and confession (Neh 9); dedicated wall of Jerusalem (Neh 12:27-43).

NEIGHBOR, NEIGHBORS (n)
one living or located near another; fellow man
Lev 19:18. . . but love your ***n*** as yourself.
Ps 15:3 . . . . . to gossip or harm their ***n-s***
Prov 24:28. . your ***n-s*** without cause;
Prov 27:10. . better to go to a ***n*** than
Jer 31:34. . . . not need to teach their ***n-s,***
Mark 12:31 . Love your ***n*** as yourself.
Luke 10:29. . And who is my ***n?***
Rom 13:8 . . . If you love your ***n,*** you will
Gal 5:14 . . . . Love your ***n*** as yourself.
Eph 4:25 . . . Let us tell our ***n-s*** the truth,
Heb 8:11 . . . not need to teach their ***n-s,***
Jas 2:8. . . . . . Love your ***n*** as yourself.

NET, NETS (n)
a meshed fabric made of ropes used for catching fish, birds, insects, or other animals
Ps 66:11 . . . . You captured us in your ***n***
Ps 141:10 . . . wicked fall into their own ***n-s,***
Hab 1:15 . . . caught in their ***n-s*** while they
Matt 4:20. . . they left their ***n-s*** at once and
Matt 13:47. . is like a fishing ***n*** that was
John 21:6 . . . Throw out your ***n*** on the

NEVER (adv)
at no time; not in any degree; not under any condition
1 Chr 29:18 . their love for you ***n*** changes.
Ps 89:33 . . . . But I will ***n*** stop loving him
Ps 111:3 . . . . His righteousness ***n*** fails.
John 14:16 . . who will ***n*** leave you.
Rom 11:29. . his call can ***n*** be withdrawn.
Rom 12:11. . ***N*** be lazy, but work hard
1 Cor 15:2 . . something that was ***n*** true

NEVER-ENDING (adj)
unceasing
1 Chr 16:17 . of Israel as a ***n*** covenant:
Ps 105:10 . . . of Israel as a ***n*** covenant:
Luke 3:17. . . burning the chaff with ***n*** fire.

NEW (adj)
fresh; original; different than before; unfamiliar
Ps 98:1 . . . . . Sing a ***n*** song to the LORD,
Jer 31:31. . . . I will make a ***n*** covenant with
Ezek 36:26. . I will give you a ***n*** heart,
Mark 16:17 . will speak in ***n*** languages.
Luke 22:20. . cup is the ***n*** covenant
Rom 6:4 . . . . we also may live ***n*** lives.
Rom 12:2. . . you into a ***n*** person
1 Cor 11:25 . cup is the ***n*** covenant
2 Cor 3:6 . . . but under the ***n*** covenant,
2 Cor 5:17 . . is gone; a ***n*** life has begun!
Gal 6:15 . . . . into a ***n*** creation.
Eph 4:24 . . . Put on your ***n*** nature,
Col 3:10 . . . . Put on your ***n*** nature,
Heb 8:8 . . . . when I will make a ***n*** covenant
Heb 9:15 . . . mediates a ***n*** covenant
Heb 12:24 . . the ***n*** covenant
2 Pet 3:13. . . ***n*** heavens and ***n*** earth he
Rev 2:17. . . . a ***n*** name that no one
Rev 21:1. . . . ***n*** heaven and a ***n*** earth,

NEWBORN (adj)
recently born
1 Pet 2:2. . . . Like ***n*** babies, you must crave

NEWS (n)
a report of recent events; "Good News": the Gospel of Jesus Christ
Isa 40:9. . . . . of good ***n***, shout from the
Matt 4:23. . . the Good ***N*** about
Mark 1:15 . . sins and believe the Good ***N!***
Luke 4:43. . . I must preach the Good ***N***
Acts 13:32 . . to bring you this Good ***N***.
Acts 14:21 . . preaching the Good ***N***
Rom 1:16. . . not ashamed of this Good ***N***
Rom 10:17. . the Good ***N*** about Christ.
Rom 15:16. . I bring you the Good ***N***
Rom 16:25. . just as my Good ***N*** says.
1 Cor 1:17 . . to preach the Good ***N***—
1 Cor 9:12 . . an obstacle to the Good ***N***
1 Cor 9:16 . . preach the Good ***N!***
1 Cor 9:23 . . to spread the Good ***N***
1 Cor 15:1 . . the Good ***N*** I preached
2 Cor 4:4 . . . glorious light of the Good ***N***.
2 Cor 9:13 . . obedient to the Good ***N***
2 Cor 11:7 . . preaching God's Good ***N***
Gal 1:7. . . . . is not the Good ***N*** at all.
Eph 6:15 . . . comes from the Good ***N***
Phil 1:27 . . . worthy of the Good ***N***
Col 1:5. . . . . heard the truth of the Good ***N***.
Col 1:23. . . . Good ***N*** has been preached
1 Thes 2:4 . . entrusted with the Good ***N***.
2 Thes 1:8 . . obey the Good ***N*** of our Lord
2 Tim 1:10. . through the Good ***N***.
2 Tim 4:5 . . . telling others the Good ***N***,
Rev 14:6. . . . the eternal Good ***N***

NIGHT, NIGHTS (n)
period of darkness between sunset and sunrise; figurative of suffering and sorrow or the reign of sin and immorality
Gen 1:16 . . . smaller one to govern the ***n***.
Exod 13:21 . provided light at ***n***
Job 35:10 . . . who gives songs in the ***n?***
Ps 1:2. . . . . . meditating on it day and ***n***.
Ps 19:2. . . . . ***n*** after ***n*** they make him
Ps 77:6 . . . . . my ***n-s*** were filled with joyful
Jonah 1:17 . . for three days and three ***n-s***.
Matt 4:2. . . . days and forty ***n-s*** he fasted
Matt 12:40. . for three days and three ***n-s***.
Luke 2:8. . . . That ***n*** there were shepherds
2 Cor 6:5 . . . endured sleepless ***n-s***, and
1 Thes 5:2 . . like a thief in the ***n***.
1 Thes 5:5 . . belong to darkness and ***n***.
Rev 21:25. . . there is no ***n*** there.

NINETY-NINE (n)
the number 99
Matt 18:13. . than over the ***n*** that didn't
Luke 15:7. . . to God than over ***n*** others

NOAH
Builder of great boat, survivor of the Flood (Gen 6–9; Matt 24:37-38; Luke 17:26-27; Heb 11:7; 1 Pet 3:20; 2 Pet 2:5); family line (Gen 5:25-32); found favor with God (Gen 6:8); enacted covenant between God and all creatures (Gen 9:1-17); made wine and became drunk (Gen 9:18-23); gave blessings and curse to descendants (Gen 9:24-27); considered righteous (Ezek 14:14, 20).

NONSENSE (n)
words or language having no meaning or intelligible ideas; things of no importance or value
Luke 24:11. . sounded like ***n*** to the men,
1 Cor 1:23 . . the Gentiles say it's all ***n***.
Col 2:8 . . . . . high-sounding ***n*** that come

NOOSE (n)
a loop with a slipknot that binds closer the more it is drawn
Job 41:1 . . . . or put a ***n*** around its jaw?

NORMAL (adj)
occurring naturally
Rom 1:27. . . ***n*** sexual relations with women,

NOSTRILS (n)
the external openings of the nose
Gen 2:7 . . . . breath of life into the man's ***n***,

NOTES (n)
melody, song; tones
1 Cor 14:7 . . harp must play the ***n*** clearly,

NOTHING (pron)
not any thing
Neh 9:21 . . . wilderness, and they lacked ***n***.
Eccl 5:5 . . . . better to say ***n*** than to make
Jas 1:4. . . . . . and complete, needing ***n***.

NOTICE (n)
a warning or intimation of something; announcement
Matt 5:31 . . . a written ***n*** of divorce.

NOTICED (v)
to treat with attention
Job 1:8 . . . . . Satan, "Have you ***n*** my servant
Job 2:3 . . . . . Satan, "Have you ***n*** my servant

NOTORIOUS (adj)
generally known and talked of; famous
Hab 1:7 . . . . They are ***n*** for their cruelty

NOURISHMENT (n)
food, nutriment; sustenance
John 4:34 . . . my ***n*** comes from doing the
Rom 11:17 . . in the rich ***n*** from the root

NUMBERED (v)
to restrict to a definite number
Ps 39:4 . . . . . Remind me that my days are ***n***
Matt 10:30 . . hairs on your head are all ***n.***

OATH (n)
an appeal to God to witness the truth of some statement

Ps 95:11 . . . . in my anger I took an *o:*
Ps 110:4 . . . . LORD has taken an *o*
Ezek 20:42 . . I promised with a solemn *o*
Heb 6:16 . . . people take an *o,* they call
Heb 7:20 . . . established with a solemn *o.*
Heb 7:21 . . . was an *o* regarding Jesus.
Jas 5:12. . . . . never take an *o,* by heaven

OBEDIENCE (n)
an act or instance of obeying; the quality or state of being obedient

Judg 2:17. . . who had walked in *o* to the
1 Sam 15:22. *O* is better than sacrifice,
Phil 2:8 . . . . humbled himself in *o* to God
Heb 5:8 . . . . learned *o* from the things he

OBEDIENT (adj)
submissive to authority; willing to obey

Luke 2:51. . . with them and was *o* to them.
Rom 16:19. . that you are *o* to the Lord.
2 Cor 9:13 . . that you are *o* to the Good
2 Cor 10:6 . . you have become fully *o,*
1 Pet 1:14. . . as God's *o* children.

OBEY, OBEYED, OBEYING, OBEYS (v)
to follow the commands or guidance of; to conform to or comply with

see also KEEP

Gen 22:18 . . because you have *o-ed* me.
Exod 20:6 . . love me and *o* my commands.
Lev 18:4. . . . be careful to *o* my decrees,
Lev 25:18. . . decrees and *o* my regulations.
Deut 4:2. . . . Just *o* the commands of the
Deut 5:27. . . we will listen and *o.*
Deut 6:17. . . diligently *o* the commands of
Deut 6:25. . . when we *o* all the commands
Deut 11:1. . . and *o* all his requirements,
Deut 11:22. . Be careful to *o* all these
Deut 13:4. . . *O* his commands, listen to his
Deut 26:16. . to *o* them wholeheartedly.
Deut 28:1. . . If you fully *o* the LORD
Deut 30:2. . . if you *o* with all your heart
Deut 30:12. . so we can hear it and *o?*
Deut 30:20. . love and *o* the LORD,
Josh 1:7 . . . . to *o* all the instructions Moses
Josh 22:5 . . . all his ways, *o* his commands,
1 Sam 7:3. . . to *o* only the LORD;
1 Kgs 8:61 . . May you always *o* his decrees
2 Kgs 17:13 . *O* my commands and
2 Kgs 18:6 . . *o-ed* all the commands
2 Kgs 23:3 . . pledged to *o* the LORD
Neh 1:5 . . . . love him and *o* his commands,
Job 36:11 . . . they listen and *o* God,
Ps 111:10 . . . All who *o* his commandments
Ps 119:17. . . I may live and *o* your word.
Ps 119:129 . . No wonder I *o* them!
Eccl 8:2 . . . . *O* the king since you vowed
Eccl 12:13 . . and *o* his commands,
Isa 11:3. . . . . delight in *o-ing* the LORD.
Jer 32:33. . . . not receive instruction or *o.*
Jer 42:6. . . . . For if we *o* him, everything
Jer 43:4. . . . . refused to *o* the LORD's
Dan 9:4 . . . . love you and *o* your commands.
Dan 9:10 . . . We have not *o-ed* the LORD
Jonah 3:3 . . . This time Jonah *o-ed* the LORD's
Mic 5:15. . . . nations that refuse to *o* me.
Matt 5:19. . . anyone who *o-s* God's laws
Matt 8:27. . . the winds and waves *o* him!
Matt 19:20. . *o-ed* all these commandments,
Matt 28:20. . to *o* all the commands
Luke 8:21. . . hear God's word and *o* it.
John 3:36 . . . who doesn't *o* the Son
John 8:51 . . . anyone who *o-s* my teaching
John 14:15 . . *o* my commandments.
Acts 4:19 . . . to *o* you rather than him?
Acts 5:29 . . . We must *o* God rather than
Rom 1:5. . . . believe and *o* him,

Rom 2:27 . . . possess God's law but don't *o*
Rom 3:28 . . . and not by ***o-ing*** the law.
Rom 6:16 . . . of whatever you choose to ***o?***
Rom 6:17 . . . wholeheartedly ***o*** this
Rom 15:31 . . in Judea who refuse to ***o*** God.
2 Cor 10:5 . . teach them to ***o*** Christ.
Gal 2:16 . . . . Christ, not by ***o-ing*** the law.
Gal 3:2 . . . . . by ***o-ing*** the law of Moses?
Gal 3:10 . . . . and ***o*** all the commands
Eph 2:2 . . . . who refuse to ***o*** God.
Eph 6:1 . . . . Children, ***o*** your parents
Eph 6:5 . . . . Slaves, ***o*** your earthly masters
2 Thes 3:14 . who refuse to ***o*** what we
1 Tim 3:4 . . . who respect and ***o*** him.
Titus 2:9. . . . Slaves must always ***o*** their
Heb 11:8 . . . that Abraham ***o-ed*** when God
Heb 11:31 . . who refused to ***o*** God.
Jas 2:8. . . . . . good when you ***o*** the royal law
1 Pet 1:2. . . . you have ***o-ed*** him and have
1 Pet 1:22. . . when you ***o-ed*** the truth,
1 Pet 2:8. . . . they do not ***o*** God's word,
1 Jn 3:22. . . . because we ***o*** him and do
Rev 22:7. . . . Blessed are those who ***o*** the

OBLIGATION (n)

something one is bound to do; duty, responsibility

Rom 1:14 . . . a great sense of ***o*** to people
Rom 8:12 . . . no ***o*** to do what your sinful
Rom 13:8 . . . except for your ***o*** to love one

OBSERVE, OBSERVES (v)

to notice or consider; to keep or comply with; to watch carefully

Exod 12:24 . descendants must ***o*** forever.
Lev 25:2. . . . the land itself must ***o*** a Sabbath
Deut 5:12. . . ***O*** the Sabbath day by keeping
Deut 16:13. . ***o*** the Festival of Shelters
Ps 33:14 . . . . From his throne he ***o-s*** all who
Acts 21:24 . . ***o*** the Jewish laws.
Gal 3:10 . . . . everyone who does not ***o***

OBSOLETE (adj)

no longer in use or no longer useful

Heb 8:13 . . . he has made the first one ***o.***

OBSTINATE (adj)

unreasonably persistent; stubborn

Isa 48:4. . . . . how stubborn and ***o*** you are
Ezek 3:8. . . . as ***o*** and hard-hearted as

OCCUPY (v)

to take or hold possession or control of; to reside in as an owner or tenant

Deut 1:8. . . . Go in and ***o*** it, for it is
Deut 4:14. . . are about to enter and ***o.***

OFFEND, OFFENDED, OFFENDS (v)

to violate, wrong, insult, or hurt; to cause difficulty, discomfort, or injury

Ps 139:24 . . . anything in me that ***o-s*** you,
1 Cor 1:23 . . the Jews are ***o-ed*** and the
Gal 5:11 . . . . Christ, no one would be ***o-ed.***
Col 3:13 . . . . forgive anyone who ***o-s*** you.

OFFENSE, OFFENSES (n)

a cause or occasion of sin; the act of displeasing

Isa 44:22. . . . I have scattered your ***o-s***
Matt 18:15 . . and point out the ***o.***
1 Cor 10:32 . Don't give ***o*** to Jews or

OFFER, OFFERED, OFFERING (v)

to present for acceptance as an act of worship or devotion; to sacrifice

Ps 4:5 . . . . . . ***O*** sacrifices in the right spirit,
Ps 116:12 . . . What can I ***o*** the LORD
Mic 6:7. . . . . Should we ***o*** him thousands of
1 Cor 10:20 . sacrifices are ***o-ed*** to demons,
Eph 5:2 . . . . He loved us and ***o-ed*** himself
Heb 7:27 . . . when he ***o-ed*** himself
Heb 9:14 . . . Christ ***o-ed*** himself to God
Heb 9:25 . . . to ***o*** himself again and again,
Heb 10:11 . . ***o-ing*** the same sacrifices again
Heb 11:17 . . that Abraham ***o-ed*** Isaac
Heb 13:15 . . let us ***o*** through Jesus
Jas 5:15. . . . . a prayer ***o-ed*** in faith will heal

OFFERING, OFFERINGS (n)

a sacrifice ceremonially offered as a part of worship; a contribution to the support of a church

Gen 22:8 . . . a sheep for the burnt ***o,***
1 Sam 13:9. . Bring me the burnt ***o***
1 Sam 15:22. burnt ***o-s*** and sacrifices
Ps 40:6 . . . . . no delight in sacrifices or ***o-s.***
Ps 141:2 . . . . hands as an evening ***o.***
Isa 53:10. . . . his life is made an ***o*** for sin,
Hos 6:6 . . . . more than I want burnt ***o-s.***
Mal 3:8. . . . . of the tithes and ***o-s***
Mark 12:33 . all of the burnt ***o-s***
Rom 15:26 . . taken up an ***o*** for the poor
Phil 2:17 . . . faithful service is an ***o***
Heb 10:5 . . . animal sacrifices or sin ***o-s.***
Heb 10:14 . . that one ***o*** he forever made
Heb 11:4 . . . Abel's ***o*** gave evidence that he

OFFICER (n)

one who holds a position of authority or command in the armed forces

Matt 8:5. . . . a Roman ***o*** came and pleaded
Luke 7:2. . . . slave of a Roman ***o*** was sick
Acts 10:1 . . . army ***o*** named Cornelius,
Acts 27:1 . . . a Roman ***o*** named Julius,

OFFSPRING (n)
children or descendants
see also DESCENDANT(S)
Gen 3:15 . . . between your ***o*** and her ***o.***
Acts 17:28 . . said, 'We are his ***o.***'

OIL (n)
liquid produced from olives used in biblical times for lamp fuel, anointing, and dressing wounds; often symbolic of the Holy Spirit
Exod 29:7 . . anointing ***o*** over his head.
Exod 30:25 . to make a holy anointing ***o.***
1 Sam 10:1 . . ***o*** and poured it over Saul's
1 Sam 16:13 . ***o*** he had brought and
Ps 23:5 . . . . . anointing my head with ***o.***
Ps 133:2 . . . . as precious as the anointing ***o***
Heb 1:9 . . . . pouring out the ***o*** of joy

OINTMENT, OINTMENTS (n)
a salve for application to the skin
Isa 1:6. . . . . . any soothing ***o-s*** or bandages.
Rev 3:18. . . . and ***o*** for your eyes so you

OLD, OLDER (adj)
dating from the remote past; advanced in years or age
1 Kgs 12:8 . . rejected the advice of the ***o-er***
2 Cor 3:11 . . So if the ***o*** way, which
1 Tim 5:2 . . . Treat ***o-er*** women as you would
Titus 2:2. . . . Teach the ***o-er*** men to exercise

OLIVE, OLIVES (n)
a Mediterranean evergreen tree with berries that ripen black; the berries of an olive tree
Gen 8:11 . . . evening with a fresh ***o*** leaf
Jer 11:16. . . . a thriving ***o*** tree, beautiful
Zech 4:3. . . . And I see two ***o*** trees,
Zech 14:4. . . the Mount of ***O-s*** will split
Matt 24:3 . . . Jesus sat on the Mount of ***O-s.***
Rom 11:17 . . of God's special ***o*** tree.
Rom 11:24 . . cut from a wild ***o*** tree.
Jas 3:12. . . . . Does a fig tree produce ***o-s,*** or
Rev 11:4. . . . prophets are the two ***o*** trees

OMEGA (n)
the last letter of the Greek alphabet
Rev 1:8. . . . . I am the Alpha and the ***O***—
Rev 21:6. . . . I am the Alpha and the ***O***—
Rev 22:13. . . I am the Alpha and the ***O,***

ONE (adj)
being a single unit or thing; being in agreement or union
2 Chr 30:12 . giving them all ***o*** heart
Phil 2:2 . . . . working together with ***o*** mind

ONE (n)
a single person or thing
Gen 2:24 . . . the two are united into ***o.***
Jas 2:10. . . . . all of the laws except ***o***

ONIONS (n)
a plant with a large pungent, edible bulb
Num 11:5 . . melons, leeks, ***o,*** and garlic

OPEN-MINDED (adj)
receptive to arguments or ideas
Acts 17:11 . . people of Berea were more ***o***

OPENED (v)
to spread out; to unfold
Isa 65:2. . . . . All day long I ***o*** my arms
Rom 10:21 . . All day long I ***o*** my arms

OPINIONS (n)
a view, judgment, or appraisal formed in the mind about a particular matter
1 Kgs 18:21 . hobbling between two ***o?***

OPPONENTS (n)
those who take an opposite position; adversaries
Prov 18:18 . . disputes between powerful ***o.***

OPPORTUNITY (n)
a favorable circumstance or advantage
2 Cor 11:12 . looking for an ***o*** to boast
Gal 6:10 . . . . have the ***o,*** we should do good
Col 4:5 . . . . . make the most of every ***o.***

OPPOSE, OPPOSED, OPPOSES (v)
to set oneself against or opposite someone or something; to resist
Exod 23:22 . ***o*** those who ***o*** you.
Ps 8:2 . . . . . . enemies and all who ***o*** you.
Ps 35:1 . . . . . ***o*** those who ***o*** me.
Acts 26:11 . . was so violently ***o-d*** to them
Gal 2:11 . . . . I had to ***o*** him to his face,
1 Tim 6:20 . . with those who ***o***
2 Tim 2:25 . . instruct those who ***o***
Titus 1:9. . . . show those who ***o*** it
Titus 2:8. . . . who ***o*** us will be ashamed
Jas 4:6. . . . . . God ***o-s*** the proud but favors
1 Pet 5:5. . . . God ***o-s*** the proud but favors
Amos 2:7. . . shove the ***o-ed*** out of the way.
Luke 4:18. . . that the ***o-ed*** will be set free,

OPPRESS, OPPRESSES, OPPRESSING (v)
to crush or burden by abuse of power or authority
Exod 22:21 . not mistreat or ***o*** foreigners
Prov 22:16 . . gets ahead by ***o-ing*** the poor
Prov 28:16 . . no understanding will ***o***

Isa 3:5. . . . . . People will *o* each other—
Isa 58:3. . . . . you keep ***o-ing*** your workers.
Ezek 18:12. . ***o-es*** the poor and helpless,
Dan 7:25 . . . defy the Most High and *o* the
Amos 5:12. . *o* good people by taking
Zech 7:10. . . Do not *o* widows, orphans,
Jas 2:6. . . . . . the rich who *o* you and drag

OPPRESSED (n)
those subject to the abuse of another's power or authority
Ps 9:9 . . . . . . a shelter for the ***o-ed,*** a refuge
Ps 14:6 . . . . . frustrate the plans of the ***o-ed,***
Ps 82:3 . . . . . uphold the rights of the ***o-ed***
Ps 146:7 . . . . He gives justice to the ***o-ed***
Prov 31:5. . . not give justice to the ***o-ed.***
Isa 1:17. . . . . Seek justice. Help the ***o-ed.***

OPPRESSION (n)
unjust or cruel exercise of power or authority
Judg 2:18. . . burdened by *o* and suffering.
Ps 72:14 . . . . redeem them from *o* and
Ps 119:134 . . Ransom me from the *o* of
Isa 58:9. . . . . Remove the heavy yoke of *o.*
Heb 11:25 . . chose to share the *o* of God's

OPPRESSORS (n)
those who abuse power or authority to crush or burden others
Ps 72:4 . . . . . and to crush their *o.*
Eccl 4:1 . . . . The *o* have great power,
Jer 22:3. . . . . rescue them from their *o.*

ORDAINED (v)
to appoint someone to a specific duty or office
see also CONSECRATE(D), DEDICATE(D)
Ezek 28:14. . I *o* and anointed you

ORDER, ORDERS (n)
a rank, class, or special group in a community or society; a command
Ps 110:4 . . . . in the *o* of Melchizedek.
Joel 2:11. . . . they follow his ***o-s.***
Mark 1:27 . . spirits obey his ***o-s!***
Heb 5:10 . . . in the *o* of Melchizedek.

ORDER (v)
to command
Ps 91:11 . . . . For he will *o* his angels
Matt 4:6. . . . He will *o* his angels

ORPHAN, ORPHANS (n)
a child deprived by death of one or usually both parents
see also FATHERLESS
Exod 22:22 . not exploit a widow or an *o.*
Deut 10:18. . ***o-s*** and widows receive
Deut 24:17. . among you and to ***o-s,***
Deut 24:19. . ***o-s,*** and widows.
Ps 10:14 . . . . in you. You defend the ***o-s.***
Ps 82:3 . . . . . justice to the poor and the *o;*
John 14:18 . . will not abandon you as ***o-s***—
Jas 1:27. . . . . caring for ***o-s*** and widows in

OUTSIDE (prep)
located on the outer side of
1 Tim 3:7 . . . Also, people *o* the church

OUTSMART (v)
to get the better of; to outwit
2 Cor 2:11 . . Satan will not *o* us.

OUTWARD, OUTWARDLY (adj or adv)
superficial, having to do with external appearance or circumstance only
1 Sam 16:7. . People judge by *o* appearance,
Matt 23:28. . ***o-ly*** you look like righteous
1 Pet 3:3. . . . concerned about the *o* beauty

OUTWEIGHS (v)
to exceed in weight, value, or importance
2 Cor 4:17 . . glory that vastly *o* them and

OVERCOME (v)
to get the better of; to overwhelm
see also CONQUER, VICTORY
Ps 119:133 . . will not be *o* by evil.
Mark 9:24 . . but help me *o* my unbelief!
John 16:33 . . because I have *o* the world.
2 Cor 2:7 . . . may be *o* by discouragement.

OVERFLOW, OVERFLOWED, OVERFLOWS (v)
to fill a space to capacity and spread beyond its limits; to flow over bounds
Ps 23:5 . . . . . My cup ***o-s*** with blessings.
Ps 65:11 . . . . even the hard pathways *o* with
Prov 3:10. . . vats will *o* with good wine.
John 15:11 . . Yes, your joy will *o!*
Rom 15:13. . you will *o* with confident
2 Cor 8:2 . . . joy, which has ***o-ed*** in rich
Phil 1:9 . . . . I pray that your love will *o*
Col 2:7. . . . . you will *o* with thankfulness.

OVERJOYED (adj)
feeling great joy
Dan 6:23 . . . The king was *o* and ordered
Acts 12:14 . . she was so *o* that,

OVERLOOKING (v)
to look past; to ignore or excuse
Prov 19:11. . they earn respect by *o* wrongs.
Mic 7:18. . . . *o* the sins of his special people?

OVERSEER(S) (KJV)
2 Chr 2:18 . . and 3,600 as ***foremen***
Neh 11:22 . . ***chief officer*** of the Levites
Prov 6:7. . . . or ***governor*** or ruler to make
Acts 20:28 . . appointed you as ***elders***
1 Tim 3:1 . . . an ***elder*** must be a man whose
1 Pet 2:25. . . Shepherd, the ***Guardian*** of

OVERSHADOW (v)
to cast a shadow over
Luke 1:35. . . power of the Most High will ***o***

OVERWHELMED, OVERWHELMING, OVERWHELMS (v)
to overpower in thought or feeling; to submerge; to overthrow
2 Sam 22:5. . waves of death ***o-ed*** me;
Job 19:27 . . . I am ***o-ed*** at the thought!
Ps 38:4 . . . . . My guilt ***o-s*** me—it is
Ps 65:3 . . . . . we are ***o-ed*** by our sins,
Ps 90:7 . . . . . we are ***o-ed*** by your fury.
Isa 61:10. . . . I am ***o-ed*** with joy in
Mark 9:15 . . they were ***o-ed*** with awe,
2 Cor 1:8 . . . We were crushed and ***o-ed***
2 Cor 3:10 . . with the ***o-ing*** glory

OWE (v)
to be under obligation to pay or repay in return for something received
Rom 13:7. . . Give to everyone what you ***o***
Phlm 1:19 . . that you ***o*** me your very soul!

OWN (adj)
belonging to oneself or itself
Luke 18:9. . . in their ***o*** righteousness
1 Cor 13:5 . . does not demand its ***o*** way.
Titus 2:14. . . to make us his very ***o*** people,

OWN (v)
to have or hold as property
Gen 28:4 . . . May you ***o*** this land

OX, OXEN (n)
a domestic bovine mammal
Deut 25:4. . . not muzzle an ***o*** to keep it
1 Kgs 7:25 . . base of twelve bronze ***o-en,***
1 Kgs 19:20 . Elisha left the ***o-en***
Isa 1:3. . . . . . ***o*** knows its owner, and a
Ezek 1:10. . . the face of an ***o*** on the left
1 Cor 9:9 . . . not muzzle an ***o*** to keep it
1 Tim 5:18 . . not muzzle an ***o*** to keep it
Rev 4:7. . . . . the second was like an ***o;***

PACT (n)
an agreement or covenant between two or more parties
1 Sam 23:18. renewed their solemn ***p*** before

PAGAN (adj)
of or relating to a pagan
1 Sam 17:26. Who is this ***p*** Philistine

PAGAN, PAGANS (n)
a follower of a false god or religion; one who delights in sensual pleasures and material goods
Ps 106:35 . . . they mingled among the ***p-s***
Isa 2:6. . . . . . have made alliances with ***p-s.***
Matt 5:47 . . . Even ***p-s*** do that.
Matt 18:17 . . treat that person as a ***p***
1 Cor 5:1 . . . something that even ***p-s*** don't
1 Cor 12:2 . . when you were still ***p-s,*** you

PAID (v)
to render payment or due return
see also PAY
1 Cor 7:23 . . God ***p*** a high price for you,
Col 3:25 . . . . be ***p*** back for the wrong
1 Tim 5:17 . . should be respected and ***p***

PAIN, PAINS (n)
physical, mental, or emotional suffering; the spasms of childbirth
Job 6:10 . . . . Despite the ***p,*** I have not
Ps 73:14 . . . . every morning brings me ***p.***
Jer 4:19. . . . . my heart—I writhe in ***p!***
Matt 24:8 . . . only the first of the birth ***p-s,***
John 16:21 . . suffering the ***p-s*** of labor.
Rom 8:22 . . . in the ***p-s*** of childbirth
Gal 4:19 . . . . going through labor ***p-s*** for
1 Thes 5:3 . . woman's labor ***p-s*** begin.
Heb 13:3 . . . as if you felt their ***p*** in your
Rev 21:4. . . . death or sorrow or crying or ***p.***

PAINFUL (adj)
feeling or giving pain
Gen 5:29 . . . the ***p*** labor of farming
Prov 17:21 . . ***p*** to be the parent of a fool;
2 Cor 2:1 . . . grief with another ***p*** visit.
Heb 12:11 . . while it is happening—it's ***p!***

PALACE, PALACES (n)
the official residence of a chief of state (as a monarch or president)
2 Sam 7:2. . . living in a beautiful cedar ***p,***
Jer 22:6. . . . . concerning Judah's royal ***p:***
Matt 11:8 . . . expensive clothes live in ***p-s.***
Luke 7:25. . . live in luxury are found in ***p-s.***

PALM, PALMS (n)
a long feathery leaf from any of various mostly tropical or subtropical trees; the part of the human hand between the base of the fingers and wrist
Isa 49:16. . . . on the ***p-s*** of my hands.
John 12:13 . . took ***p*** branches and went
Rev 7:9. . . . . and held ***p*** branches

PAMPERED (v)
to treat with extreme or excessive care and attention
Prov 29:21 . . A servant ***p*** from childhood

PANIC (n)
a sudden unreasoning terror often accompanied by mass flight
1 Sam 14:15. Suddenly, ***p*** broke out
Zech 14:13 . . by the LORD with great ***p.***

PANIC (v)
to be affected with panic
Deut 20:3. . . Do not lose heart or ***p***
Mark 13:7 . . threats of wars, but don't ***p.***

PAPERS (n)
a piece of paper containing writing or print; documents
Jer 32:16. . . . had given the ***p*** to Baruch,
2 Tim 4:13 . . books, and especially my ***p.***

PARABLE, PARABLES (n)
a brief narrative story told with earthly analogies to illustrate a spiritual truth
Ps 78:2 . . . . . I will speak to you in a ***p.***
Matt 13:35 . . I will speak to you in ***p-s.***
Luke 8:10. . . I use ***p-s*** to teach the

PARADE (n)
a public procession
1 Cor 4:9 . . . at the end of a victor's ***p,***

PARADISE (n)
an intermediate place where the souls of the righteous await resurrection and the final judgment
Luke 23:43. . you will be with me in ***p.***
2 Cor 12:4 . . that I was caught up to ***p***

PARALYZED (adj)
characterized by the inability to move
Matt 9:2. . . . Jesus said to the ***p*** man,
Mark 2:3 . . . men arrived carrying a ***p*** man
John 5:3 . . . . blind, lame, or ***p***—

PARDON, PARDONED (v)
to allow (an offense) to pass without punishment; to forgive
Num 14:19 . ***p*** the sins of this people,
Deut 29:20. . LORD will never ***p*** such
2 Kgs 5:18 . . may the LORD ***p*** me
2 Chr 30:18 . LORD, who is good, ***p***
Isa 40:2. . . . . gone and her sins are ***p-ed.***
Jer 5:7. . . . . . How can I ***p*** you?
Joel 3:21. . . . I will ***p*** my people's crimes,
Joel 3:21. . . . which I have not yet ***p-ed;***

PARENT, PARENTS (n)
one who produces and cares for offspring
see also FATHER, MOTHER
Exod 20:5 . . I lay the sins of the ***p-s*** upon
Prov 13:1. . . child accepts a ***p***'s discipline;
Jer 31:29. . . . ***p-s*** have eaten sour grapes,
Ezek 18:19. . child pay for the ***p***'s sins?
Matt 10:21 . . will rebel against their ***p-s***
Rom 1:30 . . . and they disobey their ***p-s.***
Eph 6:1 . . . . Children, obey your ***p-s***
Col 3:20 . . . . always obey your ***p-s,***

PART, PARTS (n)
portion or segment; role
see also MEMBER(S)
Rom 12:5 . . . We are many ***p-s*** of one body,
1 Cor 6:15 . . are actually ***p-s*** of Christ?
1 Cor 12:18 . each ***p*** just where he wants
1 Cor 12:28 . ***p-s*** God has appointed for
Gal 5:25 . . . . leading in every ***p*** of our
Eph 4:25 . . . we are all ***p-s*** of the same body.

PARTIAL (adj)
inclined to favor one party more than the other; of or relating to a part rather than the whole
Lev 19:15. . . or being ***p*** to the rich
1 Cor 13:10 . ***p*** things will become

PARTIALITY (n)
the quality or state of being partial
see also FAVORITES, FAVORITISM
Deut 10:17. . God, who shows no ***p*** and
Deut 16:19. . twist justice or show ***p.***
2 Chr 19:7 . . perverted justice, ***p,***

PARTICIPATE (v)
to have a part or share in something; to take part
1 Cor 10:20 . to ***p*** with demons.
Eph 5:7 . . . . ***p*** in the things these people

PARTNER, PARTNERS (n)
a person with whom one shares an intimate relationship; one associated with another, especially in action
2 Cor 6:14 . . can righteousness be a ***p***
Phil 1:5 . . . . ***p-s*** in spreading the Good
1 Pet 3:7. . . . but she is your equal ***p*** in
1 Pet 4:13. . . trials make you ***p-s*** with
3 Jn 1:8. . . . . be their ***p-s*** as they teach
Rev 1:9. . . . . your ***p*** in suffering and in God's Kingdom

PARTNERSHIP (n)
the state of being a partner
1 Cor 1:9 . . . into ***p*** with his Son,

PARTY, PARTIES (n)
a social gathering
Luke 15:24. . So the ***p*** began.
Rom 13:13 . . of wild ***p-ies*** and drunkenness,
1 Pet 4:3. . . . drunkenness and wild ***p-ies,***

PASS, PASSED (v)
to move, proceed, go; to go away; to move past
Exod 12:13 . the blood, I will ***p*** over you.
Exod 33:22 . my hand until I have ***p-ed***
1 Kgs 19:11 . there, the LORD ***p-ed***
1 Cor 7:31 . . it will soon ***p*** away.
2 Pet 3:10. . . the heavens will ***p*** away

PASSION, PASSIONS (n)
intense, driving, or overmastering feeling or conviction; ardent affection; sexual desire
Isa 59:17. . . . himself in a cloak of divine ***p.***
Zech 8:2. . . . with ***p*** for Jerusalem!
1 Cor 7:37 . . he can control his ***p,*** he does
Gal 5:24 . . . . Jesus have nailed the ***p-s***
1 Thes 4:5 . . lustful ***p*** like the pagans

PASSIONATE (adj)
capable of, affected by, or expressing intense feeling
2 Kgs 19:31 . ***p*** commitment of the LORD
Isa 9:7. . . . . . ***p*** commitment of the LORD
Isa 37:32. . . . ***p*** commitment of the LORD
Zech 1:14. . . Mount Zion is ***p*** and strong.
Zech 8:2. . . . Mount Zion is ***p*** and strong;

PASSOVER (n)
a festival that commemorated the Hebrew departure from Egypt in haste
Num 9:2 . . . celebrate the ***P***
Deut 16:1. . . celebrate the ***P*** each year
Ezra 6:19 . . . returned exiles celebrated ***P.***
Mark 14:12 . ***P*** lamb is sacrificed,
Heb 11:28 . . to keep the ***P*** and to sprinkle

PASTORS (n)
spiritual overseers
Eph 4:11 . . . and the ***p*** and teachers.

PASTURE, PASTURES (n)
land or a plot of land used for grazing
Ps 100:3 . . . . his people, the sheep of his ***p.***
John 10:9 . . . freely and will find good ***p-s.***

PATH, PATHS (n)
course, route; a way of life, conduct, or thought
1 Kgs 8:36 . . follow the right ***p,***
Ps 23:3 . . . . . He guides me along right ***p-s,***
Ps 27:11 . . . . Lead me along the right ***p,***
Prov 2:13. . . to walk down dark ***p-s.***
Prov 3:6. . . . show you which ***p*** to take.
Prov 5:21. . . examining every ***p*** he takes.
Prov 8:20. . . in ***p-s*** of justice.
Prov 14:12. . a ***p*** before each person that
Isa 48:17. . . . leads you along the ***p-s***
Hos 14:9 . . . ***p-s*** of the LORD are true
2 Tim 2:18 . . have left the ***p*** of truth,
Heb 12:13 . . Mark out a straight ***p***

PATHWAY (n)
path, course
Ps 32:8 . . . . . along the best ***p*** for your life.

PATIENCE (n)
the power or capacity to endure without complaint something difficult or disagreeable; forbearance, longsuffering
Rom 15:5 . . . May God, who gives this ***p***
Gal 5:22 . . . . joy, peace, ***p,*** kindness,
Col 1:11 . . . . endurance and ***p*** you need.
Col 3:12 . . . . humility, gentleness, and ***p.***
2 Tim 3:10 . . my faith, my ***p,*** my love,
Titus 2:2. . . . and be filled with love and ***p.***
Jas 5:10. . . . . examples of ***p*** in suffering,
2 Pet 3:15. . . Lord's ***p*** gives people time

PATIENT (adj)
bearing pains or trials calmly or without complaint; steadfast despite opposition, difficulty, or adversity; not hasty or impetuous
Rom 2:4 . . . . and ***p*** God is with you?
Rom 12:12. . Be ***p*** in trouble,
1 Cor 4:12 . . We are ***p*** with those who
1 Cor 13:4 . . Love is ***p*** and kind.
1 Thes 5:14 . Be ***p*** with everyone.
Jas 5:8. . . . . . You, too, must be ***p.***

PATIENTLY (adv)
in a patient manner
Ps 40:1 . . . . . I waited ***p*** for the LORD
1 Pet 3:20. . . God waited ***p*** while Noah
Rev 14:12. . . endure persecution ***p,***

PATTERN (n)
a form or model proposed for imitation
Exod 25:40 . according to the ***p***
Exod 26:30 . the ***p*** you were shown
2 Tim 1:13 . . Hold on to the ***p***
Heb 8:5 . . . . according to the ***p***

PAUL
Pharisee and Roman citizen (Acts 22:3); from city of Tarsus (Acts 9:11; Phil 3:5); became apostle (Gal 1) to the Gentiles (Rom 11:13); also known as "Saul" (Acts 7:58; 13:9); supported stoning of Stephen (Acts 8:1); attacked early Christians (Acts 8:1-3; 9:1-2; Gal 1:13); converted on road to Damascus (Acts 9:1-9; 22:6-16; 26:12-18); preached in Damascus (Acts 9:20-22); escaped over the wall in basket (Acts 9:23-25); escaped to Jerusalem, then to Tarsus (Acts 9:26-30); saw visions in Arabia (Gal 1:17); with Barnabas in Antioch (Acts 11:22-26); sent to Jerusalem (Acts 11:27-30); first missionary journey: Cyprus and Galatia (Acts 13–14); advocate for Gentile believers (Acts 15:1-5); testified at Jerusalem Council (Acts 15:12); split with Barnabas over John Mark (Acts 15:36-41); second missionary journey with Silas: northern

and southern Greece, western Asia (Acts 15:36–18:22); received call to Macedonia (Acts 16:6-10); Philippi, Thessalonica, Berea (Acts 16–17); Athens, Corinth (Acts 17–18); third missionary journey: returned to northern and southern Greece, western Asia (Acts 18:23–21:14); Corinth, Ephesus, Macedonia, Troas – to Jerusalem (Acts 18–21); farewell to Ephesian elders (Acts 20:13-38); journey to Rome (Acts 21–28); falsely arrested and in hands of mob (Acts 21:26–22:21); saved by Roman custody (Acts 22:22-29; 23:10); before the Jewish high council (Acts 23:1-11); relocated to Caesarea (Acts 23:12-35); trial before Felix (Acts 24); appealed to Caesar before Festus (Acts 25:1-12), before Herod Agrippa (Acts 25:13–26:32); sailed to Rome, was shipwrecked (Acts 27); arrived in Rome (Acts 28); pattern of self-denial (1 Cor 9); his gospel message (Rom 1–5; Gal 3–6); catalog of trials (2 Cor 11:22-33); his goal (Phil 3:7-15); last known written words (2 Tim 4); intervened for returning slave (Phlm 1:8-22); wrote letters: Romans through Philemon (see the first verse of each book).

PAVEMENT (n)
a surface covered firmly and solidly with material (as asphalt or concrete)
John 19:13 . . that is called the Stone ***P***

PAY (n)
something paid for a purpose and especially as a salary or wage
1 Tim 5:18 . . who work deserve their ***p!***

PAY, PAYS (v)
to suffer the consequences of an act; to requite according to what is deserved; to make due return to for services or goods rendered
see also PAID
Exod 22:3 . . A thief who is caught must ***p***
Deut 32:35 . . I will ***p*** them back.
Ps 137:8 . . . . Happy is the one who ***p-s*** you
Matt 22:17 . . to ***p*** taxes to Caesar or not?
Rom 12:19 . . I will ***p*** them back,
1 Thes 5:15 . no one ***p-s*** back evil
2 Thes 1:6 . . he will ***p*** back those who

PAYMENT (n)
the act of paying; something that is paid
Deut 15:2 . . . must not demand ***p***
Deut 27:25 . . anyone who accepts ***p***
Hos 9:7 . . . . the day of ***p*** is here.

PEACE (n)
a state of tranquility or quiet; a pact or agreement to end hostilities between those who have been at war or in a state of enmity; harmony in personal relations, especially with God; a state of security or order within a community; freedom from disquieting or oppressive thoughts or emotions
Exod 20:24 . and ***p*** offerings, your sheep
Lev 26:6 . . . . I will give you ***p*** in the land,
Num 6:26 . . his favor and give you his ***p.***
Deut 20:10 . . offer its people terms for ***p.***
1 Sam 7:14 . . there was ***p*** between Israel
1 Kgs 5:4 . . . God has given me ***p*** on every
1 Chr 22:9 . . a son who will be a man of ***p.***
2 Chr 14:7 . . has given us ***p*** on every side.
Job 3:26 . . . . I have no ***p,*** no quietness.
Job 25:2 . . . . He enforces ***p*** in the heavens.
Ps 34:14 . . . . Search for ***p,*** and work to
Ps 37:37 . . . . awaits those who love ***p.***
Ps 120:7 . . . . I search for ***p;*** but when I
Ps 147:14 . . . He sends ***p*** across your nation
Prov 12:20 . . hearts that are planning ***p!***
Eccl 3:8 . . . . for war and a time for ***p.***
Isa 9:6 . . . . . . Everlasting Father, Prince of ***P.***
Isa 32:17 . . . . righteousness will bring ***p.***
Isa 48:22 . . . . there is no ***p*** for the wicked,
Isa 52:7 . . . . . good news of ***p*** and salvation,
Jer 6:14 . . . . . give assurances of ***p*** when
Jer 46:27 . . . . return to a life of ***p*** and quiet,
Ezek 34:25 . . I will make a covenant of ***p***
Zech 8:19 . . . So love truth and ***p.***
Matt 5:9 . . . . blesses those who work for ***p,***
Mark 9:50 . . live in ***p*** with each other.
Luke 1:79 . . . guide us to the path of ***p.***
John 16:33 . . you may have ***p*** in me.
Rom 5:1 . . . . by faith, we have ***p*** with God
Rom 8:6 . . . . your mind leads to life and ***p.***
1 Cor 14:33 . God of disorder but of ***p,***
Gal 5:22 . . . . love, joy, ***p,*** patience,
Eph 2:14 . . . Christ himself has brought ***p***
Eph 2:15 . . . made ***p*** between Jews and
Eph 2:17 . . . Good News of ***p*** to you Gentiles
Eph 6:15 . . . put on the ***p*** that comes from
Phil 4:7 . . . . experience God's ***p,***
1 Thes 5:23 . God of ***p*** make you holy
2 Thes 3:16 . Lord of ***p*** himself give you
2 Tim 2:22 . . faithfulness, love, and ***p.***
Heb 13:20 . . the God of ***p***—who brought
Jas 3:17 . . . . . It is also ***p*** loving, gentle
1 Pet 3:11 . . . Search for ***p,*** and work to

PEACEFUL (adj)
quiet, tranquil; devoid of violence or force; of or relating to a state or time of peace
Ps 23:2 . . . . . leads me beside ***p*** streams.
Prov 14:30 . . A ***p*** heart leads to a healthy
1 Thes 5:3 . . Everything is ***p*** and secure,
1 Tim 2:2 . . . we can live ***p*** and quiet lives
Heb 12:11 . . a ***p*** harvest of right living
2 Pet 3:14 . . . effort to be found living ***p***

PEACEMAKER, PEACEMAKERS (n)
one who makes peace especially by reconciling parties at variance
Acts 7:26 . . . He tried to be a ***p.***
Jas 3:18 . . . . . ***p-s*** will plant seeds of peace

PEARL, PEARLS (n)
a white translucent jewel created within certain species of mollusks
Matt 7:6 . . . . throw your ***p-s*** to pigs!
Matt 13:45 . . on the lookout for choice ***p-s.***
1 Tim 2:9 . . . or by wearing gold or ***p-s***
Rev 21:21 . . . were made of ***p-s*** —
Rev 21:21 . . . each gate from a single ***p!***

PENALTY (n)
disadvantage, loss, or hardship due to some action
Job 34:36 . . . you deserve the maximum ***p***
Rom 3:24 . . . freed us from the ***p***

PENNY (n)
the smallest monetary unit
Matt 5:26 . . . you have paid the last ***p.***
Luke 12:59 . . paid the very last ***p.***

PENTECOST (n)
a Jewish feast celebrated on the 50th day after the Feast of Unleavened Bread; the day God sent the Holy Spirit after Christ's resurrection
Acts 2:1 . . . . the day of ***P*** all the believers
Acts 20:16 . . in time for the Festival of ***P.***
1 Cor 16:8 . . until the Festival of ***P.***

PEOPLE, PEOPLES (n)
human beings making up a group or assembly or linked by a common interest; clan or nation; humanity
see also NATION(S)
Exod 5:1 . . . says: Let my ***p*** go
Exod 8:23 . . between my ***p*** and your ***p.***
Exod 19:5 . . among all the ***p-s*** on earth;
Exod 19:8 . . all the ***p*** responded together,
Exod 33:13 . nation is your very own ***p.***
Lev 26:12 . . . and you will be my ***p.***
Num 14:11 . How long will these ***p***
Deut 7:6 . . . . you are a holy ***p,*** who belong
Deut 14:1 . . . are the ***p*** of the LORD
Deut 32:9 . . . For the ***p*** of Israel belong
Deut 33:29 . . ***p*** saved by the LORD?
Ruth 1:16 . . . Your ***p*** will be my ***p,***
2 Chr 7:20 . . uproot the ***p*** from this land
Neh 1:10 . . . The ***p*** you rescued by your
Neh 8:1 . . . . the ***p*** assembled with a unified
Ps 33:12 . . . . whose ***p*** he has chosen
Ps 53:6 . . . . . When God restores his ***p,***
Ps 94:14 . . . . will not reject his ***p;***
Ps 96:10 . . . . He will judge all ***p-s*** fairly.
Ps 135:14 . . . will give justice to his ***p***
Isa 2:2 . . . . . . ***p*** from all over the world
Isa 6:10 . . . . . Harden the hearts of these ***p.***
Isa 40:1 . . . . . Comfort, comfort my ***p,***
Isa 49:13 . . . . LORD has comforted his ***p***
Isa 52:6 . . . . . I will reveal my name to my ***p,***
Isa 55:4 . . . . . my power among the ***p-s.***
Jer 2:11 . . . . . Yet my ***p*** have exchanged their
Jer 2:32 . . . . . my ***p*** have forgotten me.
Jer 7:16 . . . . . Pray no more for these ***p,***
Jer 32:27 . . . . of all the ***p-s*** of the world.
Dan 8:24 . . . and devastate the holy ***p.***
Dan 9:24 . . . decreed for your ***p***
Hos 1:10 . . . You are not my ***p,***
Hos 2:23 . . . Now you are my ***p.***
Mic 4:1 . . . . . ***p*** from all over the world
Mic 4:3 . . . . . LORD will mediate between ***p-s***
Matt 4:19 . . . show you how to fish for ***p!***
Mark 7:6 . . . ***p*** honor me with their lips,
Mark 8:27 . . Who do ***p*** say I am?
Luke 1:68 . . . visited and redeemed his ***p.***
John 11:50 . . should die for the ***p***
John 18:14 . . should die for the ***p.***
Rom 9:25 . . . Those who were not my ***p,***
Rom 11:1 . . . ***p,*** the nation of Israel?
2 Cor 6:16 . . and they will be my ***p.***
Gal 6:16 . . . . they are the new ***p*** of God.
Eph 1:14 . . . purchased us to be his own ***p.***
Eph 1:18 . . . he called — his holy ***p***
Eph 2:15 . . . creating in himself one new ***p***
Eph 4:8 . . . . and gave gifts to his ***p.***
2 Tim 2:2 . . . trustworthy ***p*** who will
2 Tim 3:17 . . and equip his ***p*** to do every
Titus 2:11 . . . bringing salvation to all ***p.***
Titus 2:14 . . . make us his very own ***p,***
Heb 4:9 . . . . waiting for the ***p*** of God.
1 Pet 2:9 . . . . for you are a chosen ***p.***
1 Pet 2:10 . . . now you are God's ***p.***
Rev 5:8 . . . . . prayers of God's ***p.***
Rev 10:11 . . . again about many ***p-s,***
Rev 18:4 . . . . from her, my ***p.***
Rev 19:8 . . . . of God's holy ***p.***
Rev 21:3 . . . . home is now among his ***p!***

PERFECT (adj)
being entirely without fault or defect; corresponding to an ideal standard or abstract concept; mature, pure, complete
Deut 32:4. . . the Rock; his deeds are ***p.***
Ps 19:7 . . . . . instructions of the LORD are ***p,***
Ps 119:138 . . laws are ***p*** and completely
Matt 5:48 . . . you are to be ***p,*** even as
John 17:23 . . experience such ***p*** unity
Gal 3:3 . . . . . become ***p*** by your
Col 4:12 . . . . God to make you strong and ***p,***
Heb 2:10 . . . suffering, a ***p*** leader,
Heb 5:9 . . . . as a ***p*** High Priest,
Heb 7:19 . . . law never made anything ***p.***
Heb 9:11 . . . greater, more ***p*** Tabernacle
Heb 9:14 . . . as a ***p*** sacrifice for our sins.
Heb 10:14 . . he forever made ***p*** those
Heb 12:23 . . who have now been made ***p.***
Jas 1:25. . . . . look carefully into the ***p*** law
1 Jn 4:18. . . . because ***p*** love expels all fear.

PERFECT, PERFECTED, PERFECTS (v)
to bring to final form; to refine or improve
Ezek 16:14. . splendor and ***p-ed*** your beauty,
Heb 12:2 . . . champion who initiates and ***p-s***

PERFECTION (n)
flawlessness; maturity; an exemplification of supreme excellence
Job 37:16 . . . with wonderful ***p*** and skill?
Ps 50:2 . . . . . Mount Zion, the ***p*** of beauty,
1 Cor 13:10 . when the time of ***p*** comes,
Phil 3:12 . . . I have already reached ***p.***
Heb 7:11 . . . achieved the ***p*** God intended,
Heb 11:40 . . not reach ***p*** without us.

PERFORM, PERFORMED, PERFORMING (v)
to carry out; to do
Exod 3:20 . . ***p-ing*** all kinds of miracles
2 Sam 7:23. . You ***p-ed*** awesome miracles
John 10:41 . . John didn't ***p*** miraculous

PERFUME (n)
a substance that emits a pleasant odor
Eccl 7:1 . . . . more valuable than costly ***p.***
Mark 14:3 . . poured the ***p*** over his head.
2 Cor 2:14 . . everywhere, like a sweet ***p.***
2 Cor 2:16 . . saved, we are a life-giving ***p.***

PERISH, PERISHING (v)
to become destroyed or ruined physically or spiritually; to die
see also DESTROY, DIE
Ps 102:26 . . . They will ***p,*** but you remain
John 3:16 . . . believes in him will not ***p*** but
John 10:28 . . they will never ***p.***
2 Cor 2:15 . . by those who are ***p-ing.***
2 Cor 4:3 . . . from people who are ***p-ing.***
Jude 1:11 . . . they ***p*** in their rebellion.

PERMANENT (adj)
continuing or enduring without fundamental or marked change; lasting
Num 25:13 . a ***p*** right to the priesthood,

PERMIT, PERMITTED (v)
to consent to; to authorize; to make possible
Matt 16:19. . whatever you ***p*** on earth
Matt 18:18. . whatever you ***p*** on earth
Matt 19:8. . . "Moses ***p-ted*** divorce

PERPLEXED (adj)
unable to grasp something clearly; puzzled
Luke 21:25. . ***p*** by the roaring seas and
2 Cor 4:8 . . . ***p,*** but not driven to despair.

PERSECUTE, PERSECUTED, PERSECUTING (v)
to harass or punish in a manner designed to injure, grieve, or afflict; to cause to suffer because of belief
Ps 140:12 . . . help those they ***p;***
Matt 5:10. . . blesses those who are ***p-d***
Matt 5:11. . . when people mock you and ***p***
Matt 5:12. . . prophets were ***p-d***
Matt 5:44. . . Pray for those who ***p*** you!
Matt 13:21. . ***p-d*** for believing God's
John 15:20. . they ***p-d*** me, naturally they will ***p*** you.
Acts 9:4 . . . . Why are you ***p-ing*** me?
Rom 8:35. . . or are ***p-d,*** or hungry,
Rom 12:14. . Bless those who ***p*** you.
1 Cor 15:9 . . the way I ***p-d*** God's church.
2 Thes 1:7 . . for you who are being ***p-d***

PERSECUTION, PERSECUTIONS (n)
the condition of being persecuted, harassed, or annoyed
Mark 10:30 . along with ***p.***
2 Cor 12:10 . insults, hardships, ***p-s,***
2 Thes 1:4 . . all the ***p-s*** and hardships
2 Thes 1:5 . . God will use this ***p*** to show
2 Tim 3:11 . . You know how much ***p*** and
2 Tim 3:12. . in Christ Jesus will suffer ***p.***
Rev 13:10. . . must endure ***p*** patiently

PERSECUTORS (n)
those who persecute
Ps 142:6 . . . . Rescue me from my ***p,***

PERSEVERANCE (n)
enduring hardships with patience; steadfastness
see also ENDURANCE
1 Tim 6:11 . . along with faith, love, ***p***, and

PERSEVERE (v)
to persist in a state, enterprise, or undertaking in spite of opposition or discouragement
see also ENDURE
Rev 3:10. . . . obeyed my command to ***p***,

PERSISTENCE (n)
the action, quality, or state of continuing resolutely in the face of obstacles
Luke 11:8. . . because of your shameless ***p***.

PERSON (n)
human, individual
Ps 119:9 . . . . How can a young ***p*** stay pure?
2 Cor 5:17 . . to Christ has become a new ***p***.
Heb 9:27 . . . just as each ***p*** is destined to die

PERSUADE, PERSUADED (v)
to move by argument or entreaty to a belief, position, or course of action
Prov 25:15. . Patience can ***p*** a prince,
Acts 19:26 . . Paul has ***p-d*** many people
Acts 28:23 . . tried to ***p*** them about Jesus
Acts 28:24 . . were ***p-d*** by the things he

PERSUASIVE (adj)
tending to persuade
Prov 16:21. . and pleasant words are ***p***.
Prov 16:23. . the words of the wise are ***p***.
1 Cor 2:4 . . . clever and ***p*** speeches,

PERVERSE (adj)
corrupt; improper, incorrect; perverted
Lev 18:23. . . This is a ***p*** act.
Lev 20:12. . . They have committed a ***p*** act
Phil 2:15 . . . a world full of crooked and ***p***

PERVERT, PERVERTED (v)
to cause to turn aside or away from what is good, true, or morally right; to corrupt
1 Sam 8:3. . . bribes and ***p-ed*** justice.
Prov 17:23. . secret bribes to ***p*** the course

PETER
Leader of the twelve disciples, also known as "Simon son of John" (John 21:17) and "Cephas" (John 1:42); called to "fish for people" (Matt 4:18-20; Mark 1:16-20; Luke 5:1-11; see also John 21:3); mother-in-law healed (Matt 8:14-15; Mark 1:29-31; Luke 4:38-39); called to preach (Mark 1:36-39); brother of Andrew (Matt 10:2; Mark 3:16; Luke 6:14; Acts 1:13); present at raising of the dead (Mark 5:37; Luke 8:51); walked on water (Matt 14:22-33; Mark 6:45-52; John 6:15-21); identified Jesus as the Christ (Matt 16:13-20; Mark 8:27-30; Luke 9:18-20; see also John 6:68-69); rebuked by Jesus for lack of heavenly perspective (Matt 16:21-23; Mark 8:32-33; see also John 13:6-11); witnessed the Transfiguration (Matt 16:28–17:8; Mark 9:1-13; Luke 9:28-36; 2 Pet 1:16-20); noticed the withered fig tree (Mark 11:21; see also Matt 21:20); his denial predicted by Jesus (Matt 26:31-35; Mark 14:27-31; Luke 22:31-34; John 13:36-38); in Gethsemane (Matt 26:36-46; Mark 14:32-42; Luke 22:39-46); cut off ear of Malchus (Matt 26:51; Mark 14:47; Luke 22:50); denied Jesus – then wept (Matt 26:69-75; Mark 14:66-72; Luke 22:54-62; John 18:15-27); visited empty tomb (Luke 24:12; John 20:1-10; see also Matt 28:1-8); saw Jesus (Luke 24:34; 1 Cor 15:5); told by Jesus to shepherd his flock (John 21:15-19); in upper room before Pentecost (Acts 1:13); preached at Pentecost (Acts 2); performed miracles (Acts 3:1-10; 5:14-16; 9:32-43); preached at Temple (Acts 3:11-26); preached before Jewish high council (Acts 4:1-22); prophesied death of Ananias and Sapphira (Acts 5:1-11); preached again before Jewish high council (Acts 5:29-32); rebuked power seeker (Acts 8:14-25); healed sick (Acts 9:32-34); raised dead (Acts 9:36-43); introduced Gentiles to gospel (Acts 10–11); rescued by angel from prison (Acts 12:3-19); preached grace at Jerusalem Council (Acts 15); became pillar of the church (Gal 2:9); was correctable (Gal 2:14); wrote letters (1 Pet 1:1; 2 Pet 1:1); had believing wife (1 Cor 9:5).

PHARAOH (n)
the ruler the of ancient Egyptians
Gen 12:15 . . praises to **P**, their king,
Gen 41:14 . . went in and stood before **P**.
Exod 14:4 . . to display my glory through **P**
Exod 14:17 . will be displayed through **P**

PHARISEE, PHARISEES (n)
a religious and political party in Palestine in New Testament times known for strict observance of rites and ceremonies of the written law and for insistence on the validity of their own oral traditions concerning the law
Matt 5:20. . . ***P-s***, you will never enter
Matt 16:6. . . of the yeast of the ***P-s***
Matt 23:13. . and you ***P-s***. Hypocrites!
John 3:1 . . . . religious leader who was a **P**.
Acts 23:6 . . . **P**, as were my ancestors!

PHILIP
1. One of the twelve disciples (Matt 10:3; Mark 3:18; Luke 6:14; John 1:43-48; 12:21-22; 14:8; Acts 1:13).
2. Deacon and evangelist (Acts 6:5; Acts 8:5-25); with the Ethiopian eunuch (Acts 8:26-40); hosted Paul in Caesarea (Acts 21:8-9).
3. Son of Herod the Great and Cleopatra of Jerusalem, half-brother of Antipas and Archelaus; tetrarch of the regions north of Galilee (Luke 3:1).
4. Son of Herod the Great and Mariamne; first husband of Herodias, who left him for Herod Antipas (Matt 14:3; Mark 6:17). (He also was half-brother to Archelaus and Antipas.)

PHILISTINE, PHILISTINES (n)
a native or inhabitant of ancient Philistia
Judg 16:20 . . "Samson! The ***P-s*** have come
1 Sam 4:1 . . . was at war with the ***P-s.***
1 Sam 17:1 . . ***P-s*** now mustered their
1 Sam 17:26 . get for killing this ***P***
1 Sam 31:1 . . the ***P-s*** attacked Israel,

PHILOSOPHERS (n)
persons who seek wisdom or enlightenment
1 Cor 1:20 . . leave the ***p,*** the scholars,

PHILOSOPHIES (n)
theories underlying or regarding a sphere of activity or thought
Col 2:8 . . . . . capture you with empty ***p***

PHYSICAL (adj)
having material existence; of or relating to the body
John 1:13 . . . reborn—not with a ***p*** birth
Col 1:22 . . . . of Christ in his ***p*** body.
1 Tim 4:8 . . . ***P*** training is good, but
1 Tim 5:11 . . ***p*** desires will overpower
1 Jn 2:16 . . . . a craving for ***p*** pleasure

PICTURE (n)
a representation, image, or copy
1 Pet 3:21 . . . water is a ***p*** of baptism,

PIERCE, PIERCED (v)
to make a hole through; to stab
Exod 21:6 . . and publicly ***p*** his ear
Ps 22:16 . . . . have ***p-d*** my hands and feet.
Zech 12:10 . . me whom they have ***p-d***
Luke 2:35 . . . sword will ***p*** your very soul.
John 19:37 . . look on the one they ***p-d.***
Rev 1:7 . . . . . even those who ***p-d*** him.

PIG, PIGS (n)
a wild or domestic swine
Matt 7:6 . . . . Don't throw your pearls to ***p-s!***
Mark 5:11 . . a large herd of ***p-s*** feeding
Luke 15:15 . . his fields to feed the ***p-s.***
2 Pet 2:22 . . . washed ***p*** returns to the mud.

PIGEONS (n)
any of the family of birds with a stout body, rather short legs, and smooth and compact plumage
Lev 5:11 . . . . turtledoves or two young ***p,***
Luke 2:24 . . . turtledoves or two young ***p.***

PILATE
The procurator (Roman governor) in Palestine at the time of the crucifixion of Christ (Luke 3:1). "Pontius" was his family name; he questioned Jesus, found him innocent; later, influenced by the Jewish leaders, he sentenced him to execution (Matt 27; Mark 15; Luke 23; John 18–19).

PILGRIMS (KJV)
Heb 11:13 . . ***nomads*** here on earth
1 Pet 2:11 . . . as "temporary residents and ***foreigners"***

PILLAR, PILLARS (n)
a column or shaft standing alone as a monument or supporting a superstructure; miraculous cloud by day and fire by night; memorial pile of stones; a supporting, integral, or upstanding member of a group
Gen 19:26 . . she turned into a ***p*** of salt.
Exod 13:21 . night with a ***p*** of fire.
Exod 24:4 . . set up twelve ***p-s,*** one for
Deut 1:33 . . . by night and a ***p*** of cloud by
Judg 16:26 . . my hands against the ***p-s***
Gal 2:9 . . . . . known as ***p-s*** of the church,
1 Tim 3:15 . . ***p*** and foundation of
Rev 3:12 . . . . victorious will become ***p-s***

PINIONS (n)
the tips of a bird's wings
Deut 32:11 . . carried them safely on his ***p.***

PIOUS (adj)
marked by or showing reverence for God and devotion to worship; religious
Isa 58:2 . . . . . Yet they act so ***p!***
Col 2:18 . . . . insisting on ***p*** self-denial
Col 2:23 . . . . strong devotion, ***p*** self-denial,

PIT (n)
a hole, shaft, or cavity in the ground; a place or situation of misery, futility, or degradation
Ps 40:2 . . . . . me out of the ***p*** of despair,
Luke 14:5 . . . or your cow falls into a ***p,***

PITCH (n)
a black or dark sticky substance
Exod 2:3 . . . waterproofed it with tar and ***p.***

PITIED (v)
to feel pity for
1 Cor 15:19 . we are more to be ***p*** than

PITY (n)
sympathetic sorrow for one suffering, distressed, or unhappy
Judg 2:18 . . . For the LORD took ***p*** on
Ps 17:10 . . . . They are without ***p.***
Ps 69:20 . . . . would show some ***p;***
Ps 72:13 . . . . He feels ***p*** for the weak
Isa 27:11. . . . show them no ***p*** or mercy.
Hos 13:14 . . I will not take ***p*** on them.

PLAGUE, PLAGUES (n)
a disastrous evil, affliction, or epidemic of infectious disease, issued by God in judgment
2 Chr 6:28 . . or a ***p*** or crop disease
Luke 21:11. . will be famines and ***p-s***
Rev 21:9. . . . the seven last ***p-s*** came
Rev 22:18. . . add to that person the ***p-s***

PLAGUED (v)
to smite, infest, or afflict with disease, calamity, or natural evil
Ps 73:5 . . . . . they're not ***p*** with problems

PLAN, PLANS (n)
a detailed formulation of a program of action; goal, aim
see also PURPOSE
Ps 2:1 . . . . . . waste their time with futile ***p-s?***
Ps 33:10 . . . . frustrates the ***p-s*** of the
Ps 40:5 . . . . . ***p-s*** for us are too numerous
Isa 30:1. . . . . You make ***p-s*** that are contrary
Isa 32:6. . . . . and make evil ***p-s.***
Jer 29:11 . . . .I know the ***p-s*** I have for you
Acts 2:23 . . . his prearranged ***p*** was carried
Acts 4:25 . . . waste their time with futile ***p-s?***
Acts 7:44 . . . according to the ***p*** God had
Rom 16:25 . . ***p*** kept secret from
Eph 3:9 . . . . this mysterious ***p*** that God,
Eph 3:11 . . . This was his eternal ***p,***
2 Tim 1:9 . . . ***p*** from before the beginning

PLANNED, PLANNING (v)
to devise or project the realization or achievement of
Prov 12:20 . . hearts that are ***p-ning*** peace!
Isa 25:1. . . . . You ***p-ned*** them long ago,
Jer 23:20. . . . has finished all he has ***p-ned.***
Eph 2:10 . . . do the good things he ***p-ned***

PLANT (n)
a young tree, vine, shrub, or herb planted or suitable for planting
Matt 15:13 . . ***p*** not planted by
1 Cor 15:36 . it doesn't grow into a ***p***

PLANT, PLANTED, PLANTING, PLANTS (v)
to put or set (seeds or plants) in the ground for growth; to establish or settle
Gen 2:8 . . . . the LORD God ***p-ed*** a garden
Gen 8:22 . . . there will be ***p-ing*** and harvest,
Ps 1:3 . . . . . . like trees ***p-ed*** along the riverbank,
Ps 126:5 . . . . who ***p*** in tears will harvest
Prov 22:8. . . who ***p*** injustice will harvest
Prov 31:16 . . earnings she ***p-s*** a vineyard.
Hos 10:12 . . ***P*** the good seeds
Amos 9:15 . . I will firmly ***p*** them there
Matt 6:26 . . . They don't ***p*** or harvest or
Matt 13:3 . . . A farmer went out to ***p*** some
Matt 13:18 . . about the farmer ***p-ing***
1 Cor 3:6 . . . ***p-ed*** the seed in your hearts,
1 Cor 3:7 . . . who does the ***p-ing,***
1 Cor 9:7 . . . What farmer ***p-s*** a vineyard
1 Cor 15:42 . earthly bodies are ***p-ed***
2 Cor 9:6 . . . a farmer who ***p-s*** only a few
Jas 1:21. . . . . accept the word God has ***p-ed***
Jas 3:18. . . . . will ***p*** seeds of peace

PLANTER (n)
one who cultivates plants
John 4:36 . . . What joy awaits both the ***p*** and

PLAY, PLAYED (v)
to perform music; to engage in sport or recreation
1 Sam 16:23. David would ***p*** the harp.
Ps 87:7 . . . . . The people will ***p*** flutes
Ps 137:5 . . . . forget how to ***p*** the harp.
Isa 11:8. . . . . baby will ***p*** safely near the hole
Luke 7:32. . . so we ***p-ed*** funeral songs,

PLEA, PLEAS (n)
an earnest entreaty; appeal
1 Kgs 8:28 . . prayer and my ***p,*** O LORD
Ps 102:17 . . . He will not reject their ***p-s.***

PLEAD, PLEADING, PLEADS (v)
to entreat or appeal earnestly; to argue a case or cause
Job 9:15 . . . . I could only ***p*** for mercy.
Lam 3:56 . . . Listen to my ***p-ing!***
Hos 10:8 . . . and ***p*** with the hills,
Acts 16:9 . . . ***p-ing*** with him, "Come over
Rom 8:27 . . . the Spirit ***p-s*** for us

Rom 8:34 . . . right hand, ***p-ing*** for us.
2 Cor 5:20 . . speak for Christ when we ***p,***

PLEASANT (adj)
having qualities that tend to give pleasure; agreeable
Gen 49:15 . . and how ***p*** the land,
Ps 16:6 . . . . . given me is a ***p*** land.
Prov 16:21 . . and ***p*** words are persuasive.
Isa 5:7. . . . . . of Judah are his ***p*** garden.

PLEASE, PLEASED, PLEASES (v)
to make glad; to satisfy; to like or wish; to be the will or pleasure of
Deut 12:25. . doing what ***p-s*** the LORD.
Ps 135:6 . . . . The LORD does whatever ***p-s***
Prov 16:7 . . . people's lives ***p*** the LORD,
Isa 42:1. . . . . my chosen one, who ***p-s*** me.
Matt 12:18 . . my Beloved, who ***p-s*** me.
Luke 2:14. . . those with whom God is ***p-d.***
Luke 10:21. . Yes, Father, it ***p-d*** you to do
John 8:29 . . . I always do what ***p-s*** him.
Rom 8:8 . . . . sinful nature can never ***p*** God.
Rom 14:18 . . this attitude, you will ***p*** God,
2 Cor 5:9 . . . our goal is to ***p*** him.
Gal 6:8 . . . . . live to ***p*** the Spirit will harvest
Eph 5:10 . . . determine what ***p-s*** the
Phil 2:13 . . . power to do what ***p-s*** him.
Col 1:10 . . . . always honor and ***p*** the Lord,
Col 1:19 . . . . God in all his fullness was ***p-d***
1 Thes 2:4 . . Our purpose is to ***p*** God,
1 Thes 2:15 . They fail to ***p*** God
1 Tim 2:3 . . . is good and ***p-s*** God our
1 Tim 5:4 . . . is something that ***p-s*** God.
Heb 10:6 . . . not ***p-d*** with burnt offerings
Heb 11:6 . . . to ***p*** God without faith.
Heb 13:16 . . sacrifices that ***p*** God.
1 Pet 2:19. . . God is ***p-d*** with you when
1 Jn 2:17. . . . does what ***p-s*** God will live
Rev 4:11. . . . you created what you ***p-d.***

PLEASING (adj)
giving pleasure; agreeable
Lev 1:9. . . . . a special gift, a ***p*** aroma
Ps 19:14 . . . . of my heart be ***p*** to you,
Ps 104:34 . . . my thoughts be ***p*** to him,
Eccl 7:26 . . . who are ***p*** to God will escape
Rom 12:2. . . is good and ***p*** and perfect.
Phil 4:18 . . . is acceptable and ***p*** to God.

PLEASURE, PLEASURES (n)
desire, inclination; a source of delight or joy; sensual gratification
Ps 5:4 . . . . . . you take no ***p*** in wickedness;
Ps 16:3 . . . . . I take ***p*** in them!
Ps 16:11 . . . . the ***p-s*** of living with you
Isa 1:11. . . . . I get no ***p*** from the blood of
Luke 8:14. . . cares and riches and ***p-s***
Eph 1:9 . . . . a plan to fulfill his own good ***p.***
1 Tim 5:6 . . . widow who lives only for ***p***
2 Tim 3:4 . . . and love ***p*** rather than God.
Titus 2:12. . . living and sinful ***p-s.***
Titus 3:3. . . . slaves to many lusts and ***p-s.***
Heb 11:25 . . the fleeting ***p-s*** of sin.
Jas 4:3. . . . . . only what will give you ***p.***

PLEDGE (n)
a binding promise or agreement to do or forbear
1 Tim 5:12 . . breaking their previous ***p.***

PLENTY (n)
the full or more-than-adequate amount or supply
Ps 17:14 . . . . May their children have ***p,***
Prov 12:11 . . A hard worker has ***p*** of food,
2 Cor 8:14 . . now you have ***p*** and can help
2 Cor 9:8 . . . ***p*** left over to share with others.

PLOT, PLOTS (v)
to plan or contrive especially secretly; to scheme
Prov 3:29. . . ***p*** harm against your neighbor
Prov 6:14. . . perverted hearts ***p*** evil,
Prov 6:18. . . a heart that ***p-s*** evil,

PLOWS (v)
to turn, break up, or work with a plow
1 Cor 9:10 . . the one who ***p*** and the one

PLOWSHARES (n)
a part of a plow that cuts the furrow
Isa 2:4. . . . . . hammer their swords into ***p***
Joel 3:10. . . . Hammer your ***p*** into swords
Mic 4:3. . . . . hammer their swords into ***p***

PLUNDER (v)
to take by force (as in war)
Matt 12:29 . . like Satan and ***p*** his goods?

PLUNGE (v)
to cause to enter a state or course of action usually suddenly, unexpectedly, or violently; to act with reckless haste
1 Tim 6:9 . . . desires that ***p*** them into ruin
1 Pet 4:4. . . . no longer ***p*** into the flood of

POINT (n)
a particular place; a particular step, stage, or degree in development
Matt 4:5. . . . the highest ***p*** of the Temple,
Matt 26:38 . . grief to the ***p*** of death.

POINT (v)
to indicate the fact or probability of something specified
John 5:39 . . . But the Scriptures ***p*** to me!

POISON (n)
a substance that usually kills, injures, or impairs an organism; something destructive or harmful
2 Kgs 4:40 . . there's ***p*** in this stew!
Jas 3:8. . . . . . and evil, full of deadly ***p.***

POISONOUS (adj)
destructive, harmful; venomous
Mark 16:18 . ***p,*** it won't hurt them.

POLISHED (adj)
smooth or glossy; burnished
Dan 10:6 . . . feet shone like ***p*** bronze,
Rev 1:15. . . . feet were like ***p*** bronze refined
Rev 2:18. . . . feet are like ***p*** bronze:

POLLUTE, POLLUTES, POLLUTING (v)
to make ceremonially, physically, or morally impure
Num 35:33 . for murder ***p-s*** the land.
Prov 25:26 . . it's like ***p-ing*** a fountain
Isa 41:24. . . . who choose you ***p*** themselves.

POMEGRANATES (n)
red fruit about the size of an orange with a thick, leathery skin and many tart seeds
Exod 28:33 . Make ***p*** out of blue, purple,
Song 4:3. . . . Your cheeks are like rosy ***p***

PONDER, PONDERED (v)
to think or consider especially quietly, soberly, and deeply
see also MEDITATE
Ps 111:2 . . . . delight in him should ***p***
Ps 119:59 . . . I ***p-ed*** the direction of my life,
Ps 143:5 . . . . I ***p*** all your great works

POOR (adj)
characterized by poverty or insufficient resources; humble
Deut 15:4. . . should be no ***p*** among you,
Deut 15:11. . some in the land who are ***p.***
Deut 24:12. . If your neighbor is ***p***
1 Sam 2:7. . . The LORD makes some ***p***
Ps 35:10 . . . . protects the helpless and ***p***
Prov 10:4. . . Lazy people are soon ***p;***
Prov 13:7. . . Some who are ***p*** pretend
Prov 22:2. . . rich and ***p*** have this
Mark 12:42 . Then a ***p*** widow came and
2 Cor 8:9 . . . for your sakes he became ***p,***
Jas 2:2. . . . . another comes in who is ***p***

POOR (n)
those characterized by poverty or insufficient resources
Lev 19:10. . . Leave them for the ***p***
Job 5:16 . . . . at last the ***p*** have hope,
Ps 41:1 . . . . . those who are kind to the ***p!***
Ps 82:3 . . . . . Give justice to the ***p*** and the
Prov 14:21 . . those who help the ***p.***
Prov 17:5. . . mock the ***p*** insult
Prov 21:13 . . cries of the ***p*** will be ignored
Prov 22:22 . . Don't rob the ***p*** just because
Prov 28:27 . . Whoever gives to the ***p*** will
Prov 31:20 . . helping hand to the ***p***
Isa 3:14. . . . . things stolen from the ***p.***
Isa 14:30. . . . I will feed the ***p*** in my pasture;
Isa 32:7. . . . . They lie to convict the ***p,***
Isa 61:1. . . . . to bring good news to the ***p.***
Jer 22:16. . . . help to the ***p*** and needy,
Amos 4:1. . . who oppress the ***p*** and crush
Amos 5:11 . . trample the ***p,*** stealing their
Zech 7:10. . . foreigners, and the ***p.***
Matt 11:5 . . . is being preached to the ***p.***
Matt 19:21 . . and give the money to the ***p,***
Mark 14:7 . . You will always have the ***p***
Luke 4:18. . . to bring Good News to the ***p.***
Luke 14:13. . Instead, invite the ***p,*** the
John 12:8 . . . You will always have the ***p***
Rom 15:26 . . an offering for the ***p*** among
Jas 2:6. . . . . . you dishonor the ***p!***

PORTIONS (n)
an often limited part set off or abstracted from a whole; share
Num 18:29 . give to the LORD the best ***p***

POSITION (n)
social or official rank or status; job
Ps 109:8 . . . . let someone else take his ***p.***
Acts 1:20 . . . Let someone else take his ***p.***
1 Tim 3:1 . . . he desires an honorable ***p.***

POSSESS, POSSESSED (v)
to seize, gain, or take (control of); to own
see also INHERIT
Ps 37:11 . . . . The lowly will ***p*** the land
Ps 37:29 . . . . The godly will ***p*** the land
John 7:20 . . . You're demon ***p-ed!***
John 8:48 . . . you were ***p-ed*** by a demon?
John 8:52 . . . you are ***p-ed*** by a demon.
John 10:20 . . He's demon ***p-ed*** and out
John 10:21 . . like a man ***p-ed*** by a demon!
Phil 3:12 . . . press on to ***p*** that perfection

POSSESSION, POSSESSIONS (n)
something owned, occupied, or controlled
see also INHERITANCE, RICHES, TREASURE(S), WEALTH
Exod 6:8 . . . as your very own ***p.***
Deut 4:20. . . and his special ***p,***
Deut 32:9. . . is his special ***p.***
Zech 2:12. . . the LORD's special ***p***
Matt 19:21 . . sell all your ***p-s*** and
Mark 10:22 . for he had many ***p-s.***
1 Pet 2:9. . . . God's very own ***p.***

POSSIBLE (adj)
being within the limits of ability, capacity, or realization
Matt 19:26 . . with God everything is ***p.***
Matt 26:39 . . ***p,*** let this cup of suffering
Mark 9:23 . . Anything is ***p*** if a person
Mark 10:27 . Everything is ***p*** with God.
Mark 14:35 . if it were ***p,*** the awful hour
Heb 10:4 . . . it is not ***p*** for the blood

POTTER (n)
one who makes pottery
Isa 29:16. . . . ***p*** who made me is stupid"?
Isa 64:8. . . . . the clay, and you are the ***p.***
Zech 11:13. . threw them to the ***p***
Matt 27:7. . . to buy the ***p's*** field,
Rom 9:21 . . . a ***p*** makes jars out of clay,

POUR, POURED, POURING, POURS (v)
to move or come continuously; to supply or produce freely
Ps 42:8 . . . . . LORD ***p-s*** his unfailing love
Ps 45:7 . . . . . ***p-ing*** out the oil of joy on
Isa 32:15. . . . Spirit is ***p-ed*** out on us
Isa 44:3. . . . . I will ***p*** out my Spirit
Ezek 39:29. . I will ***p*** out my Spirit
Joel 2:28. . . . I will ***p*** out my Spirit
Zech 12:10. . I will ***p*** out a spirit of
Mal 3:10. . . . I will ***p*** out a blessing
Luke 22:20. . blood, which is ***p-ed*** out
Acts 2:17 . . . I will ***p*** out my Spirit
Acts 2:33 . . . the Holy Spirit to ***p*** out
Acts 10:45 . . Holy Spirit had been ***p-ed***
Eph 1:6 . . . . grace he has ***p-ed*** out on us
Phil 2:17 . . . ***p-ing*** it out like a liquid
Titus 3:6. . . . generously ***p-ed*** out the Spirit

POVERTY (n)
the state of one who lacks money or material possessions
Prov 6:11. . . ***p*** will pounce on you like
Prov 13:18. . end in ***p*** and disgrace;
Prov 21:5. . . hasty shortcuts lead to ***p.***
Prov 24:34. . ***p*** will pounce on you like
Prov 31:7. . . drink to forget their ***p***
2 Cor 8:9 . . . by his ***p*** he could make you
Rev 2:9. . . . . your suffering and your ***p***—

POWER, POWERS (n)
ability to act or produce an effect; possession of control, authority, or influence over others; physical might; mental or moral efficacy; a controlling group
see also STRENGTH
Exod 15:6 . . LORD, is glorious in ***p.***
Deut 8:18. . . one who gives you ***p*** to be
Ps 89:7 . . . . . angelic ***p-s*** stand in awe
Isa 40:26. . . . great ***p*** and incomparable
Jer 9:23. . . . . the powerful boast in their ***p,***
Mic 3:8. . . . . I am filled with ***p***—
Matt 16:18 . . all the ***p-s*** of hell will not
Matt 22:29 . . don't know the ***p*** of God.
Luke 1:35. . . the ***p*** of the Most High will
Luke 4:14. . . the Holy Spirit's ***p.***
Luke 9:1. . . . gave them ***p*** and authority
Luke 10:19. . over all the ***p*** of the enemy,
Luke 11:20. . demons by the ***p*** of God,
Acts 1:8 . . . . receive ***p*** when the Holy Spirit
Rom 1:16 . . . the ***p*** of God at work,
Rom 1:20 . . . his eternal ***p*** and divine
Rom 6:9. . . . Death no longer has any ***p*** over
Rom 7:23 . . . another ***p*** within me that is
Rom 8:38 . . . not even the ***p-s*** of hell can
Rom 15:13 . . the ***p*** of the Holy Spirit.
1 Cor 1:18 . . is the very ***p*** of God.
1 Cor 6:14 . . from the dead by his ***p,***
1 Cor 15:24 . ruler and authority and ***p.***
2 Cor 4:7 . . . our great ***p*** is from God,
2 Cor 13:4 . . now lives by the ***p*** of God.
Eph 6:10 . . . Lord and in his mighty ***p.***
Phil 3:10 . . . and experience the mighty ***p***
Col 1:11 . . . . with all his glorious ***p***
Col 1:29 . . . . on Christ's mighty ***p***
1 Thes 1:5 . . words but also with ***p,***
2 Tim 1:7 . . . but of ***p,*** love, and
2 Tim 3:5 . . . reject the ***p*** that could make
Heb 2:14 . . . break the ***p*** of the devil,
Jas 5:16. . . . . righteous person has great ***p***
1 Pet 1:5. . . . is protecting you by his ***p***
1 Pet 3:22. . . ***p-s*** accept his authority.
1 Pet 4:11. . . All glory and ***p*** to him
2 Pet 1:3. . . . ***p,*** God has given us everything
Jude 1:25 . . . ***p,*** and authority are his
Rev 4:11. . . . receive glory and honor and ***p.***
Rev 5:12. . . . receive ***p*** and riches and
Rev 19:1. . . . glory and ***p*** belong to our God.
Rev 20:6. . . . the second death holds no ***p,***

POWERFUL (adj)
having great power, prestige, or influence
Exod 6:6 . . . will redeem you with a ***p*** arm
Deut 5:15. . . strong hand and ***p*** arm.
Job 25:2 . . . . God is ***p*** and dreadful.
Ps 29:4 . . . . . the LORD is ***p;***
Ps 136:12 . . . strong hand and ***p*** arm.
Jer 9:23. . . . . the ***p*** boast in their power,
Jer 27:5. . . . . my great strength and ***p*** arm
Luke 24:19. . who did ***p*** miracles,
1 Cor 1:27 . . to shame those who are ***p.***

POWERLESS (adj)
devoid of strength or resources; lacking the authority or capacity to act
Num 24:13 . would be ***p*** to do anything
1 Cor 1:27 . . things that are ***p*** to shame

PRACTICE, PRACTICING (v)
to do or perform often, habitually, or customarily; to carry out, apply
Lev 19:26. . . Do not ***p*** fortune-telling
Matt 23:3. . . they don't ***p*** what they teach.
Rom 12:13 . . eager to ***p*** hospitality.
Phil 4:9 . . . . putting into ***p*** all you learned
1 Jn 1:6. . . . . we are not ***p-ing*** the truth.
1 Jn 5:18. . . . not make a ***p*** of sinning,

PRAISE, PRAISES (n)
worship; commendation; value, merit
Deut 26:19. . ***p,*** honor, and renown.
2 Sam 22:4. . LORD, who is worthy of ***p,***
2 Chr 29:30 . So they offered joyous ***p***
Ps 7:17 . . . . . I will sing ***p*** to the name
Ps 18:49 . . . . I will sing ***p-s*** to your name.
Ps 34:1 . . . . . will constantly speak his ***p-s.***
Ps 65:1 . . . . . What mighty ***p,*** O God,
Ps 81:1 . . . . . Sing ***p-s*** to God,
Ps 100:4 . . . . into his courts with ***p.***
Ps 108:1 . . . . your ***p-s*** with all my heart!
Ps 145:3 . . . . He is most worthy of ***p!***
Ps 149:6 . . . . Let the ***p-s*** of God be in
John 12:43 . . loved human ***p*** more than
Rom 2:29. . . heart seeks ***p*** from God,
Rom 15:9. . . will sing ***p-s*** to your name.
1 Thes 2:6 . . As for human ***p,***
2 Thes 1:10 . his holy people—***p*** from all
Jas 5:13. . . . . You should sing ***p-s.***

PRAISE, PRAISED, PRAISES, PRAISING (v)
to worship, commend, or give honor to
Exod 15:2 . . and I will ***p*** him—
1 Chr 16:35 . name and rejoice and ***p*** you.
2 Chr 5:13 . . together in unison to ***p*** and
2 Chr 20:21 . ***p-ing*** him for his holy
Neh 9:5 . . . . Stand up and ***p*** the LORD
Ps 9:1 . . . . . . I will ***p*** you, LORD,
Ps 12:8 . . . . . evil is ***p-d*** throughout the land.
Ps 34:1 . . . . . I will ***p*** the LORD
Ps 42:5 . . . . . I will ***p*** him again—
Ps 45:17 . . . . nations will ***p*** you forever
Ps 51:15 . . . . my mouth may ***p*** you.
Ps 63:3 . . . . . how I ***p*** you!
Ps 71:8 . . . . . I can never stop ***p-ing*** you;
Ps 71:14 . . . . I will ***p*** you more and
Ps 74:21 . . . . and needy ***p*** your name.
Ps 89:5 . . . . . angels will ***p*** you for your
Ps 96:2 . . . . . LORD; ***p*** his name.
Ps 102:18 . . . not yet born will ***p*** the
Ps 104:1 . . . . all that I am ***p*** the
Ps 115:18 . . . But we can ***p*** the LORD
Ps 135:20 . . . LORD, ***p*** the LORD!
Ps 144:1 . . . . ***P*** the LORD, who is
Ps 148:13 . . . Let them all ***p*** the name
Ps 150:2 . . . . ***p*** his unequaled greatness!
Prov 27:2. . . Let someone else ***p*** you,
Prov 27:21 . . person is tested by being ***p-d.***
Isa 63:7. . . . . I will ***p*** the LORD
Dan 2:19 . . . Daniel ***p-d*** the God of heaven.
Dan 2:20 . . . He said, "***P*** the name
Dan 4:34 . . . ***p-d*** and worshiped the Most
Matt 5:16. . . will ***p*** your heavenly Father.
Mark 11:9 . . were shouting, "***P*** God!
Luke 1:46. . . how my soul ***p-s*** the Lord.
Luke 2:13. . . armies of heaven—***p-ing*** God
Luke 2:20. . . glorifying and ***p-ing*** God for
Luke 18:43. . all who saw it ***p-d*** God, too.
Luke 19:37. . ***p-ing*** God for all the wonderful
Acts 2:47 . . . all the while ***p-ing*** God
Acts 10:46 . . in other tongues and ***p-ing*** God
1 Cor 14:16 . if you ***p*** God only in
Gal 1:24 . . . . they ***p-d*** God because of me.
Eph 1:6 . . . . we ***p*** God for the glorious
Jas 3:9. . . . . . Sometimes it ***p-s*** our Lord
Rev 19:1. . . . heaven shouting, "***P*** the LORD!

PRAY, PRAYED, PRAYING, PRAYS (v)
to address God with adoration, confession, supplication, or thanksgiving; to intercede
Gen 24:45 . . I had finished ***p-ing*** in my
1 Sam 1:12. . she was ***p-ing*** to the LORD,
2 Chr 7:14 . . humble themselves and ***p*** and
2 Chr 30:18 : King Hezekiah ***p-ed*** for
Neh 4:9 . . . . we ***p-ed*** to our God and
Job 42:8 . . . . servant Job will ***p*** for you,
Job 42:10 . . . When Job ***p-ed*** for his friends,
Ps 5:2 . . . . . . I ***p*** to no one but you.
Ps 32:6 . . . . . all the godly ***p*** to you
Ps 34:6 . . . . . In my desperation I ***p-ed,***

Dan 6:10 . . . He ***p-ed*** three times a day,
Dan 9:4 . . . . I ***p-ed*** to the LORD
Jonah 2:1 . . . Jonah ***p-ed*** to the LORD
Matt 6:5. . . . "When you ***p,*** don't be like
Matt 6:9. . . . ***P*** like this: Our Father in
Matt 26:39. . face to the ground, ***p-ing,***
Mark 11:24 . you can ***p*** for anything,
Mark 11:25 . when you are ***p-ing,*** first
Luke 3:21. . . ***p-ing,*** the heavens opened,
Luke 9:29. . . he was ***p-ing,*** the appearance
Luke 11:1. . . teach us to ***p,*** just as John
Luke 22:41. . and knelt down and ***p-ed,***
John 17:20 . . I am ***p-ing*** not only for these
Acts 6:6 . . . . apostles, who ***p-ed*** for them
Acts 9:11 . . . He is ***p-ing*** to me right now.
Acts 16:25 . . Paul and Silas were ***p-ing***
Rom 8:26. . . the Holy Spirit ***p-s*** for us
Rom 12:12. . and keep on ***p-ing.***
Rom 15:30. . join in my struggle by ***p-ing***
1 Cor 14:14 . For if I ***p*** in tongues,
2 Cor 13:9 . . We ***p*** that you will become
Eph 1:18 . . . I ***p*** that your hearts will be
Eph 3:16 . . . I ***p*** that from his glorious,
Phil 4:6 . . . . instead, ***p*** about everything.
1 Thes 1:3 . . As we ***p*** to our God and
1 Thes 5:17 . Never stop ***p-ing.***
2 Thes 1:11 . we keep on ***p-ing*** for you,
1 Tim 2:8 . . . to ***p*** with holy hands
Jas 5:13. . . . . You should ***p.***
Jas 5:16. . . . . ***p*** for each other so that
Jude 1:20 . . . ***p*** in the power of the Holy

PRAYER, PRAYERS (n)

conversation with God – in praise, thanksgiving, or intercession

2 Chr 30:27 . God heard their ***p*** from
Ps 4:1 . . . . . . mercy on me and hear my ***p.***
Ps 17:1 . . . . . Pay attention to my ***p,***
Ps 20:5 . . . . . LORD answer all your ***p-s.***
Ps 86:6 . . . . . Listen closely to my ***p,***
Prov 15:8. . . in the ***p-s*** of the upright.
Isa 1:15. . . . . Though you offer many ***p-s,***
Isa 56:7. . . . . will be called a house of ***p***
Matt 11:25 . . Jesus prayed this ***p:***
John 17:9 . . . My ***p*** is not for the world,
Acts 1:14 . . . were constantly united in ***p,***
Acts 4:31 . . . After this ***p,*** the meeting
Acts 6:4 . . . . can spend our time in ***p***
Acts 10:31 . . your ***p*** has been heard,
Acts 13:3 . . . So after more fasting and ***p,***
Eph 6:18 . . . persistent in your ***p-s*** for all
Col 4:2 . . . . . Devote yourselves to ***p*** with an
1 Pet 3:7. . . . your ***p-s*** will not be hindered.
1 Pet 3:12. . . ears are open to their ***p-s.***
Rev 5:8. . . . . are the ***p-s*** of God's people.

PREACH, PREACHED, PREACHES, PREACHING (v)

to deliver a sermon; to exhort an idea or course of action

see also PROCLAIM, TEACH

Luke 9:6. . . . ***p-ing*** the Good News and
Luke 9:60. . . go and ***p*** about the Kingdom
Acts 5:42 . . . teach and ***p*** this message:
Acts 9:20 . . . he began ***p-ing*** about Jesus
Acts 16:10 . . to ***p*** the Good News
Acts 18:5 . . . all his time ***p-ing*** the word.
Rom 1:15. . . to ***p*** the Good News.
1 Cor 9:27 . . I fear that after ***p-ing*** to
1 Cor 15:1 . . Good News I ***p-ed*** to you
2 Cor 4:5 . . . We ***p*** that Jesus Christ is Lord,
2 Cor 11:4 . . Jesus than the one we ***p,***
Gal 1:8 . . . . . than the one we ***p-ed*** to you.
Gal 1:9 . . . . . ***p-es*** any other Good News
Gal 5:11. . . . no longer ***p-ing*** salvation
Phil 1:18 . . . Christ is being ***p-ed*** either way,
Col 1:23. . . . Good News has been ***p-ed*** all
1 Tim 5:17 . . work hard at both ***p-ing*** and
2 Tim 4:17 . . might ***p*** the Good News
1 Pet 1:25. . . Good News that was ***p-ed*** to
1 Pet 3:19. . . went and ***p-ed*** to the spirits

PREACHER (n)

one who delivers sermons or proclaims the gospel

1 Tim 2:7 . . . chosen as a ***p*** and apostle
2 Tim 1:11 . . God chose me to be a ***p,***

PRECEPT(S) (KJV)

Ps 119:15 . . . study your ***commandments***
Ps 119:159 . . I love your ***commandments,***
Mark 10:5 . . this ***commandment*** only as a
Heb 9:19 . . . each of God's ***commandments***

PRECIOUS (adj)

of great value or high price; highly esteemed or cherished

Prov 31:10 . . She is more ***p*** than rubies.
Isa 28:16. . . . It is a ***p*** cornerstone
1 Pet 1:19. . . was the ***p*** blood of Christ,
2 Pet 1:4. . . . great and ***p*** promises.

PREDICTED (v)

to declare or indicate in advance; to foretell

Isa 43:12. . . . First I ***p*** your rescue,
John 12:38 . . the prophet had ***p:***
Acts 7:52 . . . ***p*** the coming of

PREDICTIONS (n)

something that is predicted; forecast

Isa 44:26. . . . I carry out the ***p*** of my
Jer 28:9. . . . . Only when his ***p*** come true

PREGNANCY (n)
the condition of being pregnant
Gen 3:16 . . . sharpen the pain of your ***p,***

PREGNANT (adj)
containing a developing unborn offspring within the body
Gen 11:30 . . was unable to become ***p***
Matt 24:19 . . How terrible it will be for ***p***
1 Thes 5:3 . . as a ***p*** woman's labor

PREPARE, PREPARED (v)
to make ready beforehand for some purpose, use, or activity; to get ready
Exod 23:20 . to the place I have ***p-d*** for
Ps 23:5 . . . . . You ***p*** a feast for me
Zeph 1:7 . . . LORD has ***p-d*** his people
Mal 3:1. . . . . he will ***p*** the way before me.
Matt 3:3. . . . '***P*** the way for the LORD's
Matt 25:34 . . inherit the Kingdom ***p-d***
John 14:2 . . . I am going to ***p*** a place
1 Cor 2:9 . . . has ***p-d*** for those who love
2 Cor 5:5 . . . God himself has ***p-d*** us for
2 Tim 4:2 . . . the word of God. Be ***p-d,***

PRESBYTERY (KJV)
1 Tim 4:14 . . ***elders of the church*** laid their hands

PRESENCE (n)
company; nearness; (symbolic of) God-with-us
Exod 25:30 . Bread of the ***P*** on the table
1 Sam 6:20 . . in the ***p*** of the LORD,
Ps 15:1 . . . . . enter your ***p*** on your holy hill?
Ps 21:6 . . . . . given him the joy of your ***p.***
Ps 23:5 . . . . . in the ***p*** of my enemies.
Ps 31:20 . . . . in the shelter of your ***p,***
Ps 89:15 . . . . walk in the light of your ***p,***
Ps 114:7 . . . . at the ***p*** of the God of Jacob.
Ps 139:7 . . . . never get away from your ***p!***
Isa 53:2. . . . . grew up in the LORD's ***p***
Jer 5:22. . . . . tremble in my ***p?***
Matt 18:10 . . always in the ***p*** of my heavenly
1 Thes 3:9 . . joy as we enter God's ***p.***

PRESENT (adj)
being in view or at hand; now existing or in progress
Lev 16:2. . . . I myself am ***p*** in the cloud
1 Cor 7:26 . . Because of the ***p*** crisis,

PRESENT, PRESENTED, PRESENTING (v)
to give or bestow formally
Gen 28:22 . . I will ***p*** to God a tenth
Matt 5:23 . . . you are ***p-ing*** a sacrifice
Rom 3:25 . . . ***p-ed*** Jesus as the sacrifice
Rom 15:19 . . fully ***p-ed*** the Good News
Eph 5:27 . . . did this to ***p*** her to himself
2 Tim 2:15 . . Work hard so you can ***p***

PRESERVE, PRESERVES (v)
to keep safe from injury, harm, or destruction
see also SAVE
Gen 45:5 . . . ahead of you to ***p*** your lives.
Deut 33:12 . . ***p-s*** them from every harm.
1 Kgs 19:18 . I will ***p*** 7,000 others
Jer 10:12. . . . he ***p-s*** it by his wisdom.

PRESS (v)
to follow through (a course of action)
Phil 3:12 . . . I ***p*** on to possess that
Phil 3:14 . . . I ***p*** on to reach the end

PRESSURE (n)
the burden of physical or mental distress
Prov 24:10 . . ***p,*** your strength is too small.

PRETEND, PRETENDED (v)
to give a false appearance of being, possessing, or performing
1 Sam 21:13. So he ***p-ed*** to be insane,
Zech 13:4. . . No one will ***p*** to be a prophet
Rom 12:9 . . . Don't just ***p*** to love

PRETENSE (n)
professed rather than real intention or purpose
Amos 5:21 . . I hate all your show and ***p***—

PREVAIL, PREVAILS (v)
to triumph
Prov 19:21 . . LORD's purpose will ***p.***
Isa 42:4. . . . . lose heart until justice ***p-s***

PRICE (n)
the quantity of one thing that is exchanged or demanded in barter or sale for another
Job 28:18 . . . ***p*** of wisdom is far above
1 Cor 6:20 . . bought you with a high ***p.***

PRIDE (n)
inordinate self-esteem or conceit; disdainful behavior or treatment of others
Ps 101:5 . . . . will not endure conceit and ***p.***
Prov 6:3. . . . Now swallow your ***p;***
Prov 8:13. . . I hate ***p*** and arrogance,
Mark 7:22 . . envy, slander, ***p,*** and
1 Jn 2:16. . . . ***p*** in our achievements and

PRIEST, PRIESTS (n)
one authorized to perform the sacred rites of sacrifice and worship; a mediator between God and humans
Exod 19:6 . . will be my kingdom of ***p-s,***
Ps 110:4 . . . . You are a ***p*** forever
Mal 1:6. . . . . Armies says to the ***p-s:***
Heb 4:14 . . . since we have a great High ***P***
Heb 5:6 . . . . You are a ***p*** forever
Heb 6:20 . . . our eternal High ***P***
Heb 8:1 . . . . a High ***P*** who sat down
1 Pet 2:5. . . . you are his holy ***p-s.***
1 Pet 2:9. . . . You are royal ***p-s,***
Rev 5:10. . . . Kingdom of ***p-s*** for our God.
Rev 20:6. . . . but they will be ***p-s*** of God

PRIESTHOOD (n)
the office, dignity, or character of a priest
Heb 7:24 . . . his ***p*** lasts forever.

PRINCE, PRINCES (n)
a son of a king; the ruler of a principality or state; a man of high rank or high standing in his class or profession
Ps 118:9 . . . . LORD than to trust in ***p-s.***
Prov 25:15 . . Patience can persuade a ***p,***
Isa 9:6. . . . . Everlasting Father, ***P*** of Peace.
Ezek 34:24 . . David will be a ***p*** among
Dan 8:25 . . . take on the ***P*** of ***p-s***
Matt 10:25 . . called the ***p*** of demons,
Luke 11:15. . the ***p*** of demons.
Acts 5:31 . . . at his right hand as ***P*** and

PRINCESS (n)
the daughter of a king; a woman having sovereign power
Ps 45:13 . . . . The bride, a ***p,*** looks glorious

PRINCIPLE, PRINCIPLES (n)
a comprehensive and fundamental law, doctrine, or assumption
Gal 4:9 . . . . . spiritual ***p-s*** of this world?
Gal 6:16 . . . . all who live by this ***p;***

PRISON, PRISONS (n)
a state of confinement or captivity; jail
Ps 142:7 . . . . Bring me out of ***p***
Isa 42:7. . . . . will free the captives from ***p,***
Matt 25:36 . . I was in ***p,*** and you visited
2 Cor 11:23 . been put in ***p*** more often,
Heb 11:36 . . were chained in ***p-s.***
Heb 13:3 . . . Remember those in ***p,***
1 Pet 3:19. . . preached to the spirits in ***p***—
Jude 1:6 . . . . chained in ***p-s*** of darkness,
Rev 20:7. . . . Satan will be let out of his ***p.***

PRISONER, PRISONERS (n)
a person deprived of liberty and kept under involuntary restraint, confinement, or custody
Ps 79:11 . . . . to the moaning of the ***p-s.***
Ps 146:7 . . . . The LORD frees the ***p-s.***
Zech 9:12. . . you ***p-s*** who still have hope!
Gal 3:22 . . . . we are all ***p-s*** of sin,
Eph 3:1 . . . . I, Paul, a ***p*** of Christ Jesus

PRIVATE (adj)
secret, not to be seen by others
Matt 6:4. . . . Give your gifts in ***p,*** and
Matt 6:6. . . . and pray to your Father in ***p.***
1 Cor 4:5 . . . and will reveal our ***p*** motives.

PRIVILEGE (n)
a right or immunity held as a peculiar benefit, advantage, or favor
Prov 25:2. . . God's ***p*** to conceal things
Rom 5:2. . . . into this place of undeserved ***p***
2 Cor 8:4 . . . for the ***p*** of sharing in

PRIZE (n)
something offered or striven for in competitions or in contests
1 Cor 9:24. . . one person gets the ***p?***
1 Cor 9:25 . . we do it for an eternal ***p.***
Phil 3:14 . . . heavenly ***p*** for which God,
2 Tim 2:5. . . cannot win the ***p*** unless
2 Tim 4:8. . . ***p*** awaits me—the crown

PRIZE (v)
to value highly, esteem
Prov 4:8. . . . If you ***p*** wisdom,

PROBLEMS (n)
sources of perplexity, distress, or vexation
Matt 13:21 . . as soon as they have ***p***
Rom 5:3. . . . we run into ***p*** and trials,

PROCESSION (n)
a group of individuals moving along in an orderly and often ceremonial way
Ps 68:24 . . . . O God—the ***p*** of my God
2 Cor 2:14 . . in Christ's triumphal ***p.***

PROCLAIM, PROCLAIMING, PROCLAIMS (v)
to declare publicly
see also PREACH
Lev 25:10. . . a time to ***p*** freedom
Deut 32:3. . . I will ***p*** the name of
1 Chr 16:8 . . and ***p*** his greatness.
Ps 2:7 . . . . . . king ***p-s*** the LORD's decree:
Ps 50:6 . . . . . heavens ***p*** his justice,
Ps 97:6 . . . . . heavens ***p*** his righteousness;
Ps 145:4 . . . . let them ***p*** your power.

Isa 61:1. . . . . to ***p*** that captives will be
Acts 28:31 . . ***p-ing*** the Kingdom of God
Col 1:25 . . . . ***p-ing*** his entire message to you.
1 Thes 3:2 . . in ***p-ing*** the Good News
Titus 1:1. . . . I have been sent to ***p*** faith
1 Jn 1:1. . . . . ***p*** to you the one who existed

PRODUCE, PRODUCES (v)
to yield, make, or manufacture
Prov 3:9. . . . best part of everything you ***p.***
Isa 55:11. . . . and it always ***p-s*** fruit.
Matt 7:18 . . . good tree can't ***p*** bad fruit,
Luke 3:9. . . . tree that does not ***p*** good fruit
John 15:8 . . . When you ***p*** much fruit,
John 15:16 . . to go and ***p*** lasting fruit,
Rom 7:4. . . . ***p*** a harvest of good deeds
Eph 5:9 . . . . light within you ***p-s*** only what
Col 1:10 . . . . lives will ***p*** every kind of good
Jas 2:17. . . . . Unless it ***p-s*** good deeds, it is

PRODUCTIVE (adj)
yielding results, benefits, or profits
2 Pet 1:8. . . . the more ***p*** and useful you will

PROFANING (v)
to treat (something sacred) with abuse, irreverence, or contempt
Neh 13:17 . . Why are you ***p*** the Sabbath

PROFESSIONAL (adj)
of, relating to, or characteristic of a profession
Amos 7:14. . I'm not a ***p*** prophet,

PROFIT (n)
gain, benefit, or usefulness
Prov 14:23. . Work brings ***p,*** but
2 Cor 2:17 . . who preach for personal ***p.***

PROFITABLE (adj)
yielding advantageous returns or results
Prov 31:18. . her dealings are ***p;***

PROGRESS (n)
a forward or onward movement (as to an objective or goal)
Phil 3:16 . . . hold on to the ***p*** we have
1 Tim 4:15 . . everyone will see your ***p.***

PROLONG (v)
to lengthen in time, extent, scope, or range
Ps 85:5 . . . . . Will you ***p*** your wrath to all

PROMISCUITY (n)
sexual excesses
see also IMMORALITY
Rom 13:13. . ***p*** and immoral living,

PROMISCUOUS (adj)
not restricted to one sexual partner
Prov 23:27. . a ***p*** woman is as dangerous

PROMISE, PROMISES (n)
a declaration that one will do or refrain from doing something specified
see also COVENANT, VOW
2 Sam 7:25. . a ***p*** that will last forever.
Neh 5:13 . . . If you fail to keep your ***p,***
Ps 91:4 . . . . . faithful ***p-s*** are your armor
Ps 116:14 . . . keep my ***p-s*** to the LORD
Ps 145:13 . . . LORD always keeps his ***p-s;***
Ps 146:6 . . . . He keeps every ***p*** forever.
Rom 4:20. . . in believing God's ***p.***
Rom 9:4. . . . receiving his wonderful ***p-s.***
Rom 15:4. . . patiently for God's ***p-s*** to be
2 Cor 1:20 . . ***p-s*** have been fulfilled
2 Cor 7:1 . . . Because we have these ***p-s,***
Eph 2:12 . . . covenant ***p-s*** God had made
Heb 6:13 . . . God's ***p*** to Abraham.
Heb 8:6 . . . . based on better ***p-s.***
Heb 10:23 . . be trusted to keep his ***p.***
Heb 11:11 . . that God would keep his ***p.***
2 Pet 3:4. . . . ***p*** that Jesus is coming again?
2 Pet 3:9. . . . being slow about his ***p,***

PROMISED, PROMISES, PROMISING (v)
to pledge to do, bring about, or provide
Exod 3:17 . . I have ***p-d*** to rescue you
Deut 15:6. . . bless you as he has ***p-d.***
Josh 23:15 . . the good things he ***p-d,***
Luke 24:49. . as my Father ***p-d.***
Acts 1:4 . . . . sends you the gift he ***p-d,***
Rom 4:21. . . able to do whatever he ***p-s.***
Gal 3:14. . . . blessing he ***p-d*** to Abraham,
1 Tim 4:8 . . . ***p-ing*** benefits in this life
Titus 1:2. . . . God—who does not lie—***p-d***
Heb 10:36 . . receive all that he has ***p-d.***
Jas 1:12. . . . . of life that God has ***p-d***
Jas 2:5. . . . . . inherit the Kingdom he ***p-d***
2 Pet 3:13. . . new earth he has ***p-d,***
1 Jn 2:25. . . . eternal life he ***p-d*** us.

PROMOTE (v)
to further; to advance
Titus 2:1. . . . ***p*** the kind of living that

PRONOUNCE (v)
to declare officially or ceremoniously
1 Chr 23:13 . to ***p*** blessings in his name

PROOF (n)
something that induces certainty or establishes validity
John 10:25 . . The ***p*** is the work I do

PROPERTY (n)
a piece of real estate owned or possessed
Acts 5:1 . . . . wife, Sapphira, sold some ***p.***

PROPHECY, PROPHECIES (n)
the spoken or written word from God; may forthtell (consoling or corrective) and/or foretell (predictive)
Matt 13:14 . . fulfills the ***p*** of Isaiah
Acts 13:29 . . all that the ***p-ies*** said about
Acts 17:3 . . . ***p-ies*** and proved that the Messiah
Acts 21:9 . . . who had the gift of ***p.***
Acts 21:10 . . who also had the gift of ***p,***
1 Cor 13:2 . . If I had the gift of ***p,***
1 Cor 13:9 . . gift of ***p*** reveals only part
1 Cor 14:6 . . knowledge or ***p*** or teaching,
Rev 22:18. . . words of ***p*** written in

PROPHESY, PROPHESIED, PROPHESIES, PROPHESYING (v)
to issue a prophecy
Num 11:25 . upon them, they ***p-ied.***
1 Sam 19:24. day and all night, ***p-ing*** in
Isa 42:9. . . . . Everything I ***p-ied*** has come
Joel 2:28. . . . sons and daughters will ***p.***
Matt 7:22. . . We ***p-ied*** in your name and
Acts 2:17 . . . sons and daughters will ***p.***
Acts 19:6 . . . in other tongues and ***p-ied.***
Rom 12:6. . . the ability to ***p,***
1 Cor 11:4 . . head while praying or ***p-ing.***
1 Cor 12:10 . the ability to ***p.***
1 Cor 14:1 . . the ability to ***p.***
1 Cor 14:3 . . one who ***p-ies*** strengthens
1 Cor 14:39 . be eager to ***p,***

PROPHET, PROPHETS (n)
an interpreter of the times and people's hearts; one who issues divinely inspired revelations
Exod 7:1 . . . Aaron, will be your ***p.***
Exod 15:20 . Miriam the ***p,*** Aaron's
Deut 13:1. . . there are ***p-s*** among you
Deut 18:18. . I will raise up a ***p*** like you
1 Sam 9:9. . . ***p-s*** used to be called seers.
1 Kgs 18:36 . Elijah the ***p*** walked up to
2 Kgs 5:8 . . . a true ***p*** here in Israel.
2 Kgs 6:12 . . Elisha, the ***p*** in Israel,
Isa 44:26. . . . the predictions of my ***p-s!***
Hos 9:7 . . . . you say, "The ***p-s*** are crazy
Amos 7:14. . I'm not a professional ***p,***
Hab 1:1 . . . . that the ***p*** Habakkuk received
Zech 7:12. . . through the earlier ***p-s.***
Mal 4:5. . . . . the ***p*** Elijah before the great
Matt 5:17. . . or the writings of the ***p-s.***
Matt 7:12. . . in the law and the ***p-s.***
Matt 10:41 . . the same reward as a ***p.***
Matt 11:9. . . Yes, and he is more than a ***p.***
Matt 12:39 . . sign of the ***p*** Jonah.
Matt 23:37 . . the city that kills the ***p-s***
Matt 26:56 . . fulfill the words of the ***p-s***
Luke 4:24. . . no ***p*** is accepted in his own
Luke 7:16. . . A mighty ***p*** has risen
Luke 11:49. . will send ***p-s*** and apostles
Luke 24:19. . ***p*** who did powerful
Luke 24:25. . all that the ***p-s*** wrote in
Luke 24:44. . law of Moses and the ***p-s***
John 1:21 . . . you the ***P*** we are expecting?
Acts 7:37 . . . a ***P*** like me from among your
Acts 10:43 . . all the ***p-s*** testified about,
Acts 13:1 . . . Among the ***p-s*** and teachers
Rom 1:2. . . . long ago through his ***p-s***
Rom 3:21 . . . Moses and the ***p-s*** long ago.
Rom 11:3. . . they have killed your ***p-s***
1 Cor 12:28 . second are ***p-s,*** third are
1 Cor 14:37 . If you claim to be a ***p*** or
Eph 2:20 . . . of the apostles and the ***p-s.***
Eph 3:5 . . . . to his holy apostles and ***p-s.***
Eph 4:11 . . . the apostles, the ***p-s,*** the
1 Pet 1:10. . . the ***p-s*** wanted to know
2 Pet 1:19. . . proclaimed by the ***p-s.***
2 Pet 1:21. . . those ***p-s*** were moved by
2 Pet 3:2. . . . what the holy ***p-s*** said long
Rev 11:10. . . death of the two ***p-s*** who
Rev 18:20. . . God and apostles and ***p-s!***

PROPHETIC (adj)
of, relating to, or characteristic of a prophet or prophecy
Ezek 37:4. . . ***p*** message to these bones
Dan 9:24 . . . to confirm the ***p*** vision,
1 Tim 1:18 . . based on the ***p*** words

PROPITIATION (KJV)
Rom 3:25. . . Jesus as the ***sacrifice*** for sin
1 Jn 2:2. . . . . the ***sacrifice that atones***
1 Jn 4:10. . . . ***sacrifice to take away*** our sins

PROSELYTE(S) (KJV)
Matt 23:15 . . and sea to make one ***convert***
Acts 2:11 . . . Jews and ***converts to Judaism***
Acts 6:5 . . . . ***convert to the Jewish faith***
Acts 13:43 . . devout ***converts to Judaism***

PROSPER, PROSPERS (v)
to achieve economic success; to become strong and flourishing
Deut 28:63. . pleasure in causing you to ***p***

Ps 37:3 . . . . . safely in the land and ***p.***
Ps 73:3 . . . . . ***p*** despite their wickedness.
Prov 16:20 . . listen to instruction will ***p;***
Prov 17:9 . . . Love ***p-s*** when a fault is forgiven,
Prov 19:8 . . . cherish understanding will ***p.***
Isa 53:10. . . . LORD's good plan will ***p***
Isa 55:11. . . . it will ***p*** everywhere I send it.
Dan 4:27 . . . then you will continue to ***p.***

PROSPERITY (n)
the condition of being successful or thriving
Gen 41:29 . . will be a period of great ***p***
Deut 28:11. . LORD will give you ***p***
Deut 30:15. . life and death, between ***p***
1 Sam 25:6. . Peace and ***p*** to you,
Ps 41:2 . . . . . He gives them ***p*** in the land
Prov 21:5 . . . and hard work lead to ***p,***
Prov 28:25 . . trusting the LORD leads to ***p.***
Jer 33:6. . . . . give it ***p*** and true peace.
Mic 4:4. . . . . will live in peace and ***p,***

PROSPEROUS (adj)
marked by success or economic well-being; flourishing
Deut 5:33. . . live long and ***p*** lives
Ps 30:6 . . . . . When I was ***p,*** I said,
Ps 34:12 . . . . a life that is long and ***p?***
Ps 128:2 . . . . How joyful and ***p*** you will be!
Ps 132:15 . . . bless this city and make it ***p;***
Jer 12:1. . . . . Why are the wicked so ***p?***

PROSTITUTE, PROSTITUTES (n)
a person who engages in promiscuous sexual relations, especially for money
Josh 6:17 . . . Rahab the ***p*** and
Prov 6:26. . . a ***p*** will bring you to poverty,
Prov 29:3 . . . hangs around with ***p-s,***
Ezek 16:15. . as a ***p*** to every man
Ezek 23:3. . . They became ***p-s*** in Egypt.
Matt 21:31 . . ***p-s*** will get into the
Luke 15:30. . your money on ***p-s,***
1 Cor 6:16 . . if a man joins himself to a ***p,***
Rev 17:1. . . . going to come on the great ***p,***

PROSTITUTING (v)
to devote to corrupt or unworthy purposes
Ezek 20:30 . . ***p*** yourselves by worshiping

PROSTITUTION (n)
the act or practice of engaging in promiscuous sexual relations especially for money
Lev 20:6. . . . who commit spiritual ***p*** by
Hos 3:3 . . . . days and stop your ***p.***

PROTECT, PROTECTED, PROTECTING, PROTECTS (v)
to cover or shield from exposure, injury, damage, or destruction; to defend
see also KEEP
Gen 15:1 . . . for I will ***p*** you,
Num 6:24 . . bless you and ***p*** you.
Josh 6:17 . . . for she ***p-ed*** our spies.
1 Sam 2:9. . . He will ***p*** his faithful ones,
Ps 23:4 . . . . . your staff ***p*** and comfort me.
Ps 27:1 . . . . . fortress, ***p-ing*** me from danger,
Ps 41:2 . . . . . LORD ***p-s*** them and keeps
Ps 116:6 . . . . LORD ***p-s*** those of childlike
Ps 127:1 . . . . Unless the LORD ***p-s*** a city,
Ps 145:20 . . . LORD ***p-s*** all those who love
Ps 146:9 . . . . LORD ***p-s*** the foreigners
Prov 2:8. . . . ***p-s*** those who are faithful
Isa 31:5. . . . . like a bird ***p-ing*** its nest.
Isa 57:1. . . . . God is ***p-ing*** them from the
John 17:11 . . now ***p*** them by the power of
Acts 26:22 . . But God has ***p-ed*** me
Gal 3:24 . . . . ***p-ed*** us until we could be
1 Pet 1:5. . . . God is ***p-ing*** you by his power
Rev 3:10. . . . I will ***p*** you from the great

PROTECTION (n)
the act of protecting; the state of being protected
see also REFUGE
2 Sam 22:3. . my rock, in whom I find ***p.***
2 Sam 22:31. look to him for ***p.***
Ps 5:11 . . . . . Spread your ***p*** over them,
Ps 31:2 . . . . . Be my rock of ***p,***
Ps 71:1 . . . . . I have come to you for ***p;***
Ps 91:4 . . . . . promises are your armor and ***p.***
Prov 19:23 . . security and ***p*** from harm.

PROTECTIVE (adj)
of or relating to protection or defense
Ezra 9:9 . . . . He has given us a ***p*** wall

PROUD (adj)
having or displaying excessive self-esteem
Ps 5:5 . . . . . . ***p*** may not stand in your
Prov 21:4. . . Haughty eyes, a ***p*** heart,
Rom 1:30. . . haters of God, insolent, ***p,***
1 Cor 13:4 . . not jealous or boastful or ***p***
1 Tim 3:6 . . . he might become ***p,***
1 Tim 6:17 . . rich in this world not to be ***p***
2 Tim 3:2. . . They will be boastful and ***p,***

PROUD (n)
those having or displaying excessive self-esteem
Prov 16:5. . . LORD detests the ***p;***
Dan 4:37 . . . he is able to humble the ***p.***
Jas 4:6. . . . . . God opposes the ***p*** but favors
1 Pet 5:5. . . . God opposes the ***p*** but favors

PROVE, PROVED, PROVING (v)
to test or establish the truth, validity, or genuineness of
Ps 51:4 . . . . . ***p-d*** right in what you say,
Isa 44:25. . . . thus ***p-ing*** them to be fools.
John 13:35 . . love for one another will ***p***
Acts 1:3 . . . . he ***p-d*** to them in many ways
Acts 17:3 . . . ***p-d*** that the Messiah
Acts 17:31 . . ***p-d*** to everyone who this is
Acts 26:20 . . ***p*** they have changed by
Rom 3:4. . . . ***p-d*** right in what you say,

PROVIDE, PROVIDED, PROVIDES (v)
to furnish or supply, implying foresight in making provision for the future
Gen 22:8 . . . God will ***p*** a sheep
Gen 22:14 . . means "the LORD will ***p***"
Ps 68:10 . . . . O God, you ***p-d*** for your needy
Isa 4:5. . . . . . the LORD will ***p*** shade
Jer 5:28. . . . . refuse to ***p*** justice to orphans
Ezek 18:7. . . and ***p-s*** clothes for the needy.
2 Cor 9:8 . . . God will generously ***p*** all you
2 Cor 9:10 . . he will ***p*** and increase your

PROVOKE (v)
to incite to anger; to stir up purposely
Eph 6:4 . . . . do not ***p*** your children to anger

PROWLS (v)
to roam over in a predatory manner
1 Pet 5:8. . . . ***p*** around like a roaring lion,

PRUDENT (adj)
marked by wisdom or judiciousness; discreet
Prov 14:8. . . ***p*** understand where they are
Prov 14:18. . the ***p*** are crowned with
Prov 22:3. . . A ***p*** person foresees danger

PRUNES (v)
to cut back or off for better shape or more fruitful growth
John 15:2. . . and he ***p*** the branches

PRUNING HOOKS
a pole bearing a curved blade for pruning plants
Isa 2:4. . . . . . their spears into ***p***.
Joel 3:10. . . . your ***p*** into spears.

PSALMS (n)
a sacred song or poem used in worship
Ps 95:2 . . . . . Let us sing ***p*** of praise
Eph 5:19 . . . singing ***p*** and hymns and
Col 3:16 . . . . Sing ***p*** and hymns and spiritual

PSYCHICS (n)
those who claim to have sensitivity to knowledge and forces that lie outside the normal human experience
Deut 18:11. . function as mediums or ***p***,
2 Kgs 21:6 . . with mediums and ***p***.
2 Kgs 23:24 . rid of the mediums and ***p***,

PUBLICAN(S) (KJV)
Matt 5:46. . . Even ***corrupt tax collectors***
Matt 9:10. . . with many ***tax collectors***
Matt 10:3. . . Matthew (the ***tax collector***),
Luke 5:30. . . and drink with ***such scum?***
Luke 18:11. . not like that ***tax collector***

PUNISH, PUNISHED, PUNISHES, PUNISHING (v)
to impose a penalty to fit the crime: from corrective measures (fines or scolding) and corporal punishment (spanking or whipping) to capital punishment and eternal damnation
Gen 15:14 . . But I will ***p*** the nation
1 Kgs 8:32 . . ***P*** the guilty as they deserve.
Prov 11:21. . people will surely be ***p-ed***,
Jer 25:14. . . . I will ***p*** them in proportion
Lam 3:39 . . . when we are ***p-ed*** for our sins?
Mark 12:40 . will be more severely ***p-ed***.
Acts 7:7 . . . . But I will ***p*** the nation
Rom 2:2. . . . God, in his justice, will ***p***
Rom 13:4. . . they have the power to ***p*** you.
Rom 13:4. . . the very purpose of ***p-ing***
2 Thes 1:9 . . ***p-ed*** with eternal destruction,
Heb 2:2 . . . . act of disobedience was ***p-ed***.
Heb 12:6 . . . he ***p-es*** each one he accepts
1 Pet 2:14. . . sent them to ***p*** those who
Rev 19:2. . . . has ***p-ed*** the great prostitute

PUNISHMENT (n)
suffering, pain, or loss that serves as retribution
Isa 53:4. . . . . troubles were a ***p*** from God,
Jer 2:19. . . . . will bring its own ***p***.
Jer 4:18. . . . . This ***p*** is bitter, piercing
Hos 5:9 . . . . On your day of ***p***, you will
Matt 25:46. . will go away into eternal ***p***,
Rom 13:5. . . not only to avoid ***p***, but also
2 Pet 2:9. . . . keeping the wicked under ***p***

PURCHASE, PURCHASED (v)
to gain or acquire; to buy
see also REDEEM
Acts 20:28 . . ***p-d*** with his own blood—
Eph 1:7 . . . . ***p-d*** our freedom with the
Eph 1:14 . . . ***p-d*** us to be his own people.
Col 1:14 . . . . who ***p-d*** our freedom

1 Tim 2:6 . . . gave his life to ***p*** freedom
Rev 14:4. . . . have been ***p-d*** from among

PURE (adj)
free of contamination or impurities; ritually clean; guileless; faultless; guiltless; chaste
see also CLEAN, HOLY
Ps 19:9 . . . . . Reverence for the LORD is ***p,***
Prov 20:9. . . I am ***p*** and free
Matt 5:8 . . . . those whose hearts are ***p,***
1 Cor 1:30 . . he made us ***p*** and holy,
Phil 4:8 . . . . right, and ***p,*** and lovely,
1 Tim 5:22 . . Keep yourself ***p.***
2 Tim 2:21 . . If you keep yourself ***p,***
Titus 1:15. . . Everything is ***p*** to those
Titus 2:5. . . . to live wisely and be ***p,***
Jas 1:27. . . . . ***P*** and genuine religion
1 Pet 3:2. . . . your ***p*** and reverent
2 Pet 3:14. . . are ***p*** and blameless
1 Jn 3:3. . . . . will keep themselves ***p,*** just as

PURIFICATION (n)
the act or an instance of purifying or of being purified
Lev 16:30. . . offerings of ***p*** will be made
Acts 21:24 . . join them in the ***p*** ceremony,

PURIFY, PURIFIED (v)
to make pure or remove (physical or moral) blemishes; to make ritually clean
see also CLEANSE
Exod 30:10 . offering made to ***p*** the people
Exod 30:15 . given to the LORD to ***p***
Num 25:13 . ***p-ied*** the people of Israel,
1 Chr 15:12 . You must ***p*** yourselves and
2 Chr 30:17 . had not ***p-ied*** themselves,
Neh 12:30 . . Levites first ***p-ied*** themselves;
Isa 52:11. . . . and ***p*** yourselves,
John 15:3 . . . pruned and ***p-ied*** by the
Heb 9:14 . . . Christ will ***p*** our consciences
Heb 9:22 . . . was ***p-ied*** with blood.
Jas 4:8. . . . . . you sinners; ***p*** your hearts,

PURIM (n)
a Jewish holiday in commemoration of the deliverance of the Jews from the massacre plotted by Haman
Esth 9:26 . . . this celebration is called ***P,***

PURITY (n)
the quality or state of being pure
Job 14:4 . . . . Who can bring ***p*** out of an
Ps 86:11 . . . . Grant me ***p*** of heart,
2 Cor 6:6 . . . by our ***p,*** our understanding,
1 Tim 4:12 . . love, your faith, and your ***p.***
1 Tim 5:2. . . younger women with all ***p***

PURPLE (adj)
of the color purple; symbolic of royalty and wealth
Prov 31:22. . fine linen and ***p*** gowns.
Mark 15:17 . They dressed him in a ***p*** robe,
Acts 16:14 . . merchant of expensive ***p*** cloth,

PURPOSE, PURPOSES (n)
something set up as an object or end to be attained; resolution, determination
see also PLAN
Exod 9:16 . . I have spared you for a ***p***—
Prov 19:21 . . the LORD's ***p*** will prevail.
Rom 8:28. . . according to his ***p*** for them.
Rom 9:11. . . according to his own ***p-s;***
Rom 9:17. . . for the very ***p*** of displaying
1 Cor 3:8 . . . with the same ***p.***
1 Cor 9:26 . . I run with ***p*** in every step.
Phil 2:2 . . . . together with one mind and ***p.***

PURSUE, PURSUES (v)
to follow in order to overtake, capture, kill, or defeat; to seek
Ps 23:6 . . . . . unfailing love will ***p*** me
Ps 119:32 . . . I will ***p*** your commands,
Prov 15:9. . . those who ***p*** godliness.
Prov 21:21 . . Whoever ***p-s*** righteousness
1 Tim 6:11 . . ***P*** righteousness and a godly
2 Tim 2:22 . . Instead, ***p*** righteous living,

QUAIL (n)
in Palestine, a migrating bird that arrives in droves along the shores of the Mediterranean Sea
Exod 16:13 . vast numbers of ***q*** flew
Num 11:31 . there were ***q*** flying

QUAKE (v)
to shake or vibrate
Ps 99:1 . . . . . the whole earth ***q!***

QUALIFICATION (n)
a condition or standard that must be complied with (as for the attainment of a privilege)
2 Cor 3:5 . . . Our ***q*** comes from God.

QUALIFIED (adj)
to declare competent or adequate
2 Cor 3:5 . . . not that we think we are ***q***

QUALITIES (n)
distinguishing attributes; characteristics; nature
Rom 1:20 . . . clearly see his invisible ***q***—

QUARREL, QUARRELS (n)
a usually verbal conflict between antagonists
Prov 10:12 . . Hatred stirs up ***q-s,***
Prov 17:14 . . Starting a ***q*** is like opening
Prov 26:20 . . ***q-s*** disappear when gossip
Prov 30:33 . . anger causes ***q-s.***
Titus 3:9. . . . ***q-s*** and fights about
Jas 4:1. . . . . . causing the ***q-s*** and fights

QUARREL, QUARRELING (v)
to find fault; to contend or dispute actively
Exod 21:18 . "Now suppose two men ***q,***
Prov 17:19 . . Anyone who loves to ***q*** loves
Prov 20:3 . . . fools insist on ***q-ing.***
Isa 58:4. . . . . keep on fighting and ***q-ing?***
1 Cor 3:3 . . . and ***q*** with each other.
2 Cor 12:20 . will find ***q-ing,*** jealousy,

QUARRELSOME (adj)
apt or disposed to quarrel in an often petty manner; contentious
Prov 19:13 . . ***q*** wife is as annoying as
Prov 21:9 . . . than with a ***q*** wife in a lovely
Prov 26:21 . . A ***q*** person starts fights
1 Tim 3:3 . . . He must be gentle, not ***q,***

QUEEN (n)
the wife or widow of a king; a female monarch
1 Kgs 10:1 . . ***q*** of Sheba heard
Ps 45:9 . . . . . your right side stands the ***q,***
Matt 12:42 . . The ***q*** of Sheba will

QUENCH (v)
to put out or extinguish
Song 8:7. . . . Many waters cannot ***q*** love,

QUICK (KJV)
Heb 4:12 . . . word of God is ***alive*** and
1 Pet 4:5. . . . the ***living*** and the dead.

QUICKEN (KJV)
Ps 80:18 . . . . ***Revive*** us so we can call on
Ps 119:37 . . . ***give*** me ***life*** through your
Rom 8:11 . . . he will ***give life*** to your mortal

QUIET (adj)
calm; gentle; peaceful, still; free from noise
Prov 11:12 . . a sensible person keeps ***q.***
Eccl 3:7 . . . . A time to be ***q*** and a time
Eccl 9:17 . . . to hear the ***q*** words of a wise
Luke 19:40 . . If they kept ***q,*** the stones
1 Thes 4:11 . to live a ***q*** life,
1 Tim 2:2 . . . peaceful and ***q*** lives marked

QUIETNESS (n)
the state of being quiet; calmness; stillness
Eccl 4:6 . . . . one handful with ***q*** than two
Isa 30:15. . . . ***q*** and confidence is
Isa 32:17. . . . it will bring ***q*** and confidence

QUIT, QUITTING (v)

to cease action; to give up

Prov 23:4 . . . wise enough to know when to ***q***.

Eccl 10:4 . . . boss is angry at you, don't ***q!***

Rev 2:3. . . . . suffered for me without ***q-ting.***

QUIVER (n)

a case for carrying or holding arrows

Ps 127:5 . . . . joyful is the man whose ***q*** is

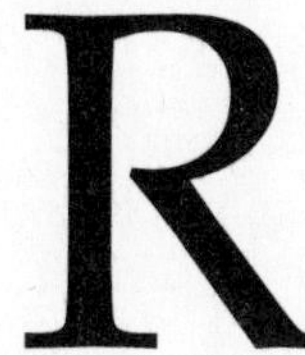

RABBI (n)
a title of honor and respect given by the Jews to a teacher of the Law
Matt 23:8 . . . anyone call you ***'R,'***
John 3:2 . . . . ***"R,"*** he said, "we all know

RACE (n)
an athletic contest; an ethnic classification
Ps 19:5 . . . . . athlete eager to run the ***r.***
Eccl 9:11 . . . doesn't always win the ***r,***
Dan 7:14 . . . people of every ***r*** and nation
1 Cor 9:24 . . that in a ***r*** everyone runs,
Gal 2:2 . . . . . running the ***r*** for nothing.
Gal 5:7 . . . . . were running the ***r*** so well.
2 Tim 4:7 . . . I have finished the ***r,***
Heb 12:1 . . . run with endurance the ***r*** God

RACE (v)
to go, move, or function at top speed or out of control
Prov 6:18 . . . feet that ***r*** to do wrong,

RADIANCE (n)
the quality or state of being radiant
Isa 60:3. . . . . will come to see your ***r.***
Luke 2:9. . . . and the ***r*** of the Lord's

RADIANT (adj)
vividly bright and shining; marked by or expressive of love, confidence, or happiness
Exod 34:29 . face had become ***r*** because
Ps 34:5 . . . . . help will be ***r*** with joy;
Ps 80:1 . . . . . display your ***r*** glory

RADIATES (v)
to spread abroad or around as if from a center; to shine brightly
Heb 1:3 . . . . The Son ***r*** God's own glory

RAGE (n)
violent and uncontrolled anger
Isa 14:6. . . . . with endless blows of ***r***
Col 3:8 . . . . . rid of anger, ***r,*** malicious

RAGING (adj)
violent, wild
Ps 42:7 . . . . . tumult of the ***r*** seas as your
Ps 65:7 . . . . . You quieted the ***r*** oceans

RAGS (n)
clothes usually in poor or ragged condition
Isa 64:6. . . . . are nothing but filthy ***r.***

RAIMENT (KJV)
Exod 12:35 . ***clothing*** and articles of silver
Deut 8:4. . . . your ***clothes*** didn't wear out
Luke 9:29. . . his ***clothes*** became dazzling

RAIN, RAINS (n)
water falling in drops from the sky
Deut 11:14. . will send the ***r-s*** in their
1 Kgs 17:1 . . no dew or ***r*** during the next
1 Kgs 18:1 . . that I will soon send ***r!***
Prov 16:15. . refreshes like a spring ***r.***
Matt 5:45 . . . and he sends ***r*** on the just
Jas 5:17. . . . . earnestly that no ***r*** would fall,
Jude 1:12 . . . land without giving any ***r.***

RAIN (v)
to fall as water in drops from the clouds
Gen 7:4 . . . . And it will ***r*** for forty days

RAINBOW (n)
an arch of colors in the sky caused by light passing through moisture in the air
Gen 9:13 . . . I have placed my ***r*** in the

RAISE, RAISED (v)
to recall from death
see also RESURRECTION
Judg 2:16 . . . the LORD ***r-d*** up judges
Luke 7:22. . . the dead are ***r-d*** to life,
John 6:39 . . . that I should ***r*** them up
Acts 2:32 . . . God ***r-d*** Jesus from the dead,
Acts 24:15 . . that he will ***r*** both the
Rom 1:4 . . . . he was ***r-d*** from the dead
Rom 6:5 . . . . we will also be ***r-d*** to life
Rom 10:9 . . . God ***r-d*** him from the dead,
1 Cor 15:4 . . he was ***r-d*** from the dead
Phil 3:10 . . . mighty power that ***r-d*** him
1 Thes 4:14 . died and was ***r-d*** to life
1 Pet 1:3. . . . because God ***r-d*** Jesus Christ

RALLY (v)
to join in a common cause
Isa 11:10. . . . The nations will ***r*** to him,

RAM, RAMS (n)
a male sheep
Gen 22:13 . . he took the ***r*** and sacrificed
1 Sam 15:22. offering the fat of ***r-s.***
Dan 8:3 . . . . I saw a ***r*** with two long
Mic 6:7. . . . . him thousands of ***r-s*** and ten

RANSOM (n)
price paid or demanded to release someone or something from captivity
Matt 20:28 . . his life as a ***r*** for many.
Mark 10:45 . his life as a ***r*** for many.
1 Pet 1:18. . . that God paid a ***r*** to save

RANSOM, RANSOMED (v)
to deliver especially from sin or its penalty; to free from captivity or punishment by paying a price
see also REDEEM(ED)
Ps 44:26 . . . . Help us! ***R*** us because of
Ps 71:23 . . . . for you have ***r-ed*** me.
Isa 35:10. . . . have been ***r-ed*** by the LORD
Hos 13:14 . . Should I ***r*** them from
Rev 5:9. . . . . your blood has ***r-ed*** people

RAVEN, RAVENS (n)
a large, black, corvine bird
Gen 8:7 . . . . and released a ***r.*** The bird
1 Kgs 17:6 . . The ***r-s*** brought him bread and
Job 38:41 . . . provides food for the ***r-s***
Ps 147:9 . . . . feeds the young ***r-s*** when they
Luke 12:24. . Look at the ***r-s.*** They don't

READ, READING, READS (v)
to receive and interpret letters or symbols by sight
Deut 17:19. . with him and ***r*** it daily
Josh 8:34 . . . Joshua then ***r*** to them
2 Kgs 23:2 . . There the king ***r*** to them
Acts 8:28 . . . carriage, he was ***r-ing*** aloud
2 Cor 3:2 . . . everyone can ***r*** it and
1 Tim 4:13 . . focus on ***r-ing*** the Scriptures
Rev 1:3. . . . . the one who ***r-s*** the words of

READY (adj)
prepared mentally or physically for some experience or action
1 Tim 6:18 . . always being ***r*** to share
1 Pet 3:15. . . always be ***r*** to explain

REAL (adj)
not artificial, fraudulent, or illusory; genuine
1 Kgs 3:26 . . who was the ***r*** mother of
1 Jn 4:2. . . . . Christ came in a ***r*** body,

REALITY (n)
a real event, entity, or state of affairs
Col 2:17 . . . . shadows of the ***r*** yet to come.

REALIZATION (n)
the state of being fully aware of
Mark 5:33 . . trembling at the ***r*** of what

REALIZE, REALIZED, REALIZING (v)
to be fully aware of; to conceive vividly as real
2 Chr 33:13 . Manasseh finally ***r-d*** that
Job 38:18 . . . Do you ***r*** the extent of
Ps 64:9 . . . . . and ***r*** all the amazing things
Song 6:12. . . Before I ***r-d*** it, my strong
Isa 61:9. . . . . Everyone will ***r*** that they are
Heb 13:2 . . . angels without ***r-ing*** it!
Jas 4:4. . . . . . Don't you ***r*** that friendship

REALMS (n)
kingdoms; spheres, domains
Eph 1:3 . . . . in the heavenly ***r*** because we
Eph 2:6 . . . . in the heavenly ***r*** because we

REAP (v)
to harvest or gather; to obtain
see also HARVEST, GATHER
Gal 6:9 . . . . . will ***r*** a harvest of blessing
Jas 3:18. . . . . ***r*** a harvest of righteousness.

REAPERS (KJV)
Ruth 2:3. . . . grain behind the ***harvesters***
2 Kgs 4:18 . . working with the ***harvesters***
Matt 13:30 . . the ***harvesters*** to sort out
Matt 13:39 . . the ***harvesters*** are the angels

REBEL, REBELLED, REBELLING, REBELS (v)
to oppose or disobey one in authority or control
Num 14:9 . . Do not ***r*** against the
Num 27:14 . of Israel ***r-led,*** you failed to
1 Sam 12:14. if you do not ***r*** against the
Ps 78:56 . . . . testing and ***r-ling*** against God
Isa 63:10. . . . But they ***r-led*** against him
Matt 10:21 . . children will ***r*** against their
Rom 13:2. . . So anyone who ***r-s*** against

REBELLION (n)
opposition to one in authority or dominance; defiance
Exod 34:7 . . forgive iniquity, ***r,*** and sin.
Ps 32:5 . . . . . I will confess my ***r*** to the
Ps 39:8 . . . . . Rescue me from my ***r.***
Ps 51:3 . . . . . I recognize my ***r;*** it haunts
Isa 53:5. . . . . was pierced for our ***r,***
Isa 53:8. . . . . for the ***r*** of my people.
Dan 9:24 . . . to finish their ***r,*** to put an
2 Thes 2:3 . . is a great ***r*** against God

REBELLIOUS (adj)
given to or engaged in rebellion
Isa 65:2. . . . . opened my arms to a ***r*** people.
Luke 1:17. . . those who are ***r*** to accept
Rom 10:21 . . were disobedient and ***r.***
1 Tim 1:9 . . . people who are lawless and ***r,***
Titus 1:6. . . . reputation for being wild or ***r.***

REBELS (n)
those who rebel or participate in a rebellion
Ps 51:13 . . . . will teach your ways to ***r,***
Isa 53:12. . . . He was counted among the ***r.***
Luke 22:37. . was counted among the ***r.***
Rom 11:30 . . Gentiles were ***r*** against God,
Rom 11:31 . . they are the ***r,*** and God's

REBUILD, REBUILT (v)
to reconstruct; to restore to a previous state
Ezra 5:2 . . . . again to ***r*** the Temple of God
Neh 2:17 . . . Let us ***r*** the wall of
Ps 102:16 . . . the LORD will ***r*** Jerusalem.
Amos 9:14 . . and they will ***r*** their ruined
Zech 1:16. . . My Temple will be ***r-t,*** says the
Acts 15:16 . . I will ***r*** its ruins and

REBUKE (n)
an expression of strong disapproval; reprimand
see also CORRECT, DISCIPLINE
Prov 17:10 . . A single ***r*** does more for
Prov 27:5. . . An open ***r*** is better than

REBUKE, REBUKED (v)
to criticize sharply; to reprimand
Prov 30:6. . . or he may ***r*** you and expose
Mark 16:14 . He ***r-d*** them for their
Luke 17:3. . . believer sins, ***r*** that person;
2 Tim 4:2. . . Patiently correct, ***r,*** and
Jas 1:5. . . . . . He will not ***r*** you for asking.

RECEIVE, RECEIVED, RECEIVES (v)
to acquire or take possession of; to welcome
Matt 7:8. . . . For everyone who asks, ***r-s.***
Matt 19:17 . . you want to ***r*** eternal life,
John 20:22 . . said, "***R*** the Holy Spirit.
Acts 1:8 . . . . But you will ***r*** power when the
Acts 2:38 . . . Then you will ***r*** the gift of
Acts 8:17 . . . they ***r-d*** the Holy Spirit.
Acts 10:47 . . they have ***r-d*** the Holy
Acts 19:2 . . . Did you ***r*** the Holy Spirit
Rom 8:15. . . Instead, you ***r-d*** God's Spirit
1 Tim 1:16 . . in him and ***r*** eternal life.
Rev 4:11. . . . our God, to ***r*** glory and honor

RECKONING (n)
a settling of accounts
Jer 51:18. . . . On the day of ***r*** they will all

RECOGNIZE, RECOGNIZED (v)
to admit as being lord or sovereign; to acknowledge or take notice of in some definite way; to perceive to be something or someone previously known
1 Chr 16:28 . of the world, ***r*** the LORD,
Ps 96:7 . . . . . of the world, ***r*** the LORD;
Jer 24:7. . . . . give them hearts that ***r*** me
Hos 4:6 . . . . refuse to ***r*** you as my priests.
John 1:26 . . . is someone you do not ***r.***
1 Cor 14:38 . But if you do not ***r*** this,
2 Cor 3:2 . . . read it and ***r*** our good work

RECOMMEND (v)
to endorse; to advise
Eccl 8:15 . . . So I ***r*** having fun, because

RECOMMENDATION (n)
something that expresses commendation
2 Cor 3:1 . . . to bring you letters of ***r,***

RECONCILED, RECONCILING (v)
to restore to friendship or harmony, especially between God and human beings
2 Cor 5:18 . . task of ***r-ing*** people to him.
Eph 2:16 . . . Christ ***r-d*** both groups to God
Col 1:20 . . . . God ***r-d*** everything to himself.
Col 1:22 . . . . now he has ***r-d*** you to himself

RECONCILIATION (n)
the action of reconciling; the state of being reconciled
Prov 14:9 . . . acknowledge it and seek ***r***.
2 Cor 5:19 . . this wonderful message of ***r***.

RECORD (n)
an official body of known or recorded facts about someone
1 Cor 13:5 . . keeps no ***r*** of being wronged.
Col 2:14 . . . . canceled the ***r*** of the charges

RECORDED (v)
to set down in writing
John 20:30 . . to the ones ***r*** in this book.

RED (adj)
of the color red
Exod 15:4 . . are drowned in the ***R*** Sea.
Ps 106:9 . . . . He commanded the ***R*** Sea to
Isa 1:18. . . . . they are ***r*** like crimson,
Isa 63:1. . . . . with his clothing stained ***r***?

REDEDICATE (v)
to devote or commit oneself or one's possessions again
Num 6:12 . . They must ***r*** themselves to

REDEEM, REDEEMED, REDEEMS (v)
to buy back; to save by payment of a ransom; to free from the consequences of sin
see also PURCHASE, RANSOM, RESCUE
Exod 6:6 . . . I will ***r*** you with a powerful
2 Sam 7:23. . have you ***r-ed*** from slavery
Ps 34:22 . . . . the LORD will ***r*** those
Ps 49:15 . . . . God will ***r*** my life.
Ps 74:2 . . . . . the tribe you ***r-ed*** as your own
Ps 103:4 . . . . He ***r-s*** me from death and
Ps 107:2 . . . . Has the LORD ***r-ed*** you?
Ps 130:8 . . . . He himself will ***r*** Israel from
Isa 35:9. . . . . Only the ***r-ed*** will walk
Isa 63:9. . . . . love and mercy he ***r-ed*** them.
Hos 7:13 . . . I wanted to ***r*** them, but they

REDEEMER (n)
one who frees or delivers another from difficulty, danger, or bondage, usually by the payment of a ransom price
Ruth 3:9. . . . for you are my family ***r***.
Ruth 4:14. . . has now provided a ***r*** for
Job 19:25 . . . I know that my ***R*** lives,
Ps 19:14 . . . . LORD, my rock and my ***r***.
Prov 23:11 . . For their ***R*** is strong;
Isa 44:6. . . . . Israel's King and ***R***, the LORD
Isa 48:17. . . . your ***R***, the Holy One of Israel:
Isa 59:20. . . . The ***R*** will come to Jerusalem

REDEMPTION (n)
the act, process, or an instance of redeeming
Ps 130:7 . . . . love. His ***r*** overflows.
Eph 4:30 . . . be saved on the day of ***r***.
Heb 9:12 . . . and secured our ***r*** forever.

REEDS (n)
any of various tall grasses that grow in wet places
Exod 2:5 . . . basket among the ***r***,
Isa 35:7. . . . . ***r*** and rushes will flourish
Isa 58:5. . . . . bowing your heads like ***r***
Ezek 29:6. . . a staff made of ***r***

REFINE, REFINED (v)
to remove impurities from metal; figurative of purifying God's people of sin
Isa 48:10. . . . I have ***r-d*** you in the furnace
Zech 13:9. . . I will ***r*** them like silver

REFINER (n)
someone or something that refines
Mal 3:3. . . . . will sit like a ***r*** of silver,

REFLECT, REFLECTS (v)
to make manifest or apparent; to think quietly and calmly
Ps 119:5 . . . . consistently ***r*** your decrees!
Ps 119:15 . . . and ***r*** on your ways.
Prov 27:19 . . the heart ***r-s*** the real person.
Isa 44:19. . . . never stops to ***r***, "Why, it's
Titus 2:7. . . . Let everything you do ***r*** the

REFRESH, REFRESHED, REFRESHES, REFRESHING (v)
to restore strength and animation to; to replenish, arouse, or stimulate
Prov 9:17 . . . Stolen water is ***r-ing;*** food
Prov 11:25 . . will themselves be ***r-ed***.
Prov 16:15 . . favor ***r-es*** like a spring rain.
Phlm 1:7 . . . has often ***r-ed*** the hearts

REFUGE (n)
shelter or protection from danger or distress
see also FORTRESS, PROTECTION, SHELTER
Deut 33:27 . . eternal God is your ***r***,
2 Sam 22:3 . . He is my ***r***, my savior,
Ps 2:12 . . . . . for all who take ***r*** in him!
Ps 5:11 . . . . . But let all who take ***r*** in you
Ps 17:7 . . . . . those who seek ***r*** from their
Ps 34:8 . . . . . those who take ***r*** in him!
Ps 46:1 . . . . . God is our ***r*** and strength,
Ps 91:2 . . . . . He alone is my ***r***, my place

REFUSE, REFUSED, REFUSING (v)
to show or express unwillingness to do or comply with
Lev 26:15... and ***r-ing*** to obey
Num 14:22 . tested me by ***r-ing*** to listen to
Josh 24:15 .. But if you ***r*** to serve the
Prov 13:19.. fools ***r*** to turn from evil
Eccl 11:10 .. So ***r*** to worry, and keep
Luke 15:29.. never once ***r-d*** to do a single
Rom 14:6... And those who ***r*** to eat
2 Thes 2:10 . because they ***r*** to love
2 Thes 3:14 . of those who ***r*** to obey
Heb 12:25 .. escape when they ***r-d*** to listen

REFUTE (v)
to prove wrong by argument or evidence
Luke 21:15.. be able to reply or ***r*** you!
Acts 9:22 ... couldn't ***r*** his proofs that

REGARDED (v)
to consider and appraise
Ps 106:31 ... has been ***r*** as a righteous

REGENERATION (KJV)
Matt 19:28.. world is ***made new*** and the
Titus 3:5.... giving us a ***new birth*** and new

REGISTERED (v)
to make or secure official entry of in a register
Luke 10:20. . your names are ***r*** in heaven.

REGRET (v)
to be very sorry for
Nah 3:7 .... Does anyone ***r*** your destruction?

REGULAR (adj)
formed, built, arranged, or ordered according to some established rule, law, principle, or type
2 Kgs 25:30 . gave him a ***r*** food allowance

REGULATIONS (n)
authoritative rules dealing with details or procedure
see also LAW(S)
Exod 21:1 .. These are the ***r*** you must
Deut 33:10.. They teach your ***r*** to Jacob;
Ps 119:30 ... determined to live by your ***r.***
Ps 119:43 ... for your ***r*** are my only hope.
Ps 119:120 .. I stand in awe of your ***r.***
Ps 119:164 .. because all your ***r*** are just.
Ps 119:175 .. and may your ***r*** help me.

REIGN, REIGNED, REIGNING, REIGNS (v)
to possess or exercise sovereign power; to rule
Exod 15:18 . The LORD will ***r*** forever
Ps 9:7...... But the LORD ***r-s*** forever,
Ps 29:10.... LORD ***r-s*** as king forever.
Ps 96:10.... The LORD ***r-s!***
Ps 146:10... The LORD will ***r*** forever.
Isa 52:7..... that the God of Israel ***r-s!***
1 Cor 4:8 ... we would be ***r-ing*** with you.
1 Cor 15:25 . For Christ must ***r*** until he
Rev 5:10.... And they will ***r*** on the earth.
Rev 11:15... and he will ***r*** forever
Rev 19:6.... our God, the Almighty, ***r-s.***
Rev 20:4.... and they ***r-ed*** with Christ
Rev 22:5.... And they will ***r*** forever

REIGNS (n)
the time during which one (as a sovereign) rules
Dan 2:44 ... During the ***r*** of those kings,

REJECT, REJECTED, REJECTING, REJECTS (v)
to refuse to accept, consider, submit to, or take for some purpose or use; to refuse to hear, receive, or admit
1 Sam 8:7... me they are ***r-ing,*** not you.
Ps 51:17.... not ***r*** a broken and repentant
Ps 118:22... stone that the builders ***r-ed***
Prov 3:11... My child, don't ***r*** the LORD's
Mal 1:3..... but I ***r-ed*** his brother,
Matt 21:42.. stone that the builders ***r-ed***
Luke 10:16.. who ***r-s*** me is ***r-ing*** God,
John 6:37... I will never ***r*** them.
John 12:48.. But all who ***r*** me and my
Rom 9:13... loved Jacob, but I ***r-ed*** Esau.
1 Thes 4:8 .. teaching but is ***r-ing*** God,
1 Tim 4:4 ... we should not ***r*** any of it
2 Tim 3:5 ... but they will ***r*** the power
Heb 6:6 .... by ***r-ing*** the Son of God, they
1 Pet 2:4.... He was ***r-ed*** by people,
1 Pet 2:7.... stone that the builders ***r-ed***

REJECTION (n)
the action of rejecting
Rom 11:15.. For since their ***r*** meant that

REJOICE, REJOICED, REJOICES, REJOICING (v)
to feel joy or great delight; to gladden
1 Chr 16:31 . glad, and the earth ***r!***
1 Chr 29:17 . ***r*** when you find integrity
Esth 8:17 ... decree arrived, the Jews ***r-d***
Ps 5:11..... who take refuge in you ***r;***
Ps 13:5..... I will ***r*** because you
Ps 35:9..... I will ***r*** in the LORD.
Ps 48:2..... the whole earth ***r-s*** to see it!
Ps 58:10.... The godly will ***r*** when they
Ps 66:6..... There we ***r-d*** in him.
Ps 68:4..... LORD—***r*** in his presence!
Ps 119:14... I have ***r-d*** in your laws

Ps 119:162 . . I *r* in your word like one
Prov 8:31 . . . I *r-d* with the human family!
Prov 17:5 . . . who *r* at the misfortune
Prov 29:2 . . . in authority, the people *r.*
Isa 9:3. . . . . . and its people will *r.*
Isa 35:1. . . . . wasteland will *r* and blossom
Isa 62:5. . . . . *r* over you as a bridegroom *r-s*
Jer 51:48. . . . the heavens and earth will *r,*
Lam 4:21 . . . Are you *r-ing* in the land
Hab 1:15 . . . while they *r* and celebrate?
Zeph 3:17 . . He will *r* over you
Zech 2:10. . . Shout and *r,* O beautiful
Luke 1:14. . . and many will *r* at his birth,
Luke 1:47. . . How my spirit *r-s* in God my
Luke 1:58. . . everyone *r-d* with her.
Luke 10:20. . But don't *r* because evil
Luke 13:17. . but all the people *r-d* at the
Acts 5:41 . . . high council *r-ing* that God
Acts 16:34 . . his entire household *r-d*
1 Cor 13:6 . . *r* about injustice but *r-s*
Phil 2:18 . . . you should *r,* and I will
Phil 3:1 . . . . and sisters, *r* in the Lord.
Phil 4:4 . . . . I say it again—*r!*
Col 2:5 . . . . . I *r* that you are living as
Rev 19:7. . . . Let us be glad and *r,* and

RELATIONSHIP (n)
a state of affairs existing between those having relations or dealings
Rom 5:11 . . . our wonderful new *r* with God
2 Jn 1:9. . . . . teaching has no *r* with God.

RELATIVES (n)
a person connected with another by blood or affinity
Lev 19:17. . . your heart for any of your *r.*
Mark 6:4 . . . among his *r* and his own
Luke 21:16. . parents, brothers, *r,* and
1 Tim 5:8 . . . who won't care for their *r,*

RELEASE (n)
relief or deliverance from restraint, sorrow, suffering, or trouble
Deut 31:10. . the Year of *R,* during the
Job 14:14 . . . eagerly await the *r* of death.

RELEASED (v)
to set free from restraint, confinement, or servitude
Isa 61:1. . . . . that captives will be *r*
Matt 18:27. . and he *r* him and forgave
Matt 27:50. . and he *r* his spirit.
Luke 4:18. . . that captives will be *r,*
John 19:30 . . his head and *r* his spirit.
Rom 7:6 . . . . we have been *r* from the law,
Rom 8:23 . . . bodies to be *r* from sin and

RELENT, RELENTED (v)
to become less severe, harsh, or strict; to give in
Ps 106:45 . . . *r-ed* because of his unfailing
Joel 2:13. . . . eager to *r* and not punish.

RELIABLE (adj)
dependable
1 Chr 9:22 . . they were *r* men.
Prov 13:17. . but a *r* messenger brings
Prov 20:6. . . find one who is truly *r?*
2 Tim 2:2 . . . by many *r* witnesses.

RELIEF (n)
removal or lightening of something oppressive, painful, or distressing
Gen 5:29 . . . he bring us *r* from our work
Ps 94:13 . . . . You give them *r* from troubled

RELIEVED, RELIEVING (v)
to free from a burden; to discharge the bladder or bowels
1 Kgs 18:27 . or is *r-ing* himself.
Acts 20:12 . . and everyone was greatly *r-d.*

RELIGION, RELIGIONS (n)
a personal set or institutionalized system of religious attitudes, beliefs, and practices; the service and worship of God or the supernatural
Matt 6:7. . . . as people of other *r-s* do.
Acts 25:19 . . something about their *r* and
Acts 26:5 . . . the strictest sect of our *r.*
Gal 1:13 . . . . I followed the Jewish *r*—
Jas 1:26. . . . . and your *r* is worthless.

RELIGIOUS (adj)
relating to or manifesting faithful devotion to God or a god
Luke 11:46. . with unbearable *r* demands,
Acts 13:50 . . the influential *r* women and
Jas 1:26. . . . . you claim to be *r* but don't

RELY, RELIED, RELIES (v)
to be dependent
2 Chr 16:8 . . time you *r-ied* on the LORD,
Ps 22:8 . . . . . one who *r-ies* on the LORD?
Ps 33:18 . . . . those who *r* on his unfailing
Prov 11:7. . . for they *r* on their own feeble
Isa 50:10. . . . the LORD and *r* on your God.
2 Cor 1:9 . . . and learned to *r* only on God,

REMAIN, REMAINED, REMAINS (v)
to stay in the same place or with the same person or group; to continue unchanged
2 Kgs 18:6 . . He *r-ed* faithful to the LORD
John 15:7 . . . But if you *r* in me and my
John 15:9 . . . loved me. *R* in my love.
Rom 11:5. . . of Israel have *r-ed* faithful

2 Tim 2:13 . . unfaithful, he ***r-s*** faithful,
2 Tim 3:14 . . But you must ***r*** faithful
2 Tim 4:7 . . . and I have ***r-ed*** faithful.
Heb 7:3 . . . . He ***r-s*** a priest forever,
Heb 10:32 . . how you ***r-ed*** faithful even
Heb 13:4 . . . and ***r*** faithful to one another
1 Pet 1:25 . . . word of the Lord ***r-s***
1 Jn 2:27 . . . . ***r*** in fellowship with Christ.

REMARRY, REMARRIES (v)
to marry again after divorce or being widowed
Rom 7:3 . . . . commit adultery when she ***r-ies.***
1 Tim 5:11 . . Christ and they will want to ***r.***

REMEMBER, REMEMBERED, REMEMBERING, REMEMBERS (v)
to bring to mind or think of again; to keep in mind for attention or consideration; to retain in the memory
Gen 9:15 . . . I will ***r*** my covenant with
Exod 2:24 . . ***r-ed*** his covenant promise
1 Chr 16:12 . ***R*** the wonders he has
Ps 49:13 . . . . though they are ***r-ed*** as being
Ps 103:14 . . . he ***r-s*** we are only dust.
Ps 106:45 . . . ***r-ed*** his covenant with them
Ps 111:5 . . . . he always ***r-s*** his covenant.
Ps 136:23 . . . He ***r-ed*** us in our weakness.
Jer 31:34. . . . never again ***r*** their sins.
Jer 32:20. . . . things still ***r-ed*** to this day!
Hab 3:2 . . . . in your anger, ***r*** your mercy.
Matt 26:13 . . will be ***r-ed*** and discussed.
Luke 1:72. . . ***r-ing*** his sacred covenant—
Luke 22:19. . Do this to ***r*** me.
1 Cor 11:24 . Do this to ***r*** me.
2 Tim 2:8 . . . Always ***r*** that Jesus
Heb 8:12 . . . never again ***r*** their sins.
2 Pet 1:15. . . you always ***r*** these things

REMIND, REMINDING (v)
to cause to remember
John 14:26 . . will ***r*** you of everything
2 Pet 1:12. . . I will always ***r*** you about
2 Pet 1:13. . . keep on ***r-ing*** you as long

REMINDER, REMINDERS (n)
something that causes to remember
Deut 6:8. . . . them on your forehead as ***r-s.***
Prov 7:3. . . . Tie them on your fingers as a ***r.***

REMISSION (KJV)
Matt 26:28 . . as a sacrifice ***to forgive***
Acts 10:43 . . sins ***forgiven*** through his
Rom 3:25 . . . he ***held back and did not punish***
Heb 9:22 . . . blood, there is no ***forgiveness***

REMNANT (n)
a usually small part, member, or trace remaining; the few people left who gathered together after God scattered them into exile
Ezra 9:8 . . . . few of us to survive as a ***r.***
Isa 6:13. . . . . a tenth—a ***r***—survive,
Isa 11:11. . . . to bring back the ***r*** of his
Jer 23:3. . . . . gather together the ***r*** of my
Zech 8:12. . . will cause the ***r*** in Judah

REMOVE, REMOVED (v)
to get rid of; to eliminate
Ps 103:12 . . . He has ***r-d*** our sins as far
Isa 6:7. . . . . . Now your guilt is ***r-d,*** and your
1 Cor 5:13 . . You must ***r*** the evil person

RENEW, RENEWED, RENEWS (v)
to restore to freshness, vigor, or perfection; to make new spiritually
Ps 23:3 . . . . . He ***r-s*** my strength.
Ps 51:10 . . . . ***R*** a loyal spirit within me.
Isa 57:10. . . . Desire gave you ***r-ed*** strength,
Eph 4:23 . . . let the Spirit ***r*** your thoughts
Col 3:10 . . . . be ***r-ed*** as you learn to know

RENOWN (KJV)
Gen 6:4 . . . . the heroes and ***famous*** warriors
Isa 14:20. . . . will never again ***receive honor***
Ezek 16:14 . . ***fame*** soon spread
Ezek 39:13 . . a ***glorious victory*** for Israel

REPAY, REPAYS (v)
to give or inflict in return or requital; to pay back (money)
Ps 62:12 . . . . Surely you ***r*** all people
Prov 17:13 . . If you ***r*** good with evil,
Prov 19:17 . . and he will ***r*** you!
Jer 51:6. . . . . he will ***r*** her in full.
Jer 51:56. . . . he always ***r-s*** in full.
Luke 6:34. . . to those who can ***r*** you,
Luke 7:42. . . neither of them could ***r*** him,
1 Tim 5:4 . . . ***r*** their parents by taking
1 Pet 3:9. . . . Don't ***r*** evil for evil.

REPENT, REPENTED, REPENTING, REPENTS (v)
to turn from sin and change one's heart and behavior; to feel regret and contrition
Matt 3:2. . . . ***R*** of your sins and turn
Matt 3:8. . . . that you have ***r-ed*** of your sins
Matt 4:17. . . began to preach, "***R*** of your
Matt 11:21 . . people would have ***r-ed*** of
Luke 3:8. . . . that you have ***r-ed*** of your sins
Luke 15:7. . . sinner who ***r-s*** and returns
Luke 15:10. . when even one sinner ***r-s.***

Acts 2:38 . . . you must ***r*** of your sins
Acts 17:30 . . everywhere to ***r*** of their sins
Acts 20:21 . . necessity of ***r-ing*** from sin
Heb 6:1 . . . . importance of ***r-ing*** from evil
2 Pet 3:9. . . . but wants everyone to ***r.***
Rev 2:5. . . . . If you don't ***r,*** I will come

REPENTANCE (n)
a turning away from sin, disobedience, or rebellion, and a turning back to God
1 Kgs 8:47 . . to you in ***r*** and pray,
Job 42:6 . . . . dust and ashes to show my ***r.***
Luke 17:3. . . if there is ***r,*** forgive.
2 Cor 7:10 . . sorrow, which lacks ***r,***

REPENTANT (adj)
penitent; expressive of repentance
see also CONTRITE
Ps 51:17 . . . . a broken and ***r*** heart, O God.

REPORT (n)
a usually detailed account or statement
Luke 16:2. . . Get your ***r*** in order,

REPRESENTATIVE (n)
one that represents another as an agent or delegate usually being invested with the authority of the principal
Col 3:17 . . . . do it as a ***r*** of the Lord

REPRIMAND, REPRIMANDED (v)
to reprove sharply or censure formally
see also CORRECT, REBUKE
1 Tim 5:20 . . sin should be ***r-ed*** in front
Titus 1:13. . . So ***r*** them sternly to make

REPROACH (n)
a cause or occasion of blame, discredit, or disgrace
1 Tim 3:2 . . . man whose life is above ***r.***

REPUTATION (n)
overall quality or character as seen or judged by people in general
see also NAME
Ps 109:21 . . . the sake of your own ***r!***
Prov 3:4. . . . you will earn a good ***r.***
Prov 22:1 . . . Choose a good ***r*** over great
Eccl 7:1 . . . . A good ***r*** is more valuable
1 Tim 3:2 . . . wisely, and have a good ***r.***
Heb 11:39 . . good ***r*** because of their

REQUIRE, REQUIRED, REQUIRES (v)
to demand as necessary or essential; to feel or be obliged
Ps 40:6 . . . . . you don't ***r*** burnt offerings
Mic 6:8. . . . . this is what he ***r-s*** of you:
Luke 12:48. . much will be ***r-d*** in return;
Luke 23:56. . they rested as ***r-d*** by the law.
Rom 1:32. . . God's justice ***r-s*** that those
Heb 8:3 . . . . high priest is ***r-d*** to offer

REQUIREMENTS (n)
something required; condition
Rom 13:8 . . . will fulfill the ***r*** of God's
Rom 13:10 . . love fulfills the ***r*** of God's

RESCUE, RESCUED, RESCUES, RESCUING (v)
to save or deliver
see also REDEEM, SAVE
2 Kgs 13:5 . . someone to ***r*** the Israelites
Ps 9:14 . . . . . rejoice that you have ***r-d*** me.
Ps 17:7 . . . . . mighty power you ***r*** those who
Ps 22:8 . . . . . let the LORD ***r*** him!
Ps 31:2. . . . . listen to me; ***r*** me quickly.
Ps 37:39 . . . . The LORD ***r-s*** the godly;
Ps 37:40 . . . . LORD helps them, ***r-ing*** them
Ps 68:20 . . . . The Sovereign LORD ***r-s*** us
Ps 72:12 . . . . He will ***r*** the poor when
Ps 145:19 . . . cries for help and ***r-s*** them.
Prov 11:8. . . godly are ***r-d*** from trouble,
Isa 56:1. . . . . coming soon to ***r*** you and
Dan 6:27 . . . He ***r-s*** and saves his people;
Zech 8:7. . . . that I will ***r*** my people from
Matt 6:13. . . but ***r*** us from the evil one.
Rom 11:26 . . The one who ***r-s*** will come
2 Cor 1:10 . . And he did ***r*** us from mortal
Gal 1:4 . . . . . in order to ***r*** us from this
Gal 3:13 . . . . But Christ has ***r-d*** us from the
Col 1:13 . . . . For he has ***r-d*** us from the
1 Thes 1:10 . the one who has ***r-d*** us
2 Pet 2:9. . . . knows how to ***r*** godly people

RESCUER (n)
one who frees from confinement, danger, or evil
Judg 3:9 . . . . raised up a ***r*** to save them.
Judg 3:15. . . raised up a ***r*** to save them.
Ps 144:2 . . . . my tower of safety, my ***r.***

RESIST (v)
to withstand the force or effect of; to counteract or defeat
Dan 11:32 . . will be strong and will ***r*** him.
Matt 5:39. . . do not ***r*** an evil person!
Jas 4:7. . . . . . ***R*** the devil, and he will flee

RESPECT (n)
a high or special regard; esteem
see also AWE, REVERENCE
Prov 11:16 . . A gracious woman gains ***r,***
Mal 1:6. . . . . the honor and ***r*** I deserve?
Titus 2:2. . . . be worthy of ***r,*** and to live

RESPECT, RESPECTED (v)
to consider worthy of high regard; to esteem
Eph 5:33 . . . the wife must ***r*** her husband.
1 Tim 3:4 . . . children who ***r*** and obey him.
1 Tim 3:8 . . . deacons must be well ***r-ed***
1 Tim 3:11 . . their wives must be ***r-ed***
1 Tim 5:17 . . work well should be ***r-ed***
1 Pet 2:17. . . Fear God, and ***r*** the king.

RESPECTFUL (adj)
marked by or showing respect or deference
1 Pet 3:16. . . a gentle and ***r*** way.

RESPONSIBILITY (n)
moral, legal, or mental accountability
1 Cor 5:12 . . certainly is your ***r*** to judge
1 Tim 5:16 . . not put the ***r*** on the church.

RESPONSIBLE (adj)
marked by or involving responsibility or accountability; liable to be called to account as the primary cause, motive, or agent
Exod 32:34 . hold them ***r*** for their sins.
Num 1:53 . . The Levites are ***r*** to stand
Ezek 33:6. . . he is ***r*** for their captivity.
Jonah 1:14 . . And don't hold us ***r*** for his
Gal 6:5 . . . . . For we are each ***r*** for our own

REST (n)
freedom from activity or labor; peace of mind or spirit; repose, sleep
see also SABBATH
Exod 31:15 . day of complete ***r,*** a holy
Exod 33:14 . and I will give you ***r***—
Ps 91:1 . . . . . Most High will find ***r*** in the
Ps 127:2. . . . for God gives ***r*** to his loved
Jer 6:16. . . . . you will find ***r*** for your
Matt 11:28. . and I will give you ***r.***
2 Thes 1:7 . . God will provide ***r*** for you
Heb 4:3 . . . . even though this ***r*** has been
Heb 4:9 . . . . a special ***r*** still waiting
Heb 4:10 . . . who have entered into God's ***r***

REST, RESTED, RESTING, RESTS (v)
to sit or lie on; to cease from action or motion; to take relief or respite
Gen 2:2 . . . . of creation, so he ***r-ed*** from all
Ps 16:9 . . . . . My body ***r-s*** in safety.
Ps 23:2 . . . . . He lets me ***r*** in green
Isa 11:2. . . . . Spirit of the Lord will ***r***
Isa 30:15. . . . and ***r-ing*** in me will you
John 1:32 . . . from heaven and ***r-ing*** upon
Heb 4:4 . . . . seventh day God ***r-ed*** from all
Rev 14:13. . . will ***r*** from their hard work;

RESTITUTION (n)
a making good of or giving an equivalent for some injury
Lev 6:5. . . . . You must make ***r*** by paying
Num 5:8 . . . relatives to whom ***r*** can be

RESTLESS (adj)
continuously moving
Isa 57:20. . . . are like the ***r*** sea, which is

RESTORE, RESTORED, RESTORES, RESTORING (v)
to give back, return; to renew
Ps 14:7 . . . . . When the Lord ***r-s*** his people,
Ps 30:2 . . . . . and you ***r-d*** my health.
Isa 58:11. . . . dry and ***r-ing*** your strength.
Jer 30:3. . . . . when I will ***r*** the fortunes of
Jer 30:18. . . . from captivity and ***r*** their
Jer 31:18. . . . Turn me again to you and ***r***
Hos 6:2 . . . . a short time he will ***r*** us,
Nah 2:2 . . . . but he will ***r*** its splendor.
Rom 5:10. . . friendship with God was ***r-d***
1 Pet 5:10. . . will ***r,*** support, and strengthen

RESURRECTION (n)
the state of one risen from the dead; the rising again to life of all the human dead before the final judgment
see also RAISE, RISE
Matt 27:53. . cemetery after Jesus' ***r,***
Mark 12:23 . will she be in the ***r?***
Luke 20:36. . children of the ***r.***
John 11:25 . . I am the ***r*** and the life.
Acts 1:22 . . . as a witness of Jesus' ***r.***
Acts 2:31 . . . speaking of the Messiah's ***r.***
Acts 4:2 . . . . there is a ***r*** of the dead.
Acts 4:33 . . . powerfully to the ***r*** of
Acts 17:32 . . Paul speak about the ***r*** of
1 Cor 15:13 . if there is no ***r*** of the
1 Cor 15:42 . way with the ***r*** of the dead.
Phil 3:11 . . . experience the ***r*** from the
2 Tim 2:18 . . claiming that the ***r*** of the
Heb 6:2 . . . . of hands, the ***r*** of the dead,
Heb 11:35 . . a better life after the ***r.***
1 Pet 3:21. . . because of the ***r*** of Jesus
Rev 20:5. . . . This is the first ***r.***

RETALIATE (v)
to repay (as an injury) in kind; to get revenge
1 Pet 2:23. . . He did not ***r*** when he

RETURN, RETURNED, RETURNING, RETURNS (v)
to go or come back again; to go back in thought, practice, or condition; to repent
2 Sam 12:23. but he cannot ***r*** to me.

2 Chr 30:9 . . if you ***r*** to the LORD,
Neh 1:9 . . . . But if you ***r*** to me and obey
Ps 35:13 . . . . my prayers ***r-ed*** unanswered.
Ps 51:13 . . . . and they will ***r*** to you.
Ps 126:6 . . . . they sing as they ***r*** with the
Isa 52:8. . . . . the LORD ***r-ing*** to Jerusalem.
Jer 24:7. . . . . for they will ***r*** to me
Hos 6:1 . . . . let us ***r*** to the LORD.
Amos 4:6. . . you would not ***r*** to me,
Matt 24:46 . . If the master ***r-s*** and finds

REVEAL, REVEALED (v)
to make known through divine inspiration; to make (something secret or hidden) publicly or generally known; to display
Exod 6:3 . . . did not ***r*** my name, Yahweh,
Deut 29:29. . all that he has ***r-ed*** to us,
Isa 40:5. . . . . the LORD will be ***r-ed,***
Isa 53:1. . . . . the LORD ***r-ed*** his powerful
Matt 10:26 . . is covered will be ***r-ed,***
Matt 11:27. . Son chooses to ***r*** him.
Luke 2:32. . . He is a light to ***r*** God
John 12:38 . . the LORD ***r-ed*** his powerful
John 14:21 . . love them and ***r*** myself
John 17:6 . . . I have ***r-ed*** you to the
Rom 8:18 . . . glory he will ***r*** to us
Rom 16:25 . . Christ has ***r-ed*** his plan
1 Cor 2:10 . . that God ***r-ed*** these things
Gal 1:16 . . . . to ***r*** his Son to me so that
Gal 2:2 . . . . . because God ***r-ed*** to me
Eph 3:3 . . . . himself ***r-ed*** his mysterious
Col 1:26 . . . . it has been ***r-ed*** to God's
2 Thes 2:3 . . man of lawlessness is ***r-ed***
Titus 2:13. . . Christ, will be ***r-ed.***
Heb 9:8 . . . . the Holy Spirit ***r-ed*** that
1 Pet 1:7. . . . when Jesus Christ is ***r-ed***

REVELATION, REVELATIONS (n)
something that is revealed by God to humans; an act of revealing or communicating divine truth
1 Cor 14:6 . . bring you a ***r*** or some
1 Cor 14:30 . person receives a ***r*** from
2 Cor 12:1 . . visions and ***r-s*** from the
2 Cor 12:7 . . wonderful ***r-s*** from God.
Gal 1:12. . . . by direct ***r*** from Jesus
Rev 1:1. . . . . This is a ***r*** from Jesus

REVELRY (n)
noisy partying or merrymaking
Exod 32:6 . . they indulged in pagan ***r.***
1 Cor 10:7 . . they indulged in pagan ***r.***

REVENGE (n)
an act or instance of retaliating in order to get even
Lev 19:18. . . Do not seek ***r*** or bear
Num 31:3 . . war of ***r*** against Midian.
Deut 32:35. . I will take ***r;*** I will
Josh 20:3 . . . relatives seeking ***r*** for
Judg 20:10. . will take ***r*** on Gibeah
Isa 34:8. . . . . day of the LORD's ***r,***
Heb 10:30 . . I will take ***r.*** I will

REVERENCE (n)
profound, adoring, awed respect
see also AWE, FEAR, RESPECT
Lev 19:30. . . of rest, and show ***r*** toward
Job 15:4 . . . . fear of God, no ***r*** for him?
Job 37:24 . . . who are wise show him ***r.***
Eph 5:21 . . . another out of ***r*** for Christ.
Heb 5:7 . . . . of his deep ***r*** for God.

REVERENT (adj)
expressing or characterized by reverence; worshipful
Col 3:22. . . . because of your ***r*** fear
1 Pet 1:17. . . must live in ***r*** fear
1 Pet 3:2. . . . your pure and ***r*** lives.

REVIVE, REVIVES, REVIVING (v)
to become active or flourishing again; to restore from a depressed, inactive, or unused state
Ps 19:7 . . . . . are perfect, ***r-ing*** the soul.
Ps 85:6 . . . . . Won't you ***r*** us again,
Ps 119:25 . . . lie in the dust; ***r*** me
Ps 119:50 . . . Your promise ***r-s*** me;
Prov 25:13. . They ***r*** the spirit of

REVOLUTIONARIES (n)
those who engage in a revolution
Mark 15:27 . Two ***r*** were crucified with

REWARD, REWARDS (n)
something that is given in return for good or evil done or received or that is offered or given for some service or attainment
Gen 15:1 . . . and your ***r*** will be
1 Sam 26:23. gives his own ***r*** for doing
Prov 12:14. . and hard work brings ***r-s.***
Isa 49:4. . . . . I will trust God for my ***r.***
Matt 5:12. . . For a great ***r*** awaits you
Matt 6:5. . . . all the ***r*** they will ever
Luke 6:23. . . For a great ***r*** awaits you
Luke 6:35. . . your ***r*** from heaven will
Phil 4:17 . . . you to receive a ***r*** for your
1 Thes 2:19 . be our proud ***r*** and crown
Heb 10:35 . . the great ***r*** it brings you!
1 Pet 1:9. . . . The ***r*** for trusting him

REWARD, REWARDED, REWARDS (v)
to give a reward to or for; to recompense
2 Sam 22:21 . The LORD ***r-ed*** me for
Prov 13:21 . . while blessings ***r*** the
Prov 25:22 . . the LORD will ***r*** you.
Jer 31:16. . . . for I will ***r*** you," says
Matt 6:18 . . . sees everything, will ***r*** you.
Luke 12:37. . for his return will be ***r-ed.***
Luke 14:14. . God will ***r*** you for
1 Cor 3:8 . . . both will be ***r-ed*** for their
Eph 6:8 . . . . the Lord will ***r*** each one
1 Tim 3:13 . . will be ***r-ed*** with respect
Heb 11:6 . . . that he ***r-s*** those who
Rev 11:18. . . the dead and ***r*** your servants

RICH (adj)
having abundant possessions and especially material wealth
Job 34:19 . . . no more attention to the ***r***
Ps 49:16 . . . . the wicked grow ***r*** and
Prov 10:4. . . poor; hard workers get ***r.***
Prov 11:18 . . Evil people get ***r*** for
Prov 13:7. . . are poor pretend to be ***r;***
Prov 21:17 . . and luxury will never be ***r.***
Prov 22:2. . . The ***r*** and poor have this
Prov 23:4. . . yourself out trying to get ***r.***
Prov 28:22 . . Greedy people try to get ***r***
Eccl 5:12 . . . But the ***r*** seldom get a
Isa 53:9. . . . . put in a ***r*** man's grave.
Matt 19:23 . . hard for a ***r*** person to enter
Luke 1:53. . . and sent the ***r*** away with
Luke 6:24. . . you who are ***r,*** for you have
Luke 16:1. . . was a certain ***r*** man who had
Luke 21:1. . . watched the ***r*** people
2 Cor 8:9 . . . Though he was ***r,*** yet for your
1 Tim 6:9 . . . who long to be ***r*** fall into
1 Tim 6:17 . . who are ***r*** in this world
Jas 1:10. . . . . those who are ***r*** should boast
Jas 2:3. . . . . . seat to the ***r*** person, but you
Jas 5:1. . . . . . Look here, you ***r*** people:

RICHES (n)
things that make one rich; wealth
see also MONEY, POSSESSIONS, TREASURE(S), WEALTH
2 Chr 1:11 . . ask for wealth, ***r,*** fame,
Ps 49:6 . . . . . wealth and boast of great ***r.***
Prov 27:24 . . for ***r*** don't last forever,
Eccl 5:13 . . . Hoarding ***r*** harms the
Jer 9:23. . . . . rich boast in their ***r.***
Luke 8:14. . . cares and ***r*** and pleasures
Rom 11:33 . . great are God's ***r*** and
2 Cor 6:10 . . give spiritual ***r*** to others.
Col 1:27 . . . . know that the ***r*** and glory

RIDER (n)
one who sits and travels on the back of an animal
Rev 6:2. . . . . Its ***r*** carried a bow, and a
Rev 19:11. . . Its ***r*** was named Faithful and

RIDICULED, RIDICULING (v)
to make fun of
2 Kgs 19:22 . you been defying and ***r-ing?***
1 Cor 4:10 . . are honored, but we are ***r.***

RIDING (v)
to sit and travel on the back of an animal that one directs
Zech 9:9. . . . is humble, ***r*** on a donkey—
Matt 21:5. . . is humble, ***r*** on a donkey—

RIGHT (adj)
being in accordance with what is good, just, or proper; being in a correct or proper state; located opposite of left; acting or judging in accordance with truth or fact
see also JUST, JUSTIFY, RIGHTEOUS, UPRIGHT
Gen 4:7 . . . . do what is ***r,*** then watch out!
Gen 18:19 . . by doing what is ***r*** and just.
Exod 15:26 . do what is ***r*** in his sight,
Num 25:13 . making them ***r*** with me.
Deut 6:18. . . Do what is ***r*** and good
Deut 25:1. . . that one is ***r*** and the other
Judg 17:6. . . whatever seemed ***r*** in their
1 Sam 12:23. what is good and ***r.***
1 Kgs 3:9 . . . difference between ***r*** and
2 Chr 12:6 . . The LORD is ***r*** in doing
Ps 19:8 . . . . . LORD are ***r,*** bringing joy
Ps 24:5 . . . . . have a ***r*** relationship with
Ps 25:8 . . . . . does what is ***r;*** he shows the
Ps 37:30 . . . . they teach ***r*** from wrong.
Ps 64:10 . . . . do what is ***r*** will praise him.
Ps 71:2 . . . . . do what is ***r.*** Turn your ear
Ps 84:11 . . . . from those who do what is ***r.***
Ps 97:11 . . . . on those whose hearts are ***r.***
Ps 106:3 . . . . and always do what is ***r.***
Ps 119:144 . . laws are always ***r;*** help me
Prov 1:3. . . . do what is ***r,*** just, and fair.
Prov 2:13. . . men turn from the ***r*** way
Prov 14:2. . . who follow the ***r*** path
Prov 14:12 . . person that seems ***r,*** but
Prov 15:21 . . stays on the ***r*** path.
Prov 15:23 . . to say the ***r*** thing at the
Prov 18:17 . . in court sounds ***r***—until
Eccl 8:5 . . . . and a way to do what is ***r,***
Eccl 9:11 . . . being in the ***r*** place at the
Isa 7:15. . . . . choose what is ***r*** and reject
Isa 16:5. . . . . be eager to do what is ***r.***
Isa 26:7. . . . . who does what is ***r,*** and you
Jer 23:5. . . . . is just and ***r*** throughout the

Ezek 18:5. . . and does what is just and ***r***.
Ezek 18:21. . and do what is just and ***r***,
Hos 14:9 . . . are true and ***r***, and righteous
Mic 3:1. . . . . to know ***r*** from wrong,
Mic 6:8. . . . . do what is ***r***, to love mercy,
Zeph 2:3 . . . to do what is ***r*** and to live
Matt 6:3. . . . hand know what your ***r*** hand
Matt 22:44. . of honor at my ***r*** hand until
Acts 2:34 . . . the place of honor at my ***r*** hand
Acts 7:55 . . . honor at God's ***r*** hand.
Acts 13:39 . . is declared ***r*** with God—
Rom 1:17. . . God makes us ***r*** in his sight.
Rom 2:13. . . doesn't make us ***r*** with God.
Rom 3:4. . . . will be proved ***r*** in what you
Rom 3:20. . . ever be made ***r*** with God by
Rom 3:22. . . We are made ***r*** with God by
Rom 3:28. . . So we are made ***r*** with God
Rom 3:30. . . makes people ***r*** with himself
Rom 4:13. . . but on a ***r*** relationship with
Rom 4:25. . . life to make us ***r*** with God.
Rom 5:1. . . . we have been made ***r*** in God's
Rom 5:16. . . being made ***r*** with God,
Rom 6:13. . . to do what is ***r*** for the glory
Rom 8:10. . . have been made ***r*** with God.
Rom 8:30. . . given them ***r*** standing,
Rom 9:30. . . they were made ***r*** with God.
Rom 10:3. . . way of getting ***r*** with God by
Rom 10:10. . you are made ***r*** with God,
1 Cor 6:11 . . you were made ***r*** with God
2 Cor 3:9 . . . which makes us ***r*** with God!
2 Cor 5:21 . . be made ***r*** with God
Gal 2:16. . . . person is made ***r*** with God by
Gal 2:17. . . . to be made ***r*** with God through
Gal 2:21. . . . law could make us ***r*** with God,
Gal 3:11. . . . can be made ***r*** with God by
Gal 3:21. . . . could be made ***r*** with God by
Gal 3:24. . . . could be made ***r*** with God
Gal 5:4. . . . . to make yourselves ***r*** with God
Eph 5:9 . . . . what is good and ***r*** and true.
Phil 4:8 . . . . honorable, and ***r***, and pure,
2 Tim 3:16 . . teaches us to do what is ***r***.
Heb 2:10 . . . it was only ***r*** that he should
Heb 12:11 . . harvest of ***r*** living for those
Jas 2:24. . . . . are shown to be ***r*** with God by
1 Jn 2:29. . . . who do what is ***r*** are God's

RIGHT, RIGHTS (n)

correct or moral behavior; something to which one has a just claim

Job 27:2 . . . . has taken away my ***r-s***, by
Ps 25:9. . . . . in doing ***r***, teaching them his
Ps 34:15. . . . those who do ***r***; his ears are
Ps 82:3. . . . . the ***r-s*** of the oppressed
Prov 29:7. . . about the ***r-s*** of the poor;
Isa 1:17. . . . . Fight for the ***r-s*** of widows.
Isa 10:2. . . . . and deny the ***r-s*** of the needy
Lam 3:35 . . . others of their ***r-s*** in
Matt 5:10. . . for doing ***r***, for the Kingdom
John 1:12. . . he gave the ***r*** to become
Rom 9:21. . . he have a ***r*** to use the same
1 Cor 9:4 . . . have the ***r*** to live in your
1 Pet 3:12. . . those who do ***r***, and his ears

RIGHTEOUS (adj)

acting in accord with divine or moral law; free from guilt or sin; morally right or justifiable

see also JUST, JUSTIFY, RIGHT, UPRIGHT

Gen 6:9 . . . . Noah was a ***r*** man, the only
Gen 15:6 . . . counted him as ***r*** because of
Gen 18:23 . . sweep away both the ***r*** and
Ps 7:8. . . . . . Declare me ***r***, O LORD, for
Ps 17:15. . . . Because I am ***r***, I will see
Ps 106:31. . . regarded as a ***r*** man ever
Ps 119:7. . . . I learn your ***r*** regulations,
Ps 119:137. . O LORD, you are ***r***,
Ps 145:17. . . The LORD is ***r*** in everything
Prov 4:18. . . The way of the ***r*** is like the
Prov 9:9. . . . Teach the ***r***, and they
Prov 29:6. . . but the ***r*** escape, shouting
Isa 26:2. . . . . to all who are ***r***; allow the
Isa 42:21. . . . Because he is ***r***, the LORD
Isa 64:6. . . . . we display our ***r*** deeds,
Jer 11:20. . . . you make ***r*** judgments, and
Jer 23:5. . . . . raise up a ***r*** descendant from
Ezek 3:20. . . None of their ***r*** acts will be
Amos 5:24. . river of ***r*** living.
Hab 2:4 . . . . But the ***r*** will live
Mal 3:18. . . . between the ***r*** and the wicked,
Matt 9:13. . . think they are ***r***, but those
Matt 13:43. . Then the ***r*** will shine
Matt 25:37. . Then these ***r*** ones will
Luke 1:6. . . . and Elizabeth were ***r*** in God's
Luke 16:15. . like to appear ***r*** in public,
Rom 1:17. . . faith that a ***r*** person has
Rom 3:5. . . . people see how ***r*** God is.
Rom 3:10. . . No one is ***r***—not even one.
Rom 4:3. . . . counted him as ***r*** because of
Rom 4:6. . . . who are declared ***r*** without
Rom 4:22. . . God counted him as ***r***.
Rom 6:19. . . be slaves to ***r*** living so that
Gal 3:6. . . . . counted him as ***r*** because of
Eph 4:24 . . . like God—truly ***r*** and holy.
Phil 1:11 . . . salvation—the ***r*** character
2 Tim 2:22. . Instead, pursue ***r*** living,
Titus 3:7. . . . he declared us ***r*** and gave us
Jas 2:23. . . . . counted him as ***r*** because of
Jas 5:16. . . . . prayer of a ***r*** person has
1 Jn 2:1. . . . . the one who is truly ***r***.
1 Jn 3:7. . . . . that they are ***r***, even as

RIGHTEOUSNESS (n)
the state or quality of being righteous
see also GODLINESS, JUSTICE
Ps 36:6 . . . . . Your *r* is like the mighty
Ps 71:15 . . . . tell everyone about your *r.*
Ps 85:10 . . . . *R* and peace have kissed!
Ps 98:2 . . . . . has revealed his *r* to every
Ps 111:3 . . . . His *r* never fails.
Prov 21:21 . . Whoever pursues *r* and
Isa 11:5. . . . . He will wear *r* like a belt
Isa 42:6. . . . . you to demonstrate my *r.*
Isa 45:8. . . . . so salvation and *r* can sprout
Isa 56:1. . . . . to display my *r* among you.
Isa 59:17. . . . He put on *r* as his body
Jer 9:24. . . . . brings justice and *r* to the
Jer 23:6. . . . . LORD Is Our *R.*
Mic 7:9. . . . . and I will see his *r.*
Mal 4:2. . . . . the Sun of *R* will rise
Matt 5:20 . . . unless your *r* is better
John 16:8 . . . and of God's *r,* and of the
Acts 24:25 . . about *r* and self-control
Rom 3:26 . . . to demonstrate his *r,* for he
Rom 5:18 . . . one act of *r* brings a right
2 Cor 6:7 . . . the weapons of *r* in the
Eph 6:14 . . . the body armor of God's *r.*
Phil 3:6 . . . . And as for *r,* I obeyed the
2 Tim 4:8 . . . the crown of *r,* which
Heb 11:7 . . . he received the *r* that comes
Jas 3:18. . . . . and reap a harvest of *r.*
2 Pet 3:13. . . filled with God's *r.*

RIPE (adj)
fully grown and developed
John 4:35 . . . are already *r* for harvest.
Rev 14:15. . . the crop on earth is *r.*

RISE, RISEN, RISES (v)
to ascend or extend above other objects; to return from death; to assume an upright position
see also RESURRECTION
Num 24:17 . A star will *r* from Jacob;
Isa 26:19. . . . bodies will *r* again!
Mal 4:2. . . . . of Righteousness will *r* with
Matt 22:30 . . when the dead *r,* they will
Matt 27:63 . . I will *r* from the dead.
Matt 28:6 . . . He is *r-n* from the dead,
Mark 8:31 . . later he would *r* from the
Mark 16:6 . . He is *r-n* from the dead!
Luke 18:33. . day he will *r* again.
Luke 24:34. . The Lord has really *r-n!*
John 5:29 . . . and they will *r* again.
John 11:24 . . when everyone else *r-s,* at
John 20:9 . . . said Jesus must *r* from the
Acts 17:3 . . . must suffer and *r* from the
1 Thes 4:16 . have died will *r* from

RIVER (n)
a natural stream of water; large or overwhelming quantities
Isa 66:12. . . . give Jerusalem a *r* of peace
Amos 5:24. . an endless *r* of righteous
Ezek 47:8. . . "This *r* flows east through
Rev 22:1. . . . showed me a *r* with the water

RIVERBANK (n)
the ground serving as an edge of a river
Ps 1:3 . . . . . . along the *r,* bearing fruit

ROAD (n)
an open way for vehicles, persons, and animals; a route or way to an end, conclusion, or circumstance
Ps 25:4 . . . . . point out the *r* for me to
Prov 22:5. . . treacherous *r;* whoever values
Isa 35:8. . . . . And a great *r* will go through
Matt 3:3 . . . . Clear the *r* for him!

ROARING (adj)
making or characterized by a sound resembling a roar
1 Pet 5:8. . . . around like a *r* lion, looking

ROB (v)
to steal from by force
Ezek 22:29. . oppress the poor, *r* the needy,

ROBBERS (n)
one who steals usually by violence or threat
John 10:8 . . . before me were thieves and *r.*

ROBBERY (n)
the act or practice of stealing by violence or threat
Isa 61:8. . . . . I hate *r* and wrongdoing.

ROBE (n)
a long, flowing outer garment
Gen 37:3 . . . for Joseph—a beautiful *r.*
Isa 6:1. . . . . . the train of his *r* filled the

ROBED (v)
clothed or covered with or as if with a robe
Ps 93:1 . . . . . LORD is *r* in majesty

ROCK (n)
a stone; a cliff; foundation, support; refuge
Exod 17:6 . . Moses struck the *r* as he was
Num 20:8 . . speak to the *r* over there,
Deut 32:13. . honey from the *r* and olive
2 Sam 22:2. . LORD is my *r,* my
Ps 18:2 . . . . . God is my *r,* in whom I
Ps 19:14 . . . . LORD, my *r* and my redeemer.
Ps 61:2 . . . . . to the towering *r* of safety,

Ps 62:7 . . . . . my refuge, a ***r*** where no enemy
Ps 92:15 . . . . He is my ***r!***
Isa 26:4. . . . . GOD is the eternal ***R***.
Matt 7:24 . . . builds a house on solid ***r***.
Matt 16:18 . . upon this ***r*** I will build
Rom 9:33 . . . stumble, a ***r*** that makes them
1 Cor 10:4 . . and that ***r*** was Christ.
1 Pet 2:8. . . . stumble, the ***r*** that makes

ROD, RODS (n)
a straight, slender stick used as a walking stick, a club or weapon, a shepherd's crook, a paddling stick, a royal scepter, or a measuring stick; figurative of divine authority
see also STAFF
2 Sam 7:14 . . him with the ***r***, like any
Ps 2:9 . . . . . . will break them with an iron ***r***
Ps 23:4 . . . . . Your ***r*** and your staff
Prov 13:24 . . spare the ***r*** of discipline
2 Cor 11:25 . times I was beaten with ***r-s***.
Rev 2:27. . . . the nations with an iron ***r***
Rev 12:5. . . . rule all nations with an iron ***r***.
Rev 19:15. . . rule them with an iron ***r***.

ROMAN (adj)
of or relating to Rome or the people of Rome
Acts 16:37 . . and we are ***R*** citizens.
Acts 22:25 . . you to whip a ***R*** citizen

ROMAN OFFICER (n)
a person of some authority in the Roman military
Matt 8:5. . . . a ***R*** came and pleaded
Luke 23:47. . the ***R*** overseeing the execution
Acts 10:22 . . sent by Cornelius, a ***R***

ROMAN SOLDIERS (n)
those actively involved in the Roman military
Mark 15:15 . over to the ***R*** to be crucified
John 18:3 . . . given Judas a contingent of ***R***

ROOSTER (n)
an adult male domestic chicken
Matt 26:34. . before the ***r*** crows, you will

ROOT, ROOTS (n)
the part of a plant usually found underground; something that is an origin or source (as of a condition or quality)
Isa 11:1. . . . . bearing fruit from the old ***r***.
Isa 53:2. . . . . green shoot, like a ***r*** in dry
Matt 3:10 . . . to sever the ***r-s*** of the trees.
Matt 13:21 . . don't have deep ***r-s***, they
Eph 3:17 . . . Your ***r-s*** will grow down
1 Tim 6:10 . . money is the ***r*** of all kinds
Jude 1:12 . . . have been pulled up by the ***r-s***.

ROPE, ROPES (n)
a large stout cord of strands twisted or braided together
Josh 2:18 . . . this scarlet ***r*** hanging from
Prov 5:22. . . they are ***r-s*** that catch
Hos 11:4 . . . with my ***r-s*** of kindness

ROT (v)
to undergo decomposition
Ps 16:10 . . . . holy one to ***r*** in the grave.
Acts 2:27 . . . Holy One to ***r*** in the grave.
Acts 13:35 . . Holy One to ***r*** in the grave.

ROYAL (adj)
of, relating to, or subject to the crown
Ps 93:5 . . . . . Your ***r*** laws cannot be
Isa 63:1. . . . . this in ***r*** robes, marching
Jas 2:8. . . . . . you obey the ***r*** law as found
1 Pet 2:9. . . . You are ***r*** priests,

RUDDER (n)
an underwater blade that steers a boat or ship
Jas 3:4. . . . . . a small ***r*** makes a huge ship

RUDE (adj)
offensive in manner or action
1 Cor 13:5 . . or ***r***. It does not demand

RUIN (n)
physical, moral, economic, or social collapse
Eccl 4:5 . . . . idle hands, leading them to ***r***.
1 Tim 6:9 . . . them into ***r*** and destruction.

RUIN, RUINED, RUINING, RUINS (v)
to damage irreparably; to subject to frustration, failure, or disaster
Prov 19:3 . . . People ***r*** their lives by
Prov 19:18 . . you will ***r*** their lives.
Prov 22:23 . . He will ***r*** anyone who ***r-s***
Isa 3:14. . . . . You have ***r-ed*** Israel,
Matt 9:17 . . . the wine and ***r-ing*** the skins.
2 Tim 2:14 . . they can ***r*** those who hear

RULE, RULES (n)
a prescribed guide for conduct or action
Isa 29:13. . . . but man-made ***r-s*** learned by
2 Tim 2:5 . . . unless they follow the ***r-s***.
Heb 13:9 . . . not from ***r-s*** about food,

RULE, RULED, RULES (v)
to exert control, direction, or influence on; to exercise authority or power over
Gen 3:16 . . . but he will ***r*** over you.
Ps 2:4 . . . . . . But the one who ***r-s*** in heaven
Ps 11:4 . . . . . LORD still ***r-s*** from heaven.
Ps 55:19 . . . . God, who has ***r-d*** forever,
Ps 66:7 . . . . . great power he ***r-s*** forever.

Ps 89:9 . . . . . You ***r*** the oceans.
Ps 103:19 . . . there he ***r-s*** over everything.
Prov 17:2. . . wise servant will ***r*** over the
Isa 9:7. . . . . . He will ***r*** with fairness
Isa 40:10. . . . He will ***r*** with a powerful
Jer 23:5. . . . . a King who ***r-s*** with wisdom.
Zech 6:13. . . honor and will ***r*** as king
Rom 5:21 . . . as sin ***r-d*** over all people
Rom 15:12. . come, and he will ***r*** over
Col 3:15 . . . . comes from Christ ***r*** in your
Rev 19:15. . . He will ***r*** them with

RULER, RULERS (n)

person with authority; tribal chief; prince or king; city magistrate; powerful spiritual beings; God himself

Judg 8:22. . . to Gideon, "Be our ***r!***
1 Sam 10:1. . to be the ***r*** over Israel,
Prov 19:6. . . favors from a ***r;*** everyone is
Prov 23:1. . . with a ***r,*** pay attention to
Jer 30:21. . . . have their own ***r*** again,
Dan 7:27 . . . all ***r-s*** will serve and obey him.
Dan 9:25 . . . until a ***r***—the Anointed One—
Mic 5:2. . . . . a ***r*** of Israel will come from
Matt 2:6. . . . for a ***r*** will come from
Matt 20:25. . that the ***r-s*** in this world
John 12:31 . . when Satan, the ***r*** of this
1 Cor 2:6 . . . or to the ***r-s*** of this world,
Eph 1:21 . . . far above any ***r*** or authority
Eph 3:10 . . . the unseen ***r-s*** and authorities
Eph 6:12 . . . but against evil ***r-s*** and
Col 1:16 . . . . as thrones, kingdoms, ***r-s,*** and
Col 2:15 . . . . disarmed the spiritual ***r-s*** and
Rev 1:5. . . . . and the ***r*** of all the kings

RUMORS (n)

a statement or report without known authority for its truth

Exod 23:1 . . must not pass along false ***r.***
Prov 18:8. . . ***R*** are dainty morsels that
Jer 51:46. . . . For ***r*** will keep coming year

RUN, RUNNING (v)

to go faster than a walk; to flee

Ps 19:5 . . . . . athlete eager to ***r*** the race.
Prov 4:12. . . when you ***r,*** you won't
Isa 40:31. . . . will ***r*** and not grow weary.
1 Cor 9:26 . . So I ***r*** with purpose in
Gal 2:2. . . . . and I was ***r-ning*** the race for
Gal 5:7. . . . . You were ***r-ning*** the race so
Phil 2:16 . . . that I did not ***r*** the race in
1 Tim 6:11 . . so ***r*** from all these evil
2 Tim 2:22 . . ***R*** from anything that
Heb 12:1 . . . let us ***r*** with endurance

RUST (n)

the reddish brittle coating formed on iron

Matt 6:19. . . them and ***r*** destroys them,

RUTH

Moabitess (Ruth 1:4); widowed daughter-in-law of Naomi (Ruth 1:18); later married Boaz (Ruth 4:10); ancestor of David and Jesus (Ruth 4:13, 21-22; Matt 1:5).

RUTHLESS (adj)

having no pity; cruel

Prov 11:16 . . gains respect, but ***r*** men gain
Isa 25:3. . . . . ***r*** nations will fear you.

S

SABAOTH (KJV)
Rom 9:29 . . . the LORD of ***Heaven's Armies***
Jas 5:4. . . . . . the LORD of ***Heaven's Armies***

SABBATH, SABBATHS (n)
cessation of activity; a holy day set aside to honor God through rest and worship
see also REST
Exod 20:8 . . to observe the *S* day by
Exod 31:14 . must keep the *S* day, for it
Lev 25:2. . . . must observe a *S* rest before
Deut 5:12. . . Observe the *S* day by
2 Chr 2:4 . . . and evening, on the *S-s,*
Isa 56:2. . . . . who honor my *S* days of rest
Isa 56:6. . . . . do not desecrate the *S* day
Isa 58:13. . . . Honor the *S* in everything
Matt 12:1. . . some grainfields on the *S.*
Luke 13:10. . One *S* day as Jesus was
Col 2:16 . . . . new moon ceremonies or *S-s.*

SACKCLOTH (KJV)
Gen 37:34 . . dressed himself in ***burlap.***
Esth 4:1 . . . . put on ***burlap*** and ashes,
Job 16:15 . . . I wear ***burlap*** to show my grief
Ps 30:11 . . . . my ***clothes of mourning*** and
Luke 10:13. . ***burlap*** and throwing ashes

SACRED (adj)
dedicated or set apart for the service or worship of a deity; entitled to reverence and respect
Lev 10:13. . . eat it in a *s* place, for
Num 4:15 . . and all the *s* articles.
2 Tim 3:2 . . . They will consider nothing *s.*

SACRIFICE, SACRIFICES (n)
worship or atonement offering; something given up or lost
Exod 12:27 . It is the Passover *s* to the
1 Sam 15:22. Obedience is better than *s,*
Ps 40:6 . . . . . no delight in *s-s* or offerings.
Ps 51:16 . . . . do not desire a *s,* or I would
Ps 51:17 . . . . The *s* you desire is
Ps 107:22 . . . offer *s-s* of thanksgiving
Prov 15:8. . . LORD detests the *s* of
Hos 6:6 . . . . to show love, not offer *s-s.*
Matt 9:13. . . to show mercy, not offer *s-s.*
Rom 3:25. . . Jesus as the *s* for sin.
Rom 8:3. . . . Son as a *s* for our sins.
Rom 12:1. . . a living and holy *s*—the
Eph 5:2 . . . . himself as a *s* for us,
Heb 5:3 . . . . he must offer *s-s* for his own
Heb 7:27 . . . need to offer *s-s* every day.
Heb 9:28 . . . time as a *s* to take away
Heb 10:5 . . . did not want animal *s-s* or sin
Heb 10:10 . . holy by the *s* of the body of
Heb 13:15 . . Jesus a continual *s* of praise
Heb 13:16 . . These are the *s-s* that please
1 Pet 2:5. . . . offer spiritual *s-s* that please
1 Jn 2:2. . . . . himself is the *s* that atones
1 Jn 4:10. . . . his Son as a *s* to take away

SACRIFICE, SACRIFICED, SACRIFICES (v)
to suffer loss of, give up, renounce, injure, kill, or destroy, especially for an ideal, belief, or end
Gen 22:2 . . . Go and *s* him as a
John 10:11 . . good shepherd *s-s* his life
John 10:15 . . I *s* my life for the sheep.
1 Cor 5:7 . . . Lamb, has been *s-d* for us.
1 Cor 13:3 . . poor and even *s-d* my body,

SACRILEGIOUS (adj)
of, relating to, or characterized by a violation of or gross irreverence toward something holy or sacred
Dan 11:31 . . and set up the *s* object that
Dan 12:11 . . stopped and the *s* object that
Matt 24:15. . about—the *s* object that
Mark 13:14 . will see the *s* object that

SAD (adj)
affected with or expressive of grief or unhappiness
Ps 42:5 . . . . . Why is my heart so *s?*
Luke 18:23. . *s,* for he was very rich.

SADDUCEES (n)
members of a Jewish faction that rejected doctrines not in the law (as resurrection, retribution in a future life, and the existence of angels)
Matt 16:6 . . . yeast of the Pharisees and *S.*
Mark 12:18 . *S*—religious leaders
Acts 23:8 . . . for the *S* say there is no

SADNESS (n)
grief or unhappiness
Ps 31:10 . . . . my years are shortened by *s.*
Eccl 7:3 . . . . *s* has a refining influence
Jas 4:9. . . . . . *s* instead of laughter

SAFE (adj)
free from harm or risk; secure from threat of danger, harm, or loss
Deut 29:19. . I am *s,* even though I am
1 Sam 30:23. has kept us *s* and helped
Ps 4:8 . . . . . . O LORD, will keep me *s.*
Ps 28:8 . . . . . He is a *s* fortress for his
Prov 2:11 . . . will keep you *s.*
Prov 4:26 . . . stay on the *s* path.
Prov 18:10 . . run to him and are *s.*
Prov 28:26 . . who walks in wisdom is *s.*
John 17:15 . . keep them *s* from the evil

SAFETY (n)
the condition of being safe from undergoing or causing hurt, injury, or loss
Deut 33:12. . and live in *s* beside him.
2 Sam 23:5. . ensure my *s* and success.
Ps 16:9 . . . . . My body rests in *s.*
Ps 59:16 . . . . my refuge, a place of *s*
Prov 11:14 . . is *s* in having many advisers.
Prov 29:25 . . trusting the LORD means *s.*
Hos 2:18 . . . live unafraid in peace and *s.*

SAINTS (KJV)
Ps 34:9 . . . . . you his ***godly people,*** for
Ps 97:10 . . . . the lives of his ***godly people***
Dan 7:18 . . . ***holy people*** of the Most High
Rom 8:27 . . . Spirit pleads for ***us believers***
1 Cor 6:2 . . . ***we believers*** will judge the

SAKE (n)
personal or social welfare, safety, or benefit; the good, advantage, or enhancement of some entity
Rom 8:36 . . . say, "For your *s* we are
2 Tim 1:8 . . . for the *s* of the Good News
Heb 11:26 . . to suffer for the *s* of Christ

SALT (n)
the mineral sodium chloride used mainly for seasoning and as a preservative
Gen 19:26 . . she turned into a pillar of *s.*
Matt 5:13 . . . You are the *s* of the earth.

SALVATION (n)
deliverance from the power and effects of sin, danger, or difficulty by God's intervention
see also SAVE
2 Sam 22:47. Rock of my *s,* be exalted!
2 Chr 6:41 . . be clothed with *s;* may your
Ps 18:46 . . . . God of my *s* be exalted!
Ps 27:1 . . . . . light and my *s*—so why should
Ps 40:16 . . . . love your *s* repeatedly shout,
Ps 51:12 . . . . joy of your *s,* and make me
Ps 62:2 . . . . . rock and my *s,* my fortress
Ps 69:13 . . . . my prayer with your sure *s.*
Ps 74:12 . . . . ages past, bringing *s* to
Ps 85:4 . . . . . us again, O God of our *s.*
Ps 89:26 . . . . and the Rock of my *s.*
Ps 91:16 . . . . long life and give them my *s.*
Ps 95:1 . . . . . joyfully to the Rock of our *s.*
Isa 25:9. . . . . rejoice in the *s* he brings!
Isa 26:18. . . . We have not given *s* to the
Isa 33:6. . . . . rich store of *s,* wisdom,
Isa 45:8. . . . . wide so *s* and righteousness
Isa 45:22. . . . the world look to me for *s!*
Isa 49:6. . . . . will bring my *s* to the ends
Isa 51:6. . . . . but my *s* lasts forever.
Isa 52:7. . . . . of peace and *s,* the news that
Isa 59:17. . . . the helmet of *s* on his head.
Isa 62:1. . . . . dawn, and her *s* blazes like
Lam 3:26 . . . wait quietly for *s* from the
Jonah 2:9 . . . For my *s* comes from the
Luke 1:77. . . to find *s* through forgiveness
Luke 2:30. . . I have seen your *s,*
Luke 3:6. . . . will see the *s* sent from
Luke 21:28. . up, for your *s* is near!
John 4:22 . . . him, for *s* comes through the
Acts 13:26 . . this message of *s* has been
Acts 13:47 . . Gentiles, to bring *s* to the
Acts 28:28 . . know that this *s* from God
Rom 11:11 . . so God made *s* available to
Rom 13:11 . . for our *s* is nearer now
2 Cor 6:2 . . . the day of *s,* I helped you.
2 Cor 7:10 . . from sin and results in *s.*
Eph 6:17 . . . Put on *s* as your helmet,
Phil 2:12 . . . show the results of your *s,*
2 Thes 2:13 . to experience *s*—a *s*
Titus 2:11. . . bringing *s* to all people.
Heb 2:3 . . . . if we ignore this great *s* that

Heb 5:9 . . . . source of eternal **s** for all
Heb 9:28 . . . but to bring **s** to all who
1 Pet 1:9. . . . will be the **s** of your souls.
1 Pet 1:13. . . to the gracious **s** that will
1 Pet 2:2. . . . into a full experience of **s.**
Rev 7:10. . . . a great roar, "**S** comes from

SAMARIA (n)
the capital city of the northern kingdom of Israel; a region in the uplands of central Palestine between Galilee and Judea
1 Kgs 16:24 . hill now known as **S** from
2 Kgs 17:6 . . Hoshea's reign, **S** fell,
John 4:4 . . . . to go through **S** on the way.

SAMARITAN (n or adj)
a native or inhabitant of Samaria
Luke 10:33. . a despised **S** came along,
Luke 17:16. . man was a **S.**
John 4:5 . . . . he came to the **S** village of
John 4:7 . . . . a **S** woman came to draw

SAMSON
Judge of Israel from tribe of Dan; defeated oppressing Philistines (Judg 14–15); killed lion with bare hands (Judg 14:6); set 300 fox tails on fire (Judg 15:4); killed 1,000 men (Judg 15:15); carried large gates to top of hill (Judg 16:3); seduced and deceived by Delilah (Judg 16:1-22); died as he destroyed many Philistines (Judg 16:23-31).

SAMUEL
Judge and prophet of Israel (Heb 11:32); prophet's birth and dedication (1 Sam 1); raised by Eli in the Temple (1 Sam 2:11, 18-21); called as a prophet (1 Sam 3); served as judge over Israel (1 Sam 7:15); warned Israel of the tyranny of kingship (1 Sam 8:10-18); anointed Saul (1 Sam 10:1); rejected Saul (1 Sam 15:23); anointed David (1 Sam 16:13); protected David from Saul (1 Sam 19:18-24); died (1 Sam 25:1); ghost of Samuel rebuked Saul (1 Sam 28:14-19).

SANCTIFY, SANCTIFIED (KJV)
Gen 2:3 . . . . and ***declared it holy***
Exod 31:13 . LORD, who ***makes you holy***
Deut 5:12. . . Sabbath day by ***keeping it holy***
John 17:19 . . myself as a ***holy sacrifice***
Heb 10:10 . . for us to ***be made holy*** by

SANCTUARY (n)
a holy place set apart for worship of God or refuge from danger
see also TABERNACLE, TEMPLE
Exod 25:8 . . build me a holy **s** so I can
Lev 19:30. . . show reverence toward my **s.**
Ps 27:5 . . . . . he will hide me in his **s.**
Ps 63:2 . . . . . you in your **s** and gazed upon
Ps 68:35 . . . . God is awesome in his **s.**
Ps 150:1 . . . . Praise God in his **s;** praise
Heb 6:19 . . . curtain into God's inner **s.**

SAND (n)
fine grains of rock that are worn away by wind and rain
Gen 22:17 . . in the sky and the **s** on
Matt 7:26. . . who builds a house on **s.**

SANDAL, SANDALS (n)
a shoe consisting of a sole strapped to the foot
Exod 3:5 . . . Take off your **s-s,** for you are
Exod 12:11 . wear your **s-s,** and carry
Deut 25:9. . . elders, pull his **s** from his
Josh 5:15 . . . Take off your **s-s,** for the
Ruth 4:7. . . . to remove his **s** and hand it
Matt 3:11. . . his slave and carry his **s-s.**

SANG (v)
to produce musical tones by means of the voice
see also SING
Exod 15:1 . . people of Israel **s** this
Exod 15:21 . And Miriam **s** this song:
Num 21:17 . the Israelites **s** this song:
Judg 5:1. . . . son of Abinoam **s** this song:
2 Sam 22:1. . David **s** this song to
Ezra 3:11 . . . and thanks, they **s** this song
Job 38:7 . . . . morning stars **s** together and
Ps 106:12 . . . Then they **s** his praise.
Matt 26:30. . Then they **s** a hymn
Rev 5:9. . . . . And they **s** a new song
Rev 5:13. . . . They **s:** "Blessing and
Rev 14:3. . . . great choir **s** a wonderful

SAPS (v)
to gradually diminish the supply or intensity of
Prov 17:22. . broken spirit **s** a person's

SARAH (SARAI)
Wife of Abraham (Abram) (Gen 11:30-31); was infertile (Gen 11:30; Rom 4:19) and very beautiful (Gen 12:11); with Abraham, deceived Pharaoh (Gen 12:10-20); dealings with Hagar and Ishmael (Gen 16); name changed (Gen 17:15); Isaac promised (Gen 18:10-15; Rom 9:9); example of faith (Heb 11:11); with Abraham, deceived Abimelech (Gen 20); Isaac born (Gen 21:1-7); Hagar and Ishmael sent away (Gen 21:8-21); died and was buried (Gen 23);

Paul's analogy using Sarah and Hagar (Gal 4:25-26).

SARDIS (n)
the capital city of Lydia in the province of Asia, in western Asia Minor (modern Turkey)
Rev 3:1. . . . . the angel of the church in *S.*

SAT (v)
to place (the buttocks) on or in a seat
see also SIT
Dan 7:9 . . . . and the Ancient One *s* down to
Mark 16:19 . into heaven and *s* down in
Heb 8:1 . . . . High Priest who *s* down in the
Heb 10:12 . . Then he *s* down in the

SATAN (n)
"adversary" of God and man; the personal name of the devil
see also DEVIL
Job 1:6 . . . . . and the Accuser, *S,* came with
Zech 3:2. . . . your accusations, *S.* Yes,
Matt 12:26 . . if *S* is casting out *S,* he
Matt 16:23 . . Get away from me, *S!*
Mark 4:15 . . only to have *S* come at once
Luke 10:18. . told them, "I saw *S* fall from
Luke 22:3. . . Then *S* entered into Judas
Rom 16:20 . . soon crush *S* under your
1 Cor 5:5 . . . him over to *S* so that his
2 Cor 11:14 . Even *S* disguises himself as
2 Cor 12:7 . . from *S* to torment
1 Tim 1:20 . . them over to *S* so they might
Rev 12:9. . . . the devil, or *S,* the one
Rev 20:2. . . . is the devil, *S*—and bound
Rev 20:7. . . . come to an end, *S* will be let

SATISFY, SATISFIED, SATISFIES, SATISFYING (v)
to make happy; to gratify to the full
Josh 22:33 . . Israelites were ***s-ied*** and
Ps 17:14 . . . . But *s* the hunger of your
Ps 17:15 . . . . you face to face and be ***s-ied.***
Ps 22:26 . . . . poor will eat and be ***s-ied.***
Ps 63:5 . . . . . You *s* me more than the richest
Ps 105:40 . . . quail; he ***s-ied*** their hunger
Ps 107:9 . . . . he ***s-ies*** the thirsty and fills
Ps 145:16 . . . your hand, you *s* the hunger
Ps 147:14 . . . and ***s-ies*** your hunger with the
Prov 5:19. . . Let her breasts *s* you always.
Prov 30:8. . . just enough to *s* my needs.
Prov 30:15. . that are never ***s-ied***—no, four
Isa 9:12. . . . . LORD's anger will not be ***s-ied.***
Mic 7:1. . . . . be found to *s* my hunger.
Luke 6:21. . . now, for you will be ***s-ied.***
Heb 13:5 . . . be ***s-ied*** with what you have.
Jas 5:5. . . . . . luxury, ***s-ing*** your every desire.

SAUL
1. First king of Israel (united kingdom), from tribe of Benjamin (1 Sam 9–11); anointed by Samuel (1 Sam 10:1); made unlawful sacrifices (1 Sam 13:1-14); warrior in battles (1 Sam 13:15–14:52); rejected as king (1 Sam 15:26); troubled by evil spirit (1 Sam 16:14-23); resentful of David and tried to kill him (1 Sam 18:5–19:22); gave Michal as wife to David (1 Sam 18:17-30); hunted David (1 Sam 22–24; 26); had priests at Nob killed (1 Sam 22:6-23); consulted medium at Endor, rebuked by Samuel's ghost (1 Sam 28:3-25); wounded in battle, then killed himself (1 Sam 31:4-6; see also 2 Sam 1:4-16); body desecrated, burned, and buried (1 Sam 31:12-13).
2. See PAUL, *also known as Saul.*

SAVE, SAVED, SAVES, SAVING (v)
to rescue or deliver from danger or harm; to deliver from sin; to preserve or guard from injury, destruction, or loss; to maintain or preserve
see also PRESERVE, RESCUE, SALVATION
2 Sam 22:3. . the power that ***s-s*** me,
1 Chr 16:23 . good news that he ***s-s.***
Ps 7:10 . . . . . is my shield, ***s-ing*** those whose
Ps 18:48 . . . . you *s* me from violent
Ps 22:8 . . . . . let the LORD *s* him!
Ps 25:5 . . . . . you are the God who ***s-s*** me.
Ps 33:16 . . . . army cannot *s* a king, nor
Ps 34:6 . . . . . LORD listened; he ***s-d*** me
Ps 44:6 . . . . . not count on my sword to *s*
Ps 68:20 . . . . Our God is a God who ***s-s!***
Ps 109:31 . . . the needy, ready to *s* them
Ps 116:6 . . . . death, and he ***s-d*** me.
Prov 2:16. . . Wisdom will *s* you from
Prov 10:2. . . right living can *s* your
Isa 25:9. . . . . trusted in him, and he ***s-d*** us!
Isa 30:15. . . . resting in me will you be ***s-d.***
Isa 35:4. . . . . He is coming to *s* you.
Isa 59:1. . . . . arm is not too weak to *s*
Isa 63:1. . . . . who has the power to ***s!***
Jer 4:14. . . . . your heart that you may be ***s-d.***
Jer 17:14. . . . if you *s* me, I will
Jer 51:9. . . . . nothing can *s* her now.
Dan 3:17 . . . we serve is able to *s* us.
Joel 2:32. . . . name of the LORD will be ***s-d,***
Mic 7:7. . . . . wait confidently for God to *s*
Zeph 1:18 . . gold will not *s* you
Matt 1:21. . . he will *s* his people
Matt 16:25. . my sake, you will *s* it.
Matt 24:13. . to the end will be ***s-d.***
Luke 17:33. . life go, you will *s* it.
Luke 19:10. . seek and *s* those who are

John 10:9 . . . in through me will be ***s-d.***
John 12:47 . . I have come to **s** the world
Acts 2:21 . . . name of the LORD will be ***s-d.***
Acts 4:12 . . . by which we must be ***s-d.***
Acts 15:11 . . we are all ***s-d*** the same way,
Acts 16:30 . . what must I do to be ***s-d?***
Rom 1:16 . . . God at work, ***s-ing*** everyone
Rom 5:9. . . . he will certainly **s** us from
Rom 10:9. . . the dead, you will be ***s-d.***
Rom 10:13 . . of the LORD will be ***s-d.***
1 Cor 1:18 . . we who are being ***s-d*** know
1 Cor 5:5 . . . himself will be ***s-d*** on the
1 Cor 7:16 . . wives might be ***s-d*** because
1 Cor 10:33 . so that many may be ***s-d.***
1 Cor 15:2 . . this Good News that ***s-s***
Eph 1:13 . . . Good News that God ***s-s*** you.
1 Thes 5:9 . . God chose to **s** us through
1 Tim 1:15 . . the world to **s** sinners
1 Tim 2:4 . . . wants everyone to be ***s-d*** and
1 Tim 2:15 . . women will be ***s-d*** through
2 Tim 1:9 . . . For God ***s-d*** us and called
Titus 3:5. . . . he ***s-d*** us, not because of the
Heb 7:25 . . . and forever, to **s** those who
Jas 5:20. . . . . sinner back will **s** that person
2 Pet 3:15. . . gives people time to be ***s-d.***

SAVING (adj)

of or relating to delivering or rescuing
Ps 40:10 . . . . faithfulness and **s** power.
Ps 67:2 . . . . . the earth, your **s** power
Ps 69:29 . . . . God, by your **s** power.
Ps 71:15 . . . . proclaim your **s** power,
Ps 98:1 . . . . . has shown his **s** power!

SAVIOR (n)

one who delivers from trouble, sin, or judgment
2 Sam 22:2. . my fortress, and my ***s;***
Ps 38:22 . . . . help me, O LORD my ***s.***
Ps 40:17 . . . . You are my helper and my ***s.***
Ps 106:21 . . . They forgot God, their ***s,***
Isa 43:11. . . . and there is no other ***S.***
Isa 45:21. . . . a righteous God and ***S.***
Isa 49:26. . . . the LORD, am your ***S*** and
Isa 62:11. . . . Look, your ***S*** is coming.
Jer 14:8. . . . . Hope of Israel, our ***S*** in
Hos 13:4 . . . for there is no other ***s.***
Zeph 3:17 . . He is a mighty ***s.***
Luke 1:47. . . rejoices in God my ***S!***
Luke 1:69. . . He has sent us a mighty ***S***
John 4:42 . . . he is indeed the ***S*** of the
Acts 5:31 . . . right hand as Prince and ***S.***
Acts 13:23 . . God's promised ***S*** of Israel!
Eph 5:23 . . . He is the ***S*** of his body,
1 Tim 2:3 . . . good and pleases God our ***S,***
1 Tim 4:10 . . who is the ***S*** of all people
Titus 2:10. . . about God our ***S*** attractive
Titus 3:4. . . . When God our ***S*** revealed his
2 Pet 3:2. . . . Lord and ***S*** commanded
1 Jn 4:14. . . . Son to be the ***S*** of the world.

SAVOUR (KJV)
2 Cor 2:16 . . a dreadful ***smell*** of death
Eph 5:2 . . . . for us, a pleasing ***aroma*** to God

SAW (v)

to perceive using the eye
see also SEE
Ps 139:16 . . . You **s** me before I was born.

SCALES (n)

the outer covering of fish or reptiles; an instrument for weighing
see also BALANCES
Lev 11:9. . . . fins and ***s,*** whether taken
Deut 25:13. . must use accurate **s** when you
Prov 11:1 . . . use of dishonest ***s,*** but he
Rev 6:5. . . . . a pair of **s** in his hand.

SCAPEGOAT (n)

a goat upon whose head the sins of the people are symbolically placed, after which he is sent into the wilderness on the Day of Atonement
Lev 16:10. . . other goat, the **s** chosen by

SCARLET (adj)

of the color of any various bright reds
Josh 2:21 . . . leaving the **s** rope hanging
Isa 1:18. . . . . sins are like ***s,*** I will make
Matt 27:28. . and put a **s** robe on him.

SCARS (n)

marks left (as in the skin) by the healing of injured tissue
Gal 6:17 . . . . on my body the **s** that show

SCATTER, SCATTERED (v)

to separate and go in various directions; to disperse
Deut 4:27. . . the LORD will **s** you
Neh 1:8 . . . . to me, I will **s** you among
Isa 11:12. . . . will gather the ***s-ed*** people
Jer 9:16. . . . . I will **s** them around
Jer 30:11. . . . where I have ***s-ed*** you, but I
Jer 31:10. . . . LORD, who ***s-ed*** his people,
Ezek 34:21 . . flock until you ***s-ed*** them to
Zech 2:6. . . . for I have ***s-ed*** you to the four
Zech 10:9. . . Though I have ***s-ed*** them like
Zech 13:7. . . sheep will be ***s-ed,*** and I will
Matt 26:31 . . of the flock will be ***s-ed.***
John 11:52 . . children of God ***s-ed*** around
Acts 8:4 . . . . were ***s-ed*** preached the Good
Jas 1:1. . . . . . Jewish believers ***s-ed*** abroad.

SCEPTER (n)
the official staff of a ruler, symbolizing his authority and power
Gen 49:10 . . The *s* will not depart from
Num 24:17 . a *s* will emerge from Israel.
Heb 1:8 . . . . rule with a *s* of justice.

SCHEME (v)
to make crafty or secret plans
Zech 8:17. . . Don't *s* against each

SCHEMERS (n)
those who plot or scheme
Job 5:12 . . . . He frustrates the plans of *s*
Prov 14:17. . things, and *s* are hated.

SCHEMES (n)
crafty or secret plans
Job 5:13 . . . . cunning *s-s* are thwarted.
Ps 37:7 . . . . . or fret about their wicked *s-s.*
Ps 140:8 . . . . let their evil *s-s* succeed,
Prov 13:11. . from get-rich-quick *s-s*
2 Cor 2:11 . . familiar with his evil *s-s.*

SCOFF (v)
to show contempt by derisive acts or language; to mock
1 Thes 5:20 . Do not *s* at prophecies,
2 Pet 2:12. . . They *s* at things they do not
Jude 1:8 . . . . defy authority, and *s* at

SCOFFERS (n)
those who scoff
2 Pet 3:3. . . . the last days *s* will come,

SCORN (n)
open dislike, disrespect, or derision often mixed with indignation
Ps 109:25 . . . they shake their heads in *s.*
Isa 51:7. . . . . not be afraid of people's *s,*

SCORN, SCORNED (v)
to reject or dismiss as contemptible or unworthy
Ps 22:6 . . . . . I am *s-ed* and despised by all!
Ps 119:22 . . . Don't let them *s* and insult
Prov 9:12. . . If you *s* wisdom, you will
Jer 6:10. . . . . They *s* the word of the LORD.

SCORNFUL (adj)
full of scorn; contemptuous
Ezek 28:24. . will Israel's *s* neighbors

SCORPION (n)
a small crawling animal with eight legs, two sets of pincers, and a tail with a poisonous stinger
Luke 11:12. . give them a *s?* Of course
Rev 9:5. . . . . pain of a *s* sting.

SCRIPTURE, SCRIPTURES (n)
the law; the writings of Moses; the entire collection of sacred books
Matt 21:16. . you ever read the *S-s?*
Matt 22:29. . you don't know the *S-s,*
Luke 24:27. . from all the *S-s* the things
Luke 24:45. . to understand the *S-s.*
John 2:22 . . . believed both the *S-s* and
John 5:39 . . . You search the *S-s* because
John 7:42 . . . the *S-s* clearly state that
John 10:35 . . know that the *S-s* cannot
Acts 8:32 . . . The passage of *S* he had
1 Cor 4:6 . . . quoted from the *S-s,* you won't
1 Tim 4:13 . . focus on reading the *S-s* to
2 Tim 3:16 . . All *S* is inspired by God
Heb 10:7 . . . written about me in the *S-s.*
2 Pet 1:20. . . no prophecy in *S* ever came
2 Pet 3:16. . . do with other parts of *S.*

SCROLL (n)
a roll (as of papyrus, leather, or parchment) for writing a document
Isa 34:4. . . . . disappear like a rolled-up *s.*
Ezek 3:1. . . . giving you—eat this *s!*
Rev 6:14. . . . sky was rolled up like a *s,*
Rev 10:8. . . . take the open *s* from the hand

SEA, SEAS (n)
a great body of salt water that covers much of the earth; a large basin used in the Temple
Exod 14:16 . middle of the *s* on dry
Deut 30:13. . not kept beyond the *s,*
1 Kgs 7:23 . . rim to rim, called the S.
Job 11:9 . . . . and wider than the *s.*
Ps 93:4 . . . . . violent raging of the *s-s,*
Ps 95:5 . . . . . The *s* belongs to him,
Eccl 11:1 . . . your grain across the *s-s,*
Isa 57:20. . . . like the restless *s,* which
Jonah 1:4 . . . wind over the *s,* causing a
Hab 2:14 . . . waters fill the *s,* the earth
Matt 18:6. . . in the depths of the *s.*
Jas 1:6. . . . . . wave of the *s* that is blown
Jude 1:13 . . . waves of the *s,* churning up
Rev 10:2. . . . right foot on the *s* and
Rev 13:1. . . . rising up out of the *s.*
Rev 20:13. . . The *s* gave up its dead,
Rev 21:1. . . . And the *s* was also gone.

SEAL, SEALS (n)
a piece of wax or clay impressed with a device such as a signet ring or cylinder engraved with the owner's name, a design, or both that certifies or authenticates a document
Rev 5:2. . . . . break the *s-s* on this scroll
Rev 6:1. . . . . the seven *s-s* on the scroll.
Rev 6:3. . . . . broke the second *s,* I heard

Rev 6:5. . . . . broke the third *s*, I heard
Rev 6:7. . . . . broke the fourth *s*, I heard
Rev 6:9. . . . . Lamb broke the fifth *s*, I saw
Rev 6:12. . . . broke the sixth *s*, and there
Rev 8:1. . . . . broke the seventh *s* on the
Rev 9:4. . . . . did not have the *s* of God

SEAL, SEALED (v)
to confirm or make secure by or as if by a seal
Dan 12:4 . . . secret; *s* up the book until
Rev 5:1. . . . . and it was ***s-ed*** with seven
Rev 22:10. . . Do not *s* up the prophetic

SEARCH, SEARCHES (v)
to investigate or examine thoroughly in an effort to find or verify something
Ps 34:14 . . . . *S* for peace, and work
Ps 139:23 . . . *S* me, O God, and know
Eccl 3:6 . . . . A time to *s* and a time to
Jer 17:10. . . . I, the LORD, *s* all hearts
1 Cor 2:10 . . Spirit ***s-es*** out everything
1 Pet 3:11. . . *S* for peace, and work

SEASHORE (n)
land adjacent to the sea
Josh 11:4 . . . like the sand on the *s*.
1 Kgs 4:29 . . vast as the sands of the *s*.

SEASON, SEASONS (n)
the period normally characterized by a particular kind of weather; a period associated with some phase or activity of agriculture (as growth or harvesting)
Gen 1:14 . . . signs to mark the ***s-s***, days,
Ps 1:3 . . . . . . bearing fruit each *s*.
Gal 4:10 . . . . or months or ***s-s*** or years.

SEASONAL (adj)
of, relating to, or varying in occurrence according to the season
Lev 26:4. . . . send you the *s* rains.

SEAT, SEATS (n)
a chair, stool, or bench intended to be sat in or on
Luke 11:43. . to sit in the ***s-s*** of honor
Luke 14:9. . . to take whatever *s* is left

SEATED (v)
to put into a sitting position; to take one's seat or place
Matt 26:64 . . Son of Man *s* in the place
Luke 22:69. . of Man will be *s* in the place
Eph 1:20 . . . the dead and *s* him in the
Eph 2:6 . . . . with Christ and *s* us with him
Heb 12:2 . . . Now he is *s* in the place of
Rev 14:14. . . a white cloud, and *s* on the

SECOND (adj)
next to the first in place or time
Job 42:12 . . . Job in the *s* half of his life
Rev 20:14. . . lake of fire is the *s* death.

SECRET (adj)
kept from knowledge or view; hidden
Ps 90:8 . . . . . before you—our *s* sins—
Jer 23:24. . . . from me in a *s* place?
Matt 10:26 . . all that is *s* will be
Rom 2:16. . . judge everyone's *s* life.
Rom 16:25 . . a plan kept *s* from the
1 Cor 13:2 . . all of God's *s* plans
1 Cor 14:25 . their *s* thoughts will be
Col 1:26 . . . . was kept *s* for centuries and

SECRET, SECRETS (n)
something kept hidden or unexplained; something kept from the knowledge of others or shared only confidentially with a few
see also MYSTERY
Deut 29:29. . God has ***s-s*** known to no
Judg 16:15. . don't share your ***s-s*** with
Ps 44:21 . . . . he knows the ***s-s*** of every
Prov 11:13. . goes around telling ***s-s***,
Dan 2:28 . . . heaven who reveals ***s-s***, and
Dan 2:29 . . . who reveals ***s-s*** has shown
Mark 4:11 . . to understand the *s*
Mark 4:22 . . and every *s* will be brought
Luke 8:10. . . to understand the ***s-s*** of
1 Cor 15:51 . reveal to you a wonderful *s*.
Phil 4:12 . . . have learned the *s* of living
Col 1:27 . . . . the *s*: Christ lives in you.

SECURE (adj)
easy in mind; free from danger or the risk of loss; trustworthy, dependable
Job 31:24 . . . felt *s* because of my gold?
Ps 30:7 . . . . . made me as *s* as a mountain.
Prov 14:26. . fear the LORD are *s*;
1 Thes 5:3 . . is peaceful and *s*," then
2 Pet 3:17. . . your own *s* footing.

SECURE, SECURED (v)
to make fast, safe, or steady
Matt 27:65. . Take guards and *s* it the
Heb 9:12 . . . and ***s-d*** our redemption

SECURITY (n)
something given, deposited, or pledged to make certain the fulfillment of an obligation; freedom from danger; protection
Deut 24:17. . widow's garment as *s* for
Ezra 9:8 . . . . has given us *s* in this holy
Prov 3:26. . . the LORD is your *s*.
Prov 19:23. . bringing *s* and protection

SEDUCE, SEDUCED (v)
to persuade to disobedience or disloyalty; to entice
Deut 4:19. . . don't be ***s-d*** into
Job 31:9 . . . . has been ***s-d*** by a woman,
Job 36:18 . . . you may be ***s-d*** by wealth.
Prov 6:25. . . her coy glances ***s*** you.

SEE, SEEING, SEES (v)
to perceive by the eye; to understand or recognize; to come to know
see also SAW
Ps 34:8 . . . . . Taste and ***s*** that the
Ps 36:2 . . . . . they cannot ***s*** how wicked
Ps 90:8 . . . . . sins—and you ***s*** them
Ps 119:82 . . . straining to ***s*** your promises
Prov 5:21. . . For the LORD ***s-s*** clearly
Prov 13:19. . pleasant to ***s*** dreams come
Eccl 3:11 . . . people cannot ***s*** the whole
Matt 6:18. . . Father, who ***s-s*** everything,
John 12:45. . you are ***s-ing*** the one who
Rom 1:20. . . can clearly ***s*** his invisible
Rom 7:13. . . So we can ***s*** how terrible sin
1 Cor 13:12 . we will ***s*** everything with
2 Cor 4:18 . . things we cannot ***s*** will last
2 Cor 5:7 . . . by believing and not by ***s-ing.***
2 Cor 8:21 . . everyone else to ***s*** that we
Phil 4:5 . . . . Let everyone ***s*** that you are
Col 1:16. . . . things we can't ***s***—such as
Rev 1:7. . . . . everyone will ***s*** him—even

SEED, SEEDS (n)
the grains of plants used for sowing
Gen 1:11. . . . These ***s-s*** will then produce
Prov 11:30. . The ***s-s*** of good deeds
Matt 13:3. . . went out to plant some ***s-s.***
Matt 13:31. . like a mustard ***s*** planted in
Matt 17:20. . as a mustard ***s,*** you could say
Mark 4:15 . . The ***s*** that fell on
Luke 8:12. . . The ***s-s*** that fell on
1 Cor 3:6 . . . I planted the ***s*** in your
2 Cor 9:6 . . . few ***s-s*** will get a small
2 Cor 9:10 . . one who provides ***s*** for the

SEED-BEARING (adj)
a plant that produces seeds
Gen 1:11 . . . every sort of ***s*** plant,

SEEK, SEEKING, SEEKS (v)
to go in search of; to try to acquire or gain
see also SOUGHT
2 Chr 7:14 . . pray and ***s*** my face and
2 Chr 15:2 . . Whenever you ***s*** him,
Prov 3:6. . . . ***S*** his will in all you do,
Prov 25:27. . not good to ***s*** honors
Prov 29:26. . Many ***s*** the ruler's favor,
Isa 55:6. . . . . ***S*** the LORD while you can
Hos 10:12. . . time to ***s*** the LORD,
Zeph 2:3. . . . ***S*** the LORD, all who are
Matt 6:33. . . ***S*** the Kingdom of God above
Matt 7:7. . . . Keep on ***s-ing,*** and you
Matt 7:8. . . . Everyone who ***s-s,*** finds.
Luke 12:31. . ***S*** the Kingdom of God
Luke 19:10. . Son of Man came to ***s*** and
Rom 3:11 . . . no one is ***s-ing*** God.
1 Cor 7:27 . . have a wife, do not ***s*** to get
Heb 11:6 . . . those who sincerely ***s*** him.

SEER (n)
one who practices divination and predicts events or developments
1 Sam 9:9. . . ask the ***s,***" for prophets

SELF-CONTROL (n)
restraint exercised over one's own impulses, emotions, or desires
Prov 5:23. . . He will die for lack of ***s;***
Prov 16:32. . better to have ***s*** than to
Acts 24:25 . . righteousness and ***s*** and the
Gal 5:23. . . . gentleness, and ***s.*** There is no
1 Tim 3:2. . . must exercise ***s,*** live wisely,
1 Tim 3:11 . . They must exercise ***s*** and be
Titus 2:2. . . . older men to exercise ***s,***
1 Pet 1:13. . . think clearly and exercise ***s.***
2 Pet 1:6. . . . and knowledge with ***s,*** and

SELF-DENIAL (n)
a restraint or limitation of one's own desires or interests
Col 2:18. . . . insisting on pious ***s*** or the
Col 2:23. . . . devotion, pious ***s,*** and severe

SELF-DISCIPLINE (n)
correction or regulation of oneself for the sake of improvement
2 Tim 1:7 . . . but of power, love, and ***s.***

SELF-INDULGENCE (n)
excessive or unrestrained gratification of one's own appetites, desires, or whims
Matt 23:25. . full of greed and ***s!***

SELFISH (adj)
seeking or concentrating on one's own advantage, pleasure, or well-being without regard for others
Matt 16:24. . turn from your ***s*** ways,
Luke 9:23. . . turn from your ***s*** ways,
Gal 5:20. . . . of anger, ***s*** ambition,
Phil 1:17 . . . They preach with ***s*** ambition,
Jas 3:14. . . . . and there is ***s*** ambition in
Jas 3:16. . . . . is jealousy and ***s*** ambition,

SELFISHNESS (n)
the act of being concerned only with oneself
2 Cor 12:20 . jealousy, anger, ***s***, slander
Jas 3:15. . . . . jealousy and ***s*** are not God's

SELL, SELLING (v)
to give up (property) to another for something of value (as money)
see also SOLD
Prov 23:23 . . truth and never ***s*** it;
Prov 31:24 . . and sashes to ***s*** to the
Mark 10:21 . and ***s*** all your possessions
Luke 17:28 . . buying and ***s-ing***, farming and
Rev 13:17. . . could buy or ***s*** anything

SEND, SENDING (v)
to direct, order, or request to go
see also SENT
Isa 6:8. . . . . . Here I am. ***S*** me.
Isa 55:11. . . . with my word. I ***s*** it out,
Mal 3:1. . . . . I am ***s-ing*** my messenger,
Matt 9:38 . . . ask him to ***s*** more workers
Mark 1:2 . . . I am ***s-ing*** my messenger
1 Cor 1:17 . . For Christ didn't ***s*** me to

SENSE (n)
sound and prudent judgment based on a simple perception of the situation or facts; intelligence
Prov 3:21 . . . common ***s*** and discernment.
Prov 8:14 . . . Common ***s*** and success
Prov 12:11 . . chases fantasies has no ***s***.
Prov 15:21 . . brings joy to those with no ***s***;
Prov 18:1 . . . they lash out at common ***s***.
Prov 24:30 . . of one with no common ***s***.

SENSIBLE (adj)
having, containing, or indicative of good sense or reason; rational, reasonable
Prov 10:23 . . brings pleasure to the ***s***.
Prov 11:12 . . a ***s*** person keeps quiet.
Prov 15:21 . . ***s*** person stays on the right
Matt 24:45 . . A faithful, ***s*** servant is one

SENSITIVE (adj)
highly responsive or susceptible
Rom 15:1 . . . those who are ***s*** about things

SENT (v)
to direct, order, or request to go
see also SEND
Exod 3:14 . . I AM has ***s*** me
Matt 10:40 . . the Father who ***s*** me.
Luke 10:16 . . God, who ***s*** me.
John 3:17 . . . God ***s*** his Son into the
John 20:21 . . As the Father has ***s*** me, so
Rom 8:3 . . . . He ***s*** his own Son in a
Rom 10:15 . . them without being ***s***?
Gal 4:4 . . . . . time came, God ***s*** his Son,

SEPARATE, SEPARATED, SEPARATES (v)
to set or keep apart; to sort
Prov 17:9 . . . on it ***s-s*** close friends.
Matt 25:32 . . a shepherd ***s-s*** the sheep
Rom 8:35 . . . Can anything ever ***s*** us
Eph 2:14 . . . of hostility that ***s-d*** us.
Col 1:21 . . . . his enemies, ***s-d*** from him

SERAPHIM (n)
six-winged angels standing in God's presence
Isa 6:2. . . . . . were mighty ***s***, each having
Isa 6:6. . . . . . Then one of the ***s*** flew to me

SERIOUSNESS (n)
a sober attitude
Titus 2:7. . . . the integrity and ***s*** of your

SERPENT (n)
a snake or crawling reptile often associated with temptation, sin, and evil; Satan
Gen 3:1 . . . . The ***s*** was the shrewdest of
Isa 27:1. . . . . ***s***, the coiling, writhing ***s***.
2 Cor 11:3 . . the cunning ways of the ***s***.
Rev 12:9. . . . the ancient ***s*** called the devil,
Rev 20:2. . . . that old ***s***, who is the devil,

SERVANT, SERVANTS (n)
one who performs tasks under the direction of another
see also SLAVE(S)
Exod 14:31 . LORD and in his ***s*** Moses.
Lev 25:55. . . They are my ***s-s***, whom I
1 Sam 3:10 . . Speak, your ***s*** is listening.
2 Kgs 17:13 . my ***s-s*** the prophets.
Job 1:8 . . . . . Have you noticed my ***s*** Job?
Ps 19:13 . . . . Keep your ***s*** from deliberate
Ps 31:16 . . . . your favor shine on your ***s***.
Ps 89:3 . . . . . with David, my chosen ***s***.
Ps 104:4 . . . . flames of fire are your ***s-s***.
Prov 14:35 . . king rejoices in wise ***s-s***
Prov 17:2. . . A wise ***s*** will rule
Prov 22:7. . . so the borrower is ***s*** to the
Prov 31:15 . . work for her ***s*** girls.
Eccl 7:21 . . . may hear your ***s*** curse you.
Eccl 10:7 . . . seen ***s-s*** riding horseback
Isa 53:11. . . . my righteous ***s*** will make it
Isa 65:8. . . . . I still have true ***s-s*** there.
Zech 3:8. . . . to bring my ***s***, the Branch.
Mal 1:6. . . . . father, and a ***s*** respects his
Matt 20:26 . . among you must be your ***s***,
Matt 24:45 . . faithful, sensible ***s*** is one
Luke 1:48. . . of his lowly ***s*** girl, and

Luke 17:10. . We are unworthy ***s-s*** who
Luke 22:26. . leader should be like a ***s***.
John 12:26 . . because my ***s-s*** must be
Rom 13:4. . . authorities are God's ***s-s,***
1 Cor 3:5 . . . are only God's ***s-s*** through
Col 1:23. . . . God's ***s*** to proclaim it.
1 Tim 4:6. . . be a worthy ***s*** of Christ
Heb 1:7 . . . . his ***s-s*** like flames of fire.
Heb 1:14 . . . angels are only ***s-s***—spirits

SERVE, SERVED, SERVES, SERVING (v)
to meet the needs of and subject one's will to that of another
Deut 10:12. . love him and ***s*** him with
Deut 11:13. . your God and ***s*** him with
Deut 28:47. . If you do not ***s*** the LORD
Deut 30:17. . drawn away to ***s*** and
Josh 24:15 . . family, we will ***s*** the LORD.
2 Chr 12:8 . . between ***s-ing*** me and
Ps 34:22. . . . redeem those who ***s*** him.
Ps 101:6 . . . . be allowed to ***s*** me.
Ps 103:21 . . . of angels who ***s*** him and do
Isa 38:3. . . . . have ***s-d*** you single-mindedly
Dan 3:17 . . . the God whom we ***s*** is able to
Matt 4:10. . . your God and ***s*** only him.
Matt 6:24. . . No one can ***s*** two masters.
Matt 20:28. . not to be ***s-d*** but to ***s***
Luke 22:27. . among you as one who ***s-s.***
John 12:2. . . Martha ***s-d,*** and Lazarus was
John 12:26 . . honor anyone who ***s-s*** me.
Rom 1:25. . . worshiped and ***s-d*** the things
Rom 12:7. . . your gift is ***s-ing*** others, ***s***
Rom 12:11. . work hard and ***s*** the Lord
Rom 13:6. . . They are ***s-ing*** God in what
Rom 14:18. . If you ***s*** Christ with
Rom 16:18. . people are not ***s-ing*** Christ
1 Cor 16:18 . to all who ***s*** so well.
Gal 5:13. . . . your freedom to ***s*** one another
Col 3:24. . . . Master you are ***s-ing*** is Christ.
1 Tim 5:10. . kind to strangers and ***s-d*** other
1 Pet 5:5. . . . all of you, ***s*** each other in

SERVICE (n)
employment as a servant; the work performed by one that serves
Num 8:11 . . dedicating them to the LORD's ***s.***
Luke 12:35. . Be dressed for ***s*** and keep
Rom 15:17. . through me in my ***s*** to God.
1 Cor 12:5 . . different kinds of ***s,*** but we

SET APART (v)
to designate or preserve for a particular use
Exod 16:23 . holy Sabbath day ***s*** for the Lord
Deut 14:2. . . ***s*** as holy to the Lord
Heb 7:26 . . . been ***s*** from sinners

SEVEN (adj)
of or relating to the number 7
Josh 6:4 . . . . around the town ***s*** times, with
Prov 6:16. . . LORD hates—no, ***s*** things
Prov 24:16. . godly may trip ***s*** times,
Isa 4:1. . . . . . so few men will be left that ***s***
Luke 11:26. . spirit finds ***s*** other spirits
Rev 1:4. . . . . John to the ***s*** churches in the
Rev 6:1. . . . . first of the ***s*** seals on the
Rev 8:2. . . . . were given ***s*** trumpets.
Rev 10:4. . . . what the ***s*** thunders said,
Rev 15:7. . . . handed each of the ***s*** angels

SEVEN (n)
the number 7
Dan 9:26 . . . period of sixty-two sets of ***s,***

SEVENFOLD (adj)
having seven units or members
Rev 4:5. . . . . This is the ***s*** Spirit of God.

SEVENTH (adj)
of or relating to the position of the number seven
Gen 2:2 . . . . On the ***s*** day God
Exod 20:10 . the ***s*** day is a Sabbath day
Exod 23:11 . uncultivated during the ***s***
Exod 23:12 . but on the ***s*** day you must
Heb 4:4 . . . . On the ***s*** day God rested

SEVENTY (adj)
of or relating to the number 70
Dan 9:24 . . . A period of ***s*** sets of seven
Matt 18:22. . Jesus replied, "but ***s*** times

SEVERE (adj)
strict in judgment, discipline, or government; inflicting physical discomfort or hardship
Rom 11:22. . God is both kind and ***s.***
1 Thes 1:6 . . in spite of the ***s*** suffering

SEWED (v)
to unite or fasten by stitches
Gen 3:7 . . . . So they ***s*** fig leaves together

SEXUAL (adj)
of, relating to, or associated with sex or the sexes; having or involving sex
Exod 22:19 . who has ***s*** relations with
Lev 18:6. . . . never have ***s*** relations with
Num 25:1 . . by having ***s*** relations with
Matt 1:25. . . did not have ***s*** relations with
Matt 15:19. . adultery, all ***s*** immorality,
Acts 15:20 . . to idols, from ***s*** immorality,
1 Cor 5:1 . . . about the ***s*** immorality going
1 Cor 5:11 . . yet indulges in ***s*** sin
1 Cor 6:9 . . . who indulge in ***s*** sin, or who
1 Cor 6:18 . . Run from ***s*** sin! No other

1 Cor 7:1 . . . to abstain from *s* relations.
1 Cor 10:8 . . not engage in *s* immorality
2 Cor 12:21 . impurity, *s* immorality,
Eph 5:3 . . . . be no *s* immorality, impurity,
Col 3:5 . . . . . to do with *s* immorality,
1 Thes 4:3 . . stay away from all *s* sin
2 Pet 2:10. . . own twisted *s* desire, and
2 Pet 2:18. . . to twisted *s* desires,
Rev 2:14. . . . and by committing *s* sin.
Rev 2:20. . . . teaches them to commit *s* sin

SEXUALLY (adv)
1 Tim 1:10 . . is for people who are *s* immoral
Rev 22:15. . . the sorcerers, the *s* immoral,

SHADE (n)
a place sheltered from the sun
Ps 121:5 . . . . you as your protective *s*.

SHADOW, SHADOWS (n)
shelter from danger or observation; an imperfect and faint representation; partial darkness or obscurity within a part of space
Ps 17:8 . . . . . me in the *s* of your wings.
Ps 36:7 . . . . . shelter in the *s* of your
Ps 39:6 . . . . . are merely moving *s-s*, and
Ps 91:1 . . . . . find rest in the *s* of the
Col 2:17 . . . . these rules are only *s-s* of
Heb 8:5 . . . . only a copy, a *s* of the real
Heb 10:1 . . . was only a *s*, a dim preview

SHADOWBOXING (v)
to box with an imaginary opponent especially as a form of training
1 Cor 9:26 . . I am not just *s*.

SHAKE, SHAKEN, SHAKING (v)
to move to and fro or up and down; to cause to quake, quiver, or tremble; to weaken
Ps 16:8 . . . . . I will not be *s-n*, for he
Ps 22:7 . . . . . They sneer and *s* their heads,
Ps 62:2 . . . . . where I will never be *s-n*.
Ps 64:8 . . . . . see them will *s* their heads
Isa 28:16. . . . believes need never be *s-n*.
Ezek 38:19. . I promise a mighty *s-ing* in the
Hag 2:6 . . . . I will again *s* the heavens
Matt 24:29. . the heavens will be *s-n*.
Mark 15:29 . abuse, *s-ing* their heads
Luke 6:38. . . pressed down, *s-n* together to
Acts 2:25 . . . I will not be *s-n*, for he is
2 Thes 2:2 . . be so easily *s-n* or alarmed
Heb 12:26 . . again I will *s* not only
Heb 12:27 . . will be *s-n* and removed,

SHAME (n)
a condition or feeling of humiliating disgrace or disrepute; something that brings censure and reproach
Lev 19:12. . . Do not bring *s* on the name
Ps 34:5 . . . . . no shadow of *s* will darken
Prov 28:7. . . wild friends bring *s* to
Dan 12:2 . . . some to *s* and everlasting
Titus 2:5. . . . not bring *s* on the word
Heb 6:6 . . . . holding him up to public *s*.
1 Jn 2:28. . . . shrink back from him in *s*.

SHAME (v)
to disgrace
1 Cor 1:27 . . in order to *s* those who
1 Cor 11:22 . church and *s* the poor?

SHAMEFUL (adj)
bringing shame
Prov 18:13. . facts is both *s* and foolish.
Hab 2:15 . . . over their *s* nakedness.
Rom 1:24. . . do whatever *s* things their
Rom 1:27. . . Men did *s* things with
2 Cor 4:2 . . . We reject all *s* deeds
2 Pet 2:2. . . . teaching and *s* immorality.

SHARE (n)
a portion belonging to or due to
Deut 10:9. . . Levites have no *s* of property
2 Kgs 2:9 . . . inherit a double *s* of your
Matt 21:34. . to collect his *s* of the crop.
Rev 22:19. . . remove that person's *s* in

SHARE, SHARED, SHARING (v)
to grant or give a share in; to partake of, use, experience, occupy, or enjoy with others; to have in common
Gen 21:10 . . to *s* the inheritance
1 Sam 30:24. We *s* and *s* alike—
Ps 41:9 . . . . . the one who *s-d* my food,
Luke 3:11. . . If you have food, *s* it with
Acts 2:42 . . . fellowship, and to *s-ing* in
Acts 2:45 . . . possessions and *s-d* the
Rom 8:17. . . we must also *s* his suffering.
Rom 11:31. . they, too, will *s* in God's
1 Cor 10:16 . aren't we *s-ing* in the blood
1 Cor 12:13 . we all *s* the same Spirit.
2 Cor 1:7 . . . as you *s* in our sufferings,
2 Cor 9:8 . . . left over to *s* with others.
Gal 4:30. . . . will not *s* the inheritance
Gal 6:6 . . . . . teachers, *s-ing* all good things
Phil 3:10 . . . suffer with him, *s-ing* in his
Col 1:12. . . . has enabled you to *s* in the
1 Thes 2:8 . . much that we *s-d* with you
2 Thes 2:14 . you can *s* in the glory
1 Tim 6:18. . ready to *s* with others.

Heb 6:4 . . . . and *s-d* in the Holy Spirit,
Heb 12:10 . . we might *s* in his holiness.
Heb 13:16 . . to *s* with those in need.
Rev 3:20. . . . and we will *s* a meal together

SHARPENS (v)
to make sharp or sharper
Prov 27:17 . . As iron *s* iron, so a

SHAVED, SHAVING (v)
to sever the hair from (the skin) close to the roots
Judg 16:17 . . my head were *s*, my strength
1 Cor 11:5 . . the same as *s-ing* her head.
1 Cor 11:6 . . her hair cut or her head *s*,

SHEARERS (n)
those who cut or clip (as hair or wool) from someone or something
Isa 53:7. . . . . silent before the *s*, he did
Acts 8:32 . . . silent before the *s*, he did

SHED, SHEDDING (v)
to spill; to cause to flow
1 Chr 22:8 . . you have *s* so much blood
Ps 106:38 . . . They *s* innocent blood,
Rom 3:25. . . his life, *s-ding* his blood.
Heb 9:22 . . . without the *s-ding* of blood,
1 Jn 5:6. . . . . by *s-ding* his blood on the cross
Rev 16:6. . . . they *s* the blood of your holy people

SHEEP (n)
a small domesticated animal, representing wealth and livelihood for many Israelites; figurative of God's people
Gen 22:8 . . . God will provide a *s* for
Num 27:17 . not be like *s* without a
Deut 17:1. . . defective cattle, *s*, or
1 Sam 15:14. bleating of *s* and goats
Ps 44:22 . . . . being slaughtered like *s*.
Ps 78:52 . . . . people like a flock of *s*,
Ps 100:3 . . . . We are his people, the *s*
Ps 119:176 . . wandered away like a lost *s*;
Isa 53:7. . . . . as a *s* is silent before
Jer 50:6. . . . . people have been lost *s*.
Matt 7:15. . . disguised as harmless *s* but
Matt 9:36. . . like *s* without a shepherd.
Matt 10:16 . . you out as *s* among wolves.
Matt 12:11 . . a *s* that fell into a well
Matt 25:32 . . separates the *s* from the
John 10:3 . . . calls his own *s* by name
John 10:7 . . . I am the gate for the *s*.
John 10:15 . . sacrifice my life for the *s*.
John 21:17 . . Then feed my *s*.
1 Pet 2:25. . . were like *s* who wandered

SHEEPFOLD (n)
a pen or shelter for sheep
John 10:1 . . . sneaks over the wall of a *s*,

SHELTER, SHELTERS (n)
something that covers or affords protection
see also REFUGE
Lev 23:34. . . the Festival of *S-s* on the
Deut 16:16. . the Festival of *S-s*.
Ps 9:9 . . . . . . LORD is a *s* for the
Ps 31:20 . . . . hide them in the *s* of your
Ps 36:7 . . . . . All humanity finds *s* in the
Ps 61:4 . . . . . safe beneath the *s* of your
Isa 4:6. . . . . . will be a *s* from daytime heat
Isa 32:2. . . . . be like a *s* from the wind
Isa 58:7. . . . . give *s* to the homeless.
Zech 14:16. . the Festival of *S-s*.

SHEPHERD, SHEPHERDS (n)
a person who tends sheep; figurative of political and religious leaders, especially those who care for God's people
Gen 48:15 . . has been my *s* all my life,
Gen 49:24 . . by the *S*, the Rock of Israel.
Num 27:17 . be like sheep without a *s*.
2 Sam 7:7. . . tribal leaders, the *s-s* of my
1 Kgs 22:17 . like sheep without a *s*.
Ps 23:1 . . . . . The LORD is my *s*;
Ps 28:9 . . . . . Lead them like a *s*, and
Isa 40:11. . . . feed his flock like a *s*.
Jer 23:1. . . . . my people—the *s-s* of my
Jer 31:10. . . . as a *s* does his flock.
Ezek 34:5. . . scattered without a *s*, and
Ezek 34:8. . . you were my *s-s*, you didn't
Ezek 34:12. . like a *s* looking for his
Zech 11:9. . . won't be your *s* any longer.
Zech 13:7. . . Strike down the *s*, and
Matt 2:6. . . . will be the *s* for my people
Matt 9:36. . . like sheep without a *s*.
Matt 26:31 . . God will strike the *S*,
John 10:11 . . I am the good *s*.
Acts 20:28 . . Feed and *s* God's flock—
Heb 13:20 . . Jesus, the great *S* of the
Jude 1:12. . . are like shameless *s-s* who care
Rev 7:17. . . . on the throne will be their *S*.

SHEWBREAD (KJV)
Exod 25:30 . Place the ***Bread of the Presence***
Num 4:7 . . . the ***Bread of the Presence*** is
1 Chr 23:29 . in charge of the ***sacred bread***
Matt 12:4. . . the ***sacred loaves of bread***
Heb 9:2 . . . . and ***sacred loaves of bread***

SHIELD (n)
a broad piece of defensive armor carried on the arm; one who protects or defends
2 Sam 22:3. . He is my *s,* the power that
2 Sam 22:36. me your *s* of victory;
Ps 3:3 . . . . . . LORD, are a *s* around me;
Ps 5:12 . . . . . them with your *s* of love.
Ps 7:10 . . . . . God is my *s,* saving those
Ps 18:2 . . . . . He is my *s,* the power that
Ps 28:7 . . . . . LORD is my strength and *s.*
Ps 33:20 . . . . is our help and our *s.*
Ps 35:2 . . . . . armor, and take up your *s.*
Ps 84:11 . . . . God is our sun and our *s.*
Ps 119:114 . . are my refuge and my *s;*
Ps 144:2 . . . . He is my *s,* and I take refuge
Prov 2:7 . . . . He is a *s* to those who walk
Eph 6:16 . . . hold up the *s* of faith

SHINE, SHINES, SHINING (v)
to emit rays of light; to be eminent, conspicuous, or distinguished; to have a bright, glowing appearance
see also SHONE
Ps 37:6 . . . . . of your cause will *s* like
Ps 50:2 . . . . . God *s-s* in glorious radiance.
Ps 112:4 . . . . Light *s-s* in the darkness for
Ps 118:27 . . . LORD is God, *s-ing* upon us.
Isa 60:1. . . . . Let your light *s* for all
Ezek 1:27. . . like a burning flame, *s-ing*
Dan 12:3 . . . righteousness will *s* like
Matt 13:43 . . the righteous will *s* like
John 1:5 . . . . The light *s-s* in the darkness,
2 Cor 4:6 . . . has made this light *s* in
Phil 2:15 . . . of God, *s-ing* like bright lights

SHIP (n)
a large seagoing vessel
Prov 31:14 . . a merchant's *s,* bringing

SHIPWRECK, SHIPWRECKED (v)
to destroy (a ship) by grounding or foundering
2 Cor 11:25 . Three times I was *s-ed.*
1 Tim 1:19 . . their faith has been *s-ed.*
Jude 1:12 . . . reefs that can *s* you.

SHONE (v)
to have a bright, glowing appearance
see also SHINE
Matt 17:2. . . his face *s* like the sun,
Rev 21:11. . . It *s* with the glory of God

SHOP (n)
a handicraft establishment; workshop
Jer 18:2. . . . . Go down to the potter's *s,*

SHORT (adj)
brief; not coming up to a measure or requirement
Ps 89:47 . . . . Remember how *s* my life is,
Rom 3:23 . . . all fall *s* of God's glorious
1 Cor 7:29 . . time that remains is very *s.*

SHORT-LIVED (adj)
not living or lasting long
Job 20:5 . . . . of the wicked has been *s*

SHORT-TEMPERED (adj)
having a quick temper
Prov 14:17. . *S* people do foolish things,

SHOULDERS (n)
the place on the human body where the arm is joined to the trunk
Isa 9:6. . . . . . government will rest on his *s.*
Luke 15:5. . . carry it home on his *s.*

SHOUT, SHOUTED, SHOUTING (v)
to utter a loud cry or in a loud voice
Job 38:7 . . . . all the angels *s-ed* for joy?
Ps 95:1 . . . . . Let us *s* joyfully to
Ps 100:1 . . . . *S* with joy to the LORD,
Isa 12:6. . . . . people of Jerusalem *s* his
Isa 40:3. . . . . someone *s-ing,* "Clear the way
Isa 40:9. . . . . *s* from the mountaintops!
Isa 42:2. . . . . He will not *s* or raise his
Zech 9:9. . . . people of Zion! *S* in triumph,
Matt 3:3 . . . . a voice *s-ing* in the wilderness,
Matt 10:27. . *s* from the housetops for

SHOW (n)
an impressive display
Matt 23:5. . . Everything they do is for *s.*

SHOW, SHOWED, SHOWN, SHOWS (v)
to cause or permit to be seen; to point out; to reveal or demonstrate; to bestow
Exod 33:18 . Then *s* me your glorious
2 Sam 22:26. To the faithful you *s*
Neh 9:19 . . . pillar of fire *s-ed* them the
Ps 4:6 . . . . . . Who will *s* us better times?
Ps 16:11 . . . . You will *s* me the way
Ps 119:132 . . Come and *s* me your
Prov 3:6. . . . he will *s* you which path
Prov 24:23 . . wrong to *s* favoritism
Eccl 9:1 . . . . God will *s* them favor.
Isa 30:18. . . . so he can *s* you his love
Hos 6:6 . . . . I want you to *s* love, not
Zech 7:9. . . . Judge fairly, and *s* mercy
Luke 24:40. . *s-ed* them his hands and his
Acts 2:28 . . . You have *s-n* me the way
Acts 10:34 . . that God *s-s* no favoritism.

Rom 3:20 . . . The law simply ***s-s*** us how
Rom 3:21 . . . But now God has ***s-n*** us a way
Rom 5:8 . . . . God ***s-ed*** his great love for us
Rom 9:22 . . . the right to ***s*** his anger
Eph 2:7 . . . . as ***s-n*** in all he has done
Jas 2:18 . . . . . I will ***s*** you my faith
1 Jn 4:9 . . . . . God ***s-ed*** how much he loved

SHOWER, SHOWERED (v)
to give in abundance
Hos 10:12 . . come and ***s*** righteousness
2 Cor 1:5 . . . more God will ***s*** us with
Eph 1:8 . . . . He has ***s-ed*** his kindness

SHOWERS (n)
something resembling a rain shower
Ezek 34:26 . . will be ***s*** of blessing.

SHREWD, SHREWDEST (adj)
marked by clever discerning awareness and hardheaded acumen
Gen 3:1 . . . . serpent was the ***s-est*** of all
Matt 10:16 . . So be as ***s*** as snakes

SHRINK (v)
to become smaller or more compacted
Matt 9:16 . . . new patch would ***s*** and rip

SHUT (v)
to close
Isa 6:10 . . . . . their ears and ***s*** their eyes.
Dan 6:22 . . . his angel to ***s*** the lions'
Amos 5:13 . . keep their mouths ***s***, for it
Heb 11:33 . . They ***s*** the mouths of lions,

SICK (adj)
affected with disease or ill health; lacking vigor
Ps 41:3 . . . . . when they are ***s*** and restores
Prov 13:12 . . deferred makes the heart ***s***,
Matt 9:12 . . . need a doctor—***s*** people do.
Matt 10:8 . . . Heal the ***s***, raise the dead,
Matt 25:36 . . I was ***s***, and you cared for
Mark 3:10 . . all the ***s*** people eagerly
1 Cor 11:30 . many of you are weak and ***s***
Jas 5:14 . . . . . Are any of you ***s***?

SICKLE (n)
a small hand tool with a curved metal blade used for cutting stalks of grain
Joel 3:13 . . . . Swing the ***s***, for the
Rev 14:14 . . . a sharp ***s*** in his hand.

SICKNESS, SICKNESSES (n)
a disordered, weakened, or unsound condition; illness
Matt 4:24 . . . whatever their ***s*** or disease,
Matt 8:17 . . . He took our ***s-es*** and removed

SIDE (n)
the right or left part of the trunk of the body
John 20:20 . . in his hands and his ***s***.

SIGHT (n)
mental or spiritual perception
Ps 51:4 . . . . . done what is evil in your ***s***.
Hab 1:13 . . . cannot stand the ***s*** of evil.
Jas 1:27 . . . . . religion in the ***s*** of God

SIGN, SIGNS (n)
something indicating the presence or existence of something else; something material or external that stands for or signifies something spiritual
Gen 9:12 . . . you a ***s*** of my covenant
Gen 17:11 . . your foreskin as a ***s*** of
Ps 105:27 . . . performed miraculous ***s-s***
Isa 55:13 . . . . be an everlasting ***s*** of
Dan 6:27 . . . he performs miraculous ***s-s***
Matt 12:38 . . a miraculous ***s*** to prove
Matt 24:3 . . . What ***s*** will signal your
Matt 24:30 . . the ***s*** that the Son of Man
Mark 16:17 . These miraculous ***s-s*** will
Luke 11:29 . . them is the ***s*** of Jonah.
John 3:2 . . . . Your miraculous ***s-s*** are
John 20:30 . . do many other miraculous ***s-s***
1 Cor 14:22 . in tongues is a ***s***, not for
2 Cor 12:12 . did many ***s-s*** and wonders
2 Thes 2:9 . . counterfeit power and ***s-s***

SIGNAL (n)
something (as a sound, gesture, or object) that conveys notice or warning
Num 10:5 . . you sound the ***s*** to move on,

SILENCE (n)
absence of speech, sound, or noise
Ps 39:2 . . . . . I stood there in ***s***—not even
Rev 8:1 . . . . . there was ***s*** throughout heaven

SILENCE, SILENCED, SILENCING (v)
to compel or reduce to silence; to cause to cease criticism
Ps 8:2 . . . . . . strength, ***s-ing*** your enemies
Titus 1:11 . . . They must be ***s-d***, because they
1 Pet 2:15 . . . honorable lives should ***s***

SILENT (adj)
mute, speechless; still
Ps 30:12 . . . . praises to you and not be ***s***.
Isa 53:7 . . . . . as a sheep is ***s*** before the
Isa 62:1 . . . . . Jerusalem, I cannot remain ***s***.
Hab 2:20 . . . the earth be ***s*** before him.
Acts 8:32 . . . And as a lamb is ***s*** before
Acts 18:9 . . . Speak out! Don't be ***s***!
1 Cor 14:34 . Women should be ***s*** during

SILVER (adj)
made of silver
Prov 25:11 . . apples in a *s* basket.
Dan 2:32 . . . and arms were *s,* its belly

SILVER (n)
a shiny gray metal valued next to gold, capable of a high polish; coin made of silver
Ps 66:10 . . . . have purified us like *s.*
Prov 3:14 . . . is more profitable than *s,*
Prov 8:10 . . . instruction rather than *s,*
Prov 22:1 . . . is better than *s* or gold.
Isa 48:10. . . . but not as *s* is refined.
Zech 11:12. . wages thirty pieces of *s.*
Zech 13:9. . . refine them like *s* and
Matt 25:15 . . two bags of *s* to another,
Matt 26:15 . . gave him thirty pieces of *s.*
Luke 7:41. . . 500 pieces of *s* to one
Acts 3:6 . . . . don't have any *s* or gold
1 Cor 3:12 . . materials—gold, *s,* jewels,

SILVERSMITH (n)
an artisan who makes articles of silver
Acts 19:24 . . with Demetrius, a *s* who had

SIMON
1. One of the twelve disciples, Simon Peter (Matt 16:16); see PETER.
2. One of the twelve disciples, Simon the Zealot (Matt 10:4; Mark 3:18; Luke 6:15; Acts 1:13).
3. Simon the sorcerer, rebuked by Peter (Acts 8:9-24).
4. Simon who had leprosy (Matt 26:6; Mark 14:3).

SIMPLE (n)
a person lacking in knowledge or expertise
Ps 19:7 . . . . . trustworthy, making wise the *s.*

SIMPLEMINDED (adj)
foolish
Prov 19:25 . . the *s* will learn a lesson;

SIN, SINS (n)
moral evil; transgression of or rebellion against God's laws
Gen 4:7 . . . . *S* is crouching at the door,
Lev 5:5. . . . . ways, you must confess your *s.*
Num 32:23 . be sure that your *s* will find
Deut 24:16. . to death for the *s-s* of their
Ps 19:13 . . . . servant from deliberate *s-s!*
Ps 32:1 . . . . . whose *s* is put out of sight!
Ps 38:18 . . . . I confess my *s-s;* I am deeply
Ps 51:1 . . . . . blot out the stain of my *s-s.*
Ps 51:2 . . . . . Purify me from my *s.*
Ps 65:3 . . . . . are overwhelmed by our *s-s,*
Ps 79:9 . . . . . Save us and forgive our *s-s*
Ps 103:12 . . . removed our *s-s* as far from
Prov 5:22. . . held captive by his own *s-s;*
Prov 10:19. . Too much talk leads to *s.*
Prov 14:21. . *s* to belittle one's neighbor;
Prov 17:19. . who loves to quarrel loves *s;*
Prov 28:13. . who conceal their *s-s* will
Prov 29:22. . commits all kinds of *s.*
Isa 1:18. . . . . your *s-s* are like scarlet,
Isa 53:6. . . . . laid on him the *s-s* of us all.
Isa 59:2. . . . . Because of your *s-s,* he has
Jer 31:30. . . . die for their own *s-s*—
Jer 31:34. . . . again remember their *s-s.*
Ezek 18:19. . pay for the parent's *s-s?*
Matt 1:21 . . . save his people from their *s-s.*
Matt 6:12. . . forgive us our *s-s,* as we
Matt 26:28 . . to forgive the *s-s* of many.
Mark 3:29 . . This is a *s* with eternal
Luke 5:24. . . on earth to forgive *s-s.*
John 1:29 . . . takes away the *s* of the world!
John 20:23 . . forgive anyone's *s-s,* they
Acts 2:38 . . . repent of your *s-s* and turn
Rom 4:25. . . because of our *s-s,* and he
Rom 6:2. . . . we have died to *s,* how can
Rom 6:11. . . the power of *s* and alive to
Rom 6:23. . . the wages of *s* is death,
Rom 7:7. . . . law that showed me my *s.*
Rom 7:25. . . nature I am a slave to *s.*
1 Cor 6:18 . . is a *s* against your own body.
1 Cor 15:3 . . died for our *s-s,* just as
1 Cor 15:56 . the law gives *s* its power.
Gal 1:4 . . . . . gave his life for our *s-s,* just
Gal 6:1 . . . . . believer is overcome by some *s,*
Eph 2:5 . . . . were dead because of our *s-s,*
1 Tim 5:22 . . share in the *s-s* of others.
Heb 2:17 . . . would take away the *s-s* of
Heb 9:28 . . . to take away the *s-s* of many
Heb 10:12 . . sacrifice for *s-s,* good for
Heb 12:1 . . . the *s* that so easily trips
Jas 1:15. . . . . when *s* is allowed to grow,
Jas 4:17. . . . . is *s* to know what you ought
Jas 5:16. . . . . Confess your *s-s* to each other
1 Pet 2:24. . . carried our *s-s* in his body
1 Pet 3:18. . . suffered for our *s-s* once for
1 Jn 1:8. . . . . claim we have no *s,* we are
1 Jn 1:9. . . . . to forgive us our *s-s* and to
1 Jn 2:1. . . . . if anyone does *s,* we have
1 Jn 3:5. . . . . take away our *s-s,* and
1 Jn 3:5. . . . . there is no *s* in him.
1 Jn 5:16. . . . a *s* that leads to death,
Rev 1:5. . . . . from our *s-s* by shedding his

SIN, SINNED, SINNING, SINS (v)

to commit an offense or fault against God; to break God's law

Exod 20:20 . will keep you from ***s-ning!***
2 Sam 12:13. I have ***s-ned*** against the
2 Chr 6:37 . . We have ***s-ned,*** done evil,
Job 1:5 . . . . . my children have ***s-ned***
Ps 51:4 . . . . . and you alone, have I ***s-ned;***
Ps 119:11 . . . I might not ***s*** against you.
Jer 14:20. . . . all have ***s-ned*** against you.
Dan 9:5 . . . . have ***s-ned*** and done wrong.
Mark 9:43 . . causes you to ***s,*** cut it off.
Luke 15:18. . I have ***s-ned*** against both
Luke 17:3. . . another believer ***s-s,*** rebuke
John 8:7 . . . . who has never ***s-ned*** throw
John 8:11 . . . Go and ***s*** no more.
Rom 1:30 . . . invent new ways of ***s-ning,***
Rom 3:23 . . . everyone has ***s-ned;*** we all
Rom 5:12 . . . When Adam ***s-ned,*** sin entered
Rom 14:23 . . is not right, you are ***s-ning.***
1 Cor 15:34 . is right, and stop ***s-ning.***
Heb 4:15 . . . we do, yet he did not ***s.***
Heb 10:26 . . deliberately continue ***s-ning***
1 Pet 2:22. . . He never ***s-ned,*** nor ever
1 Jn 1:10. . . . we have not ***s-ned,*** we are
1 Jn 3:6. . . . . who keeps on ***s-ning*** does not
1 Jn 5:18. . . . not make a practice of ***s-ning,***

SINCERE (adj)

genuine, having no intention to deceive

Prov 27:6. . . Wounds from a ***s*** friend are
2 Cor 6:6 . . . within us, and by our ***s*** love.
Jas 3:17. . . . . no favoritism and is always ***s.***
1 Pet 1:22. . . show ***s*** love to each other

SINFUL (adj)

tainted with, marked by, or full of sin; wicked

Lev 5:1. . . . . is ***s*** to refuse to testify,
1 Sam 15:23. is as ***s*** as witchcraft,
Luke 11:13. . So if you ***s*** people know
Rom 5:20. . . could see how ***s*** they were.
Rom 7:5. . . . harvest of ***s*** deeds, resulting
Rom 7:18. . . is, in my ***s*** nature.
Rom 7:25. . . because of my ***s*** nature I am
Rom 8:4. . . . follow our ***s*** nature but
Rom 8:13. . . deeds of your ***s*** nature,
Gal 5:13. . . . to satisfy your ***s*** nature.
Col 2:11. . . . away of your ***s*** nature.

SINLESS (adj)

having no moral blemish; having done nothing to incur the wrath of God

1 Pet 1:19. . . the ***s,*** spotless Lamb of God.

SING, SINGING (v)

to produce musical tones by means of the voice

Exod 15:1 . . I will ***s*** to the LORD,
Ps 5:11 . . . . . let them ***s*** joyful praises
Ps 13:6 . . . . . I will ***s*** to the LORD
Ps 47:6 . . . . . to our King, ***s*** praises!
Ps 51:14 . . . . I will joyfully ***s*** of
Ps 63:7 . . . . . my helper, I ***s*** for joy
Ps 69:30 . . . . praise God's name with ***s-ing,***
Ps 89:1 . . . . . I will ***s*** of the LORD's unfailing
Ps 95:1 . . . . . let us ***s*** to the LORD!
Ps 96:1 . . . . . ***S*** a new song to the LORD!
Ps 98:4 . . . . . praise and ***s*** for joy!
Ps 100:2 . . . . Come before him, ***s-ing*** with
Ps 101:1 . . . . I will ***s*** of your love
Ps 108:1 . . . . can ***s*** your praises with all
Ps 147:1 . . . . How good to ***s*** praises to
Isa 35:10. . . . enter Jerusalem ***s-ing***
Jer 16:9. . . . . to the happy ***s-ing*** and laughter
Acts 16:25 . . praying and ***s-ing*** hymns
1 Cor 14:15 . I will also ***s*** in words
1 Cor 14:26 . one will ***s,*** another will
Col 3:16 . . . . ***S*** psalms and hymns and
Rev 15:3. . . . And they were ***s-ing*** the song

SINGERS (n)

those who sing

2 Chr 5:13 . . trumpeters and ***s*** performed
Rev 18:22. . . of harps, ***s,*** flutes,

SINNER, SINNERS (n)

those guilty of sin

Ps 51:5 . . . . . I was born a ***s***—yes,
Prov 1:10. . . if ***s-s*** entice you, turn
Prov 23:17. . Don't envy ***s-s,*** but
Eccl 9:18 . . . one ***s*** can destroy much that
Isa 59:12. . . . we know what ***s-s*** we are.
Isa 64:5. . . . . We are constant ***s-s;*** how
Matt 9:13. . . who know they are ***s-s.***
Luke 5:8. . . . I'm too much of a ***s*** to be
Luke 15:7. . . over one lost ***s*** who repents
Luke 18:13. . to me, for I am a ***s.***
Rom 4:5. . . . faith in God who forgives ***s-s.***
Rom 5:6. . . . time and died for us ***s-s.***
1 Tim 1:15 . . into the world to save ***s-s***
Jas 5:20. . . . . whoever brings the ***s*** back
1 Pet 3:18. . . he died for ***s-s*** to bring

SISTER, SISTERS (n)

a female who has one or both parents in common with another; a female fellow Christian

Lev 18:9. . . . relations with your ***s*** or half
Matt 19:29. . or brothers or ***s-s*** or father
Mark 3:35 . . my brother and ***s*** and
1 Tim 5:2 . . . as you would your own ***s-s.***
Jas 2:1. . . . . . dear brothers and ***s-s,*** how can

SIT, SITS, SITTING (v)
to place (the buttocks) on or in a seat
Ps 110:1 . . . . to my Lord, "*S* in the place
Matt 19:28 . . Son of Man ***s-s*** upon his
Matt 20:23 . . to say who will ***s*** on my right
Col 3:1 . . . . . heaven, where Christ ***s-s*** in
Rev 3:21. . . . are victorious will ***s*** with me
Rev 4:9. . . . . to the one ***s-ting*** on the throne

SKILL (n)
a developed aptitude or ability
Heb 5:14 . . . have the ***s*** to recognize

SKILLED (adj)
having acquired mastery of or skill in something
Ps 71:15 . . . . I am not ***s*** with words.

SKILLFUL (adj)
possessed of or displaying skill
1 Kgs 7:14 . . was extremely ***s*** and talented
Ps 45:1 . . . . . the pen of a ***s*** poet.
Ps 78:72 . . . . led them with ***s*** hands.

SKY, SKIES (n)
the upper atmosphere appearing as a great vault or arch above the earth
Gen 1:8 . . . . God called the space "***s.***"
Deut 33:26. . across the ***s-ies*** in majestic
Ps 19:1 . . . . . ***s-ies*** display his craftsmanship.
Prov 30:19. . eagle glides through the ***s,***
Isa 34:4. . . . . fall from the ***s*** like withered
Jer 33:22. . . . the stars of the ***s*** cannot
Matt 24:29 . . will fall from the ***s,***
Rev 20:11. . . The earth and ***s*** fled from

SLANDER (n)
the utterance of false charges or misrepresentations that defame and damage another's reputation
Matt 15:19 . . theft, lying, and ***s.***
Mark 7:22 . . desires, envy, ***s,*** pride,
2 Cor 12:20 . selfishness, ***s,*** gossip,
Eph 4:31 . . . harsh words, and ***s,*** as
Col 3:8 . . . . . malicious behavior, ***s,***

SLANDER, SLANDERED, SLANDERING (v)
to utter slander; to malign or defame
Prov 10:18 . . ***s-ing*** others makes you a
1 Tim 3:11 . . must not ***s*** others.
2 Tim 3:3 . . . they will ***s*** others
Titus 2:3. . . . They must not ***s*** others
Titus 3:2. . . . They must not ***s*** anyone
2 Pet 2:2. . . . way of truth will be ***s-ed.***

SLANDEROUS (adj)
of, relating to, or marked by slander
Lev 19:16. . . Do not spread ***s*** gossip

SLAUGHTER (n)
the butchering of livestock for market or sacrifice
Isa 53:7. . . . . led like a lamb to the ***s.***
Jer 11:19. . . . lamb being led to the ***s.***
Acts 8:32 . . . led like a sheep to the ***s.***

SLAUGHTER, SLAUGHTERED (v)
to discredit, defeat, or demolish completely; to kill in a bloody or violent manner
Hos 6:5 . . . . to ***s*** you with my words,
Rev 5:6. . . . . looked as if it had been ***s-ed,***
Rev 5:12. . . . is the Lamb who was ***s-ed***

SLAVE, SLAVES (n)
a person bound in servitude; one who has lost his liberty and has no rights
see also SERVANT(S)
Matt 20:27 . . must become your ***s.***
John 8:34 . . . who sins is a ***s*** of sin.
John 15:15 . . longer call you ***s-s,*** because
Rom 1:1 . . . . is from Paul, a ***s*** of Christ
Rom 6:6 . . . . are no longer ***s-s*** to sin.
Rom 6:16 . . . you become the ***s*** of whatever
Rom 6:22. . . and have become ***s-s*** of God.
Rom 7:23 . . . makes me a ***s*** to the sin
1 Cor 6:12 . . not become a ***s*** to anything.
1 Cor 9:19 . . have become a ***s*** to all
1 Cor 12:13 . some are ***s-s,*** and some
Gal 3:28 . . . . Jew or Gentile, ***s*** or free,
Gal 4:7 . . . . . no longer a ***s*** but God's own
Gal 4:8 . . . . . you were ***s-s*** to so-called gods
Gal 4:30 . . . . rid of the ***s*** and her son,
Eph 6:5 . . . . ***S-s,*** obey your earthly masters
Phil 2:7 . . . . position of a ***s*** and was born
Col 3:11 . . . . barbaric, uncivilized, ***s,*** or
Col 4:1 . . . . . be just and fair to your ***s-s.***
1 Tim 1:10 . . or are ***s*** traders, liars,
Titus 3:3. . . . became ***s-s*** to many lusts
Phlm 1:16 . . no longer like a ***s*** to you.
2 Pet 2:19. . . For you are a ***s*** to whatever

SLAVERY (n)
submission to a dominating influence; the practice of slaveholding
Exod 2:23 . . under their burden of ***s.***
Rom 6:19. . . the illustration of ***s*** to help

SLEEP (n)
natural or induced state of rest; a state of lazy inactivity
Gen 2:21 . . . man to fall into a deep ***s.***
Gen 15:12 . . Abram fell into a deep ***s,***

Prov 20:13 . . If you love ***s***, you will
Prov 23:21 . . too much ***s*** clothes them
Rom 11:8 . . . has put them into a deep ***s***.

SLEEP, SLEEPING, SLEEPS (v)
to rest in a state of natural unconsciousness
Gen 28:11 . . against and lay down to ***s***.
Ps 4:8 . . . . . . peace I will lie down and ***s***,
Ps 121:4 . . . . Israel never slumbers or ***s-s***.
Prov 6:9 . . . . how long will you ***s***?
Eccl 5:12 . . . who work hard ***s*** well,
Mark 13:36 . find you ***s-ing*** when he

SLEEPER (n)
one that sleeps
Eph 5:14 . . . said, "Awake, O ***s***, rise up

SLEEPLESS (adj)
affording no sleep
2 Cor 6:5 . . . exhaustion, endured ***s*** nights,

SLING (n)
an instrument for throwing stones; slingshot
1 Sam 17:50. with only a ***s*** and a stone,

SLOTHFUL(NESS) (KJV)
Prov 15:19 . . ***lazy*** person's way is blocked
Prov 21:25 . . the ***lazy*** will come to ruin,
Eccl 10:18 . . ***Laziness*** leads to a sagging roof
Rom 12:11 . . Never be ***lazy***, but work hard
Heb 6:12 . . . ***spiritually dull and indifferent***

SLUGGARD (KJV)
Prov 6:6 . . . . a lesson from the ants, you ***lazybones***
Prov 10:26 . . ***Lazy people*** irritate their employers
Prov 13:4 . . . ***Lazy people*** want much but
Prov 20:4 . . . ***Those too lazy*** to plow
Prov 26:16 . . ***Lazy people*** consider themselves smarter

SLUMBER (n)
sleep
Prov 6:10 . . . a little more ***s***, a little

SLY (adj)
clever in concealing one's aims or ends
Prov 7:10 . . . dressed and ***s*** of heart.

SMALLEST (adj)
of little consequence
Matt 5:18 . . . not even the ***s*** detail

SMASH, SMASHES (v)
to break or crush by violence
Ps 2:9 . . . . . . rod and ***s*** them like clay
Jer 23:29 . . . . hammer that ***s-es*** a rock

SMILE (v)
to bestow approval
Num 6:25 . . May the LORD ***s*** on you and
Ps 4:6 . . . . . . Let your face ***s*** on us, LORD.
Ps 67:1 . . . . . May his face ***s*** with favor on

SMOKE (n)
the gaseous products of burning materials
Exod 19:18 . The ***s*** billowed into the sky
Isa 6:4. . . . . . building was filled with ***s***.
Joel 2:30 . . . . and fire and columns of ***s***.
Acts 2:19 . . . and fire and clouds of ***s***.
Rev 9:2. . . . . air turned dark from the ***s***.
Rev 15:8. . . . filled with ***s*** from God's

SMOKE (v)
to emit smoke
Ps 104:32 . . . the mountains ***s*** at his touch.

SMOOTH (adj)
having a continuous, even surface
Jer 31:9. . . . . ***s*** paths where they will not
Luke 3:5. . . . and the rough places made ***s***.

SMOOTH (v)
to make smooth
Isa 26:7. . . . . you ***s*** out the path ahead
Isa 40:4. . . . . and ***s*** out the rough places.

SNAKE, SNAKES (n)
any of numerous limbless scaled reptiles
Num 21:8 . . replica of a poisonous ***s*** and
Prov 23:32 . . it bites like a poisonous ***s***;
Matt 10:16 . . shrewd as ***s-s*** and harmless
Luke 3:7. . . . You brood of ***s-s***! Who warned
John 3:14 . . . lifted up the bronze ***s*** on a
Rom 3:13 . . . ***S*** venom drips from their

SNARE, SNARES (n)
something by which one is entangled, involved in difficulties, or impeded
Josh 23:13 . . they will be a ***s*** and a trap
Eccl 7:26 . . . passion is a ***s***, and her soft
Lam 4:20 . . . was caught in their ***s-s***.
Rom 11:9 . . . table become a ***s***, a trap that

SNOUT (n)
a long projecting nose (as of swine)
Prov 11:22 . . gold ring in a pig's ***s***.

SNOW (n)
precipitation in the form of small white ice crystals
Prov 25:13 . . refresh like *s* in summer.
Isa 1:18. . . . . will make them as white as *s.*
Dan 7:9 . . . . clothing was as white as *s,*

SNUFFED (v)
to extinguish
Prov 13:9. . . wicked will be *s* out.

SOAP (n)
a cleansing and emulsifying agent
Mal 3:2. . . . . like a strong *s* that bleaches

SOAR, SOARING (v)
to sail or hover in the air often at a great height
2 Sam 22:11 . flew, *s-ing* on the wings
Isa 40:31. . . . will *s* high on wings

SODOM (n)
a city at the southern end of the Dead Sea destroyed because of its wickedness
Gen 13:12 . . to a place near *S* and settled
Gen 19:24 . . the sky on *S* and Gomorrah.
Isa 1:9. . . . . . have been wiped out like *S,*
Luke 10:12. . you, even wicked *S* will be
Rom 9:29. . . have been wiped out like *S,*
Rev 11:8. . . . figuratively called "*S*"

SOIL (n)
firm land, earth
Matt 13:23 . . on good *s* represents those

SOJOURN (KJV)
Gen 12:10 . . where he ***lived as a foreigner***
Acts 7:6 . . . . descendants would ***live in a foreign land***

SOJOURNER (KJV)
Gen 23:4 . . . a stranger and a ***foreigner***
Num 35:15 . ***foreigners*** living among you
Ps 39:12 . . . . a ***traveler*** passing through

SOLD (v)
to give up (property) to another in exchange for something of value
see also SELL
1 Kgs 21:25 . *s* himself to what was evil
Matt 13:44 . . and *s* everything he owned

SOLDIER (n)
one engaged in military service
1 Cor 9:7 . . . What *s* has to pay his own
2 Tim 2:3 . . . a good *s* of Christ Jesus.

SOLID (adj)
firm; not liquid
Ps 40:2 . . . . . set my feet on *s* ground
Heb 5:12 . . . and cannot eat *s* food.

SOLOMON
King of Israel (united kingdom), second son of David and Bathsheba (2 Sam 12:24-25); chosen as successor by David (1 Kgs 1:28-40); given final advice by David (1 Kgs 2:1-9); enemies of his rule removed (1 Kgs 2:13-46); prayed for wisdom (1 Kgs 3:3-15; 4:29-34); demonstrated wisdom (1 Kgs 3:16-28); built and dedicated the Temple (1 Kgs 5–8); the LORD's second appearance (1 Kgs 9:1-9); became famous and powerful (9:10–10:29); visited by the queen of Sheba (1 Kgs 10:1-13); practiced idolatry and warned by God (1 Kgs 11:1-13); troubled by enemies (1 Kgs 11:14-40); died (1 Kgs 11:41-43); wrote many things (1 Kgs 4:32; Ps 72; 127; Prov 1:1; 10:1; 25:1; Eccl 1:1; Song 1:1); often mentioned in NT (Matt 6:29; 12:42; Luke 11:31; 12:27; Acts 7:47).

SON, SONS (n)
a parent's male child or descendant further removed; spiritual heir; relationship of Jesus to the heavenly Father
see also CHILD(REN), DESCENDANT(S)
Gen 17:19 . . birth to a *s* for you.
Gen 21:10 . . slave-woman and her *s.*
Gen 22:2 . . . Take your *s,* your only
Ruth 4:15. . . better to you than seven *s-s!*
Ps 2:7 . . . . . . You are my *s.* Today I have
Isa 7:14. . . . . birth to a *s* and will call
Dan 7:13 . . . someone like a *s* of man
Hos 11:1 . . . I called my *s* out of Egypt.
Joel 2:28. . . . *s-s* and daughters will
Matt 1:21. . . will have a *s,* and you are
Matt 2:15. . . I called my *S* out of Egypt.
Matt 3:17. . . my dearly loved *S,* who brings
Matt 4:3. . . . you are the *S* of God, tell
Matt 11:27. . truly knows the *S* except the
Matt 13:55. . the carpenter's *s,* and we
Matt 14:33. . really are the *S* of God!
Matt 16:16. . are the Messiah, the *S* of
Matt 17:5. . . my dearly loved *S,* who brings
Matt 21:9. . . God for the *S* of David!
Matt 27:54. . truly was the *S* of God!
Matt 28:19. . Father and the *S* and the
Mark 14:62 . will see the *S* of Man seated
Luke 1:32. . . be called the *S* of the Most
Luke 2:7. . . . first child, a *s.* She wrapped
Luke 9:35. . . This is my *S,* my Chosen One.
Luke 12:8. . . on earth, the *S* of Man will

Luke 15:20. . ran to his *s,* embraced him,
John 3:16 . . . his one and only *S,* so that
John 3:36 . . . doesn't obey the *S* will never
John 17:1 . . . Glorify your *S* so he
Acts 13:33 . . You are my *S.* Today I have
Rom 1:4. . . . shown to be the *S* of God
Rom 5:10. . . death of his *S* while we
Rom 8:3. . . . He sent his own *S* in a body
Rom 8:29. . . to become like his *S,* so
Rom 8:32. . . even his own *S* but gave him
1 Cor 15:28 . who gave his *S* authority
2 Cor 6:18 . . be my *s-s* and daughters,
Gal 4:4. . . . . God sent his *S,* born of a
Gal 4:30. . . . slave and her *s,* for the *s*
Heb 1:2 . . . . and through the *S* he created
Heb 1:5 . . . . You are my *S.* Today I have
Heb 7:28 . . . God appointed his *S* with an
Heb 10:29 . . trampled on the *S* of God,
1 Jn 2:23. . . . acknowledges the *S* has the
1 Jn 4:9. . . . . one and only *S* into the world
1 Jn 5:5. . . . . Jesus is the *S* of God.
Rev 1:13. . . . someone like the *S* of Man.

SONG, SONGS (n)
a short musical composition of words and music; the act of singing
Exod 15:2 . . my strength and my *s;*
Job 35:10 . . . who gives *s-s* in the night?
Ps 40:3 . . . . . given me a new *s* to sing,
Ps 63:5 . . . . . praise you with *s-s* of joy.
Ps 96:1 . . . . . Sing a new *s* to the LORD!
Ps 119:54 . . . theme of my *s-s* wherever
Ps 137:3 . . . . of those *s-s* of Jerusalem!
Ps 149:1 . . . . Sing to the LORD a new *s.*
Isa 49:13. . . . Burst into *s,* O mountains!
Isa 55:12. . . . and hills will burst into *s,*
Rev 5:9. . . . . they sang a new *s* with these
Rev 15:3. . . . God, and the *s* of the Lamb:

SOON (adv)
before long
John 13:32 . . Son, he will *s* give glory to
2 Cor 4:18 . . see now will *s* be gone,

SORCERER, SORCERERS (n)
a person who practices sorcery
Exod 7:11 . . his own wise men and *s-s,*
Acts 8:9 . . . . a *s* there for many years,
Acts 13:6 . . . a Jewish *s,* a false prophet
Rev 22:15. . . the dogs—the *s-s,* the sexually

SORCERY (n)
the use of power gained from the assistance or control of evil spirits, especially for divining
Gal 5:20. . . . idolatry, *s,* hostility, quarreling,

SORROW, SORROWS (n)
deep distress, sadness, or regret
Ps 116:3 . . . . I saw only trouble and *s.*
Isa 65:14. . . . will cry in *s* and despair.
Jer 31:12. . . . all their *s-s* will be gone.
Amos 5:18. . What *s* awaits you
Matt 18:7. . . What *s* awaits the
Matt 23:13. . What *s* awaits you
Luke 11:46. . what *s* also awaits
Rom 9:2. . . . with bitter *s* and unending
2 Cor 7:10 . . the kind of *s* God wants
Eph 4:30 . . . do not bring *s* to God's Holy
1 Tim 6:10 . . themselves with many *s-s.*
Heb 13:17 . . with joy and not with *s.*
Jude 1:11 . . . What *s* awaits them!
Rev 21:4. . . . more death or *s* or crying

SORRY (adj)
feeling sorrow, regret, or penitence; inspiring pity
Gen 6:6 . . . . So the LORD was *s* he had
2 Chr 21:20 . No one was *s* when he died.
Ps 38:18 . . . . I am deeply *s* for what I have
Mal 3:14. . . . that we are *s* for our sins?
Matt 15:32. . I feel *s* for these people.
Matt 20:34. . Jesus felt *s* for them and
Mark 8:2 . . . I feel *s* for these people.

SOUGHT (v)
to search or look for
see also SEEK
2 Chr 26:5 . . the king *s* guidance from
2 Chr 31:21 . Hezekiah *s* his God
2 Chr 33:12 . Manasseh *s* the LORD
Eccl 12:10 . . The Teacher *s* to find just
1 Thes 2:6 . . we have never *s* it from

SOUL, SOULS (n)
the inner life of a human being, the seat of emotions, and the center of human personality
Deut 6:5. . . . heart, all your *s,* and all
Deut 28:65. . fail, and your *s* to despair.
Deut 30:6. . . your heart and *s* and so you
Josh 22:5 . . . all your heart and all your *s.*
2 Kgs 23:25 . heart and *s* and strength,
Prov 3:22. . . for they will refresh your *s.*
Jer 6:16. . . . . you will find rest for your *s-s.*
Matt 10:28. . can destroy both *s* and body
Matt 11:29. . you will find rest for your *s-s.*
Matt 22:37. . all your heart, all your *s,*
Mark 8:37 . . worth more than your *s?*
Mark 12:30 . heart, all your *s,* all your
Luke 16:23. . his *s* went to the place of
Luke 21:19. . firm, you will win your *s-s.*
John 12:27 . . my *s* is deeply troubled.
Heb 4:12 . . . cutting between *s* and spirit,

SOUND (adj)
free from error, fallacy, or misapprehension
see also WHOLESOME
2 Tim 4:3 . . . listen to *s* and wholesome

SOUND (n)
a particular auditory impression
Job 39:25 . . . snorts at the *s* of the horn.
Ps 98:6 . . . . . trumpets and the *s* of the
Dan 3:10 . . . they hear the *s* of the horn,
Acts 2:2 . . . . there was a *s* from heaven

SOUND (v)
to give a summons by sound
Num 10:6 . . When you *s* the signal a
1 Cor 14:8 . . the bugler doesn't *s* a clear

SOUR (adj)
having an unpleasant, acidic taste
Ezek 18:2. . . parents have eaten *s* grapes,

SOVEREIGN (adj)
possessed of supreme power; unlimited in extent
Ps 71:16 . . . . your mighty deeds, O *S* LORD.
Isa 25:8. . . . . *S* LORD will wipe away all
Isa 40:10. . . . the *S* LORD is coming
Isa 50:4. . . . . *S* LORD has given me his
Isa 61:1. . . . . Spirit of the *S* LORD is upon

SOVEREIGNTY (n)
supreme power especially over a body politic
Dan 5:18 . . . God gave *s*, majesty, glory,
Dan 7:27 . . . the *s*, power, and greatness

SOW(ED), SOWING (KJV)
Lev 25:3. . . . you may ***plant*** your fields
Ps 126:5 . . . . Those who ***plant*** in tears
Matt 13:4. . . As he ***scattered*** them across
Luke 12:24. . the ravens. They don't ***plant***
Luke 19:21. . crops you didn't ***plant***

SOWER (KJV)
Isa 55:10. . . . producing seed for the ***farmer***
Jer 50:16. . . . all ***those who plant crops***
Matt 13:18 . . the ***farmer planting seeds***
2 Cor 9:10 . . provides seed for the ***farmer***

SPACE (n)
a blank or empty area; expanse
Gen 1:8 . . . . God called the *s* "sky."

SPANK (v)
to strike especially on the buttocks with the open hand
Prov 23:13. . won't die if you *s* them.

SPARE, SPARED, SPARES (v)
to hold back from destroying, punishing, or harming; to have left over or as margin; to rescue from the necessity of doing or undergoing something
Esth 7:3 . . . . lives of my people will be ***s-d.***
Prov 13:24. . Those who *s* the rod of
Isa 54:2. . . . . your home, and *s* no expense!
Mal 3:17. . . . as a father ***s-s*** an obedient
Rom 8:32. . . did not *s* even his own Son
Rom 11:21 . . if God did not *s* the original
2 Pet 2:4. . . . God did not *s* even the angels
2 Pet 2:5. . . . And God did not *s* the ancient

SPARKLED (v)
to glitter or shine
Rev 21:11. . . *s* like a precious stone—

SPARROW, SPARROWS (n)
any of several species of birds that eat grain and insects and gather in noisy flocks
Ps 84:3 . . . . . Even the *s* finds a home,
Matt 10:31 . . than a whole flock of ***s-s.***
Luke 12:6. . . What is the price of five ***s-s***

SPEAK, SPEAKING, SPEAKS (v)
to express thoughts, opinions, or feelings orally; to talk
see also SPOKE
Deut 18:22. . If the prophet ***s-s*** in the
Ps 15:3 . . . . . or *s* evil of their friends.
Ps 78:2 . . . . . will *s* to you in a parable.
Isa 3:8. . . . . . because they *s* out against
Isa 32:4. . . . . stammer will *s* out plainly.
Matt 12:34 . . men like you *s* what is good
Matt 15:18 . . the words you *s* come from
Acts 2:11 . . . hear these people ***s-ing*** in our
1 Cor 14:2 . . ability to *s* in tongues,
1 Cor 14:19 . I would rather *s* five
1 Pet 3:16. . . if people *s* against you,

SPEAKERS (n)
one who makes a public speech
2 Cor 8:7 . . . in your faith, your gifted *s*,

SPECK (n)
a small particle
Matt 7:3. . . . why worry about a *s* in your

SPEECH (n)
the communication of thoughts in spoken words
Prov 16:23. . a wise mind comes wise *s;*
Prov 22:11. . gracious *s* will have the king
Prov 25:15. . soft *s* can break bones.
Zeph 3:9 . . . I will purify the *s* of all
1 Cor 1:17 . . not with clever *s*, for

SPELL (n)
a state of enchantment
Gal 3:1 . . . . . cast an evil ***s*** on you?

SPEND, SPENT (v)
to use up or pay out; to exhaust or wear out
Prov 21:20 . . but fools ***s*** whatever they
Isa 55:2. . . . . Why ***s*** your money on food
Mark 5:26 . . she had ***s-t*** everything she had
2 Cor 12:15 . I will gladly ***s*** myself

SPINS (v)
to draw out and twist into yarns or threads
Prov 31:13 . . flax and busily ***s*** it.

SPIRIT, SPIRITS (n)
"wind" or "breath"; a supernatural being; the third member of the Trinity, with God the Father and Jesus the Son; an attitude, mood, or disposition; an evil presence that can possess or influence a person; invisible, nonmaterial part of humans (as opposed to body or flesh)
see also ADVOCATE, HOLY SPIRIT
Gen 1:2 . . . . the ***S*** of God was hovering
Gen 6:3 . . . . My ***S*** will not put up with
Exod 31:3 . . filled him with the ***S*** of God,
Num 11:25 . ***S*** rested upon them, they
Deut 34:9. . . full of the ***s*** of wisdom,
Judg 13:25 . . And the ***S*** of the LORD
1 Sam 16:13. And the ***S*** of the LORD
1 Sam 16:14. a tormenting ***s*** that filled
2 Kgs 2:9 . . . double share of your ***s*** and
Job 33:4 . . . . the ***S*** of God has made me,
Ps 31:5 . . . . . I entrust my ***s*** into your
Ps 34:18 . . . . those whose ***s-s*** are crushed.
Ps 51:10 . . . . Renew a loyal ***s*** within me.
Ps 51:17 . . . . you desire is a broken ***s.***
Ps 139:7 . . . . can never escape from your ***S!***
Isa 11:2. . . . . ***S*** of the LORD will rest
Isa 44:3. . . . . I will pour out my ***S*** on your
Isa 63:10. . . . him and grieved his Holy ***S.***
Ezek 11:19. . put a new ***s*** within them.
Joel 2:28. . . . I will pour out my ***S*** upon all
Zech 4:6. . . . by my ***S,*** says the LORD
Matt 3:11 . . . baptize you with the Holy ***S***
Matt 3:16. . . and he saw the ***S*** of God
Matt 4:1 . . . . was led by the ***S*** into the
Matt 28:19 . . and the Son and the Holy ***S.***
Mark 1:8 . . . baptize you with the Holy ***S!***
Mark 5:12 . . pigs," the ***s-s*** begged.
Luke 1:35. . . The Holy ***S*** will come upon
John 3:5 . . . . born of water and the ***S.***
John 6:63 . . . ***S*** alone gives eternal life.
John 14:26 . . the Holy ***S***—he will teach
John 16:13 . . When the ***S*** of truth comes,
Acts 1:8 . . . . when the Holy ***S*** comes
Acts 2:4 . . . . as the Holy ***S*** gave them this
Acts 2:17 . . . will pour out my ***S*** upon all
Acts 5:3 . . . . You lied to the Holy ***S,*** and
Acts 6:3 . . . . full of the ***S*** and wisdom.
Acts 8:15 . . . to receive the Holy ***S.***
Acts 9:17 . . . and be filled with the Holy ***S.***
Acts 11:16 . . be baptized with the Holy ***S.***
Acts 19:2 . . . receive the Holy ***S*** when you
Rom 8:5. . . . controlled by the Holy ***S*** think
Rom 8:9. . . . do not have the ***S*** of Christ
Rom 8:26. . . the Holy ***S*** prays for us
1 Cor 2:10 . . For his ***S*** searches out
1 Cor 12:1 . . abilities the ***S*** gives us.
1 Cor 12:13 . one body by one ***S,*** and we
1 Cor 14:1 . . abilities the ***S*** gives—
2 Cor 3:6 . . . covenant, the ***S*** gives life.
2 Cor 3:17 . . and wherever the ***S*** of the
2 Cor 5:3 . . . not be ***s-s*** without bodies.
Gal 3:2 . . . . . receive the Holy ***S*** by obeying
Gal 5:22. . . . But the Holy ***S*** produces this
Eph 4:4 . . . . body and one ***S,*** just as you
Eph 4:30 . . . to God's Holy ***S*** by the way
Eph 6:12 . . . and against evil ***s-s*** in the
Eph 6:17 . . . sword of the ***S,*** which is the
1 Thes 5:19 . Do not stifle the Holy ***S.***
1 Tim 3:16 . . vindicated by the ***S.***
2 Tim 1:7 . . . not given us a ***s*** of fear
1 Pet 3:4. . . . gentle and quiet ***s,*** which
1 Jn 4:1. . . . . who claims to speak by the ***S.***

SPIRITUAL (adj)
having to do with the spirit, usually God's Spirit
Jonah 4:11 . . living in ***s*** darkness, not
Rom 7:14. . . for it is ***s*** and good.
1 Cor 2:14 . . who are ***s*** can understand
1 Cor 14:37 . think you are ***s,*** you should
1 Cor 15:44 . there are also ***s*** bodies.
Eph 5:19 . . . and hymns and ***s*** songs among
1 Pet 2:5. . . . you offer ***s*** sacrifices that

SPIT (v)
to eject (as saliva) from the mouth
Matt 27:30 . . And they ***s*** on him and
Rev 3:16. . . . I will ***s*** you out of my mouth

SPLENDOR (n)
great brightness or luster; magnificence
2 Chr 20:21 . him for his holy ***s.***
Ps 29:2 . . . . . the LORD in the ***s*** of
Ps 145:5 . . . . majestic, glorious ***s*** and
Prov 20:29 . . experience is the ***s*** of
Isa 33:17. . . . see the king in all his ***s,***
Hab 3:3 . . . . brilliant ***s*** fills the heavens,

SPLINTERS (n)
thin pieces split or broken off lengthwise; slivers
Num 33:55 . will be like *s* in your eyes

SPLIT (v)
to tear or rend apart
Matt 19:6. . . let no one *s* apart what God

SPOKE, SPOKEN (v)
to express thoughts, opinions, or feelings orally
see also SPEAK
Isa 40:5. . . . . The LORD has ***s-n!***
Acts 19:37 . . and have not ***s-n*** against our
2 Pet 1:21. . . Spirit, and they *s* from God.

SPOT, SPOTS (n)
a small area visibly different (as in color, finish, or material) from the surrounding area; a taint on character or reputation
Jer 13:23. . . . leopard take away its ***s-s?***
Eph 5:27 . . . church without a *s* or wrinkle

SPOTLESS (adj)
free from impurity; unblemished
1 Pet 1:19. . . the sinless, *s* Lamb of God.

SPREAD (v)
to stretch out; to become distributed, dispersed, or scattered
Isa 25:6. . . . . Armies will *s* a wonderful
Acts 6:7 . . . . God's message continued to *s.*
Acts 13:49 . . Lord's message *s* throughout
Acts 19:20 . . about the Lord *s* widely and
Phil 1:12 . . . helped to *s* the Good News.
2 Thes 3:1 . . message will *s* rapidly and

SPRING, SPRINGS (n)
a source of water issuing from the ground
Ps 107:33 . . . and ***s-s*** of water into dry,
Jas 3:12. . . . . fresh water from a salty *s.*
2 Pet 2:17. . . useless as dried-up ***s-s*** or

SPRINKLE, SPRINKLED (v)
to scatter in drops or particles
Lev 8:30. . . . and he ***s-d*** them on Aaron
Lev 16:14. . . He must *s* blood seven
Heb 10:22 . . have been ***s-d*** with Christ's

STAFF (n)
a long stick used for walking or a weapon, often a symbol of authority and protection
see also ROD
Gen 49:10 . . nor the ruler's *s* from his
Exod 7:12 . . then Aaron's *s* swallowed up
Num 17:6 . . Aaron, brought Moses a *s.*
2 Kgs 4:29 . . travel; take my *s* and go!
Ps 23:4. . . . . Your rod and your *s* protect

STAGGER (v)
to totter
Isa 63:6. . . . . and made them *s* and fall

STAIN (n)
a soiled or discolored spot
2 Pet 2:13. . . disgrace and a *s* among you.

STAINED (v)
to discolor, soil
Isa 63:1. . . . . with his clothing *s* red?

STAIRWAY (n)
one or more flights of stairs
Gen 28:12 . . dreamed of a *s* that reached

STAND, STANDING, STANDS (v)
to remain stationary; to remain erect; to maintain one's position; to endure successfully
see also STOOD
Exod 3:5 . . . you are ***s-ing*** on holy ground.
Josh 5:15 . . . where you are ***s-ing*** is holy.
Josh 10:12 . . Let the sun *s* still
Ps 24:3 . . . . . Who may *s* in his holy
Ps 33:11 . . . . LORD's plans *s* firm
Ps 76:7 . . . . . Who can *s* before you
Ps 119:89 . . . word, O LORD, ***s-s*** firm
Prov 12:7. . . family of the godly ***s-s*** firm.
Isa 40:8. . . . . word of our God ***s-s*** forever.
Mal 3:2. . . . . be able to *s* and face him
Luke 6:48. . . that house, it ***s-s*** firm because
Rom 14:10. . all *s* before the judgment
1 Cor 10:12 . think you are ***s-ing*** strong,
1 Cor 10:13 . to be more than you can *s.*
2 Cor 5:10 . . we must all *s* before Christ
Eph 6:14 . . . *S* your ground, putting on the
Phil 1:27 . . . you are ***s-ing*** together with
2 Tim 2:19 . . But God's truth ***s-s*** firm like
1 Pet 5:9. . . . *S* firm against him, and
Rev 3:20. . . . I *s* at the door and knock.

STANDARD, STANDARDS (n)
something established by authority, custom, or general consent as a model or example; criterion
Lev 24:22. . . This same *s* applies both to
Prov 20:23. . LORD detests double ***s-s;***

STANDING (n)
a position or condition
Rom 8:33. . . us right *s* with himself.

STAR, STARS (n)
a natural luminous body visible in the sky especially at night; sometimes symbolic for angels
Gen 1:16 . . . He also made the ***s-s.***
Num 24:17 . A *s* will rise from Jacob;

Job 38:7 . . . . morning ***s-s*** sang together
Isa 14:12. . . . O shining ***s,*** son of the
Dan 12:3 . . . shine like the ***s-s*** forever.
Matt 2:2. . . . We saw his ***s*** as it rose,
2 Pet 1:19. . . the Morning ***S*** shines in
Rev 2:28. . . . also give them the morning ***s!***
Rev 22:16. . . I am the bright morning ***s.***

STARLIGHT (n)
light given by the stars
Ps 74:16 . . . . you made the ***s*** and the sun.

STARVE, STARVING (v)
to suffer extreme hunger
Job 24:10 . . . they themselves are ***s-ing.***
Prov 6:30. . . who steals because he is ***s-ing.***
Luke 15:14. . the land, and he began to ***s.***

STATUE (n)
a three-dimensional representation usually of a person, animal, or mythical being that is produced by sculpturing, modeling, or casting
Dan 3:1 . . . . made a gold ***s*** ninety feet
Rev 13:14. . . make a great ***s*** of the

STATURE (n)
quality or status gained by growth, development, or achievement
Luke 2:52. . . wisdom and in ***s*** and in favor

STATUTES (KJV)
Exod 15:26 . keeping all his ***decrees***
Deut 4:40. . . If you obey all the ***decrees*** and
1 Kgs 3:14 . . ***decrees*** and my commands
Ps 19:8 . . . . . ***commandments*** of the LORD
Ps 119:112 . . to keep your ***decrees***

STAY, STAYED (v)
to continue in a place or condition
Ps 119:9 . . . . can a young person ***s*** pure?
Luke 2:43. . . but Jesus ***s-ed*** behind in
Luke 22:28. . You have ***s-ed*** with me
Gal 5:1 . . . . . make sure that you ***s*** free,

STEDFAST (KJV)
Ps 78:37 . . . . They did not ***keep*** his covenant
1 Cor 15:58 . be ***strong*** and immovable.
Heb 3:14 . . . if we are ***faithful*** to the end,
1 Pet 5:9. . . . and be ***strong*** in your faith

STEAL, STEALING, STEALS (v)
to take the property of another wrongfully
see also STOLE
Exod 20:15 . You must not ***s.***
Lev 19:11. . . Do not ***s.***
Deut 5:19. . . You must not ***s.***
Prov 28:24. . who ***s-s*** from his father
Matt 19:18. . You must not ***s.***
Matt 27:64. . coming and ***s-ing*** his body
Rom 13:9. . . You must not ***s.***
Eph 4:28 . . . If you are a thief, quit ***s-ing.***
1 Pet 4:15. . . not be for murder, ***s-ing,***

STEPS (n)
course, way
Ps 37:23 . . . . LORD directs the ***s*** of
Prov 20:24. . LORD directs our ***s,***
1 Pet 2:21. . . you must follow in his ***s.***

STIFFNECKED (KJV)
Exod 32:9 . . how ***stubborn and rebellious***
Exod 34:9 . . ***stubborn and rebellious*** people
Deut 10:16. . stop being ***stubborn***
2 Chr 30:8 . . not be ***stubborn,*** as they
Acts 7:51 . . . You ***stubborn*** people! You are

STIFFHEARTED (KJV)
Ezek 2:4. . . . stubborn and ***hard-hearted***

STILL (adj)
devoid of or abstaining from motion; quiet, calm
Ps 46:10 . . . . Be ***s,*** and know that I am
Isa 57:20. . . . never ***s*** but continually
Mark 4:39 . . Silence! Be ***s!***

STILL (adv)
without motion
Exod 14:13 . Just stand ***s*** and watch
Josh 10:13 . . sun stood ***s*** and the moon
2 Chr 20:17 . then stand ***s*** and watch

STILLNESS (n)
the quality or state of being still
Ps 107:30 . . . What a blessing was that ***s***

STING (n)
a wound or pain caused by or as if by stinging
1 Cor 15:55 . where is your ***s?***

STIRS (v)
to provoke
Prov 10:12. . Hatred ***s*** up quarrels,

STOLE (v)
to wrongfully take the property of another
see also STEAL
Lev 6:4. . . . . give back whatever you ***s,***

STOMACH (n)
the digestive tract of the body
1 Cor 6:13 . . ***s,*** and the ***s*** for food.
Phil 4:12 . . . with a full ***s*** or empty,

STONE (adj)
of, relating to, or made of stone
Deut 4:13. . . he wrote on two *s* tablets.

STONE, STONES (n)
hardened mineral or rock; figurative of Christ or of hardened hearts
Exod 28:10 . Six names will be on each *s,*
Josh 4:3 . . . . Take twelve ***s-s*** from the very
1 Sam 17:40. picked up five smooth ***s-s***
Ps 91:12 . . . . even hurt your foot on a *s.*
Ps 118:22 . . . *s* that the builders rejected
Isa 8:14. . . . . a *s* that makes people stumble,
Isa 28:16. . . . a foundation *s* in Jerusalem,
Isa 50:7. . . . . face like a *s,* determined to
Jer 51:26. . . . Even your ***s-s*** will never again
Matt 3:9. . . . Abraham from these very ***s-s.***
Matt 7:9. . . . give them a *s* instead?
Matt 21:42. . *s* that the builders rejected
Matt 24:2. . . Not one *s* will be left
Mark 16:3 . . roll away the *s* for us from
Luke 4:3. . . . tell this *s* to become a loaf
John 8:7 . . . . sinned throw the first *s!*
1 Pet 2:5. . . . you are living ***s-s*** that God

STONED, STONING (v)
to kill by pelting with stones
2 Cor 11:25 . with rods. Once I was ***s-d.***
Heb 11:37 . . Some died by ***s-ing,*** some were

STONY (adj)
insensitive to pity or human feeling
Ezek 11:19. . away their *s,* stubborn heart

STOOD (v)
to maintain one's position
see also STAND
Josh 10:13 . . So the sun *s* still and
2 Tim 4:17 . . But the Lord *s* with me

STOP, STOPS (v)
to cease activity or operation; to pause or hesitate; to restrain or prevent
Job 37:14 . . . *S* and consider the wonderful
Prov 15:18. . cool-tempered person ***s-s***
Jer 7:5. . . . . . only if you *s* your evil
Jer 32:40. . . . I will never *s* doing good
Lam 3:49 . . . flow endlessly; they will not *s*
Dan 4:35 . . . No one can *s* him or say to
Matt 19:14. . come to me. Don't *s* them!
Eph 6:16 . . . shield of faith to *s* the

STORE (n)
a large quantity, supply, or number
Isa 33:6. . . . . a rich *s* of salvation,

STORE, STORED (v)
to lay away; to accumulate
Matt 6:19. . . Don't *s* up treasures
Matt 6:26. . . plant or harvest or *s* food
Luke 2:51. . . And his mother ***s-d*** all these

STORIES (n)
fictional narratives
2 Pet 1:16. . . making up clever *s* when

STORM (n)
a heavy fall of rain, snow, or hail sometimes accompanied by thunder and lightning; a disturbed or agitated state
see also WHIRLWIND, WIND
Ps 50:3 . . . . . and a great *s* rages around
Ps 55:8 . . . . . from this wild *s* of hatred.
Ps 107:29 . . . He calmed the *s* to a whisper
Luke 8:24. . . *s* stopped and all was calm.

STRAIN (v)
to exert (as oneself) to the utmost; to filter
Ps 119:123 . . My eyes *s* to see your
Matt 23:24 . . You *s* your water so

STRANGE (adj)
foreign; not before known, heard, or seen
see also FOREIGN
Isa 28:11. . . . who speak a *s* language!
1 Cor 14:21 . people through *s* languages
1 Pet 4:12. . . something *s* were happening

STRANGER, STRANGERS (n)
a person who is unknown or with whom one is unacquainted
see also FOREIGNER(S)
Job 31:32 . . . turned away a *s* but have
Matt 25:35. . I was a *s,* and you invited
John 10:5 . . . They won't follow a *s;*
1 Tim 5:10 . . been kind to ***s-s*** and served
Heb 13:2 . . . to show hospitality to ***s-s,*** for

STRANGLED (adj)
characterized by choking to death
Acts 15:29 . . or the meat of *s* animals,

STRATEGIES (n)
a careful and clever plan or method
Eph 6:11 . . . against all *s* of the devil.

STRAW (n)
stalks of grain after threshing
1 Cor 3:12 . . jewels, wood, hay, or *s.*

STRAYED (v)
to wander
Isa 53:6. . . . . like sheep, have *s* away.
Ezek 34:16. . lost ones who *s* away, and

STREAMS (n)
bodies of running water (as a river or brook)
Ps 23:2 . . . . . leads me beside peaceful **s**.
Jer 31:9. . . . . walk beside quiet **s** and

STRENGTH (n)
capacity for exertion or endurance; support; the power of a person or of God, measured variously in terms of wealth, wisdom, military might, or physical prowess
Exod 15:2 . . LORD is my **s** and my
Deut 6:5. . . . your soul, and all your **s**.
2 Kgs 23:25 . his heart and soul and **s**,
1 Chr 16:11 . LORD and for his **s**;
Neh 8:10 . . . of the LORD is your **s**!
Ps 23:3 . . . . . He renews my **s**. He guides me
Ps 28:7 . . . . . LORD is my **s** and shield.
Ps 33:16 . . . . nor is great **s** enough to save
Ps 46:1 . . . . . God is our refuge and **s**,
Ps 59:17 . . . . O my **S**, to you I sing
Ps 65:6 . . . . . armed yourself with mighty **s**.
Ps 84:5 . . . . . for those whose **s** comes from
Ps 139:10 . . . your **s** will support me.
Isa 31:1. . . . . depending on the **s** of human
Isa 40:26. . . . power and incomparable **s**,
Jer 27:5. . . . . With my great **s** and powerful
Mic 5:4. . . . . with the LORD's **s**, in
Hab 3:19 . . . LORD is my **s**!
Zech 4:6. . . . nor by **s**, but by my Spirit,
Mark 12:30 . your mind, and all your **s**.
1 Cor 1:25 . . the greatest of human **s**.
Phil 4:13 . . . Christ, who gives me **s**.
Heb 11:34 . . weakness was turned to **s**.
Heb 13:9 . . . Your **s** comes from God's

STRENGTHEN, STRENGTHENED, STRENGTHENS (v)
to make or become stronger
2 Chr 16:9 . . in order to **s** those whose
Isa 41:10. . . . I will **s** you and help you.
1 Cor 8:1 . . . is love that **s-s** the church.
1 Cor 14:4 . . in tongues is ***s-ed*** personally,
1 Cor 14:4 . . word of prophecy **s-s** the
1 Cor 14:5 . . whole church will be ***s-ed***.
1 Cor 14:12 . seek those that will **s** the
1 Cor 14:17 . but it won't **s** the people
1 Cor 14:26 . is done must **s** all of you.
2 Cor 13:10 . has given me to **s** you, not
Heb 12:12 . . tired hands and **s** your weak
1 Pet 5:10. . . support, and **s** you, and he

STRIKE (v)
to aim and deliver a blow, stroke, or thrust (as with the hand, a weapon, or a tool); to inflict
see also STRUCK
Zech 13:7. . . **S** down the shepherd, and
Matt 26:31 . . God will **s** the Shepherd,
Rev 19:15. . . sword to **s** down the nations.

STRIP (v)
to remove extraneous or superficial matter from
Heb 12:1 . . . let us **s** off every weight

STRIPS (n)
long, narrow pieces of a material
Luke 2:12. . . wrapped snugly in **s** of cloth,

STRIPES (KJV)
Acts 16:33 . . washed their ***wounds***
2 Cor 11:24 . gave me thirty-nine ***lashes***
1 Pet 2:24. . . By his ***wounds*** you are healed

STRONG, STRONGER, STRONGEST (adj)
having or marked by great physical power, moral or intellectual power, or great resources (as of wealth or talent); firm
Exod 6:1 . . . force of my **s** hand, he
Deut 5:15. . . you out with his **s** hand
Deut 7:8. . . . with such a **s** hand from your
Deut 31:6. . . So be **s** and courageous!
Josh 1:6 . . . . Be **s** and courageous,
Judg 16:5. . . makes him so **s** and how he
2 Sam 22:33. God is my **s** fortress, and
1 Kgs 8:42 . . and your **s** hand and your
1 Chr 28:20 . Be **s** and courageous, and
Ezra 10:4 . . . so be **s** and take action.
Ps 24:8 . . . . . The LORD, **s** and mighty;
Ps 96:7 . . . . . LORD is glorious and **s**.
Prov 18:10. . LORD is a **s** fortress;
Prov 24:5. . . wise are mightier than the **s**,
Prov 30:25. . Ants—they aren't **s**, but
Prov 31:17. . She is energetic and **s**, a
Eccl 9:11 . . . ***s-est*** warrior doesn't always
Isa 35:4. . . . . Be **s**, and do not fear,
Jer 50:34. . . . one who redeems them is **s**.
Luke 1:80. . . and became **s** in spirit.
Luke 2:40. . . grew up healthy and **s**.
Luke 11:22. . someone even ***s-er*** attacks
1 Cor 1:8 . . . keep you **s** to the end
1 Cor 1:25 . . God's weakness is ***s-er*** than
1 Cor 16:13 . Be courageous. Be **s**.
Eph 6:10 . . . final word: Be **s** in the Lord
1 Thes 3:13 . your hearts **s**, blameless,
2 Tim 2:1 . . . dear son, be **s** through the

STRUCK (v)
to inflict
see also STRIKE
Job 2:7 . . . . . presence, and he **s** Job with
Isa 53:8. . . . . But he was **s** down for the

STRUGGLE (n)
strife; a violent effort or exertion
Rom 15:30 . . to join in my *s* by praying
Heb 12:4 . . . lives in your *s* against sin.

STRUGGLE (v)
to proceed with difficulty or with great effort; to make strenuous or violent efforts in the face of difficulties or opposition
Gen 3:17 . . . will *s* to scratch a living
Col 1:29 . . . . why I work and *s* so hard,
1 Tim 4:10 . . and continue to *s,* for our

STUBBORN (adj)
unreasonably or perversely unyielding
Exod 33:5 . . You are a *s* and rebellious
Exod 34:9 . . this is a *s* and rebellious
Lev 26:41 . . . at last their *s* hearts will
Deut 10:16 . . hearts and stop being *s.*
2 Chr 36:13 . a hard and *s* man, refusing
Ps 78:8 . . . . . ancestors—*s,* rebellious,
Prov 28:14 . . the *s* are headed for serious
Ezek 36:26 . . out your stony, *s* heart and
Rom 2:5 . . . . because you are *s* and refuse

STUDENTS (n)
those who study
Matt 10:24 . . *S* are not greater than

STUDY (n)
application of the mental faculties to the acquisition of knowledge
Eccl 12:12 . . and much *s* wears you

STUDY (v)
to read in detail, especially with the intention of learning
Josh 1:8 . . . . *S* this Book of Instruction
Ezra 7:10 . . . had determined to *s* and obey

STUMBLE, STUMBLES, STUMBLING (v)
to trip or walk unsteadily; to fall into sin or waywardness
Lev 19:14 . . . or cause the blind to *s.*
Ps 37:24 . . . . Though they *s,* they will
Ps 66:9 . . . . . he keeps our feet from *s-ing.*
Ps 119:165 . . great peace and do not *s.*
Ps 121:3 . . . . He will not let you *s;*
Prov 3:23 . . . and your feet will not *s.*
Prov 24:17 . . don't be happy when they *s.*
Isa 8:14 . . . . . stone that makes people *s,*
Jer 13:16 . . . . causing you to *s* and fall
Hos 14:9 . . . paths sinners *s* and fall.
Mal 2:8 . . . . . caused many to *s* into sin.
Matt 21:44 . . Anyone who *s-s* over that
John 11:10 . . is danger of *s-ing* because
Rom 9:33 . . . that makes people *s,*
Rom 14:13 . . believer to *s* and fall.
Rom 14:20 . . makes another person *s.*
1 Cor 8:9 . . . weaker conscience to *s.*
2 Cor 6:3 . . . no one will *s* because of us,
1 Jn 2:10 . . . . does not cause others to *s.*

STUMP (n)
the part of a tree remaining attached to the root after the trunk is cut
Isa 6:13 . . . . . so Israel's *s* will be a
Isa 11:1 . . . . . Out of the *s* of David's

STUPID (adj)
lacking intelligence or reason
Ps 119:70 . . . hearts are dull and *s,*
Prov 12:1 . . . is *s* to hate correction.

STUPIDITY (n)
the quality or state of being stupid
Jer 31:19 . . . . kicked myself for my *s!*

SUBMISSION (n)
the condition of being submissive, humble, or compliant
1 Sam 15:22 . *s* is better than offering

SUBMISSIVE (adj)
submitting to others
1 Cor 14:34 . They should be *s,* just
Titus 2:5 . . . . be *s* to their husbands.

SUBMIT, SUBMITS (v)
to yield to authority or be accountable to another—God, society, or fellow believers
Ps 2:12 . . . . . *S* to God's royal son,
Rom 13:1 . . . Everyone must *s* to governing
Rom 13:5 . . . So you must *s* to them, not
Eph 5:21 . . . *s* to one another out of
Eph 5:24 . . . As the church *s-s* to Christ,
Col 3:18 . . . . Wives, *s* to your husbands,
Heb 12:9 . . . shouldn't we *s* even more

SUBTRACT (v)
to take away
Deut 4:2 . . . . Do not add to or *s* from
Deut 12:32 . . to them or *s* anything

SUBVERT (KJV)
Lam 3:36 . . . they ***twist*** justice in the courts
Titus 1:11 . . . ***turning*** whole families ***away from the truth***

SUCCEED (v)
to turn out well; to attain a desired end
Gen 39:23 . . everything he did to *s.*

Josh 1:8 . . . . prosper and *s* in all you
1 Sam 2:9 . . . No one will *s* by strength
1 Sam 18:14. continued to *s* in
2 Chr 20:20 . prophets, and you will *s*.
Ps 20:4 . . . . . and make all your plans *s*.
Prov 11:10 . . celebrates when the godly *s;*
Prov 13:13 . . respect a command will *s*.
Prov 16:3 . . . and your plans will *s*.
Prov 20:18 . . Plans *s* through good
Prov 28:12 . . When the godly *s,* everyone
Eccl 10:10 . . wisdom; it helps you *s*.

SUCCESS (n)
the attainment of wealth, favor, or eminence; favorable or desired outcome
1 Chr 12:18 . and *s* to all who help
2 Chr 26:5 . . LORD, God gave him *s*.
Prov 15:22 . . many advisers bring *s*.

SUCCESSFUL (adj)
resulting or terminating in success; gaining or having gained success
Deut 8:18 . . . gives you power to be *s,*
Deut 30:9 . . . make you *s* in everything
1 Kgs 2:3 . . . that you will be *s* in all
2 Kgs 18:7 . . Hezekiah was *s* in
1 Chr 22:13 . For you will be *s* if you
2 Chr 31:21 . result, he was very *s*.
Ps 90:17 . . . . and make our efforts *s*.
Prov 1:3 . . . . disciplined and *s* lives,
Eccl 9:11 . . . don't always lead *s* lives.

SUES (v)
to seek justice or right from (a person) by legal process
1 Cor 6:6 . . . one believer *s* another—

SUFFER, SUFFERED, SUFFERING, SUFFERS (v)
to endure death, pain, distress, or loss
Job 36:15 . . . rescues those who *s*.
Mark 8:31 . . Son of Man must *s* many
Luke 24:26. . would have to *s* all these
Luke 24:46. . Messiah would *s* and die
Rom 8:18 . . . Yet what we *s* now is nothing
1 Cor 12:26 . If one part *s-s,* all the parts
2 Cor 1:5 . . . the more we *s* for Christ,
2 Cor 12:10 . troubles that I *s* for Christ.
Phil 3:10 . . . I want to *s* with him, sharing
2 Thes 1:4 . . and hardships you are *s-ing.*
Heb 11:26 . . better to *s* for the sake
1 Pet 2:21 . . . just as Christ *s-ed* for you.
1 Pet 4:1 . . . . since Christ *s-ed* physical pain,
1 Pet 4:16 . . . is no shame to *s* for being
1 Pet 5:10 . . . So after you have *s-ed* a little
Rev 2:3 . . . . . You have patiently *s-ed* for me

SUFFERING, SUFFERINGS (n)
the state or experience of one that suffers; pain, distress
Deut 16:3 . . . the bread of *s*—so that
Job 36:15 . . . means of their *s,* he rescues
Ps 119:71 . . . My *s* was good for me,
Isa 48:10. . . . you in the furnace of *s*.
Isa 49:13. . . . on them in their *s*.
Lam 1:12 . . . if there is any *s* like mine,
Luke 22:15. . you before my *s* begins.
2 Cor 1:7 . . . as you share in our *s-s,* you
Phil 1:29 . . . the privilege of *s* for him.
Col 1:24 . . . . participating in the *s-s* of
2 Tim 2:3 . . . Endure *s* along with me,
2 Tim 4:5 . . . afraid of *s* for the Lord.
Heb 2:10 . . . through his *s,* a perfect
Heb 2:18 . . . gone through *s* and testing,
1 Pet 1:11 . . . about Christ's *s* and his
1 Pet 4:13 . . . Christ in his *s,* so that

SUMMED (v)
to summarize
Rom 13:9 . . . commandments—are *s* up in
Gal 5:14 . . . . whole law can be *s* up in this

SUN (n)
the star that sustains life on the earth, being the source of heat and light
Josh 10:13 . . So the *s* stood still and
Judg 5:31 . . . rise like the *s* in all its
Ps 84:11 . . . . God is our *s* and our shield.
Ps 121:6 . . . . The *s* will not harm you
Ps 136:8 . . . . the *s* to rule the day,
Eccl 1:9 . . . . Nothing under the *s* is truly
Isa 60:19. . . . you need the *s* to shine by
Mal 4:2. . . . . name, the *S* of Righteousness
Matt 13:43 . . shine like the *s* in their
Matt 17:2 . . . shone like the *s,* and his
Luke 23:45. . light from the *s* was gone.
Eph 4:26 . . . Don't let the *s* go down while
Rev 1:16. . . . was like the *s* in all its
Rev 21:23. . . has no need of *s* or moon,

SUNDAY (n)
the first day of the week
Matt 28:1 . . . Early on *S* morning, as

SUNLIGHT (n)
the light of the sun; sunshine
Matt 5:45 . . . he gives his *s* to both the

SUPERIOR (adj)
of higher rank, quality, or importance
Heb 8:6 . . . . that is far *s* to the old

SUPERNATURAL (adj)
of or relating to God, a spirit, or the devil
2 Pet 2:10. . . scoff at *s* beings without
Jude 1:8 . . . . and scoff at *s* beings.

SUPPER (n)
meal eaten toward the end of the day; communion (i.e., Lord's Supper)
Luke 22:20. . After *s* he took another cup of
Acts 2:42 . . . meals (including the Lord's *S*)
1 Cor 11:33 . gather for the Lord's *S*,

SUPPORT, SUPPORTS (v)
to pay the costs of; to assist or help
Lev 25:35. . . and cannot *s* himself, *s*
Ps 18:35 . . . . Your right hand *s-s* me;
Ps 139:10 . . . your strength will *s* me.
Ps 147:6 . . . . The LORD *s-s* the humble,
1 Pet 5:10. . . he will restore, *s*, and
3 Jn 1:8. . . . . we ourselves should *s* them

SUPPRESS (v)
to stop or prohibit the revelation of
Rom 1:18. . . wicked people who *s* the truth

SUPREME (adj)
highest in rank, authority, degree, or quality
Col 1:15 . . . . was created and is *s* over all
Col 1:18 . . . . is the beginning, *s* over all

SURE (adj)
admitting of no doubt; careful to remember, attend to, or find out something
Num 32:23 . you may be *s* that your sin
1 Sam 12:24. But be *s* to fear the
2 Cor 1:15 . . Since I was so *s* of your
2 Cor 9:5 . . . of me to make *s* the gift you
Eph 5:5 . . . . You can be *s* that no immoral,
2 Tim 1:12. . trust, and I am *s* that he is

SURETY (KJV)
Gen 43:9 . . . I ***personally guarantee*** his safety
Prov 17:18. . ***put up security*** for a friend
Heb 7:22 . . . Jesus is the one who ***guarantees***

SURFACE (n)
the external or superficial aspect of something
John 7:24. . . Look beneath the *s* so you can

SURGING (adj)
characterized by tossing and swelling
Ps 42:7 . . . . . your waves and *s* tides sweep

SURPASS (v)
to become better, greater, or stronger than
Prov 31:29. . world, but you *s* them all!

SURPLUS (n)
the amount that remains when use or need is satisfied
Luke 21:4. . . part of their *s*, but she,

SURPRISED (v)
to take unawares; to strike with wonder or amazement especially because it is unexpected
1 Thes 5:4 . . you won't be *s* when the day
1 Pet 4:4. . . . former friends are *s* when you
1 Jn 3:13. . . . So don't be *s*, dear brothers

SURRENDERED (v)
to yield to the power, control, or possession of another upon compulsion or demand
2 Sam 10:19. by Israel, they *s* to Israel
1 Chr 19:19 . by Israel, they *s* to David

SURROUND, SURROUNDED, SURROUNDS (v)
to envelop; to encircle
Deut 33:12. . He *s-s* them continuously
Ps 5:12 . . . . . O LORD; you *s* them with
Ps 32:10 . . . . unfailing love *s-s* those who
Ps 33:22 . . . . unfailing love *s* us, LORD,
Ps 89:7 . . . . . than all who *s* his throne.
Ps 125:2 . . . . the mountains *s* Jerusalem,
Ps 125:2 . . . . the LORD *s-s* his people,
Heb 12:1 . . . we are *s-ed* by such a huge

SUSTAINS (v)
to keep up or prolong
Heb 1:3 . . . . God, and he *s* everything by

SWADDLED, SWADDLING (KJV)
Ezek 16:4. . . salt, and ***wrapped in cloth***
Luke 2:7. . . . wrapped him ***snugly in strips of cloth***
Luke 2:12. . . baby ***wrapped snugly*** in strips

SWALLOW, SWALLOWED (v)
to take through the mouth and esophagus into the stomach; to envelop or absorb
Isa 25:8. . . . . He will *s* up death
Jonah 1:17 . . a great fish to *s* Jonah.
Hab 1:13 . . . while the wicked *s* up people
Matt 23:24. . a gnat, but you *s* a camel!
1 Cor 15:54 . fulfilled: "Death is *s-ed* up
2 Cor 5:4 . . . bodies will be *s-ed* up by life.

SWEAR (v)
to affirm by a solemn oath or binding commitment
see also SWORE, SWORN
Lev 19:12. . . using it to **s** falsely.
Isa 54:9. . . . . earth, so now I **s** that I will
Heb 6:13 . . . one greater to **s** by, God took

SWEET, SWEETER (adj)
pleasing to the taste; agreeable, gratifying
Ps 19:10 . . . . They are ***s-er*** than honey,
Ps 119:103 . . How **s** your words taste
Ps 119:103 . . they are ***s-er*** than honey.
Prov 20:17. . Stolen bread tastes **s**, but
Prov 24:14. . wisdom is **s** to your soul.
Prov 27:9. . . friend is as **s** as perfume
Song 1:2. . . . your love is ***s-er*** than wine.
Song 4:11. . . lips are as **s** as nectar,
Isa 5:20. . . . . bitter is **s** and **s** is bitter.
Ezek 3:3. . . . it tasted as **s** as honey in my

SWEET-SMELLING (adj)
of or relating to a pleasant scent
Phil 4:18 . . . They are a **s** sacrifice that

SWEETNESS (n)
the quality or state of being sweet
Song 5:16. . . His mouth is **s** itself;

SWEPT (adj)
cleaned with a broom or brush
Matt 12:44. . former home empty, **s**, and in

SWORD, SWORDS (n)
a handheld weapon with a long blade; figurative of war or persecution by government, also of God's word in spiritual warfare
Gen 3:24 . . . a flaming **s** that flashed
Deut 32:41. . my flashing **s** and begin
1 Sam 17:45. come to me with **s**, spear,
1 Sam 31:4. . Take your **s** and kill me
2 Sam 12:10. live by the **s** because you
1 Kgs 20:11 . putting on his **s** for battle
Ps 44:6 . . . . . not count on my **s** to save me.
Ps 45:3 . . . . . Put on your **s**, O mighty
Ps 64:3 . . . . . their tongues like ***s-s*** and aim
Joel 3:10. . . . plowshares into ***s-s*** and your
Amos 9:4. . . I will command the **s** to kill
Mic 4:3. . . . . will hammer their ***s-s*** into
Matt 10:34. . not to bring peace, but a **s**.
Matt 26:52. . who use the **s** will die by
Luke 2:35. . . a **s** will pierce your very
Eph 6:17 . . . take the **s** of the Spirit,
Heb 4:12 . . . sharpest two-edged **s**, cutting
Rev 1:16. . . . sharp two-edged **s** came
Rev 19:15. . . came a sharp **s** to strike

SWORE, SWORN (v)
to affirm by a solemn oath or binding commitment
see also SWEAR
Exod 33:1 . . up to the land I **s** to give
Deut 7:8. . . . the oath he had ***s-n*** to your
Deut 30:20. . land the LORD **s** to give
Isa 45:23. . . . I have ***s-n*** by my own

SYCAMORE-FIG (n)
a fig tree that has edible fruit similar but inferior to the common fig
Amos 7:14. . take care of **s** trees.
Luke 19:4. . . and climbed a **s** tree beside

SYMBOL (n)
something that stands for or suggests something else
Rom 5:14. . . Adam is a **s**, a representation

SYMPATHIZE (v)
to share in suffering or grief
1 Pet 3:8. . . . ***S*** with each other. Love each

SYNAGOGUE (n)
the house of worship and communal center of a Jewish congregation
Luke 4:16. . . to the **s** on the Sabbath
John 12:42. . expel them from the **s**.
Acts 17:2 . . . he went to the **s** service,
Rev 3:9. . . . . who belong to Satan's **s**—

T

TABERNACLE (n)
portable shrine or tent designated for the worship of God; metaphor for God dwelling among his people
see also SANCTUARY, TEMPLE
Exod 27:21 . stand in the ***T***, in front of
Exod 40:2 . . Set up the ***T*** on the first
Exod 40:34 . of the LORD filled the ***T***.
Num 3:29 . . area south of the ***T*** for their
Heb 8:5 . . . . to build the ***T***, God gave him
Heb 9:11 . . . more perfect ***T*** in heaven,
Heb 9:21 . . . blood on the ***T*** and on
Rev 15:5. . . . heaven, God's ***T***, was thrown

TABLE, TABLES (n)
a piece of furniture consisting of a smooth flat slab fixed on legs
Exod 25:23 . Then make a ***t*** of acacia
John 2:15 . . . and turned over their ***t-s***.

TABLETS (n)
flat slabs or plaques suited for or bearing an inscription
Exod 31:18 . two stone ***t*** inscribed with
Deut 10:5. . . and placed the ***t*** in the Ark
2 Cor 3:3 . . . carved not on ***t*** of stone,

TAKE, TAKEN, TAKES (v)
to exploit; to seize or capture physically; to remove; to move onto or into; to feel or experience; to lead, carry, or cause to go along to another place; to grasp or grip; to accept; to derive
see also TOOK
Gen 2:23 . . . she was ***t-n*** from 'man.'
Gen 9:6 . . . . life will also be ***t-n*** by human
Lev 25:14. . . you must not ***t*** advantage of
Num 13:30 . go at once to ***t*** the land,
Num 19:3 . . it will be ***t-n*** outside the camp
1 Chr 17:13 . I will never ***t*** my favor
Ps 2:12 . . . . . for all who ***t*** refuge in him!
Ps 5:4 . . . . . . O God, you ***t*** no pleasure in
Ps 49:17 . . . . they die, they ***t*** nothing with
Ps 51:11 . . . . and don't ***t*** your Holy Spirit
Prov 3:6. . . . show you which path to ***t***.
Jer 25:10. . . . I will ***t*** away your happy
Zech 3:4. . . . See, I have ***t-n*** away your sins,
Matt 10:38 . . refuse to ***t*** up your cross
Matt 11:29 . . ***T*** my yoke upon you. Let me
Matt 16:24 . . selfish ways, ***t*** up your cross,
Matt 24:40 . . one will be ***t-n***, the other
Matt 26:26 . . ***T*** this and eat it, for this
Matt 26:39 . . cup of suffering be ***t-n*** away
Mark 14:36 . Please ***t*** this cup of suffering
Mark 16:19 . he was ***t-n*** up into heaven
John 1:29 . . . Lamb of God who ***t-s*** away the
John 10:18 . . No one can ***t*** my life from me.
Acts 1:9 . . . . he was ***t-n*** up into a cloud
1 Tim 3:16 . . and ***t-n*** to heaven in glory.

TALK (n)
speech; pointless or fruitless discussion
Ps 5:9 . . . . . . Their ***t*** is foul, like
Prov 10:19 . . Too much ***t*** leads to
2 Tim 2:16 . . worthless, foolish ***t*** that

TALK BACK (v)
to answer impertinently
Titus 2:9. . . . They must not ***t***

TALL, TALLER (adj)
of a specified or considerable height
1 Sam 2:26 . . boy Samuel grew ***t-er*** and
1 Sam 9:2. . . and shoulders ***t-er*** than anyone
1 Sam 17:4 . . He was over nine feet ***t***!
1 Chr 11:23 . was 7½ feet ***t*** and whose

TAME (v)
to domesticate; to harness
Jas 3:7. . . . . . People can ***t*** all kinds of
Jas 3:8. . . . . . no one can ***t*** the tongue.

TANGLED (v)
to involve so as to hamper, obstruct, or embarrass; to entrap
Exod 4:10 .. and my words get ***t.***
2 Pet 2:20... Christ and then get ***t*** up and

TASK (n)
duty, function
2 Cor 2:16 .. for such a ***t*** as this?
2 Cor 5:18 .. us this ***t*** of reconciling

TASTE (n)
the act of tasting; a sample experience
Prov 24:13.. honeycomb is sweet to the ***t.***
1 Pet 2:3.... a ***t*** of the Lord's kindness.

TASTE, TASTED, TASTES (v)
to become acquainted with by experience; to ascertain the flavor of by taking a little into the mouth
Ps 34:8 ..... ***T*** and see that the LORD
Prov 9:17... eaten in secret ***t-s*** the best!
Song 2:3.... and ***t*** his delicious fruit.
Ezek 3:3.... I ate it, it ***t-d*** as sweet as
Col 2:21 .... Don't handle! Don't ***t!***

TATTOOS (n)
indelible marks or figures fixed upon the body
Lev 19:28... not mark your skin with ***t.***

TAX, TAXES (n)
a charge usually of money imposed by authority on persons or property for public purposes
Matt 17:24.. teacher pay the Temple ***t?***
Matt 22:17.. right to pay ***t-es*** to Caesar
Rom 13:7... Pay your ***t-es*** and

TAX COLLECTOR, TAX COLLECTORS (n)
one who collects tax or custom on behalf of the government
Matt 5:46... corrupt ***t-s*** do that
Matt 9:10... along with many ***t-s*** and
Matt 11:19.. a friend of ***t-s*** and other sinners
Matt 21:31.. ***t-s*** and prostitutes will get
Luke 5:27... he saw a ***t*** named Levi
Luke 18:11.. I'm certainly not like that ***t!***

TEACH, TEACHES, TEACHING (v)
to cause to know something; to instruct by precept, example, or experience
see also INSTRUCT, PREACH, TRAIN
Lev 10:11... you must ***t*** the Israelites
Deut 6:1.... commanded me to ***t*** you.
2 Chr 17:9 .. of Judah, ***t-ing*** the people.
Job 21:22 ... who can ***t*** a lesson to God,
Ps 37:30.... they ***t*** right from wrong.
Ps 51:13.... Then I will ***t*** your ways
Prov 15:33.. the LORD ***t-es*** wisdom;
Isa 2:3...... he will ***t*** us his ways,
Matt 5:19... obeys God's laws and ***t-es***
Matt 11:29.. Let me ***t*** you, because
Matt 15:9... they ***t*** man-made ideas
Matt 22:16.. You ***t*** the way of God
Matt 28:20.. ***T*** these new disciples to
Mark 10:1 .. as usual he was ***t-ing*** them.
Luke 11:1... Lord, ***t*** us to pray,
Luke 12:12.. Holy Spirit will ***t*** you
John 14:26.. he will ***t*** you everything
Acts 6:4 .... in prayer and ***t-ing*** the word.
Rom 15:4... Scriptures long ago to ***t***
Rom 15:14.. you can ***t*** each other all
1 Cor 2:16 .. knows enough to ***t*** him?
1 Cor 14:26 . another will ***t,*** another
1 Tim 2:12.. do not let women ***t*** men
1 Tim 3:2... he must be able to ***t.***
2 Tim 3:16.. is useful to ***t*** us what
2 Tim 3:16.. ***t-es*** us to do what is right.
Titus 2:15... You must ***t*** these things
Heb 5:12 ... you ought to be ***t-ing*** others.
1 Jn 2:27.... need anyone to ***t*** you what

TEACHER, TEACHERS (n)
one who teaches
Job 36:22 ... Who is a ***t*** like him?
Prov 5:13... didn't I listen to my ***t-s?***
Eccl 1:1 .... words of the ***T,*** King David's
Matt 10:24.. not greater than their ***t,***
Matt 23:10.. only one ***t,*** the Messiah.
Luke 6:40... will become like the ***t.***
Luke 20:46.. these ***t-s*** of religious law!
John 13:14.. Lord and ***T,*** have washed
Rom 12:7... If you are a ***t,*** teach well.
1 Cor 12:28 . third are ***t-s,*** then those
Gal 6:6..... should provide for their ***t-s,***
Eph 4:11 ... and the pastors and ***t-s.***
2 Tim 4:3... look for ***t-s*** who will tell
Jas 3:1...... of you should become ***t-s***
3 Jn 1:10.... the traveling ***t-s,*** he also

TEACHING, TEACHINGS (n)
something taught; doctrine
see also INSTRUCTION(S), LAW(S)
Isa 8:20..... to God's instructions and ***t-s!***
Luke 6:47... listens to my ***t,*** and then
John 7:17... whether my ***t*** is from God
John 8:31... remain faithful to my ***t-s.***
Acts 2:42... themselves to the apostles' ***t,***
Eph 4:14 ... about by every wind of new ***t.***
1 Thes 4:8 .. not disobeying human ***t*** but
2 Thes 2:15 . grip on the ***t*** we passed on
1 Tim 1:3... those whose ***t*** is contrary to

1 Tim 1:10 . . contradicts the wholesome ***t***
1 Tim 4:6 . . . and the good ***t*** you have
1 Tim 4:16 . . how you live and on your ***t.***
1 Tim 6:3 . . . people may contradict our ***t,***
2 Tim 4:2 . . . your people with good ***t.***
Titus 1:9. . . . with wholesome ***t*** and show
Titus 3:8. . . . insist on these ***t-s*** so that
Heb 6:1 . . . . stop going over the basic ***t-s***

TEAR, TEARS (n)
a drop of clear saline fluid secreted from the eye
Job 16:20 . . . I pour out my ***t-s*** to God.
Isa 25:8. . . . . will wipe away all ***t-s.***
Rev 7:17. . . . will wipe every ***t*** from their
Rev 21:4. . . . will wipe every ***t*** from their

TELL, TELLING, TELLS (v)
to divulge or reveal; to give information to
Ps 26:7 . . . . . thanksgiving and ***t-ing*** of all
Ps 71:16 . . . . I will ***t*** everyone that
Ps 118:17 . . . live to ***t*** what the LORD
Jer 1:7. . . . . . and say whatever I ***t*** you.
Jer 1:17. . . . . Go out and ***t*** them everything
John 2:25 . . . No one needed to ***t*** him what
Acts 20:20 . . shrank back from ***t-ing*** you
Rom 10:14 . . him unless someone ***t-s*** them?
2 Cor 10:12 . these other men who ***t*** you

TEMPER (n)
disposition; characteristic state of mind or of emotion; proneness to anger
Ps 37:8 . . . . . Do not lose your ***t***—it only
Prov 14:29 . . ***t*** shows great foolishness.
Prov 19:11 . . people control their ***t;***
Eccl 7:9 . . . . Control your ***t,*** for anger

TEMPLE, TEMPLES (n)
first built in Solomon's reign as a permanent worship center, which was destroyed then rebuilt under Herod's reign; figurative of the human body and of Christ
see also HOUSE, SANCTUARY, TABERNACLE
1 Kgs 6:1 . . . to construct the ***T*** of the
1 Kgs 8:10 . . cloud filled the ***T*** of the
1 Chr 29:16 . to build a ***T*** to honor your
2 Chr 36:19 . his army burned the ***T***
Ps 27:4 . . . . . meditating in his ***T.***
Isa 6:1. . . . . . train of his robe filled the ***T.***
Jer 7:8. . . . . . suffer because the ***T*** is here.
Joel 3:18. . . . forth from the LORD's ***T,***
Hab 2:20 . . . LORD is in his holy ***T.***
Hag 2:18 . . . of the LORD's ***T*** began.
Matt 12:6 . . . is even greater than the ***T!***
Matt 26:61 . . able to destroy the ***T*** of God
Matt 27:51 . . sanctuary of the ***T*** was torn
Luke 21:5. . . stonework of the ***T*** and the
John 2:14 . . . the ***T*** area he saw merchants
Acts 5:20 . . . Go to the ***T*** and give the
Acts 17:24 . . live in man-made ***t-s,***
1 Cor 3:16 . . together are the ***t*** of God
1 Cor 6:19 . . body is the ***t*** of the Holy
Eph 2:21 . . . becoming a holy ***t*** for the
1 Pet 2:5. . . . building into his spiritual ***t.***
Rev 21:22. . . and the Lamb are its ***t.***

TEMPT, TEMPTED, TEMPTING (v)
to entice to do wrong by promise of pleasure or gain; to test
Isa 13:17. . . . They cannot be ***t-ed*** by silver
Matt 4:1 . . . . wilderness to be ***t-ed*** there by
Luke 4:2. . . . where he was ***t-ed*** by the devil
Luke 4:13. . . finished ***t-ing*** Jesus, he left
1 Cor 7:5 . . . be able to ***t*** you because
1 Cor 10:13 . When you are ***t-ed,*** he will
Jas 1:13. . . . . you are being ***t-ed,*** do not say,
Jas 1:13. . . . . God is never ***t-ed*** to do wrong,

TEMPTATION, TEMPTATIONS (n)
a cause or occasion of enticement
Matt 6:13 . . . don't let us yield to ***t,***
Matt 18:7 . . . ***T-s*** are inevitable, but what
Matt 26:41 . . will not give in to ***t.***
Luke 8:13. . . fall away when they face ***t.***
1 Cor 10:13 . The ***t-s*** in your life are
1 Cor 10:13 . not allow the ***t*** to be
Gal 6:1 . . . . . fall into the same ***t*** yourself.
1 Tim 6:9 . . . to be rich fall into ***t*** and
Jas 1:12. . . . . endure testing and ***t.***

TEN (n)
the number 10
Exod 34:28 . the ***T*** Commandments—
Deut 10:4. . . wrote the ***T*** Commandments
Luke 15:8. . . a woman has ***t*** silver coins
Rev 12:3. . . . seven heads and ***t*** horns, with

TENDERHEARTED (adj)
easily moved to love, pity, or sorrow; compassionate
Deut 28:54. . The most ***t*** man among you
Eph 4:32 . . . each other, ***t,*** forgiving one
Col 3:12. . . . yourselves with ***t*** mercy,

TENDERNESS (n)
the quality or state of being gentle, fond, or loving
Jas 5:11. . . . is full of ***t*** and mercy.

TENTH (n)
one-tenth of any property or produce
see also TITHE
Gen 14:20 . . gave Melchizedek a ***t*** of all
Heb 7:2 . . . . Abraham took a ***t*** of all he

TENTMAKERS (n)
those who make tents
Acts 18:3 . . . for they were ***t*** just as he

TENTS (n)
portable housing made of cloth or skins
see also TABERNACLE
Gen 13:12 . . Lot moved his ***t*** to a place

TERRIBLE (adj)
extremely bad; terrifying
Jer 8:6. . . . . . What a ***t*** thing I have done
Zeph 1:15 . . a day of ***t*** distress and
Heb 10:31 . . It is a ***t*** thing to fall into

TERRIFY, TERRIFIED, TERRIFIES (v)
to scare, deter, or intimidate; to fill with terror
Deut 2:25. . . the earth ***t-ied*** because of you.
Deut 28:67. . you will be ***t-ied*** by the awful
1 Sam 12:18. were ***t-ied*** of the LORD
Prov 21:15. . but it ***t-ies*** evildoers.
Isa 13:8. . . . . and people are ***t-ied.*** Pangs of
Zeph 2:11 . . The LORD will ***t*** them
Matt 14:26. . on the water, they were ***t-ied.***
Matt 17:6. . . disciples were ***t-ied*** and fell
Matt 27:54. . the crucifixion were ***t-ied***
Mark 4:41 . . disciples were absolutely ***t-ied.***
Luke 21:26. . will be ***t-ied*** at what they

TERRIFYING (adj)
causing terror or apprehension
Deut 4:34. . . powerful arm, and ***t*** acts?
Deut 34:12. . Moses performed ***t*** acts in the
Judg 13:6. . . of God's angels, ***t*** to see.

TERRITORY (n)
an indeterminate geographic area
2 Cor 10:16 . done in someone else's ***t.***

TERROR, TERRORS (n)
a state of intense fear; a frightening aspect
Deut 7:19. . . Remember the great ***t-s*** the
Job 9:34 . . . . no longer live in ***t*** of his
Ps 53:5 . . . . . will grip them, ***t*** like they
Ps 91:5 . . . . . afraid of the ***t-s*** of the night,
Prov 22:8. . . their reign of ***t*** will come to
Isa 51:17. . . . the cup of ***t,*** tipping out its
Mic 7:17. . . . trembling in ***t*** at his
Luke 9:34. . . them, and ***t*** gripped them
Acts 7:32 . . . Moses shook with ***t*** and did

TEST, TESTINGS, TESTS (n)
a critical examination, observation, or evaluation
see also TRIAL(S), TROUBLE(S)
Deut 29:3. . . all the great ***t-s*** of strength,
1 Cor 10:9 . . should we put Christ to the ***t,***
1 Tim 3:10 . . If they pass the ***t,*** then let
Heb 4:15 . . . of the same ***t-ings*** we do, yet

TEST, TESTED, TESTING, TESTS (v)
to put to test or proof
Gen 22:1 . . . God ***t-ed*** Abraham's faith.
Deut 6:16. . . You must not ***t*** the LORD your
Judg 3:1. . . . land to ***t*** those Israelites
1 Kgs 10:1 . . she came to ***t*** him with hard
Job 23:10 . . . when he ***t-s*** me, I will come
Ps 17:3 . . . . . You have ***t-ed*** my thoughts
Ps 66:10 . . . . You have ***t-ed*** us,
Ps 78:18 . . . . They stubbornly ***t-ed*** God in
Ps 106:14 . . . ran wild, ***t-ing*** God's patience
Ps 139:23 . . . ***t*** me and know my anxious
Prov 17:3. . . the LORD ***t-s*** the heart.
Luke 4:12. . . You must not ***t*** the LORD your
Acts 5:9 . . . . of conspiring to ***t*** the Spirit
1 Thes 5:21 . but ***t*** everything that is said.
Heb 2:18 . . . suffering and ***t-ing,*** he is able
Heb 2:18 . . . us when we are being ***t-ed.***
Heb 3:8 . . . . they ***t-ed*** me in the wilderness.
Heb 11:17 . . when God was ***t-ing*** him.
Jas 1:3. . . . . . when your faith is ***t-ed,*** your
Jas 1:12. . . . . who patiently endure ***t-ing*** and
1 Pet 1:7. . . . It is being ***t-ed*** as fire tests
1 Jn 4:1. . . . . You must ***t*** them to see if
Rev 2:10. . . . you into prison to ***t*** you.
Rev 3:10. . . . great time of ***t-ing*** that will

TESTIFY, TESTIFIED, TESTIFIES, TESTIFYING (v)
to make a statement based on personal knowledge or belief; to give evidence or proof
Exod 20:16 . must not ***t*** falsely against
Deut 5:20. . . must not ***t*** falsely against
Prov 24:28. . Don't ***t*** against your
Luke 18:20. . You must not ***t*** falsely.
John 1:34 . . . Jesus, so I ***t*** that he is
John 5:32 . . . else is also ***t-ing*** about me,
John 15:26 . . Father and will ***t*** all about
John 18:37 . . the world to ***t*** to the truth.
John 21:24 . . one who ***t-ies*** to these events
Acts 4:33 . . . The apostles ***t-ied*** powerfully
Acts 10:43 . . the prophets ***t-ied*** about,
1 Jn 4:14. . . . own eyes and now ***t*** that the

TESTIMONY (n)
the evidence given by a witness
see also TESTIFY
Num 35:30 . to death on the ***t*** of only

John 1:7 . . . . might believe because of his *t.*
1 Tim 6:13 . . gave a good *t* before Pontius
1 Jn 5:9. . . . . Since we believe human *t,*
Rev 12:11. . . of the Lamb and by their *t.*

THANK, THANKING (v)

to express gratitude to; to acknowledge God's goodness

Ps 35:18 . . . . Then I will *t* you in front
Ps 79:13 . . . . pasture, will *t* you forever
Ps 145:10 . . . works will *t* you, LORD,
Isa 12:4. . . . . sing: "*T* the LORD!
1 Cor 10:30 . If I can *t* God for the food
Phil 4:6 . . . . and *t* him for all he has done.
1 Thes 2:13 . we never stop *t-ing* God
1 Thes 3:9 . . How we *t* God for you!

THANKFUL (adj)

conscious of benefit received; expressive of thanks

Col 3:15 . . . . And always be *t.*
Col 3:16 . . . . to God with *t* hearts.
1 Thes 5:18 . Be *t* in all circumstances,
Heb 12:28 . . let us be *t* and please God by

THANKFULNESS (n)

the quality or state of being thankful

Col 2:7 . . . . . you will overflow with *t.*

THANKS (n)

kindly or grateful thoughts; gratitude

1 Chr 16:4 . . to give *t,* and to praise
Ps 30:12 . . . . I will give you *t* forever!
Ps 107:1 . . . . Give *t* to the LORD,
Rom 1:21 . . . as God or even give him *t.*
1 Cor 11:24 . gave *t* to God for it.
Phil 1:3 . . . . of you, I give *t* to my God.
1 Tim 2:1 . . . behalf, and give *t* for them.
1 Tim 4:3 . . . be eaten with *t* by faithful
Rev 4:9. . . . . and honor and *t* to the one

THANKSGIVING (n)

a prayer expressing gratitude; a public acknowledgment or celebration of God's goodness

Ps 26:7 . . . . . singing a song of *t* and telling
Ps 28:7 . . . . . I burst out in songs of *t.*
Ps 100:4 . . . . Enter his gates with *t;* go
Isa 51:3. . . . . Songs of *t* will fill the air.

THIEF, THIEVES (n)

one who steals, especially stealthily or secretly

Prov 6:30. . . might be found for a *t*
Prov 29:24. . If you assist a *t,* you only
Jer 7:11. . . . . has become a den of *t-ves?*
Matt 6:19. . . where *t-ves* break in and steal.
Luke 19:46. . turned it into a den of *t-ves.*
John 10:1 . . . surely be a *t* and a robber!
John 10:8 . . . me were *t-ves* and robbers.
1 Cor 6:10 . . or are *t-ves,* or greedy people,
1 Thes 5:2 . . unexpectedly, like a *t* in the
Rev 16:15. . . as unexpectedly as a *t!*

THINK, THINKING, THINKS (v)

to reflect, ponder, or remember; to subject to the processes of logical thought; to have as an opinion; to conceive or reason

see also MEDITATE, THOUGHT

1 Sam 12:24. *T* of all the wonderful
Ps 8:4 . . . . . . you should *t* about them,
Ps 63:6 . . . . . I lie awake *t-ing* of you,
Ps 77:12 . . . . I cannot stop *t-ing* about your
Ps 119:97 . . . I *t* about them all day long.
Ps 119:148 . . the night, *t-ing* about your
Prov 13:16. . Wise people *t* before they
Prov 15:28. . godly *t-s* carefully before
Prov 21:29. . the virtuous *t* before they
Prov 23:7. . . are always *t-ing* about how
Prov 29:20. . who speaks without *t-ing.*
Isa 44:18. . . . are shut, and they cannot *t.*
Matt 22:42. . What do you *t* about the
Rom 11:20. . So don't *t* highly of
Phil 1:3 . . . . Every time I *t* of you, I give
Phil 2:3 . . . . Be humble, *t-ing* of others as
Phil 3:19 . . . they *t* only about this life
Heb 10:24 . . Let us *t* of ways to motivate
1 Pet 1:13. . . So *t* clearly and exercise

THINKING (n)

opinion, judgment

Rom 1:28. . . them to their foolish *t*
2 Pet 3:1. . . . wholesome *t* and refresh

THIRST (v)

to crave vehemently and urgently

Ps 42:2 . . . . . I *t* for God, the living God.
Matt 5:6 . . . . who hunger and *t* for justice,

THIRSTY (adj)

feeling a desire for liquids; having a strong desire

Ps 107:9 . . . . he satisfies the *t* and fills
Prov 25:21. . If they are *t,* give them
Isa 55:1. . . . . Is anyone *t?* Come and drink—
Matt 25:35. . I was *t,* and you gave
John 4:14 . . . will never be *t* again.
John 19:28. . Scripture he said, "I am *t.*"
Rom 12:20. . If they are *t,* give them
2 Cor 11:27 . been hungry and *t* and
Rev 7:16. . . . never again be hungry or *t;*
Rev 22:17. . . Let anyone who is *t* come.

THOMAS
One of the twelve disciples, also known as "the Twin" (Matt 10:3; Mark 3:18; Luke 6:15; Acts 1:13); willing to die with Jesus (John 11:16); queried Jesus (John 14:5); doubted Jesus' resurrection but was convinced by his appearance (John 20:24-28).

THORN, THORNS (n)
a woody plant bearing sharp impeding prickles or spines; something that causes distress or irritation
Gen 3:18 . . . It will grow ***t-s*** and thistles
Num 33:55 . in your eyes and ***t-s*** in your
Matt 13:7 . . . seeds fell among ***t-s*** that
Matt 27:29 . . wove ***t*** branches into a
2 Cor 12:7 . . I was given a ***t*** in my flesh,
Heb 6:8 . . . . a field bears ***t-s*** and thistles,

THORNBUSHES (n)
any of various spiny or thorny shrubs or small trees
Luke 6:44. . . never gathered from ***t***, nor

THOUGHT, THOUGHTS (n)
the action or process of thinking; a developed intention or plan; recollection, remembrance
Ps 77:12 . . . . They are constantly in my ***t-s***.
Ps 92:5 . . . . . And how deep are your ***t-s***.
Ps 94:11 . . . . LORD knows people's ***t-s***;
Ps 104:34 . . . May all my ***t-s*** be pleasing
Ps 139:23 . . . and know my anxious ***t-s***.
Ps 142:4 . . . . no one gives me a passing ***t***!
Isa 26:3. . . . . whose ***t-s*** are fixed on you!
Isa 55:8. . . . . My ***t-s*** are nothing like your
Matt 9:4 . . . . you have such evil ***t-s*** in your
Matt 15:19 . . heart come evil ***t-s***, murder,
1 Cor 14:25 . their secret ***t-s*** will be
Eph 4:23 . . . renew your ***t-s*** and attitudes.
Rev 2:23. . . . searches out the ***t-s*** and

THOUGHT (v)
to reflect, ponder, or remember
see also THINK
Ps 39:3 . . . . . The more I ***t*** about it,
Luke 2:19. . . in her heart and ***t*** about them
1 Cor 13:11 . I spoke and ***t*** and reasoned

THOUSAND (adj)
of the number 1,000
Ps 90:4 . . . . . For you, a ***t*** years are as
Rev 20:7. . . . When the ***t*** years come to an

THOUSANDS (n)
a very large number
Joel 3:14. . . . ***T*** upon ***t*** are waiting

THREATS (n)
expressions of intention to inflict evil, injury, or damage
Matt 24:6 . . . of wars and ***t*** of wars,

THREE (adj)
the number 3
Deut 19:15. . of two or ***t*** witnesses.
Jonah 1:17 . . ***t*** days and ***t*** nights.
Matt 12:40 . . ***t*** days and ***t*** nights,
Matt 18:20 . . where two or ***t*** gather
Matt 26:34 . . you will deny ***t*** times that
Mark 8:31 . . but ***t*** days later he would rise
1 Jn 5:7. . . . . have these ***t*** witnesses—

THRILL (v)
to cause to experience a sudden sharp feeling of excitement
Ps 92:4 . . . . . You ***t*** me, LORD,
Isa 60:5. . . . . your heart will ***t*** with joy,

THRIVING (adj)
characterized by success, prosperity, or growth
Ps 52:8 . . . . . olive tree, ***t*** in the house

THROAT (n)
the front part of the neck
Prov 23:2. . . put a knife to your ***t***;

THRONE, THRONES (n)
seat of power for a king or deity; symbolic of royal authority and the king's role as a judge
Deut 17:18. . he sits on the ***t*** as king,
2 Sam 7:16. . and your ***t*** will be secure
1 Chr 17:12 . will secure his ***t*** forever.
Job 36:7 . . . . sets them on ***t-s*** with kings
Ps 45:6 . . . . . Your ***t***, O God, endures
Ps 47:8 . . . . . nations, sitting on his holy ***t***.
Ps 89:14 . . . . are the foundation of your ***t***.
Ps 99:1 . . . . . He sits on his ***t*** between the
Ps 103:19 . . . has made the heavens his ***t***;
Isa 6:1. . . . . . He was sitting on a lofty ***t***,
Isa 66:1. . . . . Heaven is my ***t***, and the
Dan 7:9 . . . . on a fiery ***t*** with wheels
Matt 19:28 . . upon his glorious ***t***, you who
Matt 19:28 . . sit on twelve ***t-s***, judging
Acts 7:49 . . . Heaven is my ***t***, and the
Rom 15:12. . heir to David's ***t*** will come,
Col 1:16 . . . . such as ***t-s***, kingdoms, rulers,
Heb 12:2 . . . place of honor beside God's ***t***.
Rev 3:21. . . . sat with my Father on his ***t***.
Rev 4:2. . . . . and I saw a ***t*** in heaven
Rev 4:4. . . . . Twenty-four ***t-s*** surrounded
Rev 5:5. . . . . heir to David's ***t***, has won
Rev 20:11. . . a great white ***t*** and the
Rev 22:3. . . . the ***t*** of God and of the Lamb

THROUGH (prep)
by way of
Eph 2:18 . . . to the Father *t* the same Holy

THROUGHOUT (prep)
in or to every part of; during the whole course or period of
Gen 1:29 . . . seed-bearing plant *t* the
Jer 23:40. . . . be infamous *t* the ages.
Rom 10:18 . . message has gone *t* the earth,

THROW, THROWING (v)
to propel through the air by a forward motion of the hand or arm; to discard
Ps 22:18 . . . . themselves and *t* dice for my
Prov 16:33 . . We may *t* the dice,
Isa 41:9. . . . . and will not *t* you away.
Matt 27:35 . . his clothes by ***t-ing*** dice.
John 8:7 . . . . has never sinned *t* the first
John 19:24 . . apart, let's *t* dice for it.
Heb 10:35 . . do not *t* away this confident

THUNDER, THUNDERS (n)
the sound that follows a flash of lightning
Job 37:5 . . . . voice is glorious in the *t.*
Mark 3:17 . . nicknamed them "Sons of *T*"
Rev 10:3. . . . the seven ***t-s*** answered.

THUNDER, THUNDERS (v)
to give forth a sound that resembles thunder
Ps 29:3 . . . . . The God of glory ***t-s.***
Amos 1:2. . . from Zion and *t* from Jerusalem

TIE, TIED (v)
to fasten, attach, or close by means of a tie
Prov 3:3 . . . . *T* them around your neck as
Matt 18:6 . . . large millstone ***t-d*** around

TIES (n)
bonds of kinship or affection
Col 2:2 . . . . . together by strong *t* of love.

TIME, TIMES (n)
occasion; an opportune or suitable moment; an appointed, fixed, or customary moment or hour for something to happen, begin, or end; duration; conditions at present or at some specified period; added or accumulated quantities or instances
Esth 4:14 . . . just such a *t* as this?"
Ps 9:9 . . . . . . a refuge in ***t-s*** of trouble.
Ps 62:8 . . . . . trust in him at all ***t-s.***
Eccl 3:1 . . . . a *t* for every activity under
Eccl 7:14 . . . when hard ***t-s*** strike,
Dan 12:7 . . . a *t*, ***t-s,*** and half a *t.*
Amos 5:13 . . shut, for it is an evil *t.*
Matt 16:3 . . . interpret the signs of the ***t-s!***
Matt 18:21 . . sins against me? Seven ***t-s?***
Luke 12:40. . ready all the *t,* for the Son
John 4:53 . . . was the very *t* Jesus had told
John 12:23 . . the *t* has come for the Son
Acts 1:7 . . . . those dates and ***t-s,*** and they
Acts 18:5 . . . spent all his *t* preaching
1 Cor 7:29 . . The *t* that remains is very
2 Cor 6:2 . . . the "right *t*" is now.
Gal 6:9 . . . . . just the right *t* we will reap
2 Tim 1:9 . . . the beginning of *t*—to show
Heb 9:28 . . . once for all *t* as a sacrifice
Heb 10:12 . . for sins, good for all *t.*
1 Pet 4:17. . . For the *t* has come for
Rev 12:14. . . for a *t*, ***t-s,*** and half a *t.*

TIMID (adj)
lacking in courage or self-confidence
1 Thes 5:14 . Encourage those who are *t.*

TIMIDITY (n)
the quality or state of being timid
2 Tim 1:7 . . . of fear and *t,* but of power,

TIMOTHY
Paul's student and traveling companion from Lystra (Acts 16:1-3); raised by devout Jewish mother (2 Tim 1:5; 3:15); joined Paul on second missionary journey (Acts 16–20); sent to serve NT churches (1 Cor 4:17; 16:10; Phil 2:19; 1 Thes 3:5-6; 1 Tim 1:3); wrote letters with Paul (2 Cor 1:1; Phil 1:1; Col 1:1; 1 Thes 1:1; 2 Thes 1:1; Phlm 1:1); letters written to him by Paul (1 Tim 1:2; 2 Tim 1:2).

TIRED (adj)
drained of strength and energy
Exod 17:12 . became so *t* he could no
Isa 35:3. . . . . those who have *t* hands,
Gal 6:9 . . . . . let's not get *t* of doing what
2 Thes 3:13 . never get *t* of doing good.
Heb 12:12 . . new grip with your *t* hands

TITHE, TITHES (n)
one-tenth of any property or produce
see also TENTH
Num 18:21 . give them the ***t-s*** from the
Deut 12:17. . neither the *t* of your grain
2 Chr 31:12 . brought all the ***t-s*** and
Amos 4:4. . . bring your ***t-s*** every three
Mal 3:8. . . . . of the ***t-s*** and offerings due
Mal 3:10. . . . Bring all the ***t-s*** into the

TITHE (v)
to pay or give a tenth of as an offering to God
Matt 23:23 . . You should *t,* yes,
Luke 11:42. . you are careful to *t* even the

TITTLE (KJV)
Matt 5:18 . . . the ***smallest detail*** of God's law
Luke 16:17 . . the ***smallest point*** of God's law

TITUS
Young Gentile pastor and helper of Paul (Gal 2:1-3; 2 Tim 4:10); sent to Corinth (2 Cor 2:13; 7:6-14; 8:6-23; 12:18); sent to Crete (Titus 1:4-5).

TODAY (adv)
on or for this day; at the present time
Ps 2:7 . . . . . . ***T*** I have become your Father.
Ps 95:7 . . . . . listen to his voice ***t!***
Matt 6:11 . . . Give us ***t*** the food we
Luke 2:11. . . born ***t*** in Bethlehem,
Luke 23:43 . . I assure you, ***t*** you will be
Heb 1:5 . . . . ***T*** I have become your Father.
Heb 3:7 . . . . ***T*** when you hear his voice,
Heb 13:8 . . . is the same yesterday, ***t,*** and

TOGETHER (adv)
with each other; as a unit; in or into one place, mass, collection, or group
Ps 133:1 . . . . brothers live ***t*** in harmony!
Jer 3:18. . . . . will return ***t*** from exile
Zeph 3:9 . . . can worship the LORD ***t.***
Acts 1:14 . . . They all met ***t*** and were
Rom 1:12. . . When we get ***t,*** I want to
Eph 1:10 . . . bring everything ***t*** under the

TOLERANT (adj)
marked by forbearance and endurance
Rom 2:4. . . . how wonderfully kind, ***t,*** and

TOLERATE (v)
to put up with
Rev 2:2. . . . . know you don't ***t*** evil people.

TOMORROW (n)
the day after the present; the future
Prov 27:1 . . . Don't brag about ***t,*** since you
Isa 22:13. . . . and drink, for ***t*** we die!
Rom 8:38 . . . our worries about ***t***—not even
1 Cor 15:32 . and drink, for ***t*** we die!

TONGUE, TONGUES (n)
part of the mouth that enables speech; dialect or language of a people; a special gift of speech given by the Holy Spirit
see also LANGUAGE(S)
Ps 5:9 . . . . . . Their ***t-s*** are filled
Ps 34:13 . . . . keep your ***t*** from speaking
Ps 39:1 . . . . . I will hold my ***t*** when
Ps 45:1 . . . . . king, for my ***t*** is like
Ps 78:36 . . . . lied to him with their ***t-s.***
Ps 119:172 . . Let my ***t*** sing about
Ps 137:6 . . . . May my ***t*** stick to the
Prov 13:3. . . who control their ***t*** will have
Prov 15:4. . . a deceitful ***t*** crushes the
Prov 17:20 . . the lying ***t*** tumbles into
Prov 21:23 . . Watch your ***t*** and keep
Luke 16:24. . in water and cool my ***t.***
Acts 2:3 . . . . like flames or ***t-s*** of fire
Acts 10:46 . . speaking in other ***t-s*** and
Acts 19:6 . . . in other ***t-s*** and prophesied.
Rom 14:11 . . me, and every ***t*** will confess
1 Cor 14:2 . . to speak in ***t-s,*** you will
1 Cor 14:4 . . speaks in ***t-s*** is strengthened
1 Cor 14:5 . . speak in ***t-s,*** but even more
1 Cor 14:13 . speaks in ***t-s*** should pray
1 Cor 14:18 . I speak in ***t-s*** more than
1 Cor 14:27 . three should speak in ***t-s.***
1 Cor 14:39 . forbid speaking in ***t-s.***
Phil 2:11 . . . and every ***t*** confess that
Jas 3:2. . . . . . if we could control our ***t-s,*** we
Jas 3:5. . . . . . same way, the ***t*** is a small

TOOK (v)
to seize, grasp, or carry
see also TAKE
Matt 8:17 . . . He ***t*** our sicknesses and
Matt 26:26 . . eating, Jesus ***t*** some bread and
Matt 26:27 . . And he ***t*** a cup of wine and
1 Cor 11:23 . the Lord Jesus ***t*** some bread
1 Cor 11:25 . the same way, he ***t*** the cup of
Phil 2:7 . . . . he ***t*** the humble position of

TOOTH (n)
a bonelike structure in the mouth used for chewing
Exod 21:24 . eye for an eye, a ***t*** for a ***t,***
Matt 5:38 . . . eye for an eye, and a ***t*** for a ***t.***

TORMENT (n)
extreme pain or anguish of body or mind
Luke 16:28. . end up in this place of ***t.***

TORMENT, TORMENTED (v)
to cause severe, usually persistent or recurrent distress of body or mind
2 Cor 12:7 . . messenger from Satan to ***t***
Rev 20:10. . . they will be ***t-ed*** day and night

TORMENTORS (n)
those who torment
Ps 137:3 . . . . Our ***t*** insisted on a joyful

TORTURED (v)
to punish or coerce by inflicting excruciating pain
Matt 18:34 . . prison to be ***t*** until he
Heb 11:35 . . others were ***t,*** refusing to

TOSSED (v)
to fling or heave continuously about
Jas 1:6. . . . . . blown and ***t*** by the wind.

TOUCH, TOUCHED, TOUCHES (v)
to reach out or come in contact with; to lay hands upon; to have an influence upon
Gen 3:3 . . . . must not eat it or even ***t*** it;
Exod 19:12 . or even ***t*** its boundaries.
Exod 19:12 . Anyone who ***t-es*** the mountain
Isa 6:7. . . . . . this coal has ***t-ed*** your lips.
Matt 9:21 . . . If I can just ***t*** his robe,
Matt 14:36 . . who ***t-ed*** him were healed.
Luke 8:45. . . "Who ***t-ed*** me?" Jesus asked.
Luke 18:15. . so he could ***t*** and bless
Luke 24:39. . ***T*** me and make sure that
2 Cor 6:17 . . Don't ***t*** their filthy things,
Col 2:21 . . . . Don't taste! Don't ***t!***"?
1 Jn 1:1. . . . . ***t-ed*** him with our own hands.
1 Jn 5:18. . . . evil one cannot ***t*** them.

TOWER (n)
a tall building or structure typically higher than its surroundings
Gen 11:4 . . . with a ***t*** that reaches into

TRADE, TRADED (v)
to give one thing in exchange for another
Gen 25:31 . . Jacob replied, "but ***t*** me your
Ps 106:20 . . . They ***t-d*** their glorious God
Rom 1:25 . . . They ***t-d*** the truth about God

TRADERS (n)
persons whose business is buying and selling
1 Tim 1:10 . . are slave ***t,*** liars, promise

TRADITION, TRADITIONS (n)
an inherited, customary, or established pattern of thought, action, or behavior
Matt 15:6. . . for the sake of your own ***t.***
Mark 7:5 . . . disciples follow our age-old ***t?***
Mark 7:8 . . . law and substitute your own ***t.***
Mark 7:13 . . to hand down your own ***t.***
Gal 1:14 . . . . in my zeal for the ***t-s*** of my

TRAGEDY (n)
a disastrous event; misfortune
Eccl 9:12 . . . are caught by sudden ***t.***

TRAGIC (adj)
of, marked by, or expressive of tragedy
Eccl 1:13 . . . has dealt a ***t*** existence to

TRAIN (n)
a part of a gown that trails behind the wearer
Isa 6:1. . . . . . throne, and the ***t*** of his robe

TRAIN, TRAINED (v)
to form by or undergo instruction or discipline
see also TEACH
Isa 2:4. . . . . . against nation, nor ***t*** for war
Luke 6:40. . . who is fully ***t-ed*** will become
John 7:15 . . . when he hasn't been ***t-ed?***
Acts 22:3 . . . I was carefully ***t-ed*** in our
1 Tim 4:7 . . . ***t*** yourself to be godly.
Titus 2:4. . . . women must ***t*** the younger
Heb 12:11 . . those who are ***t-ed*** in this way.

TRAINING (n)
acquired skill, knowledge, or experience; the act, process, or method of one who trains
Acts 4:13 . . . men with no special ***t*** in the
1 Tim 4:8 . . . Physical ***t*** is good, but

TRAITORS (n)
those who betray another's trust, are false to an obligation or duty, or commit treason
Ps 59:5 . . . . . Show no mercy to wicked ***t.***
Ps 119:158 . . Seeing these ***t*** makes me

TRAMPLE, TRAMPLED (v)
to crush, injure, or destroy by or as if by treading
Ps 60:12 . . . . for he will ***t*** down our foes.
Ps 91:13 . . . . You will ***t*** upon lions
Amos 5:11. . You ***t*** the poor,
Amos 8:4. . . rob the poor and ***t*** down the
Mic 4:13. . . . so you can ***t*** many nations to
Mic 7:19. . . . You will ***t*** our sins under
Matt 7:6. . . . They will ***t*** the pearls,
Luke 21:24. . Jerusalem will be ***t-d*** down
Heb 10:29 . . who have ***t-d*** on the Son
Rev 14:20. . . The grapes were ***t-d*** in the

TRANCE (n)
a sleeplike state (as of deep hypnosis)
Acts 10:10 . . prepared, he fell into a ***t.***
Acts 11:5 . . . I went into a ***t*** and saw a
Acts 22:17 . . the Temple and fell into a ***t.***

TRANSFIGURED (KJV)
Matt 17:2. . . Jesus' appearance was ***transformed***
Mark 9:2 . . . Jesus' appearance was ***transformed***

TRANSFORM, TRANSFORMED (v)
to change the outward appearance of; to change in character or condition
see also CHANGE(D)
Matt 17:2. . . appearance was ***t-ed*** so that
Rom 12:2. . . let God ***t*** you into a new
1 Cor 15:51 . but we will all be ***t-ed!***

TRANSGRESSED, TRANSGRESSION (KJV)
Josh 7:11 . . . and ***broken*** my covenant
1 Chr 5:25 . . tribes were ***unfaithful***
1 Chr 10:13 . because he was ***unfaithful***
Rom 4:15 . . . to avoid ***breaking*** the law
1 Jn 3:4. . . . . sin ***is contrary to*** the law

TRAP, TRAPS (n)
something by which one is caught or stopped unawares; a position or situation from which it is difficult or impossible to escape; a device for taking game or other animals
Deut 7:25. . . will become a ***t*** to you,
Deut 12:30. . fall into the ***t*** of following
Ps 91:3 . . . . . you from every ***t*** and protect
Prov 1:17. . . a bird sees a ***t*** being set,
Prov 3:26. . . foot from being caught in a ***t.***
Prov 28:10. . into their own ***t,*** but the
Prov 29:5. . . is to lay a ***t*** for their feet.
Prov 29:25. . a dangerous ***t,*** but trusting
Isa 8:14. . . . . he will be a ***t*** and a snare.
Isa 24:17. . . . Terror and ***t-s*** and snares will
Matt 16:23. . are a dangerous ***t*** to me.
Rom 11:9. . . a snare, a ***t*** that makes them
1 Tim 3:7 . . . into the devil's ***t.***
2 Tim 2:26 . . from the devil's ***t.***

TRAP, TRAPPED, TRAPS (v)
to catch or take in or as if in a trap
Ps 7:15 . . . . . a deep pit to ***t*** others, then
Ps 9:16 . . . . . wicked are ***t-ped*** by their own
Prov 6:2. . . . if you have ***t-ped*** yourself by
Prov 12:13. . wicked are ***t-ped*** by their
Prov 18:7. . . they ***t*** themselves with
Matt 22:15. . to plot how to ***t*** Jesus into
1 Cor 3:19 . . He ***t-s*** the wise in the snare
1 Tim 6:9 . . . temptation and are ***t-ped*** by

TREACHEROUS (adj)
characterized by or manifesting treachery
Prov 11:6. . . ambition of ***t*** people traps
Prov 13:2. . . but ***t*** people have an appetite
Prov 13:15. . a ***t*** person is headed for
Prov 22:12. . ruins the plans of the ***t.***
Jer 3:8. . . . . . But that ***t*** sister Judah had

TREACHERY (n)
violation of allegiance or of faith and confidence
Acts 1:18 . . . he received for his ***t.***

TREAD, TREADING, TREADS (v)
to beat or press with the feet
Deut 25:4. . . eating as it ***t-s*** out the grain.
Isa 63:2. . . . . have been ***t-ing*** out grapes?
Joel 3:13. . . . Come, ***t*** the grapes,
1 Cor 9:9 . . . from eating as it ***t-s*** out
1 Tim 5:18 . . from eating as it ***t-s*** out

TREASURE, TREASURES (n)
wealth or a collection of precious things; something of great value
Exod 19:5 . . my own special ***t*** from
Deut 7:6. . . . to be his own special ***t.***
1 Chr 29:3 . . my own private ***t-s*** of gold
Ps 119:111 . . Your laws are my ***t;*** they
Ps 135:4 . . . . Israel for his own special ***t.***
Prov 2:4. . . . seek them like hidden ***t-s.***
Prov 18:22. . finds a wife finds a ***t,***
Song 4:10. . . delights me, my ***t,*** my bride.
Isa 10:3. . . . . Where will your ***t-s*** be safe?
Hag 2:7 . . . . the ***t-s*** of all the nations
Mal 3:17. . . . they will be my own special ***t.***
Matt 6:19. . . Don't store up ***t-s*** here on
Matt 6:21. . . Wherever your ***t*** is, there the
Matt 13:44. . Heaven is like a ***t*** that a man
Luke 12:33. . will store up ***t*** for you in
2 Cor 4:7 . . . jars containing this great ***t.***
Eph 3:8 . . . . the endless ***t-s*** available to
Col 2:3 . . . . . hidden all the ***t-s*** of wisdom
1 Tim 6:19 . . storing up their ***t*** as a good
Heb 11:26 . . to own the ***t-s*** of Egypt, for

TREASURE, TREASURED (v)
to hold or keep as precious
Job 23:12 . . . but have ***t-d*** his words more
Prov 2:1. . . . I say, and ***t*** my commands.
Prov 7:1. . . . always ***t*** my commands.
Prov 10:14. . Wise people ***t*** knowledge,

TREASURY (n)
a place in which stores of wealth are kept
Deut 28:12. . time from his rich ***t*** in the
Luke 6:45. . . things from the ***t*** of a good

TREAT, TREATED, TREATING (v)
to regard and deal with in a specified manner
Gen 18:25 . . ***t-ing*** the righteous
Eccl 8:14 . . . people are often ***t-ed*** as though
Matt 18:17. . ***t*** that person as a pagan
Eph 6:9 . . . . Masters, ***t*** your slaves in the
Heb 10:29 . . God, and have ***t-ed*** the blood
1 Pet 3:7. . . . ***T*** your wife with understanding
Heb 12:7 . . . God is ***t-ing*** you as his own

TREATY, TREATIES (n)
an agreement or arrangement made by negotiation
Exod 34:12 . to make a ***t*** with the people
Deut 7:2. . . . Make no ***t-ies*** with them and
Dan 9:27 . . . will make a ***t*** with the people

TREE, TREES (n)
woody perennial plants, many of which produce crops; highly treasured natural resource; often linked with worship of pagan gods; symbolic of a growing believer
Gen 2:9 . . . . he placed the ***t*** of life and
Deut 21:23 . . from the ***t*** overnight.
Judg 9:8 . . . . the ***t-s*** decided to choose
2 Sam 18:9 . . got caught in the ***t.***
1 Kgs 14:23 . and under every green ***t.***
Ps 1:3 . . . . . . They are like ***t-s*** planted along
Ps 52:8 . . . . . like an olive ***t,*** thriving in
Ps 92:12 . . . . like palm ***t-s*** and grow
Ps 96:12 . . . . Let the ***t-s*** of the forest
Prov 3:18 . . . Wisdom is a ***t*** of life to
Prov 11:30 . . deeds become a ***t*** of life;
Isa 55:12 . . . . and the ***t-s*** of the field
Isa 65:22 . . . . people will live as long as ***t-s,***
Jer 17:8 . . . . . They are like ***t-s*** planted along
Dan 4:10 . . . saw a large ***t*** in the middle
Mic 4:4 . . . . . and fig ***t-s,*** for there will be
Matt 3:10 . . . sever the roots of the ***t-s.***
Matt 3:10 . . . every ***t*** that does not produce
Matt 12:33 . . ***t*** is identified by its fruit.
Mark 8:24 . . look like ***t-s*** walking
Luke 19:4 . . . a sycamore-fig ***t*** beside the
Rom 11:24 . . cut from a wild olive ***t.***
Gal 3:13 . . . . everyone who is hung on a ***t.***
Jas 3:12 . . . . . Does a fig ***t*** produce olives,
Jude 1:12 . . . They are like ***t-s*** in autumn
Rev 22:2 . . . . the river grew a ***t*** of life,
Rev 22:14 . . . the fruit from the ***t*** of life.
Rev 22:19 . . . share in the ***t*** of life and

TREMBLE, TREMBLED, TREMBLES, TREMBLING (v)
to be affected with great fear or anxiety; to shake involuntarily
Exod 15:14 . hear and ***t;*** anguish grips
Exod 19:16 . horn, and all the people ***t-d.***
Exod 20:18 . a distance, ***t-ing*** with fear.
2 Sam 22:8 . . the earth quaked and ***t-d.***
1 Chr 16:30 . all the earth ***t*** before him.
Ps 2:11 . . . . . fear, and rejoice with ***t-ing.***
Ps 97:4 . . . . . The earth sees and ***t-s.***
Ps 102:15 . . . the earth will ***t*** before his
Ps 104:32 . . . The earth ***t-s*** at his glance;
Isa 66:2 . . . . . contrite hearts, who ***t*** at my
Jer 10:10 . . . . whole earth ***t-s*** at his anger.
Dan 10:10 . . and lifted me, still ***t-ing,***
Joel 2:1 . . . . . Let everyone ***t*** in fear
Nah 1:5 . . . . hills melt away; the earth ***t-s,***
Hab 3:6 . . . . the nations ***t.*** He shatters
Heb 4:1 . . . . we ought to ***t*** with fear that
Heb 12:21 . . I am terrified and ***t-ing.***

TRESPASS(ES) (KJV)
Lev 19:21 . . . a ram as a ***guilt*** offering
2 Chr 24:18 . Because of this ***sin,*** divine
Matt 6:15 . . . Father will not forgive your ***sins***
Matt 18:15 . . believer ***sins*** against you,
Eph 2:1 . . . . because of your ***disobedience***

TRIAL, TRIALS (n)
a legal proceeding based in court; a test of faith, patience, or stamina through subjection to suffering or temptation
see also TEMPTATION(S), TEST(S), TROUBLE(S)
Job 42:11 . . . all the ***t-s*** the LORD had
Ps 26:2 . . . . . Put me on ***t,*** LORD,
Ps 37:33 . . . . when they are put on ***t.***
Ps 143:2 . . . . Don't put your servant on ***t,***
Mark 13:11 . and stand ***t,*** don't worry in
Luke 22:28 . . with me in my time of ***t.***
John 16:33 . . have many ***t-s*** and sorrows.
Rom 5:3 . . . . into problems and ***t-s,*** for we
1 Pet 1:7 . . . . through many ***t-s,*** it will
1 Pet 4:12 . . . the fiery ***t-s*** you are going
2 Pet 2:9 . . . . from their ***t-s,*** even while

TRIBE, TRIBES (n)
family divisions, usually within Israel, but also of other ethnic peoples
Gen 49:28 . . are the twelve ***t-s*** of Israel,
Matt 19:28 . . the twelve ***t-s*** of Israel.
Heb 7:13 . . . a different ***t,*** whose members
Rev 5:5 . . . . . Lion of the ***t*** of Judah,
Rev 5:9 . . . . . God from every ***t*** and language
Rev 11:9 . . . . all peoples, ***t-s,*** languages,
Rev 14:6 . . . . to every nation, ***t,*** language,

TRIBULATION (n)
a period of unparalleled suffering in the last days
Rev 7:14 . . . . who died in the great ***t.***

TRIBUTE (n)
a gift or service showing respect, gratitude, or affection
Ps 76:11 . . . . Let everyone bring ***t*** to the

TRICK, TRICKED (v)
to deceive or cheat
Gen 27:35 . . and he ***t-ed*** me
Gen 29:25 . . Why have you ***t-ed*** me
Jer 29:31 . . . . has ***t-ed*** you into believing
2 Cor 4:2 . . . We don't try to ***t*** anyone
Eph 4:14 . . . people try to ***t*** us with lies

TRICKERY (n)
deception
Isa 29:21. . . . those who use *t* to pervert
2 Cor 12:16 . advantage of you by *t.*

TRIED (v)
to make an attempt at; to put to test
Ps 73:16 . . . . So I *t* to understand
Ps 95:9 . . . . . tested and *t* my patience,
Ps 119:10 . . . I have *t* hard to find
Heb 3:9 . . . . tested and *t* my patience,

TRIUMPH (n)
the joy or exultation of victory or success
Ps 118:7 . . . . I will look in *t* at those

TRIUMPH, TRIUMPHED (v)
to obtain victory
1 Sam 17:50. So David *t-ed* over the
Ps 54:7 . . . . . and helped me to *t* over my

TRIUMPHAL (adj)
of, relating to, or marked by triumph
2 Cor 2:14 . . in Christ's *t* procession.

TRIUMPHANT (adj)
victorious, conquering
Deut 33:29. . shield and your *t* sword!

TROUBLE, TROUBLES (n)
a state, condition, or cause of distress, annoyance, difficulty, or inconvenience
see also TEST(S), TRIAL(S)
Gen 41:51 . . made me forget all my *t-s*
Josh 7:25 . . . have you brought *t* on us?
2 Chr 15:4 . . they were in *t* and turned
Job 5:7 . . . . . are born for *t* as readily as
Ps 7:14 . . . . . they are pregnant with *t*
Ps 9:9 . . . . . . a refuge in times of *t.*
Ps 10:14 . . . . you see the *t* and grief
Ps 22:11 . . . . from me, for *t* is near,
Ps 27:5 . . . . . me there when *t-s* come;
Ps 32:7 . . . . . you protect me from *t.*
Ps 34:17 . . . . them from all their *t-s.*
Ps 37:39 . . . . their fortress in times of *t.*
Ps 40:12 . . . . For *t-s* surround me—
Ps 41:1 . . . . . them when they are in *t.*
Ps 46:1 . . . . . ready to help in times of *t.*
Ps 49:5 . . . . . I fear when *t* comes, when
Ps 50:15 . . . . when you are in *t,* and I will
Ps 54:7 . . . . . have rescued me from my *t-s*
Ps 55:3 . . . . . They bring *t* on me
Ps 66:14 . . . . I was in deep *t.*
Ps 81:7 . . . . . cried to me in *t,* and
Ps 86:7 . . . . . whenever I'm in *t,* and
Ps 91:15 . . . . I will be with them in *t.*
Ps 107:6 . . . . they cried in their *t,*
Ps 107:41 . . . rescues the poor from *t*
Ps 116:3 . . . . I saw only *t* and sorrow.
Ps 120:1 . . . . took my *t-s* to the LORD;
Ps 138:7 . . . . I am surrounded by *t-s,* you
Prov 6:14 . . . they constantly stir up *t.*
Prov 10:10 . . who wink at wrong cause *t,*
Prov 11:8 . . . godly are rescued from *t,*
Prov 11:29 . . Those who bring *t* on their
Prov 12:13 . . the godly escape such *t.*
Prov 12:21 . . wicked have their fill of *t.*
Prov 13:20 . . with fools and get in *t.*
Prov 25:19 . . in times of *t* is like chewing
Eccl 4:10 . . . falls alone is in real *t.*
Isa 38:14. . . . I am in *t,* LORD. Help me!
Isa 53:4. . . . . And we thought his *t-s* were
Isa 58:10. . . . and help those in *t.*
Hos 5:15 . . . as soon as *t* comes, they
Nah 1:7 . . . . strong refuge when *t* comes.
Matt 6:34 . . . Today's *t* is enough
Rom 8:35 . . . if we have *t* or calamity,
1 Cor 7:28 . . at this time will have *t-s,*
2 Cor 4:17 . . our present *t-s* are small
2 Cor 6:4 . . . We patiently endure *t-s* and
2 Cor 7:4 . . . me happy despite all our *t-s.*
2 Cor 8:2 . . . being tested by many *t-s,*
1 Thes 3:3 . . shaken by the *t-s* you were
1 Tim 6:5 . . . These people always cause *t.*
Jas 1:2. . . . . . when *t-s* come your way,
Jas 5:1. . . . . . all the terrible *t-s* ahead

TROUBLE (v)
to worry or disturb
Luke 7:6. . . . Lord, don't *t* yourself by

TROUBLED (adj)
concerned, worried
Dan 6:14 . . . the king was deeply *t,* and he
Mark 14:33 . and he became deeply *t* and
John 14:1 . . . Don't let your hearts be *t.*
John 14:27 . . So don't be *t* or afraid.

TROUBLEMAKERS (n)
those who consciously or unconsciously cause trouble
Judg 19:22 . . crowd of *t* from the town

TRUE (adj)
fully realized or fulfilled; accurate; properly so called; steadfast, loyal, honest, and just; ideal, essential; being in accordance with the actual state of affairs; legitimate, rightful
Num 11:23 . my word comes *t!*
Deut 18:22. . does not happen or come *t,*
Josh 23:14 . . your God has come *t.*
1 Sam 9:6. . . everything he says comes *t.*

1 Kgs 10:6 . . and wisdom is *t!*
2 Chr 15:3 . . without the *t* God,
Ps 7:10 . . . . . hearts are *t* and right.
Ps 19:9 . . . . . laws of the LORD are *t;*
Ps 119:142 . . instructions are perfectly *t.*
Ps 119:151 . . your commands are *t.*
Isa 45:19. . . . speak only what is *t* and
Jer 10:10. . . . is the only *t* God.
Jer 26:15. . . . it is absolutely *t* that
Jer 28:9. . . . . when his predictions come *t*
Luke 16:11. . the *t* riches of heaven?
Luke 18:31. . Son of Man will come *t.*
John 1:9 . . . . one who is the *t* light,
John 3:33 . . . can affirm that God is *t.*
John 4:23 . . . *t* worshipers will worship
John 6:32 . . . offers you the *t* bread
John 6:55 . . . my flesh is *t* food, and
John 7:28 . . . one who sent me is *t,*
John 15:1 . . . I am the *t* grapevine,
John 17:3 . . . know you, the only *t* God,
Rom 3:4 . . . . else is a liar, God is *t.*
Rom 15:8 . . . God is *t* to the promises
Eph 5:9 . . . . is good and right and *t.*
Phil 4:1 . . . . stay *t* to the Lord.
Phil 4:8 . . . . thoughts on what is *t,*
Jas 1:18. . . . . giving us his *t* word.
1 Jn 2:8. . . . . the *t* light is already
1 Jn 2:27. . . . to teach you what is *t.*
1 Jn 5:20. . . . He is the only *t* God,
Rev 19:9. . . . These are *t* words that come
Rev 22:6. . . . seen is trustworthy and *t.*

TRUMPET, TRUMPETS (n)

a wind instrument made of metal or an animal horn used to rally troops on the battlefield or by priests during sacrifices

Isa 27:13. . . . the great *t* will sound.
Matt 24:31 . . blast of a *t,* and they will
1 Cor 15:52 . when the last *t* is blown.
1 Thes 4:16 . with the *t* call of God.
Rev 8:2. . . . . they were given seven *t-s.*
Rev 8:7. . . . . angel blew his *t,* and hail
Rev 18:22. . . flutes, and *t-s* will never

TRUST (n)

assured reliance on the character, ability, strength, or truth of someone or something; hope
see also BELIEVE, FAITH

Job 31:24 . . . Have I put my *t* in money
Ps 40:3 . . . . . put their *t* in the LORD.
Ps 56:3 . . . . . I will put my *t* in you.
Isa 2:22. . . . . Don't put your *t* in mere
Jer 13:25. . . . putting your *t* in false
Jer 17:5. . . . . who put their *t* in mere
John 12:46 . . who put their *t* in me
Heb 2:13 . . . will put my *t* in him,
1 Jn 4:16. . . . have put our *t* in his love.

TRUST, TRUSTED, TRUSTING, TRUSTS (v)

to place confidence or depend; to commit or place in one's care or keeping; to rely on the truthfulness or accuracy of
see also BELIEVE, FAITH

Gen 39:8 . . . master *t-s* me with everything
Deut 1:32. . . refused to *t* the LORD
Deut 28:52. . walls you *t-ed* to protect
2 Kgs 18:5 . . Hezekiah *t-ed* in the
2 Kgs 18:19 . What are you *t-ing* in that
1 Chr 5:20 . . because they *t-ed* in him.
2 Chr 13:18 . they *t-ed* in the LORD,
Job 4:18 . . . . God does not *t* his own angels
Job 15:31 . . . fool themselves by *t-ing* in
Ps 13:5 . . . . . I *t* in your unfailing love.
Ps 21:7 . . . . . the king *t-s* in the LORD.
Ps 25:2 . . . . . I *t* in you, my God!
Ps 25:3 . . . . . No one who *t-s* in you will
Ps 31:14 . . . . I am *t-ing* you, O LORD,
Ps 33:4 . . . . . we can *t* everything he
Ps 37:3 . . . . . *T* in the LORD and do
Ps 41:9 . . . . . the one I *t-ed* completely,
Ps 44:6 . . . . . I do not *t* in my bow;
Ps 55:23 . . . . but I am *t-ing* you to save
Ps 62:8 . . . . . O my people, *t* in him at
Ps 71:5 . . . . . I've *t-ed* you, O LORD,
Ps 84:12 . . . . for those who *t* in you.
Ps 86:2 . . . . . serve you and *t* you.
Ps 112:7 . . . . confidently *t* the LORD
Ps 115:8 . . . . as are all who *t* in them.
Ps 118:8 . . . . LORD than to *t* in
Ps 119:42 . . . for I *t* in your word.
Prov 3:5 . . . . *T* in the LORD with
Prov 21:22. . fortress in which they *t.*
Prov 28:25. . *t-ing* the LORD leads to
Prov 28:26. . who *t* their own insight
Prov 29:25. . *t-ing* the LORD means safety.
Prov 31:11. . Her husband can *t* her,
Isa 12:2. . . . . I will *t* in him and
Isa 25:9. . . . . We *t-ed* in him, and he saved
Isa 26:3. . . . . peace all who *t* in you,
Isa 31:1. . . . . for help, *t-ing* their horses,
Isa 40:31. . . . who *t* in the LORD
Jer 7:14. . . . . this Temple that you *t* in
Jer 12:6. . . . . Do not *t* them, no matter
Jer 48:7. . . . . Because you have *t-ed* in your
Dan 3:28 . . . his servants who *t-ed* in him.
Dan 6:23 . . . for he had *t-ed* in his God.
Nah 1:7 . . . . to those who *t* in him.
Hab 2:4 . . . . They *t* in themselves,
Hab 2:18 . . . foolish to *t* in your own

Matt 18:6 . . . little ones who ***t-s*** in me to
John 2:24 . . . Jesus didn't ***t*** them,
John 12:44 . . you are ***t-ing*** not only me,
John 14:1 . . . in God, and ***t*** also in me.
Rom 9:32 . . . instead of by ***t-ing*** in him.
Rom 9:33 . . . But anyone who ***t-s*** in him will
Rom 10:11 . . Anyone who ***t-s*** in him will
Rom 15:13 . . peace because you ***t*** in
1 Cor 2:5 . . . so you would ***t*** not in
1 Cor 7:25 . . wisdom that can be ***t-ed,***
Eph 3:17 . . . hearts as you ***t*** in him.
Phil 1:29 . . . the privilege of ***t-ing*** in Christ
Col 2:12 . . . . because you ***t-ed*** the mighty
1 Tim 6:17 . . not to ***t*** in their money,
2 Tim 1:12 . . the one in whom I ***t,***
2 Tim 3:15 . . that comes by ***t-ing*** in Christ
Heb 10:22 . . hearts fully ***t-ing*** him.
Heb 10:23 . . God can be ***t-ed*** to keep his
1 Pet 1:9 . . . . reward for ***t-ing*** him will be
1 Pet 2:6 . . . . anyone who ***t-s*** in him will
1 Pet 2:7 . . . . you who ***t*** him recognize

TRUSTWORTHY (adj)
worthy of confidence; dependable
see also FAITHFUL, LOYAL
2 Kgs 22:7 . . honest and ***t*** men.
Ps 19:7 . . . . . of the LORD are ***t,***
Ps 119:86 . . . All your commands are ***t.***
Ps 119:138 . . perfect and completely ***t.***
Prov 11:13 . . those who are ***t*** can keep
Dan 6:4 . . . . responsible, and completely ***t.***
Titus 2:10 . . . to be entirely ***t*** and good.
Heb 6:19 . . . a strong and ***t*** anchor

TRUTH, TRUTHS (n)
the property (as of a statement) of being in accord with fact or reality (natural and spiritual); sincerity in action, character, and utterance
Ps 15:2 . . . . . speaking the ***t*** from sincere
Ps 25:5 . . . . . Lead me by your ***t*** and teach
Ps 26:3 . . . . . lived according to your ***t.***
Ps 43:3 . . . . . light and your ***t;*** let them
Ps 45:4 . . . . . defending ***t,*** humility, and
Ps 86:11 . . . . live according to your ***t!***
Ps 119:160 . . essence of your words is ***t;***
Prov 8:7 . . . . for I speak the ***t*** and detest
Prov 12:17 . . honest witness tells the ***t;***
Prov 12:22 . . in those who tell the ***t.***
Prov 23:23 . . Get the ***t*** and never sell
Isa 45:23 . . . . I have spoken the ***t,***
Isa 59:15 . . . . Yes, ***t*** is gone,
Jer 4:2 . . . . . . do so with ***t,*** justice,
Jer 9:3 . . . . . . to stand up for the ***t.***
Dan 10:21 . . written in the Book of ***T.***
Dan 11:2 . . . . I will reveal the ***t*** to you.
Amos 5:10 . . people who tell the ***t!***
Zech 8:16 . . . Tell the ***t*** to each other.
Zech 8:19 . . . So love ***t*** and peace.
Luke 1:4 . . . . can be certain of the ***t***
John 4:23 . . . Father in spirit and in ***t.***
John 7:18 . . . him speaks ***t,*** not lies.
John 8:32 . . . the ***t*** will set you free.
John 8:44 . . . there is no ***t*** in him.
John 14:6 . . . way, the ***t,*** and the life.
John 14:17 . . who leads into all ***t.***
John 15:26 . . Advocate—the Spirit of ***t.***
John 16:13 . . the Spirit of ***t*** comes,
John 17:17 . . your word, which is ***t.***
John 18:37 . . to testify to the ***t.***
Acts 20:30 . . distort the ***t*** in order
Acts 21:34 . . find out the ***t*** in all
Acts 24:8 . . . can find out the ***t*** of our
Rom 1:18 . . . who suppress the ***t*** by their
Rom 1:25 . . . They traded the ***t*** about God
Rom 2:8 . . . . to obey the ***t*** and instead
Rom 2:20 . . . complete knowledge and ***t.***
1 Cor 2:13 . . to explain spiritual ***t-s.***
2 Cor 6:7 . . . We faithfully preach the ***t.***
2 Cor 13:8 . . always stand for the ***t.***
Gal 2:5 . . . . . wanted to preserve the ***t***
Gal 5:7 . . . . . back from following the ***t?***
Eph 1:13 . . . also heard the ***t,*** the Good
Eph 4:15 . . . will speak the ***t*** in love,
Eph 6:14 . . . the belt of ***t*** and the body
2 Thes 2:10 . ***t*** that would save them.
2 Thes 2:12 . rather than believing the ***t.***
1 Tim 2:4 . . . and to understand the ***t.***
1 Tim 3:15 . . and foundation of the ***t.***
1 Tim 4:3 . . . people who know the ***t.***
1 Tim 6:5 . . . their backs on the ***t.***
2 Tim 2:15 . . explains the word of ***t.***
2 Tim 3:7 . . . able to understand the ***t.***
Titus 1:14 . . . turned away from the ***t.***
Heb 10:26 . . received knowledge of the ***t,***
Jas 3:14 . . . . . don't cover up the ***t*** with
Jas 5:19 . . . . . wanders away from the ***t***
1 Pet 1:22 . . . you obeyed the ***t,*** so now
2 Pet 1:12 . . . standing firm in the ***t***
2 Pet 2:2 . . . . the way of ***t*** will be
1 Jn 1:8 . . . . . and not living in the ***t.***
1 Jn 2:20 . . . . all of you know the ***t.***
1 Jn 3:19 . . . . belong to the ***t,*** so we
1 Jn 4:6 . . . . . Spirit of ***t*** or the spirit
1 Jn 5:6 . . . . . Spirit, who is ***t,*** confirms
2 Jn 1:2 . . . . . because the ***t*** lives
2 Jn 1:3 . . . . . who live in ***t*** and love.
3 Jn 1:3 . . . . . living according to the ***t.***
3 Jn 1:8 . . . . . partners as they teach the ***t.***

TRUTHFUL (adj)
telling or disposed to tell the truth
Ps 5:9 . . . . . . cannot speak a ***t*** word.
Prov 12:19 . . ***T*** words stand the test
John 8:26 . . . and he is completely ***t***.

TRUTHFULNESS (n)
the quality or state of being truthful
Rom 3:7 . . . . highlights his ***t*** and brings
Rom 9:1 . . . . I speak with utter ***t***.

TURMOIL (n)
a state or condition of extreme confusion, agitation, or commotion
Prov 15:16 . . treasure and inner ***t***.

TURN, TURNED, TURNING, TURNS (v)
to convert or change allegiance; to return or change direction; to face toward or away; to divert one's attention from; to become or transform; to shape or bend
Deut 28:14 . . You must not ***t*** away from
Deut 30:10 . . if you ***t*** to the LORD
1 Kgs 11:4 . . old age, they ***t-ed*** his heart
2 Chr 7:14 . . seek my face and ***t*** from
2 Chr 34:33 . they did not ***t*** away from
Esth 9:22 . . . sorrow was ***t-ed*** into gladness
Ps 14:3 . . . . . no, all have ***t-ed*** away; all
Ps 30:11 . . . . You have ***t-ed*** my mourning
Ps 40:1 . . . . . and he ***t-ed*** to me and
Ps 119:59 . . . I ***t-ed*** to follow your
Ps 119:102 . . I haven't ***t-ed*** away from
Prov 3:7 . . . . fear the LORD and ***t*** away
Prov 28:13 . . confess and ***t*** from them,
Isa 17:7. . . . . Creator and ***t*** their eyes to
Isa 54:8. . . . . anger I ***t-ed*** my face away
Isa 55:7. . . . . Let them ***t*** to the LORD
Isa 59:2. . . . . he has ***t-ed*** away and will
Jer 14:7. . . . . We have ***t-ed*** away from you
Jer 31:13. . . . I will ***t*** their mourning into
Jer 31:19. . . . I ***t-ed*** away from God,
Lam 3:40 . . . Let us ***t*** back to the LORD.
Mal 4:6. . . . . preaching will ***t*** the hearts
Matt 3:8 . . . . your sins and ***t-ed*** to God.
Matt 18:3 . . . truth, unless you ***t*** from your
Mark 4:12 . . Otherwise, they will ***t*** to me
Mark 8:34 . . must ***t*** from your selfish
Luke 1:17. . . He will ***t*** the hearts of
Luke 17:4. . . ***t-s*** again and asks forgiveness
Luke 22:32. . you have repented and ***t-ed***
John 12:40 . . and they cannot ***t*** to me
John 16:20 . . will suddenly ***t*** to wonderful
Acts 3:19 . . . of your sins and ***t*** to God,
Acts 7:42 . . . Then God ***t-ed*** away from
Acts 26:18 . . so they may ***t*** from darkness
Rom 1:26 . . . Even the women ***t-ed*** against
Rom 2:4 . . . . to ***t*** you from your sin?
Rom 3:12 . . . All have ***t-ed*** away;
Gal 1:6 . . . . . that you are ***t-ing*** away so
2 Tim 2:19 . . LORD must ***t*** away from
Titus 2:12. . . instructed to ***t*** from godless
Heb 10:38 . . in anyone who ***t-s*** away.
1 Pet 2:25. . . But now you have ***t-ed*** to

TURTLEDOVES (n)
any of several small wild pigeons noted for plaintive cooing
Lev 12:8. . . . must bring two ***t*** or two young
Luke 2:24. . . a pair of ***t*** or two young

TWELVE (adj)
of or relating to the number 12
Gen 35:22 . . names of the ***t*** sons of Jacob:
Gen 49:28 . . These are the ***t*** tribes of
Matt 10:1 . . . Jesus called his ***t*** disciples
Luke 9:17. . . picked up ***t*** baskets of
Rev 21:12. . . names of the ***t*** tribes of
Rev 21:14. . . names of the ***t*** apostles of
Rev 21:21. . . The ***t*** gates were made of

TWINS (n)
two offspring produced at a birth
Gen 25:24 . . she did indeed have ***t!***
Gen 38:27 . . that she was carrying ***t***.

TWIST, TWISTED (v)
to distort or pervert
Exod 14:25 . He ***t-ed*** their chariot wheels,
Exod 23:8 . . righteous person ***t*** the truth.
Deut 16:19. . You must never ***t*** justice or
Job 34:12 . . . will not ***t*** justice.
Isa 24:5. . . . . have ***t-ed*** God's instructions,
Lam 3:36 . . . if they ***t*** justice in the courts—
Ezek 7:13. . . whose life is ***t-ed*** by sin
Gal 1:7 . . . . . who deliberately ***t*** the truth
2 Pet 3:16. . . unstable have ***t-ed*** his letters

TWO-EDGED (adj)
marked by having two cutting edges
Heb 4:12 . . . sharpest ***t*** sword, cutting
Rev 1:16. . . . a sharp ***t*** sword came from
Rev 2:12. . . . with the sharp ***t*** sword:

UNAFRAID (adv)
in a manner not filled with fear
Hos 2:18 . . . you can live ***u*** in peace

UNBELIEF (n)
incredulity or skepticism in matters of religious truth
see also UNFAITHFUL
Matt 13:58 . . there because of their ***u.***
Mark 6:6 . . . he was amazed at their ***u.***
Mark 9:24 . . help me overcome my ***u!***
Mark 16:14 . them for their stubborn ***u***
Rom 11:23 . . Israel turn from their ***u,***
1 Tim 1:13 . . it in ignorance and ***u.***
Heb 3:19 . . . because of their ***u*** they

UNBELIEVER, UNBELIEVERS (n)
one who does not believe; a non-Christian
Matt 6:32. . . dominate the thoughts of ***u-s,***
Luke 12:30. . the thoughts of ***u-s*** all over
1 Cor 6:6 . . . right in front of ***u-s!***
1 Cor 14:22 . for believers, but for ***u-s.***
2 Cor 6:15 . . a partner with an ***u?***
1 Tim 5:8 . . . people are worse than ***u-s.***
Rev 21:8. . . . But cowards, ***u-s,*** the corrupt,

UNBELIEVING (adj)
marked by unbelief
1 Pet 2:12. . . among your ***u*** neighbors.

UNBREAKABLE (adj)
not capable of being broken
Num 18:19 . an eternal and ***u*** covenant

UNCHANGEABLE (adj)
not changing or to be changed; immutable
Heb 6:18 . . . two things are ***u*** because

UNCIRCUMCISED (adj)
not circumcised; spiritually impure
Jer 9:26. . . . . of Israel also have ***u*** hearts.
1 Cor 7:18 . . man who was ***u*** when he
Gal 5:6 . . . . . being circumcised or being ***u.***
Col 3:11 . . . . circumcised or ***u,*** barbaric,

UNCLEAN (adj)
morally or spiritually impure; prohibited by ritual law for use or contact
Lev 10:10. . . is ceremonially ***u*** and what is
Lev 11:4. . . . it is ceremonially ***u*** for you.
Lev 17:15. . . remain ceremonially ***u*** until
Lev 27:11. . . vow involves an ***u*** animal—
Isa 52:11. . . . everything you touch is ***u.***
Acts 10:14 . . have declared impure and ***u.***
Acts 10:15 . . not call something ***u*** if God

UNDERGROUND (adj)
beneath the surface of the earth
Gen 8:2 . . . . The ***u*** waters stopped

UNDERMINE (v)
to weaken or ruin by degrees
Jer 38:4. . . . . will ***u*** the morale of
Ezek 13:11. . A heavy rainstorm will ***u*** it

UNDERSTAND (v)
to grasp the meaning or reasonableness of; to be thoroughly familiar with
see also UNDERSTOOD
Job 5:9 . . . . . things too marvelous to ***u.***
Job 36:26 . . . is greater than we can ***u.***
Ps 73:16 . . . . tried to ***u*** why the wicked
Ps 119:27 . . . Help me ***u*** the meaning of
Ps 119:125 . . then I will ***u*** your laws.
Ps 119:130 . . so even the simple can ***u.***
Prov 2:5. . . . will ***u*** what it means to fear
Prov 2:9. . . . you will ***u*** what is right,
Prov 28:5. . . the LORD ***u*** completely.
Prov 30:18. . things that I don't ***u:***
Eccl 7:25 . . . and to ***u*** the reason
Isa 6:9. . . . . . carefully, but do not ***u.***
Isa 40:21. . . . you heard? Don't you ***u?***

Jer 9:24. . . . . truly know me and ***u*** that
Hos 14:9 . . . who are wise ***u*** these things.
Matt 13:11 . . permitted to ***u*** the secrets
Matt 13:23 . . truly hear and ***u*** God's
Luke 19:42. . people would ***u*** the way
Luke 24:45. . minds to ***u*** the Scriptures.
Acts 8:30 . . . Do you ***u*** what you are
Rom 7:15. . . I don't really ***u*** myself,
Rom 15:21 . . never heard of him will ***u.***
1 Cor 2:14 . . and they can't ***u*** it,
1 Cor 14:14 . but I don't ***u*** what I am
2 Cor 3:14 . . they cannot ***u*** the truth.
Gal 1:11 . . . . you to ***u*** that the gospel
Eph 1:18 . . . you can ***u*** the confident
Eph 5:17 . . . thoughtlessly, but ***u*** what
Phil 1:10 . . . want you to ***u*** what really
Phil 4:7 . . . . exceeds anything we can ***u.***
Col 2:2. . . . . that they ***u*** God's mysterious
1 Tim 2:4 . . . saved and to ***u*** the truth.
2 Tim 2:7 . . . will help you ***u*** all these
Heb 11:3 . . . By faith we ***u*** that the entire
2 Pet 3:16. . . are hard to ***u,*** and those

UNDERSTANDABLE (adj)

marked by being able to understand; comprehendible

1 Cor 14:19 . rather speak five ***u*** words

UNDERSTANDING (n)

comprehension; explanation, interpretation; sympathy

Job 28:12 . . . Where can they find ***u?***
Job 28:28 . . . to forsake evil is real ***u.***
Ps 119:32 . . . for you expand my ***u.***
Ps 119:34 . . . Give me ***u*** and I will
Ps 119:104 . . commandments give me ***u;***
Prov 3:5. . . . not depend on your own ***u.***
Prov 10:13 . . lips of people with ***u,***
Prov 14:29 . . People with ***u*** control
Prov 15:32 . . correction, you grow in ***u.***
Prov 16:21 . . wise are known for their ***u,***
Prov 18:2. . . Fools have no interest in ***u;***
Prov 19:8. . . who cherish ***u*** will prosper.
Prov 20:5. . . a person with ***u*** will draw
Prov 28:16 . . ruler with no ***u*** will oppress
Isa 40:28. . . . the depths of his ***u.***
Isa 50:4. . . . . opens my ***u*** to his will.
Jer 10:12. . . . With his own ***u*** he stretched
Mark 12:33 . heart and all my ***u*** and all
Luke 2:47. . . were amazed at his ***u*** and his
1 Cor 14:20 . but be mature in ***u*** matters
2 Cor 6:6 . . . purity, our ***u,*** our patience,
Eph 1:8 . . . . along with all wisdom and ***u.***
Phil 1:9 . . . . growing in knowledge and ***u.***
Col 1:9 . . . . . you spiritual wisdom and ***u.***
2 Thes 3:5 . . a full ***u*** and expression
1 Tim 6:4 . . . is arrogant and lacks ***u.***
1 Pet 3:7. . . . your wife with ***u*** as you live
2 Pet 1:20. . . from the prophet's own ***u,***
1 Jn 5:20. . . . he has given us ***u*** so that

UNDERSTOOD (v)

to comprehend the meaning of

see also UNDERSTAND

Neh 8:12 . . . God's words and ***u*** them.
Ps 73:17. . . . I finally ***u*** the destiny
1 Cor 13:2 . . and if I ***u*** all of God's

UNDERWORLD (n)

place of destruction (Hebrew Sheol*)*

see also HELL

Job 26:6 . . . . The ***u*** is naked in God's

UNDESERVED (adj)

of, relating to, or being that which one does not deserve

Rom 5:2. . . . place of ***u*** privilege where

UNDISCIPLINED (adj)

marked by or possessing no discipline

Prov 29:15 . . disgraced by an ***u*** child.

UNDIVIDED (adj)

not directed or moved toward conflicting interests, states, or objects

2 Chr 19:9 . . faithfulness and an ***u*** heart.
2 Cor 11:3 . . your pure and ***u*** devotion

UNFADING (adj)

not losing freshness, value, or effectiveness

1 Pet 3:4. . . . the ***u*** beauty of a gentle

UNFAILING (adj)

constant, everlasting, inexhaustible, sure

see also FAITHFUL

Exod 15:13 . With your ***u*** love you
Ps 6:4 . . . . . . because of your ***u*** love.
Ps 13:5 . . . . . trust in your ***u*** love.
Ps 17:7 . . . . . Show me your ***u*** love in
Ps 18:50 . . . . you show ***u*** love to your
Ps 25:6 . . . . . compassion and ***u*** love,
Ps 31:16 . . . . In your ***u*** love, rescue
Ps 32:10 . . . . but ***u*** love surrounds
Ps 33:5 . . . . . the ***u*** love of the LORD
Ps 33:22 . . . . Let your ***u*** love surround
Ps 36:7 . . . . . precious is your ***u*** love,
Ps 36:10 . . . . Pour out your ***u*** love
Ps 48:9 . . . . . meditate on your ***u*** love
Ps 51:1 . . . . . because of your ***u*** love.
Ps 52:8 . . . . . trust in God's ***u*** love.
Ps 57:10 . . . . For your ***u*** love is
Ps 85:7 . . . . . Show us your ***u*** love,

Ps 90:14 .... morning with your *u* love,
Ps 117:2 .... he loves us with *u* love;
Ps 119:41 ... give me your *u* love,
Ps 119:76 ... let your *u* love comfort
Ps 147:11 ... hope in his *u* love.
Isa 55:3. .... the *u* love I promised
Isa 63:7. .... the LORD's *u* love.
Lam 3:32 ... greatness of his *u* love.
Mic 7:18. ... in showing *u* love.

UNFAIR (adj)
marked by injustice, partiality, or deception
Job 31:13 ... If I have been *u* to my male
Rom 3:5. ... Isn't it *u,* then, for him
Rom 9:14. .. then, that God was *u?*
1 Pet 2:19. .. endure *u* treatment.

UNFAITHFUL (adj)
marked by stubborn disbelief and disloyalty; adulterous
see also TREACHEROUS, UNBELIEF
Ps 78:8 ..... rebellious, and *u,* refusing
Prov 23:28 .. eager to make more men *u.*
Jer 3:20. .... you have been *u* to me,
Matt 5:32. .. unless she has been *u,*
Rom 3:3. ... some of them were *u;* but
2 Tim 2:13 .. If we are *u,* he remains

UNFORGIVING (adj)
unwilling or unable to forgive
2 Tim 3:3 ... will be unloving and *u;*

UNGODLY (adj)
sinful, wicked
see also GODLESS, WICKED
Eph 5:12 ... the things that *u* people do
2 Pet 2:6. ... will happen to *u* people.
Jude 1:15 ... of all the *u* things they

UNHOLY (adj)
showing disregard for what is holy; wicked
Matt 7:6. ... people who are *u.* Don't throw
Heb 10:29 .. were common and *u,* and have

UNION (n)
an act or instance of uniting two or more things into one
2 Cor 6:16 .. And what *u* can there be
Col 2:10. ... through your *u* with Christ,

UNITED (v)
to become one or as if one; in one accord or spirit
Gen 2:24 ... the two are *u* into one.
Mark 10:8 .. the two are *u* into one.
Rom 6:5. ... we have been *u* with him
Rom 7:4. ... now you are *u* with the one
1 Cor 6:16 .. The two are *u* into one.
Eph 4:3 .... to keep yourselves *u* in the
Eph 5:31 ... the two are *u* into one."

UNITY (n)
the quality or state of oneness or harmony
John 17:23 .. perfect *u* that the world
Eph 4:13 ... come to such *u* in our faith

UNIVERSE (n)
the whole body of things created; cosmos
Eph 4:10 ... the entire *u* with himself.
Heb 1:2 .... the Son he created the *u.*
Heb 11:3 ... the entire *u* was formed at

UNJUST (adj)
characterized by injustice
Ps 82:2 ..... you hand down *u* decisions
Matt 5:45. .. the just and the *u* alike.

UNKIND (adj)
harsh, cruel
1 Pet 2:1. ... and all *u* speech.

UNKNOWN (adj)
not known or well-known
1 Cor 12:28 . who speak in *u* languages.

UNLEAVENED (adj)
characterized by being without yeast
Exod 12:17 . this Festival of *U* Bread,
Deut 16:16. . the Festival of *U* Bread,

UNLOVING (adj)
characterized by lack of affection
2 Tim 3:3 ... be *u* and unforgiving;

UNMARRIED (adj)
not married
1 Cor 7:8 ... it's better to stay *u,*
1 Cor 7:32 .. An *u* man can spend his

UNPUNISHED (adj)
to not pay the consequences for a fault, offense, or violation
Exod 20:7 .. let you go *u* if you misuse
Deut 5:11. .. let you go *u* if you misuse
Prov 6:29. .. embraces her will not go *u.*
Prov 19:5. .. false witness will not go *u,*
Jer 49:12. ... You will not go *u!*
Amos 1:3. .. will not let them go *u!*

UNRELIABLE (adj)
not dependable
Prov 25:19. . confidence in an *u* person
1 Tim 6:17. . money, which is so *u.*

UNSTABLE (adj)
not firm, fixed, or constant; unsteady
2 Pet 2:14. . . They lure ***u*** people into sin,
2 Pet 3:16. . . ignorant and ***u*** have twisted

UNTHANKFUL (adj)
showing no gratitude
Luke 6:35. . . those who are ***u*** and wicked.

UNTHINKING (adj)
not having the power of thought
2 Pet 2:12. . . like ***u*** animals, creatures

UNTIE (v)
to free from something that ties, fastens, or restrains
Mark 1:7 . . . a slave and ***u*** the straps
Luke 13:15. . Don't you ***u*** your ox or

UNTRUSTWORTHY (adj)
not worthy of confidence; undependable
Luke 16:11. . if you are ***u*** about worldly

UNWORTHILY (adv)
in an undeserving manner
1 Cor 11:27 . this cup of the Lord ***u***

UPHOLD (v)
to give support to
Ps 82:3 . . . . . ***u*** the rights of the oppressed

UPRIGHT (adj)
marked by strong moral integrity
see also GODLY, RIGHT, RIGHTEOUS
Deut 32:4. . . how just and ***u*** he is!
Prov 3:33. . . blesses the home of the ***u.***
Prov 15:8. . . in the prayers of the ***u.***

UPROOT (v)
to displace from a country or traditional habitat
Ps 52:5 . . . . . and ***u*** you from the land of
Matt 13:29. . 'you'll ***u*** the wheat if you do.

URGE (n)
a continuing impulse
Deut 12:20. . you have the ***u*** to eat meat,

URGE, URGED, URGES (v)
to solicit or entreat; to impel
Job 32:18 . . . spirit within me ***u-s*** me on.
Matt 15:23. . ***u-d*** him to send here away.
Rom 15:30. . I ***u*** you in the name of our
1 Cor 4:16 . . I ***u*** you to imitate me.
1 Thes 2:12 . encouraged you, and ***u-d*** you
2 Tim 4:1 . . . I solemnly ***u*** you in the

URGENCY (n)
a force or impulse that impels
Exod 12:11 . meal with ***u,*** for this is

USE (v)
to put into action or service
2 Tim 2:21 . . for the Master to ***u*** you
1 Pet 2:16. . . don't ***u*** your freedom as an

USEFUL (adj)
serviceable for an end or purpose
2 Tim 3:16 . . inspired by God and is ***u*** to
2 Pet 1:8. . . . productive and ***u*** you will be

USELESS (adj)
having or being of no use; ineffectual, inept
John 15:6 . . . thrown away like a ***u*** branch
Acts 26:14 . . It is ***u*** for you to fight
1 Cor 13:8 . . knowledge will become ***u.***
1 Cor 15:14 . ***u,*** and your faith is ***u.***
1 Cor 15:58 . do for the Lord is ever ***u.***
2 Tim 2:14 . . Such arguments are ***u,*** and
Titus 1:10. . . who engage in ***u*** talk and
Heb 7:18 . . . because it was weak and ***u.***

UTTERMOST (KJV)
Isa 24:16. . . . songs of praise from the ***ends of the earth***
Acts 1:8 . . . . and to the ***ends of the earth***

VAIN (adj)
marked by futility or ineffectualness
Isa 65:23. . . . will not work in *v,* and

VALID (adj)
well-grounded or justifiable
John 8:14 . . . claims are *v* even though

VALLEY, VALLEYS (n)
a depression in the earth's surface between ranges of mountains, hills, or other uplands
Ps 23:4 . . . . . through the darkest *v,* I will
Song 2:1. . . . lily of the *v.*
Isa 40:4. . . . . Fill in the *v-s,* and level
Joel 3:14. . . . waiting in the *v* of decision.
Luke 3:5. . . . The *v-s* will be filled, and

VALUABLE (adj)
having desirable or esteemed characteristics or qualities; of great use or service
Job 28:17 . . . Wisdom is more *v* than gold
Ps 119:72 . . . instructions are more *v*
Prov 8:11. . . is far more *v* than rubies.
Prov 20:15. . words are more *v* than
Matt 10:31 . . you are more *v* to God than
Luke 12:24. . are far more *v* to him than
Phil 3:7 . . . . these things were *v,* but now

VALUE (n)
monetary worth of something; relative worth, utility, or importance
Matt 13:46 . . a pearl of great *v,* he sold
1 Cor 3:13 . . a person's work has any *v.*
Phil 3:8 . . . . the infinite *v* of knowing

VALUED (v)
to estimate or assign the monetary worth of
Zech 11:13. . sum at which they *v* me!

VANISHING (adj)
disappearing
Prov 21:6. . . lying tongue is a *v* mist

VANITY, VANITIES (KJV)
Deut 32:21. . with their ***useless idols***
Ps 144:4 . . . . For we are like ***a breath of air***
Eccl 12:8 . . . Everything is ***meaningless***
Acts 14:15 . . turn from these ***worthless things***
Eph 4:17 . . . they are ***hopelessly confused***

VEGETABLES (n)
a plant or its edible part
Rom 14:2. . . conscience will eat only *v.*

VEIL (n)
a facial covering
Exod 34:33 . covered his face with a *v.*
2 Cor 3:14 . . same *v* covers their minds
2 Cor 3:18 . . have had that *v* removed can

VENGEANCE (n)
punishment inflicted in retaliation for an injury or offense
1 Sam 25:26. taking *v* into your own
1 Sam 25:33. carrying out *v* with my
Ps 94:1 . . . . . O LORD, the God of *v,*
Isa 66:6. . . . . the LORD taking *v* against
Luke 21:22. . be days of God's *v,* and the

VENOM (n)
poisonous matter secreted by some animals
Ps 140:3 . . . . a snake; the *v* of a viper
Rom 3:13. . . Snake *v* drips from their

VERILY (KJV)
Ps 58:11 . . . . There ***truly*** is a reward
John 16:20 . . ***I tell you the truth***

VICIOUS (adj)
dangerously aggressive
Matt 7:15 . . . but are really *v* wolves.
Acts 20:29 . . teachers, like *v* wolves,

VICTORIOUS (adj)
of, relating to, or characteristic of victory; having won a victory
see also OVERCOME
2 Sam 8:6. . . made David *v* wherever he
Isa 53:12. . . . of a *v* soldier, because he
Matt 12:20 . . cause justice to be *v.*
Rev 2:11. . . . Whoever is *v* will not be
Rev 2:17. . . . everyone who is *v* I will give
Rev 2:26. . . . To all who are *v,* who obey
Rev 3:5. . . . . All who are *v* will be clothed
Rev 3:21. . . . Those who are *v* will sit with
Rev 21:7. . . . All who are *v* will inherit

VICTORY, VICTORIES (n)
the overcoming of an enemy, antagonist, or struggle
see also OVERCOME
Exod 15:2 . . he has given me *v.*
2 Sam 22:51. You give great ***v-ies*** to your
Ps 18:50 . . . . You give great ***v-ies*** to your
Ps 20:5 . . . . . we hear of your *v* and
Ps 21:1 . . . . . because you give him *v.*
Ps 35:3 . . . . . I will give you *v!*
Ps 44:4 . . . . . You command ***v-ies*** for Israel.
Ps 48:10 . . . . right hand is filled with *v.*
Ps 62:1 . . . . . for my *v* comes from him.
Ps 98:3 . . . . . have seen the *v* of our God.
Ps 118:14 . . . he has given me *v.*
Ps 149:4 . . . . crowns the humble with *v.*
Isa 12:2. . . . . he has given me *v.*
Isa 52:10. . . . see the *v* of our God.
Rom 8:37 . . . overwhelming *v* is ours
1 Cor 15:54 . Death is swallowed up in *v.*
Col 2:15 . . . . publicly by his *v* over them
Rev 5:5. . . . . David's throne, has won the *v.*

VILLAGE (n)
a settlement usually smaller than a town
Mark 6:6 . . . Jesus went from *v* to *v,*

VINDICATED (v)
shown to be without blame; prove right
1 Tim 3:16 . . body and *v* by the Spirit.

VINE (KJV)
Gen 49:11 . . He ties his foal to a ***grapevine***
Deut 8:8. . . . and barley; of ***grapevines***
Ps 80:8 . . . . . from Egypt like a ***grapevine***
John 15:5 . . . I am the ***vine;*** you are the branches

VINEGAR (n)
a liquid made from wine that has been soured or overfermented
Prov 10:26 . . employers, like *v* to the

VINEYARD (n)
a plantation of grapevines
1 Kgs 21:1 . . who owned a *v* in Jezreel
Prov 31:16 . . earnings she plants a *v.*
Song 1:6. . . . for myself—my own *v.*
Isa 5:1. . . . . . beloved had a *v* on a rich
1 Cor 9:7 . . . farmer plants a *v* and

VIOLATE, VIOLATED, VIOLATES, VIOLATING (v)
to do harm to the person or especially the chastity of; to fail to show proper respect for; to break or disregard
Lev 18:7. . . . Do not *v* your father
Lev 18:8. . . . for this would *v* your father.
Lev 18:10 . . . this would *v* yourself.
Lev 18:14 . . . Do not *v* your uncle,
Lev 18:16 . . . this would *v* your brother.
Lev 20:11 . . . If a man ***v-s*** his father by
Lev 20:20 . . . he has ***v-d*** his uncle.
Lev 20:21 . . . He has ***v-d*** his brother, and
Num 15:30 . who brazenly *v* the LORD's
Deut 22:30. . for this would *v* his father.
Deut 27:20. . for he has ***v-d*** his father.
Isa 24:5. . . . . instructions, ***v-d*** his laws,
Mal 2:10. . . . each other, ***v-ing*** the covenant

VIOLATION (n)
infringement, transgression
Heb 2:2 . . . . firm, and every *v* of the law

VIOLENCE (n)
exertion of physical force so as to injure or abuse
Gen 6:11 . . . and was filled with *v.*
Ps 12:5 . . . . . I have seen *v* done to the
Ps 72:14 . . . . them from oppression and *v,*
Isa 60:18. . . . *V* will disappear from your
Jonah 3:8 . . . and stop all their *v.*
Mic 2:2. . . . . take it by fraud and *v.*

VIOLENT (adj)
emotionally agitated to the point of loss of self-control
1 Tim 3:3 . . . a heavy drinker or be *v.*
Titus 1:7. . . . not be a heavy drinker, *v,*

VIPER (n)
a particular species of venomous snakes
Ps 140:3 . . . . venom of a *v* drips from

VIRGIN (n)
an unmarried woman who has not had sexual intercourse
Gen 24:16 . . but she was still a *v.*
Isa 7:14. . . . . The *v* will conceive a child!
Matt 1:18 . . . while she was still a *v,* she
Matt 1:23 . . . The *v* will conceive a child!
Luke 1:34. . . this happen? I am a *v.*

VIRGINITY (n)
the quality or state of being virgin
Deut 22:15. . proof of her *v* to the elders

VIRTUE (KJV)
Phil 4:8 . . . . things that are ***excellent***
2 Pet 1:5. . . . provision of ***moral excellence***

VIRTUOUS (adj)
morally excellent; righteous
Prov 31:10 . . Who can find a *v* and
Prov 31:29 . . There are many *v* and

VISION, VISIONS (n)
a visual form of divine revelation, including dreams, that consists of symbolic images, often accompanied by their interpretation
Num 12:6 . . would reveal myself in *v-s.*
2 Sam 7:17 . . LORD had said in this *v.*
Dan 9:24 . . . the prophetic *v,* and to
Dan 10:1 . . . that the *v* concerned events
Joel 2:28. . . . your young men will see *v-s.*
Hab 2:3 . . . . This *v* is for a future time.
Acts 2:17 . . . Your young men will see *v-s,*
Acts 26:19 . . I obeyed that *v* from heaven.
Col 2:18 . . . . they have had *v-s* about these

VOICE (n)
verbal communication by human and divine means
Isa 40:3. . . . . the *v* of someone shouting,
Mark 1:3 . . . He is a *v* shouting in the
John 10:3 . . . sheep recognize his *v* and
John 12:28 . . a *v* spoke from heaven,
Rev 3:20. . . . If you hear my *v* and open

VOMIT (n)
matter disgorged from the stomach
Prov 26:11 . . returns to its *v,* so a fool
2 Pet 2:22. . . A dog returns to its *v.*

VOMIT (v)
to eject violently or abundantly
Lev 18:28. . . it will *v* out the people

VOW, VOWS (n)
a binding promise or pledge
see also COVENANT, PROMISE
Num 6:2 . . . the special *v* of a Nazirite,
Judg 11:30 . . Jephthah made a *v* to the
Ps 110:4 . . . . and will not break his *v:*
Matt 5:34 . . . do not make any *v-s!*
Heb 7:21 . . . and will not break his *v:*

VOWED (v)
to promise solemnly
Eccl 8:2 . . . . since you *v* to God that
Mark 7:11 . . For I have *v* to give to

VULGAR (adj)
lewdly or profanely indecent
Ps 101:3 . . . . at anything vile and *v.*

VULNERABLE (adj)
capable of being physically or emotionally wounded
2 Tim 3:6 . . . the confidence of *v* women

VULTURES (n)
any of various large birds that subsist chiefly or entirely on dead flesh
Matt 24:28 . . gathering of *v* shows there
Rev 19:17. . . shouting to the *v* flying high

WAGE, WAGES (n)

payment for labor or services; compensation

Hag 1:6 . . . . Your *w-s* disappear as though
Zech 11:12. . give me my *w-s,* whatever
Mal 3:5. . . . . cheat employees of their *w-s,*
Matt 20:2. . . the normal daily *w* and
Rom 4:4. . . . their *w-s* are not a gift,
Rom 6:23 . . . For the *w-s* of sin is death,

WAGE (v)

to engage in or carry on

2 Cor 10:3 . . but we don't *w* war

WAILING (v)

the act of expressing sorrow audibly

Amos 5:17. . There will be *w* in every

WAIT, WAITED, WAITING (v)

to look forward expectantly; to stay in place in expectation of

Ps 40:1 . . . . . I *w-ed* patiently for the Lord
Ps 62:5 . . . . . that I am *w* quietly before
Ps 69:3 . . . . . *w-ing* for my God to help me.
Isa 30:18. . . . Blessed are those who *w* for
Mic 7:7. . . . . I *w* confidently for God to
Hab 3:16 . . . I will *w* quietly for the
Luke 12:37. . who are ready and *w-ing*
Rom 8:19 . . . all creation is *w-ing* eagerly
Rom 8:23 . . . We, too, *w* with eager hope
Heb 9:28 . . . are eagerly *w-ing* for him.

WAKE (v)

to rouse from or as if from sleep

see also AWAKE

Prov 6:22. . . When you *w* up, they will
Rev 3:3. . . . . If you don't *w* up, I will

WAKENS (v)

to wake

Isa 50:4. . . . by morning he *w* me and

WALK, WALKED, WALKING (v)

to roam, traverse, or advance by steps; to pursue a course of action or way of life

Gen 3:8 . . . . God *w-ing* about in the garden.
Lev 26:12. . . I will *w* among you;
Deut 11:22. . God by *w-ing* in his ways
Deut 26:17. . promised to *w* in his ways,
Josh 22:5 . . . God, *w* in all his ways,
Ps 23:4 . . . . . when I *w* through the
Ps 89:15 . . . . they will *w* in the light
Prov 4:12. . . When you *w,* you won't
Prov 6:22. . . When you *w,* their counsel
Isa 2:3. . . . . . we will *w* in his paths.
Isa 40:31. . . . They will *w* and not
Isa 43:2. . . . . When you *w* through the
Jer 6:16. . . . . godly way, and *w* in it.
Dan 3:25 . . . *w-ing* around in the fire
Amos 3:3. . . two people *w* together
Mic 6:8. . . . . to *w* humbly with your God.
Mal 2:6. . . . . they *w-ed* with me, living good
Matt 14:29. . boat and *w-ed* on the water
Mark 2:9 . . . pick up your mat, and *w*
John 8:12. . . have to *w* in darkness,

WALL, WALLS (n)

a thick, high, continuous structure of stones or brick that formed a defensive barricade around an ancient city

Josh 6:20 . . . Suddenly, the *w-s* of Jericho
Neh 2:17 . . . rebuild the *w* of Jerusalem
Isa 58:12. . . . as a rebuilder of *w-s* and
Heb 11:30 . . and the *w-s* came crashing
Rev 21:12. . . city *w* was broad and high,

WANDER, WANDERED, WANDERS (v)

to follow a winding course; to stray

Num 32:13 . them *w* in the wilderness
Ps 119:10 . . . don't let me *w* from your
Ps 119:67 . . . I used to *w* off until you

Ps 119:176 . . I have *w-ed* away like a
Matt 18:12 . . one of them *w-s* away
Eph 4:18 . . . *w* far from the life God
1 Tim 6:10 . . have *w-ed* from the true
Jas 5:19. . . . . someone among you *w-s*
1 Pet 2:25. . . like sheep who *w-ed* away.
2 Pet 2:15. . . They have *w-ed* off the

WANT, WANTED, WANTS (v)

to desire or wish

Gen 3:6 . . . . she *w-ed* the wisdom it would
Job 23:13 . . . Whatever he *w-s* to do,
Ps 51:16 . . . . do not *w* a burnt offering.
Ps 119:58 . . . heart I *w* your blessings.
Prov 13:4. . . Lazy people *w* much but
Eccl 6:2 . . . . they could ever *w*, but then
Mic 7:3. . . . . get what they *w*, and together
Matt 5:42. . . from those who *w* to borrow.
Matt 14:20 . . as they *w-ed*, and afterward,
Matt 19:21 . . If you *w* to be perfect,
Matt 23:37 . . I have *w-ed* to gather your
Luke 19:14. . We do not *w* him to be
John 3:8 . . . . blows wherever it *w-s*.
John 7:17 . . . Anyone who *w-s* to do the
John 15:7 . . . ask for anything you *w*,
Acts 20:27 . . all that God *w-s* you to know.
Rom 7:15 . . . I *w* to do what is right,
1 Cor 12:18 . part just where he *w-s* it.
2 Cor 8:5 . . . just as God *w-ed* them to do.
2 Cor 8:10 . . the first who *w-ed* to give,
2 Cor 12:14 . you have—I *w* you.
Eph 1:5 . . . . This is what he *w-ed* to do,
Eph 5:17 . . . what the Lord *w-s* you to do.
1 Tim 2:4 . . . who *w-s* everyone to be saved
Heb 10:5 . . . did not *w* animal sacrifices
Heb 13:18 . . is clear and we *w* to live
1 Pet 1:10. . . the prophets *w-ed* to know
1 Pet 3:17. . . if that is what God *w-s*,

WAR, WARS (n)

armed conflict with an opposing military force; a state of hostility, conflict, or antagonism

Josh 11:23 . . finally had rest from *w*.
Ps 46:9 . . . . . He causes *w-s* to end
Ps 68:30 . . . . nations that delight in *w*.
Ps 120:7 . . . . peace, they want *w!*
Ps 144:1 . . . . He trains my hands for *w*
Isa 2:4. . . . . . nor train for *w* anymore.
2 Cor 10:3 . . we don't wage *w* as humans
1 Pet 2:11. . . that wage *w* against your
Rev 12:7. . . . Then there was *w* in heaven.
Rev 19:11. . . and wages a righteous *w*.

WARN, WARNED, WARNING (v)

to give notice to beforehand especially of danger or evil; to counsel

Gen 2:16 . . . God *w-ed* him, "You may
Gen 31:24 . . told him, "I'm *w-ing* you—
Gen 31:29 . . to me last night and *w-ed* me,
Exod 19:21 . down and *w* the people
Num 16:40 . This would *w* the Israelites
1 Sam 8:9. . . but solemnly *w* them about
1 Kgs 2:42 . . LORD and *w* you not to
2 Kgs 17:13 . and seers to *w* both Israel
2 Chr 19:10 . must *w* them not to sin
Ezek 3:18. . . If I *w* the wicked,
Ezek 33:3. . . the alarm to *w* the people.
Matt 16:6. . . "Watch out!" Jesus *w-ed* them.
Luke 16:28. . I want him to *w* them so
Acts 4:17 . . . must *w* them not to speak
1 Cor 4:14 . . to *w* you as my beloved
1 Cor 10:11 . written down to *w* us who
Col 1:28 . . . . *w-ing* everyone and teaching
1 Thes 4:6 . . solemnly *w-ed* you before.
1 Thes 5:14 . urge you to *w* those who
2 Thes 3:15 . but *w* them as you would
Heb 3:13 . . . You must *w* each other

WARNING, WARNINGS (n)

something that warns or serves to warn; the act of warning

Ps 19:11 . . . . They are a *w* to your servant,
Ps 81:8 . . . . . while I give you stern *w-s*.
Jer 6:8. . . . . . Listen to this *w*, Jerusalem,
Jer 42:19. . . . Don't forget this *w* I have
Zeph 3:7 . . . they will listen to my *w-s*.
1 Cor 10:6 . . happened as a *w* to us,
1 Tim 5:20 . . as a strong *w* to others.
Titus 3:10. . . give a first and second *w*.

WARRIOR, WARRIORS (n)

a man engaged or experienced in warfare

Gen 6:4 . . . . and famous *w-s* of ancient
Exod 15:3 . . LORD is a *w;* Yahweh
Josh 1:14 . . . strong *w-s*, fully armed,
1 Chr 28:3 . . for you are a *w* and
Ps 45:3 . . . . . your sword, O mighty *w!*
Jer 20:11. . . . beside me like a great *w*.

WASH, WASHED (v)

to cleanse—of physical, ceremonial, or spiritual significance

see also BAPTIZE(D), CLEANSE

Ps 51:7 . . . . . *w* me, and I will be whiter
John 13:5 . . . he began to *w* the disciples'
John 13:10 . . does not need to *w*, except
Acts 22:16 . . Have your sins *w-ed* away
Eph 5:26 . . . holy and clean, *w-ed* by the
Titus 3:5. . . . He *w-ed* away our sins,

Heb 10:22 . . bodies have been *w-ed*
Jas 4:8. . . . . . *W* your hands, you sinners;
2 Pet 2:22. . . *w-ed* pig returns to the mud.
Rev 7:14. . . . They have *w-ed* their robes in
Rev 22:14. . . those who *w* their robes.

WASHBASIN (n)
a large bowl for water that is used to wash
Exod 30:18 . Make a bronze *w* with a

WASTE, WASTED (v)
to spend or use carelessly or inefficiently
Ps 127:1 . . . . work of the builders is *w-d.*
Prov 29:3 . . . prostitutes, his wealth is *w-d.*
Prov 31:3 . . . do not *w* your strength
Luke 15:13. . there he *w-d* all his money
John 6:12 . . . so that nothing is *w-d.*
Gal 2:2. . . . . all my efforts had been *w-d*

WATCH (n)
the act of keeping awake to guard, protect, or attend
Matt 24:42. . you, too, must keep *w!*
Acts 20:31 . . my constant *w* and care

WATCH, WATCHES, WATCHING (v)
to diligently wait or keep guard; to observe closely
Judg 18:6. . . the LORD is *w-ing* over
Job 14:16 . . . my steps, instead of *w-ing*
Job 34:21 . . . God *w-es* how people live;
Ps 1:6 . . . . . . For the LORD *w-es* over the
Ps 17:11 . . . . and surround me, *w-ing* for
Ps 61:7 . . . . . faithfulness *w* over him.
Ps 121:3 . . . . one who *w-es* over you will
Prov 2:11 . . . Wise choices will *w* over
Prov 31:27. . carefully *w-es* everything
Eccl 11:4 . . . If they *w* every cloud,
Jer 24:6. . . . . I will *w* over and care for
Jer 31:10. . . . gather them and *w* over
Acts 1:9 . . . . while they were *w-ing,* and
Eph 6:6 . . . . just when they are *w-ing* you.
Heb 13:17 . . is to *w* over your souls,
1 Pet 1:12. . . eagerly *w-ing* these things
1 Pet 3:12. . . eyes of the Lord *w* over

WATCHER (n)
one who watches
Job 7:20 . . . . you, O *w* of all humanity?

WATCHMAN (n)
a person who keeps watch; guard
Ezek 3:17. . . you as a *w* for Israel.
Ezek 33:6. . . hold the *w* responsible
Ezek 33:7. . . you a *w* for the people

WATER, WATERS (n)
precious resource for drink and irrigation, usually associated with blessing; a body of water
Exod 7:20 . . struck the *w* of the Nile.
Exod 17:1 . . there was no *w* there for
Num 20:2 . . was no *w* for the people
2 Sam 23:15. good *w* from the well
Ps 42:1 . . . . . streams of *w,* so I long
Prov 25:21. . give them *w* to drink.
Song 8:7. . . . Many *w-s* cannot quench
Isa 11:9. . . . . for as the *w-s* fill the sea,
Isa 32:2. . . . . like streams of *w* in the
Isa 43:2. . . . . through deep *w-s,* I will be
Isa 49:10. . . . lead them beside cool *w-s.*
Jer 17:8. . . . . reach deep into the *w.*
Jonah 2:3 . . . The mighty *w-s* engulfed me;
Hab 2:14 . . . For as the *w-s* fill the sea,
Zech 14:8. . . life-giving *w-s* will flow
Matt 14:25 . . them, walking on the *w.*
John 3:5 . . . . born of *w* and the Spirit.
John 4:10 . . . would give you living *w.*
John 7:38 . . . Rivers of living *w* will
1 Jn 5:6. . . . . his baptism in *w* and by
Rev 7:17. . . . springs of life-giving *w.*
Rev 21:6. . . . springs of the *w* of life.

WATERED, WATERING (v)
to moisten, sprinkle, or soak with water
Joel 3:18. . . . *w-ing* the arid valley of acacias.
1 Cor 3:6 . . . hearts, and Apollos *w-ed* it,
1 Cor 3:7 . . . planting, or who does the *w-ing.*

WATERPROOF (v)
to cover or treat with a material to prevent permeation by water
Gen 6:14 . . . cypress wood and *w* it with

WAVE, WAVES (n)
a moving ridge or swell on the surface of a liquid (as of the sea)
Matt 8:27. . . the winds and *w-s* obey him!
Jas 1:6. . . . . . unsettled as a *w* of the

WAVER, WAVERED, WAVERING (v)
to fluctuate in opinion, allegiance, or direction
Rom 4:20. . . Abraham never *w-ed* in believing
Jude 1:22 . . . to those whose faith is *w-ing.*

WAY, WAYS (n)
characteristic, regular, or habitual manner or mode of being, behaving, or happening; manner or method of doing or happening; a course of action; route
Exod 33:13 . let me know your *w-s*
Deut 26:17. . to walk in his *w-s,* and

Deut 30:16. . by walking in his *w-s.*
Josh 22:5 . . . walk in all his *w-s,* obey
2 Sam 22:31. God's *w* is perfect.
Ps 77:13 . . . . O God, your *w-s* are holy.
Ps 86:11 . . . . Teach me your *w-s,* O LORD,
Prov 2:9. . . . find the right *w* to go.
Prov 4:11. . . teach you wisdom's *w-s*
Eccl 8:6 . . . . and a *w* for everything,
Isa 2:3. . . . . . teach us his *w-s,* and we will
Isa 40:3. . . . . Clear the *w* through the
Jer 6:16. . . . . old, godly *w,* and walk in
Mic 4:2. . . . . teach us his *w-s,* and we will
Mal 3:1. . . . . prepare the *w* before me.
Matt 3:3. . . . Prepare the *w* for the
Matt 3:8. . . . Prove by the *w* you live
Luke 7:27. . . prepare your *w* before you.
John 14:6 . . . I am the *w,* the truth,
Acts 9:2 . . . . followers of the *W* he
Acts 24:14 . . I follow the *W,* which
Rom 1:30. . . invent new *w-s* of sinning,
1 Cor 10:13 . will show you a *w* out
1 Cor 12:31 . show you a *w* of life
Col 1:10. . . . Then the *w* you live will
Heb 10:20 . . and life-giving *w* through

WAYWARD (adj)
following one's own capricious, wanton, or depraved inclinations
Jer 3:14. . . . . Return home, you *w* children,
Jer 3:22. . . . . will heal your *w* hearts.

WEAK, WEAKER, WEAKEST (adj)
lacking strength; not able to withstand temptation or persuasion
Ps 72:13 . . . . pity for the *w* and the
Ps 103:14 . . . he knows how *w* we are;
Isa 59:1. . . . . arm is not too *w* to save
Matt 12:20. . will not crush the *w-est* reed
Matt 26:41. . but the body is *w!*
Rom 14:1. . . who are *w* in faith,
1 Cor 8:9 . . . others with a *w-er* conscience
1 Cor 9:22 . . bring the *w* to Christ.
1 Cor 11:30 . many of you are *w* and
1 Cor 12:22 . of the body that seem *w-est*
2 Cor 12:10 . For when I am *w,* then
1 Thes 5:14 . care of those who are *w.*

WEAKNESS, WEAKNESSES (n)
the quality or state of being weak
Ps 136:23 . . . He remembered us in our *w.*
Isa 53:4. . . . . it was our *w-es* he carried;
Rom 8:3. . . . the *w* of our sinful nature.
Rom 8:26. . . Spirit helps us in our *w.*
1 Cor 1:25 . . God's *w* is stronger than
1 Cor 2:3 . . . I came to you in *w*—timid
2 Cor 12:5 . . boast only about my *w-es.*
2 Cor 12:10 . take pleasure in my *w-es,*
2 Cor 13:4 . . he was crucified in *w,*
Heb 5:2 . . . . is subject to the same *w-es.*

WEALTH (n)
abundance of valuable material possessions or resources
see also MONEY, POSSESSIONS, RICHES, TREASURE(S)
2 Chr 1:11 . . not ask for *w,* riches,
Job 36:18 . . . you may be seduced by *w.*
Ps 39:6 . . . . . We heap up *w,* not knowing
Ps 62:10 . . . . if your *w* increases, don't
Prov 3:9. . . . the LORD with your *w*
Prov 10:2. . . Tainted *w* has no lasting
Prov 13:11. . *w* from hard work grows
Prov 21:20. . wise have *w* and luxury,
Prov 29:3. . . prostitutes, his *w* is wasted.
Eccl 4:8 . . . . gain as much *w* as he can.
Luke 19:8. . . give half my *w* to the poor,
Eph 2:7 . . . . of the incredible *w* of his
1 Tim 6:6 . . . contentment is itself great *w.*
Jas 5:3. . . . . . The very *w* you were counting

WEALTHY (adj)
characterized by abundance
Prov 11:24. . freely and become more *w;*
Eccl 2:26 . . . sinner becomes *w,* God takes
1 Cor 1:26 . . or *w* when God called you.

WEAPON, WEAPONS (n)
something used to injure, defeat, or destroy
Prov 26:18. . shooting a deadly *w*
Eccl 9:18 . . . have wisdom than *w-s* of war,
2 Cor 6:7 . . . use the *w-s* of righteousness

WEARY (adj)
exhausted in strength, endurance, or vigor
Isa 40:31. . . . They will run and not grow *w.*
Isa 50:4. . . . . know how to comfort the *w.*
Matt 11:28. . you who are *w* and carry
2 Cor 5:2 . . . We grow *w* in our present
Heb 12:3 . . . won't become *w* and give up.

WEDDING, WEDDINGS (n)
a marriage ceremony usually with its accompanying festivities
Matt 11:17. . We played *w* songs, and
Matt 22:11. . the proper clothes for a *w.*
Matt 24:38. . parties and *w-s* right up
Rev 19:7. . . . for the *w* feast of the Lamb,

WEEDS (n)
undesirable growth surrounding a plant
Matt 13:25. . and planted *w* among the

WEEK (n)
a seven-day cycle
1 Cor 16:2 . . of each *w*, you should

WEEPING (n)
shedding of tears out of grief or sadness
Jer 31:15. . . . deep anguish and bitter *w-ing*.
Matt 2:18 . . . heard in Ramah—*w-ing* and
Matt 8:12 . . . will be *w-ing* and gnashing

WEEP, WEEPING (v)
to cry aloud, often linked with prayer and repentance
2 Sam 1:26 . . How I *w* for you,
Ps 126:6 . . . . They *w* as they go to
Jer 31:16. . . . Do not *w* any longer,
Jer 50:4. . . . . will come *w-ing* and seeking
Luke 6:21. . . blesses you who *w* now,
Luke 22:62. . the courtyard, *w-ing* bitterly.
Luke 23:28. . don't *w* for me, but *w*
Rom 12:15 . . and *w* with those who *w*.

WEIGHED, WEIGHS (v)
to oppress or depress; to measure weight
Ps 146:8 . . . . up those who are *w-ed* down.
Prov 12:25 . . Worry *w-s* a person down;
Isa 53:4. . . . . our sorrows that *w-ed* him
Dan 5:27 . . . *Tekel* means '*w-ed*'—you

WEIGHT, WEIGHTS (n)
a piece of material (as metal) of known specified weight for use in weighing articles; burden, hindrance
Lev 19:36. . . Your scales and *w-s* must be
Prov 11:1 . . . he delights in accurate *w-s*.
Heb 12:1 . . . strip off every *w* that slows

WELCOME (n)
the state of being accepted with pleasure
Prov 25:17. . you will wear out your *w*.

WELCOMED, WELCOMES, WELCOMING (v)
to greet hospitably and with courtesy or cordiality
Matt 18:5. . . And anyone who *w-s* a little
Mark 9:37 . . Anyone who *w-s* a little child
John 13:20 . . who *w-s* my messenger
John 13:20 . . *w-s* me is *w-ing* the Father
Acts 28:7 . . . He *w-d* us and treated us

WELL (adj)
completely cured or healed (physically or spiritually)
Isa 38:9. . . . . King Hezekiah was *w* again,
Matt 15:31 . . the crippled were made *w*,
Matt 17:18 . . that moment the boy was *w*.
Mark 5:34 . . your faith has made you *w*.
Jas 5:15. . . . . the Lord will make you *w*.

WELL (adv)
in a prosperous or affluent manner; in a kindly or friendly manner
Deut 6:18. . . all will go *w* with you.
Eph 6:3 . . . . things will go *w* for you,
1 Tim 3:7 . . . church must speak *w* of him

WEPT (v)
to cry aloud
see also WEEP
Ps 137:1 . . . . we sat and *w* as we thought
John 11:35 . . Then Jesus *w*.

WEST (n)
the general direction of the sunset
Ps 103:12 . . . as the east is from the *w*.
Ps 107:3 . . . . from east and *w*, from north

WHEAT (n)
a cereal grain that yields a fine white flour
Matt 3:12. . . gathering the *w* into his barn
Matt 13:25. . among the *w*, then slipped
Mark 4:28 . . the heads of *w* are formed,
Luke 22:31. . sift each of you like *w*.
John 12:24 . . a kernel of *w* is planted in

WHEELS (n)
circular frames of hard material capable of turning on an axle
Ezek 1:16. . . All four *w* looked alike

WHIPPED (v)
to strike with a lash or rod
2 Cor 11:23 . been *w* times without

WHIRLWIND (n)
a small rotating windstorm, sometimes violent and destructive
see also STORM, WIND
2 Kgs 2:1 . . . to heaven in a *w*,
Job 38:1 . . . . answered Job from the *w*:
Hos 8:7 . . . . and will harvest the *w*.
Nah 1:3 . . . . in the *w* and the storm.

WHISPER (n)
a minor or softer reflection of the original noise; hint, trace
1 Kgs 19:12 . sound of a gentle *w*.
Job 26:14 . . . merely a *w* of his power.
Ps 107:29 . . . calmed the storm to a *w*

WHISPER (v)
to speak softly with little or no vibration of the vocal cords
Matt 10:27 . . What I *w* in your ear,

WHITE, WHITER (adj)
free from color; of the color white
Ps 51:7 . . . . . I will be ***w-r*** than snow.
Isa 1:18. . . . . make them as *w* as snow.
Dan 7:9 . . . . clothing was as *w* as snow,
Matt 28:3 . . . clothing was as *w* as snow.
Rev 1:14. . . . like wool, as *w* as snow.
Rev 6:2. . . . . saw a *w* horse standing
Rev 19:11. . . a *w* horse was standing
Rev 20:11. . . saw a great *w* throne

WHITE (n)
the absence of color; free from spot or blemish
Rev 3:4. . . . . will walk with me in *w,*
Rev 7:13. . . . who are clothed in *w?*

WHITEWASHED (adj)
glossed over with whitewash
Matt 23:27 . . are like *w* tombs—

WHOLE (adj)
entire; complete, unmodified; undivided
1 Sam 1:28 . . LORD his *w* life.
1 Sam 17:46. the *w* world will know
1 Chr 28:9 . . him with your *w* heart
Ps 72:19 . . . . Let the *w* earth be filled
Ps 103:1 . . . . with my *w* heart, I will
Prov 4:22. . . healing to their *w* body.
Eccl 12:13 . . That's the *w* story.
Isa 6:3. . . . . . The *w* earth is filled
Isa 14:26. . . . plan for the *w* earth,
Dan 2:35 . . . covered the *w* earth.
Zeph 1:18 . . For the *w* land will be
Matt 6:22. . . eye is good, your *w* body
Matt 16:26 . . gain the *w* world but lose
Matt 24:14 . . throughout the *w* world,
John 21:25 . . I suppose the *w* world
Acts 17:26 . . throughout the *w* earth.
1 Cor 12:17 . Or if your *w* body were
Gal 5:3 . . . . . regulation in the *w* law of

WHOLEHEARTEDLY (adv)
in a completely and sincerely devoted, determined, or enthusiastic manner
Num 32:11 . they have not obeyed me *w.*
Deut 11:18. . commit yourselves *w* to
Deut 26:16. . careful to obey them *w.*
Josh 14:8 . . . For my part, I *w* followed
Josh 24:14 . . LORD and serve him *w.*
1 Chr 29:9 . . had given freely and *w*
2 Chr 25:2 . . sight, but not *w.*
2 Chr 31:21 . sought his God *w.*
Jer 29:13. . . . look for me *w,* you will
Jer 32:41. . . . faithfully and *w* replant
Phil 2:2 . . . . happy by agreeing *w* with

WHOLESOME (adj)
promoting health or well-being of mind or spirit
see also SOUND
1 Tim 1:10 . . contradicts the *w* teaching
1 Tim 6:3 . . . these are the *w* teachings
Titus 1:9. . . . others with *w* teaching and
Titus 2:1. . . . that reflects *w* teaching.
2 Pet 3:1. . . . stimulate your *w* thinking

WHORE (KJV)
Lev 21:7. . . . woman ***defiled by prostitution***
Deut 23:18. . the earnings of a ***prostitute***
Prov 23:27 . . ***prostitute*** is a dangerous trap
Hos 4:14 . . . sinning with ***whores***
Rev 17:1. . . . ***prostitute,*** who rules over

WICKED (adj)
morally very bad
Gen 13:13 . . area were extremely *w* and
Ps 7:9 . . . . . . those who are *w,* and defend
Prov 10:7. . . name of a *w* person rots
Prov 26:23 . . may hide a *w* heart, just
Jer 35:15. . . . Turn from your *w* ways,
Ezek 18:21 . . But if *w* people turn away
Ezek 21:25 . . you corrupt and *w* prince
Ezek 33:8. . . that some *w* people are sure
Hos 10:9 . . . not right that the *w* men of
Jonah 1:2 . . . I have seen how *w* its people
Luke 6:35. . . who are unthankful and *w.*
1 Jn 5:17. . . . All *w* actions are sin,

WICKED (n)
those who practice evil
2 Sam 22:27. but to the *w* you show
Ps 1:1 . . . . . . the advice of the *w,* or stand
Ps 10:13 . . . . Why do the *w* get away with
Ps 12:8 . . . . . though the *w* strut about,
Ps 14:6 . . . . . The *w* frustrate the plans
Ps 18:26 . . . . but to the *w* you show
Ps 37:1 . . . . . worry about the *w* or envy
Ps 82:2 . . . . . by favoring the *w?*
Ps 101:8 . . . . ferret out the *w* and free
Ps 139:19 . . . you would destroy the *w!*
Ps 146:9 . . . . the plans of the *w.*
Prov 4:14. . . Don't do as the *w* do,
Prov 9:7. . . . who corrects the *w* will
Prov 10:28 . . expectations of the *w* come
Prov 12:5. . . of the *w* is treacherous.
Prov 29:7. . . the *w* don't care at all.
Isa 5:23. . . . . to let the *w* go free,
Isa 11:4. . . . . mouth will destroy the *w.*

Isa 26:10. . . . the *w* keep doing wrong
Isa 48:22. . . . no peace for the *w*,
Mal 4:1. . . . . arrogant and the *w* will be

WICKEDNESS (n)
the quality or state of being wicked; something wicked
Lev 16:21. . . it all the *w*, rebellion,
Lev 19:29. . . with prostitution and *w*.
Deut 9:4. . . . because of the *w* of the other
Ps 73:3 . . . . . them prosper despite their *w*.
Jer 3:2. . . . . . your prostitution and your *w*.
Jer 14:16. . . . out their own *w* on them.
Jer 14:20. . . . we confess our *w* and that
Ezek 33:19. . turn from their *w* and do
Luke 11:39. . of greed and *w!*
Rom 1:18. . . the truth by their *w*.
Rom 1:29. . . every kind of *w*, sin, greed,
Rom 2:8. . . . and instead live lives of *w*.
2 Cor 6:14 . . be a partner with *w?*
Heb 8:12 . . . I will forgive their *w*,

WIDE-OPEN (adj)
having virtually no limits or restrictions
1 Cor 16:9 . . a *w* door for a great

WIDE (adj)
fully opened; having great extent
Ps 81:10 . . . . Open your mouth *w*, and I
Matt 7:13. . . its gate is *w* for the
Eph 3:18 . . . should, how *w*, how long,

WIDOW, WIDOWS (n)
a woman whose husband has died
Deut 10:18. . orphans and *w-s* receive
Ps 68:5 . . . . . defender of *w-s*—this is God,
Ps 146:9 . . . . for the orphans and *w-s*, but
Isa 1:17. . . . . Fight for the rights of *w-s*.
Luke 21:2. . . Then a poor *w* came by and
Acts 6:1 . . . . that their *w-s* were being
1 Cor 7:8 . . . aren't married and to *w-s*—
1 Tim 5:3. . . Take care of any *w* who
1 Tim 5:16 . . care for the *w-s* who are
Jas 1:27. . . . . for orphans and *w-s* in their

WIFE (n)
the female partner in a marriage
see also WIVES
Gen 2:24 . . . and is joined to his *w*,
Gen 19:26 . . But Lot's *w* looked back
Exod 20:17 . covet your neighbor's *w*,
Lev 20:10. . . his neighbor's *w*, both
Deut 5:21. . . not covet your neighbor's *w*.
Deut 24:5. . . happiness to the *w* he has
Prov 5:18. . . Rejoice in the *w* of your
Prov 12:4. . . A worthy *w* is a crown
Prov 18:22. . man who finds a *w*
Prov 19:13. . a quarrelsome *w* is as
Prov 21:9. . . a quarrelsome *w* in a
Prov 31:10. . a virtuous and capable *w?*
Mal 2:14. . . . vows you and your *w* made
Matt 1:20. . . to take Mary as your *w*.
Matt 19:3. . . to divorce his *w* for just
Luke 17:32. . happened to Lot's *w!*
Luke 18:29. . up house or *w* or brothers
1 Cor 7:2 . . . should have his own *w*,
1 Cor 7:15 . . the husband or *w* who isn't
1 Cor 7:33 . . and how to please his *w*.
Eph 5:23 . . . head of his *w* as Christ
Eph 5:33 . . . love his *w* as he loves
1 Tim 3:12. . be faithful to his *w*,
Titus 1:6. . . . be faithful to his *w*,
1 Pet 3:7. . . . Treat your *w* with
Rev 21:9. . . . bride, the *w* of the Lamb.

WILD (adj)
not tame or domesticated; growing without human aid; uncontrolled, unruly
Gen 1:25 . . . made all sorts of *w* animals,
Gen 8:1 . . . . and all the *w* animals
Luke 15:13. . his money in *w* living.
Rom 11:17. . branches from a *w* olive

WILDERNESS (n)
any desolate, barren, or unpopulated area, usually linked with danger
see also DESERT
Num 16:13 . kill us here in this *w*,
Num 26:65 . all die in the *w*.
Num 32:13 . wander in the *w* for forty
Deut 8:16. . . manna in the *w*, a food
Deut 29:5. . . led you through the *w*,
Ps 78:19 . . . . give us food in the *w*.
Ps 78:52 . . . . safely through the *w*.
Isa 32:15. . . . *w* will become a fertile
Isa 35:6. . . . . will gush forth in the *w*,
Matt 3:3. . . . the *w*, 'Prepare the way
Luke 5:16. . . withdrew to the *w* for
Rev 12:6. . . . fled into the *w*, where God

WILDFLOWERS (n)
the flower of a wild or uncultivated plant
Ps 103:15 . . . like grass; like *w*, we bloom
Matt 6:30. . . so wonderfully for *w* that are

WILL (n)
desire, wish
Ps 40:8 . . . . . in doing your *w*, my God,
Ps 143:10 . . . me to do your *w*, for you
Prov 3:6. . . . Seek his *w* in all you do,
Matt 6:10. . . May your *w* be done on
Matt 7:21. . . who actually do the *w*

Matt 12:50 . . does the *w* of my Father
Matt 18:14 . . heavenly Father's *w* that
Matt 26:39 . . want your *w* to be done,
Matt 26:42 . . I drink it, your *w* be done.
John 5:30 . . . carry out the *w* of the one
John 6:38 . . . heaven to do the *w* of God
Rom 12:2 . . . learn to know God's *w*
1 Thes 5:18 . this is God's *w* for you
Heb 10:7 . . . come to do your *w*, O God—
Heb 13:21 . . need for doing his *w*.
1 Pet 4:2. . . . to do the *w* of God.

WILLING (adj)
inclined or favorably disposed in mind; done, borne, or accepted by choice or without reluctance
1 Chr 28:9 . . heart and a *w* mind.
Ps 51:12 . . . . and make me *w* to obey you.
Dan 3:28 . . . command and were *w* to die
Matt 26:41 . . spirit is *w*, but the body
Rom 9:3 . . . . I would be *w* to be forever

WIN (v)
to be the victor in
1 Jn 5:5. . . . . who can *w* this battle
Rev 6:2. . . . . rode out to *w* many battles

WIND, WINDS (n)
a natural movement of air
see also STORM, WHIRLWIND
Ps 1:4 . . . . . . chaff, scattered by the *w*.
Eccl 2:11 . . . like chasing the *w*.
Hos 8:7 . . . . have planted the *w* and
Mark 4:41 . . Even the *w* and waves
John 3:8 . . . . The *w* blows wherever
Eph 4:14 . . . blown about by every *w*
Heb 1:7 . . . . his angels like the *w-s*,
Jas 1:6. . . . . . and tossed by the *w*.

WINDOW, WINDOWS (n)
an opening in the wall of a building
Josh 2:21 . . . rope hanging from the *w*.
Mal 3:10. . . . will open the *w-s* of heaven
2 Cor 11:33 . a basket through a *w*

WINDOWSILL (n)
the edge at the bottom of a window opening
Acts 20:9 . . . sitting on the *w*, became

WINE (n)
the fermented juice of grapes, linked positively with blessings and negatively with drunkeness
Ps 104:15 . . . *w* to make them glad,
Prov 31:6. . . and *w* for those in bitter
Song 1:2. . . . love is sweeter than *w*.
Isa 28:7. . . . . who reel with *w* and stagger
Mark 15:36 . with sour *w*, holding it
John 2:3 . . . . The *w* supply ran out
Rom 14:21 . . to eat meat or drink *w*
Eph 5:18 . . . Don't be drunk with *w*,
1 Tim 5:23 . . drink a little *w* for
Rev 16:19. . . was filled with the *w*

WINEBIBBER(S) (KJV)
Prov 23:20 . . not carouse with ***drunkards***
Matt 11:19 . . glutton and a ***drunkard***, and
Luke 7:34. . . glutton and a ***drunkard***, and

WINEPRESS (n)
a vat in which the juice from grapes is pressed in the process of making wine
Rev 19:15. . . juice flowing from a *w*.

WINESKINS (n)
a bag used for holding wine, made from the skin of an animal
Matt 9:17. . . stored in new *w* so that
Luke 5:37. . . new wine into old *w*.

WINGS (n)
feathered appendages of a bird, figurative of freedom, strength, and protection from God
Exod 19:4 . . carried you on eagles' *w*
Ps 17:8 . . . . . in the shadow of your *w*.
Ps 91:4 . . . . . shelter you with his *w*.
Isa 6:2. . . . . . each having six *w*.
Isa 40:31. . . . high on *w* like eagles.
Mal 4:2. . . . . rise with healing in his *w*.
Luke 13:34. . chicks beneath her *w*,
Rev 4:8. . . . . living beings had six *w*,

WIPE, WIPED (v)
to clean or dry by rubbing; to expunge completely
Isa 25:8. . . . . will *w* away all tears.
Luke 7:38. . . she ***w-d*** them off with her
Acts 3:19 . . . your sins may be ***w-d*** away.
Rev 7:17. . . . And God will *w* every tear
Rev 21:4. . . . He will *w* every tear

WISDOM (n)
knowledge, insight, judgment
Gen 3:6 . . . . she wanted the *w* it would
1 Kgs 4:29 . . gave Solomon very great *w*
1 Kgs 10:24 . to hear the *w* God had
2 Chr 1:10 . . Give me the *w* and
Job 11:6 . . . . *w*, for true *w* is not
Job 42:3 . . . . that questions my *w* with such
Ps 51:6 . . . . . teaching me *w* even there.
Prov 2:6 . . . . the LORD grants *w!*
Prov 3:13. . . the person who finds *w*,
Prov 8:11. . . *w* is far more valuable

Prov 11:2. . . with humility comes *w.*
Prov 16:16 . . better to get *w* than gold,
Prov 23:23 . . also get *w,* discipline,
Prov 29:3. . . man who loves *w* brings joy
Eccl 10:10 . . the value of *w;* it helps
Isa 11:2. . . . . on him—the Spirit of *w*
Isa 50:4. . . . . me his words of *w,* so that
Luke 2:52. . . Jesus grew in *w* and in
Acts 6:3 . . . . full of the Spirit and *w.*
1 Cor 1:21 . . him through human *w,* he
Eph 1:17 . . . you spiritual *w* and insight
Col 2:3 . . . . . treasures of *w* and knowledge.
Col 3:16 . . . . with all the *w* he gives.
2 Tim 3:15 . . given you the *w* to receive
Titus 2:12. . . world with *w,* righteousness,
Jas 1:5. . . . . . If you need *w,* ask our
Rev 5:12. . . . riches and *w* and strength

WISE, WISER, WISEST (adj)

marked by deep understanding, keen discernment, and a capacity for sound judgment

1 Kgs 3:12 . . you a *w* and understanding
Job 9:4 . . . . . God is so *w* and so mighty.
Ps 14:2 . . . . . anyone is truly *w,* if anyone
Ps 19:7 . . . . . are trustworthy, making *w* the
Ps 119:100 . . I am even ***w-r*** than my
Prov 4:7. . . . wisdom is the ***w-st*** thing
Prov 9:8. . . . correct the *w,* and they
Prov 10:1. . . A *w* child brings joy to
Prov 11:30 . . a *w* person wins friends.
Prov 12:16 . . a *w* person stays calm
Prov 12:18 . . of the *w* bring healing.
Prov 13:1. . . A *w* child accepts a parent's
Prov 13:10 . . who take advice are *w.*
Prov 13:20 . . Walk with the *w* and
Prov 15:5. . . learns from correction is *w.*
Prov 16:23 . . From a *w* mind comes *w*
Prov 18:4. . . wisdom flows from the *w*
Prov 19:25 . . they will be all the ***w-r.***
Prov 24:5. . . *w* are mightier than the
Prov 28:7. . . who obey the law are *w;*
Eccl 8:5 . . . . who are *w* will find a time
Eccl 9:17 . . . quiet words of a *w* person
Matt 2:1 . . . . some *w* men from eastern
Matt 11:25 . . who think themselves *w*
Matt 25:2. . . foolish, and five were *w.*
Rom 3:11. . . No one is truly *w;* no one
1 Cor 1:19 . . wisdom of the *w* and
1 Cor 1:25 . . plan of God is ***w-r*** than
1 Cor 12:8 . . ability to give *w* advice;
Jas 3:13. . . . . If you are *w* and understand

WITCHCRAFT (n)

the use of sorcery or magic

Lev 19:26. . . practice fortune-telling or *w.*
Deut 18:10. . omens, or engage in *w,*
Rev 21:8. . . . those who practice *w,* idol

WITHDRAW, WITHDREW (v)

to remove; to retreat

Ps 66:20 . . . . or *w* his unfailing love from
Luke 5:16. . . But Jesus often ***w-ew*** to the

WITHER, WITHERS (v)

to shrivel and lose vitality, force, or freshness

Job 14:2 . . . . like a flower and then *w.*
Ps 1:3 . . . . . . leaves never *w,* and they
Isa 40:7. . . . . grass ***w-s*** and the flowers
Isa 64:6. . . . . autumn leaves, we *w* and fall,
1 Pet 1:24. . . grass ***w-s*** and the flower

WITHHELD (v)

to refrain from granting, giving, or allowing

Gen 22:12 . . You have not *w* from me

WITNESS, WITNESSES (n)

a person who gives testimony; one asked to be present at a transaction so as to be able to testify to its having taken place

Deut 19:15. . of two or three ***w-es.***
Prov 19:5. . . A false *w* will not go
Prov 21:28 . . but a credible *w* will be
Matt 18:16 . . by two or three ***w-es.***
John 1:8 . . . . simply a *w* to tell about
Acts 1:8 . . . . will be my ***w-es,*** telling people
1 Tim 5:19 . . by two or three ***w-es.***
1 Jn 5:7. . . . . we have these three ***w-es***—

WITNESSED (v)

to have personal or direct cognizance of

Mal 2:14. . . . the LORD *w* the vows

WIVES (n)

the female partner in marriage

see also WIFE

Eph 5:22 . . . For *w,* this means submit
Eph 5:25 . . . this means love your *w,*
1 Pet 3:1. . . . way, you *w* must accept

WOE (KJV)

Isa 6:5. . . . . . ***It's all over!*** I am doomed
Matt 18:7. . . ***What sorrow awaits*** the world
Matt 23:13 . . ***What sorrow awaits*** you
1 Cor 9:16 . . ***How terrible*** for me if I didn't
Rev 8:13. . . . ***Terror, terror, terror*** to all who

WOLVES (n)

any of several wild, predatory animals that resemble large dogs

Matt 7:15. . . but are really vicious *w.*
Matt 10:16 . . you out as sheep among *w.*

WOMAN (n)
an adult female person
see also WOMEN
Gen 2:22 . . . God made a *w* from the rib,
Gen 3:6 . . . . The *w* was convinced.
Gen 3:12 . . . It was the *w* you gave me
Gen 3:16 . . . he said to the *w,* "I will
Exod 3:22 . . Every Israelite *w* will ask
Lev 12:2. . . . If a *w* becomes pregnant
Lev 15:19. . . a *w* has her menstrual
Lev 15:25. . . a *w* has a flow of blood
Num 5:29 . . If a *w* goes astray and defiles
Judg 4:9. . . . be at the hands of a *w.*
Judg 16:4. . . love with a *w* named Delilah,
Ruth 3:11. . . knows you are a virtuous *w.*
2 Sam 11:2. . he noticed a *w* of unusual
2 Sam 20:16. But a wise *w* in the town
Prov 11:16. . A gracious *w* gains respect,
Prov 11:22. . A beautiful *w* who lacks
Prov 14:1. . . A wise *w* builds her
Prov 30:19. . how a man loves a *w.*
Prov 30:23. . a bitter *w* who finally gets
Prov 31:30. . *w* who fears the LORD
Matt 5:28. . . looks at a *w* with lust
Matt 9:20. . . Just then a *w* who had
Matt 26:7. . . was eating, a *w* came in
Mark 7:25 . . Right away a *w* who had
Luke 7:39. . . what kind of *w* is touching
John 4:7. . . . Soon a Samaritan *w* came to
John 8:3. . . . Pharisees brought a *w* who
Rom 7:2. . . . when a *w* marries, the law
1 Cor 7:2 . . . and each *w* should have
1 Cor 7:34 . . a married *w* has to think
1 Cor 11:3 . . the head of *w* is man, and
1 Cor 11:6 . . shameful for a *w* to have
1 Cor 11:13 . it right for a *w* to pray
Gal 4:4. . . . . born of a *w,* subject to the
Gal 4:31. . . . are children of the free *w.*
Rev 12:1. . . . I saw a *w* clothed with the
Rev 12:13. . . he pursued the *w* who had
Rev 17:3. . . . There I saw a *w* sitting on a

WOMB (n)
uterus
Ps 139:13 . . . together in my mother's *w.*
Prov 31:2. . . O son of my *w,* O son
Jer 1:5. . . . . . you in your mother's *w.*
Luke 1:44. . . baby in my *w* jumped for joy.
John 3:4 . . . . into his mother's *w* and be

WOMEN (n)
adult female persons
see also WOMAN
Gen 6:2 . . . . saw the beautiful *w* and took
Song 1:3. . . . all the young *w* love you!
Mark 15:41 . Many other *w* who had
Luke 1:42. . . you above all *w,* and your
Luke 23:27. . many grief-stricken *w.*
Rom 1:26. . . Even the *w* turned against
1 Cor 7:25 . . the young *w* who are not
1 Tim 2:9. . . I want *w* to be modest in
2 Tim 3:6. . . of vulnerable *w* who are
Titus 2:3. . . . teach the older *w* to live in
Titus 2:4. . . . train the younger *w* to love
1 Pet 3:5. . . . how the holy *w* of old made

WON (v)
to gain victory
see also WIN
1 Kgs 20:11 . warrior who has already *w.*
1 Pet 3:1. . . . They will be *w* over
1 Jn 2:13. . . . you have *w* your battle

WONDERFUL (adj)
marked by a marvelous, amazing, or extraordinary quality
1 Chr 16:9 . . about his *w* deeds.
Job 37:14 . . . consider the *w* miracles
Ps 16:6 . . . . . What a *w* inheritance!
Ps 17:7 . . . . . unfailing love in *w* ways.
Ps 71:17 . . . . about the *w* things you
Ps 72:18 . . . . does such *w* things.
Ps 75:1 . . . . . tell of your *w* deeds.
Ps 105:2 . . . . about his *w* deeds.
Ps 118:23 . . . it is *w* to see.
Ps 119:18 . . . to see the *w* truths in
Ps 119:27 . . . meditate on your *w* deeds.
Ps 119:129 . . Your laws are *w.*
Ps 139:6 . . . . knowledge is too *w* for
Ps 145:5 . . . . and your *w* miracles.
Eccl 11:9 . . . Young people, it's *w* to be
Isa 9:6. . . . . . be called: *W* Counselor,
Isa 12:5. . . . . he has done *w* things.
Isa 25:1. . . . . You do such *w* things!
Matt 21:15. . saw these *w* miracles
Matt 21:42. . and it is *w* to see.
Luke 13:17. . rejoiced at the *w* things
Acts 2:11 . . . about the *w* things God has
Acts 20:24 . . News about the *w* grace of
2 Cor 10:12 . we are as *w* as these
Titus 2:13. . . hope to that *w* day when

WONDERS (n)
mighty works, miracles
1 Chr 16:12 . Remember the *w* he has
Ps 26:7 . . . . . and telling of all your *w.*
Ps 31:21 . . . . has shown me the *w* of his
Ps 77:14 . . . . are the God of great *w!*
Ps 89:5 . . . . . your great *w,* LORD;
Mark 13:22 . perform signs and *w* so
Acts 2:19 . . . will cause *w* in the heavens

Acts 5:12 . . . signs and *w* among the people.
2 Cor 12:12 . signs and *w* and miracles
Heb 2:4 . . . . signs and *w* and various

WORD, WORDS (n)

something that is said; special revelation from God; commands

Deut 8:3. . . . live by every *w* that comes
Deut 11:18. . to these *w-s* of mine. Tie
Job 38:2 . . . . with such ignorant *w-s?*
Ps 19:3 . . . . . speak without a sound or *w;*
Ps 52:4 . . . . . others with your *w-s,* you liar!
Ps 119:9 . . . . pure? By obeying your *w.*
Ps 119:11 . . . hidden your *w* in my heart,
Ps 119:103 . . How sweet your *w-s* taste
Ps 119:160 . . essence of your *w-s* is
Ps 119:162 . . I rejoice in your *w* like
Prov 12:19. . Truthful *w-s* stand the test
Prov 12:25. . an encouraging *w* cheers
Prov 16:24. . Kind *w-s* are like honey—
Prov 17:27. . wise person uses few *w-s;*
Prov 26:23. . Smooth *w-s* may hide a
Isa 40:21. . . . deaf to the *w-s* of God—
Jer 15:16. . . . your *w-s,* I devoured
Jer 23:29. . . . Does not my *w* burn like
Amos 8:13. . for the LORD's *w.*
Matt 4:4. . . . but by every *w* that comes
Matt 15:6. . . you cancel the *w* of God
Matt 24:35. . *w-s* will never disappear.
John 1:1 . . . . the beginning the **W** already
John 6:68 . . . the *w-s* that give eternal life.
John 15:7 . . . and my *w-s* remain in you,
John 17:17 . . teach them your *w,* which
Rom 10:18 . . the *w-s* to all the world.
1 Cor 2:1 . . . use lofty *w-s* and impressive
1 Cor 2:13 . . do not use *w-s* that come
1 Cor 14:9 . . to people in *w-s* they don't
1 Cor 14:19 . than ten thousand *w-s* in
2 Cor 2:17 . . We preach the *w* of God
2 Cor 4:2 . . . or distort the *w* of God.
Eph 6:17 . . . which is the *w* of God.
Phil 2:16 . . . firmly to the *w* of life;
2 Tim 2:15 . . explains the *w* of truth.
Titus 2:5. . . . shame on the *w* of God.
Heb 4:12 . . . For the *w* of God is
Heb 5:12 . . . things about God's *w.*
Jas 1:22. . . . . listen to God's *w.*
1 Pet 1:23. . . eternal, living *w* of God.
1 Pet 2:8. . . . not obey God's *w,* and so
1 Pet 3:1. . . . to them without any *w-s.*
2 Pet 3:5. . . . the heavens by the *w* of
Rev 19:13. . . title was the **W** of God.
Rev 22:19. . . of the *w-s* from this book

WORK, WORKS (n)

one's occupation; physical or creative effort

see also DEEDS

Gen 2:2 . . . . finished his *w* of creation,
Exod 20:9 . . week for your ordinary *w,*
Deut 5:13. . . week for your ordinary *w,*
Ps 77:12. . . . about your mighty *w-s.*
Ps 107:24. . . impressive *w-s* on the
Ps 127:1 . . . . *w* of the builders is wasted.
Ps 150:2. . . . Praise him for his mighty *w-s;*
Prov 21:5. . . planning and hard *w* lead
Eccl 2:19 . . . my skill and hard *w* under
Eccl 5:19 . . . To enjoy your *w* and accept
John 4:34 . . . and from finishing his *w.*
John 5:36 . . . Father gave me these *w-s* to
John 10:32 . . have done many good *w-s.*
Acts 13:2 . . . for the special *w* to which
Acts 20:24 . . finishing the *w* assigned
Rom 4:5. . . . not because of their *w,* but
1 Cor 3:5 . . . the *w* the Lord gave us.
Gal 6:4 . . . . . attention to your own *w,* for
Eph 4:12 . . . people to do his *w* and build
Eph 4:16 . . . part does its own special *w,*
Eph 4:28 . . . your hands for good hard *w,*
Phil 1:6 . . . . began the good *w* within you,
1 Tim 6:18 . . rich in good *w-s* and
2 Tim 3:17 . . people to do every good *w.*
Heb 10:24 . . acts of love and good *w-s.*
Jas 2:26. . . . . faith is dead without good *w-s.*
Rev 15:3. . . . marvelous are your *w-s,*

WORK, WORKED, WORKING (v)

to exert oneself physically or mentally

Prov 13:4. . . but those who *w* hard will
Eccl 5:12 . . . who *w* hard sleep well,
Matt 6:28. . . They don't *w* or make their
Matt 12:30. . anyone who isn't *w-ing* with
Luke 10:7. . . who *w* deserve their pay.
Luke 13:24. . **W** hard to enter the narrow
Rom 4:6. . . . righteous without *w-ing* for
Rom 8:28. . . to *w* together for the good
Rom 12:11. . Never be lazy, but *w* hard
1 Cor 15:10 . I have *w-ed* harder than
1 Cor 15:58 . Always *w* enthusiastically
2 Cor 11:27 . I have *w-ed* hard and
Eph 6:7 . . . . you were *w-ing* for the Lord
1 Thes 4:11 . and *w-ing* with your hands,
2 Thes 3:10 . unwilling to *w* will not
1 Tim 5:18 . . Those who *w* deserve their
1 Tim 6:2. . . slaves should *w* all the harder
Heb 6:10 . . . how hard you have *w-ed* for
2 Pet 1:10. . . *w* hard to prove that you

WORKER, WORKERS (n)
one who works; laborer
Prov 10:4 . . . poor; hard *w-s* get rich.
Prov 12:11 . . A hard *w* has plenty of
Prov 22:29 . . see any truly competent *w-s?*
Prov 27:18 . . *w-s* who protect
Prov 31:17 . . and strong, a hard *w.*
Matt 9:37 . . . great, but the *w-s* are few.
Matt 20:1 . . . one morning to hire *w-s* for
1 Cor 3:9 . . . For we are both God's *w-s.*
2 Tim 2:15 . . Be a good *w,* one who does

WORLD (n)
the earth and its inhabitants; the human race; the current age and its value system
Ps 33:9 . . . . . he spoke, the *w* began!
Ps 50:12 . . . . for all the *w* is mine
Ps 96:13 . . . . judge the *w* with justice,
Isa 13:11 . . . . will punish the *w* for its
Matt 16:26 . . you gain the whole *w* but
John 1:29 . . . away the sin of the *w!*
John 3:16 . . . God loved the *w* so much
John 8:12 . . . I am the light of the *w.*
John 13:35 . . prove to the *w* that you
John 16:33 . . I have overcome the *w.*
John 17:5 . . . shared before the *w* began.
John 17:14 . . And the *w* hates them
John 18:36 . . Kingdom is not of this *w.*
Rom 3:19 . . . the entire *w* is guilty
1 Cor 1:27 . . things the *w* considers
1 Cor 2:7 . . . glory before the *w* began.
1 Cor 3:1 . . . you belonged to this *w* or
1 Cor 3:19 . . of this *w* is foolishness
1 Cor 6:2 . . . to judge the *w,* can't you
2 Cor 5:19 . . reconciling the *w* to himself,
Eph 2:12 . . . lived in this *w* without God
Eph 4:9 . . . . also descended to our lowly *w.*
Phil 2:15 . . . lights in a *w* full of crooked
Titus 1:2 . . . them before the *w* began.
Heb 9:26 . . . ever since the *w* began.
Jas 2:5 . . . . . . poor in this *w* to be rich
Jas 4:4 . . . . . . a friend of the *w,* you make
1 Jn 2:2 . . . . . the sins of all the *w.*
1 Jn 2:15 . . . . Do not love this *w* nor
1 Jn 5:4 . . . . . defeats this evil *w,* and

WORLDLY (adj)
belonging to the sphere of human existence only; affected by sin; corrupt
Luke 16:9 . . . Use your *w* resources to benefit
2 Cor 7:10 . . *w* sorrow, which lacks repentance,
2 Cor 10:4 . . not *w* weapons, to knock down
1 Pet 2:11 . . . *w* desires that wage war

WORRY, WORRIES (n)
mental distress or agitation resulting from concern; anxiety
Prov 12:25 . . *W* weighs a person down;
Matt 6:27 . . . Can all your *w-ies* add a single
Luke 21:34 . . and by the *w-ies* of this life.
1 Pet 5:7 . . . . Give all your *w-ies* and cares

WORRY, WORRIED, WORRYING (v)
to feel or experience concern or anxiety
Deut 20:8 . . . anyone here afraid or *w-ied?*
Ps 37:1 . . . . . Don't *w* about the wicked
Isa 7:4 . . . . . . Tell him to stop *w-ing.*
Matt 6:25 . . . I tell you not to *w* about
Matt 10:19 . . don't *w* about how to
Luke 6:41 . . . And why *w* about a speck in
Acts 27:33 . . You have been so *w-ied* that
Phil 4:6 . . . . Don't *w* about anything;

WORSE (adj)
of more inferior condition
Matt 12:45 . . that person is *w* off than
2 Pet 2:20 . . . they are *w* off than

WORSHIP (n)
reverent devotion and allegiance pledged to God or a god
1 Cor 10:14 . flee from the *w* of idols.

WORSHIP, WORSHIPED, WORSHIPING, WORSHIPS (v)
to regard with great respect, honor, or devotion
Gen 12:8 . . . and he *w-ed* the LORD.
Gen 13:4 . . . and there he *w-ed* the LORD
Gen 21:33 . . and there he *w-ed* the LORD,
Gen 26:25 . . there and *w-ed* the LORD.
Deut 12:30 . . and *w-ing* their gods.
2 Kgs 17:36 . But *w* only the LORD,
Ps 29:2 . . . . . *W* the LORD in the splendor
Ps 95:6 . . . . . Come, let us *w* and bow down.
Isa 44:19 . . . . bow down to *w* a piece of
Jer 16:11 . . . . *w-ed* other gods and served
Dan 3:28 . . . die rather than serve or *w* any
Hos 9:1 . . . . like prostitutes, *w-ing* other
Hos 9:10 . . . as vile as the god they *w-ed.*
Hos 13:1 . . . Ephraim sinned by *w-ing* Baal
Zeph 3:9 . . . everyone can *w* the LORD
Zech 14:17 . . to Jerusalem to *w* the King,
Matt 2:2 . . . . we have come to *w* him.
Matt 4:9 . . . . kneel down and *w* me.
Matt 15:25 . . she came and *w-ed* him,
Matt 28:9 . . . grasped his feet, and *w-ed*
Luke 23:47 . . he *w-ed* God and said,
John 4:24 . . . *w* in spirit and in truth.
1 Cor 5:11 . . is greedy, or *w-s* idols,
Heb 9:14 . . . we can *w* the living God.

WORST (adj)
most corrupt, bad, or evil
1 Tim 1:15 . . I am the *w* of them all.

WORTHLESS (adj)
valueless, useless, contemptible
1 Sam 12:21 . worshiping *w* idols that
Prov 6:12. . . *w* and wicked people
1 Cor 3:20 . . he knows they are *w*.
Eph 5:11 . . . part in the *w* deeds of evil
Titus 1:16. . . *w* for doing anything good.
Jas 5:3. . . . . . and silver have become *w*.

WORTHY (adj)
having sufficient merit or importance; estimable, honorable
Gen 32:10 . . I am not *w* of all the
Prov 12:4. . . A *w* wife is a crown
Matt 8:8. . . . Lord, I am not *w* to have
Matt 10:37. . are not *w* of being mine;
Matt 22:8. . . I invited aren't *w* of the
Luke 15:19. . I am no longer *w* of being
1 Cor 15:9 . . I'm not even *w* to be called
Eph 4:1 . . . . lead a life *w* of your calling,
Phil 1:27 . . . a manner *w* of the Good News
Rev 5:5. . . . . He is *w* to open the scroll

WOUNDS (n)
injuries to the body
Isa 30:26. . . . and cure the *w* he gave them.
Zech 13:6. . . what about those *w* on your
John 20:20 . . he showed them the *w* in
1 Pet 2:24. . . By his *w* you are healed.

WRAP (v)
to fold cloth, paper, etc., around something, especially in order to cover it
Exod 29:9 . . ***W*** the sashes around
Num 4:12 . . *w* them in a blue cloth

WRAPPINGS (n)
something used to wrap an object
John 20:5 . . . saw the linen *w* lying there,

WRATH (n)
extreme displeasure, anger, or hostility; God's response to sin
Isa 13:13. . . . Armies displays his *w* in
Rev 6:16. . . . and from the *w* of the Lamb.
Rev 16:19. . . the wine of his fierce *w*.

WREATH (n)
a band of intertwined flowers or leaves worn as a mark of honor or victory
Prov 4:9. . . . will place a lovely *w* on your

WRESTLED (v)
to engage in a violent or determined struggle
Gen 32:24 . . man came and *w* with him

WRITE, WRITING (v)
to inscribe or engrave; to record
see also WRITTEN
Deut 10:2. . . I will *w* on the tablets
Prov 3:3. . . . ***W*** them deep within your
Prov 7:3. . . . ***W*** them deep within your
Eccl 12:12 . . for ***w-ing*** books is endless,
Jer 31:33. . . . I will *w* them on their hearts.
1 Tim 3:14 . . I am ***w-ing*** these things to
Heb 8:10 . . . I will *w* them on their hearts.
Rev 3:12. . . . I will *w* on them the name of

WRITHE (v)
to twist (the body or body part) in pain
Jer 4:19. . . . . my heart—I *w* in pain!

WRITTEN (v)
to enscribe or engrave; to record
see also WRITE
Deut 28:58. . that are *w* in this book,
Josh 1:8 . . . . to obey everything *w* in it.
Isa 49:16. . . . See, I have *w* your name
Dan 12:1 . . . whose name is *w* in the book
Mal 3:16. . . . scroll of remembrance was *w*
Luke 24:44. . everything *w* about me in
John 20:31 . . these are *w* so that you
John 21:25 . . the books that would be *w*.
Rom 2:15. . . law is *w* in their hearts,
1 Cor 10:11 . They were *w* down to warn
Heb 12:23 . . names are *w* in heaven.
Rev 21:27. . . whose names are *w* in the

WRONG (adj)
incorrect, sinful, immoral, or improper
Prov 14:2. . . who take the *w* path
Rom 7:19. . . don't want to do what is *w*,
Rom 12:9. . . Hate what is *w*. Hold tightly
Rom 14:14. . of itself, is *w* to eat.
2 Tim 3:16 . . make us realize what is *w*

WRONG (adv)
in an unsuccessful or unfortunate way
Prov 15:22. . Plans go *w* for lack

WRONG (n)
an injurious, unfair, or unjust act; something wrong, immoral, or unethical
Exod 23:2 . . the crowd in doing *w*.
Deut 32:4. . . faithful God who does no *w*;
Job 34:10 . . . The Almighty can do no *w*.
Ps 141:9. . . . snares of those who do *w*.
Isa 53:9. . . . . done no *w* and had never

Rom 13:10 . . Love does no *w* to others,
Rom 16:19 . . to stay innocent of any *w.*
1 Cor 6:9 . . . those who do *w* will not
Jas 1:13. . . . . God is never tempted to do *w,*
1 Pet 3:17. . . to suffer for doing *w!*

WRONGDOING (n)
evil or improper behavior or action
Prov 26:26 . . their *w* will be exposed
Isa 61:8. . . . . justice. I hate robbery and *w.*
Acts 18:14 . . some *w* or serious crime,
Gal 3:13 . . . . the curse for our *w.*

WRONGED (v)
to injure or harm; to malign or discredit
Num 5:7 . . . to the person who was *w.*
Isa 42:3. . . . . to all who have been *w.*
1 Cor 13:5 . . keeps no record of being *w.*

XERXES

Persian king (486–465 B.C.); mentioned in the books of Ezra, Esther, and Daniel (9:1, where he is called Ahasuerus)

Ezra 4:6 . . . . later when *X* began his reign,
Esth 1:1 . . . . in the days of King *X*, who
Esth 1:9 . . . . in the royal palace of King *X*.
Esth 1:19 . . . from the presence of King *X*,
Esth 2:16 . . . Esther was taken to King *X*
Esth 3:1 . . . . later King *X* promoted Haman
Esth 6:2 . . . . plotted to assassinate King *X*.
Esth 8:7 . . . . King *X* said to Queen Eshter
Esth 10:3 . . . with authority next to that of King *X* himself

YAHWEH (n)
"I Am Who I Am" or "I Will Be What I Will Be"; the personal name of God revealed to Moses in the burning bush
see also Lord
Gen 22:14 . . named the place ***Y***-Yireh
Exod 3:15 . . ***Y,*** the God of your ancestors
Exod 6:2 . . . I am ***Y***—'the Lord'
Exod 15:3 . . warrior; ***Y*** is his name!
Exod 17:15 . there and named it ***Y***-nissi
Exod 33:19 . I will call out my name, ***Y,***
Exod 34:5 . . called out his own name, ***Y.***
Judg 6:24 . . . there and named it ***Y***-Shalom

YEAR, YEARS (n)
the period of about 365 days; a period having special significance; a measure of age or duration
Gen 1:14 . . . the seasons, days, and ***y-s.***
Exod 12:40 . lived in Egypt for 430 ***y-s.***
Exod 16:35 . manna for forty ***y-s*** until
Exod 34:23 . Three times each ***y*** every
Lev 16:34 . . . the Lord once each ***y.***
Lev 25:11 . . . During that ***y*** you must
Job 36:26 . . . His ***y-s*** cannot be counted.
Ps 90:4 . . . . . a thousand ***y-s*** are as a
Luke 3:23 . . . about thirty ***y-s*** old when
Heb 10:1 . . . again and again, ***y*** after ***y,***
Heb 10:3 . . . of their sins ***y*** after ***y.***
2 Pet 3:8 . . . . like a thousand ***y-s*** to the
Rev 20:2 . . . . in chains for a thousand ***y-s.***

YEAST (n)
a fungus used for making alcohol and bread
Exod 12:8 . . and bread made without ***y.***
Exod 12:15 . bread made with ***y*** during
Matt 16:6 . . . Beware of the ***y*** of the
1 Cor 5:6 . . . a little ***y*** that spreads

YESTERDAY (adv)
on the day preceding today
Heb 13:8 . . . same ***y,*** today, and forever.

YIELD, YIELDS (v)
to produce; to surrender or submit
Prov 30:33 . . beating of cream ***y-s*** butter
Matt 6:13 . . . don't let us ***y*** to temptation,
Luke 11:4 . . . don't let us ***y*** to temptation.
Jas 3:17 . . . . . willing to ***y*** to others.

YOKE (n)
a wooden crossbar linking two load-pulling animals together; figurative of bondage or linkage between people
Hos 11:4 . . . lifted the ***y*** from his neck,
Matt 11:29 . . Take my ***y*** upon you.

YOUNG, YOUNGER (adj)
being in the first or an early stage of life, growth, or development
2 Chr 10:14 . counsel of his ***y-er*** advisers.
Ps 119:9 . . . . How can a ***y*** person stay pure?
Prov 20:29 . . The glory of the ***y*** is their
Joel 2:28 . . . . your ***y*** men will see visions.
Acts 2:17 . . . Your ***y*** men will see visions,
Acts 7:58 . . . feet of a ***y*** man named Saul.
1 Tim 5:1 . . . Talk to ***y-er*** men as you
Titus 2:4 . . . . must train the ***y-er*** women to
Titus 2:6 . . . . encourage the ***y*** men to live
1 Pet 5:5 . . . . same way, you ***y-er*** men must
1 Jn 2:13 . . . . you who are ***y*** in the faith

YOUTH (n)
the period between childhood and maturity
Ps 103:5 . . . . My ***y*** is renewed like the
Eccles 12:1 . . Honor him in your ***y*** before

YOUTHFUL (adj)
of, relating to, or characteristic of youth
2 Tim 2:22 . . that stimulates ***y*** lusts.

Z

ZEAL (n)
eagerness and ardent interest in pursuit of something
Num 25:13 . in his *z* for me, his God,
Rom 10:2 . . . but it is misdirected *z.*
Gal 1:14 . . . . *z* for the traditions of my ancestors

ZEALOT (n)
a Jewish revolutionary who sought liberation from Roman rule near and during the time of Christ
Matt 10:4 . . . Simon (the *z*), Judas Iscariot,
Mark 3:18 . . Thaddaeus, Simon (the *z*),
Acts 1:13 . . . Simon (the *Z*), and Judas (son